Inside Terrorism

Columbia Studies in Terrorism and Irregular Warfare

Columbia Studies in Terrorism and Irregular Warfare
Bruce Hoffman, Series Editor

This series seeks to fill a conspicuous gap in the burgeoning literature on terrorism, guerrilla warfare, and insurgency. The series adheres to the highest standards of scholarship and discourse and publishes books that elucidate the strategy, operations, means, motivations, and effects posed by terrorist, guerrilla, and insurgent organizations and movements. It thereby provides a solid and increasingly expanding foundation of knowledge on these subjects for students, established scholars, and informed reading audiences alike.

Inside Terrorism

THIRD EDITION

Bruce Hoffman

Columbia University Press   *New York*

Columbia University Press
Publishers Since 1893
New York   Chichester, West Sussex
cup.columbia.edu
Copyright © 2017 Bruce Hoffman
All rights reserved

Library of Congress Cataloging-in-Publication Data
Names: Hoffman, Bruce, 1954– author.
Title: Inside terrorism / Bruce Hoffman.
Description: Third Edition. | New York : Columbia University Press, [2017] |
    Series: Columbia studies in terrorism and irregular warfare | Revised edition
    of the author's Inside terrorism, 2006. | Includes bibliographical references
    and index.
Identifiers: LCCN 2017003659 | ISBN 9780231174763 (cloth : alk. paper) |
    ISBN 9780231174770 (pbk. : alk. paper) | ISBN 9780231544894 (e-book)
Subjects: LCSH: Terrorism.
Classification: LCC HV6431 .H626 2017 | DDC 363.325—dc23
LC record available at https://lccn.loc.gov/2017003659

Columbia University Press books are printed on permanent
    and durable acid-free paper.
Printed in the United States of America

Cover design: Lisa Hamm
Cover images (*clockwise from the upper-left corner*): From the author's
    collection (1–3); Anky/Shutterstock.com (4); Shutterstock.com (5);
    Nate Derrick/Shutterstock.com (6); Shutterstock.com (7)

For my children—M, N, S, and A

Contents

Preface to the Third Edition

Twenty years ago, I set out to write a book on terrorism that would fill what I believed was a serious gap in the literature. At the time, there was no single work that addressed this increasingly vexatious issue of domestic and international security in an authoritative, yet accessible, way. My intention had been to produce a book that would appeal to student and scholar alike, and to general as well as more specialized audiences. That *Inside Terrorism* has remained in print ever since and indeed is still required reading in undergraduate, graduate, executive education, and other professional intelligence, military, and law enforcement courses taught throughout the world, clearly attests both to the book's continued relevance as well as to its enduring contribution to the field.

Persons familiar with the first edition will recall its main thesis that the nature and character of terrorism was changing. New adversaries with different rationales and often transcendent motivations had emerged to challenge the conventional wisdom about terrorists and terrorism. We were therefore at the dawn of a new era of terrorist violence, I had argued—one that would likely be even bloodier and more destructive than before.

The attacks on September 11, 2001, clearly validated that conclusion, and also created the need for a revised and updated edition of *Inside Terrorism*, which was published five years later. Today, a variety of new developments—the rise of the Islamic State in Iraq and Syria (ISIS, also known as ISIL, or Daesh); the use of social media for terrorist recruitment and the availability of encrypted applications for operational planning and communications; the large number of Salafi-Jihadi foreign volunteers fighting in Syria and Iraq, Yemen and Libya, and Mali and Afghanistan, among other places; as well as the proliferation of increasingly violently inclined homegrown extremists and lone wolf terrorists—have again necessitated a new edition with all the additional information and fresh insight and analysis that may be found throughout this thoroughly amended and revamped volume.

This latest iteration of *Inside Terrorism* may be read as the third of a succession of treatises that have charted terrorism's evolution and growth from its ancient origins to the end of the Cold War (the first edition, published in 1998); from the epochal September 11 attacks through the wars in Afghanistan and Iraq (the second edition published in 2006); and now to ISIS's sanguinary emergence, al-Qaeda's patient rebuilding, and the seemingly unmitigated litany of heinous beheadings, mass annihilations, and alarming urban assaults that have convulsed Paris and Brussels, Baghdad and Berlin, San Bernardino and Orlando, and Nice and Istanbul.

Yet another installment of *Inside Terrorism*, however, also sadly reflects the intractability of this timeless phenomenon and, in turn, the immense interest among students, scholars, government officials, and the general public to better understand why this violence occurs and how it can be stopped. These same questions have both preoccupied and perplexed me throughout a professional career spent studying these issues that now exceeds four decades. I would therefore be remiss not to acknowledge the help and assistance from the many persons and institutions that have facilitated, supported, and encouraged my intellectual inquiries into this subject.

For the past dozen years, I have been extremely fortunate to teach at Georgetown University's world-renowned Security Studies Program, one of eight master's-level programs in that university's School of Foreign Service. From my time as an adjunct professor to my appointment as a tenured full professor, and indeed for the past seven years as the program's director, my own knowledge and understanding of terrorists and terrorism has been appreciably enhanced by both my colleagues and the hundreds of students I have taught in SEST-500 Theory and Practice of Security, SEST-546 Terrorism and Counterterrorism, and SEST-520 Insurgency and Counterinsurgency. For their tremendous friendship and support, I would like to thank Jeffrey Anderson, Elizabeth Arsenault, Jacques Berlinerblau, Daniel Byman, Christine Fair, the late Carol Lancaster, Robert Lieber, David Maxwell, Tom McNaugher, Elizabeth Stanley, and James Reardon-Anderson. It is a special pleasure as well to acknowledge the superb research assistance in the preparation of this book provided by Joseph Bernard, Jenny Abarbanel, Sarah Maksoud, Natalia Peña, Siobhan Steel, and Christopher Wall.

Since 2003, I have also had the privilege of being the George H. Gilmore Senior Fellow at the U.S. Military Academy's Combating Terrorism Center (CTC) in West Point, New York. The CTC's mission is to ensure that future U.S. Army officers are thoroughly knowledgeable about the theory and practice of terrorism and counterterrorism, as well as insurgency and counterinsurgency. I am continually humbled and honored by the opportunity to teach, and indeed learn, from these outstanding young men and women who go from class to serve on the front lines of a war on terrorism that shows no signs of abating. I should therefore like to thank the Gilmore family for their generous support of the fellowship billet I proudly occupy and the succession of CTC executive directors and social sciences department chairs with whom I have worked: Reid Sawyer, Kip McCormick, Joe Felter, Liam Collins, and Bryan Price, as well as Russell Howard, Michael Meese, Cindy Jebb, and Suzanne Nielsen.

Nearly a quarter of a century ago, Professor Paul Wilkinson and I cofounded the Centre for the Study of Terrorism and Political Violence (CSTPV) in the School of International Relations at St. Andrews University, Scotland. That this paragon of scholarship and teaching has flourished to become the world's leading academic institution for the rigorous, objective study of terrorism is a fitting tribute to Paul and a source of great pride and satisfaction for me. Accordingly, I value all the more my continuing relationship with St. Andrews and the CSTPV as a part-time, visiting professor of terrorism studies. I would therefore like to thank Timothy Wilson, the current interim director, and Richard English, the former director, for their continued friendship and support; Nick Rengger and Anthony Lang, the former and current heads of the School of International Relations; Louise Richardson, the previous principal and vice-chancellor; and, as always, my beloved friend of many decades, Alison Watson.

I have also benefited enormously from my interactions with colleagues and students associated with both the master's degree and executive education programs at the Interdisciplinary Center's International Institute for Counter-Terrorism in Herzliya, Israel, where I am also a visiting professor. I would like to thank Boaz Ganor, Eitan Azani, Stevie Weinberg, Orit Shamash-Wieksza, and especially Assaf Moghadam for including me in their efforts to improve our knowledge of terrorism and the means with which to most effectively counter it.

Finally, completion of this revised edition of *Inside Terrorism* would not have been possible without the time I was able to spend on sabbatical during fall semester 2016 as the William F. Podlich Distinguished Fellow at Claremont McKenna College (CMC) in Claremont, California. I am thus very grateful to Hiram Chodosh, CMC's president; Peter Uvin, vice president and dean of faculty; Shana Levin, associate dean of faculty for research and her predecessor, Ronald Riggio; and, Andrew Busch and William Ascher of the Government Department, for inviting me to Claremont and welcoming me into the CMC community. I was very lucky to be assigned an office on the second floor of CMC's stunning Kravis Center building, where I benefited greatly from the many discussions with, and friendship of, Gary Gilbert, Alex Rajczi, and George Thomas, as well as Robert von Hallberg. My greatest debt, however, is to my old friend of nearly thirty years, Jenny Taw, also of CMC's Government Department, who did everything she could to ensure me this extraordinarily happy and productive respite in southern California.

Various other friends, former students, and colleagues have contributed to this new edition in ways that they may not be aware of. Foremost among them are Robert Art, Peter Bergen, David Brannan, Peter Chalk, Mark Cochrane, Dan Darling, Daveed Gartenstein-Ross, John Gannon, Mary Habeck, Seth Jones, Jytte Klausen, Robert Litwak, Ellen McHugh, Peter Neumann, Ami Pedahzur, Arie Perliger, Dennis Pluchinsky, Michael Rainsborough, Fernando Reinares, William Rose, Anders Strindberg, and Amy Sturm. Their insights, and especially their friendship, have immeasurably enhanced both my work and my life.

Nearly twenty years ago, Walter Laqueur, one of the founding fathers of terrorism studies, was kind enough to write an endorsement for the first edition of *Inside Terrorism*. When I subsequently moved to Washington, D.C., he and his lovely wife, Susi, were among the first to welcome us. Since that time, they have become cherished friends and mentors. And, needless to say, my many discussions with Walter about terrorism and counterterrorism have enormously influenced and strengthened this book.

It is also incumbent upon me to acknowledge an entirely different set of people without whom this work would not have been possible. Sincere thanks are therefore due to Andrew Umhau, John Gualtieri, Bruce Kressel, Assil Saleh, and Hisham Barakat.

I have benefited from what is now a decades-long professional association with Taylor and Francis Publishers in my role as editor in chief of the premier scholarly journal in the field, *Studies in Conflict and Terrorism*. I would like to thank Claire Cusak, Lauren Jackson, and Taylor and Francis, not least, of course, for permission to adapt some material for this book from articles I had previously written that first appeared in *Studies in Conflict and Terrorism*.

This new edition of *Inside Terrorism* would not have been possible without the tremendous interest and enthusiastic support of my editor at Columbia University Press, Anne Routon. She and I had a truly unique working relationship for the past fifteen years, where Anne was variously muse, tireless exponent, and bureaucratic slayer par excellence. Together, we created the thriving series on terrorism and irregular warfare—to which this book is the latest addition—and a succession of authors, like myself, could always be absolutely confident that we were in the best possible hands with so extraordinarily attentive and effective an editor as Anne. My sadness at her departure from the press is only somewhat compensated by the fact that the third edition of *Inside Terrorism* was among Anne's last projects at Columbia. My gratitude to you, Anne, is incalculable.

I am similarly indebted to Sean Magee, who has been my trusted editor, valued counselor, and cherished friend for more than three decades. Sean first persuaded me of the need for a book like *Inside Terrorism* over lunch on a dreary autumn day in Scotland twenty-one years ago and later gave it this memorable name. He epitomizes the rare good fortune and happy fate that bonds author to editor and seamlessly combines work with pleasure.

I was very fortunate to have Sue Sakai copyedit the manuscript. Her sharp eye and stylistic adjustments appreciably improved this edition. Thanks to both Erin Davis and Kathryn Jorge for their patience and attention to detail in overseeing the manuscript through publication. Miriam Grossman was an enthusiastic supporter of this third edition from the start and, as always, provided superb support and advice throughout the entire publication process.

Finally, for most authors, our successes and accomplishments are often entirely predicated on the love, support, patience, and equanimity of our spouses and children. It is no different for me. Indeed, my wife, as always, deserves special praise for her good humor and fortitude despite the mood swings and vicissitudes inherent to writing. When all is going well, there are few pursuits more satisfying and rewarding than the melding of research with prose. But when that process goes temporarily awry, pity those in close proximity to the frustrated writer. My wife, however, has always been there to offer endless assurance, comfort, and encouragement. And for all that, I remain deeply and eternally grateful. The same is true of my children, whose lifelong memories of their father I fear are of too much time spent reading, writing, researching, and traveling and too little time spent at home with them. This edition, very appropriately, is therefore for them—with all the love and gratitude possible from an ever doting and devoted father.

BRUCE HOFFMAN
Washington, D.C.
March 2017

Inside Terrorism

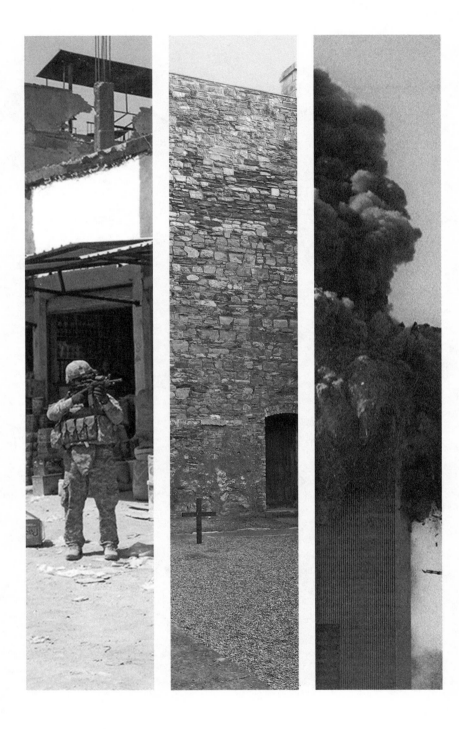

Chapter 1

Defining Terrorism

What is terrorism? Few words have so insidiously worked their way into our everyday vocabulary. Like "social media"—another grossly overused term that has similarly become an indispensable part of the argot of the early twenty-first century—most people have a vague idea or impression of what terrorism is, but lack a more precise, concrete, and truly explanatory definition of the word. This imprecision has been abetted partly by the modern media, whose efforts to communicate an often complex and convoluted message in the briefest amount of airtime or print or online space possible have led to the promiscuous labeling of a range of violent acts as "terrorism." Upon picking up a newspaper, accessing a website, or turning on the radio or television—even within the same broadcast or on the same page—one can find such disparate acts as the bombing of a building, the assassination of a head of state, the massacre of civilians by a military unit, the poisoning of produce on supermarket shelves, or the hacking of a Hollywood studio's e-mail server and public exposure of its employees' personal data, all described as incidents of terrorism.[1] Indeed, virtually any especially abhorrent act of violence perceived as directed against society—whether it involves the activities of antigovernment dissidents or governments themselves, organized-crime syndicates, common criminals, rioting mobs, people engaged in militant protest, individual psychotics, or lone extortionists—is often labeled "terrorism."

Dictionary definitions offer little help. The preeminent authority on the English language, the much-venerated *Oxford English Dictionary* (*OED*), is disappointingly unobliging when it comes to providing edification on this subject, its interpretation at once too literal and too historical to be of much contemporary use:

> **Terrorism**: A system of terror. 1. Government by intimidation as directed and carried out by the party in power in France during the revolution of 1789–94; the system of "Terror." 2. *gen.* A policy intended to strike with terror those against whom it is adopted; the employment of methods of intimidation; the fact of terrorizing or condition of being terrorized.[2]

These definitions are wholly unsatisfying. In the first instance, rather than learning what terrorism is, one instead finds a somewhat pedestrian historical description, and with respect to the modern accepted usage of the term, one that is uselessly anachronistic. The second definition offered is only slightly more helpful. While accurately communicating the fear-inducing quality of terrorism, the definition is still so broad as to apply to almost any action that scares ("terrorizes") us. Though an integral part of "terrorism," this definition is still insufficient for the purpose of accurately defining the phenomenon that is today called "terrorism."

A slightly more satisfying elucidation may be found in the *OED*'s definition of the perpetrator of the act than in its efforts to come to grips with the act itself. In this respect, a "terrorist" is defined thus:

> 1. As a political term: a. Applied to the Jacobins and their agents and partisans in the French Revolution, esp. to those connected with the Revolutionary tribunals during the "Reign of Terror," b. Any one who attempts to further his views by a system of coercive intimidation; *spec*, applied to members of one of the extreme revolutionary societies in Russia.[3]

This is appreciably more helpful. First, it immediately introduces the reader to the notion of terrorism as a *political* concept. As will be seen, this key characteristic of terrorism is absolutely paramount to understanding its aims, motivations, and purposes, and is critical in distinguishing it from other types of violence.

Terrorism, in the most widely accepted contemporary usage of the term, is fundamentally and inherently political. It is also ineluctably about power: the pursuit of power, the acquisition of power, and the use of power to achieve political change. Terrorism is thus violence—or, equally important, the threat of violence—used and directed in pursuit of, or in service of, a political aim. With this vital point clearly illuminated, one can appreciate the significance of the additional definition of "terrorist" provided by the *OED*: "Any one who attempts to further his views by a system of coercive intimidation." This point is especially noteworthy since it underscores clearly the other fundamental characteristic of terrorism: that it is a planned, calculated, and indeed systematic act. Finally, implicit in the *OED*'s definition is the long-standing, normative understanding of terrorism as a phenomenon of political violence perpetrated by individuals (e.g., "any one who attempts . . ." rather than "any government" or "any state that attempts . . .") belonging to an organization or ideological movement dedicated to revolutionary change—change that they fervently believed can only be effected through violence or the threat of violence (e.g., coercive intimidation).

Given this relatively straightforward elucidation, why, then, is terrorism so difficult to define? The most compelling reason perhaps is because the meaning of the term has changed so frequently over the past two hundred-plus years.[4]

The Changing Meaning of Terrorism

The word "terrorism" was first popularized during the French Revolution. In contrast to its contemporary usage, at that time terrorism had a decidedly *positive* connotation. The system, or *régime de la terreur*, of 1793–1794—from which the English word came—was adopted as a means to establish order during the transient anarchical period of turmoil and upheaval that followed the uprisings of 1789, and indeed many other subsequent revolutions. Hence, unlike the term "terrorism" as it is commonly understood today, meaning a *revolutionary* or antigovernment activity undertaken by nonstate or subnational entities, the *régime de la terreur* was an instrument of governance wielded by the recently established revolutionary *state*. It was designed to consolidate the new government's power by intimidating counterrevolutionaries, subversives, and all other dissidents whom the new regime regarded as "enemies of the people." The Committee of General Security and the Revolutionary Tribunal ("People's Court" in the modern vernacular) were thus accorded wide powers of arrest and judgment, publicly putting to death by guillotine those convicted of treasonous (i.e., reactionary) crimes. In this manner, a powerful lesson was conveyed to any and all who might oppose the revolution or grow nostalgic for the ancien régime.

Ironically, perhaps, terrorism in its original context was also closely associated with the ideals of virtue and democracy. The revolutionary leader Maximilien Robespierre firmly believed that virtue was the mainspring of a popular government at peace, but that during the time of revolution virtue must be allied with terror for democracy to triumph. He appealed famously to "virtue, without which terror is evil; terror, without which virtue is helpless" and proclaimed: "Terror is nothing but justice, prompt, severe and inflexible; it is therefore an emanation of virtue."[5]

Despite this divergence from its subsequent meaning, the French Revolution's "terrorism" still shared at least two key characteristics with its modern-day variant. First, the *régime de la terreur* was neither random nor indiscriminate, as terrorism is often portrayed today, but was organized, deliberate, and systematic. Second, its goal and its very justification—like that of contemporary terrorism—was the creation of a "new and better society" in place of a fundamentally corrupt and undemocratic political system. Indeed, Robespierre's vague and utopian exegeses of the revolution's central goals are remarkably similar in tone and content to the equally turgid, millenarian manifestos issued by many revolutionary—primarily left-wing, Marxist-oriented—terrorist organizations during the latter decades of the twentieth century. For example, in 1794 Robespierre declared, in language eerily presaging the communiqués issued by groups such as Germany's Red Army Faction and Italy's Red Brigades nearly two centuries later: "We want an order of things . . . in which the arts are an adornment to the liberty that ennobles them, and commerce the source of wealth for the public and not of monstrous opulence for a few families. . . . In our country we desire morality instead of selfishness, honesty and not mere 'honor,' principle and not mere custom, duty and not mere propriety, the sway of reason rather than the tyranny of fashion, a scorn for vice and not a contempt for the unfortunate."[6]

Like many other revolutions, the French Revolution eventually began to consume itself. On 8 Thermidor, year two of the new calendar adopted by the revolutionaries (July 26, 1794), Robespierre announced to the National Convention that he had in his possession a new list of traitors. Fearing that their own names might be on that list, extremists joined forces with moderates to repudiate both Robespierre and his *régime de la terreur.* Robespierre and his closest followers themselves met the same fate that had befallen some forty thousand others: execution by guillotine. The Terror was at an end; thereafter, "terrorism" became a term associated with the abuse of office and power—with overt "criminal" implications.[7] Within a year of Robespierre's demise, the word had been popularized in English by Edmund Burke, who, in his famous polemic against the French Revolution, described the "Thousands of those Hell hounds called Terrorists . . . let loose on the people."[8]

One of the French Revolution's more enduring repercussions was the impetus it gave to antimonarchical sentiment elsewhere in Europe. Popular subservience to rulers who derived their authority from God through divine right of rule rather than from their subjects was increasingly questioned by a politically awakened Continent. The advent of nationalism, and with it notions of statehood and citizenship based on the common identity of a people rather than the lineage of a royal family, were resulting in the unification and creation of new nation-states such as Germany and Italy. Meanwhile, the massive socioeconomic changes engendered by the Industrial Revolution were creating new universalist ideologies (such as communism/Marxism), born of the alienation and exploitative conditions of nineteenth-century capitalism. From this milieu a new era of terrorism emerged, in which the concept had gained many of the familiar revolutionary, antistate connotations that it holds today. Its chief progenitor was arguably the Italian republican extremist Carlo Pisacane, who had forsaken his birthright as duke of San Giovanni only to perish in 1857 during an ill-fated revolt against Bourbon rule. A passionate advocate of federalism and mutualism, Pisacane is remembered less on this account than for the theory of "propaganda by deed,"[9] which he is credited with defining—an idea that has exerted a compelling influence on rebels and terrorists alike ever since. "The propaganda of the idea is a chimera," Pisacane wrote. "Ideas result from deeds, not the latter from the former, and the people will not be free when they are educated, but educated when they are free."[10] Violence, he argued, was necessary not only to draw attention to or generate publicity for a cause, but also to inform, educate, and ultimately, rally the masses behind the revolution. The didactic purpose of violence, Pisacane argued, could never be effectively replaced by pamphlets, wall posters, or assemblies.

Perhaps the first organization to put into practice Pisacane's dictum was the Narodnaya Volya, or People's Will (sometimes translated as "People's Freedom"), a small group of Russian constitutionalists that had been founded in 1878 to challenge czarist rule. For the Narodnaya Volya, the apathy and alienation of the Russian masses afforded few alternatives besides resorting to daring and dramatic acts of violence designed to attract attention to the group and its cause. However, unlike the many contemporary terrorist organizations that have cited the principle of "propaganda by deed" to justify the wanton targeting of civilians to assure them publicity through the shock and horror produced by wholesale bloodshed, the Narodnaya Volya displayed an almost quixotic attitude toward the violence it wrought. To this group, "propaganda by deed" meant the selective targeting of specific individuals whom the group considered the embodiment of the autocratic, oppressive state.[11] Hence, the victims—the czar, leading members of the royal family, senior government officials—were deliberately chosen for their "symbolic" value as the dynastic heads and subservient agents of a corrupt and tyrannical regime. An intrinsic element in the group's collective beliefs was that "not one drop of superfluous blood" should be shed in pursuit of aims, however noble or utilitarian they might be.[12] Even having selected their targets with great care and the utmost deliberation, group members still harbored profound regrets about taking the life of a fellow human being. Their unswerving adherence to this principle is perhaps best illustrated by the failed attempt on the life of Grand Duke Sergei Alexandrovich made by a successor organization to the Narodnaya Volya in 1905. As the royal carriage came into view, the terrorist tasked with the assassination saw that the grand duke was unexpectedly accompanied by his children and therefore aborted his mission rather than risk harming the intended victim's family. The grand duke was killed in a subsequent attack. By comparison, the midair explosion caused by a terrorist bomb on Pan Am Flight 103 over Lockerbie, Scotland, in December 1988 indiscriminately claimed the lives of all 259 people on board—innocent men, women, and children alike—plus 11 inhabitants of the village where the plane crashed.

Ironically, the Narodnaya Volya's most dramatic accomplishment also led directly to its demise. On March 1, 1881, the group assassinated Czar Alexander II.[13] The failure of eight previous plots had led the conspirators to take extraordinary measures to ensure the success of this attempt. Four volunteers were given four bombs each and deployed along the alternative routes followed by the czar's cortege. As two of the bomber-assassins stood in wait on the same street, the sleighs carrying the czar and his Cossack escort approached the first terrorist, who hurled his bomb at the passing sleigh, missing it by inches. The whole entourage came to a halt as soldiers seized the hapless culprit and the czar descended from his sleigh to check on a bystander wounded by the explosion. "Thank God, I am safe," the czar reportedly declared—just as the second bomber emerged from the crowd and—presaging today's suicide terrorists, whose own deaths are intrinsic to the success of their attacks—detonated his weapon, killing both himself and his target. The full weight of the czarist state now fell on the heads of the Narodnaya Volya. Acting on information provided by the arrested member, the secret police swept down on the group's safe houses and hideouts, rounding up most of the plotters, who were quickly tried, convicted, and hanged. Further information from this group led to subsequent arrests, so that within a year of the assassination, only one member of the original executive committee was still at large. She, too, was finally apprehended in 1883, at which point the first generation of Narodnaya Volya terrorists ceased to exist, although various successor organizations subsequently emerged to carry on the struggle.[14]

At the time, the repercussions of the czar's assassination could not have been known or appreciated by either the condemned or their comrades languishing in prison or exiled to Siberia. But in addition to precipitating the beginning of the end of czarist rule, the group also deeply influenced individual revolutionaries and subversive organizations elsewhere. To the nascent anarchist movement, the "propaganda by deed" strategy championed by the Narodnaya Volya provided a model to be emulated.[15] Within four months of the czar's murder, a group of radicals in London convened an "anarchist conference," which publicly applauded the assassination and extolled tyrannicide as a means to achieve revolutionary change. In hopes of encouraging and coordinating worldwide anarchist activities, the conferees decided to establish the Anarchist International (or Black International). Although this idea, like most of their ambitious plans, came to naught, the publicity generated by even a putative Anarchist International was sufficient to create a myth of global revolutionary pretensions and thereby stimulate fears and suspicions disproportionate to its actual impact or political achievements. Disparate and uncoordinated though the anarchists' violence was, the movement's emphasis on individual action or operations carried out by small cells of like-minded radicals made detection and prevention by the police particularly difficult, thus further heightening public fears—a precursor of the "lone wolf" phenomenon and leaderless resistance and leaderless jihad strategies pursued by many terrorist movements today. For example, following the assassination of U.S. president William McKinley in 1901 by Leon Czolgosz, who, while not a regular member of any anarchist organization, was nonetheless influenced by the philosophy, Congress swiftly enacted legislation barring known anarchists or anyone "who disbelieves in or is opposed to all organized government" from entering the United States. And, over a century before Edward Snowden's revelations of the U.S. National Security Agency's (NSA) mass surveillance and data mining of international telephone calls, text messages, and e-mails, the legendary Pinkerton National Detective Agency advocated that anarchists, suspected anarchists, and other known "Reds" "should all be marked and kept under constant surveillance and on the slightest excuse be made harmless."[16]

However, while anarchists were responsible for an impressive string of assassinations of heads of state and a number of particularly notorious bombings from about 1878 until the second decade of the twentieth century,[17] in the final analysis, other than stimulating often exaggerated fears, anarchism made little tangible impact on either the domestic or the international politics of the countries affected. It does, however, offer an interesting historical parallel to the information revolution that today has made the means and methods of bomb making and other types of terrorist activity more readily available electronically, especially through digital copies of terrorist online magazines such as al-Qaeda in the Arabian Peninsula's (AQAP) *Inspire* publication and *Dabiq*, produced by the terrorist movement known variously as the Islamic State (IS), the Islamic State in Iraq and Syria (ISIS), the Islamic State in Iraq and the Levant (ISIL), or simply by its Arabic acronym, Daesh. Indeed, more than a century ago, one of anarchism's flourishing cottage industries was the widespread printing and distribution of similar sorts of "how-to" or "do-it-yourself" hard-copy manuals and pamphlets on violence and mayhem.[18]

Meanwhile, another series of developments was unfolding on the other side of Europe that would exert a similarly profound influence on future terrorist strategy and tactics. In this instance, the motivation was neither antimonarchical nor anarchist, but nationalist and separatist. Although Britain's rule of Ireland already had a centuries-long history of restiveness and rebellion, in the mid-nineteenth century the locus of revolutionary activities had expanded from Ireland to include the United States as well. Among the mass of Irish emigrants who had fled the failure of successive potato crops and the resultant famine was a group of radical nationalists who in 1858 founded a secret society called the Fenian Brotherhood. The Fenians—and their Ireland-based offshoot, the Irish Revolutionary Brotherhood (IRB)—were at once as daring and determined as they were impatient and incompetent. Their motto "revolution sooner or never"[19] accurately describes a string of half-baked plots that purported to kidnap the Prince of Wales,[20] invade Canada, and orchestrate a popular uprising in Ireland. So successful were British efforts to penetrate the organization, and so abject were the Fenians' failed grand schemes, that the movement fell into desuetude within a decade of its founding.[21] But the Fenians' unswerving commitment to both Irish republicanism and the use of violence to attain it created a legacy that subsequently inspired successive generations of Irish revolutionaries.[22]

Thus, by 1873 a new organization, calling itself the Clan na Gael (United Irishmen), had taken up the Fenians' mantle. Its driving force was a firebrand named Jeremiah O'Donovan Rossa. Sentenced to life imprisonment for sedition in 1865, O'Donovan Rossa was released only six years later after a commission of inquiry substantiated his claims of mistreatment. The abuse inflicted on imprisoned terrorists such as O'Donovan Rossa in the nineteenth century actually bears a disquieting resemblance to the treatment meted out to detainees during the United States' own war on terrorism following the September 11, 2001, attacks.[23] As punishment, O'Donovan Rossa was stripped naked and kept in a dark cell where he subsisted on a meager ration of bread and water.[24] Exiled to the United States, O'Donovan Rossa quickly resumed his subversive activities. He was assisted in these endeavors by Patrick Ford, the editor of the *Irish World*, a newspaper that became the main platform for Clan na Gael propaganda and incitement. Together, they developed a new strategy for the republican movement. "We are not now advising a general insurrection," Ford explained in a December 4, 1875, column. "On the contrary, we should oppose a general insurrection in Ireland as untimely and ill advised. But we believe in action nonetheless. The Irish cause requires Skirmishers. It requires a little band of heroes who will initiate and keep up without intermission a guerrilla warfare."

In words that accurately presaged the advent of a form of transnational terrorism that has become a permanent fixture of our time, Ford also described how these "Skirmishers" would "fly over land and sea like invisible beings—now striking the enemy in Ireland, now in India, now in England itself as occasion may present."[25]

O'Donovan Rossa and Ford displayed an uncommon understanding of the terrorist dynamic that went beyond even this early recognition of the media's power to communicate and amplify a violent message. Remarkably, both men grasped that just as money lubricates commerce, a solid financial base is required to sustain an effective terrorism campaign. It was thus not long before advertisements began to appear in the *Irish World* soliciting contributions on behalf of a "skirmisher fund."[26] By March 1877, $23,350 had been collected—a sum equivalent to over half a million dollars in 2016.[27] O'Donovan Rossa appears to have also fully appreciated terrorism's asymmetric virtues with regard to the disproportionate economic losses and damage that could be inflicted on the enemy state and the flood of contributions that a series of successful attacks might engender. "England," he explained in the *Irish World*, "will not know how or where she is to be struck. A successful strike that will do her half a million dollars' worth of damage will bring us enough funds to carry on the work."[28]

Four years later, the Skirmishers commenced operations. On January 14, 1881, they bombed the Salford Infantry Barracks in Manchester. Their choice of target reflected yet another now-familiar pattern of contemporary terrorism: attacks on buildings or other inanimate objects designed to commemorate, and thereby draw attention to, some event of historic significance to the perpetrators. In this instance, the Salford Barracks was where three Fenians—the so-called Manchester Martyrs—had been hanged in 1867. Up until this point, the Irish terrorists seem to have differed only slightly from their Russian counterparts. Both attacked targets symbolizing their enemy—inanimate objects in the case of the Skirmishers and representatives of the czar by the Narodnaya Volya. Both also believed fervently in terrorism's didactic potential—whether directed toward the landless Irish or the Russian peasant.[29] But two years later, the Irish campaign diverged significantly from the highly discriminate terrorism practiced by the Narodnaya Volya to something both more sinister and consequential. The principal weapons in the Russians' campaign, as we have seen, were the handgun and the nineteenth-century equivalent of the hand grenade, employed in acts of individual assassination deliberately calculated to avoid death or injury to all but their intended target. By comparison, the Skirmishers had already spilled innocent blood: a seven-year-old boy had been killed and three other people were injured in the Salford Barracks blast.[30] Still more innocent blood, however, was soon to be shed.

In 1883, the Clan na Gael and a rebranded IRB, now known as the Irish Republican Brotherhood, formed a tactical alliance and together embarked on a bombing campaign directed against the London Underground and mainline railway stations in both the United Kingdom's capital and other cities.[31] Although the bombers' intention was not to wantonly or deliberately kill or harm innocent persons, but instead to throttle Britain's economy and dramatically call attention to themselves and their cause,[32] their choice of both weapon (homemade bombs consisting of gunpowder detonated by primitive time-delay fuses) and target (locations in congested urban areas and public transportation) ensured that the effects of their operations could be neither constrained nor controlled. And while it is true that these bombings claimed the lives of fewer than a dozen passersby or rail passengers, given that some of the explosive devices contained more than twenty pounds of commercial dynamite, this was more likely the result of luck and happenstance than any effort on the part of the bombers to limit by timing or placement the effect of their attacks.[33]

The "dynamite campaign," as this spasm of Victorian-era urban terrorism came to be known, lasted until 1887.[34] It spread beyond London to Liverpool and Glasgow before collapsing under the weight of intensified police surveillance, heightened border and port control, the effective use of informants, and unprecedented national and even international cooperation and liaison among hitherto entirely parochial law enforcement agencies. Indeed, the advances in police investigative, intelligence, and preemptive operations necessitated by the bombings led that same year to the formal establishment of Scotland Yard's famed Special Branch—the first such police unit dedicated specifically to political crime and counterterrorism.[35] More significant for our purposes, however, is the impact that nineteenth-century Irish political violence had on terrorism's evolution and development. In retrospect, we can see that it was at this time that patterns and modi operandi first appeared that would become standard terrorist operating procedures decades later. The Irish groups, for example, were among the first to recognize the importance of establishing a foreign base beyond the reach of their enemy to better sustain and promote a protracted terrorist campaign. They were also ahead of their time in understanding the value of such a sanctuary not only for planning and logistical purposes but also for the effective dissemination of propaganda and the critical solicitation of operational funds. Their use of time-delayed explosive devices so that the perpetrator could easily effect escape, and thereby ensure the terrorist campaign's sustainment, was another important innovation that became a standard feature of twentieth-century terrorism. Finally, terrorist targeting of mass transport—and especially subway systems—along with an almost callous, if not even casual, disregard of innocent life have now become commonplace. The July 2005 suicide attacks on London's transit system, which killed 52 people and wounded nearly 800 others, and the ten near-simultaneous bombings of commuter trains arriving at Madrid's Atocha rail station in March 2004, which killed 191 people and wounded hundreds more, are especially apposite, and tragic, examples. "At the grand strategic level," Lindsay Clutterbuck cogently notes, the Clan na Gael and IRB's

> ideas enabled terrorism to move away from being a phenomenon consisting of a single event, or at best a loosely connected series of events, and to evolve into sustained campaigns underpinned by their own well-developed sense of timing and tempo. There was a quantum leap beyond the limited aim of assassinating an individual to achieve their objectives and into operational scenarios where terrorism could persist for years and encompass the deaths of thousands of people.[36]

On the eve of World War I, terrorism still retained its revolutionary connotations. By this time, growing unrest and irredentist ferment had already welled up within the decaying Ottoman and Hapsburg empires. In the 1880s and 1890s, for example, militant Armenian nationalist movements in eastern Turkey pursued a terrorist strategy against continued Ottoman rule of a kind that would later be adopted by most of the post–World War II ethnonationalist/separatist movements. The Armenians' objective was simultaneously to strike a blow against a despotic, alien regime through repeated attacks on its colonial administration and security forces to rally indigenous support, and to attract international attention, sympathy, and support.[37]

Around the same time, the Inner Macedonian Revolutionary Organization (IMRO) was active in the region overlapping present-day Greece, Bulgaria, and Serbia.[38] Although the Macedonians did not go on to suffer the catastrophic fate that befell the Armenians during World War I—when an estimated one million people perished in what is considered to be the first officially implemented genocide[39] of the twentieth century—IMRO never came close to achieving its aim of an independent Macedonia and thereafter degenerated into a mostly criminal organization of hired thugs and political assassins.

The events immediately preceding World War I in Bosnia are of course more familiar because of their subsequent cataclysmic impact on world affairs. There, similar groups of disaffected nationalists—intellectuals, university students, and even schoolchildren, collectively known as Mlada Bosna, or Young Bosnia—arose against continued Hapsburg suzerainty. While it is perhaps easy to dismiss the movement, as some historians have, as comprising "frustrated, poor, dreary and maladjusted"[40] adolescents— much as many contemporary observers similarly denigrate modern-day terrorists as mindless, obsessive, and maladjusted—it was a member of Young Bosnia, Gavrilo Princip, who is widely credited with having set in motion the chain of events that began on June 28, 1914, when he assassinated the Hapsburg archduke Franz Ferdinand in Sarajevo, which culminated in World War I. Whatever its superficially juvenile characteristics, the group was nonetheless passionately dedicated to the attainment of a federal South Slav political entity—uniting Slovenes, Croats, and Serbs— and resolutely committed to assassination as the vehicle with which to achieve that aim. In this respect, Young Bosnia perhaps had more in common with the radical republicanism of Giuseppe Mazzini, one of the most ardent exponents of Italian unification in the nineteenth century, than with groups such as the Narodnaya Volya—despite a shared conviction in the efficacy of tyrannicide. An even more significant difference, however, was the degree of involvement in, and external support provided to, Young Bosnia activities by various shadowy Serbian nationalist groups. Principal among these was the pan-Serbian secret society, the Srpska Narodna Obrana (Serbian National Defense).[41]

The Srpska Narodna Obrana had been established in 1908, originally to promote Serbian cultural and national activities. It subsequently assumed a more subversive orientation as the movement became increasingly involved with anti-Austrian activities—including terrorism—mostly in neighboring Bosnia and Herzegovina. Although the Srpska Narodna Obrana's exclusionist pan-Serbian aims clashed with Young Bosnia's less parochial South Slav ideals, its leadership was quite happy to manipulate and exploit the Bosnians' emotive nationalism and youthful zeal for its own purposes. To this end, the Srpska Narodna Obrana actively recruited, trained, and armed young Bosnians and Herzegovinians from movements, such as Young Bosnia, who were then deployed in various seditious activities against the

Hapsburgs. As early as four years before the archduke's assassination, a Herzegovinian youth, trained by a Serbian army officer with close ties to the Srpska Narodna Obrana, had attempted to kill the governor of Bosnia. But while the Srpska Narodna Obrana included among its members senior Serbian government officials, it was not an explicitly government-controlled or directly state-supported entity. Whatever hazy government links it maintained were further and deliberately obscured when a radical faction left the Srpska Narodna Obrana in 1911 and established the Ujedinjenje ili Smrt (the Union of Death, or Death or Unification)—more popularly known as the Crna Ruka, the Black Hand.[42] This more militant and appreciably more clandestine splinter group has been described by one historian as combining

> the more unattractive features of the anarchist cells of earlier years— which had been responsible for quite a number of assassinations in Europe and whose methods had a good deal of influence via the writings of Russian anarchists upon Serbian youth—and of the [American] Ku Klux Klan. There were gory rituals and oaths of loyalty, there were murders of backsliding members, there was identification of members by number, there were distributions of guns and bombs. And there was a steady traffic between Bosnia and Serbia.[43]

Although ostensibly a secret society, like many contemporary terrorist groups the Black Hand also cultivated a public persona in the form of a highly stylized and evocative logo and recognizable insignia. In this respect, it was unique in embracing the entire panoply of terrorism's symbolic accoutrements: evidencing a skull and crossbones surrounded by a knife, a phial of poison, and a bomb.[44]

This group, which continued to maintain close links with its parent body, was largely composed of Serbian military officers. It was led by Lieutenant Colonel Dragutin Dmitrievich (known by his pseudonym, Apis), himself the chief of the Intelligence Department of the Serbian general staff.[45] With this key additional advantage of direct access to military armaments, intelligence, and training facilities, the Black Hand effectively took charge of all Serb-backed clandestine operations in Bosnia.[46]

Although there were obviously close links between the Serbian military, the Black Hand, and Young Bosnia, it would be a mistake to regard the relationship as one of direct control, much less outright manipulation. Clearly, the Serbian government was well aware of the Black Hand's objectives and the violent means the group employed in pursuit of them; indeed, the Serbian crown prince, Alexander, was one of the group's benefactors.

But this does not mean that the Serbian government was necessarily as committed to war with Austria as the Black Hand's leaders were, or that it was prepared to countenance the group's more extreme plans for fomenting cross-border, anti-Hapsburg terrorism. There is some evidence to suggest that the Black Hand may have been trying to force Austria's hand against Serbia and thereby plunge both countries into war by actively abetting the Young Bosnia plot to assassinate the archduke.[47] Indeed, according to one revisionist account of the events leading up to the murder,[48] even though the pistol used by Princip had been supplied by the Black Hand from a Serbian military armory in Kragujevac, and even though Princip had been trained by the Black Hand in Serbia before being smuggled back across the border for the assassination, at the eleventh hour Dmitrievich had apparently bowed to intense government pressure and tried to stop the assassination. According to this version, Princip and his fellow conspirators would hear nothing of it and stubbornly went ahead with their plans. Contrary to popular assumption, therefore, the archduke's assassination may not have been specifically ordered or even directly sanctioned by the Serbian government.[49] However, the obscure links between high government officials and their senior military commanders and ostensibly independent, transnational terrorist movements, and the tangled web of intrigue, plots, clandestine arms provision and training, intelligence agents, and cross-border sanctuary that these relationships inevitably involved provide a pertinent historical parallel to the contemporary phenomenon known as "state-sponsored" terrorism—that is, the active and often clandestine support, encouragement, and assistance provided by a foreign government to a terrorist group.[50] This nexus was made clearly evident in the Austrian ultimatum delivered to Serbia following the assassination in which the words "terrorism" and "terrorist" appear multiple times.[51]

By the 1930s, the meaning of "terrorism" had changed again. It was now used less to refer to revolutionary movements and violence directed against governments and their leaders and more to describe the practices of mass repression that totalitarian states and their dictatorial leaders employed against their own citizens. Thus, the term regained its former connotations of governmental abuse of power, and it was applied specifically to the authoritarian regimes that had come to power in Fascist Italy, Nazi Germany, and Stalinist Russia. In Germany and Italy, respectively, the accession to office of Hitler and Mussolini had depended in large measure on the "street"—the mobilization and deployment of gangs of brown- or black-shirted thugs to harass and intimidate political opponents and root out other scapegoats for public vilification and further victimization. "Terror? Never," Mussolini insisted, demurely dismissing such intimidation as "simply . . . social hy-giene, taking those individuals out of circulation like a doctor would take out a bacillus."[52] The most sinister dimension of this form of "terror" was that it became an intrinsic component of Fascist and Nazi governance, ex-ecuted at the behest of, and in complete subservience to, the ruling political party of the land—which had arrogated to itself complete, total control of the country and its people. A system of government-sanctioned fear and coercion was thus created whereby political brawls, street fights, and wide-spread persecution of Jews, communists, and other declared "enemies of the state" became the means through which complete and submissive compli-ance was ensured. The totality of party control over, and perversion of, gov-ernment was perhaps most clearly evinced by a speech given by Hermann Göring, the newly appointed Prussian minister of the interior, in 1933. "Fel-low Germans," he declared, "my measures will not be crippled by any judi-cial thinking. My measures will not be crippled by any bureaucracy. Here I don't have to worry about Justice; my mission is only to destroy and exter-minate, nothing more. This struggle will be a struggle against chaos, and such a struggle I shall not conduct with the power of the police. A bourgeois State might have done that. Certainly, I shall use the power of the State and the police to the utmost, my dear Communists, so don't draw any false con-clusions; but the struggle to the death, in which my fist will grasp your necks, I shall lead with those there—the Brown Shirts."[53]

The "Great Terror" that Stalin was shortly to unleash in Russia both resembled and differed from that of the Nazis. On the one hand, drawing inspiration from Hitler's ruthless elimination of his own political oppo-nents, the Russian dictator similarly transformed the political party he led into a servile instrument responsive directly to his personal will, and the state's police and security apparatus into slavish organs of coercion, en-forcement, and repression. But conditions in the Soviet Union of the 1930s bore little resemblance to the turbulent political, social, and economic up-heaval afflicting Germany and Italy during that decade and the previous one. On the other hand, therefore, unlike either the Nazis or the Fascists, who had emerged from the political free-for-alls in their own countries to seize power and then had to struggle to consolidate their rule and retain their unchallenged authority, by the mid-1930s the Russian Communist Party had been firmly entrenched in power for more than a decade. Stalin's purges, in contrast to those of the French Revolution, and even to Russia's own recent experience, were not "launched in time of crisis, or revolution and war . . . [but] in the coldest of cold blood, when Russia had at last reached a comparatively calm and even moderately prosperous condition."[54] Thus, the political purges ordered by Stalin became, in the words of one of his biographers, a "conspiracy to seize total power by terrorist action,"[55] resulting in the death, exile, imprisonment, or forcible impressment of millions.

Certainly, similar forms of state-imposed or state-directed violence and terror against a government's own citizens continue today. The use of death squads (often off-duty or plainclothes security or police officers) in conjunction with blatant intimidation of political opponents, human rights and aid workers, student groups, labor organizers, journalists, and others has been a prominent feature of the right-wing military dictatorships that took power in Argentina, Chile, and Greece during the 1970s, and even of elected governments in El Salvador, Guatemala, Colombia, and Peru during the upheavals that afflicted those countries, particularly in the 1980s. But these state-sanctioned or explicitly ordered acts of *internal* political violence directed mostly against domestic populations—that is, rule by violence and intimidation by those *already* in power against their own citizenry—are generally termed "terror" to distinguish that phenomenon from "terrorism," which is traditionally understood to be violence committed by non-state entities.

Following World War II, in another swing of the pendulum of meaning, "terrorism" regained the revolutionary connotations with which it is most commonly associated today. At that time, the term was used primarily in reference to the violent revolts then being prosecuted by the various indigenous nationalist/anticolonialist groups that emerged in Asia, Africa, and the Middle East during the late 1940s and 1950s to oppose continued European rule. Countries as diverse as Israel, Kenya, Cyprus, and Algeria, for example, owe their independence at least in part to nationalist political movements that employed terrorism against colonial powers. It was also during this period that the appellation "freedom fighters" came into fashion as a result of the political legitimacy that the international community—whose sympathy and support were actively courted by many of these movements—accorded to struggles for national liberation and self-determination. Sympathy and support for the rebels extended to segments of the colonial state's own population as well, creating a need for less judgmental and more politically neutral language than "terrorist" and "terrorism" to describe these revolutionaries and the violence they committed in what were considered justified "wars of liberation."[56] Many newly independent Third World countries and Communist-bloc states in particular also adopted this vernacular, arguing that anyone or any movement that fought against "colonial" oppression, Western domination, or both should not be described as "terrorists" but were properly deemed to be "freedom fighters." This position was perhaps most famously explained by Palestine Liberation Organization (PLO) chairman Yasir Arafat when he addressed the United Nations General Assembly in November 1974. "The difference between the revolutionary and the terrorist," Arafat stated, "lies in the reason for which each fights. For whoever stands by a just cause and fights for the freedom and liberation of his land from the invaders, the settlers and the colonialists, cannot possibly be called terrorist."[57]

During the late 1960s and 1970s, terrorism continued to be viewed within a revolutionary context. However, this usage now expanded to include nationalist and ethnic separatist groups outside a colonial or neocolonial framework as well as radical, entirely ideologically motivated organizations. Disenfranchised or exiled nationalist minorities—such as the PLO, the Quebecois separatist group FLQ (Front de Libération du Québec), the Basque ETA (Euskadita Askatasuna, or Freedom for the Basque Homeland), and even a hitherto unknown South Moluccan irredentist group seeking independence from Indonesia—adopted terrorism as a means to draw attention to themselves and their respective causes, in many instances with the specific aim, like their anticolonial predecessors, of attracting international sympathy and support. Around the same time, various left-wing political extremists—drawn mostly from radical student organizations and Marxist/Leninist/Maoist movements in Western Europe, Latin America, and the United States—began to form terrorist groups opposing American intervention in Vietnam and what they claimed were the irredeemable social and economic inequities of the modern capitalist liberal-democratic state.

Although the revolutionary cum ethnonationalist/separatist and ideological exemplars continue to shape our most basic understanding of the term, it was not long before "terrorism" was being used to denote broader, less distinct phenomena. In the early 1980s, for example, terrorism came to be regarded as a calculated means to destabilize the West as part of a vast global conspiracy. Books such as *The Terror Network* by Claire Sterling propagated the notion to a receptive American presidential administration and similarly susceptible governments elsewhere that the seemingly isolated terrorist incidents perpetrated by disparate groups scattered across the globe were in fact linked elements of a massive clandestine plot, orchestrated by the Kremlin and implemented by its Warsaw Pact client states, to destroy the Free World.[58] By the middle of the decade, however, a series of suicide bombings directed mostly against American diplomatic and military targets in the Middle East was focusing attention on the rising threat of state-sponsored terrorism. Consequently, this phenomenon—whereby various renegade foreign governments such as the regimes in Iran, Iraq, Libya, and Syria became actively involved in sponsoring or commissioning terrorist acts—replaced communist conspiracy theories as the main context within which terrorism was viewed. Terrorism thus became associated with a type of covert or surrogate warfare whereby weaker states could confront larger, more powerful rivals without the risk of retribution.[59]

In the early 1990s, the meaning and usage of the term "terrorism" were further blurred by the emergence of two new buzzwords: "narco-terrorism" and the so-called gray area phenomenon.[60] The former term revived the Moscow-orchestrated terrorism conspiracy theories of previous years while introducing the critical new dimension of narcotics trafficking. Thus, "narco-terrorism" was defined by one of the concept's foremost propagators as the "use of drug trafficking to advance the objectives of certain governments and terrorist organizations"—identified as the "Marxist-Leninist regimes" of the Soviet Union, Cuba, Bulgaria, and Nicaragua, among others.[61] The emphasis on "narco-terrorism" as the latest manifestation of the communist plot to undermine Western society,[62] however, had the unfortunate effect of diverting official attention away from a bona fide emerging trend. To a greater extent than ever in the past, entirely criminal (that is, violent, *economically* motivated) organizations were now forging strategic alliances with terrorist and guerrilla organizations or were themselves employing violence for specifically political ends. The growing power of the Colombian cocaine cartels, their close ties with left-wing terrorist groups in Colombia and Peru, and their repeated attempts to subvert Colombia's electoral process and undermine successive governments constitute perhaps the best-known example of this continuing trend.[63]

Those who drew attention to this "gray area phenomenon" were concerned less with grand conspiracies than with highlighting the increasingly fluid and variable nature of subnational conflict in the post–Cold War era. Accordingly, in the 1990s, "terrorism" began to be subsumed by some analysts within the "gray area phenomenon." Thus, the latter term came to be used to denote "threats to the stability of nation states by non-state actors and non-governmental processes and organizations";[64] to describe violence affecting "immense regions or urban areas where control has shifted from legitimate governments to new half-political, half-criminal powers";[65] or simply to group together in one category the range of conflicts across the world that no longer conformed to traditionally accepted notions of war as fighting between the armed forces of two or more established states, but instead involved irregular forces as one or more of the combatants.[66] Terrorism had shifted its meaning again from an individual phenomenon of subnational violence to one of several elements, or part of a wider pattern, of nonstate conflict.

The terrorist attacks on September 11, 2001, inevitably, redefined "terrorism" yet again. On that day, nineteen terrorists belonging to a group calling itself al-Qaeda (or al-Qa'ida) hijacked four passenger aircraft soon after they took off from airports in Boston, Newark (New Jersey), and Washington, D.C. Two of the planes were then deliberately flown into the Twin Towers of New York City's World Trade Center. Both structures collapsed shortly afterward. A third aircraft similarly smashed into the Pentagon, where the U.S. Department of Defense is located, severely damaging the southwest portion of that building. Meanwhile, passengers on board the fourth aircraft learned of the other attacks and struggled to subdue the hijackers. In the ensuing melee, the plane spun out of control and crashed into a field in rural Pennsylvania. A total of nearly three thousand people were killed in the attacks.[67] To put that death toll in perspective, in the entirety of the twentieth century only thirty-four terrorist incidents had killed more than one hundred people.[68] And until 9/11, no terrorist operation had ever killed more than five hundred people.[69] Among the dead were citizens of some eighty different countries,[70] although the largest number of fatalities by far were U.S. citizens. Indeed, more than twice as many Americans perished on 9/11 than had been killed by terrorists since 1968[71]—the year acknowledged as marking the advent of modern, international terrorism.

Such a massive and consequential terrorist onslaught required nothing less than an equally comprehensive and far-reaching response. "This is a new kind of evil . . . [and we] will rid the world of the evildoers," President George W. Bush promised just days later. "Our nation was horrified," he continued, "but it's not going to be terrorized."[72] Yet when the president addressed a special joint session of the U.S. Congress on September 20, 2001, he repeatedly invoked the word "terror"—that is, the "state of being terrified or greatly frightened," according to the *OED*'s definition[73]—rather than the specifically political phenomenon "terror*ism*." "Our war on terror," the president famously declared, "begins with al-Qaida, but it does not end there."[74] The consequences of his semantic choice, whether deliberate or not, nonetheless proved as portentous as they were significant: heralding a virtually open-ended struggle against anyone and anything that arguably scared or threatened Americans. The range of potential adversaries thus expanded beyond Osama bin Laden, al-Qaeda's leader, and his minions, who, the president explained, "hate us . . . [and] our freedoms,"[75] to include "rogue" states arrayed in an "axis of evil" (e.g., Iraq, Iran, and North Korea)[76] and especially heinous Middle East dictators thought to possess weapons of mass destruction (WMD). As Professor Sir Michael Howard, the world's leading authority on strategy and military history, later reflected, "President Bush's declaration of a 'war on terror' was generally seen abroad as a rhetorical device to alert the American people to the dangers facing them, rather than as a statement to be taken seriously or literally in terms of international law. But further statements and actions by the Bush Administration have made it clear that the President's words were intended to be taken literally."[77]

The implications of this policy were clearly demonstrated by the relationship that the president and his advisers believed existed between al-Qaeda and Saddam Hussein. Although White House suspicions that Iraq was somehow behind 9/11 never completely faded,[78] they were eventually eclipsed by growing concerns about terrorists acquiring WMD from Iraqi stockpiles.[79] Indeed, it was precisely this fear that President Bush cited to justify the March 2003 invasion. The Bush administration's conflation of terrorism and WMD was specifically cited by Richard Dearlove, then head of MI6, Britain's Secret Intelligence Service, in his report to Prime Minister Tony Blair of high-level U.S.–U.K. consultations held in Washington, D.C., seven months before the invasion. "Military action was now seen as inevitable," notes of Dearlove's meeting with the prime minister stated. "Bush wanted to remove Saddam, through military action, justified by the conjunction of terrorism and WMD."[80] The chain of events that began on 9/11 and the declaration of a "war on terror" that thereafter set America on the path to war with Iraq thus prompted Michael Howard again to note how it was evidently "not enough" for Americans

> to be at war with an abstract entity described by their president as "Terror." They need a specific adversary who embodies the spirit of evil against whom national sentiment can be mobilised, as it was mobilised against Hitler in 1941. Osama bin Laden proved too evasive and evanescent a figure to provide the necessary catharsis, but prominent among the usual suspects was Saddam Hussein. There was little evidence to link him with this particular crime, but he was a bad guy, with whom many members of the Bush administration had unfinished business. . . . He was, in short, the most powerful and dangerous figure among the declared enemies of the US, which in itself gave them the right—indeed the duty—to destroy him.[81]

The "war on terror" thus became, in President Bush's infelicitous choice of words, as much a "crusade"[82] against evil as it was an unwavering reaction to the multiplicity of new security threats confronting the nation—and therefore accounts for the way terrorism was redefined in the early twenty-first century, according to Stanford University linguist Geoffrey Nunberg, to "encompass both the dark forces that threaten 'civilization' and the fears they arouse."[83]

Why Is Terrorism So Difficult to Define?

Not surprisingly, as the meaning and usage of the word have changed over time to accommodate the political vernacular and discourse of each successive era, terrorism has proved increasingly elusive in the face of attempts to construct one consistent definition. At one time, the terrorists themselves were far more cooperative in this endeavor than they are today. The early practitioners didn't mince their words or hide behind the semantic camouflage of more anodyne labels such as "freedom fighter" or "urban guerrilla." The nineteenth-century anarchists, for example, unabashedly proclaimed themselves to be terrorists and frankly proclaimed their tactics to be terrorism.[84] The members of Narodnaya Volya similarly displayed no qualms in using these same words to describe themselves and their deeds.[85] Such frankness did not last, however. Although the Jewish terrorist group of the 1940s known as Lehi (the Hebrew acronym for Lohamei Herut Yisrael, the Freedom Fighters for Israel), but more popularly called the Stern Gang after its founder and first leader, Abraham Stern, would admit to its effective use of terrorist tactics, its members never considered themselves to be terrorists.[86] It is significant, however, that although Lehi may have been far more candid than its latter-day counterparts, it nevertheless chose as the name of the organization not Terrorist Fighters for Israel but the far less pejorative Freedom Fighters for Israel. Similarly, although more than twenty years later the Brazilian revolutionary Carlos Marighela displayed little compunction about openly advocating the use of "terrorist" tactics,[87] he still insisted on depicting himself and his disciples as "urban guerrillas" rather than "urban terrorists." Indeed, it is clear from Marighela's writings that he was well aware of the word's undesirable connotations and strove to displace them with positive resonances. "The words 'aggressor' and 'terrorist,'" Marighela wrote in his famous *Handbook of Urban Guerrilla War* (also known as the "Mini-Manual"), "no longer mean what they did. Instead of arousing fear or censure, they are a call to action. To be called an aggressor or a terrorist in Brazil is now an honour to any citizen, for it means that he is fighting, with a gun in his hand, against the monstrosity of the present dictatorship and the suffering it causes."[88]

This trend toward ever more convoluted semantic obfuscations to sidestep terrorism's pejorative overtones has, if anything, become more entrenched in recent decades. Terrorist organizations almost without exception now regularly select names for themselves that consciously eschew the word "terrorism" in any of its forms. Instead, these groups actively seek to evoke images of

- freedom and liberation (e.g., the National Liberation Front, the Popular Front for the Liberation of Palestine, Freedom for the Basque Homeland);
- armies or other military organizational structures (e.g., the National Military Organization, the Popular Liberation Army, the Fifth Battalion of the Liberation Army);
- actual self-defense movements (e.g., the Afrikaner Resistance Movement, the Shankhill Defence Association, the Organization for the Defence of the Free People, the Jewish Defense Organization);
- righteous vengeance (the Organization for the Oppressed on Earth, the Justice Commandos of the Armenian Genocide, the Palestinian Revenge Organization)

—or else deliberately choose names that are decidedly neutral and therefore bereft of all but the most innocuous suggestions or associations (e.g., the Shining Path, Front Line, al-Dawa [the Call], Alfaro Lives—Damn It!, Kach [Thus], al-Gamat al-Islamiya [the Islamic Organization], the Lantaro Youth Movement, and especially al-Qaeda [the Arabic word for the "base of operation"[89] or "foundation"—meaning the base or foundation from which worldwide Islamic revolution can be waged—or, as other translations have it, the "precept" or "method"]).[90] Nowadays, this semantical evasiveness manifests itself in terrorist organizations adopting for themselves the mantle of responsible governance and putative statehood, and in the case of one even more radical al-Qaeda offshoot, styling themselves variously as the Islamic *State* in Iraq, the Islamic *State* in Iraq and Syria (aka the Islamic *State* in Iraq and Levant), or simply as *the* Islamic *State*.

What all these examples suggest is that terrorists clearly do not see or regard themselves as others do. "Above all I am a family man," the archterrorist Carlos "the Jackal" described himself to a French newspaper following his capture in 1994.[91] Similarly, when the infamous KSM—Khalid Sheikh Mohammed, mastermind of the 9/11 attacks whom bin Laden called simply "al Mukhtar" (Arabic for "the chosen one")—was apprehended in March 2003, a photograph of him with his arms around his two young sons was found next to the bed in which he had been sleeping.[92] Cast perpetually on the defensive and forced to take up arms to protect themselves and their real or imagined constituents, terrorists perceive themselves as reluctant warriors, driven by desperation—and lacking any viable alternative—to violence against a repressive state, a predatory rival ethnic or nationalist group, or an unresponsive international order. Bin Laden himself revealed precisely this mind-set when, in a 2002 interview, he explained:

> America has made many accusations against us and many other Muslims around the world. Its charge that we are carrying out acts of terrorism is an unwarranted description. . . . [We act in] self-defense, in defense of our brothers and sons in Palestine, and to liberate our sacred religious sites. If inciting people to do that is terrorism, and if killing those who kill our sons is terrorism, then let history be witness that we are terrorists.[93]

This perceived characteristic of self-denial also distinguishes the terrorist from other types of political extremists as well as from people similarly involved in illegal, violent avocations. A communist or a revolutionary, for example, would likely readily accept and admit that he is in fact a communist or a revolutionary. Indeed, many would doubtless take particular pride in claiming either of those appellations for themselves. Similarly, even a person engaged in illegal, wholly disreputable, or entirely selfish violent activities, such as robbing banks or carrying out contract killings, would probably admit to being a bank robber or a murderer for hire. The terrorist, by contrast, will *never* acknowledge that he is a terrorist, and moreover will go to great lengths to evade and obscure any such inference or connection. Terry Anderson, the American journalist who was held hostage for almost seven years by the Lebanese terrorist organization Hezbollah, relates a telling conversation he had with one of his guards. The guard had objected to a newspaper article that referred to Hezbollah as terrorists. "We are not terrorists," he indignantly stated, "we are fighters." Anderson replied, "Hajj, you are a terrorist, look it up in the dictionary. You are a terrorist, you may not like the word and if you do not like the word, do not do it."[94]

The terrorist will always argue that it is society or the government or the socioeconomic "system" and its laws that are the *real* "terrorists," and moreover that if it were not for this oppression, he would not have felt the need to defend either himself or the population he claims to represent.[95] Another revealing example of this process of obfuscation-projection may be found in the book *Invisible Armies*, written by Sheikh Muhammad Hussein Fadlallah, the spiritual leader of the Lebanese terrorist group responsible for Anderson's kidnapping. "We don't see ourselves as terrorists," Fadlallah explains, "because we don't believe in terrorism. We don't see resisting the occupier as a terrorist action. We see ourselves as *mujihadeen* [holy war-riors] who fight a Holy War for the people."[96] Indeed, Hezbollah's efforts to distance itself entirely from any terrorist associations and appellations have only intensified in the years since it first entered mainstream Lebanese pol-itics.[97] Given its domination of Lebanese politics and the significant role that Hezbollah has played in that country's governance for more than a decade, including exercising effective veto power in the post-2008 national unity government, the group's spokespersons have consistently argued that it is a bona fide political party, cum "resistance movement."[98]

On one point, at least, everyone agrees: "Terrorism" is a pejorative term.[99] It is a word with intrinsically negative connotations that is generally applied to one's enemies and opponents, or to those with whom one disagrees and would otherwise prefer to ignore. "What is called terrorism," Brian Jenkins has written, "thus seems to depend on one's point of view. Use of the term implies a moral judgement; and if one party can successfully attach the label *terrorist* to its opponent, then it has indirectly persuaded others to adopt its moral viewpoint."[100] Hence, the decision to call someone or label some organization "terrorist" becomes almost unavoidably subjective, depending largely on whether one sympathizes with or opposes the person/group/cause concerned. If one identifies with the victim of the violence, for example, then the act is terrorism. If, however, one identifies with the perpetrator, the vio-lent act is regarded in a more sympathetic, if not positive (or, at the worst, ambivalent) light, and it is not terrorism.

The implications of this associational logic were perhaps most clearly demonstrated in the exchanges between Western and non-Western mem-ber states of the United Nations (UN) following the 1972 Munich Olympics massacre, in which eleven Israeli athletes were killed. The debate began with the proposal by the UN secretary-general, Kurt Waldheim, that the UN should not remain a "mute spectator" to the acts of terrorist violence then occurring throughout the world but should take practical steps that might prevent further bloodshed.[101] While a majority of the UN member states supported the secretary-general, a disputatious minority—including many Arab states and various African and Asian countries—derailed the discus-sion, arguing (much as Arafat would do two years later in his own address to the General Assembly) that "people who struggle to liberate themselves from foreign oppression and exploitation have the right to use all methods at their disposal, including force."[102]

The Third World delegates justified their position with two arguments. First, they claimed that all bona fide liberation movements are invariably decried as "terrorists" by the regimes against which their struggles for free-dom are directed. The Nazis, for example, labeled as terrorists the resistance groups opposing Germany's occupation of their lands, the Mauritanian ambassador Moulaye el-Hassen pointed out, just as "all liberation movements are described as terrorists by those who have reduced them to slavery." Therefore, by condemning "terrorism" the UN was endorsing the power of the strong over the weak and of the established entity over its nonestablished challenger—in effect, acting as the defender of the status quo. According to Chen Chu, the deputy representative of the People's Republic of China, the UN thus was proposing to deprive "oppressed nations and peoples" of the only effective weapon they had with which to oppose "imperialism, colonialism, neo-colonialism, racism and Israeli Zionism."[103] Second, the Third World delegates argued forcefully that it is not the violence itself that is germane but its "underlying causes"—that is, the "misery, frustration, grievance and despair"—that produce the violent acts.[104] As the Mauritanian representative again explained, the term "terrorist" could "hardly be held to apply to persons who were denied the most elementary human rights, dignity, freedom and independence, and whose countries objected to foreign occupation."[105] When the issue was again raised the following year, Syria objected on the grounds that "the international community is under legal and moral obligation to promote the struggle for liberation and to resist any attempt to depict this struggle as synonymous with terrorism and illegitimate violence."[106] The resultant definitional paralysis subsequently throttled UN efforts to make any substantive progress on international cooperation against terrorism beyond very specific agreements on individual aspects of the problem (concerning, for example, diplomats and civil aviation).

The opposite approach, in which identification with the victim determines the classification of a violent act as terrorism, is evident in the conclusions of a parliamentary working group of the North Atlantic Treaty Organization (NATO; an organization comprising long-established, status quo Western states). The final report of the 1989 North Atlantic Assembly's Subcommittee on Terrorism states: "Murder, kidnapping, arson and other felonious acts constitute criminal behavior, but many non-Western nations have proved reluctant to condemn as terrorist acts what they consider to be struggles of national liberation."[107] In this reasoning, the defining characteristic of terrorism is the act of violence itself, not the motivations or justification for or reasons behind it. After decades of debate and resistance, the UN itself finally embraced this rationale by adopting the International Convention for the Suppression of Terrorist Bombings. The convention outlawed the unlawful delivery, placement, discharge, or detonation of an "explosive or other lethal device in, into or against a place of public use, a State or government facility, a public transportation system or an infrastructure facility with the intent to cause death or serious bodily injury; or with the intent to cause extensive destruction of such a place, facility or system, where such destruction results in or is likely to result in major economic loss."[108]

This came into force just four months before the 9/11 attacks.[109] Indeed, this approach has long been espoused by analysts such as Jenkins who argue that terrorism should be defined "by the nature of the act, not by the identity of the perpetrators or the nature of their cause."[110] But this is not an entirely satisfactory solution either, since it fails to differentiate clearly between violence perpetrated by states and by nonstate entities, such as terrorists. Accordingly, it plays into the hands of terrorists and their apologists who would argue that there is no difference between the "low-tech" terrorist pipe bomb placed in the rubbish bin at a crowded market that wantonly and indiscriminately kills or maims everyone within a radius measured in tens of feet and the "high-tech" precision-guided ordnance dropped by air force fighter-bombers from a height of twenty thousand feet or more that achieves the same wanton and indiscriminate effects on the crowded marketplace far below. This rationale thus equates the random violence inflicted on enemy population centers by military forces—such as the Luftwaffe's raids on Warsaw and Coventry, the Allied firebombings of Dresden and Tokyo, and the atomic bombs dropped by the United States on Hiroshima and Nagasaki during World War II, and indeed the countervalue strategy of the postwar superpowers' strategic nuclear policy, which deliberately targeted the enemy's civilian population—with the violence committed by substate entities labeled "terrorists," since both involve the infliction of death and injury on noncombatants.[111] Indeed, following the 1972 Munich Olympics massacre, this was precisely the point made during the above-mentioned UN debates by the Cuban representative, who argued that "the methods of combat used by national liberation movements could not be declared illegal while the policy of terrorism unleashed against certain peoples [by the armed forces of established states] was declared legitimate."[112]

It is a familiar argument. Terrorists, as we have seen, deliberately cloak themselves in the terminology of military jargon. They consciously portray themselves as bona fide (freedom) fighters, if not soldiers, who—though they wear no identifying uniform or insignia—are entitled to treatment as prisoners of war (POWs) if captured, and therefore should not be prosecuted as common criminals in ordinary courts of law. Terrorists further argue that because of their numerical inferiority, far more limited firepower, and paucity of resources compared with an established nation-state's massive defense and national security apparatus, they have no choice but to operate clandestinely, emerging from the shadows to carry out dramatic (i.e., bloody and destructive) acts of hit-and-run violence to attract attention to, and ensure publicity for, themselves and their cause. The bomb in the rubbish bin, in their view, is merely a circumstantially imposed "poor man's air force":[113] the only means with which the terrorist can challenge—and get the attention of—the more powerful state. "How else can we bring pressure to bear on the world?" one of Arafat's political aides once inquired. "The deaths are regrettable, but they are a fact of war in which innocents have become involved. They are no more innocent than the Palestinian women and children killed by the Israelis and we are ready to carry the war all over the world."[114]

But rationalizations such as these ignore the fact that although national armed forces have been responsible for far more death and destruction than terrorists might ever aspire to bring about, there is nonetheless a fundamental qualitative difference between the two types of violence. Even in war there are rules and accepted norms of behavior that prohibit the use of certain types of weapons (e.g., hollow-point or "dum-dum" bullets, CS tear gas, and chemical and biological warfare agents) and proscribe various tactics and outlaw attacks on specific categories of targets. Accordingly, in theory, if not always in practice, the rules of war—as observed from the early seventeenth century when they were first proposed by the Dutch jurist Hugo Grotius and subsequently codified in the famous Geneva and Hague Conventions on Warfare of the 1860s, 1899, 1907, and 1949—not only grant civilian noncombatants immunity from attack but also

- prohibit taking civilians as hostages;
- impose regulations governing the treatment of captured or surrendered soldiers (POWs);
- outlaw reprisals against either civilians or POWs;
- recognize neutral territory and the rights of citizens of neutral states; and
- uphold the inviolability of diplomats and other accredited representatives.

Even the most cursory review of terrorist tactics and targets over the past fifty years reveals that terrorists have violated all these rules. They not infrequently have

- taken civilians as hostages, and in some instances then brutally executed them (e.g., the former Italian prime minister Aldo Moro and the German industrialist Hans Martin Schleyer, who, respectively, were taken captive and later murdered by the Red Brigades and the Red Army Faction in the 1970s, Daniel Pearl, a *Wall Street Journal* reporter, and Nicholas Berg, an American businessmen, who were kidnapped by radical Islamist terrorists in Pakistan and Iraq, respectively in 2002 and 2004, and grotesquely beheaded), and, more recently, the American journalists James Foley and Steven Sotloff who suffered the same fate in Syria at the hands of the so-called Islamic State, aka ISIS;

- similarly abused and murdered kidnapped military officers—even when they were serving on UN-sponsored peacekeeping or truce supervisory missions (e.g., the American Marine Lieutenant Colonel William Higgins, the commander of a UN truce-monitoring detachment, who was abducted by Lebanese Shi'a terrorists in 1989 and subsequently hanged);
- undertaken reprisals against wholly innocent civilians, often in countries far removed from the terrorists' ostensible locus of conflict, thus disdaining any concept of neutral states or the rights of citizens of neutral countries (e.g., the brutal 1986 machine-gun and hand-grenade attack on Turkish Jewish worshipers at an Istanbul synagogue carried out by the Palestinian Abu Nidal Organization (ANO) in retaliation for an Israeli raid on a guerrilla base in southern Lebanon); and
- repeatedly attacked embassies and other diplomatic installations (e.g., the bombings of the U.S. embassies in Nairobi and Dar es Salaam in 1998 and in Beirut and Kuwait City in 1983 and 1984, and the mass hostage taking at the Japanese ambassador's residence in Lima, Peru, in 1996–1997), as well as deliberately targeting diplomats and other accredited representatives (e.g., the British ambassador to Uruguay, Sir Geoffrey Jackson, who was kidnapped by leftist terrorists in that country in 1971, and the fifty-two American diplomats taken hostage at the Tehran legation in 1979).

Admittedly, the armed forces of established states have also been guilty of violating some of the same rules of war. However, when these transgressions do occur—when civilians are deliberately and wantonly attacked in war or taken hostage and killed by military forces—the term "war crime" is used to describe such acts and, as imperfect and flawed as both international and national judicial remedies may be, steps nonetheless are often taken to hold the perpetrators accountable for the crimes. By comparison, one of the fundamental raisons d'être of international terrorism is a refusal to be bound by such rules of warfare and codes of conduct. International terrorism disdains any concept of delimited areas of combat or demarcated battlefields, much less respect for neutral territory. Accordingly, terrorists have repeatedly taken their often parochial struggles to other, sometimes geographically distant, third-party countries and there deliberately enmeshed people completely unconnected with the terrorists' cause or grievances in violent incidents designed to generate attention and publicity.

Reporting on terrorism by the news media, which have been drawn into the semantic debates that divided the UN in the 1970s and continue to influence all discourse on terrorism, has further contributed to the obfuscation of the terrorist/"freedom fighter" debate, enshrining imprecision and implication as the lingua franca of political violence in the name of objectivity and neutrality. In striving to avoid appearing either partisan or judgmental, the venerable BBC (British Broadcasting Corporation) effectively bans the use of the word "terrorist" by its editors and reporters—a term it describes as "a barrier rather than an aid to understanding."[115] In the wake of the January 2015 attack on the offices of the French satirical weekly newsmagazine *Charlie Hebdo* by two gunmen professing allegiance to an al-Qaeda affiliate, in which a dozen persons lost their lives, the head of the BBC's Arabic language broadcasting justified this rationale, explaining: "We know what political violence is, we know what murder, bombings and shootings are and we describe them. That's much more revealing than a word like terrorist which people will see as value-laden."[116]

The U.S. media has embraced a similar rationale. It has resorted to describing terrorists—often in the same report—variously as "guerrillas," "gunmen," "raiders," "commandos," and even "soldiers." A random sample of American newspaper reports of Palestinian terrorist activities between June and December 1973, found in the terrorism archives and database formerly maintained by the RAND Corporation,[117] provides striking illustrations of this practice. Out of eight headlines of articles reporting the same incident, six used the word "guerrillas" and only two used "terrorists" to describe the perpetrators. An interesting pattern was also observed: those accounts that immediately followed a particularly horrific or tragic incident—that is, involving the death and injury of innocent people (in this instance, a 1973 attack on a Pan Am airliner at the Rome airport, in which thirty-two passengers were killed)—tended to describe the perpetrators as "terrorists" and their act as "terrorism" (albeit in the headline in one case only, before reverting to the more neutral terminology of "commando," "militants," and "guerrilla attack" in the text) more frequently than did reports of less serious or nonlethal incidents.[118] One *New York Times* editorial, however, was far less restrained than the stories describing the actual incident, describing it as "bloody" and "mindless" and using the words "terrorists" and "terrorism" interchangeably with "guerrillas" and "extremists."[119] Only six months previously, however, the same newspaper had run a story about another terrorist attack that completely eschewed the terms "terrorism" and "terrorist," preferring "guerrillas" and "resistance" (as in "resistance movement") instead.[120] The *Christian Science Monitor*'s reports of the Rome Pan Am attack similarly avoided "terrorists" and "terrorism" in favor of "guerrillas" and "extremists";[121] an Associated Press story in the next day's *Los Angeles Times* also stuck with "guerrillas,"[122] while the two *Washington Post* articles on the same incident opted for the terms "commandos" and "guerrillas."[123]

This slavish devotion to terminological neutrality, which David Rapoport first observed nearly forty years ago,[124] has persisted. A telling illustration of the semantics of terrorism reportage can be found in some of the press coverage of the terrorist violence that afflicted Algeria during the 1990s and claimed the lives of an estimated hundred thousand people. An article appearing in the *International Herald Tribune* (a Paris-based newspaper then published in conjunction with the *New York Times* and the *Washington Post*) reported a 1997 incident in Algeria in which thirty people had been killed by perpetrators who were variously described as "terrorists" in the article's headline, less judgmentally as "extremists" in the lead paragraph, and as the still more ambiguous "Islamic fundamentalists" in the article's third paragraph.[125] In a country where terrorist-inflicted bloodshed was endemic, one might think that the distinctions between "terrorists," mere "extremists," and ordinary "fundamentalists" would be clearer. Equally interesting was the article that appeared on the opposite side of the same page of the newspaper that described the "decades of sporadic *guerrilla* [my emphasis] warfare by the IRA [Irish Republican Army]" in Northern Ireland.[126] Yet fifty years earlier this newspaper apparently had fewer qualms about using the word "terrorists" to describe the two young Jewish men in preindependence Israel who, while awaiting execution after having been convicted of attacking British military targets, committed suicide.[127] Other press accounts of the same period in the *Times* of London and the *Palestine Post* similarly had no difficulties, for example, in describing the 1946 Jewish terrorist bombing of the British military headquarters and government secretariat located in Jerusalem's King David Hotel as a "terrorist" act perpetrated by "terrorists."[128] And, in perhaps the most specific application of the term, the Communist terrorists against whom the British fought in Malaya throughout the late 1940s and 1950s were routinely referred to as "CTs"—for "Communist terrorists." As Rapoport warned in the 1970s, "In attempting to correct the abuse of language for political purposes, our journalists may succeed in making language altogether worthless."[129]

The coverage given by the *Washington Post* and the *New York Times* to the barricade-and-hostage situation that unfolded at a Beslan, North Ossetia, school in September 2004 underscored these continuing semantic ambiguities. Even in the immediate post-9/11 era, few terrorist attacks had evoked quite the horror and revulsion that the fifty-two-hour ordeal and its deliberate targeting of children produced. According to official Russian figures, at least 331 hostages—including more than 172 children—were killed, although many believe the actual numbers to be much higher. Yet the perpetrators, an indisputably cruel and ruthless group of Chechen terrorists, were repeatedly described in far more neutral and anodyne terms by both of the United States' national newspapers of record. The *Washington Post*'s initial report of the seizure and its account of the rescue operations, for example, did not use the words "terrorism" and "terrorists" at all, except in the context of direct quotations or statements made by an aide to Russian president Vladimir Putin, various other Russian official spokespersons, or President Bush himself. Instead, a variety of other adjectives were employed in the two articles sampled, including "guerrillas" (seventeen references), "hostage takers" (eleven), "rebels" (six), "fighters" (three), and "separatists" (two).[130]

The *New York Times*'s reporting and rhetorical choices were not much different. Admittedly, its first article detailing the incident used the word "terrorist" twice, in both instances independently of quotes or statements made by Russian officials. But more inoffensive terms such as "guerrillas" (seventeen references), "fighters" (nine), "insurgents" (six), "rebels" (six), and "hostage takers" (two) predominated in both this story and the report of the siege's grisly denouement.[131] The word "terrorist" again appeared twice in the second piece, but only when quoting Russian president Vladimir Putin and his spokesman.[132] Indeed, the "unrelenting use of such euphemistic language" in the *Washington Post*'s reporting of the Beslan incident prompted one reader to ask in a letter to the editor, "Why can't your editors just identify these people for what they are . . . terrorists?"[133] The *New York Times*'s first public editor, Daniel Okrent, devoted a column to the subject after readers similarly complained about the paper's reluctance to use the words "terrorist," "terrorism," and "terror." His explanation was that the *Times* in fact has no policy governing the use of such words—except to eschew them as much possible.[134]

A decade later, this same unstated policy continues. A 2016 *New York Times* report on airport security breaches, for instance, recalled the infamous hijacking forty-six years earlier of five passenger aircraft by "militants" belonging to the Popular Front for the Liberation of Palestine (PFLP), whose demands, the article explained, included the release of fellow imprisoned "activists."[135] Omitted from the story was how three of the planes were diverted to a disused British Royal Air Force landing strip in Jordan known as Dawson's Field, where their 310 passengers were held hostage. Although most were released two days later, a group of 56 passengers nonetheless remained captive for another two weeks——after which time they were freed and the aircraft was dramatically blown up, despite the terrorists' previous promise not to do so.[136] These serial acts of violence, inflicted on completely innocent persons, followed by the wanton destruction of property valued at millions of dollars, belie such anodyne descriptions of terrorists as mere "activists" or "militants."

The cumulative effect of this proclivity toward equivocation is that today there is no one widely accepted or agreed-upon definition for terrorism. The most pernicious effect of this "failure to craft an agreed upon definition of terrorism," Anthony Richards argues in his book devoted to this subject, is the creation of a conceptual "vacuum for actors, whether they be state or non-state, to define terrorism in ways that serve their own perceived political and strategic interests."[137]For instance, different departments or agencies of even the same government will themselves often have very different definitions for it. According to one authoritative survey, the U.S. government alone utilizes more than twenty definitions of this phenomenon, differentiating between its international and domestic characteristics, and whether it is a federal or other form of crime. To complicate this matter further, the U.S. State Department changed its own definition of terrorism at least seven times between 1982 and 2004.[138] It currently uses the definition of terrorism contained in Title 22 of the United States Code, Section 2656f(d): "premeditated, politically motivated violence perpetrated against noncombatant targets by subnational groups or clandestine agents."

An accompanying explanation notes: "The term 'non-combatant,' which is referred to but not defined in 22 USC 2656f(d)(2), is interpreted to mean, in addition to civilians, military personnel (whether or not armed or on duty) who are not deployed in a war zone or a war-like setting."[139]

The U.S. Federal Bureau of Investigation (FBI) defines terrorism as "the unlawful use of force or violence against persons or property to intimidate or coerce a Government, the civilian population, or any segment thereof, in furtherance of political or social objectives."[140]

For the FBI, "terrorism" is legally interpreted to include

Acts intended to be a means of

- Intimidating/coercing civilian populations;
- Influencing policy through intimidation/coercion;
- Affecting the conduct of government by mass destruction, assassination, or kidnapping.[141]

According to the Department of Homeland Security (DHS), "terrorism" is

Any act of violence that is dangerous to human life or potentially destructive of critical infrastructure or key resources committed by a group or individual based and operating entirely within the United States or its territories without direction or inspiration from a foreign terrorist group. The act is a violation of the criminal laws of the United States or of any state or other subdivision of the United States and appears to be intended to intimidate or coerce a civilian population, to influence the policy of a government by intimidation or coercion, or to affect the conduct of a government by mass destruction, assassination, or kidnapping.[142]

And the U.S. Department of Defense defines it as, "The unlawful use of violence or threat of violence, often motivated by religious, political, or other ideological beliefs, to instill fear and coerce governments or societies in pursuit of goals that are usually political."[143]

Not surprisingly, each of the above definitions reflects the priorities and particular interests of the specific agency involved. The State Department's emphasis is on the premeditated and planned or calculated nature of terrorism in contrast to more spontaneous acts of political violence. Its definition is also the only one of the four to emphasize both the ineluctably political nature of terrorism and the perpetrators' fundamental "subnational" characteristic. The State Department's approach is also noteworthy in that it expands the definition of a terrorist act beyond the usual, exclusive focus on civilians to include "noncombatant targets." This broad category encompasses not only assassinations of military attachés and military forces deployed on peacekeeping missions, but also attacks on cafes, discotheques, and other facilities frequented by off-duty service personnel, as well as on military installations and armed personnel—"whether or not armed or on duty" provided that they "are not deployed in a war zone or a war-like setting." Under this rubric, incidents such as the 1983 suicide truck bombing of the U.S. Marine barracks at Beirut International Airport; the similar attack thirteen years later against a U.S. Air Force housing complex in Khobar, Saudi Arabia; and the October 2000 seaborne suicide assault on a U.S. Navy destroyer, the USS *Cole* while it was at anchor in Aden, Yemen, are defined as terrorist acts.[144] The State Department definition is deficient, however, in failing to consider the psychological dimension of terrorism. Terrorism is as much about the threat of violence as the violent act itself and, accordingly, is deliberately conceived to have far-reaching psychological repercussions beyond the actual target of the act among a wider, watching, "target" audience. "Terrorism," as Jenkins succinctly observed two decades ago, "is theatre."[145]

Given the FBI's mission of investigating and solving crimes—both political (e.g., terrorism) and other—it is not surprising that its definition focuses on different elements. Unlike the State Department's, this definition does address the psychological dimensions of the terrorist act described above, laying stress on terrorism's intimidatory and coercive aspects. The FBI definition also identifies a much broader category of terrorist targets than only "noncombatants," specifying not only governments and their citizens but also inanimate objects, such as private and public property. Its emphasis is on "the use of force intended to influence or instigate a course of action that furthers a political or social goal."[146] Accordingly, politically motivated acts of vandalism and sabotage are included, such as attacks on:

- abortion clinics by militant opponents of legalized abortion in the United States;
- retail businesses and stores by antiglobalists, anarchists, or both;
- medical research facilities by groups opposing experimentation on animals, such as the Animal Liberation Front (ALF); and
- ski resorts, condominium vacation developments, commercial logging operations, or automobile dealerships by radical environmentalists associated with the Earth Liberation Front (ELF).[147]

Although the FBI definition recognizes social objectives alongside political ones as fundamental terrorist aims, it offers no clear elucidation of the differences between them to explain this distinction. The DHS definition clearly reflects its mission, concentrating on attacks to critical infrastructure and key national resources that could have grave societal consequences.

The Department of Defense definition of terrorism is arguably the most complete of the four. It highlights the terrorist threat as much as the actual act of violence and focuses on terrorism's targeting of whole societies as well as governments. Curiously, unlike the State Department definition, it does not include the deliberate targeting of individuals for assassination and makes no attempt to distinguish between attacks on combatant and noncombatant military personnel. The Defense Department definition, significantly, also cites the religious and ideological aims of terrorism alongside its fundamental political objectives—but omits the social dimension found in the FBI's definition.

It is not only individual agencies within the same governmental apparatus that cannot agree on a single definition of terrorism. Experts and other long-established scholars in the field are equally incapable of reaching a consensus. In the first edition of his magisterial survey, *Political Terrorism: A Research Guide*, published in 1984,[148] Alex P. Schmid devoted more than a hundred pages to examining more than a hundred different definitions of terrorism in an effort to discover a broadly acceptable, reasonably comprehensive explication of the word. Four years and a second edition later, Schmid was no closer to the goal of his quest, conceding in the first sentence of the revised volume that the "search for an adequate definition is still on."[149] When he resumed his elucidatory odyssey in 2011, Schmid found that there were now hundreds more definitions of terrorism in use. The 250 that he compiled in *The Routledge Handbook of Terrorism Research* thus represent only a sample of the diverse approaches and foundational differences that, Schmid laments, have rendered terrorism "a 'contested concept' in the

Table 1.1 Frequencies of Definitional Elements in 109 Definitions of "Terrorism"

Element	Frequency (%)
Violence, force	83.5
Political	65
Fear, terror emphasized	51
Threat	47
(Psychological) effects and (anticipated) reactions	41.5
Victim-target differentiation	37.5
Purposive, planned, systematic, organized action	32
Method of combat, strategy, tactic	30.5
Extranormality, in breach of accepted rules, without humanitarian constraints	30
Coercion, extortion, induction of compliance	28
Publicity aspect	21.5
Arbitrariness; impersonal, random character; indiscrimination	21
Civilians, noncombatants, neutrals, outsiders as victims	17.5
Intimidation	17
Innocence of victims emphasized	15.5
Group, movement, organization as perpetrator	14
Symbolic aspect, demonstration to others	13.5
Incalculability, unpredictability, unexpectedness of occurrence of violence	9
Clandestine, covert nature	9
Repetitiveness; serial or campaign character of violence	7
Criminal	6
Demands made on third parties	4

SOURCE: Alex P. Schmid and Albert J. Jongman, *Political Terrorism: A New Guide to Actors, Authors, Concepts, Data Bases, Theories, and Literature* (New Brunswick, N.J.: Transaction Books, 1988), 5–6.

sense that people find it difficult to agree on its meaning or the scope of that meaning."[150]

Indeed, Walter Laqueur had previously despaired of defining terrorism in both editions of his monumental work on the subject, maintaining that it is neither possible to do so nor worthwhile to make the attempt.[151] "Ten years of debates on typologies and definitions," he responded to a survey on definitions conducted by Schmid in the early 1980s, "have not enhanced our knowledge of the subject to a significant degree."[152] Laqueur's contention is supported by the 22 different word categories occurring in the 109 different definitions that Schmid identified in his first survey of the subject (see table 1.1). At the end of this exhaustive exercise, Schmid wondered "whether the above list contains all the elements necessary for a good definition. The answer," he suggests, "is probably 'no.' "[153]

If it is impossible to define terrorism, as Laqueur argues, and fruitless to attempt to cobble together a truly comprehensive definition, as Schmid admits, are we to conclude that terrorism is impervious to precise, much less an accurate, definition? Not entirely. If we cannot define terrorism, then we can at least usefully distinguish it from other types of violence and identify the characteristics that make it the distinct phenomenon of political violence that it is.

Distinctions as a Path to Definition

Guerrilla warfare and insurgency are good places to start, not least since both terms are often used in lieu of terrorism and indeed are often the preferred nomenclature since they are regarded as less pejorative and less judgmental.[154] In actual practice, guerrillas and insurgents often employ the same tactics (assassination, kidnapping, hit-and-run attack, bombings of public gathering places, hostage taking, etc.) for the same purposes (to intimidate or coerce, thereby affecting behavior through the arousal of fear) as terrorists.[155] In addition, terrorists as well as guerrillas and insurgents wear neither uniform nor identifying insignia and thus are often indistinguishable from noncombatants. However, despite the inclination to lump terrorists, guerrillas, and insurgents into the same catchall category of "irregulars," there are nonetheless fundamental differences among the three.

"Guerrilla," for example, in its most widely accepted usage, is taken to refer to a numerically larger group of armed individuals who operate as a military unit, attack enemy military forces, and seize and hold territory (even if only ephemerally during daylight hours), while also exercising some form of sovereignty or control over a defined geographical area and its population. As Laqueur noted, "The distinction is of more than academic importance; there have been guerrilla units of ten thousand men and women but an urban terrorist unit seldom, if ever, comprises more than a few people and urban terrorist 'movements' rarely consist of more than a few hundred members."[156]

"Insurgents" share these same characteristics; however, their strategy and operations transcend hit-and-run attacks to embrace what in the past has variously been called "revolutionary guerrilla warfare,"[157] "modern revolutionary warfare," or "people's war"[158] but is today commonly termed "insurgency." Thus, in addition to the irregular military tactics that characterize guerrilla operations, insurgencies typically involve coordinated informational (e.g., propaganda) and psychological warfare efforts designed to mobilize popular support in a struggle against an established national government, imperialist power, or foreign occupying force.[159] Terrorists, however, do not function in the open as armed units, generally do not attempt to seize or hold territory, deliberately avoid engaging enemy military forces in combat, are constrained both numerically and logistically from undertaking concerted mass political mobilization efforts, and exercise no direct control or governance over a populace at either the local or the national level.[160]

It should be emphasized that none of these are pure categories and considerable overlap exists. Older terrorist groups such as Hezbollah, FARC (Revolutionary Armed Forces of Colombia), and the LTTE (Liberation Tigers of Tamil Eelam, or Tamil Tigers), for example, are also often described as guerrilla movements because of their size, tactics, and control over territory and populace. Indeed, nearly a third of the thirty-seven groups on the U.S. State Department's "Designated Foreign Terrorist Organizations" list could just as easily be categorized as guerrillas.[161] The insurgency waged in Iraq against U.S. and coalition military forces between 2003 and 2010 contributed to this semantic confusion. The 2003 edition of the State Department's *Global Patterns of Terrorism*, for instance, specifically cited the challenge of making meaningful distinctions between these categories, noting that the "line between insurgency and terrorism has become increasingly blurred as attacks on civilian targets have become more common."[162] Accordingly, the State Department generally considered attacks against U.S. and coalition military forces as insurgent operations and incidents such as the August 2003 suicide vehicle-borne bombings of the UN headquarters in Baghdad and the Jordanian embassy in that city, the assassinations of Japanese diplomats, and kidnapping and murder of aid workers and civilian contractors as terrorist attacks.[163] The definitional rule of thumb was therefore that secular Ba'athist Party loyalists and other former regime elements who staged guerrilla-like hit-and-run assaults or carried out attacks using roadside IEDs (improvised explosive devices) were deemed "insurgents," whereas foreign fighters and domestic Islamic extremists who belonged to groups such as ISIS's precursor, al-Qaeda in Iraq,[164] founded and led by the late Abu Musab al-Zarqawi, and who were responsible for most of the suicide attacks and the videotaped beheadings of hostages, were labeled terrorists. And ISIS itself defies easy categorization. Unlike most terrorist groups, it displays characteristics of a true conventional military force.[165] As a result of fighting against Syrian military forces loyal to Bashar al-Assad during the first half of 2014, it seized large stockpiles of weapons, equipment, and cash.[166] Then, in June 2014, ISIS launched a series of successive battalion-sized assaults into Iraq, defeating some thirty thousand American-trained Iraqi soldiers. As the defenders fled, they left behind approximately three divisions worth of equipment,[167] including American-made Humvees and M1 Abrams tanks costing tens of millions of dollars, which ISIS fighters gleefully added to its burgeoning arms stockpiles and deployed in subsequent battles.[168] The size, weapons, and tactics of the ISIS forces, combined with their ability to seize and hold terrain, are thus unique among terrorist groups and may signal the emergence of a new kind of hybrid force combining elements of terrorism, guerrilla warfare, and insurgency with formidable conventional fighting capabilities.

It is also useful to distinguish terrorists from ordinary criminals. Like terrorists, criminals use violence as a means to attain a specific end. However, while the violent act itself may be similar—kidnapping, shooting, and arson, for example—the purpose or motivation clearly is different. Whether the criminal employs violence as a means to obtain money, to acquire material goods, or to kill or injure a specific victim for pay, he is acting primarily for selfish, personal motivations (usually material gain). Moreover, unlike terrorism, the ordinary criminal's violent act is not designed or intended to have consequences or create psychological repercussions beyond the act itself. The criminal may, of course, use some short-term act of violence to "terrorize" his victim, such as waving a gun in the face of a bank clerk during a robbery to ensure the clerk's expeditious compliance. In these instances, however, the bank robber is conveying no "message" (political or otherwise) through his act of violence beyond facilitating the rapid handing over of his "loot." The criminal's act therefore is not meant to have any effect reaching beyond either the incident itself or the immediate victim. Furthermore, the violence is neither conceived nor intended to convey any message to anyone other than the bank clerk himself, whose rapid cooperation is the robber's only objective. Perhaps most fundamentally, the criminal is not concerned with influencing or affecting public opinion; he simply wants to abscond with his money or accomplish his mercenary task in the quickest and easiest way possible so that he may reap his reward and enjoy the fruits of his labors. By contrast, the fundamental aim of the terrorist's violence is ultimately to change "the system"—about which the ordinary criminal, of course, couldn't care less.[169]

The terrorist is also very different from the lunatic assassin, who may use identical tactics (e.g., shooting, bombing) and perhaps even seeks the same objective (e.g., the death of a political figure). However, while the tactics and targets of terrorists and lone assassins are often identical, their purpose is different. Whereas the terrorist's goal is again ineluctably *political* (to change or fundamentally alter a political system through his violent act), the lunatic assassin's goal is more often intrinsically idiosyncratic, completely egocentric, and deeply personal. John Hinckley, who tried to kill President Reagan in 1981 to impress the actress Jodie Foster, is a case in point. He acted not from political motivation or ideological conviction but to fulfill some profound personal quest (killing the president to impress his screen idol). Such entirely *apolitical* motivations can in no way be compared to the rationalizations used by the Narodnaya Volya to justify its campaign of tyrannicide against the czar and his minions, nor even to the Irish Republican Army's (IRA) efforts to assassinate Prime Minister Margaret Thatcher or her successor, John Major, in hopes of dramatically changing British policy toward Northern Ireland. Furthermore, just as one person cannot credibly claim to be a political party, so a lone individual cannot be considered to constitute a terrorist group. In this respect, even though Sirhan Sirhan's assassination of presidential candidate and U.S. senator Robert Kennedy in 1968 had a political motive (to protest U.S. support for Israel), it is debatable whether the murder should be defined as a terrorist act since Sirhan belonged to no organized political group and there is no evidence that he was either directly or indirectly influenced or inspired by an identifiable political or terrorist movement. Rather, Sirhan acted entirely on his own, out of deep personal frustration and a profound animus.[170] These characteristics distinguish Sirhan from the contemporary threat posed by "lone wolf" terrorists, discussed below.

Indeed, unlike the ordinary criminal or the lunatic assassin, the terrorist is not pursuing purely egocentric goals; he is not driven by the wish to line his own pocket or satisfy some personal need or grievance. The terrorist is fundamentally an *altruist*: he believes that he is serving a "good" cause designed to achieve a greater good for a wider constituency—whether real or imagined—that the terrorist and his organization purport to represent. The criminal, by comparison, serves no cause at all, just his own personal aggrandizement and material satiation. Indeed, a "terrorist without a cause (at least in his own mind)," the RAND Corporation's distinguished terrorism analyst Konrad Kellen argued, "is not a terrorist."[171] Yet the possession or identification of a cause is not a sufficient criterion for labeling someone a terrorist. In this key respect, the difference between terrorists and political extremists is clear. Many people, of course, harbor all sorts of radical and extreme beliefs and opinions, and many of them belong to radical or even illegal or proscribed political organizations. If they do not use violence in the pursuit of their beliefs, however, they cannot be considered terrorists. The terrorist is fundamentally a *violent intellectual*, prepared to use and, indeed, committed to using force in the attainment of his or her goals.

A final important, although increasingly controversial, distinction is that terrorism is most commonly understood to be violence perpetrated by sub-national or nonstate actors and not by states. This statement is not meant to ignore or deny that states——through their military forces and intelligence services——have never committed acts of violence that deliberately and wantonly targeted civilians. Nor is it meant to absolve states from the fear and panic that their violence has at times deliberately sown, or the far-reaching psychological damage and repercussions that such violence has indubitably caused. Rather, this specifically contextual differentiation between nonstate and state violence accepts the long-standing, normative meaning of "terrorism": it is a necessary step to bring analytical precision to a term that, as this chapter argued earlier, more than ever seems to be so promiscuously and expansively applied.[172] Embracing such a distinction is not, as critical terrorism studies scholars maintain, in servile obeisance to the perpetuation of Western hegemony,[173] rigid adherence to an outmoded statist outlook,[174] or a ploy to "legitimize US 'counterterrorism' policy."[175] It is instead a reflection of terrorism's broadest and most customary usage.

In the past, terrorism was arguably far easier to define than it is today. To qualify as terrorism, violence had to be perpetrated by an individual acting at the behest of or on behalf of some existent organizational entity or movement with at least some conspiratorial structure and identifiable chain of command. This criterion, however, is no longer sufficient. In recent years, a variety of both foreign and domestic terrorist movements have increasingly adopted a strategy of "leaderless networks" or encouraged "lone wolves" to engage in individual acts of violence against common enemies to thwart law enforcement and intelligence agency efforts to penetrate these organizations and preempt or prevent attack.[176]

Craig Rosebraugh, the publicist for a radical environmentalist group calling itself the Earth Liberation Front (ELF), for instance, described the movement in a 2001 interview as a deliberately conceived "series of cells across the country with no chain of command and no membership roll . . . only a shared philosophy." It is designed this way, he continued, so that "there's no central leadership where [the authorities] can go and knock off the top guy and [the movement then] will be defunct."[177] Indeed, an ELF recruitment video narrated by Rosebraugh advises, "Individuals interested in becoming active in the Earth Liberation Front to . . . form your own close-knit autonomous cells made of trustworthy and sincere people. Remember, the ELF and each cell within it are anonymous not only to one another but to the general public."[178] As a senior FBI official conceded, the ELF is "not a group you can put your fingers on" and thus is extremely difficult to infiltrate.[179]

This type of networked adversary is a new and different breed of terrorist entity to which traditional organizational constructs and definitions do not neatly apply. It is populated by individuals who are ideologically motivated, inspired, and animated by a movement or a leader, but who neither formally belong to a specific, identifiable terrorist group nor directly follow orders issued by its leadership and are therefore outside any established chain of command. It is a structure and approach that al-Qaeda has also sought to implement. Ayman al-Zawahiri, who succeeded bin Laden as al-Qaeda's emir following the latter's death as a result of a U.S. military operation in May 2011, had previously extolled this strategy in his seminal clarion call to jihad (Arabic for "striving," but also "holy war"), *Knights Under the Prophet's Banner: Meditations on the Jihadist Movement*, published just three months after the September 11, 2001, attacks. The chapter, titled "Small Groups Could Frighten the Americans," explains:

> Tracking down Americans and the Jews is not impossible. Killing them with a single bullet, a stab, or a device made up of a popular mix of explosives or hitting them with an iron rod is not impossible. Burning down their property with Molotov cocktails is not difficult. With the available means, small groups could prove to be a frightening horror for the Americans and the Jews.[180]

In point of fact, it was not until the rise of ISIS, following its split from al-Qaeda, that al-Zawahiri's original summons acquired the impact, impetus, and momentum that he had hoped. The statement issued in September 2014 by ISIS's chief spokesperson, Abu Muhammad al-Adnani, subsequently proved much more effective in inciting random acts of violence worldwide than al-Qaeda's previous entreaties to achieve the same end.[181] In language strikingly reminiscent of al-Zawahiri's over a decade before, al-Adnani assured ISIS's actual and would-be sympathizers and supporters that they did not have to travel to the battlefields of either Syria or Iraq to contribute to ISIS's struggle, but could do so at home in their own communities. "Do not let his battle pass you by wherever you may be," he declared.

You must strike the soldiers, patrons, and troops of the [unbelievers]. Strike their police, security, and intelligence members, as well as their treacherous agents. Destroy their beds. Embitter their lives for them and busy them with themselves. If you can kill a disbelieving American or European—especially the spiteful and filthy French—or an Australian, or a Canadian, or any other disbeliever from the disbelievers waging war, including the citizens of the countries that entered into a coalition against the Islamic State, then rely upon Allah, and kill him in any manner or way however it may be. Do not ask for anyone's advice and do not seek anyone's verdict. Kill the disbeliever whether he is civilian or military, for they have the same ruling. Both of them are disbelievers. . . .

If you are not able to find an IED or a bullet, then single out the disbelieving American, Frenchman, or any of their allies. Smash his head with a rock, or slaughter him with a knife, or run him over with your car, or throw him down from a high place, or choke him, or poison him. . . .

If you are unable to do so, then burn his home, car, or business. Or destroy his crops.[182]

Within days of al-Adnani's message, ISIS claimed responsibility for an attack in Melbourne, Australia, where a man stabbed two police officers after being summoned for questioning in connection with his public display of an ISIS flag. Then, just weeks later, two separate ISIS-inspired lone wolf attacks took place in Canada in October 2014. The individuals implicated in both incidents were found to have had direct contact with the group and had sought to leave Canada to become foreign fighters with ISIS in Syria or Iraq before deciding instead to carry out entirely domestic terrorist attacks. And that same month, ISIS took credit for the series of attacks by a hatchet-wielding perpetrator in Queens, New York City, in October 2014, who was subsequently found to have large amounts of jihadi material in his home.

Whether termed "leaderless resistance," "phantom cell networks," "autonomous leadership units,"[183] "autonomous cells," a "network of networks,"[184] or "lone wolves," this new conflict paradigm conforms to what John Arquilla and David Ronfeldt nearly twenty years ago called "netwar":

an emerging mode of conflict (and crime) at societal levels, short of traditional military warfare, in which the protagonists use network forms of organization and related doctrines, strategies, and technologies attuned to the information age. These protagonists are likely to consist of dispersed organizations, small groups, and individuals who communicate, coordinate, and conduct their campaigns in an internetted manner, often without precise central command.[185]

Unlike the hierarchical, pyramidal structure that typified terrorist groups of the past, this new type of organization is looser, flatter, and more linear. Although there is a leadership of sorts, its role may be more titular than actual, with less a direct command and control relationship than a mostly inspirational and motivational one.[186]

As part of this "leaderless" strategy, autonomous local terrorist cells plan and execute attacks independently of one another or of any central command authority, but through their individual terrorist efforts seek the eventual attainment of a terrorist organization or movement's wider goals. Although these ad hoc terrorist cells and lone individuals may be less sophisticated and therefore less capable than their more professional, trained counterparts who are members of actual established terrorist groups, these "amateur" terrorists can be just as bloody-minded. The brutal murder of an off-duty British soldier outside his London barracks in 2013 is an especially heinous example of this new type of threat. The soldier was run over by two men in a car who then alighted and proceeded to stab and hack him to death. One of the assailants had previously been arrested in Kenya while trying to join a terrorist group affiliated with al-Qaeda.

A 2004 FBI strategic planning document presciently described lone wolves as the "most significant domestic terrorism threat" that the United States faces. "They typically draw ideological inspiration from formal terrorist organizations," the 2004–2009 plan stated, "but operate on the fringes of those movements. Despite their ad hoc nature and generally limited resources, they can mount high-profile, extremely destructive attacks, and their operational planning is often difficult to detect."[187] This assessment accurately presaged the attack on a county government office facility in San Bernardino, California, nearly a decade later by a married couple claiming allegiance to ISIS—but with no direct or discernible connection to that organization. Fourteen persons were killed and more than twenty others were wounded.

Conclusion

By distinguishing terrorists from other types of criminals and irregular fighters and terrorism from other forms of crime and irregular warfare, we come to appreciate that terrorism is

- ineluctably political in aims and motives;
- violent—or, equally important, threatens violence;
- designed to have far-reaching psychological repercussions beyond the immediate victim or target;

- conducted *either* by an organization with an identifiable chain of command or conspiratorial cell structure (whose members wear no uniform or identifying insignia) or by individuals or a small collection of individuals influenced, motivated, or inspired by the ideological aims or example of some existent terrorist movement or its leaders, or both; and
- perpetrated by a subnational group or nonstate entity.

We may therefore now attempt to define terrorism as the deliberate creation and exploitation of fear through violence or the threat of violence in the pursuit of political change. All terrorist acts involve violence or the threat of violence. Terrorism is specifically designed to have far-reaching psychological effects beyond the immediate victim(s) or object of the terrorist attack. It is meant to instill fear within, and thereby intimidate, a wider "target audience" that might include a rival ethnic or religious group, an entire country, a national government or political party, or public opinion in general. Terrorism is designed to create power where there is none or to consolidate power where there is very little. Through the publicity generated by their violence, terrorists seek to obtain the leverage, influence, and power they otherwise lack to effect political change on either a local or an international scale.

Chapter 2

The End of Empire and the Origins of Contemporary Terrorism

lthough terrorism motivated by ethnonationalist/separat-
ist aspirations had emerged from within the moribund
Ottoman and Hapsburg empires during the three decades
immediately preceding World War I, it was only after 1945 that this phenomenon became a more pervasive global force. Two separate, highly symbolic
events that had occurred early in World War II abetted its subsequent development. At the time, the repercussions for postwar anticolonial struggles of the fall of Singapore and the proclamation of the Atlantic Charter
could not possibly have been anticipated. Yet both, in different ways, exerted
a strong influence on indigenous nationalist movements, demonstrating as
they did the vulnerability of once-mighty empires and the hypocrisy of wartime pledges of support for self-determination.

On February 15, 1942, the British Empire suffered the worst defeat in its
history when Singapore fell to the invading Japanese forces. Whatever Singapore's strategic value, its real significance—according to the foremost
military strategist of his day, Basil Liddell Hart—was as the

outstanding symbol of Western power in the Far East. . . . Its easy capture
in February 1942 was shattering to British, and European, prestige in Asia.
No belated re-entry could efface the impression. The white man had lost
his ascendancy with the disproof of his magic. The realisation of his vulnerability fostered and encouraged the post-war spread of Asiatic revolt
against European domination or intrusion.[1]

Indeed, within weeks Japan had also conquered the Dutch East Indies (Indonesia) and Burma. Hong Kong had already capitulated the previous Christmas, and more than a year earlier Japan had imposed its rule over French Indochina. Thus, when the American garrison holding out on Corregidor in the Philippines finally surrendered in May 1942, Japan's conquest of Southeast Asia—and the destruction of the British, French, Dutch, and American empires there—was complete.

The long-term impact of these events was profound. Native peoples who had previously believed in the invincibility of their European colonial overlords hereafter saw their former masters in a starkly different light. Not only had the vast British Empire been dealt a crushing blow, but American pledges of peace and security to its Pacific possessions had been similarly shattered. France's complete impotence in the face of Japanese bullying over Indochina had greatly undermined its imperial stature among the Vietnamese, and in Indonesia, Japanese promises of independence effectively negated any lingering feelings of loyalty to the Dutch. In the blink of an eye, the European powers' prewar arguments that their variegated Asian subjects were incapable of governing themselves were swept aside by Japan's policy of devolving self-government to local administrations and nominal independence to the countries they now occupied. Paradoxically, in many places it was the natives who now ruled the interned Europeans—many of whom found themselves forced to perform the most menial and backbreaking tasks. It is not surprising, therefore, that even as the tide of war shifted in the Allies' favor over the following years, almost all these peoples resolved never again to come under European imperial rule.

It was not only the Asian subjects of these declining colonial powers who clamored for independence and self-determination. The litany of humiliating defeats had struck responsive chords in other places also, everywhere challenging the myth of European—indeed, Western—power and military superiority, if not omnipotence. In the Middle East as well as in Africa, India, the Mediterranean, and North Africa, indigenous peoples chafed at the prospect of returning to their prewar colonial status quo. They were encouraged, however unintentionally, by promises of independence and self-determination made by the Allies early in World War II.[2] Even before the United States had entered the war in 1941, President Franklin D. Roosevelt had met with Britain's prime minister, Winston Churchill, on a warship off the coast of Newfoundland to formulate both countries' postwar aims. The result was an eight-point document known as the Atlantic Charter, whose main purpose, one historian has observed, was to "impress enemy opinion with the justice of the western cause."[3] Its effects, however, went far beyond that lofty aim.

The charter's first point innocuously affirmed that both countries sought no "aggrandisement, territorial or other" from the war; it was the next two points that would be the source of future difficulties for the European powers. The second point declared unequivocally that neither Britain nor the United States desired to "see . . . territorial changes that do not accord with the freely expressed wishes of the peoples concerned," while the third point further pledged both countries to "respect the right of all peoples to choose the form of government under which they will live."[4] These principles were embodied in the "Declaration of the United Nations," agreed to by Britain and the United States on January 1, 1942, and subsequently signed by all the governments at war with Germany, thus committing their countries to respect promises that in some instances they had no intention of keeping. Although on the first anniversary of the charter's signing Churchill attempted to qualify and restrict the terms of the original agreement—arguing that it was not intended that these principles should apply to either Asia or Africa, and especially not to India and Palestine, but only to those peoples in hitherto sovereign countries conquered by Germany, Italy, and Japan[5]— the damage had already been done. Indeed, all subsequent efforts by the European colonial powers to redefine or reinterpret the charter in ways favorable to the prolongation of their imperial rule for the most part fell on deaf ears.

The situation in postwar Algeria was perhaps typical of the bitterness, engendered by broken promises and misplaced hopes, that nurtured intractable conflict. In 1943, shortly after the Allied landings had liberated North Africa from Vichy rule, a delegation of Algerian Muslims sought an audience with the newly installed Free French commander, General Henri Giraud. Their request amounted to nothing more than recognition of the rights and freedoms that had been so loftily proclaimed in the Atlantic Charter, of which, of course, the French government-in-exile was a signatory. Giraud's reply was dismissively brusque. "I don't care about reforms," he thundered. "I want soldiers first."[6] The ever-compliant Algerians obligingly provided these volunteers—much as they had some thirty years before, but they did so now in the expectation, shared by other European powers' colonial subjects elsewhere, that their loyalty would be rewarded appropriately at the war's end. As was the case in at least a dozen other colonial settings, however, their anticipation was to be disappointed. Indeed, by 1947, the future leader of the anti-British guerrilla campaign in Cyprus, General George Grivas—a Greek Cypriot who had fought beside the Allies—had already despaired in the face of repeated prevarications concerning Britain's own wartime promises of self-determination. "More and more," he recalled, "it seemed to me that only a revolution would liberate my homeland."[7] The

Algerians were rapidly coming to the same conclusion. They were further encouraged by the catastrophic defeat inflicted by the Vietnamese on the French at Dien Bien Phu in 1954 and by France's subsequent ignominious withdrawal from Indochina. Meanwhile, a revolt against British rule had broken out in Palestine, waged by two small Jewish terrorist organizations—the Irgun Zvai Le'umi (National Military Organization, or Irgun) and the Lohamei Herut Yisrael (Freedom Fighters for Israel), known to Jews by its Hebrew acronym, Lehi, and to the British as the Stern Gang. The Irgun's campaign was the more significant of the two, in that it established a revolutionary model that thereafter was emulated and embraced by both anti-colonial- and postcolonial-era terrorist groups around the world.[8]

Postwar Palestine

Palestine had, of course, long been the scene of numerous riots and other manifestations of intercommunal violence that between 1936 and 1939 had culminated in a full-scale rebellion by its Arab inhabitants. In 1937, a new element was added to the country's incendiary landscape when the Irgun commenced retaliatory terrorist attacks on the Arabs. The group expanded its operations to include British targets in 1939 following the government's promulgation of a White Paper in May that imposed severe restrictions on Jewish immigration to Palestine, thereby closing one of the few remaining avenues of escape available to European Jews fleeing Hitler. But the Irgun's inchoate revolt against British rule was short-lived. Less than three months after it began, Britain was at war with Germany. Confronted by the prospect of the greater menace of a victorious Nazi Germany, the Irgun declared a truce and announced the suspension of all anti-British operations for the war's duration. Like the rest of the Jewish community in Palestine, who had also pledged to support the British war effort, the Irgun hoped that this loyalty would later result in the recognition of Zionist claims to statehood.

In May 1942, a young private attached to General Wladyslaw Anders's Polish army-in-exile arrived in Palestine. Menachem Begin's journey had been a circuitous one. Born in 1913 in Brest Litovsk, Poland, the future prime minister of Israel (1977–1983) had first become involved in Zionist politics as a teenager when he joined Betar, a right-wing nationalist Jewish youth group. By the time he had received his law degree from Warsaw University in 1936, Begin was head of the group's Organization Department for Poland. Three years later he was appointed its national commander. When Germany invaded Poland in September 1939, however, Begin was forced to flee to Lithuania. A year later, Russian secret police arrested him and charged him with being "an agent of British imperialism." After spending nine months in a local jail, Begin was sentenced to eight years of "correctional labor." In June 1941, when Germany invaded Russia, he was on a Russian ship carrying political prisoners to a Stalinist labor camp in Siberia. A reprieve came in the form of an offer to join the Polish Army or continue his journey. Begin chose the former and found himself in a unit ordered to Palestine. Shortly after his arrival, he established contact with the Irgun high command.

Since the suspension of its revolt, the Irgun had fallen into disarray. The deaths of its ideological mentor, Vladimir Jabotinsky, in August 1940 and its military commander, David Raziel, nine months later had deprived the group of leadership and direction at a time when its self-imposed dormancy required someone at the top with the vision and organizational skills necessary to hold it together. Throughout 1943, Begin met with the Irgun's surviving senior commanders to discuss the group's future. As the war against Germany moved decisively in the Allies' favor, they became convinced that the Irgun should resume its revolt. Four dominant considerations influenced this decision. First and foremost was news of the terrible fate that had befallen European Jewry under Nazi domination. Second, the expiration in March 1944 of the White Paper's rigidly enforced five-year immigration quota would likely choke off all future Jewish immigration to Palestine. Third, the Irgun's leaders agreed that the reasoning behind the self-imposed truce they had declared four years before—that harming Britain might help Germany—was no longer tenable since the course of World War II had now virtually assured an Allied victory. Finally, by renewing the revolt, the Irgun's revamped high command sought to position themselves and their organization at the vanguard of the active realization of the Jews' political and nationalist aspirations.

On December 1, 1943, Begin formally assumed command of the group and finalized plans for the resumption of anti-British operations. As a lowly enlisted man in an exile army with only the bare minimum of formal military training, Begin was an unlikely strategist. But he possessed an uncanny analytical ability to cut right to the heart of an issue and an intuitive sense about the interplay of violence, politics, and propaganda that ideally qualified him to lead a terrorist organization. Begin's strategy was simple. The handful of men and the few weapons that in 1943 constituted the Irgun could never hope to challenge the British Army on the battlefield and win. Instead, the group would function in the setting and operate in the manner that best afforded the terrorist with means of concealment and escape. Based in the city, its members would bury themselves within the surrounding community, indistinguishable from ordinary, law-abiding citizens. At the appropriate moment, they would emerge from the shadows to strike, then disappear back into the anonymity of Palestine's urban neighborhoods, remaining safely beyond the reach of the authorities. The Irgun's plan, therefore, was not to defeat Britain militarily but to use terrorist violence to undermine the government's prestige and control of Palestine by striking at symbols of British rule. "History and our observation," Begin later recalled, "persuaded us that if we could succeed in destroying the government's prestige in Eretz Israel [Hebrew: literally, 'Land of Israel'], the removal of its rule would follow automatically. Thenceforward, we gave no peace to this weak spot. Throughout all the years of our uprising, we hit at the British Government's prestige, deliberately, tirelessly, unceasingly."[9]

In contrast to other colonial rebellions that either had sought decisive military victories in actual battle or had relied on a prolonged strategy of attrition, the Irgun adopted a strategy that involved the relentless targeting of those institutions of government that unmistakably represented Britain's oppressive rule of Palestine. Thus, the Irgun recommenced operations in February 1944 with the simultaneous bombings of immigration department offices in Palestine's three major cities—Jerusalem, Tel Aviv, and Haifa. Subsequent attacks were mounted against the government land registry offices, from which the White Paper's provisions restricting Jewish land purchase were administered; the department of taxation and finance, responsible for collecting the revenue used to fund the government's repressive policies; and of course the security forces—the police and army—that were charged with enforcement of the White Paper of 1939.

The Irgun's most spectacular operation was without doubt its bombing in July 1946 of Jerusalem's King David Hotel. Although much has been written about this controversial incident, it is worth recalling that the King David was no ordinary hotel. On six floors of its southern wing (beneath which the explosives were placed), the hotel housed the nerve center of British rule in Palestine: the government secretariat and headquarters of British military forces in Palestine and Transjordan. The attack's target, therefore, was neither the hotel itself nor the people working or staying in it, but the government and military offices located there. Nor was its purpose random, indiscriminate carnage. Unlike many terrorist groups today, the Irgun's strategy was not deliberately to target or wantonly harm civilians. At the same time, though, the claim of Begin and other apologists that warnings were issued to evacuate the hotel before the blast cannot absolve either the group or its commander from responsibility for the ninety-one people killed and forty-five others injured—men and women, Arabs, Jews, and Britons alike. Indeed, whatever nonlethal intentions the Irgun may or may not have had, the fact remains that a tragedy of almost unparalleled magnitude was inflicted at the King David Hotel, so that to this day the bombing remains one of the world's single most lethal terrorist incidents of the twentieth century.

Despite—or perhaps because of—the tragic loss of life, as far as the Irgun was concerned, the bombing achieved its objective: attracting world-wide attention to the group's struggle and the worsening situation in Palestine. Editorials in all the British newspapers focused on the nugatory results of recent military operations against the terrorists that had been previously trumpeted as great successes. Typical of these was the *Manchester Guardian*'s observation that the bombing "will be a shock to those who imagined that the Government's firmness had put a stop to Jewish terrorism and had brought about an easier situation in Palestine. In fact, the opposite is the truth."[10] These reactions accorded perfectly with Begin's plan to foster a climate of fear and alarm in Palestine so pervasive as to undermine confidence both there and in Britain in the government's ability to maintain order. Indeed, in these circumstances, the government could respond only by imposing on Palestine a harsh regimen of security measures encompassing a daily routine of curfews, roadblocks, snap checks, cordon-and-search operations and, for a time, even martial law. The failure of these measures to stop the Irgun's unrelenting terrorist campaign would, Begin hoped, have the effect of further underscoring the government's weakness. He also banked on the fact that the massive disruptions caused to daily life and commerce by the harsh and repressive countermeasures that the British were forced to take would further alienate the community from the government, thwart British efforts to obtain the community's cooperation against the terrorists, and create in the minds of the Jews an image of the army and the police as oppressors rather than protectors. Moreover, the more conspicuous the security forces seemed, the stronger the terrorists appeared.

At the foundation of this strategy was Begin's belief that the British, unlike the Germans who during the war had carried out wholesale reprisals against civilians, were incapable of such barbarity.[11] "We knew," he explained, "that Eretz Israel, in consequence of the revolt, resembled a glass house. The world was looking into it with ever-increasing interest and could see most of what was happening inside. . . . Arms were our weapons of attack; the transparency of the 'glass' was our shield of defence."[12] By compelling a liberal democracy like Britain to take increasingly repressive measures against the public, the terrorists sought to push Britain to the limit of its endurance. In this respect, the Irgun did not have to defeat Britain militarily; it had only to avoid losing. Accordingly, British tactical "successes" did nothing to change the balance of forces or bring the security forces any closer to victory. Rather, measures such as massive cordon-and-search operations and the imposition of martial law proved to bring only ephemeral benefits, bought at the cost of estranging the population from the government. Nearly a quarter of a century later, the Brazilian revolutionary theorist Carlos Marighela would advocate the same strategy in his famous "Mini-Manual," the *Handbook of Urban Guerrilla War*.[13]

In sum, this was not a war of numbers. Success was measured not in terms of casualties inflicted (between 1945 and 1947, the worst years of the conflict, just under one hundred fifty British soldiers were killed) or assets destroyed, but—precisely as Begin had wanted—by psychological impact. In place of a conventional military strategy of confrontation in battle, Begin and his lieutenants conceived operations that were designed less to kill than to tarnish the government's prestige, demoralize its security forces, and undermine Britain's resolve to remain in Palestine. Explaining his strategy, Begin argued: "The very existence of an underground must, in the end, undermine the prestige of a colonial regime that lives by the legend of its omnipotence. Every attack which it fails to prevent is a blow at its standing. Even if the attack does not succeed, it makes a dent in that prestige, and that dent widens into a crack which is extended with every succeeding attack."[14] Thus, even though the British forces outnumbered the terrorists by twenty to one—so that there was, according to one account, "one armed soldier to each adult male Jew in Palestine"[15]—even with this overwhelming numerical superiority, the British were still unable to destroy the Irgun and maintain order in Palestine.

Finally, an integral and innovative part of the Irgun's strategy was Begin's use of daring and dramatic acts of violence to attract international attention to Palestine and thereby publicize simultaneously the Zionists' grievances against Britain and their claims for statehood. In an era long before the advent of CNN and instantaneous satellite-transmitted news broadcasts, the Irgun deliberately attempted to appeal to a worldwide audience far beyond the immediate confines of the local struggle, beyond even the ruling regime's own homeland. In particular, the Irgun—like its nonviolent and less violent Zionist counterparts—sought to generate sympathy and marshal support among powerful allies such as the Jewish community in the United States and its elected representatives in Congress and the White House, as well as among the delegates to the fledgling United Nations, to bring pressure to bear on Britain to grant Jewish statehood. The success of this strategy, Begin claims, may be seen in the paucity of global coverage afforded to the civil war that had erupted in Greece after World War II, compared to that devoted to events in Palestine. Palestine, he wrote, had undeniably become a "centre of world interest. The revolt had made it so. It is a fact," Begin maintains, that no partisan struggle had been so publicized throughout the world as was ours. . . . The reports on our operations, under screaming headlines, covered the front pages of newspapers everywhere, particularly in the United States. . . . The interest of the newspapers is the measure of the interest of the public. And the public—not only Jews but non-Jews too—were manifestly interested in the blows we were striking in Eretz Israel.[16]

In this respect, pro-Irgun Jewish American lobbyists were noticeably successful in obtaining the passage of resolutions by the U.S. Congress condemning "British oppression" and reaffirming American support for the establishment of a Jewish state in Palestine.[17] These activities, which presaged the efforts undertaken by Irish American activists on behalf of Sinn Fein ("We Ourselves," an Irish nationalist political party) and the IRA prior to the 1998 Good Friday Agreement, had similarly corrosive effects on Anglo-American relations more than half a century ago.

By 1947, the Irgun had, in fact, achieved its objectives. Reporting on the situation to Washington, the American consul general in Jerusalem observed:

with [British] officials attempting to administrate from behind masses of barbed wire, in heavily defended buildings, and with the same officials (minus wives and children evacuated some time ago) living in pathetic seclusion in "security zones," one cannot escape the conclusion that the Government of Palestine is a hunted organization with little hope of ever being able to cope with conditions in this country as they exist today.[18]

Indeed, each successive terrorist outrage illuminated the government's inability to curb, much less defeat the terrorists. Already sapped by World War II, Britain's limited economic resources were further strained by the cost of deploying so large a military force to Palestine to cope with the tide of violence submerging the country. Public opinion in Britain, already ill disposed to the continued loss of life and expenditure of effort in an unwinnable situation, was further inflamed by incidents such as the King David Hotel bombing and the Irgun's hanging in July 1947 of two British Army sergeants in retaliation for the government's execution of three convicted Irgun terrorists. As the renowned British historian of the Middle East Elizabeth Monroe has noted with respect to the hangings: "The British public had taken Palestine in its stride . . . and had looked upon 'disturbances' and 'violence' there much as it viewed 'the troubles' in Ireland—as an unpleasant experience that was part of the white man's burden." All this changed, however, with the cold-blooded murder of the sergeants. Photographs of the grim death scene—depicting the two corpses just inches above the ground, the sergeants' hooded faces and bloodied shirts—were emblazoned across the front pages of British newspapers under headlines decrying their execution as an act of "medieval barbarity." As inured to the almost daily reports of the death and deprivation suffered by the army in Palestine as the British public was, the brutal execution of the two sergeants made a deep and unalterable impression on the national psyche. "All home comment on that deed," Monroe continued, was "different in tone from that on earlier terrorist acts, many of which caused greater loss of life—for instance, the blowing up of the officers' club or of the King David Hotel."[19] For both the British public and the press, the murders seemed to demonstrate the futility of the situation in Palestine and the pointlessness of remaining there any longer than was absolutely necessary.

At the time, Britain was also, of course, coming under intense pressure from the United States and other quarters regarding the admission to Palestine of tens of thousands of Jewish displaced persons still languishing throughout liberated Europe and was itself trying to stem the flood of illegal Jewish immigrants attempting to enter Palestine. In addition, throughout the summer of 1947 the Special Committee on Palestine (UNSCOP) appointed by the UN General Assembly was completing its investigations regarding the country's future.[20] It is a measure of the Irgun's success that Begin was twice granted audiences with members of the committee to explain the group's aims, motivations, and vision for a Jewish state in Palestine. The committee's unanimous recommendation calling for the immediate termination of British rule and granting of independence to Palestine finally forced the government's hand.[21] In September, the colonial secretary, Arthur Creech Jones, announced that Britain would no longer be responsible for governing Palestine and that all civilian and military personnel would be evacuated as soon as was practicable.

A decade and a half after the event, Creech Jones cited four pivotal considerations that influenced the government's decision. First, there were the irreconcilable differences between Palestine's Arab and Jewish communities; second, the drain on Britain's shrinking financial resources imposed by the country's heavy military commitment in Palestine; third, the force of international, American, and parliamentary opinion; and finally—and, he believed, most significant—the public outcry in Britain that followed the Irgun's hanging of the two sergeants. Describing the confluence of events that compelled the government to surrender the mandate, the former colonial secretary recalled specifically, "Terrorism was at its worst and the British public seemed unable to stand much more." Hence, with "accelerating speed," Creech Jones explained, "the Cabinet was pushed to the conclusion that they could [no] longer support the Mandate."[22] On May 15, 1948, Britain's rule over Palestine formally ended and the establishment of the State of Israel was proclaimed. In a communiqué issued that same day by the Irgun, Begin declared:

> After many years of underground warfare, years of persecution and suffering . . . [the] Hebrew revolt of 1944–48 has been crowned with success. . . . The rule of enslavement of Britain in our country has been beaten, uprooted, has crumbled and been dispersed. . . . The State of Israel has arisen. And it has arisen "Only Thus": through blood, fire, a strong hand and a mighty arm, with suffering and sacrifices.[23]

The Anticolonial Struggles of the 1950s: Cyprus and Algeria

The Irgun's revolt provided a template for subsequent anticolonial uprisings elsewhere. Indeed, the most effective irredentist struggles of the immediate postwar era were those that emulated Begin's strategy and deliberately sought to appeal to—and thereby attract the attention and sympathy of— an international audience. "Our intention," explained General George Grivas, the founder and commander of EOKA (Ethniki Organosis Kyprion Agoniston, or National Organization of Cypriot Fighters), in his memoirs, "was to focus the eyes of the world on Cyprus and force the British to fulfil their promises."[24] Similarly, the 1954 proclamation of revolt against French rule of Algeria by the FLN (Front de Liberation Nationale, or National Liberation Front) prominently cited the "internationalism of the Algerian problem" as among its principal goals.[25]

In pursuit of this end, both groups also made a conscious effort to appeal directly to the United Nations for help. EOKA's own proclamation of revolt, for example, was specifically addressed to "Diplomats of the World." It called upon them to "Look to your duty. It is shameful that, in the twentieth century, people should have to shed blood for freedom, that divine gift for which we too fought at your side and for which you, at least, claim that you fought against Nazism."[26] In Algeria, FLN offensives, general strikes, and other demonstrations were timed to occur when the UN General Assembly reconvened or was already scheduled to discuss the conflict. In January 1957, the fabled Battle of Algiers, immortalized by the 1966 Gillo Pontecorvo film of the same name, when the FLN unleashed its campaign of mass urban terrorism, was deliberately choreographed to coincide with the General Assembly's annual opening session. The FLN communiqué announcing the strike that accompanied the new terrorist offensive candidly admitted to this timing, announcing its desire to "bestow an incontestable authority upon our delegates at the United Nations in order to convince those rare diplomats still hesitant or possessing illusions about France's liberal policy."[27] To a large extent, therefore, the success of both EOKA and the FLN in ending foreign rule of their respective countries was predicated on their ability to attract external attention to their respective struggles, much as the Irgun had a decade before.

In Cyprus, from the very start, Grivas appreciated the necessity of reaching out to an audience beyond the immediate geographical boundaries of his group's struggle. "The enlightenment of international public opinion," he recognized, "was bound to play an important part in bringing home to all concerned the Cypriot people's demand for self-determination. It is a fact that there were many foreigners and even United Nations representatives who were completely ignorant of why we were demanding our freedom."[28] Accordingly, Grivas enshrined this principle in the "Preparatory General Plan" that he had formulated in 1953—two years before the campaign actually began—whose opening paragraph clearly states the fundamental objective "to arouse international public opinion . . . by deeds of heroism and self-sacrifice which will focus attention on Cyprus until our aims are achieved."[29] Although an English-language translation of *The Revolt* had been published in London and New York in 1951, there is no evidence that Grivas ever read Begin's book or studied the Irgun's campaign, the parallels between the two struggles are unmistakable. Grivas's strategy, like Begin's, was not to win an outright military victory against the numerically superior British forces but to rely on dramatic, well-orchestrated, and appropriately timed acts of violence to focus international attention on the situation in Cyprus and the Greek Cypriots' demand for *enosis*—unification with Greece.

"My small force was outnumbered by more than a hundred to one," Grivas later recalled, "but, as I have said, this made no difference to the type of subversive warfare I was planning."[30] His plan was to deploy the majority of EOKA forces in the island's urban centers, where they were organized into individual terrorist cells numbering no more than eight to ten men each. Their mission was to tie up as many British troops as possible on static guard duties in the cities, thereby allowing EOKA to consolidate its control over the rest of the island. In words reminiscent of Begin's, Grivas explained in his treatise on guerrilla warfare:

> Our strategy consisted in turning the whole island into a single field of battle in which there was no distinction between front and rear, so that the enemy should at no time and in no place feel himself secure. The enemy never knew where and when we might strike. . . . This strategy

achieved the dispersal, intimidation and wearing down of the enemy's forces and especially serious consequences resulting from our use of surprise.[31]

By concentrating on urban operations, as the Irgun had in Palestine, EOKA also gained immediate access to the news media dispatched to the island to cover the escalating violence. Had EOKA, like traditional guerrilla forces, confined its operations to the island's rugged and isolated rural areas and mountain ranges, it would arguably have lost this access and forfeited the exposure so critical to Grivas's strategy. The urban terrorist campaign was thus pivotal in securing the propaganda platform required by the group to broadcast its cause to the world. In this respect, Grivas was able to derive great satisfaction from the fact that within five months of the revolt's proclamation, EOKA had succeeded in attaining what a decade of patient diplomacy and insistent lobbying had failed to achieve: UN consideration of the Greek Cypriots' nationalist claims. Hitherto, the General Assembly had upheld British arguments that the situation in Cyprus was an entirely *internal* matter and therefore outside the organization's purview. Now, for the first time, Cyprus had been placed on the UN's agenda. "This proved," Grivas later recalled, "that inside this international body the idea was beginning to penetrate that something must be done about the Cyprus question."[32]

Indeed, by the end of 1955, Grivas had succeeded in plunging the island into complete disorder. An average of two British soldiers or policemen were being killed each week. The security forces had been thrown on the defensive, kept off balance by repeated EOKA hit-and-run attacks and unable to mount any effective offensive operations. Like Begin, Grivas also calculated that the unrelenting terrorist onslaught would sap the morale of British forces and compel them to overreact with counterproductive, self-defeating measures directed against the law-abiding Greek-Cypriot community. "The 'security forces' set about their work in a manner which might have been deliberately designed to drive the population into our arms," Grivas recalled. "These attempts to frighten the people away from EOKA always had exactly the opposite effect to that intended: the population were merely bound more closely to the Organisation."[33] Once again, the fundamental asymmetry between the terrorists' apparent ability to strike anywhere, at any time, and the security forces' inability to protect all conceivable targets, all the time, was glaringly demonstrated. As in Palestine, the more visible and pervasive the security forces in Cyprus became, the greater the public frustration caused by disruption to daily life, and the more powerful and omnipresent the terrorists appeared. At the height of the conflict, British security forces on Cyprus totaled nearly 40,000 men, arrayed against a hard core of fewer than 400 active terrorists, backed by some 750 "auxiliaries."[34] Again, as in Palestine, this was not a war of numbers. The massive deployment of British troops had little overall impact on the situation. As Grivas later reflected about his opponent commanding the British forces, Field Marshal Sir John Harding: "He underrated his enemy on the one hand, and overweighted his forces on the other. But one does not use a tank to catch field mice—a cat will do the job better."[35]

Throughout the campaign, Grivas coordinated his underground campaign with the aboveground diplomatic efforts of Archbishop Makarios III (Michael Christodoros Mouskos). As the appointed head of the Ethnarchy (Church Council) of Cyprus, Makarios was also the Greek-Cypriot community's de facto political leader. He and Grivas had met as early as 1950 to plan the general outline of the revolt, and prelate and soldier worked closely together throughout the struggle to achieve their shared goal of enosis. Thus, the symbiotic relationship that is believed to have existed between Sinn Fein and the IRA has a historical parallel in that between the Ethnarchy and EOKA thirty years earlier, with Makarios playing the role allegedly performed by Gerry Adams, Sinn Fein's president since 1983. Like Adams, Makarios was also interned, and in 1956 he was exiled to the Seychelles, being allowed to return to Cyprus two years later as a condition for Greek-Cypriot participation in British-sponsored multiparty talks on the island's future. It was not until February 1959 that agreement was reached.

Under intense pressure from Greece, Makarios reluctantly accepted the proposal for the creation of an independent republic of Cyprus, with Britain being allowed to retain two strategic bases on the island. Fears that Turkey would otherwise forcibly impose partition (as in fact occurred fifteen years later) led Makarios to acquiesce in the arrangement despite Grivas's vehement opposition. The revolt officially ended a month later, when EOKA surrendered a large enough quantity of arms to satisfy the government that the peace agreement could be implemented. Although enosis was never achieved, British rule was forcibly ended and Cyprus was granted its independence. The fruits of the terrorists' labors were also apparent in the new republic's general election: Makarios was elected the country's first president, polling 67 percent of the popular vote.[36]

At the other end of the Mediterranean, the revolt against French rule over Algeria between 1954 and 1962 was the last of the immediate postwar anticolonial struggles. For that reason, perhaps, it had the most direct and discernible impact on many later ethnonationalist terrorist campaigns. Yasir Arafat, for example, in his authorized biography, cites the pivotal influence that the FLN had on the PLO's struggle and the critical material assistance that Algeria later provided to the Palestinians. "I started my contacts with the Algerian revolutionaries in the early 1950s," he recalled. "I stayed in touch with them and they promised they would help us when they had achieved their independence. I never doubted for one moment that they would win, and that their victory would be very important for us."[37] In his own candid memoir, Nelson Mandela similarly identifies the seminal influence that the FLN's struggle had on the decades-long effort of the African National Congress (ANC) to end minority white rule of South Africa. "The situation in Algeria," Mandela wrote, "was the closest model to our own in that the rebels faced a large white settler community that ruled the indigenous majority." Accordingly, the ANC studied the Algerian conflict closely, deriving the main lesson that a pure military victory was impossible to achieve in such circumstances. Instead, Mandela assiduously applied the advice given to him by an Algerian revolutionary that "international opinion . . . is sometimes worth more than a fleet of jet fighters."[38] It was a lesson that the FLN itself had learned only belatedly.

By the middle of 1956, the rebellion against French rule had been raging for nearly two years; the FLN, however, had precious few tangible achievements to show for its efforts, and recent advances by the security forces in the countryside had seriously undermined the group's rural insurgent strategy. Accordingly, the FLN embarked on a new strategy that would, for the first time, focus on the country's capital, Algiers, and thereby apply pressure to France by appealing directly to international opinion. The architect of this new strategy, first unveiled during the August 1956 summit convened at Soummam, Morocco, in hopes of reversing the FLN's declining fortunes, was Ramdane Abane, a leading figure in the movement until his execution the following year during an internecine power struggle. As the group's chief theoretician, he was also its most potent intellect. From an impoverished background and entirely self-educated, Abane was as completely unsentimental as he was ruthless, maintaining an unalterable faith in the efficacy of violence. This was clearly evident in his famous directive number nine, wherein he succinctly explained not just the purpose of the FLN's new strategy but the elementary logic behind urban terrorism. "Is it preferable for our cause to kill ten enemies in an oued [dry riverbed] of Telergma when no one will talk of it," he rhetorically asked, "or a single man in Algiers which will be noted the next day by the American press?"[39]

The chain of events that led to the FLN's full-scale urban terrorist campaign, however, had actually begun two months earlier, in June, with the execution by guillotine of two convicted FLN fighters. As had occurred countless times elsewhere (Palestine and Cyprus included), such attempts by the ruling regime to deter further violence with a particularly harsh exemplary punishment backfired catastrophically. The recipients of this lesson, rather than serving as abject examples, as often as not become martyrs: emblematic rallying points for the revolutionary cause around which still greater sacrifice and still further bloodshed and destruction are demanded and justified. Thus, it was in Algeria, where the FLN announced that for every FLN fighter executed, a hundred Frenchmen would meet a similar fate. Hitherto, the group could boast that its campaign in the capital had been deliberately nonlethal, its bombs directed against inanimate "symbols" of French rule—government offices and buildings, military cantonments and police stations—but not deliberately against people. This now changed with Abane's instructions to the FLN's urban cadres to unleash a reign of unprecedented bombings and terror. Within seventy-two hours, forty-nine French civilians had been gunned down. Then, in August, as a result of the new strategic direction approved that same month at Soummam, the bombings began.

The campaign was spearheaded not by the group's hardened male fighters but by its attractive young female operatives—whose comely bearing and European looks, as Saadi Yacef, the group's operations officer in Algiers (who later reprised his real-life role in the famed 1966 Gillo Pontecorvo film *The Battle of Algiers*), correctly guessed, would arouse far less suspicion than their male counterparts. Their targets, moreover, were neither military nor even governmental, but the crowded seaside milk bar frequented by *pied noir* (French colonist) families after a day at the beach; a cafeteria particularly favored by European university students; and the downtown Air France passenger terminal. The coordinated operations killed three people and injured some fifty others—including several children, some of them among the dozen or so victims requiring surgical amputation of mangled limbs. Throughout it all, Abane was unmoved. Drawing the same analogy between the terrorist bomb in the dustbin and the "poor man's air force" cited in chapter 1, Abane is said to have dismissively observed, "I see hardly any difference between the girl who places a bomb in the Milk-Bar and the French aviator who bombards a *mechta* [village] or who drops napalm on a *zone interdite* [interdiction, or free-fire, zone]."[40]

The urban campaign continued throughout the remainder of the year, climaxing on December 28, 1956, with the assassination of the mayor of Algiers. Widespread anti-Muslim rioting broke out, only to be followed by a new round of FLN assassinations. This was the last straw. In despair over the deteriorating situation, the governor-general called out the army. On January 7, 1957, General Jacques Massu, commander of the elite Tenth Parachute Division, assumed complete responsibility for maintaining order in the city. The FLN responded by declaring a general strike for January 28, to coincide, as noted above, with the UN's annual opening session. Its purpose—and that of the terrorist attacks that accompanied it: to focus international attention on Algeria. Once again, Yacef's bombers set about their work with startling efficiency. The FLN's target set now expanded to include popular bars and bistros, crowded city streets, and sports stadiums packed with spectators. Within two weeks, 15 people had been killed and 105 others were wounded.

Massu went on the offensive. Having fought in Indochina, he and his senior commanders prided themselves on having acquired a thorough understanding of revolutionary warfare and how to counter it. Victory, they were convinced, would be entirely dependent on the acquisition of intelligence. "The man who places the bomb," declared Colonel Yves Godard, Massu's chief of staff and later one of his sector commanders, "is but an arm that tomorrow will be replaced by another arm"; the key was to find the individual commanding the arm. Accordingly, Godard and his men set out to uproot and destroy the FLN's urban infrastructure. Their method was to build up a meticulously detailed picture of the FLN's apparatus in Algiers that would home in relentlessly on the terrorist campaign's mastermind. Godard's approach, dramatically depicted onscreen by Pontecorvo, was described by the British historian Alistair Horne as a "complex *organigramme* [that] began to take shape on a large blackboard, a kind of skeleton pyramid in which, as each fresh piece of information came from the interrogation centres, another name (and not always necessarily the right name) would be entered."[41] That this system proved effective, there is no doubt. The problem was that it also depended on, and therefore encouraged, widespread abuses, including torture, for Massu and his men were not particularly concerned about *how* they obtained this information. Torture of both terrorists and *suspected* terrorists became routine. The French Army in Algeria found it easy to justify such extraordinary measures, given the extraordinary conditions. The prevailing exculpatory philosophy among the Tenth Parachute Division can be summed up by Massu's terse response to complaints, that "the innocent [that is, the next victims of terrorist attacks] deserve more protection than the guilty."[42]

The brutality of the army's campaign, however, completely alienated the native Algerian Muslim community. Hitherto mostly passive or apathetic, it was now driven into the arms of the FLN, swelling the organization's ranks and increasing its popular support. Domestic public opinion in France was similarly outraged, undercutting popular backing for continuing the struggle and creating deep fissures in French civil–military relations. Massu and his men stubbornly consoled themselves that they had achieved their mission and defeated the rebels' attempt to seize control of Algiers, but this military victory was bought at the cost of eventual political defeat. Five years later, the French withdrew from Algeria and granted the country its independence.

For decades, Massu remained unrepentant, maintaining that the ends justified the means used to destroy the FLN's urban insurrection. He later had second thoughts. In 2000, for instance, Massu told an interviewer that France should acknowledge that torture was routinely employed in Algeria and officially condemn it.[43] The officer under Massu's command at the time, retired general Paul Aussaresses, who was directly responsible for implementing this policy, however, has never softened. "For my part, I do not repent," Aussaresses told the same interviewer. "Torture never pleased me but I was resolute when I arrived in Algiers. At the time it was already widespread. If it were done again, it would piss me off, but I would do the same thing because I do not believe that one can do it differently."[44] Respect for the rule of law and the niceties of legal procedure, much less international conventions governing the rights of combatants, he argued, were totally irrelevant given the crisis situation enveloping Algeria in 1957. "Only rarely were the prisoners we had questioned during the night still alive the next morning," Aussaresses explained in his memoir, *The Battle of the Casbah*: "Whether they had talked or not they generally had been neutralized. It was impossible to send them back to the court system; there were too many of them and the machine of justice would have become clogged with cases and stopped working altogether. Furthermore, many of the prisoners would probably have managed to avoid any kind of punishment."[45]

Thus, the battle was won and the terrorists' indiscriminate bombing campaign ended. Extraordinary measures were legitimated by extraordinary circumstances—all of which Aussaresses maintains is beside the point. As torturers before and since have claimed, he too contends, "I don't think I ever tortured or executed people who were innocent. I was mainly dealing with terrorists who had been involved in attacks."[46]

At the same time, there is no doubt that this "success" cut both ways. The FLN's tactical defeat in the city resulted in yet another complete reassessment of its strategy. Large-scale urban terrorism was now abandoned alongside the FLN's belief that France could be defeated militarily. The group's high command also concluded that the struggle could not be won inside Algeria alone; accordingly, the rebels relocated their operational bases to Tunisia, from which they pursued a rural hit-and-run strategy, making cross-border raids from their newly established sanctuaries. But the Battle of Algiers remains perhaps the most significant episode in bringing about the FLN's subsequent triumph, in that it succeeded in focusing world attention on the situation in Algeria, just as Abane had calculated. By provoking the government to overreact with torture, summary executions, and other repressive tactics, the FLN also revealed the bankruptcy of French rule, thereby hastening the complete destruction of Algérie Française.

Conclusion

The ethnonationalist insurrections that followed World War II had a lasting influence on subsequent terrorist campaigns. Although governments throughout history and all over the world always claim that terrorism is ineffective as an instrument of political change, the examples of Israel, Cyprus, and Algeria, and of Begin, Makarios, and Ahmed Ben Bella (the FLN's leader, who became Algeria's first president), provide convincing evidence to the contrary. Admittedly, the establishment of these independent countries was confined to a distinct period of time and was the product, in some cases, of powerful forces other than terrorism. At the same time, however, it is indisputable that, at the very least, the tactical "successes" and political victories won through violence by groups such as the Irgun, EOKA, and the FLN clearly demonstrated that—notwithstanding the repeated denials of the governments they confronted—terrorism does "work." Even if this "success" did not always manifest itself in terms of the actual acquisition of power in government, the newfound respectability accorded to terrorist organizations hitherto branded as "criminals" in forums such as the United Nations and their success in attracting attention to themselves and their causes, in publicizing grievances that might otherwise have gone overlooked, and perhaps even in compelling governments to address issues that, if not for the terrorists' violence, would have largely been ignored, cannot be disregarded.

In sum, the anticolonial terrorism campaigns are critical to understanding the evolution and development of modern, contemporary terrorism. They were the first to recognize the publicity value inherent in terrorism and to choreograph their violence for an audience far beyond the immediate geographical loci of their respective struggles. The Irgun directed its message to New York and Washington, D.C., as much as to London and Jerusalem. EOKA similarly appealed to opinion in New York and London, as well as in Athens and Nicosia. And the FLN was especially concerned with influencing policy not only in Algiers but in New York and Paris as well. The ability of these groups to mobilize sympathy and support outside the narrow confines of their actual theaters of operation thus taught a powerful lesson to similarly aggrieved peoples elsewhere, who now saw in terrorism an effective means of transforming hitherto local conflicts into international issues. Thus, the foundations were laid for the transformation of terrorism in the late 1960s from a primarily localized phenomenon into a security problem of global proportions.

Chapter 3

The Internationalization of Terrorism

T he advent of what is considered modern, international terrorism occurred on July 22, 1968. On that day, three armed
Palestinian terrorists, belonging to the Popular Front for
the Liberation of Palestine (PFLP), one of the six groups that then constituted the Palestine Liberation Organization (PLO), hijacked an Israeli El Al
commercial flight en route from Rome to Tel Aviv. Although commercial
aircraft had been hijacked before—this was the twelfth such incident in 1968
alone—the El Al hijacking differed from all previous ones. First, its purpose
was not simply the diversion of a scheduled flight from one destination to
another, as had been happening since 1959 with a seemingly endless succession of homesick Cubans or sympathetic revolutionaries from other countries commandeering domestic American passenger aircraft simply as a
means to travel to Cuba. This hijacking was a bold political statement. The
terrorists who seized the El Al flight had done so with the express purpose
of trading the passengers they held hostage for Palestinian terrorists imprisoned in Israel. Second, unlike previous hijackings, in which the origin or
nationality of the aircraft that was being seized did not matter so long as
the plane itself was capable of transporting the hijacker(s) to a desired destination, El Al—as Israel's national airline and by extension, therefore, a
readily evident national symbol of the Israeli state—had been specifically
and deliberately targeted by the terrorists. Third, by engineering a crisis in
which the consequences of a government's ignoring or rejecting the terrorists'

demands could prove catastrophic, leading to the destruction of the aircraft and the deaths of all people on board, the terrorists succeeded in forcing their avowed enemy, Israel, to communicate directly with them and therefore with the organization to which they belonged, despite the Israeli government's previous declarations and policy pronouncements to the contrary. Finally, through the combination of dramatic political statement, "symbolic" targeting, and crisis-induced de facto recognition, the terrorists discovered that they had the power to create major media events—especially when innocent civilians were involved. As Zehdi Labib Terzi, the PLO's chief observer at the United Nations, reflected in a 1976 interview, "The first several hijackings aroused the consciousness of the world and awakened the media and world opinion much more—and more effectively—than twenty years of pleading at the United Nations."[1]

Many of the postwar anticolonial terrorist campaigns, as previously noted, also had a prominent international orientation. With the El Al hijacking, however, the nature and character of terrorism demonstrably changed. For the first time, terrorists began to travel regularly from one country to another to carry out attacks. In addition, they also began to target innocent civilians from other countries who often had little if anything to do with the terrorists' cause or grievance, simply to endow their acts with the power to attract attention and publicity that attacks against their declared or avowed enemies often lacked. Their intent was to shock and, by shocking, to stimulate worldwide fear and alarm. These dramatic tactical changes in terrorism were facilitated by the technological advances of the time that had transformed the speed and ease of international commercial air travel and vastly improved both the quality of television news footage and the promptness with which that footage could be broadcast around the globe. Accordingly, terrorists rapidly came to appreciate that operations perpetrated in countries other than their own and directly involving or affecting foreign nationals were a reliable means of attracting unparalleled attention to themselves and their cause.

At the forefront of this transformation were the constituent groups of the PLO. Between 1968 and 1980, Palestinian terrorist groups were indisputably the world's most active, accounting for more *international* terrorist incidents than any other movement.[2] The success achieved by the PLO in publicizing the Palestinians' plight through the "internationalization" of its struggle with Israel has since served as a model for similarly aggrieved ethnic and nationalist minority groups everywhere, demonstrating how longstanding but hitherto ignored or forgotten causes can be resurrected and dramatically thrust onto the world's agenda through a series of wellorchestrated, attention-grabbing acts. To understand how revolutionary a development this was, it is necessary to briefly review the Palestinians' modern history and to appreciate the depths of obscurity and international neglect from which the PLO emerged.

The PLO and the Internationalization of Terrorism

The end of the First Arab-Israeli War in 1949 introduced two new factors into Middle Eastern politics: the Jewish State of Israel and the Palestinian refugees exiled from it. During the war, many of Palestine's Arab inhabitants had fled their homes for the safety of neighboring countries. Some had left voluntarily; others had been forcibly expelled by the advancing Israeli forces. The exodus of Palestinian Arabs, however, did not end with the cessation of fighting. Fears of Israeli reprisals, coupled with the hope that the defeated Arab armies would shortly regroup and renew the fight against Israel, had convinced many Palestinians that they were better off becoming temporary exiles in the countries of their Arab brethren than remaining in the new Jewish state. The number of these displaced people soon climbed beyond 700,000—although some estimates put the figure as high as 950,000.

Crowded into decrepit refugee camps in Jordan, Syria, Lebanon, and Egypt, the Palestinians dreamed of the day when the Arab armies would arise to destroy Israel and return them to their homes. The Arab states, however, disheartened by the crushing defeat inflicted on them by the numerically inferior Israeli forces, had no desire to launch another war. Furthermore, in the wretched conditions of the Palestinians' exile, the region's Arab leaders seized on an issue that could be exploited for their own ends. On the one hand, the Palestinian cause was a useful means by which to marshal international opprobrium against Israel and also to generate support among Arab states for greater regional unity against the common Zionist enemy; on the other, the refugee issue offered a convenient way to deflect attention from domestic problems by focusing popular discontent outward, against Israel, for the injustice done to the Palestinians. In any event, what the Palestinian refugees had once hoped would be a brief absence from their land evolved into indefinite displacement.

Meanwhile, inside the refugee camps, groups of desperate and disgruntled Palestinians were slowly banding together and establishing new political movements and associations. Out of these groups emerged new leaders, men who were untainted by the humiliation of the 1948–1949 defeat and had not been party to the broken promises of their Arab hosts. These leaders argued that the Palestinians must henceforth rely on no one but themselves if they were ever to reclaim their homeland. Small groups of fedayeen (Arabic for "commandos") began to sneak out of the refugee camps to carry out cross-border hit-and-run attacks inside Israel. At a time when Egypt, like all other frontline Arab states, was militarily unprepared for another major war, its president, Gamal Abdel Nasser, saw in the raids a means by which he could both harass Israel and simultaneously advance his claim to leadership of the Arab world. Accordingly, Egypt began actively to train and arm the fedayeen. By 1953, Palestinian marauding had become both sufficiently frequent and sufficiently lethal to provoke repeated Israeli military reprisals. Thereafter, a deadly cycle of raid and retaliation followed, culminating in the 1956 Suez crisis and providing Israel with the excuse it sought to invade the Sinai peninsula and eliminate the Egyptian bases supporting the fedayeen operations. Nearly a decade later, an almost identical tit-for-tat pattern of terrorist attack and Israeli reprisal set in motion a similar chain of events that resulted in the 1967 Six Day War.[3]

Yet although Palestinian terrorist activities precipitated a significant international crisis (Suez) and eleven years later led to a major regional war—notwithstanding the plight of hundreds of thousands of Palestinian refugees, many of whom were still living in the abject poverty of squalid refugee camps nearly two decades after their exile had begun—few outside the region took any notice of, much less cared about, the Palestinians. In fact, it was not until after 1968, when the fedayeen took their campaign against Israel outside the Middle East and began deliberately to enmesh citizens from more distant countries in their struggle, that the Palestinians discovered an effective means of broadcasting their cause to the world and attracting its attention and sympathy. "When we hijack a plane it has more effect than if we killed a hundred Israelis in battle," PFLP founder and leader George Habash explained in a 1970 interview—echoing the same point made a decade earlier by the FLN's Ramdane Abane. "For decades world opinion has been neither for nor against the Palestinians," Habash noted. "It simply ignored us. At least the world is talking about us now."[4]

The premier example of terrorism's power to rocket a cause from obscurity to renown, however, was without doubt the murder of eleven Israeli athletes seized by Palestinian terrorists at the 1972 Munich Olympic Games. The purpose of the operation, according to Fuad al-Shamali, one of its architects, was to capture the world's attention by striking at a target of inestimable value (a country's star athletes), in a setting calculated to provide the terrorists with unparalleled exposure and publicity (the top global sporting event). "Bombing attacks on El Al offices do not serve our cause," al-Shamali had argued. "We have to kill their most important and most famous people. Since we cannot come close to their statesmen, we have to kill artists and sportsmen."[5]

The incident began on September 5, 1972, shortly before 5:00 A.M., when eight terrorists belonging to the PLO's Black September Organization (BSO) burst into the Israelis' dormitory, killing two athletes immediately and taking nine others hostage. As news of the attack spread and police rushed to the scene, the site was cordoned off and the terrorists issued their demands. They offered to exchange the hostages for 236 Palestinians imprisoned in Israeli jails and 5 other terrorists being held in Germany—including Andreas Baader and Ulrike Meinhof, the founders of the radical left-wing West German terrorist group the Red Army Faction—and they wanted a guarantee of safe passage to any Arab country (except Lebanon or Jordan). They also threatened to begin killing one hostage every two hours if their demands were not met. Fifteen hours of negotiations followed until a deal, brokered by the West Germans, was struck. The terrorists and their hostages, it was agreed, would be transported in two helicopters to the air base at Fürstenfeldbruck, where they would then board a Lufthansa 727 aircraft and depart for Cairo. Once in Egypt, the exchange of prisoners would be effected and the terrorists allowed to proceed wherever they wished. The Egyptians, however, later changed their minds and decided to refuse the aircraft landing rights.

At 10:35 P.M., the two helicopters touched down at the German air base. Two terrorists emerged and went to inspect the airliner parked nearby. Two others took up positions outside the helicopters. The remaining four terrorists stayed inside, guarding the nine Israelis. Suddenly, shots rang out. As part of a prearranged rescue plan, five West German police sharpshooters had opened fire. Three of the four terrorists outside the helicopters were cut down: the survivor, Mohammad Masalhah, the group's commander, took cover. The other terrorists immediately began to return fire and, according to some accounts, started to kill the hostages. A tense standoff now ensued as appeals were broadcast over loudspeakers in Arabic, German, and English to the remaining five terrorists to release their hostages and surrender. The terrorists again responded with gunfire. Finally, just after midnight, as German police prepared to mount a rescue assault, a terrorist leaped from one of the helicopters and tossed a hand grenade back into the cabin behind him. Pandemonium broke out when the grenade exploded. In the firefight that erupted, two more terrorists, including Masalhah, were killed. The three remaining terrorists, however, kept police at bay until roughly 12:30 A.M., when they finally surrendered and were taken into custody. All nine hostages lay dead, along with a West German policeman.[6]

Both operations—the hostage seizure and the rescue attempt—were colossal failures. The Palestinians had not only failed to obtain their principal stated demand—the release of terrorists imprisoned in Israel and West

Germany—but, to many observers, had irredeemably tarnished the righteousness of their cause in the eyes of the world. Indeed, international opinion was virtually unanimous in its condemnation of the terrorists' operation. The grisly denouement on the airfield tarmac, broadcast via television and radio throughout the world, was initially regarded as disastrous to the Palestinian cause: a stunning failure and a grave miscalculation, generating revulsion rather than sympathy and condemnation instead of support.

As for the failure to save the hostages, for many other countries as well as for West Germany the botched rescue attempt provided stark evidence of how serious a threat international terrorism had become and how woefully inadequate their own counterterrorist capabilities were. The embarrassed West Germans lost little time in establishing a special antiterrorist detachment of their border police, known as GSG-9 (Grenzschutzgruppe Neun). Five years later, it acquitted itself brilliantly in Mogadishu, Somalia, rescuing all eighty-six hostages on board a Lufthansa flight hijacked en route from Mallorca by a mixed team of Palestinian and West German terrorists. In this incident, in marked contrast to the debacle at Fürstenfeldbruck, the GSG-9 commandos killed three of the hijackers and captured the fourth before they could harm any of the hostages (one GSG-9 officer was wounded in the rescue assault, as well as four hostages). In France, the Groupe d'Intervention de la Gendarmerie Nationale (GIGN) was created within the Gendarmerie Nationale as that country's dedicated counterterrorist unit; in Britain, the elite Special Air Services Regiment (SAS) was given permission to establish the Counter-Revolutionary Warfare detachment with a specific counterterrorism mission. In 1980, these SAS units successfully resolved the six-day siege at the Iranian embassy in Princes Gate, London, rescuing nineteen of the twenty-one hostages (two died during the rescue operation) and killing five of the six terrorists. Curiously, at the time the United States decided *not* to follow the example of its European allies and established no special, elite counterterrorist unit of its own—thus courting the disaster that came eight years later in the failed attempt to rescue the fifty-two Americans held hostage at the U.S. embassy in Tehran. Instead, President Richard Nixon ordered the formation of the special Inter-Departmental Working Group on Terrorism, chaired by Secretary of State Henry Kissinger, and elected to concentrate on diplomatic initiatives in the UN and elsewhere, focusing on the adoption of international conventions against terrorism.

The real lesson of Munich, however, was a somewhat counterintuitive one. The Olympic tragedy provided the first clear evidence that even terrorist attacks that fail to achieve their ostensible objectives can nonetheless still be counted successful provided that the operation is sufficiently dramatic to capture the attention of the media. In terms of the publicity and exposure accorded the Palestinian cause, Munich was an unequivocal success—a point conceded by even the most senior PLO officials. According to Abu Iyad, the organization's intelligence chief at the time, longtime confidant of Arafat and cofounder with him of al-Fatah, the Black September terrorists admittedly "didn't bring about the liberation of any of their comrades imprisoned in Israel as they had hoped, but they did attain the operation's other two objectives: World opinion was forced to take note of the Palestinian drama, and the Palestinian people imposed their presence on an international gathering that had sought to exclude them."[7]

Indeed, despite the worldwide condemnation of the terrorists' actions at the time, it soon became apparent that for the Palestinians, Munich was in fact a spectacular publicity coup. The undivided attention of some four thousand print and radio journalists and two thousand television reporters and crew already in place to cover the Olympics was suddenly refocused on Palestine and the Palestinian cause.[8] An estimated nine hundred million people in at least a hundred different countries saw the crisis unfold on their television screens.[9] According to one observer, "If one includes other forms of media it is safe to say that over a quarter of the world's population was at least aware of Black September's attack."[10] It seems fair to suppose that few viewers who tuned in to watch the games would forget the image emblazoned on their television screens of a terrorist, his face concealed by a balaclava, standing on the balcony of the Israeli suite at the Olympic village, preening in front of the cameras. Henceforth, those people throughout the world who before the games had neither known of the Palestinians nor been familiar with their cause were no longer as ignorant or dismissive. As an elderly Palestinian refugee remarked to a British reporter shortly after the attack, "From Munich onwards nobody could ignore the Palestinians or their cause."[11]

Furthermore, the brutal dimensions of the operation, and its perpetrators' desperate plea for attention and recognition, convinced many across the world that the Palestinians were now a force to be reckoned with and possessed a cause that could no longer justifiably be denied. Black September was jubilant. In a communiqué published in a Beirut newspaper a week after the attack, the group proudly announced:

> In our assessment, and in light of the result, we have made one of the best achievements of Palestinian commando action. A bomb in the White

House, a mine in the Vatican, the death of Mao Tse-Tung, an earthquake in Paris could not have echoed through the consciousness of every man in the world like the operation at Munich. The Olympiad arouses the people's interest and attention more than anything else in the world. The choice of the Olympics, from the purely propagandistic view-point, was 100 percent successful. It was like painting the name of Palestine on a mountain that can be seen from the four corners of the earth.[12]

During the weeks that followed the incident, thousands of Palestinians rushed to join the PLO's constituent terrorist organizations.[13] It is perhaps not entirely coincidental, then, that eighteen months after Munich, the PLO's leader, Yasir Arafat, was invited to address the UN General Assembly and shortly afterward the PLO was granted special observer status in that international body. Indeed, by the end of the 1970s the PLO, a nonstate actor, had formal diplomatic relations with more countries (eighty-six) than the actual established nation-state of Israel (seventy-two). It is doubtful whether the PLO could ever have achieved this success had it not resorted to international terrorism. Within four years, a handful of Palestinian terrorists had overcome a quarter century of neglect and obscurity. They had achieved what diplomats and statesmen, lobbyists and humanitarian workers had persistently tried and failed to do: focusing world attention on the Palestinian people and their plight. They had also provided a powerful example to similarly frustrated ethnic and nationalist groups elsewhere, and within the decade, the number of terrorist groups either operating internationally or committing attacks against foreign targets in their own country to attract international attention had more than quadrupled. According to the international terrorism incident database formerly maintained by the RAND Corporation,[14] the number of organizations engaged in *international* terrorism grew from only eleven in 1968 (of which just three were ethnonationalist/separatist organizations, and the remainder were radical Marxist-Leninist or left-wing groups) to an astonishing fifty-five in 1978. Of this total, more than half (thirty, or 54 percent) were ethnonationalist/separatist movements, all seeking to copy or capitalize on the PLO's success. They ranged from large international communities of displaced persons with profound historical grievances, such as the Armenian diaspora, to minuscule self-contained entities like the obscure expatriate South Moluccan community in the Netherlands. What they all had in common, however, was a burning sense of injustice and dispossession, and a belief that through *international* terrorism they too could finally attract worldwide attention to themselves and their causes.

The Palestinians as Model:
The Rise of Ethnonationalist Terrorism

The Armenians, as noted in chapter 1, had waged an inchoate armed struggle against Ottoman rule during the 1880s and 1890s in hopes of eliciting Western sympathy and intervention. Their revolt had culminated in 1896 with the daring but ill-fated seizure of the Ottoman Bank in Constantinople. This event was followed by three days of intense anti-Armenian rioting and bloodshed during which untold numbers of Armenians lost their lives. Thereafter, most overt manifestations of Armenian nationalism lapsed into temporary abeyance, and those that did surface were forcibly suppressed. Nationalist activity was rekindled, however, during World War I, mostly as a result of Russian efforts to foment Armenian unrest and thereby undermine the common enemy, Turkey. Ottoman suspicions of their Armenian subjects' loyalty, already aggravated by these Russian interventions, were further inflamed by the Armenians' refusal to support the Turkish war effort. Accordingly, in 1915, Taalat Pasha, the Ottoman interior minister, ordered the Armenians' expulsion from their traditional homelands in eastern Turkey to Syria and Iraq. Although the exact number of Armenians who perished at this time of widespread war and upheaval remains a matter of considerable debate, the figure most commonly cited is 1.5 million people—roughly 60 percent of Turkey's Armenian population. The events of 1915, therefore, are often cited as the first state genocide of the twentieth century.

Despite the magnitude of this catastrophe, for sixty years thereafter the Armenians' tragic history remained either ignored or forgotten. This began to change in 1975 when two Armenian terrorist groups—known as ASALA (the Armenian Army for the Secret Liberation of Armenia) and the JCAG (Justice Commandos of the Armenian Genocide)—emerged from the civil war then engulfing Lebanon. When asked to account for the sudden reemergence of Armenian terrorism, Hagop Hagopian, ASALA's founder and leader, unhesitatingly cited the Palestinian example. "There are substantially two factors to be taken into consideration," he stated in a 1975 interview, namely, the "general discovery as to the failure of the policy of the traditional Armenian parties [to publicize the Armenians' cause and grievances] . . . and the fact that many Armenians since 1966 participated in the Palestinian Arab struggle from which they learned many things."[15] Indeed, so important was the Palestinians' influence, and so close were their relations with the Armenian community in Lebanon, that ASALA can claim direct descent from both George Habash's PFLP and an even more radical splinter group of that organization, the PFLP Special Operations Group, led by Dr. Wadi Haddad.[16]

The similarities and circumstances of these two dispossessed peoples' respective plights had an almost hypnotic effect on young Armenians living in Beirut. Indeed, nearly twenty years later, the Palestinian influence still burned bright for a new generation of young Armenians fighting for control over the Caucasus enclave of Nagorno Karabakh. As one observer noted in 1994 after meeting with these men while on a visit to Yerevan, most of them "viewed the 'Palestinian cause' as a model that had attracted world wide attention. Palestinians were seen as people like themselves—persecuted without a homeland."[17] In ASALA's case, the relationship between the two peoples was solidified through the PFLP's generous provision of arms, training, and other forms of assistance.

It was ASALA's early success in reinvigorating the Armenian cause that prompted the formation of a rival group, the JCAG. Although the two differed in their ideology—ASALA was avowedly Marxist-Leninist, adhering to the PFLP's global revolutionary orientation, while the JCAG tended to represent more mainstream Armenian nationalist views—both had the same three goals: to exact revenge for the events of 1915, to force the present Turkish republic to recognize the genocide committed by its Ottoman predecessors and thereby accept responsibility for it, and to compel the Turkish government to make reparations payments to the survivors and their descendants. In pursuit of these ends, between 1975 and 1985 more than forty Turkish diplomats and members of their families were murdered by Armenian terrorists. Whereas the JCAG (and its splinter group, the Armenian Revolutionary Army) preferred individual assassinations of Turkish diplomats or nonlethal bombings of Turkish diplomatic and airline facilities, ASALA tended to employ more indiscriminate tactics and weapons, evincing little concern about who was killed or injured, Turk and non-Turk alike, so long as the operation succeeded in attracting attention. In July 1983, for example, ASALA bombed the Turkish airline's ticket counter at Orly Airport in Paris, killing seven people and wounding fifty-six others. A month later, an ASALA attack at Ankara's Esenboga Airport killed nine people and injured seventy-eight, while an assault mounted in Istanbul's Grand Bazaar killed two and wounded twenty-seven. Indeed, ASALA's brutal tactics and desperate bids for attention drew comparisons with the ruthlessness of the Palestinian Black September Organization in general and the Olympics massacre in particular.[18] It was even reported that Hagopian himself had participated in the Munich operation.[19]

By the early 1980s, the Armenians' use of terrorism had apparently paid off. "Thus it is true that the re-emergence of the Armenian question in the news—and especially of the Armenian genocide—is largely owing to Armenian terrorists," wrote Gerard Chaliand, a French Armenian scholar and one of the world's foremost authorities on terrorism and guerrilla warfare, in 1983.[20] A year earlier, in a study of the Armenian terrorist movements, Andrew Corsun, one of the U.S. State Department's leading analysts of terrorism, similarly argued that "by resorting to terrorism, Armenian extremists were able to accomplish in 5 years what legitimate Armenian organizations have been trying to do for almost 70 years—internationalize the Armenian cause."[21] However, while publicity and exposure proved to be easily gained through terrorism, the Armenian groups also found that attention does not necessarily translate into more tangible gains. For example, a detailed empirical study of American network news coverage of Armenian terrorism between 1968 and 1983 concluded that while the terrorist campaign had certainly increased public name recognition of the Armenians, it had not engendered any meaningful awareness or sensitivity about the Armenians' cause, their historical condition, or their political aims.[22] More critical, perhaps, was the fact that, unlike the Palestinians, the vast majority of the worldwide Armenian diaspora did not rally to, much less actively support, the terrorists. Despite expressions of understanding of the terrorists' goals and motivations, the Armenian community offered them little overt assistance and became increasingly alienated by the violent acts committed in its name. What minimal actual support did exist began to dry up following the 1983 Orly Airport attack, to the point that, by the end of the decade, none of the Armenian terrorist groups was still actively engaged in international terrorism.

The tiny South Moluccan expatriate community in the Netherlands is yet another example of an ethnonationalist group that sought to duplicate the Palestinians' success during the period following the Munich Olympics attack. Some fifteen thousand South Moluccans had emigrated to the Netherlands in 1951 from their native Indonesia, following the incorporation of their Republic of the South Moluccas into the Indonesian state of Negara Indonesia Timur. For more than twenty years, they nursed increasingly futile hopes of returning to their homeland and reestablishing their independent nation. In 1977, militant elements within the mainstream Free South Moluccan Organization lost patience and prepared to embark on a campaign of terrorism designed to internationalize their cause and realize their nationalist goals. In June of that year, two groups of terrorists, respectively, hijacked a Dutch passenger train and seized a nearby schoolhouse, taking hostages in both cases. They had, in fact, gotten their idea of seizing the train from press coverage of a similar operation attempted by Palestinian terrorists.[23] Both hostage seizures were successfully resolved by Royal Dutch

Marine commandos who stormed both the train (killing six of the nine terrorists, and tragically, two of the fifty-one hostages) and the schoolhouse, where all four terrorists were apprehended without bloodshed. Like the Armenians, the South Moluccans discovered the difficulties of converting publicity into actual political achievement. While the train and schoolhouse seizures brought the Moluccans more attention and publicity than they could otherwise ever have hoped to obtain, in the end this exposure did nothing to advance their cause or bring them any closer to obtaining their nationalist goals.

As a universally applicable model, therefore, the Palestinian archetype seems wanting. Nonetheless, nearly twenty years later, the Palestinian example continued to loom large for ethnonationalist/separatist groups seeking international recognition and self-determination. During the 1990s, for example, Kurds fighting for autonomy in southeastern Turkey reportedly debated whether to adopt the Palestinian model for their own struggle. To date, the Kurdish Workers Party (PKK)—which renamed itself Kongra-Gel (KGK) in 2003—has largely eschewed *international* terrorism as a means to advance its nationalist claims, concentrating instead on an internal campaign of rural guerrilla warfare coupled with occasional acts of urban terrorism inside Turkey only. But its failure to win the international attention and stature that other, similar movements such as the PLO enjoy had reportedly led to increasing discontent among younger Kurdish militants. "Proponents of terrorism," one account from that time noted, argue that "the Palestinians have embassies in more than 100 countries while the Kurds, a far larger minority, have none."[24] Accordingly, they pressed for the adoption of an aggressive campaign of international terrorism—against the advice of their more moderate elders, who argued that such a strategy would ultimately deprive their cause of both credibility and international sympathy.

The Palestinians as Mentors: The Rise of Revolutionary Left-Wing Terrorism

The "internationalization" of terrorism that occurred in the late 1960s and early 1970s was not solely a product of Palestinian influence and success. Outside the Middle East, a combination of societal malaise and youthful idealism, rebelliousness and antimilitarism/anti-imperialism was rapidly transforming the collective political consciousness among the more affluent countries of Western Europe and North America. Perhaps the unprecedented economic prosperity of these years allowed the luxury of introspection and self-criticism that, in more radical political circles, generated a revulsion against the socioeconomic inequities endemic to the modern, industrialized capitalist state. "All they can think about," Ulrike Meinhof, the political activist and radical newspaper columnist turned Red Army Faction (RAF) terrorist, once dismissively remarked of her fellow Germans, "is some hairspray, a vacation in Spain, and a tiled bathroom."[25]

The sharp contrast between the highest and the lowest domestic levels of wealth and consumer consumption was further accentuated by the growing economic disparity between the developed world and the undeveloped world—as it came to be called, the "Third World." This was attributed by radicals as much to the "neocolonialist" ethos and economic exploitation inherent in capitalism as to the interventionist foreign policy championed by the United States under the banner of fighting the spread of communism. Thus, by the late 1960s, opposition to America's involvement in Indochina had emerged as the principal rallying cry for politically engaged, disaffected youth everywhere. "Anti-imperialism meant first of all the protest against the Vietnam war, but also [against] the American predominance over most countries of the Third World," the former RAF terrorist Christoph Wackernagel explained in a 1995 speech recounting his own experience.[26]

Indeed, to a great extent, the Red Army Faction (in German, Rote Armee Fraktion, more popularly known as the Baader-Meinhof Group) and its sister terrorist organization, the Second of June Movement, encapsulated the revolutionary spirit and antiestablishment attitudes typical of left-wing terrorists in other Western countries at the time. Both groups emerged from the communes and student associations that were part of the counterculture in late-1960s West Germany, and it was consequently impossible to separate their radical politics from their alternative lifestyles. Revolution and armed struggle went hand in hand with sexual promiscuity and drug use. "You must understand," Astrid Proll, a member of the RAF's first generation, later explained, "that then the most fantastic thing in the world was not to be a rock star, but a revolutionary."[27] Michael "Bommi" (the nickname given to him because of his penchant for bombing) Baumann, a leading member of the Second of June Movement, similarly describes in his memoir how

> with me it all began with rock music and long hair. . . . It was like this: if you had long hair, things were suddenly like they are for the Blacks. Do you understand? They threw us out of joints, they cursed at us and ran after us—all you had was trouble. . . . So you start building contact with a few people like yourself, other dropouts, or whatever you want to call them. You begin to orient yourself differently.[28]

Yet it would be a mistake to dismiss Proll and Baumann simply as apolitical narcissists or mere dropouts from society. Like many of their generation, they too were animated by a profound sense of social injustice coupled with an intense enmity toward what they perceived as worldwide American militarism and domination. "To my mind, it wasn't simply an international question," the German terrorist Hans Joachim Klein recalled in a 1978 interview,[29] "but also an internal problem. The B-52s stopped over at Wiesbaden on their way from Vietnam."[30] The pervasive influence of the Vietnam War on German terrorism can be seen in several of the contemporary Second of June statements reproduced in Baumann's autobiography,[31] as well as in RAF communiqués issued long after the war and American involvement in Indochina ended. The RAF's first *actual* terrorist operation (that is, other than bank robberies) was in retaliation for the U.S. Air Force's mining of North Vietnam's Haiphong harbor. The target was the U.S. Fifth Army Corps officers' mess at Frankfurt: one person was killed and thirteen others were injured in the bomb attack. As Brigitte Monhaupt, who later emerged as one of the group's key leaders, explained to a German court in 1976, "The strategic concept as developed by the RAF . . . was directed against the U.S. military presence in the Federal Republic. . . . The concept was enveloped by us all in the collective discussion process."[32]

With the end of the Vietnam War, the German terrorists in both the RAF and other groups needed to find a new cause. Their choice again reflected the international orientation of West German radical politics: common cause was now to be made with the Palestinians. In his book, Baumann described the logic behind this decision. "Since Vietnam is finished," the argument ran, "people should get involved with Palestine. It is actually much closer to us, which is apparent today with the oil business, and has more to do with us here in the European cities than does Vietnam. This was to become the new framework to carry on the struggle here."[33]

The Palestinians were in fact the obvious candidates. As far back as 1968, the PLO—and Habash's PFLP especially—had welcomed terrorists from around the world to its guerrilla camps in Jordan for training, indoctrination, and the general building of transnational revolutionary bridges. In this respect, the Palestinians pioneered the networking dimension of international terrorism and multinational operational attack teams still in evidence among many groups today. In 1969, the Palestinians had welcomed the first delegation of West German terrorists—Baumann's comrades in the "Blues" group, an early precursor of the Second of June Movement—to their guerrilla training camps in Jordan. "They got some training there: how to shoot; how to make bombs; how to fight," Baumann recalled. "But the Palestinians told them to go back to Germany and make propaganda for them. That was all they were hot for—they offered no weapons."[34] The following year, another party of German terrorists—including Andreas Baader, Gudrun Ensslin, Ulrike Meinhof, and six of their colleagues—secretly made their way to Beirut and then to Palestinian terrorist camps in Jordan, as much to escape the police dragnet closing in on them at home as to receive training as urban guerrillas. Although relations between the Germans and their Palestinian hosts were strained to the point that, after two months, the group was asked to leave, Baader and company had by this time learned enough to enable them formally to establish their own terrorist group—the RAF. According to terrorism scholar David Rapoport, this development marked a significant milestone in the history of terrorism, since it was probably the first time that one terrorist group had trained another.[35]

Thereafter, the relationship between the German and Palestinian groups flourished. Combined teams of German and Palestinian terrorists were involved in the 1975 seizure of the OPEC (Organization of Petroleum Exporting Countries) oil ministers' conference in Vienna, the 1976 hijacking of an Air France flight to Entebbe, Uganda, and the hijacking (mentioned previously) of a Lufthansa flight to Somalia in 1977. The Germans also reportedly provided critical logistical assistance to the Palestinian Black September terrorists responsible for the Munich massacre. Although the closest ties were forged with the PFLP, Arafat's comparatively more moderate al-Fatah organization played a particularly important role in supplying the RAF with weapons. Its political agents in Germany, assigned primarily to fund-raising activities, operated a profitable business on the side selling handguns to the RAF. Indeed, according to leading German-Israeli counterterrorism analyst David Schiller, without the assistance provided by the Palestinian terrorists to their German counterparts the latter could not have survived.[36]

The profound influence exercised by the Palestinians over the Germans was perhaps never more clear than in 1985, when the RAF joined forces with the French left-wing terrorist organization Direct Action (in French, Action Directe, thus AD), in hopes of creating a PLO-like umbrella "anti-imperialist front of Western European guerrillas" that would include Italy's Red Brigades (RB) and the Belgian Communist Combatant Cells (CCC) as well. But just as the Armenians' and South Moluccans' attempts to replicate the PLO's success had foundered, so did the efforts of German and French organizations. Within two years, the promised campaign of "Euroterrorism" against NATO's politico-military structure had fizzled out. The global conditions that had produced and nurtured these organizations—that indeed had endowed them with their fundamental raison d'être—were changing more rapidly than they could adapt, thus threatening to turn them into hopeless anachronisms. Crippled by the arrests of the leading members of the French and Belgian groups, the "anti-imperialist front" fell into disarray. Not surprisingly, perhaps, the Red Brigades shortly afterward drifted into complete lassitude. The forty-year revolutionary struggle it had so proudly proclaimed for the Italian people less than a decade earlier had run out of steam before even a generation had passed. In Germany, meanwhile, the RAF disconsolately carried on, despite the political revolutions then transforming the Soviet Union and Eastern Europe. The fall of the Berlin Wall in 1989 and the national reunification that followed deprived the group of its ideological resilience as well as a convenient cross-border sanctuary. Politically marginalized and bereft of either patron or safe haven, the RAF finally collapsed in 1992 under the weight of its own exhaustion and the indifference of those in the newly united Germany whom the group still purported to represent.

Thus, of the four radical movements that only a few decades ago attempted collectively to realize the revolution that they believed was inevitable, none remains. Yet more than sixty years after its founding, the PLO—though still short of its ultimate goal of true sovereignty over a bona fide Palestinian state—has nonetheless survived expulsions and dislocations, internal rivalry and external enmity, to continue the struggle begun long ago in an equally transformed political environment.

Conclusion

The PLO, as a terrorist movement, is arguably unique in history. Not only was it the first truly international terrorist organization, it also consistently embraced a far more internationalist orientation than most other terrorist groups. Some accounts suggest that by the early 1980s, at least forty different terrorist groups—from Asia, Africa, North America, Europe, and the Middle East—had been trained by the PLO at its camps in Jordan, Lebanon, and Yemen, among other places. The Palestinians' purpose in this tutelary role was not entirely philanthropic. The foreign participants in these courses were reportedly charged between five thousand and ten thousand U.S. dollars each for a six-week program of instruction. In addition, many of them were later recruited to participate in joint operations alongside Palestinian terrorists. Thus, according to Israeli defense sources, the PLO in 1981 had active cooperative arrangements with some twenty-two different terrorist organizations that had previously benefited from Palestinian training, weapons supply, and other logistical support.[37]

The PLO was also one of the first terrorist groups actively to pursue the accumulation of capital and wealth as an organizational priority. By the mid-

1980s, it was estimated to have established an annual income flow of some $600 million, of which some $500 million was derived from investments.[38] The amassing of so vast a fortune is all the more astonishing given the fact that when the PLO was established in 1964, it had no funds, no infrastructure, and no real direction. It was not until Arafat's election as chairman in 1968 that the PLO started to become the major force in international politics that it remains today. As renowned former *Sunday Times* journalist and authority on terrorism James Adams has observed: "As the PLO has grown in complexity and its income has risen accordingly, the organisation has had to adapt to a changing role and an altered image of itself. While the world still viewed the PLO as a bunch of terrorist fanatics robbing banks and blowing up aircraft to boost their cause, the secret side of the organisation was being rapidly transformed."[39]

Thus, the attention that the PLO has received, the financial and political influence and power that it has amassed, and the stature that it has been accorded in the international community continues to send a powerful message to aggrieved peoples throughout the world. Ironically, this "success" has also had a profound effect on the PLO's commitment to terrorism. It can be argued that despite the fiery rhetoric, even an international terrorist organization such as the PLO does not necessarily have an overriding interest in upsetting the international order of which it yearns to become an accepted part. This is not entirely surprising, given the PLO's unique international orientation. But what makes this process especially noteworthy is that the PLO's internationalist efforts had long since expanded beyond the narrow goal of forging tactical alliances with other terrorist groups. Indeed, from the mid-1970s, al-Fatah in particular—but also the mainstream PLO in general—has actively sought to establish relations with as many countries as possible, regardless of their form of government or concern with the Palestinian cause. In pursuit of this policy, the PLO often abjured from committing certain types of operations against non-Israeli targets, attempted to impose restrictions on the geographical range of terrorist acts committed by its constituent groups (as, for example, in Arafat's 1988 prohibition of Palestinian terrorist activities outside of Israel and the occupied territories and his previous 1974 edict banning terrorist operations in Europe), and frequently tried to cover up its involvement in or sponsorship of terrorist incidents that violated these declared self-imposed restraints. Over time, therefore, the most radical of its aims have been forsaken in favor of what the moderate leadership has defined as the organization's "national interest." Or, as Abu Iyad more dourly described this process: "What we feared most of all . . . has happened. Our movement has become bureaucratized. What it gained in respectability it lost in militancy. We have acquired a taste for dealing with governments and men of power."[40] Indeed, the PLO, as the ruling party in the Palestine Authority on the West Bank and Gaza until the January 2006 elections, had to deal with the same daily complaints of incompetence, lethargy, inefficiency, and corruption faced by governments the world over.[41]

Chapter 4

Religion and Terrorism

A few hours after the first American air strikes against Afghanistan began on October 7, 2001, a prerecorded videotape was broadcast around the world. A tall, skinny man with a long, scraggly beard, wearing a camouflage fatigue jacket and the headdress of a desert tribesman, with an AK-47 assault rifle at his side, stood before a rocky backdrop. In measured yet defiant language, Osama bin Laden once again declared war on the United States. Like all his previous statements, bin Laden's message that day was unmistakably religious in tone and content. "Praise be to God and we beseech him for help and forgiveness," it began.

> We seek refuge with the Lord of our bad and evildoing. He whom God guides is rightly guided but he whom God leaves to stray, for him wilt thou find no protector to lead him to the right way.
>
> I witness that there is no God but God and Muhammad is his slave and prophet.
>
> God Almighty hit the United States at its most vulnerable spot. He destroyed its greatest buildings. Praise be to God.
>
> Here is the United States. It was filled with terror from its north to its south and from its east to its west. Praise be to God.

In thanking his god for the death and destruction that al-Qaeda wrought on 9/11, bin Laden clearly had cast his struggle in incontrovertibly theological terms. "As for the United States," he concluded, "I tell it and its people these few words: I swear by Almighty God, who raised the heavens without pillars, that neither the United States nor he who lives in the United States will enjoy security before we can see it as a reality in Palestine and before all the infidel armies leave the land of Muhammad, may God's peace and blessing be upon him."[1]

Throughout history, many terrorist groups have evidenced a strong religious component, mostly by dint of their membership. Anticolonial, nationalist movements such as the Jewish terrorist organizations active in preindependence Israel and the Muslim-dominated FLN in Algeria come readily to mind, as do more recent examples such as the overwhelmingly Catholic IRA; its Protestant counterparts, arrayed in various loyalist paramilitary groups such as the Ulster Freedom Fighters, the Ulster Volunteer Force, and the Red Hand Commandos; and the predominantly Muslim PLO. In all these groups, however, it is the political rather than the religious aspect of their motivation that is dominant; the preeminence of their ethnonationalist or irredentist aims, or both, is incontestable.

But for others such as al-Qaeda, however, the religious motive is overriding, and indeed, the religious imperative for terrorism has become the most important defining characteristic of terrorist activity today. The consequences of the revolution that transformed Iran into an Islamic republic in 1979 played a crucial role in the resurgence of this strand of terrorism, but the modern advent of religious terrorism has not been confined exclusively to Iran, much less to the Middle East or to Islam or indeed to al-Qaeda: since the 1980s, it has involved elements of all the world's major religions and, in some instances, smaller sects or cults as well. "I have no regrets," said Yigal Amir, the Jewish extremist who in 1995 assassinated Israeli prime minister Yitzhak Rabin, to the police. "I acted alone and on orders from God."[2] Today, Amir's words could just as easily have come from the mouths of the ISIS fanatics whose violence in 2015 claimed the lives of more than six thousand persons—Sunnis, Shi'a, Sufis, Druze, Kurds, Alawites, and Yazidis, as well as Christians and Jews;[3] the Hamas and Palestine Islamic Jihad (PIJ) terrorists responsible for the wave of suicide bombings of civilian buses and public gathering places that convulsed Israel between 2000 and 2005; the young Dutch-Moroccan Muslim who brutally murdered controversial filmmaker Theo van Gogh in November 2004;[4] the Japanese followers of Shoko Asahara in the Aum Shinrikyo sect who perpetrated the March 1995 nerve gas attack on the Tokyo subway in hopes of hastening a new millennium; the militant Sikh movement that embarked on a bloody but inchoate campaign of international terrorism during the 1980s; or the American Christian white supremacist Patriot movement, which, acting on an even more complex and less comprehensible mixture of seditious, millenarian, paranoiac, and anti-government beliefs, has waged a campaign of bombing and assassination in the United States. As will become apparent, terrorism motivated either in whole or in part by a religious imperative, where violence is regarded by its practitioners as a divine duty or sacramental act, embraces markedly different means of legitimation and justification than that committed by secular terrorists, and these distinguishing features lead, in turn, to yet greater bloodshed and destruction.

The connection between religion and terrorism is not new. More than two thousand years ago, the first acts of what we now describe as terrorism were perpetrated by religious fanatics. Indeed, some of the words we use in the English language to describe terrorists and their actions are derived from the names of Jewish, Hindi, and Muslim terrorist groups active long ago. The etymology of the word "zealot,"[5] for example, which to us means an "immoderate partisan" or a "fanatical enthusiast," can be traced back to a millenarian Jewish sect of the same name that fought in A.D. 66–73 against the Roman Empire's occupation of Israel. The Zealots waged a ruthless campaign of assassination, mostly of individuals, relying on the *sica*, a primitive dagger. The Zealot would emerge from the anonymous obscurity of a crowded marketplace, draw the *sica* that had been concealed beneath his robes, and in plain view of those present, dramatically slit the throat of a Roman legionnaire or a Jewish citizen who had been judged by the group guilty of betrayal, apostasy, or both. Thus, in an era long before 24/7 television news and the transmission of instantaneous live satellite images, the Zealots' dramatic public acts of violence—precisely like those of terrorists today—were designed to have psychological repercussions far beyond the immediate victim(s) of the terrorist attack and thereby to send a powerful message to a wider, watching target audience, namely, the Roman occupation administration and Jews who collaborated with the invaders. The Zealots are also reputed to have employed a primitive form of chemical warfare, poisoning wells and granaries used by the Romans and even sabotaging Jerusalem's water supply.[6]

Similarly, the word "thug," now used to describe "a vicious or brutal ruffian,"[7] is derived from a seventh-century religious cult that terrorized India until its suppression in the mid-nineteenth century. The Thugs engaged in acts of ritual murder designed to serve the Hindu goddess of terror and destruction, Kali. On specified holy days throughout the year, group members would forsake their daily occupations and lie in wait for innocent travelers, who would be ritually strangled as sacrificial offerings to Kali. According to some accounts, the Thugs killed as many as a million people during their twelve-hundred-year existence, or more than eight hundred individuals every year, a murder rate rarely equaled by their modern-day counterparts armed with far more efficient and destructively lethal weaponry.[8]

Finally, the word "assassin"—"one who undertakes to put another to death by treacherous violence"[9]—was the name of a radical offshoot of the Muslim Shi'a Ismaili sect, which between A.D. 1090 and 1272 fought to repel the Christian crusaders attempting to conquer present-day Syria and Iran. Literally translated, "assassin" means "hashish eater," a reference to the ritual intoxication that, as legend has it, the Assassins supposedly undertook before embarking on their missions of murder. Violence for the Assassins was a sacramental act, a divine duty, commanded by religious text and communicated by clerical authorities. Accordingly, the Assassins' violence was meant not only to vanquish the sect's Christian enemies but also to hasten the dawn of a new millennium as well. An important additional motivation for an Assassin was the promise that, should he himself perish in the course of carrying out his attack, he would ascend immediately to a glorious heaven. This same ethos of self-sacrifice and suicidal martyrdom can be seen in many Islamic—and indeed other religious—terrorist organizations today.

Until the nineteenth century, in fact, as David Rapoport points out in his seminal study of what he terms "holy terror," religion provided the only justification for terrorism.[10] Many of the political developments of this era discussed in chapter 1—including the end of divine, monarchical rule in Europe at the beginning of the nineteenth century, followed by the emergence of new concepts redefining the role of both citizen and state, alongside emergent notions of nationalism and self-determination—account for the shift in motivation and emphasis that then took place. The growing popularity of various schools of radical political thought, embracing Marxist ideology (or its subsequent Leninist and Maoist interpretations), anarchism, and nihilism, completed the transformation of terrorism from a mostly religious to a predominantly secular phenomenon. This process of "secularization" was given fresh impetus by the anticolonialist/national liberation movements that arose after World War II to challenge continued Western rule in Asia, the Middle East, and Africa, and subsequently exerted so profound an influence on ethnonationalist/separatist and ideological terrorist organizations in the late 1960s and early 1970s.

While terrorism and religion share a long history, for the past century this particular manifestation has mostly tended to be overshadowed by ethnonationalist/separatist and ideologically motivated terrorism. For example, none of the eleven *identifiable* international terrorist groups active in 1968—the year, as previously noted, credited with marking the advent of modern, international terrorism—could be classified as religious: that is, having aims and motivations reflecting a predominant religious character or influence.[11] This, perhaps, was only to be expected at the height of the Cold War, when the majority of terrorist groups (eight) were left-wing, revolutionary Marxist-Leninist ideological organizations, and the remaining three—including the various constituent groups of the PLO—reflected the emergence of the first postcolonial, ethnonationalist/separatist organizations. Not until 1980—as a result of the repercussions of the revolution in Iran the previous year—did the first modern religious terrorist groups appear. Even so, despite the large increase in the total number of identifiable international terrorist groups from eleven to sixty-four and the concomitant tenfold increase (from three to thirty-two) in ethnonationalist/separatist organizations (for reasons described in chapter 3), only two of the sixty-four groups active in 1980 could be classified as predominantly religious in character and motivation: the Iranian-backed Shi'a organizations al-Dawa and the Committee for Safeguarding the Islamic Revolution.

However, while the reemergence of modern religious terrorism was initially closely associated with the Islamic revolution in Iran, within a decade of that event none of the world's major religions could claim to be immune to the same volatile mixture of faith, fanaticism, and violence. Twelve years later, in 1992, the number of religious terrorist groups had increased exponentially (from two to eleven groups) and moreover had expanded to embrace major world religions other than Islam, as well as various obscure religious sects and cults.

It is interesting to note that as the number of religious terrorist groups was increasing, the number of ethnonationalist/separatist terrorist groups declined appreciably. One explanation for this trend may be that many ethnonationalist/separatist groups, suddenly finding themselves at the end of the Cold War enmeshed in bitter conflict and civil wars over their respective homelands—in Bosnia, Chechnya, Nagorno Karabakh, and other parts of the Balkans, Eastern Europe, and the former Soviet Union, for example—consequently had little time or energy to engage in international terrorism. Another plausible explanation is that at a time when the rigid bipolar structure of the Cold War that had throttled the United Nations for nearly half a century was breaking down and new nations were obtaining sovereignty and rapidly gaining admission to the international community, there was perhaps less reason to resort to international terrorism to have one's own irredentist claims recognized. Also, in circumstances where previous impediments to UN membership no longer existed, many groups may have come to regard the use of international terrorism not only as an embarrassment that could potentially vitiate their case for joining the community of nations but as counterproductive. Finally, it is also interesting to note that notwithstanding the end of the Cold War and the demise of the Soviet

Union and the Warsaw Pact, the number of groups espousing Marxist-Leninist-Maoist dogma (or some idiosyncratic interpretation of those ideological elements) remained unchanged, thus further challenging the Cold War myth of a global terrorist conspiracy directed by, and dependent upon, Moscow and its communist minions.

Significantly, during the 1990s the growth in the number of religious terrorist groups as a proportion of all active international terrorist organizations increased significantly. In 1994, for example, a third (sixteen) of the forty-nine identifiable international terrorist groups active that year could be classified as religious in character or motivation, or both, and in 1995, their number grew yet again, to account for nearly half (twenty-six, or 46 percent) of the fifty-six known active international terrorist groups. A decade later, it was perhaps not surprising to find that this trend not only continued but solidified. In 2004, for instance, nearly half (fifty-two, or 46 percent) of the terrorist groups active that year were religious, while thirty-two (28 percent) were left-wing groups, and twenty-four (21 percent) were ethnonationalist/separatist organizations. And, in 2016, an astonishing three-quarters, or forty-four of the fifty-nine, groups designated Foreign Terrorist Organizations (FTOs) by the U.S. State Department can be classified as having a salient religious motivation or justification for their violence.[12]

It is perhaps not surprising that religion should become a far more popular motivation for terrorism in the post–Cold War era as old ideologies lie discredited by the collapse of the Soviet Union and irrelevance of communist ideology, and the promise of munificent benefits from the liberal-democratic, capitalist state, once apparently triumphant at what Francis Fukuyama termed the "end of history," failed to materialize in many countries throughout the world. The "public sense of insecurity" engendered by these changes[13]—which has affected both the most economically disadvantaged and the most prosperous—has been deepened by other societal factors, including accelerated population growth, rapid urbanization, and the breakdown of local services (e.g., medical care, housing, social welfare programs, and education), typically provided by the state.

The salience of religion as the major driving force behind international terrorism in the decade preceding 9/11 is further evidenced by the fact that the most serious terrorist acts of that era—whether reckoned in terms of political implications and consequences or numbers of fatalities caused—all had a significant religious dimension or motivation, or both. They included:

- the March 1995 sarin nerve gas attack on the Tokyo subway system, perpetrated by an apocalyptic Japanese religious cult, which killed 12 people and wounded 3,796 others,[14] along with reports that the group also planned to carry out identical attacks in the United States;[15]

- the August 1998 simultaneous suicide car and truck bombings of the U.S. embassies in Nairobi, Kenya, and Dar es Salaam, Tanzania, by al-Qaeda, in which 301 people were killed and more than 5,000 wounded;
- the bombing of a shopping mall in Zamboanga, Philippines, that same December by Muslim extremists belonging to the Abu Sayyaf Group, wounding 60 Christians who were Christmas shopping;
- the April 1995 bombing of an Oklahoma City federal office building by individuals influenced by Christian Patriot ideology, where 168 people perished;
- the 1993 bombing of New York City's World Trade Center by Islamic radicals who deliberately attempted to topple one of the Twin Towers onto the other;
- the assassination in November 1995, as previously mentioned, of Israeli premier Yitzhak Rabin by a Jewish religious extremist, intended as only the first step in a campaign of mass murder designed to disrupt the peace process;
- the June 1996 truck bombing of a U.S. Air Force barracks in Dhahran, Saudi Arabia, where 19 people perished, by religious militants opposed to the reigning al-Saud regime;
- the string of bloody attacks by Hamas suicide bombers that turned the tide of Israel's national elections, killing 60 people, between February and March 1996;
- the brutal machine-gun and hand-grenade attack carried out by Egyptian Islamic militants on a group of Western tourists, killing 18, outside their Cairo hotel in April 1996;
- the November 1997 massacre of 58 foreign tourists and 4 Egyptians by terrorists belonging to the Gamat al-Islamiya (Islamic Group) at the Temple of Queen Hatshepsut in Luxor, Egypt;
- the series of thirteen nearly simultaneous car and truck bombings that shook Bombay (now Mumbai), India, in February 1993, killing 400 people and injuring more than 1,000 others, in reprisal for the destruction of an Islamic shrine in that country;
- the December 1994 hijacking of an Air France passenger jet by Islamic terrorists belonging to the Algerian Armed Islamic Group (GIA), who plotted—as in the 9/11 attacks that would follow seven years later— to crash the aircraft and the 283 passengers on board into downtown Paris;[16]
- the wave of bombings unleashed by the GIA between the following July and October, in metro trains, outdoor markets, cafes, schools,

and popular tourist spots, during which 8 people were killed and more than 180 others wounded; and,

- the unrelenting bloodletting by Islamic extremists in Algeria itself, which has claimed the lives of more than 100,000 people there since 1992.

As this list suggests, terrorism motivated in whole or in part by religious imperatives has often led to more intense acts of violence that have produced considerably higher levels of fatalities than the relatively more discriminating and less lethal incidents of violence perpetrated by secular terrorist organizations. Although religious terrorists committed only 6 percent of recorded terrorist incidents between 1998 and 2004, their acts were responsible for 30 percent of the total number of fatalities recorded during that time period.[17] The direct relationship between the religious motive for terrorism and higher numbers of deaths is even more dramatically depicted by the record of violence perpetrated by Shi'a Islamic terrorists during the 1980s and by al-Qaeda specifically between 1998 and 2004. Although Shi'a groups committed only 8 percent of all international terrorist incidents between 1982 and 1989, they nonetheless were responsible for 30 percent of the total number of fatalities arising from those incidents.[18] And while al-Qaeda perpetrated only 0.1 percent of all terrorist attacks between 1998 and 2004, it was responsible for nearly 19 percent of total fatalities from terrorist attacks during that time period.[19]

Core Characteristics of Religious Terrorism

The reasons that terrorist incidents perpetrated for religious motives result in so many more deaths may be found in the radically different value systems, mechanisms of legitimation and justification, concepts of morality, and worldviews embraced by the religious terrorist and his secular counterpart.

For the religious terrorist, violence is first and foremost a sacramental act or divine duty executed in direct response to some theological demand or imperative. Terrorism thus assumes a transcendental dimension, and its perpetrators therefore often disregard the political, moral, or practical constraints that may affect other terrorists. Whereas secular terrorists, even if they have the capacity to do so, have rarely attempted indiscriminate killing on a truly massive scale because such tactics are not consonant with their political aims and therefore are regarded as counterproductive, if not immoral, religious terrorists often seek the elimination of broadly defined categories of enemies and accordingly regard such large-scale violence not only as morally justified but as necessary expedients for the attainment of their goals. Religion—conveyed by sacred text and imparted via clerical authorities claiming to speak for the divine—therefore critically serves as a means to explain contemporary events and, in turn, as a legitimating force justifying violence. This explains why clerical sanction is so important to religious terrorists and why religious figures are often required to bless (i.e., approve or sanction) terrorist operations before they are executed.

Finally, religious and secular terrorists also have starkly different perceptions of themselves and their violent acts. Whereas secular terrorists regard violence either as a way of instigating the correction of a flaw in a system that is basically good or as a means to foment the creation of a new system, religious terrorists see themselves not as components of a system worth preserving but as outsiders seeking fundamental changes in the existing order. This sense of alienation also enables the religious terrorist to contemplate far more destructive and deadly types of terrorist operations than secular terrorists, indeed to embrace a far more open-ended category of enemies for attack—that is, anyone who is not a member of the terrorists' religion or religious sect. This explains the rhetoric common to "holy terror" manifestos describing those outside of the terrorists' religious community in denigrating and dehumanizing terms as, for example, "infidels," "dogs," "children of Satan," and "mud people." The deliberate use of such terminology to condone and justify terrorism is significant, for it further erodes constraints on violence and bloodshed by portraying the terrorists' victims as either subhuman or unworthy of living.

Islamic Groups

These core characteristics, while common to religious terrorists of all faiths, have nonetheless often been most closely associated with Islamic terrorist groups in general and Iranian-inspired ones and al-Qaeda and ISIS and their respective affiliates, franchises, and branches in particular.

The revolution that transformed Iran into an Islamic republic in 1979 played a crucial role in the modern advent of religious terrorism. At the root of the Iranian-backed Islamic terrorist campaign was the aim of extending the fundamentalist interpretation of Islamic law espoused in Iran to other Muslim countries. "We must strive to export our Revolution throughout the world," the Ayatollah Khomeini declared on the occasion of the Iranian new year in March 1980, less than a year after the establishment of the Islamic Republic in Iran, and must abandon all idea of not doing so, for not only does Islam refuse to recognize any difference between Muslim countries, it is the champion of all oppressed people. . . . We must make plain our stance toward the powers and superpowers and demonstrate to them despite the arduous problems that burden us. Our attitude to the world is dictated by our beliefs.[20]

The Islamic revolution in Iran has been held up as an example to Muslims throughout the world, exhorting them to reassert the fundamental teachings of the Qur'an and to resist the intrusion of Western—particularly U.S.—influence into the Middle East. This stance reflects the beliefs and history of Shi'a Islam as interpreted by Khomeini and subscribed to by his followers in Iran and other Middle Eastern countries. It begins with the notion of the Shi'a as a centuries-old minority within Islam, persecuted because of its special, revealed knowledge, but it further entails an unswerving conviction of the inherent illegitimacy of all secular government. Under this rationale, legitimacy can be conferred only through the adoption of Islamic law. Accordingly, since Iran was the only state to have begun the process of redemption by creating a "true" Islamic state, it must be the advocate for the oppressed and aggrieved everywhere. Not only are violence and coercion permissible to achieve the worldwide spread of Islamic law, but they are also a necessary means to this divinely sanctioned end.

The sense of alienation and of the necessity for far-reaching changes in the world order is apparent in the works of a number of Shi'a theologians. "The world as it is today is how others shaped it," wrote Grand Ayatollah Baqer al-Sadr, a leading Iraqi Shi'a cleric. "We have two choices: either to accept it with submission, which means letting Islam die, or to destroy it, so that we can construct the world as Islam requires." Mustafa Chamran, the Islamic Republic's first defense minister who would subsequently die a martyr during the 1980–1988 Iran-Iraq War, once explained: "We are not fighting within the rules of the world as it exists today. We reject all those rules." Similarly, Hussein Mussawi, the former leader of Lebanon's Hezbollah ("Party of God") who was the victim of an Israeli helicopter-borne assassination in 1992, maintained: "We are not fighting so that the enemy recognizes us and offers us something. We are fighting to wipe out the enemy."[21]

These statements also reflect the Shi'a perception of encirclement and concomitant predatory defensiveness. "We, the sons of the community of Hezbollah,"[22] a 1985 communiqué from the Lebanese Shi'a terrorist group of the same name declared, "consider ourselves a part of the world Islamic community, attacked at once by the tyrants and the arrogant of the East and the West. . . . Our way is one of radical combat against depravity, and America is the original root of depravity."[23] That Hezbollah perceives itself as fighting an entirely self-defensive struggle, sanctioned if not commanded by God, is also evident in the pronouncements of the group's first spiritual leader, the late Sheikh Muhammad Hussein Fadlallah. "We do not hold in our Islamic belief that violence is the solution to all types of problems," he once told an interviewer. "Rather, we always see violence as a kind of surgical operation that a person should use only after trying all other means, and only when he finds his life imperiled. . . . The violence began as the people, feeling themselves bound by impotence, stirred to shatter some of that enveloping powerlessness for the sake of liberty." In this context, Fadlallah pointed out, Israel's invasion of Lebanon in 1982 was the embodiment of the West's hostility to revolutionary Islam:

> This invasion was confronted by the Islamic factor, which had its roots in the Islamic Revolution in Iran. And throughout these affairs, America was the common denominator. America was generally perceived as the great nemesis behind the problems of the region, due to its support for Israel and many local reactionary regimes, and because it distanced itself from all causes of liberty and freedom in the area.[24]

Fadlallah unhesitatingly justified Islamic terrorism on the grounds of self-defense. "We are not preachers of violence," he declared in a 1996 interview. "Jihad in Islam is a defensive movement against those who impose violence."[25] For Hezbollah, then, the struggle against Israel's occupation of southern Lebanon between 1982 and 2000 was nothing less than divinely ordained. "The Resistance is not led by commanders," one local cleric proclaimed. "It is directed by the tenets of Islam."[26]

The role of clerical authority in sanctioning terrorist operations has always been critical to both Shi'a and Sunni organizations. The fatwa (a legal ruling or statement of legal issues, given by a mufti—a qualified jurist—at the request of a religious court)[27] issued in 1989 by the Ayatollah Khomeini imposing the death sentence on the author Salman Rushdie is precisely a case in point. Similarly, the Sunni extremists who bombed New York City's World Trade Center in 1993 specifically obtained a fatwa from Sheikh Omar Abdel-Rahman (the blind Egyptian cleric who died in 2017 while imprisoned in the United States) before planning their attack. Muslim clerics have also lent their support and encouraged as well as given their blessing even to self-martyrdom—though suicide is forbidden by Islamic law. For example, immediately after the 1983 suicide attacks on the U.S. Marines and French paratroop headquarters, Hussein Mussawi said: "I proclaim loud and clear that the double attack of Sunday is a valid act. And I salute, at Death's door, the heroism of the kamikazes, which they are; they are now under the protection of the All Powerful one and of the angels."[28]

Nor are such sentiments restricted to radical Shi'a only. Militant Sunni fundamentalist organizations portray their struggle in similarly uncompromising terms. According to Antar Zouabri, a leader of the GIA's struggle in the 1990s to establish an Islamic republic in Algeria who was killed by security forces in 2002, there could never be either dialogue or truce in his organization's struggle against the illegitimate, secular Algerian government. The word of God, he argued, is immutable on this point. God, Zouabri explained to an interviewer in 1996, does not negotiate or engage in discussion. Zouabri further couched the GIA's campaign in terms of an all-out war. Its ineluctable mission, he said, is to "found a true Islamic state": should innocents perish in the course of achieving this divinely commanded aim, then so be it. In the first instance, Zouabri explained, the killing of apostates, or those not a part of the Islamic movement, is a duty for him and his followers. In any event, the Prophet excuses the murder of innocents, as revealed in a verse from the Qur'an that Zouabri quoted: "I am innocent of those killed because they were associated with those who had to be fought."[29]

The struggle being waged against Israel by the Islamic Resistance Movement (Harakat al-Muqawama al-Islamiya), better known by its Arabic acronym, Hamas (which also means zeal),[30] is similarly cast in terms of an all-out war from which there can be no respite until the enemy is vanquished. The Hamas Covenant, for example, bluntly states, "Israel will exist and will continue to exist until Islam will obliterate it, just as it obliterated others before it,"[31] a view reflected in the words of a leader of the group's political wing, who told American scholar Mark Juergensmeyer that "Palestine is not completely free"—not in reference to the truncated sovereignty exercised by that group over the Gaza Strip or by Mahmoud Abbas's (Abu Mazen) Palestine Authority (PA) over the West Bank,[32] but "until it is an Islamic state."[33] Moreover, the Hamas Covenant's Article 7 displays clear millenarian overtones, declaring: "The time [of Redemption] will not come until the Muslims fight the Jews and kill them, and until the Jews hide behind rocks and trees when the call is raised: 'Oh Muslim, here is a Jew hiding! Come and kill him.'"[34] The religious terrorist's preoccupation with the elimination of an almost open-ended category of enemies is further illustrated in the sermon preached at a Gaza City mosque in 1987 by Hamas's founder and spiritual leader, Imam Sheikh Ahmad Ibrahim Yassin (who was killed in 2004 by an Israeli air strike). Driving home the point that Hamas's war is not only against Israel, but against all Jews, Yassin reportedly declared: "Six million descendants of monkeys [i.e., Jews] now rule in all the nations of the world, but their day, too, will come. Allah! Kill them all, do not leave even one."[35]

Bin Laden deliberately framed al-Qaeda's struggle in similarly stark, un-compromisingly theological terms. At a time when the impersonal forces of economic determinism and globalization were thought to have submerged the ability of a single man to affect the course of history, bin Laden effec-tively melded the strands of religious fervor, Muslim piety, and a profound sense of grievance into a powerful ideological force. "All men dream: but not equally," T. E. Lawrence, the legendary Lawrence of Arabia, once wrote. "Those who dream by night in the dusty recesses of their minds wake in the day to find that it was vanity: but the dreamers of the day are dangerous men, for they may act on their dream with open eyes, to make it possible."[36] Bin Laden was indeed one of the dangerous men that Lawrence described. He repeatedly defined al-Qaeda's fundamental raison d'être in terms of the "clash of civilizations" religious typology that the United States and its al-lies in the war on terrorism labored so hard to avoid. "These events," bin Laden declared in his October 7, 2001, statement, quoted at the beginning of this chapter, "have divided the world into two sides—the side of believers and the side of infidels. . . . Every Muslim has to rush to make his religion victorious. The winds of faith have come."[37] In a videotaped speech broad-cast over al-Jazeera television on November 3, 2001, he reiterated this mes-sage, stating: "This is a matter of religion and creed, it is not what Bush and Blair maintain, that it is a war against terrorism. There is no way to forget the hostility between us and the infidels. It is ideological, so Muslims have to ally themselves with Muslims."[38]

During the late 1990s, bin Laden set the stage for this clash as the author/architect of two major fatwas.[39] The first, issued on August 23, 1996, was a lengthy and turgid diatribe. Titled "Declaration of War Against the Ameri-cans Occupying the Land of the Two Holy Places: A Message from Usama bin Muhammad bin Laden Unto His Muslim Brethren All Over the World Generally, and in the Arab Peninsula Specifically," it presented bin Laden's seminal analysis of Islam under siege. In this respect, it also evidenced the perennial terrorist characteristic, described in chapter 1, of the reluctant warrior, thrown perpetually on the defensive with no option but to embrace violence in response to the transgressions of some aggressive, predatory enemy. "Praise be to Allah," bin Laden began.

We seek His help and ask for his pardon. We take refuge in Allah from our wrongs and bad deeds. . . . I bear witness that there is no God except Allah, no associates with Him and I bear witness that Muhammad is His slave and messenger. . . .

It should not be hidden from you that the people of Islam had suffered from aggression, inequity and injustice imposed on them by the Zionist-Crusaders alliance and their collaborators; to the extent that the Muslims blood became the cheapest and their wealth as loot in the hands of the enemies. Their blood was spilled in Palestine and Iraq. The horrifying pictures of the massacre of Qana, in Lebanon are still fresh in our memory. Massacres in Tajikistan, Burma, Cashmere [Kashmir], Assam, Philippine, Fatani, Ogadin [sic], Somalia, Eritrea, Chechnya and in Bosnia and Herzegovina took place, massacres that send shivers in the body and shake the conscience. All of this and the world watch and hear, and not only didn't respond to these atrocities, but also with a clear conspiracy between the USA and its allies and under the cover of the iniquitous United Nations the dispossessed people were even prevented from obtaining arms to defend themselves. . . .

The walls of oppression and humiliation cannot be demolished except in a rain of bullets. . . .

Without shedding blood no degradation and branding can be removed from the forehead I remind the youths of the Islamic world, who fought in Afghanistan and Bosnia Herzegovina with their wealth, pens, tongues and themselves that the battle had not finished yet [sic].[40]

Although widely dismissed and ignored at the time as inflated rhetoric or posturing braggadocio, the 1996 fatwa was an unambiguous clarion call to battle for Muslims everywhere. "My Muslim Brothers of The World," bin Laden concluded, "Your brothers in Palestine and in the land of the two Holy Places are calling upon your help and asking you to take part in fighting against the enemy your enemy and their enemy the Americans and the Israelis. [T]hey are asking you to do whatever you can, with one['s] own means and ability, to expel the enemy, humiliated and defeated, out of the sanctities of Islam. Exalted be to Allah [sic]."[41]

The second fatwa, styled as a "Statement of the World Islamic Front: Jihad Against Jews and Crusaders," was issued on February 23, 1998. Although the basic message was the same, it differed from the 1996 iteration in that bin Laden was now only one of five signatories. The others were Ayman al-Zawahiri, the emir of the Jihad Group in Egypt who would later succeed bin Laden as al-Qaeda's leader following the latter's killing in 2011; Abu Yasir Rifa'I Ahmad Taha, head of the Egyptian Islamic Group; Sheikh Mir Hamza, secretary of the Jamiat-ul-Ulema-e-Pakistan; and Fazlur Rahman, emir of the Jihad Movement in Bangladesh. After obeisantly paying homage to "God, who revealed the Book, controls the clouds, defeats factionalism . . . and peace be upon our Prophet, Muhammad Bin-'Abdallah, who said: I have been sent with the sword between my hands to ensure that no one but God is worshipped, God who put my livelihood under the shadow of my spear and who inflicts humiliation and scorn on those who disobey my orders,"[42] the fatwa explained how the

> crimes and sins committed by the Americans are a clear declaration of war on God, his messenger, and Muslims. And ulema ["the legal scholars of Islam, 'guardians of the faith'"[43]] have throughout Islamic history agreed that the jihad is an individual duty if the enemy destroys the Muslim countries. . . .
>
> On that basis, and in compliance with God's order, we issue the following fatwa to all Muslims:
>
> The ruling to kill the Americans and their allies—civilians and military—is an individual duty for every Muslim who can do it in any country in which it is possible to do it, in order to liberate the al-Aqsa Mosque and the holy mosque [Mecca] from their grip, and in order for their armies to move out of all the lands of Islam, defeated and unable to threaten any Muslim. This is in accordance with the words of Almighty God, "and fight the pagans all together as they fight you all together," and "fight them until there is no more tumult or oppression, and there prevail justice and faith in God."[44]

It was duly executed six months later with the simultaneous suicide attacks on the U.S. embassies in Kenya and Tanzania. A statement released that same day by the "International Islamic Front," reiterated and justified the previous calls for jihad:

> Oh Muslims, the Israeli cancer in Palestine and the American cancer in the land Hijaz (i.e., Saudi Arabia) must be uprooted. Islam obliges us to liberate all Muslim land from occupiers whoever they may be whether American, Israeli or other forces. . . .
>
> Oh Muslims, yours is an Ummah [worldwide community of Muslims] for whom jihad is the spearhead of its ideology whose creed is built upon a firm foundation with unshakeable belief that victory is from Allah and that Allah has promised authority, victory and domination which will undoubtedly be fulfilled God willing.[45]

The February 1998 fatwa also exemplified one of bin Laden's major theological accomplishments: interpreting the imperative of jihad as an individual responsibility incumbent upon Muslims everywhere.[46] This henceforth became a familiar theme of bin Laden's declarations, articulated with increasing fervor in a succession of uncompromising exhortations. In his "Message to the Youth of the Muslim Ummah [worldwide community]" of December 9, 2001, for instance, bin Laden detailed how jihad

> has become fard-ain [obligatory] upon each and every Muslim. . . . The time has come when all the Muslims of the world, especially the youth, should unite and soar against the kufr [nonbeliever] and continue jihad till these forces are crushed to naught, all the anti-Islamic forces are wiped off the face of this earth and Islam takes over the whole world and all other false religions.[47]

The above statement, in fact, encapsulates precisely bin Laden's preeminent objective: the restoration of a pan-Islamic caliphate that is at once as idealized as it is venerated.[48] The caliphate, which disappeared with the demise of the Ottoman Empire in 1924, is recalled by Muslims as a "golden age of Islam,"[49] when the theocratic "structure of law and governance bequeathed by the Prophet Mohammed to his successors" reigned and divinely revealed Sacred Law took precedence over arbitrary secular or natural law.[50] Ayman al-Zawahiri, cosigner of the aforementioned February 1998 fatwa and a physician by training who was the founder and leader of Egyptian Islamic Jihad[51] and before bin Laden's killing al-Qaeda's deputy emir,[52] also invoked this long-lamented desideratum in a fatwa he personally issued that same year. Al-Qaeda's goal, al-Zawahiri wrote, was as immutable as it was straightforward: to "unite all Muslims and establish a government that follows the rule of the Caliphs."[53] Three years later, as he fled with bin Laden from Afghanistan, pursued by the Afghan Northern Alliance and the combined might of the American and coalition militaries, al-Zawahiri stubbornly clung to his belief that that day would still come. While the "establishment of a Muslim state in the heart of the Islamic world," he conceded, "is not an easy goal or an objective that is close at hand . . . it constitutes the hope of the Muslim nation to reinstate its fallen caliphate and regain its lost glory."[54]

The United States was seen by both bin Laden and al-Zawahiri as willfully impeding this goal. They described the United States as the "far enemy" that must be defeated both because of America's alleged opposition to Islam and the active support that it gives to the so-called near enemy—the corrupt, reprobate, and authoritarian anti-Islamic regimes in the Middle East, Central Asia, South Asia, and Southeast Asia that could not otherwise remain in power.[55] In a May 1998 interview with ABC News, bin Laden explained his profound enmity toward the United States: "We believe that the worst thieves in the world today and the worst terrorists are the Americans. . . . We do not differentiate between those dressed in military uniforms and civilians: they are all targets."[56] On al-Jazeera television the following year, bin Laden used similar words to make the same point: "Our enemy . . . is every American male, whether he is directly fighting us or paying taxes."[57] Indeed, during the years immediately preceding the 9/11 attacks, bin Laden often lauded the men who bombed the New York City World Trade Center in 1993 as "role models" and repeatedly beseeched Muslims to "take the fighting to America."[58]

In recent years, however, ISIS, an especially extreme and brutal terrorist movement that was once affiliated with al-Qaeda, has been at the forefront of this ongoing struggle. Like al-Qaeda, ISIS also seeks to restore the caliphate and thereby ensure that a rigidly fundamentalist interpretation of Islam becomes the only accepted religion and sharia, the legal system based on Islamic religious precepts drawn from the Qur'an and Hadith, the only law.[59] In June 2014, ISIS's leader, Abu Bakr al-Baghdadi (real name: Ibrahim Awad al-Badri), dramatically upstaged al-Qaeda when he formally declared himself the caliph of a newly proclaimed caliphate—henceforth to be called the Islamic State.[60] With this bold move, al-Baghdadi aimed to achieve what bin Laden had only promised: nothing less than redrawing the map of the Middle East, erasing the artificial states and contrived borders created by the Western powers following World War I, while resurrecting the Muslim empire that once stretched from Spain across North Africa, through the Middle East and the Caucasus, into South and Southeast Asia. A distinguishing feature of al-Baghdadi's Islamic State has been its uncompromising enmity toward a variety of Islam's minority sects, including Sufis, Druze, Kurds, Alawites, and Yazidis, alongside an unremitting hostility to the Shi'a, the West, and to Christians, Jews, and other nonbelievers.[61]

It should be noted, however, that the differences between ISIS and al-Qaeda have thus far been more in style and tone than in substance and ideology. Both movements' overarching worldviews are firmly rooted in the principles of resistance to Western influence and encroachment and the unstinting defense of Muslim lands most forcefully expounded three decades ago by the leading jihadi theorist and propagandist of his time, Abdullah Azzam.[62] Born near Jenin, Palestine, in 1941, Azzam studied Islamic law as an undergraduate in Syria before obtaining his doctorate in Islamic jurisprudence at Cairo's al-Azhar University, one of the world's most famous and renowned Islamic institutions of higher education.[63] While in Cairo, Azzam befriended the family of the prominent Egyptian Islamist martyr, Sayyid Qutb, and fervently embraced both Qutb's strident defense of Islam and profound antipathy to the West and Western cultural values as articulated in the latter's seminal work, *Milestones*.[64] After being fired from his university teaching post in Jordan and expelled from that country because of his radical views,[65] Azzam moved to Saudi Arabia, where he found employment at King Abdul Aziz University in Jeddah.[66] Among his most devoted students was an impressionable young man named Usama bin Laden.[67]

Following the Soviet Union's invasion of Afghanistan in 1979, Azzam decided to dedicate his efforts to the jihad in Afghanistan.[68] In this context, he argued that it was obligatory for Muslims everywhere to come to the defense of their brethren wherever they were in danger. A charismatic orator with a commanding presence, Azzam exerted a powerful impact on the audiences he addressed as he traveled around the world preaching jihad.[69] The thrust of his argument was the distinction that Azzam drew between the religious concepts of *fard kifaya* and *fard ayn*. The former principle, he explained, was a collective religious obligation incumbent upon Muslims—a communal duty—such as daily prayer and ritual fasting. The latter, however, Azzam described as an individual obligation to come to the aid of all Muslims anywhere they are threatened. It was therefore *fard ayn*, a compulsory duty, Azzam argued, to repulse the infidel invasions of Muslim lands.[70]

Indeed, Azzam's influence over the Salafi-Jihadi movement continues to this day despite his assassination in 1989. Azzam's fundamental thesis that an aggressive, predatory war is being waged against Islam by its enemies, including the Western democratic liberal state; corrupt, repressive Western-backed local apostates; the Shi'a; and, other Muslim minorities—has become a staple of the inevitablility of the epic confrontations variously described by bin Laden, al-Zawahiri, and al-Baghdadi, among others.[71] The need for global jihad to defeat these enemies is thus as integral an aspect of ISIS's mind-set as it is of al-Qaeda's.[72] Both movements, moreover, share the same view that the Western liberal state system is inimical to Islam. ISIS, for instance, regularly inveighs against democracy as that "wicked methodology"[73]—thus reflecting al-Qaeda's long-standing denigration of this particular form of governance. Like al-Qaeda, ISIS also rails against the West's exploitation and expropriation of the Muslims' most precious natural resources—its oil and natural gas fields—and the established order's creation and support of corrupt, compliant local regimes that facilitate the ongoing plundering of the Muslim world. At the height of its popularity and power, in late 2015/early 2016 ISIS reportedly could claim the allegiance of fifty affiliates in some twenty-one different countries and thirty-three actual "official provinces" (*wilayets*) in eleven of those countries.[74]

Jewish Extremism

Significantly, the same characteristics attributed to Islamic terrorist groups—
the legitimation of violence by reference to religious precepts, the sense of
alienation, the existence of a terrorist movement in which the activists are
the constituents, and a preoccupation with the elimination of a broadly
defined category of "enemies"—are equally apparent among the Jewish terrorist movements that have surfaced in Israel since the early 1980s. To a
great extent, many of the members of these groups draw their inspiration
from the late Rabbi Meir Kahane.[75] A native New Yorker, Kahane preached
a liturgy of virulent hatred of Arabs that simultaneously extolled the virtues of Jewish aggressiveness and combativeness. He was a prolific author,[76]
sermonizer, public speaker, and newspaper columnist[77] who founded his
own (long outlawed) Israeli political party/vigilante organization, Kach
(Thus), to disseminate his extreme, uncompromising views.[78] Kahane's
overriding obsession was to reverse the mythical image of the Jew as victim. From this flowed his conviction that Jews were enmeshed in a continual
struggle against an inherently anti-Semitic world, surrounded by hatemongers and closet anti-Semites in the United States and predatory, blood-
thirsty Arabs both inside and encircling Israel. "And, above all," he wrote in
1971 and reiterated throughout his life, "let us understand that people, in
the very best of times, do not like Jews."[79] Kahane's prescription in the face
of this eternally bleak Jewish condition was simple: a militant aggressiveness, portrayed as nothing more than the inalienable right of self-defense,
which evoked images of Frantz Fanon's philosophy of the catharsis of
violence.[80] "Never again," Kahane declared, "means that we have had it in the
concept of being beaten and not hitting back. No one will respect us, and no
one in the end will love us, if we don't respect ourselves."[81]

When Kahane and his family emigrated to Israel in 1971, he began to apply his program of strident self-assertion to the "Palestinian problem." This
entailed repeated and vitriolic denunciations of governmental policies with
respect both to the peace and to its alleged soft approach to countering Palestinian terrorism. In 1980, for example, Kahane openly called upon the
Israeli government to establish an official "Jewish terrorist group" whose sole
purpose would be to "kill Arabs and drive them out of Israel and the Occupied Territories."[82] For more than a decade afterward, he unceasingly
called for the forced expulsion of all Arabs from Eretz Israel—the Land of
Israel, that is, the biblical lands of Greater Israel, embracing both the current state's territory as well as the ancient biblical lands of Judea and Samaria
(e.g., the occupied West Bank of the Jordan River)—or for their physical annihilation if they refused to leave. In a speech before university students in

a Los Angeles suburb in 1988, Kahane described the Arabs as "dogs," as people who "multiply like fleas" who must be expelled from Israel or eliminated.[83] In this manner, Kahane sought to dehumanize Arabs completely and thus make his odious policy prescriptions more tolerable and acceptable to Jews. "I don't intend to sit quietly by while Arabs intend to liquidate my state—either by bullets or by having babies," he declared. "It's important that you know what the name 'Kahane' means to the Arabs. It means terror."[84]

Kahane's concerns, however, went far beyond practical matters of security to embrace mystical Judaic notions that condoned and justified ill treatment of—and violence against—Arabs. In this respect, the responsibility of all Jews to work actively to hasten redemption became immutably aligned with the "sin" of returning to the Arabs the biblical lands (Judea and Samaria) that God gave to Israel. "Is there no longer a G-d in Israel?" Kahane asked in 1981.

> Have we so lost our bearings that we do not understand the ordained historical role of the State of Israel, a role that ensures that it can never be destroyed and that no further exile from it is possible? Why is it that we do not comprehend that *it is precisely our refusal to deal with the Arabs according to halakhic* [Jewish religious law] *obligation that will bring down on our heads terrible sufferings, whereas our courage in removing them will be one of the major factors in the hurrying of the final redemption?*[85]

When a Jewish yeshiva (religious school) student was murdered by Arabs two years later, a group of Kahane's followers in the ultranationalist West Bank settler movement Gush Emunim (Bloc of the Faithful) decided to take action. Their plan was to attack an Islamic college in Hebron in the Israeli-occupied West Bank at a time of day calculated to inflict the maximum casualties. Significantly, like their Islamic counterparts, the Jewish settlers sought the specific approval and sanction of their own clerical authorities for the operation. Indeed, among the group it was axiomatic that they would not—indeed, that they could not—act without rabbinical blessing. Having secured this dispensation, the terrorists struck: opening fire with machine guns on the Muslim students as they emerged from their classrooms for the noontime recess, killing three and wounding another thirty-three.

Emboldened by the success of this operation—and armed once again with rabbinical sanction—the terrorists set in motion plans for an even more ambitious attack. They now plotted the simultaneous bombings of five Arab buses at a day and time when they were guaranteed to be packed with passengers but the roads were likely to be empty of Jews. The plan was to

attach explosive devices to the gas tanks of the buses, setting them to detonate on a Friday evening, after the Jewish Sabbath had begun. However, just
as the group was about to act, its members were arrested. Only then did information come to light that for the preceding four years they had also
been plotting to blow up Jerusalem's Dome of the Rock—the third holiest
shrine of Islam—which occupies the same grounds as the most sacred site
in the Jewish religion, the Second Temple, which was destroyed in A.D. 70.[86]

The so-called Temple Mount operation represented a dramatic escalation
in the terrorists' campaign, propelling it on a violent trajectory from simple
vengeance wrought against mere mortals to genuine millenarian dimensions. The twenty-eight precision bombs that the terrorist cell had constructed were to them not mere instruments of death and destruction but
the means by which miracles were to be attained.[87] Their goal was not just
to destroy a Muslim holy place for reasons of blind hatred or petulant revenge but to facilitate the resurrection of a Jewish Third Temple and thereby
enable the Messiah's return. They were convinced that through their actions
they could themselves hasten redemption. Even more alarming, though, was
the terrorists' ancillary motive. By obliterating so venerated an Islamic
shrine, they also sought to spark a cataclysmic war between Israel and the
Muslim world. The terrorists' vision was that a beleaguered Jewish state, attacked on all sides by enraged, unrelenting, savage forces, would have no
option but to unleash its nuclear arsenal. The result would be the complete
annihilation of Israel's Muslim enemies,[88] and the establishment on earth
of a new "Kingdom of Israel"—a theocracy governed by a divinely anointed
Jewish king and held in judgment by a true "Supreme Court."[89] As with the
terrorists' previous operations, this grand scheme was again entirely dependent on obtaining clerical approval.

The same volatile combination—messianic visions of redemption, legitimated by clerical dispensation and achieved through direct action entailing
indiscriminate mass murder—was also evident a decade later in the 1994
Cave of the Patriarchs massacre and the assassination of Rabin the following year.[90] The first incident occurred on February 25, 1994, at a holy site revered and shared by both Jews and Muslims. Dr. Baruch Goldstein, an
American-born, ultranationalist, orthodox Jew and ardent disciple of Kahane, entered the Ibrahim Mosque, located at the Cave, and opened fire on
Muslim worshipers who had gathered there for Friday prayers. His attack
was timed to coincide not only with the middle of Islam's holy month of
Ramadan—when the mosque was certain to be filled to capacity—but also
with the Jewish festival of Purim. Purim celebrates how a Jew named Mor-
decai, living in fifth-century B.C. Persia, single-handedly saved his people
from their archenemy, Haman. Seeking to play the role of a modern-day

savior, Goldstein fired 119 bullets from his M-16 assault rifle into the crowd, killing 29 and wounding 150 before he was set upon by the stunned congregants, who beat him to death. Goldstein's grave has become a shrine, guarded and revered by the ultrareligious nationalists who share his intense animus toward secular Israeli government and regard the peace accords as a blasphemous plan to hand over to the Palestinians the biblical lands that God gave to the Jewish people. Like the Temple Mount plotters, Goldstein had sought to place himself in the vanguard of the actualization of the Jews' destiny. His mission, like theirs, was no less than to hasten redemption through the cataclysmic forces that his violent act was meant to unleash. This, Goldstein was certain, would ensure not only Israel's perennial possession of its biblical birthright but the coming of the Messiah as foretold by Kahane.

The assassination in 1995 of Prime Minister Rabin exuded the same uncompromising blend of religious fervor coupled with intense enmity toward Israel's secular government, its elected leaders, and the peace process that would return God-given lands to the Jews' most implacable opponents. Like Goldstein, Amir believed that he was fulfilling God's will. Invoking the *halakhic* decree of the "law of the pursuer" (*Din Rodef*), he explained to his police interrogators that he was completely justified in murdering the person he considered the architect of the Jewish people's doom. "The minute a Jew betrays his people and country to the enemy," Amir maintained, "he must be killed."[91] Amir appears to have been greatly influenced by extremist rabbis who had repeatedly condemned Rabin to death as a mortal enemy of the Jewish people.[92] He, accordingly, felt a moral obligation—what Amir himself described as a "mystical" urge—to kill a person declared by his religious authorities to pose so grave a danger to the Jewish people. "Perhaps physically I acted alone," he proclaimed during his trial, "but it was not only my finger on the trigger but the entire nation which for two thousand years dreamed about this country and spilled its blood for it."[93] Indeed, information that came to light after the assassination revealed that Amir had tried to murder Rabin on at least two previous occasions. The assassination, moreover, was intended by Amir and his alleged confederates to be only the first step in a campaign of mass murder, including car bombings to avenge Palestinian attacks as well as the murder of Palestinian terrorists released from Israeli jails as part of the peace process.

Any hope that these uncompromisingly violent sentiments—backed and indeed encouraged by clerical decree—might have dissipated in the furor and national soul-searching that followed Rabin's assassination was dispelled by the call from an extremist rabbi in April 1997 for Jews to emulate Hamas and launch suicide attacks of their own against Arabs. "Suicide during wartime is permissible for the sake of the victory of Israel," wrote the rabbi from the West Bank settlement of Tapuah, advocating Jewish self-martyrdom in an article titled "Sacrificing Oneself for God." "A man who volunteers for such operations," he proclaimed, "will be called a hero and a martyr."[94]

Sikh Militants

The radical Sikh movement as it crystallized in the early 1980s also conforms to the pattern and the characteristics of terrorism motivated by religion discussed in this chapter.[95] Unlike previous campaigns for Sikh autonomy, the activists behind this new, more aggressive militancy were also far more religious than their mostly secular predecessors.[96] This shift in emphasis thus elevated the irredentist struggle for self-determination in the Punjab, the Sikh's traditional homeland straddling present-day India and Pakistan, to the imperative of creating a separate, ethnically, culturally, and religiously homogeneous Sikh nation called Khalistan, the "Land of the Pure."[97] As K. P. S. Gill, who, as director general of police in the Punjab, led the government's counterterrorist operations against the militants, recalled, "All the evil they did was in the name of God. Every instrument and strategy was adopted to perpetuate the myth, to authenticate it . . . anything that could drive a wedge between communities; anything that could incite a slaughter of the Hindus in the state, and a retaliatory pogrom against the Sikhs in the rest of India."[98]

A charismatic rural preacher named Jarnail Singh Bhindranwale, a disciple of the eighteenth-century hallowed Sikh martyr, Baba Deep Singh, had emerged as the modern movement's leader.[99] Bhindranwale's fusion of religious devotion with strident nationalism was most clearly exemplified by his preaching of the Sikh concept of *miri-piri*: whereby spiritual and temporal power are inextricably linked—thus reflecting a distinctly Manichean mindset that recognizes extremes of absolute good and absolute evil with no middle gradation, nuance, or subtlety. According to Bhindranwale, this struggle for the preservation of the Sikh nation required nothing less than the unyielding prosecution of a war against the Indian state "for our faith . . . [and] for the oppressed."[100] Although the Sikh religion expresses nonviolence and condemns the taking of human life, Bhindranwale argued that violence was both justifiable and necessary given these dire circumstances to break the domination imposed over the Sikhs by India's Hindu majority.[101] Bhindranwale was also strident in his condemnation of those whom he described as "the enemies of religion"—that is, moderate Sikhs who did not share the revitalized movement's hard-line position and who were therefore decried as heretics and traitors to the Sikh people.[102]

Significantly, the Sikh extremists who answered Bhindranwale's summons to battle also regarded martyrdom—the selfless, altruistic surrender of one's life to preserve one's culture and religion, and the existence of one's kith and kin against a powerful, aggressive state and its predatory majority populace—as the highest accolade that a warrior for Khalistan could be paid.[103] The final statement of two Sikh militants sentenced to die for their assassination of an Indian general illustrates this unswerving commitment. In words reminiscent of terrorists from other religious traditions, the men described the hangman's noose awaiting them "as the embrace of a lover"; explaining that they "longed for death as for the marital bed" from which their "dripping blood . . . [would] fertilize the fields of Khalistan."[104]

Thereafter, a bloody campaign commenced to cleanse the Punjab of all "foreign influences."[105] Bands of young Sikhs started locally, indiscriminately killing Hindus, but it was not long before the violence escalated to include the hijacking in 1981 of an Air India passenger aircraft to Pakistan.[106] Two years of unrelenting terrorism in the Punjab followed, prompting commentators to term 1983 "The Year of the Armageddon."[107] By the spring of 1984, India's prime minister, Indira Gandhi, had enough. On June 5, 1984, she ordered Indian military forces to assault the Golden Temple in Amritsar, the Sikh religion's holiest shrine, which Bhindranwale had turned into his headquarters. Code-named "Operation Bluestar," the attack by some ten thousand infantry, paratroops, and police backed by armor and artillery, was neither swiftly nor efficiently executed. It took two days of brutal fighting to clear the compound of Sikh fighters. Bhindranwale was among the first to die and thereafter attained the venerated status as a fallen martyr to the Sikh cause.[108] Less than six months later, the Sikhs avenged what they regarded as a blasphemous assault on their religion's most sacred place as well as the death of their revered leader, when two of Mrs. Gandhi's Sikh bodyguards assassinated her. The prime minister's murder sparked a new round of intercommunal tensions that exploded the following day, when rampaging mobs in Delhi and elsewhere killed more than two thousand Sikhs.[109] This, in turn, set in motion a new cycle of sectarian bloodletting and antistate violence that drew into its maelstrom the Sikh Diaspora in both Canada and the United States.[110] The result was the tragic midair bombing of an Air India commercial aircraft en route from Montreal to Delhi via London on June 23, 1985.[111] Until the September 11, 2001, attacks, this mostly forgotten incident held the nefarious distinction as the most deadly act of international terrorism in history.[112] Less than an hour before the blast that destroyed flight number 185 over international waters off the coast of Ireland, another bomb had exploded——but this time prematurely, as baggage was being transferred at Tokyo's Narita Airport from a Canadian Pacific flight that had just arrived from Vancouver to a waiting Air India plane. Two airport workers were killed and four others wounded in the blast.[113] Both incidents were blamed on a radical Sikh separatist group called Babbar Khalsa ("Tigers of the True Faith").[114]

An estimated twenty thousand persons were killed in the Punjab as a result of the violent campaign that continued into the 1990s.[115] Bombs concealed in transistor radios were routinely placed in crowded urban locations and marketplaces, and on buses.[116] Although the majority of victims were Hindus, Sikhs suffered as well. The attacks, one contemporary observer noted, were almost always "entirely indiscriminate in nature," with crowded passenger trains a favorite target. One hundred Hindu passengers, for instance, were killed and seventy injured in two such incidents in 1991[117]—before the violence was finally suppressed two years later.[118]

American Christian White Supremacists

Half a world away from the Middle East and South Asia, in the very heartland of the United States, the use of violence is similarly justified by theological imperative as a means to overthrow a reviled secular government and attain both racial purification and religious redemption. The bombing of the Alfred P. Murrah Federal Office Building in Oklahoma City in April 1995 suddenly shed unaccustomed light on an indigenous, violent, Christian white supremacist and antifederalist movement that had been active long before this tragedy.

In June 1997, a Denver federal court convicted Timothy McVeigh, a twenty-eight-year-old U.S. Army veteran, of perpetrating the attack. Sentenced to death by lethal injection, McVeigh was executed four years later. An antigovernment, right-wing extremist, McVeigh engineered the attack with the help of three friends, Terry L. Nichols and Michael and Lori Fortier, to commemorate the second anniversary of the FBI's bloody assault on the Branch Davidians' compound in Waco, Texas, during which seventy-four people, including twenty-one children, were killed.[119] He and his alleged accomplices were apparently obsessed by the idea that the Waco assault—and a similar FBI siege of a reputed white supremacists' rural cabin at Ruby Ridge, Idaho, the previous year[120]—represented the opening salvo in U.S. government plans to outlaw and seize all privately held firearms. There were other motivations as well—including vengeance, protest, and armed resistance[121]—which, it transpired, were shared by the members of the well-armed, militantly antigovernment "citizens' militias" with whom McVeigh mixed. Zealous exponents, like those linked to the Oklahoma City bombing, of the American Constitution's Second Amendment, which provides for a well-regulated civilian militia and upholds the right to bear arms, many of these groups also evince the same combination of seditious, anti-Semitic, and racist views that is common to the broader American Christian Patriot (white supremacist) movement. In this respect, the militias have been described as part of a longer "conveyor belt," to use a phrase coined by Leonard Zeskind, the director of the Kansas City–based Institute for Research and Education of Human Rights, an organization dedicated to social and economic justice. The metaphor is intended to depict a process whereby individuals are initially recruited into groups like the militias on the basis of their opposition to legislation outlawing firearms, but gradually come to embrace increasingly extreme and violent positions that, in turn, are legitimated by appeals to scripture and theological imperatives.

Although organized hate groups and other bodies similarly preoccupied with far-fetched conspiracy theories have existed in the United States for decades, the advent of extremist white supremacist "citizens' militias" and related Christian Patriot paramilitary groups oriented toward survivalism, outdoor skills, guerrilla training, and outright sedition is a relatively more recent development. Thus, while the various militia movements have surfaced only within the past twenty-five years or so, they are in fact but the latest manifestations of a radical right-wing and white supremacist movement that has repeatedly repackaged itself in a bid to attract new recruits and a larger number of adherents and supporters. With the militias, the wider antigovernment movement discovered a powerful way of attracting people—like McVeigh—who were not only vehemently opposed to gun control but also subscribed to a variety of fantastic conspiracy theories that invariably involved the Clinton administration in some master plan to seize all firearms held by American citizens and thereby proscribe fundamental individual liberties. According to Michael Fortier, a close friend of McVeigh's, who testified for the prosecution at McVeigh's trial, "We both believed that the United Nations was actively trying to form a one-world government, disarm the American public, take away our weapons."[122] The imposition of a so-called "New World Order" was a particular preoccupation of the militia movement throughout the 1990s.[123] "This is the coming of a New World Order," the late Linda Thompson, an Indiana attorney cum self-styled "adjunct general" of an entity claiming to be the Unorganized Militia of the United States, used to claim.

> A one-world government, where, in order to put the new government in place, we must all be disarmed first. To do that, the government is deliberately creating schisms in our society, funding both anti-abortion/pro-

choice sides, the antigun/pro-gun issues, black-white riots, gay/anti-gay hysteria, trying to provoke a riot that will allow martial law to be implemented and all the weapons to be seized, while "dissidents" are put safely away.[124]

The Michigan Militia, a paramilitary survivalist organization which at one time claimed to have twelve thousand members and to which McVeigh and Nichols were believed to have been connected,[125] maintained that the U.S. government had initiated a program to intervene in the affairs of every American. "The Government is [already] in control," Ray Southwell, the group's cofounder and information officer explained in a 1994 interview. "And if you push back, if you cross the Government, they will come down on you hard. We are preparing to defend our freedom. The way things are going, I think bullets might be as valuable as gold and silver one day soon."[126] Accordingly, throughout the 1990s the militia trained in guerrilla warfare and survivalist techniques to resist what it maintained were plans by the Clinton administration to deploy UN forces armed with cast-off Soviet military equipment or hordes of Communist Chinese troops, backed by Latino and African American inner-city street gangs, to crush any opposition. Stripped bare of its conspiratorial explanations, the Michigan Militia's purpose appeared to be sedition, plain and simple: its other cofounder and commander, Norman E. Olson, made no bones about that. "My goal is not to plan a revolution," he boasted in a 1994 message posted over the Internet— the favored means of communication of militia members and other white supremacists even back then—"for revolution will come. . . . My goal is to establish the Republican Provisional Government."[127] The Michigan Militia's website in 2016 reiterated its purpose to "Defend Against Disaster, Crime, Invasion, Terrorism and Tyranny."[128]

At one time, an estimated eight hundred other similarly oriented militias—with a total membership claimed to be more than five million, though more realistically put at no more than one hundred thousand—had reportedly organized in almost every state of the Union.[129] By 2007, however, there were fewer than fifty such groups. But a combination of both the subsequent economic recession and President Barack Obama's election the following year triggered renewed growth with a sixfold expansion in the number of militia groups. The Southern Poverty Law Center identified 276 existing groups in its annual survey of militia activity in the United States for 2015—a 37 percent increase over the previous year's figure.[130]

The difficulty in gauging even the rough dimensions of the American militia movement is a product not only of its geographical pervasiveness and its then-unimpeded growth but also of critical differences between the two different types of militias that had emerged. On the one hand, there are the so-called talking militias (also known as "out-front" militias), to which the vast majority of the movement's adherents belong. The members of these groups are primarily concerned with opposing antigun legislation rather than with fomenting revolution, and consequently they are neither especially nor explicitly violent. Their politics therefore tend to reflect the entirely secular conspiracy theories that have long been associated with various Far Right American groups parodied in films such as Stanley Kubrick's *Dr. Strangelove*. The "marching" militias (also referred to as "up-front" militias), on the other hand, are actively involved in violent, seditious activities, embracing the combination of revolutionary, racist, and anti-Semitic doctrines inherent in the wider American Christian Patriot movement. It is this more radical element of the militia phenomenon who fervently believed in an impending UN invasion and takeover of the United States and therefore had resolved to take violent action to prevent it from occurring. At the height of this movement's popularity in the 1990s, it numbered no more than a dedicated hard core of perhaps ten thousand members.[131]

Among the more prominent of the "marching" militia groups that came to light following the Oklahoma bombing was the Militia of Montana, or MOM. This organization embraced the same revolutionary principles and harbored the same profound fears as its counterparts in Michigan and elsewhere. "Gun control is people control,"[132] its founders, brothers John and David Trochmann, declared in a 1995 interview. MOM's more than twelve thousand claimed members accordingly trained in guerrilla warfare, survivalist techniques, and other unconventional tactics in preparation for withstanding the inevitable federal government onslaught to seize their weapons and deprive them of their inalienable right to bear arms, presaged by the Branch Davidian raid. The group also marketed its own range of do-it-yourself manuals and tapes that not only explained how to manufacture bombs but exhorted listeners to prepare for the coming apocalypse that was sure to engulf the United States in retribution for its "sins against God."[133] A posting on its website from the late-1990s explained in ambiguous language:

> We, at the Militia of Montana, are dedicated to ensuring that all Americans are educated to make an informed decision as to which direction America should go. Along with being physically prepared to withstand the onslaught which will erupt no matter where we end up, we must at all costs, keep reaching those who have not had the opportunity to decide for themselves. The Militia of Montana has been, and continues to be, a national focal point for assisting [*sic*] Americans in forming their own

grass roots organization dedicated to American's [*sic*] sovereignty and status as an independent nation among the nations of the world.[134]

In recent years, MOM has turned to Facebook to publicize itself and its cause. The group's current mission statement declares: "Its [*sic*] time for militias to step forward. If you come to my house wanting to confiscate my legally owned weapons, someone will leave in a body bag. I will fight to the death against tyranny, if you don't believe me come on."[135]

Montana was also home to other prominent Far Right groups, including the North American Volunteer Militia and the Almost Heaven survivalist compound. While the North American Volunteer Militia railed against the "mess" created by the U.S. government and warned, "We need cleansing . . . we need blood to cleanse us,"[136] the millenarian Almost Heaven residents awaited the inevitable Armageddon. Founded in 1994 and led by James "Bo" Gritz, formerly a presidential candidate for an extreme right-wing party and a U.S. Special Forces Vietnam veteran (supposedly the model for Sylvester Stallone's "Rambo" character), this group embraced the same zealous advocacy of firearms possession and antigovernment sentiments as the militias, but also believed in a coming apocalypse, for which it prepared by stockpiling weapons, food, and valuables, and training in survivalist techniques and guerrilla warfare.[137] Gritz left the compound and moved to Nevada in 1999. Some of his followers then formed their own militia group, known as the Idaho Mountain Boys, which was later implicated in a plot to kill a U.S. District judge and blow up a propane storage facility near Sacramento, California.[138] In April 1996, a tense standoff between the FBI and yet another Montana militia, known as the Freemen, was defused and a repetition of the Branch Davidian debacle was avoided when eighty-one days of negotiations led to the voluntary surrender of two of the group's members for whom federal arrest warrants had been issued. The subsequent trial, conviction, and imprisonment of its founder and leader, LeRoy M. Schweitzer, and several of his followers, on a variety of federal charges, effectively ended the group's existence.[139]

To the south, the Texas-based Big Star One claimed a decade ago to have a military "division-sized" following, with separate "units" deployed across the northern part of the state and into Oklahoma and New Mexico; the Texas Constitutional Militia boasted a membership in the thousands and chapters in some forty counties; and a third militia, known as the Republic of Texas, prosecuted what it described as a "campaign of paper terrorism"— attempting to throttle state courts with bogus land claims and bad checks— claiming that the United States illegally annexed Texas in 1845 and therefore has no jurisdiction over the state. The group was involved in a weeklong siege with law enforcement authorities that was resolved peacefully despite threats by the militia to "wage an Alamo-style fight to the death."[140] A website posting from 2012 quotes a Big Star One member boasting how he and his compatriots were "primarily training in guerrilla warfare" and had "learned a lot from the Viet Cong. There will be no Waco in this area."[141]

And in the Midwest, the Indiana Militia, as it existed in the 1990s, was described by observers as a particularly militant anti–gun control organization. Its members proudly once proclaimed that they were "sick and tired of being raped and pillaged by the bunch of thieves that run the federal government" and clamored to take matters into their own hands.[142]

Both the militia and broader Christian Patriot movement's violent ambitions have been clearly illuminated by the nearly three dozen attacks, plots, and serious conspiracies uncovered by federal authorities over the course of the two decades since the Oklahoma City bombing. Among them are the following:

- In 1995, seven members of the West Virginia Mountaineer Militia were arrested and charged with plotting to blow up the FBI's computer center in that state.
- Twelve members of an Arizona group known as the Viper Militia were arrested in 1996,[143] of whom six were later charged with illegal possession of explosives and machine guns along with conspiracy to promote civil disorder. The group is alleged to have plotted for more than two years to blow up seven federal office buildings in Phoenix and to this end had carried out detailed reconnaissance, including videotaping of potential target sites. It was in the process of building up a stock of ammonium nitrate fertilizer—such as that used to construct the bomb that destroyed the Murrah Building—for this purpose. At the time of the arrest, the Vipers had amassed 1,900 pounds of the fertilizer;[144] the Oklahoma City bomb contained an estimated 4,800 pounds mixed with high-powered racing fuel.[145]
- Agents of the Bureau of Alcohol, Tobacco, and Firearms (BATF) arrested three members of the so-called Militia-at-Large for the Republic of Georgia in 1996. The three were subsequently convicted of conspiring to wage "war against the government," with plans including the assassination of senior elected officials and possibly even attacks at the then forthcoming Olympic Games in Atlanta.[146]
- A group of white supremacists, describing themselves as members of the "Phineas Priesthood," were also arrested in 1996 in connection with a string of bombings and bank robberies in Spokane, Washington. Four either pled guilty or were convicted.

- Four Ku Klux Klansmen were arrested in 1997 and subsequently convicted of plotting to blow up a natural gas processing plant to divert attention from a robbery that they were planning to finance seditious activities.
- Members of a militia group based in both Kansas and Texas were also arrested in 1997 and convicted on weapons charges pertaining to a series of planned attacks on U.S. military bases.
- A plot by members of the Michigan-based North American Militia to kill federal agents and unleash a bombing campaign was uncovered during 1997 and 1998, and the conspirators were arrested and convicted on explosives, weapons, and conspiracy charges.
- In 1998, members of a white supremacist group, the New Order, were convicted of plotting to rob banks, bomb public buildings, poison municipal water supplies, and murder federal judges and other government officials.
- Two white supremacists were convicted of planning to instigate a "race war" in 2001 by destroying Jewish and African American landmarks.
- In 2003, two antigovernment extremists were convicted of amassing a "huge arsenal of illegal weapons and explosives in Tyler, Texas, including suitcase bombs and a working chemical weapon."[147] They apparently possessed sufficient quantities of sodium cyanide to kill some six thousand people and had stockpiled half a million rounds of ammunition and sixty pipe bombs.[148]
- The following year, a father and son embarked on what law enforcement officials termed a "self-proclaimed mission to revenge Waco."[149] They killed an armed guard in the course of a robbery in Tulsa, Oklahoma, meant to fund their intended terrorist campaign.
- In 2009, a man alleged to have ties with the antifederalist Sovereign Citizens movement killed Dr. George Tiller, the director of an abortion clinic in Witchita, Kansas.
- That same year, a known white supremacist killed a security guard and wounded another person at the U.S. Holocaust Museum in Washington, D.C.
- In 2010, a man with militant antifederalist and antitax views deliberately crashed a small aircraft into an Internal Revenue Service (IRS) office building in Austin, Texas.
- Four men belonging to a Georgia group calling itself the Forever Enduring Always Ready (FEAR) Militia killed two individuals in 2011 as part of a series of plots that included the bombing of a Savannah park, an attack on the U.S. Army's Fort Stewart facility, and assassination of leading political figures.

- The following year, a white supremacist shot six people to death at a Sikh temple in Wisconsin.
- Also in 2012, four members of a Sovereign Citizens group ambushed and killed two police officers in northern Louisiana.
- Frazier Glenn Cross, a founder of the Carolina Knights of the Ku Klux Klan and the now defunct White Patriot Party, was convicted and sentenced to death for the 2014 shootings at a Kansas City Jewish Center, in which three persons died.
- A white supremacist named Dylann Roof killed nine people in a shooting at Charleston, South Carolina's historic black Emmanuel AME Church in 2015.[150]

In 1995 and again in 2011, American law enforcement agencies uncovered three separate plots involving persons who had connections to various American Christian white supremacist organizations who had sought to obtain deadly toxins and contaminants for use in terrorist attacks. In March 1995, two members of the Minnesota Patriots Council, a militia group, were convicted of stockpiling enough ricin to kill at least 129 people,[151] allegedly as part of a plan to murder IRS agents, U.S. marshals, and local deputy sheriffs. According to the FBI, ricin is ranked as the third most toxic known substance, behind only plutonium and botulism: a minute amount can kill in minutes if inhaled, ingested, or absorbed through the skin. Two months later, a man described as a certified microbiologist—who also had links to the Aryan Nations—was able to order a quantity of bubonic plague agent through the mail from a Maryland chemical supply firm. He had obtained three vials of *Yersinia pestis*—a bacterium credited with having wiped out one-third of the population of fourteenth-century Europe. In addition to the bacterium, police found in his home a dozen assault rifles, smoke grenades, blasting caps—and white supremacist literature.[152] And in December 1995, an Arkansas resident with reputed ties to white supremacist survivalist groups in that state was arrested at his farm on charges of having attempted to smuggle 130 grams of ricin into the United States from Canada. Canadian customs officials also discovered in the man's car four guns and more than twenty thousand rounds of ammunition. When U.S. authorities searched the man's Arkansas farm, they found copies of the commercially available *Poisoner's Handbook*, which explains how to extract ricin from castor beans, and *Silent Death*, which describes how to use toxic compounds to poison people.[153] The most recent plot involved four members of a Georgia militia who conspired to use ricin to kill government employees in an attack allegedly planned for Washington, D.C. They had also developed a backup plan to use explosives to destroy a federal office building just "like Timothy McVeigh," the ringleader of the cell boasted.[154]

Given this proliferation of plots, plans, and actual incidents,[155] it is not surprising that when American law enforcement agencies were asked in 2014 to identify the most serious violent extremist threats they face in their respective jurisdictions, three-quarters cited right-wing, antigovernment extremists; followed by al-Qaeda–inspired violent extremism (which was present in the jurisdictions of 40 percent of the respondents); radical environmentalists (present in one-third); and racist violent extremism (present in one-quarter).[156] The fact that twenty-five law enforcement officials have been slain in the United States by right-wing extremists since 2000, doubtless accounts for the respondents' ranking the presence of right-wing, antigovernment extremists and racists in their communities as the most serious threat they face. Indeed, according to the Global Terrorism Database maintained by the University of Maryland's START Center (National Consortium for the Study of Terrorism and Responses to Terrorism), right-wing extremists are responsible for more than twice as many attacks (65) that have occurred in the United States since September 11, 2001, compared to their Islamic counterparts (24).[157] Viewed from another perspective, more people have been killed in terrorist acts committed by the Far Right in the United States since 2001 (48) than by Muslim extremists.[158] Dylann Roof's twisted intent to spark a race war with the Charleston church shootings coupled with sentiments such as Victor Gerhard's proclamation that "WE should be blowing up NYC and DC, not waiting for a bunch of camel jockeys to do it for us" neatly encapsulate this entirely homegrown terrorist movement's extremely violent proclivities.[159]

The perpetrators and plotters of these acts consider themselves "minutemen": ordinary citizens and patriots ready to take up arms at a moment's notice to defend their inalienable rights; self-styled heirs of the tradition of the American Revolution. It is therefore significant that the Oklahoma City bombing took place on the date that the American Revolution commenced in Boston 220 years earlier. Indeed, McVeigh actually used this analogy to describe himself and the reasons behind his actions. "Any able-bodied adult male, any patriot," he told a British journalist, "is responsible for defending his liberty. Just like the Minutemen of the revolution."[160]

Although the militias are the latest iteration to this distinctly American radicalist phenomenon, their pedigree can be traced directly to the Posse Comitatus (Latin for "power of the county") movement founded during the 1970s and its 1980s offshoot—with which McVeigh is also believed to have had ties—the Arizona Patriots. These groups strenuously reject any form of government above the county level and specifically oppose federal and state income taxes, the existence of the Federal Reserve system, and the supremacy of the federal judiciary over local courts. Over the past four decades, local chapters of the Posse Comitatus have been founded in almost every state in the United States. The group became increasingly violent, particularly in the American Midwest and the far Northwest during the 1980s, with members attacking local, state, and federal law enforcement officers who were attempting to serve subpoenas or otherwise enforce the law. An attempt to serve a subpoena on North Dakota Posse Comitatus member Gordon Kahl in 1983 resulted in the first of many armed confrontations between the authorities and the radical right. In the ensuing shoot-out, Kahl killed two federal marshals before he himself was shot to death.[161] Undeterred by Kahl's death, in December 1986 six members of the Arizona Patriots were arrested and subsequently convicted on charges of plotting to bomb an IRS office in Ogden, Utah; the Los Angeles Federal Building (specifically, the FBI offices located there); and a synagogue in Phoenix, Arizona. A second generation of Arizona Patriots attempted to carry on their predecessors' campaign. Nightly shortwave radio broadcasts by Patriot leader William Cooper exhorted members to forcibly resist the imposition of the "new world order" epitomized by institutions such as the United Nations and treaties such as the General Agreement on Tariffs and Trade, but he attracted a meager following and the group eventually folded.

It would be a mistake, however, to view either the militias or the older Posse Comitatus and moribund Arizona Patriots organizations as simply militant antifederalist or extremist tax resistance movements. The aims and motivations of many of these extremist groups in fact span a broad spectrum of antifederalist and seditious beliefs coupled with religious hatred and racial intolerance, masked by a transparent veneer of religious precepts. Those that also embrace religious and racial intolerance are bound together by the ethos of the broader Christian Patriot movement, which includes

- hostility to any form of government above the county level;
- the vilification of Jews and nonwhites as children of Satan;
- an obsession with achieving the religious and racial purification of the United States;
- belief in a conspiracy theory of powerful Jewish interests controlling the government, banks, and the media;
- advocacy of the overthrow of the U.S. government, or the ZOG (Zionist Occupation Government), as the Patriot and militia groups disparagingly refer to it.

Many militia groups' "field manuals" (literally, recycled and repackaged versions of U.S. military training handbooks and genuine field manuals) and other literature quote liberally from Christian scripture in support of their violent activities and use biblical liturgy to justify their paranoid call to arms. A militia recruit recalled in an interview his initiation into the movement in a rural Missouri church: "It was odd. It was extremely religious. There were people standing along the aisles carrying weapons, rifles, a few with pistols. We all stood up and walked to the front of the church in this strange procession. We were told that it was part of the ritual of becoming 'God's soldiers' in this 'holy war.' One of the organizers of the event then mounted the pulpit declaring, 'Soon we will be asked to kill, but we will kill with love in our hearts because God is with us.'"[162]

The connecting thread in this seemingly diverse and disparate collection of citizens' militias, tax resisters, antifederalists, bigots, and racists is the white supremacist religious dogma espoused by the Christian Identity movement, which is itself based on the "Anglo-Israelism" movement that emerged in Britain during the mid-nineteenth century. The core belief of Anglo-Israelism was that the ten lost tribes of ancient Israel were composed of Anglo-Saxons, not Jews. However, in marked contrast to the present-day Christian Identity movement in the United States, nineteenth-century Anglo-Israelism embraced an entirely pacifist doctrine. The basic tenets of the contemporary American version of the Identity movement include the beliefs that

- Jesus Christ was not a Semite but an Aryan;
- the lost tribes of Israel are composed not of Jews but of "blue-eyed Aryans";
- white Anglo-Saxons and not Jews are the true "Chosen People"; and
- the United States is the "Promised Land."

In this context, Jews are viewed as impostors and children of Satan who had to be exterminated.

Identity theology, combined with militant tax resistance and a form of regressive populism, figures prominently in the Christian Patriotism doctrine subscribed to by the "marching" militia groups today. The ideological heir to the Posse Comitatus with its hard-line antifederalist principles, Christian Patriotism goes one step further by embracing a salient theological component that combines Identity interpretation of scripture with the myth of the Illuminati—the global conspiracy theory first promulgated in the late eighteenth century with respect to Freemasons and later adapted to include the Jews, worldwide banking interests, and other dark, mystical forces. According to its modern-day American interpretation, the "two seed" theory embraced by Christian Patriotism, there are two races on earth: one godly and one satanic—the former comprising white Anglo-Saxon Christians and the latter, Jews and all nonwhites. The movement further believes in the moral and legal force of a form of "common law" derived from a synthesis of the Magna Carta, the original articles of the U.S. Constitution, and the American Bill of Rights, and it also regards all paper money as "fraudulent" and holds that gold and silver are the only legitimate means of trade. McVeigh, it should be noted, openly admitted to interviewers his belief in Christian Patriotism and involvement in Patriot activities.[163]

At the nexus of Identity, Christian Patriotism, and the militia movements was once the organization called the Aryan Nations. An extremist, anti-Semitic, neo-Nazi group of white supremacists, survivalists, and militant tax resisters, the Aryan Nations had its headquarters on a secluded, fenced-in forty-acre site at the edge of the Coeur d'Alene National Forest in Hayden Lake, Idaho. It was founded in 1974 by the Reverend Richard Girnt Butler, a former aeronautical engineer from California who had moved to Idaho the previous year. Under his direction, the Aryan Nations performed a function similar to that of the PLO, acting as an umbrella group for like-minded organizations, providing a coordinating and liaison function. To this end, Aryan Nations congresses were held almost every year between 1973 and the 1990s—except for 1985, when widespread arrests of members of a radical splinter group, calling itself the Order, dealt a stunning, albeit temporary blow to the white supremacist movement. MOM's leader, John Trochmann, for example, was a featured speaker at the 1990 event.

The Aryan Nations, however, collapsed more than a decade ago as a result of the dual blows of Butler's death in 2004 and a lawsuit filed four years earlier that forced the movement to pay $6.3 million in damages to Victoria and Jason Keenan. The Keenans, who had been assaulted by Aryan Nations security guards, also took possession of the organization's Hayden Lake compound. They subsequently sold the property to a philanthropist, who then donated it to a local community college.[164] Thereafter, the Aryan Nations struggled to maintain what it claimed were some seventeen local chapters across the United States.[165] Its hate-filled website was active until around 2005. One statement from that time, declared that "all means are justified to restore Aryan honor," calling for a racial "holy war" that "can only end in total victory or total defeat,"[166] while another statement elucidated how Christian theology justifies its own variant of jihad, citing biblical text in support of its theological arguments for a religious war.[167] Today, neither is active. Instead a plaintive message on the group's defunct website mourns Butler and "the noble and honorable organization . . . [that] no longer exists with the veracity that it once had."[168]

The Aryan Nations ideology, however, continues to inspire bigots, anti-Semites, hatemongers, and antifederalists across the United States. This is because its core beliefs evidence the same mixture of racist and seditious dicta that is common throughout the American Christian Patriot movement. "*WE BELIEVE,*" a 1980s-era brochure titled *This Is Aryan Nations*, explained:

> There is a battle being fought this day between the children of darkness (today known as Jews) and the children of light (God), the Aryan race, the true Israel of the Bible. . . .
>
> *WE BELIEVE* in the preservation of our race individually and collectively as a people as demanded and directed by God. We believe a racial nation has a right and is under obligation to preserve itself and its members. . . . As His divine race, we have been commissioned to fulfill His divine purpose and plans. . . .
>
> *WE BELIEVE* that there is a day of reckoning. The usurper will be thrown out by the terrible might of Yahweh's people as they return to their roots and their special destiny.[169]

Indeed, the "Aryan National State Platform" from that time cites as Article 8: "A ruthless war must be waged against any whose activities are injurious to the common interest."[170]

This "cleansing" of the United States forms an immutable point of reference for the Christian Patriots' ideology as well. "Aliens are pouring over as a flood into *each* of our ancestral lands," Butler had warned, "threatening dispossession of the heritage, culture, and very life blood of our posterity. . . . We know that as we return to our Father's natural Life Order, all power, prosperity, and liberty again comes to us as our possession, to establish justice forever on earth."[171] In promotional literature from its heyday in the 1980s, the group proclaims its desire to "make clear to ourselves and our enemies what we intend to do: We will have a national racial state at whatever price in blood is necessary. Just as our forefathers purchased their freedom in blood, so must we." The leaflet went on to decry "the leadership of malicious, bastardizing politicians . . . [in] modern, decadent America [where] millions of whites watch in abject dismay and hopelessness as their great culture, heritage and civilization evaporates in the steaming stinking, seething milieu of so many alien races, cultures and gods."[172] Robert Matthews, the deceased leader of the Order, once declared that to stem this tide, all Jews, blacks, Hispanics, and other "mud people," along with white "race traitors," must be exterminated in what he described as "a racial and religious Armageddon."[173]

It is particularly alarming that the Christian Patriots' expressed raison d'être—the cocktail of racism, anti-Semitism, and sedition—is justified and legitimated on theological grounds. It is at once a political and a grassroots religious movement. The leaders of individual groups within it have often been clergymen—such as the Michigan Militia's founder and "general," Pastor Norman Olson; the Idaho-based Aryan Nations' leader, Reverend Richard Girnt Butler; and the Ku Klux Klan's Pastor Thomas Robb—who deliberately flaunted their clerical titles to endow their organizations with a theological veneer that condones and justifies violence. In an article from the 1980s titled "An All White Nation?—Why Not?," Reverend Roy B. Masker, for example, explained how Aryan Nations members "are in disobedience to our Father and God, Yahwey, for allowing the Nation He gave us to become the mongrelized cesspool in which we now find ourselves. . . . Indeed, it is incumbent upon us to BUILD A NEW, ALL-WHITE NATION! We are under command to do so! All scripture demands it!" Masker concludes with the admonition "Woe to those who stand in the way of the Aryan juggernaut!"[174]

The Christian Patriots do not appear to recognize any of the political, moral, or practical considerations that constrain most other terrorist groups from causing mass death and destruction. There are, in fact, striking parallels between these groups and religiously motivated Islamic Sunni and Shi'a extremists or the messianic Jewish fanatics in the Middle East or Sikh militants in South Asia. All of these groups transform abstract political ideologies and objectives into a religious imperative. Violence is not merely sanctioned; it is divinely decreed. The killing of those described as "infidels" by the Shi'a, "dogs" by the Jews, or "children of Satan" by the Christian Patriots becomes a sacramental act.

Indeed, in the 1980s, evidence came to light that at least some of the movement's key figures had laid plans to engage in mass, indiscriminate killing. For example, an indictment handed down by a U.S. federal grand jury in 1987 alleged that fifteen representatives of groups from throughout the United States and Canada had met at the Aryan Nations headquarters in Idaho in 1983 to plot the forcible overthrow of the federal government and the creation of a separate Aryan nation within the United States. The indictment stated that they planned to "carry out assassinations of federal officials, politicians and Jews, *as well as bombings and polluting of municipal water supplies* [emphasis added]."[175] Any doubts of their seriousness of purpose were dispelled when police and federal agents raided a white supremacist compound in rural Arkansas in April 1984 and discovered a stockpile of some thirty gallons of cyanide to be used to poison reservoirs in Chicago, Illinois, and Washington, D.C.[176]

An identical scenario, in fact, is detailed in the novel *The Turner Diaries*,[177] written by the late William Pierce under the pseudonym Andrew MacDonald, which has been cited as "the Bible" of the Christian Patriots[178] and as a major influence on McVeigh in his planning of the Murrah Building bombing.[179] The book describes a chain of events that begins with a white supremacist revolution in 1991 and culminates two years later in "an all-out race war" and worldwide nuclear conflagration. A terrorist group called the Order embarks on a ruthless campaign of violence involving the assassination of public officials and prominent Jews, the shooting down of commercial airliners, the poisoning of water supplies, and bombings of public utilities. The book reaches its climax when the terrorists seize the U.S. nuclear arsenal and obliterate several American cities before turning the weapons on targets in Israel and the former Soviet Union.

As incredible and lunatic as the events described in *The Turner Diaries* may seem, the strategy of the inchoate terrorist campaign waged in the United States between 1983 and 1984 by Robert Matthews and the real-life Order was based entirely on the battle plan detailed in the book. In another example of life imitating art, MOM's two-hundred-page manual from the 1990s reportedly read exactly like a blueprint for battle copied out of *The Turner Diaries*, detailing plans to

- paralyze America's entire economy, including its agricultural and industrial sectors as well as transport and communications systems;
- assassinate prominent "artists and sports figures" and other leading personalities as a "useful form of propaganda for the revolutionary and patriot principles";
- eliminate spies and traitorous government officials; and
- generally foment "an air of nervousness, discredit, insecurity, uncertainty, and concern on the part of government."[180]

The bizarre apocalyptic vision of *The Turner Diaries* has long formed an integral part of the beliefs of white supremacists, Christian Patriots, and militia adherents. Whereas most people, for example, harbor deep fears of a nuclear war, many white supremacists appeared to welcome the prospect as an opportunity to eliminate their avowed "enemies" and permit the fulfillment of their objectives to create a new world order peopled exclusively by the white race. The self-described purpose of the Covenant, the Sword, and the Arm of the Lord's former compound at Mountain Home, Arkansas (where the cyanide was discovered), was "to build an Ark for God's people during the coming tribulations on the earth."[181] Accordingly, the hundred or so men, women, and children who lived in the compound in the early 1980s prepared themselves for the coming Armageddon by stockpiling weapons, food, and valuables and undergoing training in survivalist techniques and guerrilla warfare. As Pastor Terry Noble, a spokesman for the group, once explained, "We are Christian survivalists who believe in preparing for the ultimate holocaust. . . . The coming war is a step toward God's government."[182]

The influence that apocalyptic revelations and millenarian imperatives exerted over many of these groups may be seen in the "DIY [do-it-yourself] apocalypse kit" once marketed by MOM. The kit reportedly contained such detailed instructions as the need to build at least two concealed and well-protected "fall-out" shelters, stockpile enough food to last for at least a year, and arm oneself with, at the very minimum, a Colt AR-15 assault rifle and six hundred rounds of .223 ammunition, as well as at least one 9 mm-type Beretta automatic pistol with no fewer than two hundred bullets. A can opener, a toothbrush, and thermal underwear were the other recommended essentials—with MOM having offered for sale such additional optional gear as a military surplus NBC (nuclear, biological, and chemical) protective suit (available in green only) for fifty dollars.[183]

These beliefs involving the inevitability of Armageddon are actively encouraged by proselytizers of Dominion theology, a reinterpretation of Christian Identity doctrine popular within some Christian Patriot circles. Dominion theology has been described by one knowledgeable observer as a "post-millennial Bible-based doctrine" incorporating the main tenets of Identity dogma. Thus, in addition to anti-Semitism and racism, Dominionists believe that it is incumbent upon each individual to hasten redemption by working actively to ensure the return of the Messiah—in the Dominionists' vision, Christ. Only by accelerating the inevitable apocalypse, Dominionists contend, will the tribulations that currently afflict the American Christian white man end. The apocalypse will be followed by a thousand-year period of rule by Christians, at the end of which Christ will return to earth.[184]

The abiding link between religion and violence was most clearly demonstrated at the conference sponsored by a leading Identity and Dominionist figure, Reverend Pete Peters,[185] in Estes Park, Colorado, in October 1992.[186] At that meeting, Louis Beam—one of the preeminent figures in American white supremacism—defined the violent strategy of "leaderless resistance" for the militia movement. Beam, a Vietnam veteran and former Grand Dragon of the Texas Ku Klux Klan, whose close ties with Butler once led to his appointment as the Aryan Nations' ambassador-at-large, has long been at the cutting edge of white supremacist violent activism. It was he who, in the early 1980s, pioneered the use of computer bulletin boards as a means for like-minded hatemongers both to communicate with one another and to circulate literature and information otherwise outlawed by the U.S. and Canadian postal services. Beam was thus well positioned to take the American white supremacist movement into the twenty-first century, making full use of the advanced capabilities of the Internet and the World Wide Web. Information and literature from obscure organizations that was once difficult to obtain therefore has been made readily available over the Internet to millions. Beam's concept of "leaderless resistance" was designed to avoid the mistakes of the past, when traditional-type terrorist groups such as the Order were created to prosecute the white-race revolution, only to be undermined and ultimately neutralized by arrests and informants. Accordingly, Beam proposed that "phantom cell networks" or "autonomous leadership units" (ALUs) be established that would operate completely independently of one another, but through their individual terrorist acts, would eventually join together to create a chain reaction leading to a nationwide white supremacist revolution.

The object of "leaderless resistance," Beam explained, is to "defeat state tyranny."[187] The concept is taken from the white supremacist adventure novel *Hunter*, William Pierce's sequel to *The Turner Diaries* (again written under the pseudonym Andrew MacDonald). The impact of the strategy on the militia movement has been profound. For example, the "field manual" produced by "the Free Militia" in Wisconsin—typical of the genre in the 1990s—stated:

THE FUNDAMENTAL RULE GUIDING THE ORGANIZATION OF THE FREE MILITIA IS [NOT] GENERALIZED PRINCIPLES AND PLANNING BUT DECENTRALIZED TACTICS AND ACTION.

What is meant by this key statement is that the whole Militia must be committed to the same cause and coordinated in their joint defense of a community. . . . The way a balance between these competing concerns is achieved in the Free Militia is to organize all elements into "cells."[188]

Similarly, in an address to a meeting of the Washington State Militia in January 1996, MOM's John Trochmann was quoted as saying: "If the enemy forces have no idea what's . . . in store for them if they come to our backyard . . . leave the element of surprise on your side. Not everyone has to stand up publicly. Go with the cell structure in some of your areas—have a ball. Let them guess what's going on for a change, instead of us."[189]

A subsequent incarnation of the fusion of religion and hate is believed to be the previously mentioned shadowy militant Christian Patriot activist-warriors known as the Phineas Priesthood—a movement that the *Washington Post* characterized as "an anti-Semitic, anti-multiculturalism affiliation that opposes biracial relationships, same-sex marriage, taxation and abortion."[190] The name is taken from the Old Testament (Numbers 25), which recounts how a man named Phineas became an avenger priest by murdering a Midianite whom he discovered having sex with her Israelite (Jewish) lover. The biblical tale is taken by some modern-day Christian antiabortion extremists cum Identity adherents as a decree against "race mixing" and a summons to "strike down those who are viewed as enemies of the pure white race."[191] The Phineas Priests' self-appointed mission is allegedly to impose what they believe is "God's law" on earth, that is, the enforcement of prohibitions against interracial marriage, homosexuality, and abortion, and an end to the federal banking system. They are reported to be highly secretive: a loose association of like-minded individuals adhering to the wider movement's "leaderless resistance" or "phantom cells" strategy.[192] Joe Roy, the director of Klanwatch, a project of the Southern Poverty Law Center that is now called Hatewatch, has described the Phineas Priests as "zealots who truly believe they are commanded by God to carry out a revolution in the United States to restore 'God's law.'"[193] To this end, in November 2014, Larry McQuilliams was shot to death by police after he opened fire on the Austin, Texas, police headquarters, a federal courthouse, and the Mexican consulate (which he also attempted to set on fire). The police found in a rental van he used for the attacks a copy of the book *Vigilantes of Christendom: The History of the Phineas Priesthood* by Richard Kelly Hoskins.[194]

A clear convergence of religious terrorism and violence against homosexuals and abortion clinics and their staffs has also been evident on several occasions over the past few decades.[195] In 1994, for example, a Christian fundamentalist minister named Paul Hill shot to death a clinic doctor and his bodyguard in Pensacola, Florida. In his book *Should We Defend Born and Unborn Children with Force?*, Hill cited Phineas's biblical mission and writes of the need for a vigilante underground to punish all who "disobey God's law" on abortion or homosexuality and engage in other forms of blasphemous behavior.[196] Christian Patriots also invoked the Priesthood in defense of the slaying of three customers at a gay bookstore in Shelby, North Carolina, in 1991, and it surfaced again in connection with a series of bank robberies and bombings that took place between April and July 1996 in Spokane, Washington. Three men were subsequently convicted of bombing a Planned Parenthood clinic (where abortions are performed), a local newspaper's offices, and a bank, as well as twice robbing the same bank of $108,000 (a sum that was never recovered). At the scene of some of their attacks the gang left a two-page printed document, signed with the mark of the "Phineas Priests." The document espoused both Dominionist and Identity theology, before concluding with the warning:

> Let the high praises of Yahweh [God] be in their mouth, and a two-edged sword in their hand; to execute vengeance upon the heathen, and punishments upon the people: To bind their kings with chains, and their nobles with fetters of iron: To execute upon them the judgment written. . . .
>
> Flee you usurer from the face of our land, and all that would not that the Master should reign over them, for the end of Babylon is come. Praise Yahweh![197]

The uncompromising antigovernment fervor, aggressive racism, and strident anti-Semitism espoused by the American Christian Patriot movement have not been confined to the United States. The racist British group Combat 18 (which takes its name from the first and eighth letters of the alphabet—Adolf Hitler's initials), for example, modeled itself on the American militias and Christian Patriot movements, advocating attacks on the police and other symbols of governmental authority.[198] In Australia, militia groups patterned on the American model have reportedly been established using an organizational blueprint provided by MOM.[199] And perhaps the most significant atrocity committed by a white supremacist since the 1995 bombing of the Murrah federal office building in Oklahoma City was the July 2011 bombing and shooting rampage that took place in Oslo and Utøya, Norway, by a then thirty-two-year-old Norwegian named Anders Behring Breivik.[200]

Despite the deaths and imprisonment of past leaders and key members alongside the sometimes wild fluctuations in the number of nationwide chapters and overall membership, the two characteristics of the American white supremacist movement and its various antigovernment and tax resistance derivations that have remained constant are its enormous capacity for reinvention as a means to attract new and more diverse constituencies and its proclivity for sharp, sudden spasms of violence. The FBI today, as noted in chapter 1, is especially concerned about the threat from "lone wolf" terrorism—whether by individuals claiming allegiance to ISIS, such as Syed Rizwan Farook and Tashfeen Malik, the aforementioned married couple, who in December 2015 attacked a regional government center in San Bernardino, California, or violent right-wing extremists such as Timothy

McVeigh and Eric Rudolph, neither of whom actually belonged to a white supremacist group, much less any existing terrorist organization, but who, like Farook and Malik, were nevertheless clearly motivated and inspired by the ideology of such movements to commit murder.[201] Rudolph pled guilty in April 2005 to killing two people and injuring 150 others in a series of bombings that included the 1996 Olympics and a gay club in Atlanta, Georgia, as well as an abortion clinic in Birmingham, Alabama.[202] Like McVeigh, Rudolph shared the beliefs and positions of the white supremacist movement on issues such as legalized abortion and hatred of global institutions such as the Olympic Games, which to his mind, promoted the "despicable ideals [of] global socialism."[203]

The fact that the American Christian Patriot movement, according to one analyst, "is now larger than at any time in the 1990s"—with 1,360 identifiable groups active as recently as 2012 compared with 858 in 1996—attests to the remarkable resiliency and durability of this twisted mélange of extremist views and conspiratorial theorizing.[204] In this respect, the growth of the so-called Sovereign Citizen Movement (SCM) is perhaps the latest iteration of this ideological continuum. The FBI describes the movement's adherents, known as "Sovereign Citizens," as "anti-government extremists who believe that even though they physically reside in this country, they are separate or 'sovereign' from the United States. As a result, they believe that they don't have to answer to any government authority, including courts, taxing entities, motor vehicle departments or law enforcement."[205] Sovereign Citizens hence disdain the authority of courts, judges, juries, law enforcement, and elected officials; believe they should not have to pay taxes; and maintain that which laws someone chooses to obey is an entirely personal choice. It should be emphasized that bogus liens and frivolous lawsuits brought against public officials are the Sovereign Citizens' preferred weapons—not guns and bombs.[206] But their capacity for violence cannot be completely discounted either. Persons claiming allegiance to the movement, for instance, have committed murder and physical assaults; threatened judges, public officials, and law enforcement personnel with physical violence; impersonated police officers and diplomats; used fake currency, passports, license plates, and drivers' licenses; and perpetrated a variety of mortgage fraud and so-called redemption schemes.[207] Among the most notorious incidents have been the slayings in 2003 of two South Carolina police officers over a land dispute; the 2010 killing of two Arkansas policemen during a routine traffic stop; and the ambush death of a deputy sheriff in Florida in 2010.[208] The FBI accordingly classifies the Sovereign Citizens more extreme and violently inclined members "as comprising a domestic terrorist movement."[209]

The difficulty in gauging the threat from the SCM is a reflection of its amorphous membership, deliberately unorganized nature, local leadership, and ambiguous, broadly inclusive ideology. The Southern Poverty Law Center, for example, hypothesized that a reasonable estimate of sovereign believers in 2011 was in the range of 100,000 dedicated adherents, with perhaps another 200,000 persons at various stages of personal commitment. Although the movement has long styled itself as an exclusionist white, Anglo-Saxon, Christian entity with strong racist and anti-Semitic beliefs, there are nonetheless many African American, Asian, and other persons of different races and religions who identify themselves as Sovereign Citizens. According to David Brannan, a former police officer and expert on American religious and political extremism, "Some of the biggest developments on the Right have been in the Sovereign Citizen's Movement moving AWAY from a specific Christian Identity focus/context." Indeed, the SCM's growing prominence and popularity is part of a broader makeover that has fundamentally transformed the violent American Far Right during the first two decades of the twenty-first century. "The neo-Nazi types of the late 1980s to 2000," Brannan points out, "are being replaced by Nationalists concerned with immigration—and they are wearing suits and square rimmed glasses rather than combat boots and red suspenders."[210]

Cults

The special potential of terrorism motivated by a religious imperative to cause mass indiscriminate killing has been perhaps most clearly demonstrated by the ominous activities of various religious cults and sects in the United States, Japan, and elsewhere since the 1980s. While the attention of law enforcement officials, government intelligence agencies, and security services was focused firmly on the more visible threat presented by familiar terrorist adversaries in the traditional ideological, ethnonationalist/separatist and more mainstream religiously inspired groups, members of these other, often uniquely idiosyncratic movements were already poised to cross the threshold of terrorist use of either weapons of mass destruction (WMD) or mass annihilation.

In 1984, for example, a nonlethal but disturbingly portentous incident occurred in the small Oregon town of The Dalles. Followers of the Bhagwan Shree Rajneesh, an ascetic Indian mystic who, in addition to amassing a collection of ninety-three Rolls-Royce automobiles, had established a large religious commune nearby, contaminated the salad bars of ten restaurants with salmonella bacteria in hopes of debilitating the local populace and thereby rigging a key municipal election in the cult's favor. Although their plot to gain power in this way failed,[211] 751 people did become ill, 45 of whom required hospitalization. Moreover, evidence subsequently came to light that the restaurant contaminations were in fact a test run for a more ambitious plot to poison the town's water supply.[212] The Rajneeshis' successful cultivation and effective dispersal of the bacteria clearly suggested the ease with which lethal agents could potentially be produced and disseminated in even larger population centers.[213]

The release of deadly nerve gas on the Tokyo underground in March 1995 not only confirmed those fears but also marked a significant historical watershed in terrorist tactics and weaponry. Previously, most terrorists had shown an aversion to the esoteric and exotic weapons of mass destruction popularized in fictional thrillers or depicted in action-hero films and television shows. Radical in their politics, the majority of terrorists were equally conservative in their methods of operation. Indeed, from the time of the late-nineteenth-century Russian revolutionaries and the Fenian dynamiters who terrorized Victorian-era London, terrorists have continued to rely almost exclusively on the same two weapons: the gun and the bomb. The sarin-induced deaths of a dozen Tokyo commuters and the injuries inflicted on nearly four thousand others may have changed that forever.

The Aum Shinrikyo (Aum "Supreme Truth" sect)[214] arguably still represents a new kind of terrorist threat, posed not by traditional secular adversaries but by a mass religious movement motivated by a mystical, almost transcendental, divinely inspired imperative. The group was founded in 1987 by Shoko Asahara. A partially blind, hitherto unexceptional purveyor of supposedly medicinal herbs, who in 1982 was fined eight hundred dollars and sentenced to twenty days' incarceration after conviction for selling fake cures, and owner of a chain of yoga schools in Japan, Asahara had emerged as a self-anointed prophet after a trip to the Himalayas the previous year. His messianic inclinations were subsequently encouraged by a vision he had while meditating on a beach after returning to Japan. According to Asahara, the Shiva God sent a "message" to him that he had been chosen to "lead God's army." Asahara believed that he had been ordained an *Abiraketsu no mikoto*, an ancient "light god," and given the divine task of establishing the "Kingdom of Shambhala"—a utopian community populated only by those who had achieved psychic powers.[215] Not long after this experience, Asahara fortuitously fell into conversation with an eccentric historian he met at a mountainside spiritual retreat. The historian told him that Armageddon would come at the end of the century, that "only a merciful, godly race will survive," and that "the leader of this race will emerge in Japan." Asahara immediately knew that he was the person destined to be that leader. Transformed by this revelation, he changed his name from the plain-sounding Chizuo Matsumoto to the apparently more suitably spiritual Shoko Asahara.[216]

Shortly afterward, with just ten followers, Asahara opened the first Aum office. The new sect grew rapidly, tapping into a peculiarly Japanese fascination with mystical, obscure religious sects that combine the spiritual with the supernatural. Indeed, according to one account, at that time approximately 183,000 different religious cults already existed in Japan.[217] Aum's highly idiosyncratic mixture of Buddhism and Hinduism fused with notions of apocalyptic redemption exerted a powerful attraction for young, intelligent Japanese alienated by society's preoccupation with work, success, technology, and making money. Hence, by the end of 1987, Aum had fifteen hundred members with branches in several Japanese cities,[218] and by 1989, double that number.[219] In less than a decade, it would have some ten thousand members, organized within twenty-four branches scattered throughout Japan, alongside an estimated twenty to thirty thousand followers in Russia alone,[220] with an additional ten to twenty thousand converts in at least six other countries[221] and offices in New York, Germany, Australia, and Sri Lanka.

From the start, Asahara preached about the inevitability of an impending apocalypse, stressing his unique messianic mission and variously describing himself as "Today's Christ," "the saviour of This Century,"[222] and "the one and only person who had acquired supreme truth."[223] By 1994, these delusions of power and authority had led Asahara to believe that he should be king of Japan, claiming the mantle of Zhu Yuanzhang, a fourteenth-century Chinese religious leader who created the Ming dynasty.[224] Particular emphasis was given to the Hindu god of destruction and subsequent regeneration, Shiva, whose fifteen-foot visage dominated the entrance to the Satian-7 laboratory where the group manufactured the sarin nerve gas used in the subway attack. To round out his preoccupation with prophesied cataclysmic events, Asahara also borrowed Judeo-Christian notions of Armageddon and frequently cited the apocalyptic predictions of the sixteenth-century French astrologer Nostradamus, whose recently translated works had become best-sellers in Japan. According to Asahara, the world would end—but he was never sure exactly when, variously fixing 1993, 1997, 1999, 2000, and 2003 as likely times. Whatever the date, Asahara was certain that Armageddon would be caused by a Third World War. Citing his otherworldly abilities of both "astral vision and intuitive wisdom," he proclaimed before an Aum conference in 1987 that nuclear war was "sure to break out" between 1999 and 2003. This catastrophe could be averted, Asahara assured his followers, provided that they worked actively to establish an

Aum branch in every country in the world. "Spread the training system of Aum on a global scale and scatter Buddhas over the world," he advised. "Then we can avoid World War III for sure. I guarantee it."[225] From these apocalyptic predictions sprang Asahara's obsession with American enmity toward the Japanese in general and himself in particular. "As we move toward the year 2000," an Aum pamphlet warned, "there will be a series of events of inexpressible ferocity and terror. The lands of Japan will be transformed into a nuclear wasteland. Between 1996 and January 1998, America and its allies will attack Japan, and only 10 percent of the population of the major cities will survive."[226] Indeed, Asahara regularly blamed the United States for all of Japan's economic and social problems, as well as for attempting to destroy his own health. According to the testimony of Aum's former director of intelligence, Yoshihiro Inoue, Asahara had stated that after overthrowing the Japanese government and seizing power, the movement's real challenge would be to deal with the U.S. military forces stationed in the country.[227] An intrinsic element of all these claimed plots was Asahara's fascination with nerve gas. "I come under a gas attack wherever I travel," he reportedly once declared, drawing a connection between the "jet fighters from the US forces [that] fly for exercises around Mt Fuji" and his alleged medical problems.[228]

Asahara thus deliberately fostered a climate of paranoiac expectation within the cult, driven by the same Manichean worldview embraced by other religious terrorist movements, who see the world as a battleground between good and evil. The sect's avowed enemies gradually expanded to include not only the predatory U.S. government and its minions in the Japanese government (who, Asahara alleged, were responsible for causing the January 1995 Kobe earthquake), but also a mysterious international cabal of Freemasons, Jews, and financiers. Asahara's adherence to the same far-fetched conspiracy theories promulgated by the American Christian Patriot movement is perhaps not entirely surprising given that he was also an unabashed admirer of Hitler and a fervent believer in the conspiratorial fantasies spun by such well-known anti-Semitic works as the turn-of-the-century forgery *Protocols of the Elders of Zion*.

In books such as *Disaster Approaches the Land of the Rising Sun: Shoko Asahara's Apocalyptic Predictions*, Asahara warned that Armageddon would be precipitated by a poisonous gas cloud dispatched from the United States that would engulf Japan.[229] Thereafter, a cataclysmic global conflict would erupt—involving both nerve gas and nuclear weapons—that, in words reminiscent of Hitler's proclaimed thousand-year Reich, would lead to a thousand years of peace, after which the appearance of a new messiah would create a paradise on earth.[230] In 1993, however, Asahara suddenly began to proclaim that the forthcoming apocalypse could be averted if Aum took proper action. "We need a lot of weapons to prevent Armageddon," he reportedly told his closest aides. "And we must prepare them quickly."[231]

Thus, Aum embarked on its program to acquire an array of conventional and unconventional weaponry that would effectively dwarf the arsenals of most established nation-states. To achieve this goal, the group recruited scientists and technical experts from Japan, Russia (including two nuclear scientists), and other countries. In contrast to Asahara's lack of higher education—in 1977 he failed to win a place at Japan's best university, the University of Tokyo, and therefore immersed himself more fervently in yoga and his Eastern medical practice[232]—these individuals brought to Aum's projects superb credentials, including advanced degrees from their respective countries' most prestigious universities and research institutions. Among the Japanese recruited to Aum, for instance, was Seiichi Endo, Aum's minister of public health. Endo was a veterinarian and then a PhD student at Kyoto University, considered the country's best university in the natural sciences, where he studied virology and genetic engineering. At Aum, he led the team of scientists tasked with developing biological weapons, including botulinum and anthrax.[233] Ikuo Hayashi, the minister of medicine and one of the five perpetrators of the subway nerve gas attack, had studied medicine at Keio University, one of Japan's best private universities. He subsequently held appointments as a heart specialist at the Keio University hospital and at the Henry Ford Heart and Vascular Institute in Detroit, Michigan. Hayashi was director of the Department of Circulatory Organs at the Japanese National Sanatorium when he joined the cult and was made director of Aum's own hospital. His responsibilities included administering drugs—including powerful hallucinogens and electroshock therapy—to brainwash recalcitrant group members and make them more compliant.[234] Another prominent Aum physician, Tomomasa Nakagawa, according to the American psychiatrist and author, Robert J. Lifton, "became a visionary planner of large-scale killing" for Asahara. And Fumihiro Joyu, a telecommunications specialist who had been employed by Japan's space agency, became the cult's spokesperson.[235] What all the Japanese recruits had in common, according to Harvard University's Mayuka Yamazaki, was that

> before joining Aum, they had questions about their lives. Some of them knew they were not outstanding enough to reach the pinnacle of Japanese society, some realized the limitations of their occupation and some were frustrated with their surroundings which [were] either boring or unfair. Aum effectively approached these young, intelligent but depressed elites, proposing to provide status, money, facilities and the tremendous

opportunities to allow them to explore their potential capability to the maximum, and made them believe they could find themselves in Aum.[236]

Moreover, with its vast financial reserves—Aum's assets exceeded an estimated $1 billion,[237] and when the police searched Asahara's office, they reportedly discovered twenty pounds of gold and about £5 million in cash[238]—the sect was able to purchase whatever additional knowledge and resources its members lacked. Prime vendors in this respect were the Russian KGB's (Komitet Gosudarstvennoi Bezopanosti) elite Alpha Group, the equivalent of the British SAS or American Delta Force, whose expertise in counterterrorist tactics (the group was established as a direct result of the Munich Olympics incident) and clandestine warfare (including sabotage, assassination, kidnapping, and intelligence and counterintelligence techniques) was imparted to Aum activists. Additional personnel from Russia's other military special operations force, known as Spetsnaz, reportedly provided further training in martial arts, escape and evasion techniques, and the use of various small arms, including rocket launchers and assault rifles. Aum is also thought to have purchased large quantities of small arms from KGB stocks and to have been in the market for such advanced weaponry as T-72 tanks, MiG-29 jet fighters, an SL-13 Proton rocket launcher, and even a nuclear bomb. What is known is that Aum succeeded in obtaining a surplus twin-turbine Mi-17 helicopter, complete with chemical spray dispersal devices. The group had ambitious plans—and had already acquired sophisticated robotic manufacturing devices—to produce at least one thousand knockoff versions of Russia's world-famous AK-47 assault rifle, along with one million bullets. It had also perfected the manufacture of TNT and the central component of plastic explosives, RDX.[239] The group spent 90 million yen (about $9 million) on its manufacturing facilities for automatic weapons and another 34 million yen (about $3.4 million) to construct the Satian-7 facility.[240]

Aum's intentions, however, went far beyond a revolution facilitated by conventional armaments alone: it also armed itself with a panoply of chemical and biological warfare agents, and even harbored nuclear aspirations. When the police raided the sect's laboratories after the nerve gas attack on the Tokyo underground, they found potentially enough sarin to kill an estimated 4.2 million people. In addition, Aum either had already produced or had plans to develop other nerve gases such as VX, tabun, and soman; chemical warfare agents such as mustard gas and sodium cyanide; and biological warfare agents that included anthrax, the highly contagious disease known as Q-fever, and possibly the deadly Ebola virus as well.[241] Authorities also found 100 grams of the psychedelic drug LSD—the equivalent of one million doses—and 3 kilograms of mescaline, among other hallucinatory and stimulant drugs.[242] As previously noted, these drugs, as well as electro-shock therapy, were administered to punish cult members either for at-tempting to leave the cult or for even making contact with outsiders. These "brainwashing" treatments involved massive doses of LSD, which in some instances resulted in severe memory loss and other psychological dysfunction.[243]

Aum's most ambitious project was without doubt its attempt to develop a nuclear capability. To this end, the group had purchased the 500,000-acre Banjawarn sheep station in a remote part of Western Australia. There, they hoped to mine uranium, which was to be shipped back to Aum's laborato-ries in Japan, where scientists using laser enrichment technology would convert it into weapons-grade nuclear material. The reason for a massive explosion that occurred near Aum's Australian holdings on May 28, 1993, which lit up the sky for miles and caused shock waves felt hundreds of miles away, is still unexplained but may have been related to Aum's nuclear research and development activities.

"With the use of sarin we shall eradicate major cities," Asahara had de-clared, and on the morning of March 20, 1995, his disciples put his deadly plan into action. The date was much sooner than had been expected because Aum informants inside the National Police Agency had warned that the po-lice were about to search the cult's compounds and so Asahara suddenly ordered the planned attack to be brought forward in hopes of thwarting the impending raids and completely derailing the intensifying police investiga-tion into Aum's activities.[244] At approximately eight o'clock on Monday morning, in the midst of rush hour, selected Aum cadres placed eleven pack-ages containing sarin nerve gas on five subway trains on the Eidan Chi-yoda, Hibiya, and Marunouchi lines. The trains were scheduled to converge within four minutes of one another at Kasumigaseki central station, the ter-minus at the heart of the Japanese government, used daily by the thousands of office workers employed in the country's most important ministries—including the National Police Agency. Eyewitnesses reported that some of the containers appeared to be ordinary lunch boxes or soft-drink flasks, while others were nylon trash bags wrapped in newspaper. In at least one instance, a man was observed stabbing his package with the sharpened tip of an umbrella, thus releasing the nerve gas. Almost immediately, passen-gers were affected by the noxious fumes: some were quickly overcome; others were afflicted with nosebleeds, oral hemorrhaging, uncontrollable cough-ing fits, or convulsions. In all, fifteen stations and three separate subway lines were affected. The casualties might even have been far greater had not favorable weather conditions fortuitously combined with hastened—and therefore perhaps botched—preparations that likely reduced the sarin's potency.

Amazingly, this was neither the first nor the last Aum attack to employ chemical or biological warfare agents. In April 1990, the group had attempted to realize one of Asahara's dire prophecies of an impending catastrophe by staging an attack with botulinum toxin. Using an aerosol device developed by Aum's scientists to disperse the poison over a wide area, the sect targeted downtown Tokyo, and specifically, the Diet (parliament) building. The toxin, however, proved ineffective. Another attempt to disperse botulinum in downtown Tokyo failed in June, as did a suspected Aum plot to spread anthrax the following month. Then, in June 1994, the group had tried to kill three judges presiding over a civil suit brought against Aum in the rural resort town of Matsumoto. The plan was to spray sarin into a block of flats where the judges were sleeping. Seven people were killed, and more than 250 others were admitted to the hospital with nerve gas–induced symptoms. Although they became seriously ill, the judges survived. Incredible as it seems, a report previously issued by a special unit of the Tokyo metropolitan police department's criminal investigation laboratory pointing to the presence of the nerve gas apparently went ignored— despite repeated local complaints of strange odors emanating from the sect's nearby compound, alongside various unexplained disappearances of former Aum members and other persons who had attempted to investigate the sect's activities. Instead, the man who first reported the incident was branded as the culprit and accused of accidentally mixing some noxiously fatal concoction of weed killer.[245] Finally, in a last spasm of activity designed to avert the governmental onslaught directed at Aum in the wake of the underground attacks, members of the sect attempted to stage a chemical attack using hydrogen cyanide—more infamously known as Zyklon B, the same type of gas used by the Nazis at Auschwitz during World War II to murder tens of thousands of people—on May 5, 1995, the national "Children's Day" holiday.

Aum's objective, however, was not, as many have described it, wanton, mass indiscriminate murder as an end in itself, but the acquisition and unimpeded exercise of political power. Theological treatise and religious imperatives clearly played a preeminent role in the justification behind and motivation for Aum's campaign of violence and subversion. But killing for the sake of killing was not the engine driving Asahara's and the movement's grandiose ambitions. Indeed, it was Asahara's frustrations in pursuing legal, democratic means of change and influence that arguably drove him to embrace terrorism. As an adolescent, he had boasted of his desire to become the prime minister of Japan one day.[246] And in 1989 he presaged his entry into politics, explaining in *Mahayana*, Aum's magazine, "We have to complement what we cannot achieve religiously by [a] political approach."[247] In 1990, accordingly, together with twenty-five other Aum members, Asahara stood for election to Japan's House of Representatives as members of the Shinri Tou (Supreme Truth) Party.[248] Asahara was certain that he would win,[249] and he became deeply embittered by his defeat, claiming that the Japanese government had interfered to deprive him of the victory he had rightly won. Thereafter, he became obsessed with exacting revenge by seizing power.[250]

On December 15, 1995, the Japanese prime minister, invoking a 1952 antisubversion law, ordered Aum disbanded and seized all its assets. Although a court later ruled that the Anti-Subversive Activities Act did not apply to religious movements such as Aum, new legislation—the "Regulation Against the Group Which Conducted Indiscriminate Massive Murder Attack" (*Dantai Kisei Ho*)—was enacted in 1999 that provided the authorities with additional, strengthened powers to monitor and curtail the activities of groups like Aum.[251] Asahara and his lieutenants were charged with a variety of crimes, and in February 2004 a Tokyo district court sentenced Asahara to death. The Aum movement, however, still exists. In 2000, Aum renamed itself Aleph, and under a new leader, Fumhiro Joyu, its former spokesman, the group attracted some fifteen hundred members.[252] Aleph has sought to distance itself from Aum's infamous past, portraying Asahara as its spiritual founder only, eschewing any theology that could be interpreted as justifying violence and murder, and making reparations payments to victims of the sarin attack.[253] A letter from the Aleph executive posted on the group's website in March 2005 evidenced this remorse: "It is 10 years since that tragic day. The world has gone through great changes which people could not have imagined and so has our group. However, whenever we think of the people who have lived with sorrow, our mind always go [sic] back to the day. Here, again, we express our deepest condolence on the people who died of the incident and give our greatest apology to what we did. As the best we can do, we will continue paying reparation from now. We will never repeat such a mistake."[254]

Conclusion

The emergence of obscure, idiosyncratic millenarian movements, zealously nationalist religious groups, militantly antigovernment, Far Right paramilitary organizations, and a transnational network of religious extremists that seeks the restoration of theocratic rule over what was once a vast pan-Islamic empire arguably represents a different and potentially far more lethal threat than traditional terrorist adversaries—and, in many cases, a far more amorphous and diffuse one. The members of the Aum sect in Japan, the fanatical Jewish groups in Israel, the Christian Patriots in America, the violent Islamist organizations active in Afghanistan, Algeria, Iraq, Lebanon, Libya, Mali, Pakistan, Palestine, the Sinai, Somalia, and Yemen among other places as part of either the al-Qaeda network or ISIS's transnational caliphate, do not conform to our traditional stereotypes of the secular terrorist organization. Those groups had a defined set of conventional—and thereby potentially attainable—political, social, or economic objectives, and however disagreeable or distasteful their aims and motivations may have been, their ideology and intentions were at least constrained and comprehensible—albeit politically radical and personally fanatical.

In terms of the countermeasures that the government, military, police, and intelligence and security services can employ against these theologically motivated and inspired adversaries, the first and most immediate challenge is often identifying them. These ethereal, sometimes deliberately amorphous entities—especially if they embrace lone wolf or leaderless strategies—will lack the footprint or modus operandi of an actual, existing terrorist organization, making it more difficult for intelligence, law enforcement, and other security specialists to get a firm idea or build a complete picture of their intentions and capabilities, much less their capacity for violence, before they strike. A second challenge is unraveling why mainstream religious traditions become radicalized and co-opted by violent extremists and why fringe movements or hitherto peaceful religious cults suddenly embark on lethal campaigns of indiscriminate terrorism.

Traditional counterterrorism approaches and policies may not be relevant, much less effective, in the face of religious terrorism. Strategies that have been used successfully in the past—including political concessions, financial rewards, amnesties, and other personal inducements—would be not only irrelevant but impractical, given both the religious terrorists' fundamentally alienated worldviews and their often extreme, resolutely uncompromising demands. Above all, the profound sense of alienation and isolation of these cults and religious movements needs to be vigorously counteracted. A bridge needs to be found between mainstream society and these violent and violently inclined militants so that they do not feel threatened and forced to withdraw psychologically into aggressive defensive stances used to justify violence or physically into heavily armed, seething compounds, or feel driven to undertake preemptive acts of violence directed against what they regard as a menacing, predatory society. The nonviolent resolution of the eighty-one-day standoff between the Freemen, a Montana militia organization, and the FBI in April 1996 provides a marked contrast to the debacle three years before involving the assault on the Branch Davidians' compound in Waco, Texas. By skillfully employing the tactics of negotiation and the nonconfrontational approaches developed during previous encounters with antigovernment and white supremacist groups, the authorities defused a potentially explosive situation, obtained the surrender of sixteen heavily armed Freemen who had barricaded themselves in the isolated ranch they had dubbed Justus Township, and avoided the bloodshed that had accompanied previous incidents.[255]

But while patient negotiation and minimum force have an important role to play in specific instances, particularly sieges, there is a more widespread problem of intense, often paranoiac, antigovernment sentiments in many pockets of the American hinterland. Here, the challenge is surely one of developing preemptive educational programs to mitigate grassroots alienation and polarization, and to stop the spread of seditious and intolerant beliefs before they take hold and become exploited by demagogues and hatemongers. Across the United States, progress can also be seen in this respect. A number of community groups and political action committees are attempting to counter the spread of ignorance, hate, and simplistic conspiracy theories that are used to explain complex economic phenomena and thus acquire new recruits to the antifederalist movement. Through a series of town hall meetings featuring plainspoken commonsense presentations that communicate important lessons in a vernacular as accessible and relevant to the local populace as that peddled by the conspiracy theorists, people gain a more critical perspective from which they can challenge the assertions of the sophists and refute the homespun ideologies that lie at the core of their odious belief systems.

The immense challenge of countering religious and religion-inspired terrorism among homegrown groups in the United States is eclipsed, of course, by that of ameliorating anti-American sentiment abroad. The tremendous international outpouring of sympathy and support that followed the 9/11 attacks has since been vitiated to a great extent by opposition to the United States–led invasion of Iraq and continuing controversy over America's prosecution of the war on terrorism.[256] The revelations about prisoner abuse at Abu Ghraib and the indefinite detention of enemy combatants at the Guantánamo Bay U.S. military base[257] have further sharpened the existing friction between the United States and the Muslim world. "This is the most dangerous, fiercest, and most savage crusade war launched against Islam," bin Laden said in a statement broadcast by al-Jazeera on December 27, 2001. "God willing the end of America is imminent."[258] His undiminished popularity in the years following the 2001 attacks among the populations of such key American allies as Pakistan (where in 2004 he was viewed favorably by 65 percent of those polled), in Jordan (55 percent), and in Morocco (45 percent) underscores the intense antipathy felt toward the United States in North Africa, the Middle East, and South and Southeast Asia. Such sentiments remain in some countries with large Muslim populations today—such as Egypt, Jordan, the Palestinian territories, Lebanon, and Turkey.[259] This perception of Islam under attack by the United States has been eagerly exploited and expertly manipulated by bin Laden, al-Zawahiri, and al-Baghdadi, among others.

The rise of ISIS combined with al-Qaeda's intractable persistence clearly demonstrates the resiliency and continued resonance of this message. Both these groups attain relevancy and legitimacy from a widespread perception of Islam under siege: threatened by an ineluctably bellicose Western-dominated world order. In this respect, the use of U.S. military force—even in self-defense or to prevent terrorist attacks—is seen not only by Muslims but by many others as symptomatic of a heavy-handed foreign policy. This perhaps explains the shift in emphasis from the global war on terrorism waged by the Bush administration to the strategy of countering violent extremism (CVE) pursued by President Obama. In contrast to the reliance on military force embraced by the United States following the 9/11 attacks, CVE seeks to address "the underlying grievances and conflicts that feed extremism," including measures such as building community awareness to identify the drivers of radicalization and indicators of terrorist recruitment; the countering of extremist narratives through grassroots-directed and implemented efforts; and community-led interventions designed to disrupt and prevent terrorist radicalization.[260]

The above proposed policy adjustment notwithstanding, the resurgence of this ancient breed of adversary, the religious terrorist, actually means that nothing less than a sea change is required in our thinking about terrorism and the policies needed to counter it. Perhaps the most sobering realization in confronting religious terrorism is that the threat—and the problems that fuel it—can never be eradicated completely. The complexity, diversity, and often idiosyncratic nature of religious terrorism imply that there is no magic bullet—no single superior solution—that can be applied to all cases. Yet this fact only reinforces the need for multiple creative solutions, if not to resolve, then at least to ameliorate, both the underlying causes of religious terrorism and its violent manifestations. Only by expanding our range of possible responses will we be able to target our resources prudently and productively in ways that will have the greatest positive effect.[261]

Chapter 5

Suicide Terrorism

I
n no area of contemporary terrorism has religion had a greater impact than in propelling the vast increase of suicide attacks that have occurred since 9/11. The years from 2001 to 2005 alone account for 78 percent of all the suicide terrorist incidents perpetrated between 1968 and 2005. And the dominant force behind this trend is religion.[1] Moreover, of the 25 identifiable terrorist organizations employing suicide tactics in 2015 (the last year for which complete data is available), 96 percent (24 of 25) were Islamist.[2] A decade ago these movements were themselves responsible for some 80 percent of all suicide attacks, thus confirming the trend observed by Mia Bloom in her 2005 study of suicide terrorism, *Dying to Kill*, that "there is an increasing and disturbing trend towards Islamic suicide terrorism."[3] The Tel Aviv-based Institute for National Security Studies reached an identical conclusion in assessing the continued rise in suicide terrorist incidents for both 2014 and 2015.[4]

According to the National Consortium for the Study of Terrorism and Responses to Terrorism, in 2015, 907 suicide attacks took place in some 25 countries—more than twice as many incidents in as many countries as had occurred in 2005.[5] Iraq, Afghanistan, Nigeria, Syria, Yemen, Pakistan, Libya, Somalia, and Cameroon accounted for the majority. And virtually all the perpetrators were Salafi-Jihadi terrorist organizations such as ISIS, Nigeria's ISIS-affiliate Boko Haram, the Taliban, the TTP (Tehrik-i-Taliban Pakistan), AQAP, and al-Qaeda's Syrian and Somali franchises—Jabhat al-Nusra (also known as the Nusra Front) and al-Shabaab. ISIS itself was responsible for over 3,000 deaths from suicide attacks, and Boko Haram for well over a 1,000—thus themselves accounting for over half the 8,353 persons who were killed in suicide terrorist operations during 2015.[6]

At the dawn of the modern era of religious terrorism some thirty years ago, by comparison, this phenomenon was confined exclusively to two countries: Lebanon and Kuwait. Toward the end of the 1980s, however, suicide terrorism began to spread beyond the Middle East—first to Sri Lanka, but then, as the 1990s unfolded, to India, Argentina, Israel, Saudi Arabia, Kenya, and Tanzania. It was also initially embraced by only a couple of terrorist groups: al-Dawa, an Iraqi Shi'a group, and the Lebanese Shi'a organization Hezbollah (mostly using its cover name, Islamic Jihad). Hezbollah's example of successfully driving the United States out of Lebanon with suicide attacks subsequently inspired other groups to adopt this tactic, specifically the Liberation Tigers of Tamil Eelam (LTTE or the Tamil Tigers), Hamas, the Palestine Islamic Jihad (PIJ), and eventually, al-Qaeda. Even secular, ethnonationalist movements that later resorted to suicide attacks have either deliberately cultivated religious imagery—such as al-Fatah in calling its special suicide unit the al-Aqsa Martyrs Brigade—combining "al-Aqsa," referring to the mosque in Jerusalem that, together with the adjacent Dome of the Rock, is Islam's third holiest shrine, and the word "martyr," among the most potent religious images—or, like the Tamil Tigers, evidenced characteristics like the single-minded devotion to, and veneration of, a leader—in this case, its founder and supreme commander for some three decades, Velupillai Prabhakaran—that arguably have more in common with a religious cult such as Aum than with stereotypical nationalist-separatist groups such as the IRA or the Basque ETA.

Core Characteristics of Suicide Terrorism

Terrorists have become increasingly attracted to suicide attacks because of their unique tactical advantages compared to those of more conventional terrorist operations. Suicide tactics are devastatingly effective, lethally efficient, have a greater likelihood of success, and are relatively inexpensive and generally easier to execute than other attack modes. The terrorist decision to employ this tactic is therefore neither irrational nor desperate, as is sometimes portrayed; rather, it is an entirely rational and calculated choice, consciously embraced as a deliberate instrument of warfare—the "strategic logic" to which Robert Pape refers.[7] Indeed, as Rashmi Singh explains, "Suicide attacks are both acts of strategic experience and practical reason as well

as acts that are simultaneously symbolic, ritualistic, and communicative . . .
a complex combination of expressive and instrumental violence."[8] For radical Islamic terrorist groups in particular, religious and theological justification plays an additionally critical role: it ensures a flow of recruits to these
organizations that is needed to sustain suicide operations.

Suicide terrorism differs from all other terrorist operations because the
perpetrator's own death is an essential requirement for the attack's success.[9]
The suicide terrorist is the "ultimate smart bomb," a human missile relentlessly homing in on its target but with flexibility in timing and access. The
suicide terrorist thus has the ability to effect last-minute changes in his or
her attack plan on the basis of ease or difficulty of approach, the paucity or
density of people in or around the target, and whether or not security personnel are present or other countermeasures are visible. Suicide terrorist
operations are also inexpensive to mount. According to one estimate, the
total cost of a typical Palestinian suicide operation during what has been
variously called the al-Aqsa Intifada (Arabic for "uprising" or more literally,
"shaking off") or the Second Intifada, which lasted from 2000 to 2005,[10] was
about $150.[11] Yet this modest sum yields a very attractive return: on aver-
age, suicide operations worldwide kill about four times as many people as
other kinds of terrorist attacks; in Israel, however, the average has been even
higher, inflicting six times the number of deaths and roughly twenty-six
times more casualties than other acts of terrorism.[12] These attacks are also
less complicated and compromising than other terrorist operations, since
no escape plan is needed: if the attack is successful, there is no assailant to
capture and interrogate. The very fact that it is a suicide attack obviates the
need to formulate a plan for the perpetrator(s) to get away—often the most
complicated and complex aspect of a terrorist operation—and therefore
greatly enhances its simplicity.

Suicide terrorism, moreover, is guaranteed to provide media coverage,
given its irresistible combination of savagery and bloodshed. Suicide terrorist attacks are also an especially powerful psychological weapon.[13] With the
exception perhaps of only WMD terrorism, no other terrorist tactic arguably induces the same fear and paralysis in the terrorists' target audience.
This is, of course, precisely the terrorists' purpose: to intimidate government
and citizens alike and create a climate of profound fear and insecurity that
the terrorists seek to manipulate and exploit to their advantage. The suicide
terrorist attack is thus deliberately conceived by its practitioners to have far-
reaching and profound psychological effects and repercussions well beyond
the immediate victims or object of the attack.

These core characteristics of suicide terrorism were all clearly evident on
9/11. First, the operation's success, of course, was completely dependent on

the nineteen hijackers' willingness to martyr themselves.[14] Each, accordingly, not only was handpicked by bin Laden himself but also was then asked to swear an oath of loyalty, pledging to carry out a suicide operation. Then, in addition to the training that the hijackers underwent in preparation for the attack, each was filmed for a martyrdom video to be released after his death.[15] According to Khalid Sheikh Mohammed (KSM), all but one of the nineteen hijackers made such a tape. The lone exception, whom KSM never publicly named, was excused after he explained his fear that "it might be hypocritical and Allah, then, might not accept his sacrifice."[16]

Second, the plan itself was a masterful act of deception that sought to turn ordinary passenger aircraft into human cruise missiles and hence the ultimate smart bomb.[17] The 9/11 Commission Report specifically noted this aspect of the operation, describing its chief architect, KSM, as having used "his imagination, technical aptitude, and managerial skills to hatching and planning an extraordinary array of terrorist schemes," including the "use of aircraft as missiles guided by suicide operatives."[18]

Third, the 9/11 attacks were relatively inexpensive to mount. According to the 9/11 Commission, al-Qaeda spent between $400,000 and $500,000 to finance the operation.[19] Its effects on both the U.S. and the global economy, as well as the vast expenditures on security measures worldwide that followed, have, of course, been disproportionately immense. Bin Laden himself specifically lauded the cost-effectiveness of the 9/11 attacks in the videotaped message released just before the U.S. national elections on October 29, 2004. After citing a statement made at a conference held by the venerable London-based Royal Institute of International Affairs that al-Qaeda "spent $500,000 on the event while America, in the incident and its aftermath lost—according to the lowest estimate—more than $500 billion," bin Laden crowed that this meant "every dollar of al-Qaida defeated a million dollars by the permission of Allah, besides the loss of a huge number of jobs." He then credited the attacks with setting in motion America's subsequent budget deficit problems, stating that this sum had "reached record astronomical numbers estimated to total more than a trillion dollars."[20] Previous major al-Qaeda attacks reflected an equally handsome return on investment. According to the CIA, for example, the 1998 East Africa embassy bombings required no more than $10,000—and succeeded in killing 301 people and injuring 5,000 others.[21] And the leader of a radical Egyptian jihadist terrorist group was quoted a month after the October 2000 maritime suicide attack on the USS Cole, a U.S. Navy destroyer anchored in Aden, Yemen, as stating that that operation similarly cost al-Qaeda no more than $10,000.[22] In addition to claiming the lives of 17 American sailors and wounding 39 others, it resulted in $250 million in damage to the vessel.[23]

Fourth, in terms of lethality and destruction, the 9/11 operation exceeded even al-Qaeda's grandest expectations. "I was the most optimistic of them all," bin Laden boasted in a videotape discovered by American troops in Kandahar, Afghanistan. "I was thinking that the fire from the gas in the plane would melt the iron structure of the building and collapse the area where the plane hit and all the floors above it only. This is all that we had hoped for."[24] Al-Zawahiri also credited the attack's suicide dimension with its astonishing infliction of death and destruction. "It was the mujahideen's desire for martyrdom that was the unique advantage," he explained in an audiotape released on the first anniversary of the attack, "which resulted in the stealthy raids on New York and Washington—by the grace of Allah. Nineteen mujahideen who desired death were able to inflict damage upon America, such as it had never before witnessed in its history."[25]

Fifth, the 9/11 attacks had an indisputably powerful psychological impact on the American psyche. They shattered the country's sense of well-being and invulnerability that had been predicated on both America's unrivaled superpower status and its relative geographical isolation, separated from the rest of the world by two vast oceans.[26] With the attacks, al-Qaeda sought to depict the United States not only as the "paper tiger" that bin Laden called it[27] but also as dangerously exposed and therefore vulnerable in the face of continued suicide onslaught.[28] "We love this kind of death for Allah's cause as much as you like to live," bin Laden warned CNN's Peter Arnett in a 1997 interview. "We have nothing to fear. [Death] is something we wish for."[29] Less than a month after the 9/11 attacks, al-Qaeda's chief spokesman, Suleimain Abu Ghaith, invoked exactly the same image of unrelenting, future attacks to torment the United States. "The Americans must know that the storm of airplanes will not stop, God willing," he said. "And there are thousands of young people who are as keen about death as Americans are about life."[30] Al-Zawahiri similarly raised the specter of endless waves of suicide attackers a year later. "It is the love of death in the path of Allah," he declared, "that is the weapon that will annihilate this evil empire of America by the permission of Allah. The mujahid youth will compete with each other to die in the path of Allah, to destroy the myth of 'great' America, by the permission of Allah."[31] That these threatened follow-on attacks have yet to materialize has done little to mitigate the fears of many Americans about likely future attacks.

Finally, that no escape plan was required and that the 9/11 attacks were doubtless the most media-covered news story of our time are both self-evident. It remains only to consider briefly the role that religion played in inspiring and motivating the hijackers. This is most clearly evidenced by the suicide note that Mohammad Atta, the operation's ringleader and one of the four pilots, wrote to his confederates. It was found at Boston's Logan Airport seven days after the attack, in a flight bag belonging to Atta that had missed its connecting flight from Portland, Maine, onto the ill-fated Los Angeles–bound American Airlines Flight 11.[32] "Be happy, optimistic, calm," Atta advised his fellow hijackers,

> because you are heading for a deed that God loves and will accept [as a good deed]. It will be the day, God willing, you spend with the women in paradise.
> Smile in the face of hardship young man / For you are heading toward eternal paradise. . . .
> Pray for yourself and all of your brothers that they may be victorious and hit their targets and . . . ask God to grant you martyrdom facing the enemy, not running away from it, and for him to grant you patience and the feeling that anything that happens to you is for him.[33]

This same unflinching dedication and determination to martyring oneself can be seen in the preattack videotape made by Ibrahim Ahmed al-Haznawi, one of the terrorists who provided the "muscle" aboard American Airlines Flight 77, which crashed into the Pentagon shortly after departing from Washington, D.C.'s Dulles Airport. "O Allah, I sacrifice myself for your sake, accept me as a martyr," al-Haznawi pleads. "We shall meet in the eternal Paradise with the prophets, honest people, martyrs, and righteous people."[34]

Although al-Qaeda is the first terrorist group to have successfully conducted suicide attacks on land, at sea, and in the air, throughout both the 1990s and the first decade of the twenty-first century, the LTTE and Palestinian terrorist movements—such as Hamas,[35] PIJ,[36] the al-Aqsa Martyrs Brigade,[37] and some of the Palestinian Popular Front organizations[38]—were among this tactic's foremost exponents. They not only eclipsed the earlier record established by Hezbollah but each during that time had perpetrated more suicide attacks than all other terrorist groups combined—including al-Qaeda. Indeed, since the LTTE first adopted this tactic in 1987 until the group's decisive defeat and demise in 2009, its suicide cadres were reported to have been responsible for over two hundred attacks.[39] The LTTE's elite suicide units comprised men, women[40] and children,[41] operated on both land and sea,[42] and, according to some reports, had also aspired to develop an airborne suicide attack capability.[43] The various Palestinian terrorists organizations employing this tactic have together similarly been credited with carrying out more than two hundred suicide attacks since 1993.[44]

The resort to suicide terrorism by the Tamils and the Palestinians has often been portrayed in terrorist propaganda and world press accounts alike as two sides of the same coin: intense outbursts of violence born of frustration, occupation, desperation, and humiliation, caused by the intransigence and brutality of the Sri Lankan and Israeli governments. Such explanations, however, give a distorted view of the rationale that underlies suicide terrorism. While such grievances are real and help ensure a steady stream of recruits, the organizational employment of suicide operations, as previously described, is an instrumental decision. Suicide terrorism in this respect is seen by its adherents as a particularly effective way to communicate a violent message. High-profile attacks are thus conducted for the purpose of demonstrating the terrorist organization's ability and determination to use violence to achieve its political objectives.[45] This motivation was particularly strong in the case of the LTTE and Hamas, which, as up-start organizations challenged by older, well-entrenched political rivals, were forced to distinguish themselves—in the eyes of both their state opponents and their would-be supporters—in an already crowded political field. Suicide terrorism thus became the chosen instrument for achieving this objective, designed to impress their friends, strike fear into the hearts of their enemies, and catapult them to the forefront of their respective national struggles.

Given that the LTTE and these Palestinian movements together arguably account for the vast majority of suicide terrorist incidents committed respectively before and since 9/11, both case studies are well suited to closer examination to better comprehend the dynamics of and motivations behind suicide terrorism.

The "Tamil Tigers" and Suicide Terrorism

From its founding, the LTTE sought to develop the image of an elite, professional, and ruthlessly dedicated fighting force. This image was designed initially as much to distinguish the LTTE from other, better-established Tamil separatist groups as to intimidate its principal set of opponents: the government of Sri Lanka and the country's predominantly Buddhist ethnic Sinhalese majority. During its opening period of operations, the organization's tactic of choice was assassination. The LTTE's targeting efforts were directed principally against rival Tamils and Tamil and Sinhala government officials and security forces. Later, as an almost logical extension of these calculated political killings, suicide bombing became the LTTE's signature mode of attack, further reinforcing its image as a distinctive and elite strike force. Indeed, a novel feature of this tactic was the group's heavy reliance on women as a suicide cadre.[46] Although women and girls accounted for perhaps only one-third of all LTTE fighters, they comprised 60 percent of its suicide cadre.[47] In this, as in every other aspect of the group's existence, the overriding influence and vision of its now deceased founder and leader, Velupillai Prabhakaran, reigned supreme. The histories of Prabhakaran and the LTTE are inextricably linked. It is therefore necessary to know the one to understand the other.

The LTTE emerged in the mid-1970s in the midst of a period of renewed intercommunal tensions that was rapidly descending into violence. Twenty years earlier, the recently formed Ceylonese government had enacted highly discriminatory legislation that gave preference to Sinhalese over Tamils in government hiring, university admissions, and the attainment of key professional qualifications.[48] Although these laws were deeply resented, Tamil opposition was largely kept in check until 1972, when the legislation was reinforced and further institutionalized in the Republican Constitution of the newly renamed state of Sri Lanka.[49] The Sinhala ascendancy over the Tamils was now complete. Long-standing sectarian tensions resurfaced as Tamil anger mounted over this latest act of discrimination and disenfranchisement. Among the comparatively well-educated Tamil youth living in and around Jaffna, the historical center of the community's cultural heritage, the passage of the Standardization of Education Act two years before had already triggered intense resentment and acts of civil disobedience. In the face of growing discrimination in university admissions quotas, a group of activists formed the Tamil Students Front in 1970, one of the first groups to specifically advocate violence to regain Tamil civil rights. In a relatively short span of time, this single movement initiated a militant ethnonationalist awakening that eventually resulted in the creation of thirty-six different extremist Tamil separatist groups.[50]

One of these groups was a new Tamil political party called the Tamil United Liberation Front (TULF). The TULF quickly emerged as the leading political force within the Tamil community. Its hard-line nationalist platform, which called for the establishment of an independent, ethnically separate Tamil state in the northern and adjacent northeastern and eastern regions of Sri Lanka, helped distinguish it from its more conciliatory parent organization, the Tamil United Front (TUF). A more important distinction, however, was the fact that in addition to engaging in legal, overt political activities, as the TUF did, the TULF was also preparing for war. Unwilling to put its trust in a political system that had long demonstrated its bias against basic Tamil civil rights, the TULF sought to hedge its bets by establishing a parallel, clandestine organization to recruit radical young Tamils who believed that the only solution to their political problems would be found at the point of a gun. Prabhakaran, who joined the TULF in 1972, was among these recruits.[51]

Little is known conclusively about Prabhakaran's background. Most commentators agree, however, that he was born in 1954 and was the son of a tax commissioner—not the progeny of a smuggler, as is sometimes reported.[52] His grandfather is believed to have been a postman. Unlike many rural Tamils at the time, his family would thus have had both an interest in learning and the means to acquire at least some formal, if rudimentary, education. Prabhakaran has claimed that his own political and ethnic consciousness was awakened when he was nine or ten years old, after hearing stories told to him by his relatives about the bloody history of Tamil-Sinhalese relations over the course of the previous decade.[53] The increasing militancy of Tamil nationalism unfolding during the mid-1970s closely mirrored the development of Prabhakaran's own strident views. Given his developing radicalism, it might have been expected that he would be gradually drawn toward one of the more extreme offshoots of the TULF, the Tamil New Tigers (TNT).[54] The TNT at that time was led by its founder, Chetti Thanabalsingham, who had established the organization in 1974 for the purpose of silencing progovernment Tamils,[55] eliminating Tamil police informants and their Sinhalese police handlers, and staging armed demonstrations against the Sinhalese government. Prabhakaran was quickly promoted to serve as Thanabalsingham's deputy.[56]

The TNT gained particular notoriety in 1975, when its gunmen murdered the Tamil mayor of Jaffna, Alfred Duraiyappah.[57] The group suffered a mortal blow the following year, however, when Thanabalsingham was arrested. Never one to repine, Prabhakaran immediately stepped in and assumed command on May 5, 1976. He renamed the group the Liberation Tigers of Tamil Eelam and set about reshaping it in his own image. Prabhakaran's immediate challenge was to distinguish the LTTE from its thirty-plus rivals.[58] His solution was to refashion the old TNT/new LTTE into an elite, ruthlessly efficient, and highly professional fighting force. According to Rohan Gunaratna, an expert on the LTTE, "Prabhakaran insisted on keeping [his] numbers small, maintaining a high standard of training, [and] enforcing discipline at all levels."[59] The end result was a cadre that was unswervingly dedicated to winning a Tamil homeland, Tamil Eelam. The groundwork was thus laid early in LTTE's history for the culture of individual self-sacrifice that eventually manifested itself in the employment of suicide tactics. At the time, this culture proved especially successful not only as a means of attracting popular support but also as a means of intimidating the group's Tamil and Sinhalese opponents. As the LTTE's reputation—and its leader's appetite for power—grew, so did its strength. Actual and potential rivals were now systematically eliminated both within and outside the Tiger organization. Power was ruthlessly and relentlessly consolidated to ensure the movement's preeminence.[60] By the end of the decade, Prabhakaran had completed his ascent to power, and the LTTE had become the preeminent political and military force within the Tamil community.[61]

The next watershed in the development of the LTTE was the widespread ethnic riots that convulsed Sri Lanka in July 1983.[62] The riots were sparked by an LTTE land mine ambush that killed thirteen SLAF (Sri Lanka Armed Forces) soldiers in Jaffna. Throughout the country, the disorders escalated rapidly into the bloodiest attacks perpetrated by Sinhalese mobs against Tamils since Sri Lanka (then Ceylon) had achieved its independence from Britain in 1948. Hundreds of Tamils were killed and thousands injured. Destruction of homes, businesses, and other property was especially widespread. The riots proved to be a boon to the LTTE and other militant groups, for thousands of young Tamils who previously had shunned violence now flocked to the various guerrilla movements. LTTE propaganda hammered home the point that the Tamil community could feel truly secure only if they had a land of their own. In the wake of the devastation, many who had previously resisted the group's entreaties now found themselves drawn to Prabhakaran's uncompromising message. Attempts by moderates from both communities to restore ethnic amity were rebuffed. This was reinforced by unthinking government policies that in the riots' aftermath were viewed as unresponsive, nonconciliatory, and even hostile.[63]

The LTTE meanwhile worked actively to continue to sow discord in an effort to complete the isolation of the Tamil population from the central government. These acts included allegedly provoking the government into carrying out misdirected retaliatory attacks against Tamil targets in order to reinforce the growing ethnic divide. One way in which the LTTE sought to capitalize on these developments was to draw recruits from the families of those who had suffered at the hands of the security forces or the Sinhalese mobs, offering them a venue through which to strike back. Later on, the LTTE's efforts to recruit individuals into its suicide units would also focus specifically on the families of those who had been victimized by the authorities.[64] According to Father Harry Miller, an American Jesuit priest who has lived in Sri Lanka for nearly seven decades and in 2014 was awarded a prestigious international peace prize, "The abuse that ordinary people suffer[ed] at the hands of the army [was] the primary motivating factor to join the Tigers." One such candidate, quoted in the same newspaper article, was a twenty-two-year-old man named Mahendran. "I am thinking of joining [the

LTTE]," he explained. "The harassment that I and my parents have suffered at the hands of the army makes me want to take revenge."[65] The Tamil Tigers were only too happy to oblige.

In 1983, in an effort to capitalize on the momentum generated by these events, as well as to further distinguish the group from its nationalist rivals, Prabhakaran decreed that henceforth every LTTE fighter—male and female alike—would be required to wear a glass capsule containing potassium cyanide—a highly toxic chemical asphyxiant—around his or her neck. Prabhakaran's order was unambiguous: any LTTE cadre who was in danger of being arrested was obligated to bite down on the glass vial, which would lacerate the gums and send the deadly poison into the system, for a quick death. Prabhakaran thus commanded his fighters to kill themselves rather than risk capture and subsequent interrogation by the authorities.[66] The LTTE's rank and file responded with alacrity. The cyanide capsule, which was typically suspended on a leather strap around each fighter's neck, became a badge of honor[67] and a source of pride among LTTE cadres, each of whom received the capsule amid great ceremony at passing out exercises. Prabhakaran and other senior LTTE commanders also adopted the practice. Photographs of the Tigers' supreme leader often revealed the capsule worn prominently around his own neck.

The most significant turning point in the LTTE's history, however, was still to come. Sometime around the mid-1980s, Prabhakaran decided to steer the group down an even more violent path that would greatly increase its international notoriety. Hezbollah's 1983 suicide attack on the U.S. Marine compound in Lebanon reportedly made a deep impression on Prabhakaran and the Tigers' senior leadership.[68] A small and little-known terrorist group was able to offset its relative weakness and in a single devastating attack strike decisively at the world's leading superpower. The same tactic, Prabhakaran is believed to have concluded, could be employed by the LTTE to offset its own numerical and material disadvantages against the Sri Lankan state. Indeed, it has been suggested that Prabhakaran became convinced that if the LTTE did not significantly step up its campaign by resorting to suicide attacks, it would never achieve its goal of winning a Tamil homeland in his lifetime. "With perseverance and sacrifice," Prabhakaran is said to have argued, "Tamil Eelam can be achieved in 100 years. But if we conduct Black Tiger [suicide] operations, we can shorten the suffering of the people and achieve Tamil Eelam in a shorter period of time."[69]

Prabhakaran's real genius, however, was in creating a historical narrative for the LTTE and the Tamil people that was tailored to support suicide terrorism. Two themes, in particular, were actively incorporated into Tiger lore. The first, as illustrated by Prabhakaran's own words just quoted, was the belief that extreme sacrifices would have to be made to secure an independent future for the Tamil nation. The cornerstone of the LTTE's self-identity became the principle of self-sacrifice and, ultimately, martyrdom, for the greater good of the Tamil race. This was reflected in the Tamil word *thatkodai* (to give yourself), which was used in lieu of the word *thatkolai* (suicide) to describe the group's suicide operations. According to Suppayya Paramu Thamilselvan who, until his death in 2007 as a result of a Sri Lankan airstrike was the political head of the LTTE, these operations were regarded by the movement's suicide cadres as a "gift of the self," a "selfgift," an "oath to the nation," that [was] offered in the name of Tamil Eelam.[70]

The second theme that Prabhakaran incorporated into the movement's constructed mythology was that of "determination and invincibility."[71] This theme both supported and was, in turn, supported by his decision to turn to suicide operations in 1987. The first of the attacks was carried out on May 5 by "Captain Millar," who subsequently became one of the movement's most important martyrs. The target, in this case, was a former Tamil high school that had been taken over by elements of the Sri Lankan army.[72] It was a textbook vehicular assault, closely resembling Hezbollah's attack on the Marine barracks four years earlier. Seventy-five people were killed in the attack, the news of which radiated throughout Sri Lanka, generating widespread shock and horror. The incident not only represented a significant military and political setback for the Sri Lankan government, it also proved to be a significant psychological blow to the Sinhalese population, endowing the LTTE with an aura of unstoppable fanaticism. The group had worked to reinforce and capitalize on that fanatical image until its demise in 2009.

Since the organization was intent on cultivating an image of invincibility, it was natural that the LTTE would confer a special status to its "Black Tiger" suicide units. Those who had volunteered to join the Black Tigers were accordingly required to demonstrate an even higher level of skill, dedication, and motivation than traditional LTTE cadres. While everyone had to be willing to fight, in Prabhakaran's view only a very few had what it took to intentionally sacrifice themselves to destroy the enemy.[73] "Our strength is our willingness to make the supreme sacrifice," declared Gena, the thirty-year-old leader of the female "Black Tigresses" (also known as the Birds of Freedom) in a 1998 interview.[74] "This is the most supreme sacrifice I can make," said a seventeen-year-old Tamil recruit named Vasantha. "The only way we can achieve our eelam [homeland] is through arms. That is the only way anybody will listen to us. Even if we die."[75] Proof of this commitment could be found in the laminated identification cards carried by suicide cadres on missions in Colombo. The cards show a photograph of the suicide

bomber and his or her name. Written in both English and Sinhala, and emblazoned with the symbolic warning of a skull and crossbones, the card
states: "I am filled with a huge explosive. If my journey is blocked I will explode it. Let me go."[76] Although decades of fighting and combat losses had
forced the group to adopt a much more liberal—even coercive—recruitment
policy, the elite units within the LTTE (e.g., reconnaissance and intelligence
cadres as well as the group's various suicide squads) continued to be carefully selected and trained to a high mental and physical standard.[77]

From its inception, the development and strategic evolution of the LTTE
was inexorably guided by Prabhakaran's domineering leadership and omnipresent influence. Prabhakaran exercised direct control over virtually every
aspect of organizational life, imposing a strict, ascetic regimen on LTTE
cadres that was based on unquestioned loyalty to their leader and the goal
of Tamil Eelam.[78] This subjugation of individual will was evidenced by the
degree of control that the LTTE exerted over the personal affairs of its rank
and file. Sexual contact or relationships among unmarried cadres, for example, were strictly forbidden and harshly punished. LTTE cadres could
marry only after they had reached a specific age determined by Prabhakaran,
and then only with their commanders' approval.[79] Prabhakaran's pivotal role
and unchallenged influence over the organization were reinforced in a daily
ceremony in which cadres pledged allegiance to Prabhakaran the man,
rather than to the organization or to the Tamil people or their homeland.[80]
These and similar internal policies further contributed to the group's carefully cultivated "brand" as an elite fighting force.

Although Prabhakaran is not believed to have ever received any formal
military training, many of his followers deemed him a military genius. His
knowledge of strategy, tactics, weapons, logistics, and military administration was reportedly derived from his voracious reading of history and military affairs. Prabhakaran's idea to create a maritime guerrilla commando
unit, for example, was reported to have come from reading a history of the
famed Special Boat Squadron (SBS), an elite unit of the Royal Marines that
is Britain's counterpart to the U.S. Navy SEALs ("Sea, Air, Land" teams).[81]
It was his own idea to turn the unit into a suicide force, which he named the
Sea Tigers.[82] Prabhakaran was also described as a film buff, with a strong
preference for war movies and other action thrillers. Once again, he was always prepared to borrow a good idea when he saw one. Prabhakaran's idea
to design a suicide vest that would allow an attacker to approach his or her
target without being detected is said to have come from viewing a *Death
Wish*–like movie, released for the South Asian film market. In the movie, a
beautiful girl apparently presents a bouquet of flowers to the president of

the United States. As she offers the bouquet, she kills herself and the president with a bomb concealed beneath her clothing.[83] The 1991 assassination of former Indian prime minister Rajiv Gandhi by a female LTTE suicide terrorist was carried out in a similar manner, as were the attempted assassinations of Sri Lanka's female president, Chandrika Kumaratunga, in 1999 and Douglas Devananda, the minister of social services and welfare, in 2007.[84]

Whatever the source of Prabhakaran's strategic insights, it is clear that the LTTE waged a determined and, at times, quite successful military campaign. At one time, the group was able to field a fighting force of some eighteen thousand men and women. Indeed, at its peak in 2004, the LTTE[85] constituted one of the best trained and equipped nonstate military forces in the world—complete with armored and artillery units, its own blue-, green-, and brown-water navies, an embryonic air capability, comprising light aircraft, a commando and special reconnaissance force, portable surface-to-air missiles, and last but not least, the aforementioned suicide attack units. Women, as previously noted, played a uniquely dominant role in the group's suicide operations.[86] Hence, by 2005 the LTTE had fought the Sri Lankan government to a standstill in a conflict that had cost more than sixty thousand lives since it began in 1983. When faced by a previous battlefield deadlock, Colombo had in 2001 decided to enter negotiations with the LTTE. In the view of many knowledgeable observers, however, it was the threat posed by LTTE's suicide campaign that had then driven the regime to the bargaining table. Such attacks, one former Sri Lankan diplomat argued, have had their intended effect. "We have been cowed. We have been intimidated by suicide terrorism. It is that simple. The fear caused by this tactic has made us cave in to them."[87]

Over the years, LTTE suicide attacks were carried out to support two distinctly different campaigns: a rural campaign and an urban campaign. In the case of the group's rural operations, suicide tactics were employed primarily against the Sri Lanka Armed Forces, often as part of a larger operational plan involving guerrilla and semiconventional forces. In the case of the group's urban campaign, numerous and often highly dramatic suicide attacks were carried out against critical national infrastructure and what the Tigers referred to expansively as VIPs, such as senior elected government leaders, prominent political figures, other high-level government officials, senior military and police commanders, and even lower-ranking military and police intelligence officers whose competence had attracted the attention of the Tigers.[88] Since many of these latter actions occurred in and around Colombo and at times caused significant numbers of collateral casualties, LTTE attacks against nonmilitary targets were never claimed.

The Tigers always insisted that "it is not the policy of the LTTE to attack civilian targets."[89] "By adopting such a position," Gunaratna explains, the group "seeks to project to the international community that it is a liberation movement that targets only military personnel, and not a terrorist group."[90] The LTTE, for example, has never taken credit for the suicide truck bombing of the Central Bank of Sri Lanka in January 1996 that killed ninety people and wounded fourteen hundred others or for the November 1994 assassination of presidential candidate Gamini Dissanayake, which claimed the lives of fifty-four people and injured seventy-two. In 1991, as previously noted, the group also used a suicide bomber to assassinate former Indian prime minister Rajiv Gandhi. Two years later, a deep penetration mole wearing a suicide bodysuit similar to that worn by the female cadre who killed Gandhi succeeded in killing Sri Lankan president Ranasinghe Premadasa. Neither assassination was ever claimed. Government efforts to ascribe such attacks to the LTTE resulted in denials and the counterclaim that the regime was trying to whip up anti-Tamil sentiment.

In summary, suicide terrorism became a central tactic in LTTE planning. The purpose of adopting this tactic was twofold: first, to distinguish the group from its many better-established political challengers within the Tamil resistance and attract a solid base of popular support, and second, to achieve a perceptual force multiplier that would allow the LTTE to level the playing field with the Sri Lankan government. To achieve these objectives, the LTTE worked very deliberately to cultivate an image of elitism, professionalism, invincibility, and fanatical single-mindedness. The use of suicide tactics to demonstrate these qualities was a central element of this policy. Prabhakaran and his senior commanders, as we have seen, were inspired to experiment with this tactic in the wake of Hezbollah's stunning attack against the U.S. Marine barracks in Lebanon in 1983. The use of suicide operations was subsequently institutionalized to the point that it became a hallmark of the Tamil Tigers, symbolizing the determination of the organization, its membership, and its supreme leader. Prabhakaran's faith in the transformative power of this tactic, however, proved grievously misplaced. By 2009, the three-year old Sri Lankan military campaign to eliminate the LTTE, named "Eelam IV," was closing in on the movement's leader and his remaining senior commanders. On May 17, the LTTE conceded that their long and bloody struggle had "reached its bitter end." The following day, Prabhakaran and 250 of his fighters were killed in the final assault by the SLAF to seize the last remaining corner of LTTE-held territory. "We have successfully ended the war," the country's defense secretary triumphantly declared as an uneasy peace, the first in more than a quarter of a century, settled over that embattled island.[91]

The Palestinian Use of Suicide Terrorism

From the time of its founding in 1987, Hamas faced the same problem that had confronted the LTTE: devising a means of carving out a distinctive niche in an already crowded field of competing militant groups. Hamas's challenge, however, was considerably more formidable. As a latecomer to an already well-established Palestinian liberation movement with deep popular roots, Hamas not only had to distinguish itself from competing terrorist organizations, some of which had been fighting for decades,[92] but it also had to differentiate itself from a long-standing and powerful representative body—the PLO—which had become the preeminent force in Palestinian politics. That in 2005 Hamas reportedly could claim the support of upward of 70 percent of the Palestinians on the West Bank and Gaza,[93] and by 2006 was the dominant, ruling political party in Gaza, is testament to the group's success in overcoming its initial disadvantages. As in the case of the LTTE, Hamas's eventual adoption of suicide terrorism as a signature mode of attack was pivotal to this process.

Although Hamas can trace its ideological lineage to the Muslim Brotherhood,[94] the group itself arguably owes its existence to a fatal traffic accident that took place in the Gaza Strip on December 8, 1987. That day, an otherwise unremarkable collision involving an Israeli truck and some other vehicles resulted in the deaths of several Palestinian workers. Without warning, the mishap triggered an explosion of Palestinian rioting. The disorders were initially dismissed by Palestinians and Israelis alike as an ephemeral outburst of frustration. Within days, however, it was clear that events had taken on a dynamic of their own and that the riots were spreading throughout the occupied areas. Palestinians began to describe this outpouring of popular anger as an intifada. The uprising was not even a week old when, on December 14, the Muslim Brotherhood distributed a leaflet calling for sustained resistance.[95] This leaflet is credited as marking the birth of Hamas.

From the beginning, Hamas's young, predominantly university-educated leadership[96] consciously sought to distance themselves and their new organization from the mainstream, secular PLO and its affiliated terrorist and nationalist groups. Most had attended Palestinian universities where the Muslim Brotherhood had been particularly active and were greatly influenced by the movement's doctrine combining religion with politics.[97] Accordingly, Hamas's fundamental raison d'être became the liberation of Palestine and the establishment of an Islamic state in all Palestine (that is, Israel as well as the West Bank and Gaza Strip). Such a liberation could be achieved, they argued, only by means of a popular jihad. Jihad in this context referred not only to a collective struggle, as it is commonly understood, but also to the belief that the use of organized violence was the "sole legitimate way to retrieve Palestine in its entirety." Once this territorial imperative was achieved, Islamic social and moral norms would then be rigorously enforced in the new state.[98] Hamas's religious ideology and "maximalist" political aims were thus resolutely opposed to the "minimalist" aims pursued by the PLO.

To more clearly define its agenda and delineate itself from its mainstream Palestinian competitors, Hamas also adopted the motto of "not [ceding] one inch" of land, thus further emphasizing its uncompromising opposition to dialogue, much less a negotiated settlement, with Israel.[99] One leaflet, distributed during the intifada's first year, neatly encapsulated the group's doctrinal platform. Titled *Islamic Palestine from the [Mediterranean] Sea to the [Jordan] River*, it declared: "Muslims have had a full—not a partial—right to Palestine for generations, in the past, present and future. . . . No Palestinian generation has the right to concede the land, steeped in martyr's blood. . . . You must continue the uprising and stand up against the usurpers wherever they may be, until the complete liberation of every grain of the soil of . . . Palestine, all Palestine, with God's help."[100] In both word and deed, Hamas has always disdained in equal measure the PLO and the traditional, local Palestinian ruling elite in Gaza and the West Bank, along with its declared enemy, Israel. The group, moreover, was neither impressed nor intimidated by the strength of the much-vaunted IDF (Israel Defense Forces).[101]

Nonetheless, the intifada's early years were characterized more by Palestinian youths' throwing stones and general rioting and popular unrest than by any sustained campaign of outright terrorism.[102] The use of *bayanat*, the Arabic word for leaflets, was one of the principal ways in which Hamas publicized and sought to differentiate itself and its fundamentalist religious orientation from the secular groups involved in the intifada.[103] In addition to declaring its own strike days—apart from those proclaimed by the United National Command of the Intifada, the umbrella organization directing the uprising—Hamas also endeavored to set itself up as a social welfare organization. Accordingly, the movement's leaflets during this period dealt as much with the range of issues affecting Palestinian daily life—such as work, health, transport, education, and religious instruction—as they did with the need for resistance and rebellion.[104]

By 1989, however, the intifada's momentum was ebbing.[105] Hamas, moreover, was losing ground to its rivals, which now included not only long-standing secular nationalist Palestinian groups but a new religious group—the Palestine Islamic Jihad (PIJ). Confronted by this situation, according to Israeli scholars Shaul Mishal and Avraham Sela, "Hamas's turn to violence was a matter of necessity." Its opening actions, however, were unimpressive. Lacking a bona fide military wing with the attendant organizational ability to recruit and train fighters, obtain arms, and plan and control serious operations, Hamas activists were able to carry out just ten attacks during its first year of dedicated operations. While the movement managed to increase this number to thirty-two attacks the following year, the campaign was still having little effect on its targeted constituents, who continued to favor the group's better-established, secular rivals.[106] The only significant attention Hamas seems to have attracted during this opening period was from Israeli security forces who came down hard on the organization in a series of operations between late 1990 and early 1991 that effectively stripped it of its emerging military potential.[107]

This all changed, however, with the establishment of a proper military wing in 1991, the Battalions of Izz al-Din al-Qassam, named after a revered cleric turned guerrilla leader whose rebellion against British rule of Palestine ended when he was shot to death by police in 1935.[108] The new unit began modestly enough, with the systematic execution of Palestinian collaborators in the Gaza Strip. By the following year, it had graduated to the murder of Israeli settlers and the use of car bombs, and was well on its way to becoming a force in Palestinian politics. Hamas's increasingly violent successes spawned both imitation and competition from other Palestinian militants, especially those who shared the group's religious orientation. The PIJ in particular was driven to strike out in new directions, forging ties with Hezbollah and participating in attacks on IDF forces in south Lebanon.[109] The climax to this phase of the intifada came between October and December 1992, when a series of terrorist attacks claimed the lives of five IDF soldiers and a member of the Israeli Border Police. The incident proved to be the last straw for Israeli prime minister Itzhak Rabin, who ordered the deportation to Lebanon of 415 Islamic Palestinian activists—the vast majority of whom belonged to Hamas.[110] The deportation proved to be a serious miscalculation. Deposited in the middle of winter in rough country in south Lebanon, the deportees quickly became a cause célèbre, attracting international media attention and sympathy.[111] Hamas bore the fruits of its leaders' suffering, attaining a level of support among both Palestinians and foreigners that it might not otherwise have achieved. Included among the exiles were doctors, clerics, teachers, engineers, judges, and professors, thus supporting Hamas's claims that it was a true community and social welfare organization and not a terrorist group.[112]

More significantly, during the nearly ten months they were in Lebanon, the Hamas exiles were able to establish the organization's first ties with

Hezbollah. The PIJ, whose members were also among the exiles, benefited doubly, forging tighter relations with Iran while significantly enhancing its military capabilities under Hezbollah's tutelage.[113] The impact of this exile on Hamas, however, was ultimately more profound. Mishal and Sela are unequivocal in stating that the "deportation of 415 Islamic activists by Israel to Lebanon in December 1992 was a milestone in Hamas's decision to use car bombs and suicide attacks as a major modus operandi against Israel." A direct cause and effect, they argue, is clearly evident in the exiles' return to Gaza and the West Bank the following year and Hamas's decision to adopt suicide tactics. "Thus, it was no coincidence," they write, "that Hamas's first suicide operation was carried out shortly after the deportees had returned to the occupied territories."[114]

The deportations also had a third major unintended consequence: with almost the entire established Hamas political leadership in exile, the movement did not collapse, as Israel hoped it would. Instead, the leadership vacuum was filled by the exiles' more violent-minded, younger followers. This new generation was concerned less with the ideological and theological Islamization of Palestinian society, which had been the focus of much of the organization's initial efforts, than with the active promotion of the violent dimension of Hamas's struggle. Emulating the militarism of historical Palestinian guerrilla groups like al-Fatah, they pushed an even harder line of no compromise/no surrender with Israel and focused their efforts on increased attacks in the hope of pressuring Israel to withdraw from the Occupied Territories.[115] The net result was that the influence of the al-Qassam wing grew within Hamas while the group's overall prestige among Palestinians also increased.[116]

Hamas was now well positioned to escalate its military campaign against Israel and consolidate the political gains it was beginning to achieve over the PLO and other rivals. These imperatives acquired new urgency in the fall of 1993 with the conclusion of the Oslo Accords and the commencement of formal negotiations between the PLO and Israel. The entire process was anathema to Hamas. Not only did negotiations entail de facto recognition of Israel and the cessation of the Palestinian military struggle, but also the parameters of the Israeli-Palestinian Declaration of Principles (DOP) guiding the discussions called for the eventual implementation of UN Security Council Resolutions 242 and 338, leading to formal Palestinian recognition of Israel's right to exist.[117]

Confronted by this existential challenge to its raison d'être, freedom of operations, and very existence, Hamas decided to challenge simultaneously the entire DOP framework, PLO chairman Yasir Arafat's leadership, and the PLO's authority within the Occupied Territories.[118] As Hamas's greatest concern was the deleterious effect that any peace process would have on the continuation of a popular jihad against Israel,[119] the movement arguably had no option but to ratchet up its armed operations. The Israeli decision to allow the Hamas and PIJ deportees to return to the West Bank and the Gaza Strip in late 1993 fortuitously strengthened Hamas just as it was poised to strike.[120]

Within a month of the signing of the Oslo Accords, Hamas initiated a new round of bombings. Three attacks alone killed twenty-six Israelis and wounded scores of others. The message Hamas was communicating to Israel and the PLO alike was clear: there would be no peace and security[121] "unless and until Hamas [was] recognized and its demands [were] met."[122] While these incidents were impressive in their own right, they did little to change the basic constellation of forces between either Hamas and the PLO or between Hamas and Israel. Indeed, in the context of this decades-old conflict, the latest wave of bombings was neither especially significant nor extraordinary. Both sides in the struggle had become conditioned to worse violence. Hamas was still nothing more than a nuisance to Israel—an increasingly violent nuisance, to be sure, but a comparatively minor nuisance nevertheless. At this critical juncture, Hamas's challenge—much as it was only a few years earlier for Prabhakaran and the LTTE—was to find an operational profile that was sufficiently unique and dramatic so as to alter the strategic balance between Palestine and Israel once and for all. The solution that Hamas, like the LTTE, embraced was suicide bombing.[123] Indeed, violence, according to Singh, was already "an established mechanism of ensuring survival for Hamas" much as it had been for the LTTE.[124] Accordingly, their mutual adoption of suicide attacks was the next logical step in Hamas's and the LTTE's uniquely violent trajectories.

Hamas carried out its first suicide attack on April 6, 1994. The incident, which killed eight people and wounded thirty-four others, occurred in the northern Israeli city of Afula. It was timed to coincide with the end of the Islamic period of mourning that had begun on February 25, when, as previously mentioned, Dr. Baruch Goldstein, an ultranationalist orthodox Jew, had killed twenty-nine Palestinian worshipers at the Ibrahim Mosque in Hebron. The attack was also meant to derail the talks between Israel and the PLO on implementing the Oslo Accords.[125] Thereafter, another series of suicide bombings followed, including attacks in Hadera on April 13 that killed five people; at the Dizengoff Shopping Center in Tel Aviv in October, which claimed the lives of twenty-two others; and at Nezarim Junction less than a month later where three people perished.[126] According to the late professor Ehud Sprinzak, an Israeli scholar and one of the world's foremost authorities on terrorism, these incidents were decisive in "erod[ing] Israel's collective confidence in the peace process," which, in turn, "played right into the hands of extremist Hamas clerics who opposed negotiations with Israel."[127]

Hamas's inauguration of suicide tactics also sharpened its rivalry with the numerically inferior and less consequential PIJ. Fearing its own complete eclipse, the PIJ now got into the act, too, killing twenty Israeli soldiers in a suicide bombing near Netanya on January 22, 1995. In all these incidents—for Hamas and the PIJ alike—Hezbollah's influence, example, and training are evident.[128] Khaled Meshal, Hamas's political leader, was quite candid about this during an interview he gave in July 2000. "We always have the Lebanese experiment before our eyes," he explained. "It was a great model of which we are proud."[129] Indeed, according to Mishal and Sela, these early suicide operations were textbook Hezbollah attacks—both groups, they point out, adopted the "same procedure [for] finding a candidate for a suicide operation, training and preparing him psychologically, writing a farewell letter, and making a videotape before his mission."[130] At least seven years before, Dr. Fathi Shiqaqi, the PIJ's founder and leader, had developed a plan for what he termed "exceptional" martyrdom operations involving human bombs that was based on Hezbollah's theological justification for these acts.[131] Within the context of suicide terrorism as deception, Hamas also appears to have borrowed a leaf from the LTTE's book on the subject, similarly insisting publicly that despite its attacks on shopping malls and buses, the group "opposed any action that hurt civilians."

The suicide attacks and the carnage that they wrought were designed to elicit an aggressive response from Israel. By doing so, Hamas sought to lock Israel into an upward spiral of violence that would enable the group to portray its violence as defensive and also more effective than that of its rival Palestinian counterparts.[132] Israel's decision to target Palestinian leaders who were believed to be directly engaged in planning suicide operations fed this dynamic almost exactly as Hamas had planned. In October 1995, Israeli agents are thought to have assassinated Fathi Shiqaqi in Malta. Three months later they achieved an even more important success when they managed to kill Hamas's master bomb maker, Yahya Ayyash. Ayyash, whose expertise had earned him the sobriquet "the Engineer"—bestowed by no less a personage than Israeli prime minister Rabin—is credited with having first proposed that Hamas engage in suicide bombing.[133] He also reputedly built the bombs that were used in the 1994 Afula and Hadera attacks. Altogether, he was believed to have been responsible for the deaths of 130 Israelis and injuries to nearly 500 others.[134] Rather than ending the suicide attacks, however, Ayyash's assassination triggered the most dramatic escalation in this campaign to date. After six months of relative quiet, Hamas suicide bombers struck five times in two weeks, killing a total of 59 Israelis. Their targets included public buses, populated bus stops, and Tel Aviv's Dizengoff Shopping Center—for the second time in seventeen months.

The death toll from these attacks alone was nearly half the total amassed by suicide bombers over the preceding two years.[135] This wave of terrorism is also widely credited with affecting the outcome of Israel's national elections in May 1996. The right-wing Likud coalition's Benjamin Netanyahu was elected prime minister over the Labor Party candidate and sitting premier, Shimon Peres. In the wake of these attacks, Netanyahu's hard-line stance on negotiations and campaign promises of increased security proved to be more attractive to Israeli voters than Peres's pledge to continue the peace process begun by his assassinated predecessor, Itzhak Rabin. Even at the time, it was clear that this was precisely Hamas's intent: to use suicide attacks to polarize the Israeli polity and thereby scuttle the peace process. Hamas believed that Netanyahu's election would not only undermine the Oslo Accords but would have the secondary advantage of checking the political ascendancy of the PLO.[136] For the Israeli military, Hamas's violent retribution, despite the loss of one of its key operational planners, provided disquieting evidence of the group's strategic depth and organizational resiliency. The IDF now judged Hamas to be "militarily the strongest Palestinian organization."[137] The head of Israeli military intelligence, Brigadier General Ya'acov Amidor, publicly conceded that Hamas had now become a serious challenge to Israeli security. "You can trim its branches," he suggested, but it was going to be difficult to "pull out its roots."[138]

Thereafter, however, the pace of Palestinian terrorist operations began to wane. Two suicide attacks were conducted in August and September 1996, and three attacks were carried out between March and September 1997. Hamas's relative quiescence during this period, until the final collapse of the Oslo Accords that followed the abortive Camp David meetings in the summer of 2000, reflected a variety of internal Palestinian political developments. The first appears to have been the establishment of a tenuous modus vivendi between Hamas and the governing Palestinian Authority (PA). Hamas agreed to limit its attacks on Israeli targets in return for the Palestinian Authority's refusal to cave in to Israeli pressure to proscribe Hamas's political activities. The second reason was a product of the short-lived, but for the moment, ongoing, optimism in both Palestine and Israel about the prospects for a stable peace that persisted despite Netanyahu's premiership. The late 1990s were an albeit evanescent time of close cooperation between PA security forces and their Israeli counterparts—often brokered and overseen by U.S. government representatives.[139] Not only were Hamas and PIJ terrorists apprehended and imprisoned by the PA, but even leading Hamas commanders such as Muhammad Daif were swept up in the dragnet and jailed.

Finally, there was Hamas's policy of "controlled violence."[140] The rational basis of this policy was clearly articulated in late 1995 by one of the group's senior leaders based in Gaza, Mahmud al-Zahar. In an interview given to the East Jerusalem daily *al-Quds*, al-Zahar made a point of explaining how Hamas's use of violence was a carefully calculated means to an end. It was not, as its critics suggested, an end in itself. In every case, he argued, the group's decision to use force was subordinated to its larger political objectives. If the prevailing political climate made it necessary for Hamas to put its military option on the shelf, it was prepared to do so, at least for a period of time. "We must calculate the benefit and cost of continued armed operations," al-Zahar said. "If we can fulfill our goals without violence, we will do so. Violence is a means, not a goal. Hamas's decision to adopt self-restraint does not contradict our aims, including the establishment of an Islamic state instead of Israel. . . . We will never recognize Israel, but it is possible that a truce could prevail between us for days, months, or years."[141]

That self-restraint ended on October 30, 2000, when a Hamas suicide bomber killed 15 people in Jerusalem. Less than a month before, the visit of prime ministerial candidate Ariel Sharon to Jerusalem's al-Haram al-Sharif or Temple Mount, triggered what has come to be known as the al-Aqsa, or Second Intifada, and the escalation of violence that continued for another five years. The appreciably greater number of suicide attacks during this phase of the long-standing Israeli-Palestinian conflict attests to the growing salience and importance of this tactic. According to the database maintained by Haifa University's National Security Studies Center, there were a total of 23 suicide attacks between December 31, 1993, and September 30, 2000 (e.g., the start of the al-Aqsa Intifada)—an average of 0.24 per month. During the first 15 months of the al-Aqsa Intifada, that is, from October 1, 2000, to December 31, 2001, there were 39 attacks—an average of 2.6 per month. And during the entirety of 2002, when, as of January, the Second Intifada entered a far more violent and dangerous phase as the al-Aqsa Martyrs Brigade began its own campaign of suicide bombings, a total of 59 incidents were recorded—an average of 4.9 per month. Viewed from another perspective, there were nearly as many suicide attacks carried out against Israeli targets during 2002 as during the previous eight years combined (62).[142]

Four explanations account for this dramatic upsurge of Palestinian suicide attacks:

- First, the terrorist organization's shared conviction that the sustained and unrelenting use of suicide attacks would achieve results that could not be matched by using other tactics;

- Second, the inverted sense of normality that the Palestinian terrorist organizations had created within the Palestinian community given the resulting approval that was bestowed on their employment of suicide tactics;
- Third, the use of religion and theological justification—communicated and encouraged by Muslim clerical authorities—both to sustain popular support of these tactics and to ensure a continued flow of new recruits eager to undertake suicide operations into the ranks of the terrorist organizations; and,
- Fourth, the entrenched rivalries between the Palestinian terrorist organizations themselves that produced a deadly competition to determine which group was able to mobilize and deploy the largest number of suicide terrorists in order to win the support of the Palestinian population and undermine its rivals.[143]

Suicide Terrorism as an Instrument of War

It is clear that the leadership of Hamas and the PIJ entered the al-Aqsa Intifada during the fall of 2000 with the belief that a sustained suicide bombing campaign would have the desired political effect on both the Israeli government and their own political base that would be significantly greater than what they could expect to achieve through more conventional terrorist attacks. Here again, as with the LTTE, the Hezbollah model loomed large. Only four months earlier, the IDF had completed its withdrawal from south Lebanon. The primary reason for this policy reversal, in the opinion of both Hezbollah[144] and Palestinian[145] observers, was Israel's inability to deal effectively with the threat posed by Hezbollah's sustained use of suicide tactics. As the leader of the PIJ, Ramadan Shalah, explained in late 2001:

> The shameful defeat that Israel suffered in southern Lebanon and which caused its army to flee in terror was not made on the negotiations table but on the battlefield and through jihad and martyrdom, which achieved a great victory for the Islamic resistance and Lebanese People. . . . We would not exaggerate if we said that the chances of achieving victory in Palestine are greater than in Lebanon. . . . If the enemy could not bear the losses of the war on the border strip with Lebanon, will it be able to withstand a long war of attrition in the heart of its security dimension and major cities?[146]

Moreover, to Hamas's thinking, suicide attacks were the next step in a logical progression of escalating violence. "Like the intifada in 1987," Hamas's

Khaled Meshal told the BBC, "the current intifada has taught us that we should move forward normally from popular confrontation to the rifle to suicide operations. This is the normal development."[147]

The decision to rely heavily on suicide bombings during the Second Intifada thus was neither irrational nor desperate,[148] but rational and calculated. As the terrorist organizations themselves acknowledge, suicide bombings are both inexpensive and effective. "It is easy and costs us only our lives," Shalah told one interviewer. "Human bombs," he further averred, "cannot be defeated, not even by nuclear bombs."[149] The logic behind these operations was explained by a leading Gaza Muslim activist interviewed on Israeli television in 1994. His exposition of this phenomenon accurately captured the strategic logic of suicide terrorism as an especially effective weapon of the weak in confronting a stronger and exponentially more powerful opponent. "We lack the arms possessed by the enemy," he said.

> We have no planes or missiles, not even artillery with which to fight evil. The most effective instrument for inflicting harm with a minimum of losses is this type of operation. This is a legitimate technique based on martyrdom. Through such action, the "martyr" acquires the right to enter heaven and liberate himself from all the pain and suffering of this world.[150]

Using almost identical terminology, a member of Hamas's al-Qassam brigades explained to Nasra Hassan, an international relief worker posted to Gaza who had closely followed the suicide terrorism phenomenon since it had emerged in the mid-1990s: "We do not have tanks or rockets, but we have something superior—our exploding Islamic human bombs. In place of a nuclear arsenal, we are proud of our arsenal of believers."[151]

As the preceding clearly evidence, these three Palestinian terrorist movements regarded suicide attacks as a legitimate means to offset a numerically superior, better-armed, and better-equipped opponent. Indeed, the material and technological inferiority of the Palestinian resistance was often to justify this tactic. The Palestinians, as one Israeli scholar has observed, "are fighting with the only tools they possess."[152] Shalah offered an identical justification for PIJ suicide operations: "Our enemy possesses the most sophisticated weapons in the world and its army is trained to a very high standard. We have nothing with which to repel killing and thuggery against us except the weapon of martyrdom."[153] Another PIJ official maintained that suicide terrorism was necessary to achieve a "balance of terror"[154]—a logic expressed by a fellow militant who declared, "If our wives and children are not safe from Israeli tanks and rockets, theirs will not be safe from our human bombs."[155]

Part and parcel of these justifications are two ancillary, but critical, beliefs. The first is related to the effectiveness argument cited above. According to this line of reasoning, suicide terrorism is the only way to convince Israeli decision makers that the Palestinian people will never yield to coercion. The second, derivative belief is that in adopting suicide tactics, the Palestinian resistance had finally found Israel's Achilles' heel. Drawing again on the Hezbollah model, Meshal, for instance, claims, "The Zionist enemy . . . only understands the language of Jihad, resistance and martyrdom; that was the language that led to its blatant defeat in South Lebanon and it will be the language that will defeat it on the land of Palestine."[156] Similarly, more than a decade earlier, Shiqaqi had argued that suicide tactics would prove to be the most efficacious means of wearing down Israel's will. This would be achieved, he explained, "through the explosion, which forces the mujahid not to waver, not to escape; to execute a successful operation for religion and jihad; and to destroy the morale of the enemy and plant terror in the people."[157]

Suicide terrorism is thus embraced as a psychological weapon that is capable of paralyzing their hated opponent. "The Israelis . . . will fall to their knees," said Sheikh Ahmad Yassin, the spiritual leader of Hamas[158] until his death in an Israeli air strike in 2004. "You can sense the fear in Israel already; they are worried about where and when the next attacks will come. Ultimately, Hamas will win."[159] The reason, according to another Hamas leader, Ismail Haniya, who was famously quoted in both a *Washington Post* article and a Thomas Friedman *New York Times* column in March 2002, is that with suicide attacks, the Palestinian people—after years of struggle— have finally discovered Israel's greatest vulnerability. In words reminiscent of bin Laden, Haniya said that Jews "love life more than any other people, and they prefer not to die."[160] Lest such claims be dismissed as terrorist hyperbole or braggadocio, no higher authority than the preeminent Muslim religious figure in Palestine, the then-Mufti of Jerusalem, Ikrama Sa'id Sabri, explicitly endorsed this view. "Look at the society of the Israelis," he told journalist Jeffrey Goldberg in a 2001 interview. "It is a selfish society that loves life. These are not people who are eager to die for their country and their God. The Jews will leave this land rather than die, but the Muslim is happy to die."[161]

This is what is known in the Middle East as the "spiderweb" theory. It is the conclusion drawn by Hezbollah about Israel's withdrawal from south Lebanon and has since been embraced by the Palestinians and others in the region as well. The phrase itself is derived from a verse of the Qur'an about the inherent weakness of nonbelievers. "The parable of those who take guardians besides Allah," verse 29.41 states, "is as the parable of the spider that makes for itself a house; and surely the frailest of the houses is the spider's house did they but know." It was applied in the context of Israel's frailty by Hezbollah's spiritual leader, Sheikh Hassan Nasrallah, who described the Jewish state as a formidable military power, but one that is rooted in a civil society that has become materialistic and lazy, with self-satisfied, comfortable, and pampered citizens who have gone soft. This view was echoed by the then-IDF chief of staff, Lieutenant General Moshe "Boogie" Ya'alon, who explained in an interview published in *Ha'aretz* in August 2002 that the perception on the part of Israel's enemies is that

> the Israeli army is strong, Israel has technological superiority and is said to have strategic capabilities, but its citizens are unwilling any longer to sacrifice lives in order to defend their national interests and national goals. Therefore, Israel is a spider-web society: it looks strong from the outside, but touch it and it will fall apart.[162]

The IDF high command, for its part, does not dispute the popularity of this argument among Israel's enemies or the pernicious influence of the "spider-web" theory on Palestinian thinking. "If you ask why this crisis [the al-Aqsa Intifada] erupted four months after IDF withdrew from Lebanon," a senior IDF strategist observed, "the answer is yes. There was clear encouragement. . . . Lebanon is not the West Bank, but the Palestinians were influenced."[163]

Inverted Sense of Normality and Societal Imprimatur

The Palestinian terrorist organizations have also worked hard to endow suicide operations with a positive social imprimatur and to ensure the support for this tactic by the Palestinian people. They have deliberately created an inverted sense of normality throughout much of Palestinian society whereby suicide—the senseless taking of one's life, an act that is usually negatively regarded as aberrant, if not abnormal—becomes something routinely accepted and applauded, and indeed endowed with demonstrably positive connotations.[164] The veneration routinely accorded martyrs reinforces this view. The images of suicide terrorists emblazoned on murals and wall posters, calendars and key chains, and postcards and pennants are but one manifestation of these efforts.[165] Similarly, the suddenly elevated and now highly respected status accorded their families—is another.[166] The proud parents of Palestinian martyrs, for instance, publish announcements of their progeny's accomplishments in local newspapers not on the obituaries page but in the section announcing weddings.[167] Finally, the terrorist organizations—and their supporters through financial contributions—provide material as well as spiritual encouragement to both the suicide terrorists and their families. According to one authoritative account, until at least 2001, Hamas paid the families of suicide terrorists a death benefit of $3,000 to $5,000[168]—more than double the financial compensation paid to families of terrorists killed in other, nonsuicidal attacks.[169] Later, during the al-Aqsa Intifada, this amount increased to $10,000 and then, courtesy of then–Iraqi dictator Saddam Hussein's largesse, to $25,000.[170] There were additional material benefits as well, including nicer living accommodations and gifts of consumer goods—"appliances, rugs and stuffed furniture . . . gaudy wall clocks, even . . . [a] bracelet and rings"[171]—bestowed on the families of martyrs.

Videotapes of martyrs before their operations are routinely circulated by the terrorist organizations as a means to call attention to the organization and its determined fighters, to cultivate an image of invincibility and the inevitability of victory, and to attract further recruits.[172] The wedding announcements cited earlier are further evidence of the recalibration of Palestinian societal values engineered by the terrorist organizations.[173] The reaction in Palestinian neighborhoods in Gaza when news of a successful suicide strike is broadcast illustrates this. Typically, candy is distributed in the streets and women respond with traditional shrieks of joy. "Martyrdom has become an ambition for our children," Sadl Abu Hein, a psychology lecturer from Gaza, has sadly observed.[174] It is not surprising, therefore, to find that opinion polls taken in 2002 reported that more than 70 percent of Palestinians support suicide attacks against Israel.[175]

Use of Religion and Theological Justification

Religion and theological justification communicated and encouraged by Muslim clerical authorities has also played an important role in positively framing popular attitudes toward suicide operations and encouraging voluntarily acts of self-sacrifice on behalf of their community. The sermon given by Sheikh Ibrahim Madhi on April 12, 2001, at the Gaza City mosque, which was broadcast live on Palestinian television demonstrates the power of clerical sanction in support of these attacks. "Anyone who does not attain martyrdom in these days should wake in the middle of the night," the sheikh declared, "and say: 'My God, why have you deprived me of martyrdom for your sake? For the martyr lives next to Allah.'" He then called on Allah to "accept our martyrs in the highest heavens . . . show the Jews a black day . . . annihilate the Jews and their supporters . . . [and] raise the flag of Jihad across the land."[176]

Such messages are reinforced by Palestinian television channels, which have regularly aired promotional spots extolling the virtues of martyrdom operations and actively encouraging Palestinian youth to volunteer. One such segment broadcast in 2003 depicted the image of a young Palestinian couple out for a walk when suddenly IDF troops open fire, shooting the woman in the back and killing her. While visiting her grave, her boyfriend is also shot dead by the IDF. He is then shown ascending to heaven, where he is welcomed by his girlfriend, who is seen dancing with dozens of other female martyrs, portraying the seventy-two virgins—the promised "Maidens of Paradise"—who reputedly await the male martyr in heaven.[177] The clip is thus cleverly designed to appeal to would-be male and female martyrs alike.[178] In fact, just two days before the August 18, 2003, suicide bombing of a bus in Jerusalem by a Hamas terrorist that killed eighteen people, a music video version of this same spot aired on the Palestinian Authority's television station. In commentary provided on the same station the day before the blast, an Islamic scholar explained: "When the Shahid [martyr] meets his Maker, all his sins are forgiven from the first gush of blood. He is exempted from the 'torments of the grave' (Judgment); he sees his place in paradise, he is shielded from the great shock, and marries Dark Eyed Virgins. He is a heavenly advocate for 70 members of his family, on his head is placed a crown of honor, one stone of which, is worth more than all there is in this world."[179]

Theological arguments are regularly invoked both by the organizations responsible for the attacks and by the community that approvingly supports them.[180] The Qur'an, however, expressly forbids suicide. Indeed, it is considered one of the greatest wrongs that a Muslim can commit, according to Abu Ruqaiyah, an Islamic philosopher and author of a detailed treatise addressing the religious legitimacy of suicide terrorism.[181] Accordingly, a semantical distinction has been devised, similar to that used by the Tamil Tigers, which differentiates suicide—the taking of one's own life—from martyrdom, in which the perpetrator's death is a requirement for the attack's success and is thus justified and morally acceptable. Suicide terrorism therefore becomes the ultimate expression of selflessness and altruism. "The ideal of sacrificing one's life for the sake of the community or God," Dr. Eyad Sarraj, a Gaza-based Palestinian psychiatrist, writes,

is deeply rooted and glorified in this part of the World. . . . A person who would die for his country or tribe is glorified, even sanctified and blessed.

Islam is a powerful message and the Quran is the most beautifully written Arab script, with overwhelming appeal. In the Quran, God says: "and don't think that those who are killed in the battle for God, are dead. Sure they are alive and looked after by God." Our life on earth life [sic] is the lower one, but the life after is the higher and the true. . . .

In the next life you will be rewarded for your goodness or will be punished for your badness. You will either go to heaven or you to hell [sic]. Heaven is profusely described through Quran as the place of eternal joy, beauty and happiness. The quest of Muslims in this earthly life is to secure a place in heaven through total surrender to God.[182]

The perpetrators of this violence are thus accorded a special status and are revered as *shaheed batal*—"martyr heroes"[183] or *istishahadi*—"he who martyrs himself."[184] As Ruqaiyah notes, "It is important to know that suicide is forbidden [in Islam] because of its evil objectives; such as impatience, desperation or any other bad and evil objects." In the context of the *istishahadi*, however, he explains, "The Qur'an evidences that such assaults are Islamically legitimate." Ruqaiyah goes on to cite ten Islamic theologians/philosophers who have endorsed this justification of suicide terrorism and the four essential motivations that permit such attacks:

1. Desiring martyrdom
2. Hurting the enemy
3. Encouraging fellow Muslims
4. Weakening the enemy's spirit and morale

In conclusion, Ruqaiyah states, "evidences from the Qur'an and the Sunnah . . . [have] clearly demonstrated that the 'Islamic-bombing assault' or the 'martyrdom attack' is Islamically legitimate as far as it is within the framework of Islam."[185] Similar pronouncements have been made by prominent Muslim clerics, and in some instances have been promulgated as fatwas.[186] Among the most prominent was the declaration by the Ayatollah Khomeini, who once declared that he knew of no command "more binding to the Muslim than the command to sacrifice life and property to defend and bolster Islam."[187]

In the specific context of Palestine, Sheikh Yusuf al Qardawi, a well-known Egyptian-born theologian, published an article in 1996 that began: "Suicide bombings in occupied Palestine represent one of the highest forms of jihad in the name of Allah." He maintained: "To call these operations suicide attacks would be a mistake and misleading. These are examples of heroic sacrifice, as utterly outside the bounds of suicide as the acts of martyrs. A suicide takes his life. . . . But what we are talking about is killing yourself for your religion and your people. A suicide is someone tired of himself and Allah, but a mujahadin [holy warrior] is imbued with faith in Allah's grace and generosity."[188]

Indeed, Sheikh Yassin had reportedly justified suicide terrorism by citing Sura 2, verses 190–91 of the Qur'an, which state: "Fight in the way of Allah against those who fight against you. . . . And slay them wherever ye find them and drive them out of the place when they drove you out, for persecution is worse than slaughter."[189]

The language and terminology are, of course, reminiscent of the medieval Assassins' doctrine, invoking the paradise that awaits the holy warrior. This heaven is described today just as it was more than seven hundred years ago, as a place with "rivers of milk and wine . . . lakes of honey, and the services of seventy-two virgins," where the martyr will see the face of Allah and later be joined by seventy chosen relatives.[190] Indeed, the pleasures of alcohol—which all Muslims are forbidden in their lives on earth—and sex, according to some accounts of interpretations—are permitted in this glorious afterlife, in which the commandments of the sharia do not apply.[191] Not surprisingly, perhaps, from the time of the first Islamic suicide bomb attacks in the early 1980s, witnesses and survivors have often recounted how the bombers were seen smiling just before blowing themselves and their victims up. The U.S. Marine corporal standing guard outside the barracks at Beirut International Airport on the morning of October 23, 1983, for example, remembered how the truck bomb's driver, a young man with bushy black hair and a mustache, "looked right at me . . . and smiled."[192] This is known as the *bassamat al-farah*, the "smile of joy"—a tradition of the Shi'a denoting the joy of martyrdom. It is just as prevalent among Sunni terrorists. The statement issued by Hamas following the Israeli assassination of the group's master bomber, Yahya Ayyash, "the Engineer," reiterated the virtues of self-sacrifice.[193] "Our valiant Palestinian people," it declared,

> Your militant movement, Hamas, while bringing you glad tidings that its leader hero Yahya Ayyash has ascended to heaven, congratulates its hero leader on winning the honor of martyrdom for the sake of God, and recalls the long series of sacrifices which were given as cheap offerings for the sake of God and the freedom of the homeland and the people. . . .
>
> Martyrdom has been Yahya's long-pursued wish. It is the hope pursued by Hamas's heroes every hour.[194]

These sentiments were confirmed by Ayyash's own father, who observed: "If he is dead, then God bless his soul. If he has acquired martyrdom, then congratulations."[195] The Pulitzer Prize winner and *New York Times* reporter and editor Joseph Lelyveld recounts a conversation he had with the mother of a twenty-three-year-old Palestinian suicide bomber who, only days before his university graduation, had killed himself and two IDF soldiers. Asked how she reacted to news of her son's death, the mother similarly replied: "I was very happy when I heard. To be a martyr, that's something. Very few people can do it. I prayed to thank God. In the Koran it's said that a martyr does not die. I know my son is close to me. It is our belief."[196]

One reason perhaps that the parents and other relatives of suicide bombers applaud and praise the violent deaths of their progeny and relatives may be because of their own impending salvation. For instance, it is widely believed that by becoming a martyr the suicide terrorist is able to intercede with God and ensure that seventy members of his family enter heaven.[197] Barbara Victor, an American journalist, recalls in her book on female Palestinian suicide bombers a conversation she had in January 2003 with Sheikh 'Abd-Salan Abu Shukheudem, the chief mufti of the Palestine Authority Police Force—a position akin to the official chaplain of a British or American police force. Sheikh Abu Shukheudem detailed for Victor the seven rewards that, according to Islamic tradition, are bestowed on the martyr for his or her act of self-sacrifice. "From the moment the first drop of blood is spilled," he explained,

> the martyr does not feel the pains of his injury, and is absolved of all his bad deeds; he sees his seat in Paradise; he is saved from the torture of the grave; he is saved from the fear of the Day of Judgment; he marries seventy-two beautiful black-eyed women; he is an advocate for seventy of his relatives to reach Paradise; he earns the Crown of Glory, whose precious stone is better than all this world and everything in it.[198]

In an interview four years earlier in the Palestinian Authority's newspaper, *al Hayat al Jadida*, Sheikh Abu Shukheudem had made the exact same point.[199]

Nasra Hassan writes of a meeting she had in 1999 with a young Hamas-affiliated imam, a graduate of Cairo's prestigious al Azhar University, who was similarly eloquent in his depiction of the afterlife that awaits the martyr. "He explained that the first drop of blood shed by a martyr during jihad washes away his sins instantaneously. On the Day of Judgment, he will face no reckoning. On the Day of Resurrection, he can intercede for seventy of his nearest and dearest to enter Heaven; and he will have at his disposal seventy-two houris, the beautiful virgins of Paradise."[200] Indeed, an almost identical formulation was used by Sheikh Isma'il al-Radhwan, who was quoted in a sermon he delivered in 2001 promising:

> The martyr, if he meets Allah, is forgiven with the first drop of blood; he is saved from the torments of the grave; he sees his place in Paradise; he is saved from the Great Horror (of the day of judgment); he is given

72 black-eyed women; he vouches for 70 of his family to be accepted to Paradise; he is crowned with the Crown of glory, whose precious stone is better than all of this world and what is in it.[201]

As these various statements illustrate, such ethereal promises, repeated by Muslim clerics, are readily accepted by the martyrs and would-be martyrs, and believed by parents and other family members who, though saddened by the death of their relative, arguably are nonetheless comforted by their own future ascension to heaven.[202] Thus, the Palestinian terrorist organizations have created a recruitment and support mechanism of both compelling and attractive incentives, based on theological justification and interpretation of sacred text, which sustains their suicide bombing campaign by appealing as much to the would-be bomber as to his or her family. In this manner, the families of both male and female bombers are co-opted into supporting—if not encouraging—their relations' homicidal self-destruction by the promise of an assured place in heaven as well.[203]

Rivalry and Competition Between Terrorist Groups

Finally, rivalries between the various Palestinian terrorist organizations also spawned intense competition. The struggle for both political preeminence and popular support has long characterized Hamas-PLO/PA relations.[204] A new element was introduced into this equation in November 2001 with the formation within Fatah and the irregular militias under its command, known as the Tanzim, with the creation of the al-Aqsa Martyrs Brigade as its specially dedicated suicide terrorist unit. Fears of Hamas's growing popularity and enhanced prestige among Palestinians had persuaded the PLO/PA leadership that it now had to compete directly with its rival.[205] External as well as internal considerations likely figured prominently in this decision. First was the dangerous erosion of morale among the PLO/PA's fighters, who watched as Hamas's power and influence increased as that of their organization eroded. Second was the faith now placed in suicide tactics as a means to reinvigorate the PLO/PA and check Hamas's ascendance. Third was the hope that the PLO/PA would attract the same surge in recruits by embracing suicide operations that both Hamas and the PIJ had experienced.[206] And finally, there was the belief that sustained suicide attacks would bring to the PLO/PA the power and prestige that both Hamas and the PIJ had reaped. Indeed, Fatah's creation of the al-Aqsa Martyrs harkened back thirty years, to the similar decision to establish the previously discussed and similarly clandestine Black September Organization as a means to counteract the success and publicity generated by the PFLP's brazen airline hijackings and newfound power and popularity that this upstart group had garnered.

In November 2001, Fatah signaled its entry into the realm of suicide terrorism by launching a joint operation with the PIJ. Two terrorists from each group—one of whom was a member of the Palestinian Authority's police force, based in Jericho—blew themselves up on a bus near Hadera.[207] Israel's seizure two months later of the *Karine-A*, a cargo ship transporting some fifty tons of arms and explosives to the PLO,[208] greatly accelerated the frequency of al-Aqsa Martyrs Brigades attacks. Now deprived of the means to wage a more conventional terrorist campaign of its own choosing and now even more fearful of being eclipsed by Hamas, al-Fatah was driven to intensify al-Aqsa Martyrs operations. Indeed, it is probably no coincidence that within weeks of the loss of the *Karine-A* shipment, the first female suicide bomber appeared. Her name was Wafa Idris, a twenty-eight-year-old divorcée who worked as a medical secretary for the Palestinian Red Crescent. She was recruited and deployed on a suicide bombing mission to Jerusalem in the name of the al-Aqsa Martyrs Brigade. One person, an eighty-one-year-old man, was killed, and 114 others were wounded.[209]

The al-Aqsa Martyrs operations challenged Hamas and the PIJ, and set in motion an almost macabre competition among them of who could mobilize and deploy the largest number of and the most effective "martyrs." The succession of terrorist incidents that convulsed Israel during the first part of 2002 was likely fueled by this competition. Indeed, by any measure, 2002 was an astonishing year for Israel in terms of suicide bombings. There were on average five successful suicide attacks per month in 2002, nearly double the number of successful attacks during the first fifteen months of the al-Aqsa Intifada—which itself is a figure more than ten times the monthly average since 1993. The distribution of groups claiming credit for suicide attacks during 2002 is revealing. Of the fifty-nine incidents recorded that year, the al-Aqsa Martyrs Brigade led with 25 (42 percent), followed by Hamas with 16 (27 percent), and the PIJ with 12 (2 percent). Significantly, this intergroup competition was so febrile that in just one year the al-Aqsa Martyrs Brigades staged nearly two-thirds the number of suicide attacks that Hamas had perpetrated during the previous three years combined.[210]

Conclusion

As this discussion of Tamil and Palestinian so-called martyrdom operations demonstrates, suicide attacks are an instrumental strategy consciously embraced by terrorist organizations because of their effectiveness. Thus, the decision to adopt this tactic has significantly less to do with the presumed anger, desperation, or frustration of the individuals who carry out these attacks than with the strategic requirements of the organizations behind them.[211] In a widely read account of Palestinian martyrs published shortly after 9/11 in the *New Yorker*, Nasra Hassan observed that none of the 250 or so suicide bombers and their handlers that she interviewed conformed to the typical suicidal personality. "None of them were uneducated, desperately poor, simple-minded, or depressed," Hassan observed. "Many were middle class and, unless they were fugitives, held paying jobs." Among them were the sons of two millionaires.[212] This misconception about suicide terrorism being a product of economic deprivation and lack of education and career opportunities has also been debunked empirically by the economist Claude Berrebi. In his study of the relationship between education and poverty with terrorism among Palestinians belonging to Hamas and PIJ, Berrebi concluded, "Both higher education and standard of living appear to be *positively* associated with membership in terror organizations such as Hamas or PIJ and with becoming a suicide bombing."[213] Suicide tactics have thus been adopted by a growing number of terrorist organizations around the world precisely because they are shocking, deadly, cost-effective, and difficult to stop. The only operational requirement that an organization must satisfy to get into the game, therefore, is the ability to recruit persons with a willingness to kill and a willingness to die.

Suicide terrorism, accordingly, is not a product of intense personal frustration or desperation but an organizational imperative that on the one hand increases the likelihood of a successful terrorist attack and on the other is intrinsically appealing to terrorists because of its profoundly unsettling psychological effects on the societies against which it is directed. The suicide aspect of the 9/11 attacks on the World Trade Center and the Pentagon, for instance, was essential to the success of those operations and, indeed, to their undeniably stunning impact. Moreover, the increased likelihood of success that attracts terrorists to suicide attacks is precisely what prompted Timothy McVeigh to consider turning his 1995 bombing of the Alfred P. Murrah Federal Office Building in Oklahoma City into a suicide operation. Not once, but four times in his quasi-autobiography, *American Terrorist*, McVeigh discusses how he contemplated employing this tactic for this very reason until he identified a plan that satisfied his intentions but did not require him to surrender his life in the process.[214]

Any hopes that the United States could remain immune to the global trend in suicide terrorism after 9/11 was dispelled in 2009 when information of a plot to stage simultaneous suicide bombings on the New York

City subway system, to coincide with the eighth anniversary of the 2001 attack came to light. The ringleader of the al-Qaeda–directed terrorist cell was an Afghan-born Green Card holder named Najibullah Zazi. Both Zazi and two fellow conspirators had been trained at an al-Qaeda camp in Pakistan. Three senior Core al-Qaeda commanders—the late Rashid Rauf and Saleh al-Somali, who were respectively killed in U.S. drone strikes in 2008 and 2009, together with Adnan al-Shukrijumah, who remains at large—had overseen and directed the plot, which was also linked to two other ambitious sets of attacks planned for April 2009 in Manchester, England, and July 2010 in Scandinavia.[215] Moreover, Zazi was easily able to purchase the ingredients needed to construct the bombs and then, following the instructions given to him by his al-Qaeda handlers from Pakistan, was able to produce a crude but potentially devastatingly lethal weapon. In their book, *Enemies Within*, the Pulitzer Prize winning journalists, Matt Apuzzo and Adam Goldman, explain how Zazi set about to fulfill his mission. "For weeks he'd been visiting beauty supply stores," they write,

> filling his carts with hydrogen peroxide and nail polish remover. At the Beauty Supply Warehouse, among the rows of wigs, braids, and extensions, the manager knew [Zazi] as Jerry. He said his girlfriend owned hair salons. There was no reason to doubt him.
>
> On pharmacy shelves, in the little brown plastic bottles, hydrogen peroxide is a disinfectant, a sting-free way to clean scrapes. Beauty salons use a more concentrated version to bleach hair or activate hair dyes. At even higher concentrations, it burns the skin. It is not flammable on its own, but when it reacts with other chemicals, it quickly releases oxygen, creating an environment ripe for explosions. . . . Even with a cheap stove, it's easy to simmer water out of hydrogen peroxide, leaving behind something more potent. It takes time, and he had plenty of that.

Preparing the explosive initiator was only slightly more complicated, but considerably more dangerous. Hence, Zazi had to be especially careful. "He added the muriatic acid and watched as the chemicals crystallized," the account continues.

> The crystals are known as triacetone triperoide, or TATP. A spark, electrical current, even a bit of friction can set off an explosion. . . .
> The white crystal compound had been popular among Palestinian terrorists. It was cheap and powerful, but its instability earned it the nickname "Mother of Satan". . . .

When he was done mixing, he rinsed the crystals with baking soda and water to make his creation more stable. He placed the finished product in a wide-rimmed glass jar about the size of a coffee tin and inspected his work. There would be enough for three detonators. Three detonators inside three backpacks filled with a flammable mixture and ball bearings—the same type of weapon that left 52 dead in London in 2005. . . .

He was ready for New York.[216]

Nor was this the first suicide terrorist plot directed against the New York City subway system. Four years before 9/11, two Palestinians living in Brooklyn had plotted such an attack. Their 1997 plan to bomb the B subway line, running from the northern tip of Manhattan to Coney Island on the south shore of Brooklyn, was foiled only because an informant told the police. When the two would-be bombers were arrested, they were probably less than a day away from attacking; according to law enforcement authorities, five bombs had been primed. Although the pair were never formally linked to any identifiable terrorist organization and appeared to have concocted the plot entirely on their own, there was no doubting their determination. "I always dreamed to be a martyr," one of them reportedly declared.[217] Both men resisted arrest when police officers and FBI agents raided their apartment, and both were shot and wounded in the struggles that ensued, one while attempting to detonate the explosives. "I wouldn't call them sophisticated," Howard Safir, the commissioner of the New York City police at the time, observed, "but they certainly were very dangerous."[218] That suicide bombers don't need to be sophisticated is precisely what makes them so dangerous. Indeed, it is the ease and simplicity of suicide bombings that makes it so appealing to organizations behind them. The means of attack, moreover, can vary widely:

- using aircraft as human cruise missiles (as we saw with the 9/11 attacks) or boats as human torpedoes (for instance, the 2000 attack on the USS *Cole*);
- involving vehicular bombs with a driver and explosive-laden cars or trucks (such as in the 1998 simultaneous attacks on the U.S. embassies in Kenya and Tanzania); or
- using pedestrians—individual attackers wearing a specially designed vest or belt or carrying a backpack or small handheld bag containing explosives and connected to a manual or remote-control detonator (as Zazi and his two confederates plotted).

Similarly, the potential targets of these attacks can be equally diverse, embracing

- high-value symbolic targets such as buildings or installations that necessarily involve the infliction of mass casualties—such as the World Trade Center and the Pentagon on 9/11;
- high-value human targets with the goal of assassinating leading government figures and other prominent persons—as the LTTE regularly did; and
- deliberately lethal attacks specifically targeting the public—whether on buses, trains, and subways, shopping malls, cinema, sports stadiums, pedestrian malls, or any public venue where people gather.

The potential perpetrators of such attacks in the United States could range from domestic right-wing extremists (such as McVeigh) to militant nationalists (such as the two Palestinians involved in the 1997 New York City subway attack plot) to radical Salafi-Jihadis (such as Zazi and his two accomplices), and even to lone individuals without any organizational affiliation (such as the gunman who staged a suspected suicide attack at Los Angeles International Airport on July 4, 2002). As the last incident suggests, bombs and explosives are not the only weapons in an act of suicide terrorism; firearms, knives, and other weapons can be involved. The most consequential suicide attacks, however, in terms of casualties and effect, would doubtless be those involving a weapon capable of causing mass casualties, most likely a bomb or explosive device, or a means of attack designed to generate some wider conflagration.

The challenge in responding to suicide terrorism is not to fall victim to the psychological paralysis and sense of defenselessness or powerlessness that the terrorists hope to achieve. As Ehud Sprinzak had long argued, "Contrary to popular belief, suicide bombers can be stopped—but only if security authorities pay more attention to their methods and motivations." The experience of a country like Israel, for example, shows that despite the significant death toll inflicted by suicide attacks initially, with the proper attention, focus, preparations, and training, this threat can be effectively countered. Israel in fact has achieved remarkable success in dramatically reducing the number of successful suicide attacks. Various authoritative Israeli government sources maintain that the countermeasures adopted since 2002 have prevented at least 80 to 85 percent of all attempts.[219] A special report produced by the Israeli security establishment summarizing that country's struggle against terrorism, for example, cites a 30 percent decrease in the number of Palestinian terrorist attacks—including suicide attacks—against Israeli targets in 2003, compared with 2002, as well as a 50 percent decrease in the number of casualties.[220] A senior Israeli counterterrorism official identified three key reasons for the success of these countermeasures:

- First, quite good intelligence and understanding of the situation, as well as analysis of information in a fast and effective way;
- Second, when we have intelligence, we can send units and engage quickly; and
- Third, we have been able to close up the "operational circle"—that is, when we have information, we are able to deploy the right unit and weapons quickly.[221]

Although the challenges of defending against and effectively countering this threat are vastly more complex for countries that, unlike Israel, are not enmeshed in permanent states of war with enemies poised immediately across national borders and that have exponentially larger territory and populations, precautions can be adapted from Israel's experience and best practices applied to reduce the threat of suicide terrorist attack. Perhaps most important is the realization that suicide terrorism is an instrument of warfare whose use has only increased and become more pervasive in the decade and a half since the 9/11 attacks. Suicide operations are thus rational acts undertaken by terrorist organizations as part of a deliberately calculated and orchestrated campaign to undermine confidence in government and leadership, crush popular morale, and spread fear and intimidation. Responding to suicide terrorism must therefore be equally calculated and planned, and instrumental in its reactions. The police, the military, and intelligence agencies can take steps that work from the outside in, beginning far ahead in time and distance from a potential attack and ending at the moment and the site of an actual attack. Although the importance of these steps is widely recognized, they have been implemented unevenly by many countries, including the United States. Among the key lessons are:

- *Understand the terrorists' mind-set and their operational environment.* Know their modus operandi and targeting patterns. Suicide bombers are rarely lone outlaws; they are preceded by long logistical trails. Focus not just on suspected bombers but on the infrastructure required to launch and sustain suicide bombing campaigns. This is the essential spadework. It will be for nothing, however, if concerted efforts are not made to circulate this information quickly and systematically within police forces, across regional jurisdictions (especially the adjacent and surrounding suburbs of a metropolitan area), and among other government authorities charged with protection and defense against terrorist attack.
- *Develop strong confidence-building ties with the communities from which terrorists are most likely to come or hide in, and mount communications campaigns to eradicate support for violent extremism from these*

communities. The most effective and useful intelligence comes from places where terrorists conceal themselves and seek to establish and hide their infrastructure. Law enforcement officers should actively encourage and cultivate cooperation by building strong ties with community leaders, including elected officials, civil servants, clerics, businessmen, and teachers, among others, and thereby enlist their assistance and support.

• *Encourage businesses from which terrorists can obtain bomb-making components to alert authorities if they notice large or unusual purchases— the acquisition, for example, of ammonium nitrate fertilizer or of pipes, batteries, and wires or chemicals commonly used to fabricate explosives.* Information about customers who simply inquire about any of these materials can also be extremely useful to police officers. Companies that either sell or distribute materials that can be used in the construction of a terrorist device must be made aware and instructed on identifying and reporting suspicious activity to the authorities.[222]

• *Force terrorists to pay more attention to their organizational and personal security than to planning and carrying out attacks.* Terrorist groups do not attack people or places without planning and reconnaissance. The greatest efficiencies arguably come from the effective disruption of preattack operations. Given the highly fluid international threat that the United States faces alongside the potential for entirely homegrown adversaries to launch such attacks, specialized counterterrorism units, dedicated specifically to identifying and targeting the intelligence-gathering and reconnaissance activities of terrorist organizations, should be established within existing law enforcement agencies. These units should be especially aware of the means and venues where potential recruitment might occur, such as community centers, social clubs, schools, and religious institutions.

• *Make sure that ordinary materials don't become shrapnel. Some steps to build up physical defenses were taken after 9/11—reinforcing park benches, erecting Jersey barriers around vulnerable buildings, and the like.* More precautions are needed, such as ensuring that windows on buses and subway cars are shatterproof and that seats and other accoutrements are not easily dislodged or splintered. Buses can be outfitted, as in Israel, with barriers to make entry through rear exit doors impossible and to enable the driver to stop a suspicious person from entering the bus from the front door.

• *Civil defense and public efforts that enlist the help and support of citizens in remaining alert for strange or suspicious behavior of people in areas in and around likely attack sites (i.e., on buses and subways, at historical landmarks, near embassies or consulates, or particularly well-known buildings) and being aware of packages or bags left unattended at public venues*. During the IRA's bombing campaign in London from the 1970s to the 1990s, residents and visitors to that city were reminded of the need for vigilance through posters and other advertisements containing basic instructions on both what to look for and whom to contact. Israel's populace is similarly indoctrinated on the need for eternal vigilance and the appropriate action to take when suspicion is aroused or a terrorist attack occurs. Although public awareness campaigns of this type have been instituted in some cities in the United States, in many cases they are either insufficiently advertised or simply warn citizens to be aware and provide a toll-free telephone number but do not advise specifically what citizens should be aware of or sufficiently educate them to the extent that is done in Israel today and that was done in London in the past.[223]

• *Teach law enforcement awareness—what to do at the moment of an attack or an attempt.* Prevention comes first from the cop on the beat, who will be forced to make instant life-and-death decisions affecting those nearby. Training is required for ordinary law enforcement officers to identify a potential suicide bomber, confront a suspect, and to respond and secure the area around the attack site in the event of an explosion. Is the officer authorized to take action upon sighting a suspected bomber, or must he or she call a supervisor or special unit first? Policies and procedures must be established. In the aftermath of a blast, the police must determine when emergency medical crews and firefighters may enter the site without risk to themselves; concerns about a follow-up attack may dictate that first responders be held back until the area is secured. The ability to make such lightning-quick determinations requires training, protocols, and experience from simulations and real-life exercises.[224]

In sum, an effective defense against suicide terrorism must be nimble, flexible, and adaptive. It must be as dynamic and fluid as terrorist operational planning, reconnaissance, and attack execution are. Accordingly, law enforcement plans, procedures, and policies cannot rest on past laurels or previous successes achieved in deterring, preventing, or responding to terrorist threats or attacks, or both, but must be familiar with existing, historical, emergent, and probable future terrorist targeting patterns and modi operandi.

In this respect, that our enemies are marshaling their own resources to continue the struggle that crystallized on 9/11 is beyond doubt. Whether it will materialize in the same shape or form as the suicide bombing campaigns directed against Sri Lanka and Israel remains to be seen. But in his 2001 book, *Knights Under the Prophet's Banner*, al-Zawahiri laid down a blueprint for how al-Qaeda envisions this struggle will unfold: "We must move the battle to the enemy's ground to burn the hands of those who ignite fire in our countries," he wrote. This entails, al-Zawahiri continued:

1. The need to inflict the maximum casualties against the opponent, for this is the language understood by the west, no matter how much time and effort such operations take.
2. The need to concentrate on the method of martyrdom operations as the most successful way of inflicting damage against the opponent and the least costly to the mujahidin in terms of casualties.
3. The targets as well as the type and method of weapons used must be chosen to have an impact on the structure of the enemy and deter it enough to stop its brutality, arrogance, and disregard for all taboos and customs. It must restore the struggle to its real size.[225]

Indeed, the call to violence from ISIS's chief spokesperson, Abu Muhammad al-Adnani, quoted in chapter 1, has already proven more effective in inciting precisely this type of violence worldwide than over a decade's worth of similar entreaties from both bin Laden and al-Zawahiri to achieve the same end. Some persons have answered al-Adnani's call in their own countries on their own initiative, while others have been explicitly guided by ISIS operatives, either in person or over the Internet and social media.[226] The suicide attacks that convulsed Paris in November 2015 and Brussels the following March are examples of the latter and clearly demonstrate the continuing appeal of these tactics to terrorist organizations such as ISIS. In Paris, three teams of three terrorists each launched a dozen unsparingly lethal attacks. Three suicide bombers struck the national sports stadium during a soccer match between France and Germany attended by President Francois Hollande. A fourth blew himself up in a cafe on the Boulevard Voltaire, while two more detonated their explosives-filled vests as police stormed the Bataclan Theatre, where the terrorists had begun to shoot the hundred or so concertgoers they had seized as hostages. One hundred and thirty persons were killed and nearly four hundred others were wounded. The attacks in Brussels four months later involved two suicide bombers who attacked the unsecured departures area at that city's international airport and a third who targeted the city's metro system. A fourth, unexploded device, abandoned by another bomber was later found at the Brussels Airport. Thirty-two persons perished and more than three hundred were injured.

In the years immediately following the 9/11 attacks, when the greatest military onslaught in history against a terrorist movement was arguably at its zenith, al-Zawahiri defiantly proclaimed in February 2004: "Bush, reinforce your security measures. . . . The Islamic nation which sent you the New York and Washington brigades has taken the firm decision to send you successive brigades to sow death and aspire to paradise."[227] Although al-Qaeda has yet to make good on al-Zawahiri's threat—and it remains unclear whether ISIS has the capability to do so—it is a warning and a potentiality that we cannot afford to dismiss or ignore given the continued salience of suicide terrorist attacks across the globe.

Chapter 6

The Old Media, Terrorism, and Public Opinion

The goals and motivations of terrorists, as we have seen in previous chapters, vary widely, from such grand schemes as the total remaking of society along fundamentalist religious or doctrinaire ideological lines, and even the fulfillment of some divinely inspired millenarian imperative, to comparatively more distinct aims such as the reestablishment of a national homeland or the unification of a divided nation. Still other terrorists are motivated by very issue-specific causes, such as the banning of abortion, animal rights, or environmental concerns, and seek to apply direct pressure on both the public and its representatives in government to either enact or repeal legislation directly affecting their particular interest. Despite these many differences, however, all terrorist groups have one trait in common: they do not commit actions randomly or senselessly. Each wants maximum publicity to be generated by its actions and, moreover, aims at intimidation and subjection to attain its objectives. In the words of the late Dr. Frederick Hacker, a psychiatrist and noted authority on terrorism, terrorists seek to "frighten and, by frightening, to dominate and control. They want to impress. They play to and for an audience, and solicit audience participation."[1]

Terrorism, therefore, may be seen as a violent act that is conceived specifically to attract attention and then, through the publicity it generates, to communicate a message. "There is no other way for us," a leader of the United Red Army (the parent group of the Japanese Red Army), a left-wing terror-

ist group active in Japan during the early 1970s, once explained. "Violent actions . . . are shocking. We *want* to shock people, everywhere. . . . It is our
way of communicating with the people."[2] This is why Anthony Richards describes terrorism as a means of "violent propaganda through which to deliver a message or an advert for a cause that would otherwise never receive
such exposure."[3]

The modern news media, as the principal conduit of information about
such acts, thus play a vital part in the terrorists' calculus. Indeed, without
the media's coverage, the act's impact is arguably wasted, remaining narrowly confined to the immediate victim(s) of the attack rather than reaching the wider "target audience" at whom the terrorists' violence is actually
aimed. Only by spreading the terror and outrage to a much larger audience
can the terrorists gain the maximum potential leverage that they need to
effect fundamental political change. "Terrorism is theatre," Brian Jenkins
famously declared in his seminal 1974 paper, explaining how "terrorist attacks
are often carefully choreographed to attract the attention of the electronic
media and the international press."[4]

Just as often, the media respond to these overtures with almost unbridled alacrity, proving unable to ignore what has been accurately described
as "an event . . . fashioned specifically for their needs."[5] The American media coverage of the hijacking of TWA (Trans World Airlines) Flight 847 by
Lebanese Shi'a terrorists in 1985 amply confirms that observation. Three terrorists belonging to Hezbollah had hijacked the aircraft en route from
Rome to Cairo on June 14. The hijackers originally demanded the release of
776 Shi'a held in Israeli jails, although they later reduced that number. The
commandeered aircraft was flown first to Beirut, then to Algiers, then back
to Beirut. At each stop, passengers who were not U.S. citizens, along with
the women and children on board, were released, until only thirty-nine
American men remained. After the aircraft landed in Beirut for the second
time, the hostages were spirited into hiding and scattered throughout the
city to thwart any attempted rescue operation by U.S. military forces. During the seventeen-day crisis, while the Americans were held hostage in Beirut,
nearly 500 news segments—an average of 28.8 per day[6]—were broadcast by
the three major U.S. television networks of that time: ABC, the American
Broadcasting Corporation; NBC, the National Broadcasting Corporation;
and CBS, the Columbia Broadcasting System. Indeed, on average, two-thirds
of their daily early evening flagship news shows—14 out of 21 minutes—
focused on the hostage story,[7] and their regularly scheduled programs were
interrupted at least 80 times over those 17 days with special reports or news
bulletins.[8] This intense coverage was made possible by the small army of
reporters, field producers, editors, camera crews, and sound technicians

that the three networks rushed to the scene of the breaking story: within days, a total of 85 people representing the three networks were in Beirut.[9] The message that they imparted to their viewers was clear: no news of any significance was occurring anywhere except that which concerned the hostages and their anxious families back home.

More disconcerting, perhaps, was the tenor of the coverage. As the hostage crisis dragged on day after day, at times with seemingly little or no progress toward a resolution, the vast media resources deployed for just this one story had to find or create news to justify the expense and continued presence of the media personnel, even if no real news was occurring. A gross imbalance therefore emerged: soft, human-interest feature stories predominated (mostly interviews with the hostages and their families), accounting for slightly more than a third of all reports, with fewer than half as many stories addressing real issues, such as the U.S. government's reactions to various developments in the crisis or the Reagan administration's persistent efforts to reach a resolution.[10] The cloying and meretricious content of the reporting was clearly revealed in a contemporary *Washington Post* article. "In the race for on-the-air scoops, which ABC-TV News seems to have won to date," it began, "the interview Friday morning between anchorman Dan Rather of *CBS Evening News* and TWA flight 847's hostage media star, Allyn Conwell, was distinctive."[11] In possibly the most egregious perversion of news reporting during this episode, the "news presenters" rather than the "news makers" had become the story!

However, the most pernicious effect of the crisis was its validation of terrorism as a tactic. The Reagan administration, driven by intense domestic pressure generated by the hostages' plight, in turn compelled Israel to accede to the hijackers' demands and release 756 imprisoned Shi'a. The terrorists, in return, duly freed their thirty-nine American captives. The line of distraught hostage family members that paraded before the three networks' cameras ensured that there was no letup of pressure. "Should the Reagan administration press Israel to release its Shi'a prisoners?" the son of one hostage was asked on a morning news show. "That's what I'd like to see," came the reply.[12] The networks professed little or no concern that they had moved beyond reporting the news to actively helping to determine policy. At times, presenters assumed for themselves the responsibility of negotiating with the terrorists. "Any final words to President Reagan this morning?" the congenial host of ABC's *Good Morning America* asked the leader of one Lebanese group.[13] Justifying this type of active intervention in a story, CBS White House correspondent Lesley Stahl explained, "We are an instrument for the hostages. . . . We force the Administration to put their lives above policy."[14]

Those responsible for determining and implementing that policy understandably took a very different view. Reflecting on a state of affairs where public emotions were seen to determine government policy, the late congressman Tom Lantos lamented that "focusing on individual tragedies, interviewing the families of people in anguish, in horror, in nightmare, completely debilitates national policymakers from making rational decisions in the national interest."[15] His complaint was echoed by former U.S. secretary of state Henry Kissinger and Zbigniew Brzezinski, President Carter's national security adviser during the Tehran hostage crisis. Both agreed that there was little doubt that the febrile television coverage afforded to hijackings and hostage situations involving American citizens complicated, and even undermined, governmental efforts to obtain their release.[16]

That terrorism had indeed become a perverted form of show business is borne out by the experiences of other journalists who dealt with the hostage-takers' official spokesmen, and therefore witnessed firsthand the terrorists' polished PR campaign. "These guys are so sophisticated about the way they are getting through to the American viewer," a senior Associated Press editor marveled. "These guys are street fighters [yet] they're making ground rules for the media."[17] According to John Bullock, a British journalist who covered the story, throughout the crisis the terrorists knew exactly what they were doing. Their deft manipulation of the U.S. networks, he recalls, "was done quite consciously. There were graduates of media studies from American colleges at meetings at Nabih Berri's house in West Beirut while ['spin doctoring'] tactics were being worked out."[18]

The fruit of the hijackers' labors may be seen in the abject capitulation of the American television networks to the terrorists' point of view. On-air commentary repeatedly and unthinkingly equated the wanton kidnapping of entirely innocent airline passengers—who were targeted only because of the nationality of the passport they carried—with Shi'a militiamen and suspected terrorists detained by Israeli troops during fighting in southern Lebanon. These invidious and inaccurate comparisons were all the more odious considering that one of the hostages, a U.S. Navy diver named Robert Dean Stethem, had been mercilessly beaten to death on board the aircraft shortly after the hijacking began. As one critic noted, "It's a cliché now that the Shi'ites got the networks to carry their political message back to America. When the TV coverage is replayed, it's clear just how well the Shi'ite line was delivered." Indeed, so obvious was this perceived bias on the part of some reporters that it was said to be a standing joke among journalists in Beirut that the initials "ABC" stood for the "Amal Broadcasting Company" in recognition of the attention it showered on one of the Lebanese militias purportedly helping to effect the hostages' release, while "NBC" denoted the "Nabih Berri Company," the name of that militia's leader.[19]

While the American networks' response to the TWA Flight 847 crisis was among the most glaring examples of terrorism's ability to capture media attention and manipulate and exploit it in ways amenable to the terrorists' cause, the problem is endemic to all democratic countries with open and unrestricted press reporting. So pervasive was the influence exerted by West German terrorists over coverage of the 1972 deal that freed a kidnapped West Berlin politician, Peter Lorenz, in exchange for five imprisoned terrorists, one executive was driven to admit that "for seventy-two hours we lost control of our medium."[20] In 1978, the same blanket coverage, to the exclusion of almost all other news, that would later be afforded the TWA hijacking was evident in Italy throughout the fifty-five-day state crisis engendered by the Red Brigades' kidnapping of former prime minister Aldo Moro. According to one analysis, during that time only two articles appeared on the front pages of Italy's newspapers that did not have to do with the Moro case.[21] During the 1990s, complaints were voiced in Britain over the stranglehold exercised by Sinn Fein spokesmen on behalf of their IRA masters over reporting in Northern Ireland. Henry McDonald, BBC Northern Ireland security correspondent between 1994 and 1996, contends that the terrorists and their apologists orchestrated a public relations campaign that imposed a "politically correct culture" on the reporting of both British and Irish print and electronic media. "It is a culture," McDonald claims, "where the commentators and opinion-formers blame [then British prime minister] John Major for resumed IRA violence, rather than the IRA itself."[22]

Given that terrorism is inherently about attracting attention and publicity, and that in even its earliest manifestations centuries ago the Zealots and the Assassins deliberately played to an audience far beyond the immediate victims of their attacks, why is it only comparatively recently that the media have been blamed for serving as the terrorists' willing apologists? The answer may be found in two technological advances in mass communication that occurred nearly one hundred years apart, respectively, altering the way that news is transmitted and making it accessible to exponentially larger audiences. These developments, in turn, have been ruthlessly and successfully exploited by terrorists.

Terrorism and the Transformation of Reporting

The invention of the steam-powered printing press in 1830 began the modern era of mass media and communication: within three years, the first mass circulation newspaper was being produced in the United States. Subsequent technological refinements led to the introduction of the even more efficient rotary press the following decade. News became more timely because of the speed with which newspapers could now be printed and more accessible as the economics of technological innovation created a more widely affordable product. By the 1870s, the newspaper business had been completely transformed by the advent of electric power coupled with the development of curved stereotype printing plates, together resulting in the automatic rotary cylinder press—and the capability to print on both sides of a continuous roll of paper. The revolution in mass communication, begun less than fifty years earlier, was now complete, offering abundant new opportunities to communicate on a vaster scale than ever before. I have already noted that terrorists were quick to recognize the potential of this new mass communications technology. It suffices simply to add here that the symbiotic relationship between terrorism and the media was forged during this era by both the Russian constitutionalists in the Narodnaya Volya and their anarchist contemporaries who, through "propaganda by deed," deliberately sought to communicate their revolutionary message to a wide audience.

The second great revolution in mass communication that directly affected terrorism occurred in 1968. That year marked not only, as previously noted, the birth of international terrorism—when Palestinian terrorists began to hijack airliners in Europe—but also the launching by the United States of the first television satellite. Now stories could be transmitted from local studios back to network news headquarters for editing and broadcast far more rapidly than was previously possible. It is perhaps not entirely coincidental that from this time forward, the United States became the number-one target of terrorists throughout the world. Throughout the following thirty years, terrorists attacked American citizens and interests more than those of any other country.[23] While there are various reasons terrorists find American targets so attractive,[24] a salient consideration has always been the unparalleled opportunities for publicity and exposure that terrorists the world over know they will get from the extensive U.S. news media. This was made especially clear during the TWA Flight 847 crisis when a British correspondent assigned to the story discovered that the hostage-takers paid no attention to "non-American and non-television journalists."[25] In retrospect, therefore, the U.S. satellite launch was the first, critical step in facilitating the American news media's worldwide predominance through its ability to reach a numerically vast audience. Ironically, it was also this development that made the same audience exponentially more attractive to terrorists than that of any other nation.

By the early 1970s, the effect of this technological leap was further enhanced by the availability of three critical pieces of television equipment that made possible the reporting of events in real time. These were the minicam— the portable, lightweight video camera; the equally portable battery-powered video recorder, and the time-base—which converts video footage into transmittable output, which in turn can be broadcast over the airwaves. With this combination of technologies, live television transmissions could now be made directly from remote locations throughout the world and beamed instantaneously into the homes of viewers everywhere.[26] The dramatic potential of this breakthrough was, as previously described, spectacularly demonstrated at the 1972 Munich Olympics when Palestinian terrorists were able to monopolize the attention of a global television audience that had tuned in expecting to watch the Games.

The emergence of these broadcast technologies has had equally profound consequences for the content of the news and its impact on government. The ability to transmit a breaking story live spawned intense competition among rival networks to "scoop" one another (as was illustrated by the *Washington Post* article that commented on the network news organizations during the TWA Flight 847 hostage situation). This could be accomplished basically in one of two ways: by being the first on the scene or by being the first to report some hitherto undisclosed information. The main problem with the former is that even though it is the most sought-after prize of television journalism, it is also an inherently evanescent advantage. Hence, having broken the story and captured viewers' attention, the priority becomes to hold that attention with equally gripping follow-on reports. Accordingly, for the duration of an important story's life, the media's focus invariably shifts from the reporting of the limited, and often dwindling, quantity of "hard" news to more human-interest sorts of "feature" stories, mostly involving exclusive interviews (e.g., the aforementioned Rather-Conwell exchange) or the breathless revelation of some previously unknown or undocumented item of related news—no matter how trivial or irrelevant.

For the media-savvy terrorist, these conditions are ripe for exploitation. The networks' capability to broadcast instantaneously, coupled with the intense pressure to scoop competitors, has meant that the responsibilities once exercised by a studio editor—with the attendant opportunities for sober reflection or considered judgment—have long since passed in the rush to "go live on air."[27] The television medium thus presents itself as a vacuum waiting to be filled; a void of rolling cameras and open mikes susceptible to terrorist exploitation and manipulation. Indeed, in this key respect, the terrorists' and the networks' interests are identical: having created the story, both are resolved to ensure its longevity. The overriding objective for the terrorists is to wring every last drop of exposure, publicity, and coercive power from the incident, while the networks' goal is to squeeze from the story every additional ratings point that their coverage can provide. "Capturing the audience's attention may be easy," political psychologists Jeffrey Z. Rubin and Nehemia Friedland note, "but terrorist organizations need a flair for the dramatic to sustain that interest."[28] Precisely the same can be said of television correspondents and field producers.

The quest to keep a story alive leads inevitably to a disproportionate fixation on the human-interest angle: most often, the grief and anguish of family and friends of terrorist victims or hostages. In this manner, the vicarious dimension of a terrorist incident—the stimulation of thoughts in the minds of millions of television viewers and newspaper readers everywhere that "there but for the grace of God go I"—is effectively and efficiently mined by terrorist and journalist alike. Beyond any doubt, the American networks during the TWA crisis served this diet on a platter to a waiting and watching public at home, made hungry both for every scrap of information on the hostages themselves and for each morsel doled out on the plight of their worried loved ones back home. This sort of coverage dovetailed perfectly with the terrorists' wish to apply the maximum pressure possible on the Reagan administration to force Israel to accede to the hijackers' demands. Day in and day out, as the hostages' uncertain fate was played out in the glare of the camera's lens, the administration was progressively compelled to abandon its publicly stated policy of refusing to negotiate with terrorists, undermine its relations with a close regional ally, embrace the recovery of the hostages as its only goal, and believe that its sole option was the safe return of the thirty-nine American hostages in exchange for the release of the more than seven hundred Shi'a imprisoned in Israel. "What the Shi'ite terrorists in Beirut achieved is spin control beyond the wildest dreams of any politician," the American columnist Fred Barnes wrote in the wake of the crisis. "How did this happen?" he asked rhetorically. "Easy," came the reply: "The terrorists exploited the normal lust of the media—particularly TV—for breaking events of international impact, and for high drama and a human dimension to the news. . . . Media competition, always brutal, is especially fierce in this atmosphere, partly because the public is more attentive, partly because media stardom may be at stake for some."[29]

It will be recalled that the leading late-night American television news show *Nightline* grew out of the need to report at the end of each day, as viewers prepared for sleep, some new tidbit of information from Tehran during the previous 444-day hostage crisis of 1979–1980. This approach not only made the show's presenter, Ted Koppel, a media star[30] but also spawned dozens of imitators in other countries.

One additional, even paramount, consideration influencing television news coverage that has emerged in recent years is its cost. A once finite number of privately owned or state-run broadcasting corporations now must contend with heightened competition not only from their traditional network rivals but also from a virtually unlimited array of upstart cable and satellite channels. Moreover, news is now broadcast over such diverse media as the Internet, e-mail, faxes, local telephone servers, and social media. Therefore today, on top of increasingly constrained news budgets—already an issue that had emerged more than two decades ago—foreign network news coverage, especially, must increasingly justify itself and its vast expense by winning larger audience shares. According to one veteran network foreign correspondent writing in the late 1990s, the daily cost of the typical international television news team "begins at around $3,000 a day. Air fare and excess baggage charges can easily reach $12,000"—in addition to the costs of satellite uplinks and transmittal time.[31] Accordingly, network executives exhibit a discernible proclivity to look more to the bottom line than to journalistic priorities for guidance, and hence to emphasize entertainment value over good reporting. "They've got us putting more fuzz and wuzz on the air," Dan Rather lamented in a 1993 speech, "cop show stuff, so as to compete not with other news programs but with entertainment programs—including those posing as news programs—for dead bodies, mayhem and lurid tales."[32] This view was reiterated by one of Rather's contemporaries, Garrick Utley, a former chief foreign correspondent for NBC and ABC television news and a contributor to CNN, in a lead article in *Foreign Affairs*.[33] Immediacy, exclusivity, and drama—the more violent or life-threatening, the better—thus become the essential hooks with which to reel in viewers and ensure a flow of advertising revenue. Terrorist incidents, inherently dramatic, replete with human interest, and often of prolonged duration—whether the wrenching daily ordeal of hostages or reports on postattack cleanup and repercussions in the aftermath of bombings—thus occupy center stage in network television's entertainment/ news calculations. The result is a trivialization of television news that inevitably emphasizes aspects of the story that the wider viewing audience can relate to,[34] rather than genuine analysis or probing to gain an understanding of the background of a particular issue. The camera becomes tightly focused on the human drama at the expense of the bigger picture that is what the story is really about. In essence, what is broadcast is the big picture writ so small that the average television viewer can understand it, the story deliberately packaged to suit the typical audience's short attention span.[35] "Mindless gaga and emotional gush seem the mainstays of the moment," the *Washington Post*'s Pulitzer Prize–winning television critic Tom Shales opined in the midst of the TWA crisis, bemoaning the debasement of broadcast news.[36]

This trend in American television news was by no means an inconsequential development, given that by 1978 television had become the primary source of news information for a majority (67 percent) of Americans and the *only* source of news for 34 percent.[37] The emphasis on entertainment and, in turn, the violence and "blood and guts" aspects of news stories were demonstrated in a study of the three major American networks' reporting on Armenian terrorism between 1975 and 1983. It concluded that while the coverage had indeed (as noted in chapter 3) provided unparalleled exposure to the terrorists and their cause, the "networks tended to reduce Armenians to terrorists (not freedom fighters) shooting an American woman in the back as she tried to flee, taunting the police by holding a small child at gun point, and killing a young French boy with a gasoline bomb." In this respect, virtually no attention was paid to the historical background, political context, or attendant wider issues that would have shed light on the terrorists' reasoning and motivations.[38]

Unfortunately, the approach to terrorism coverage embraced by broadcast journalists is often emulated by their print counterparts. "As the television media trivialise the news," James Adams, former CEO of United Press International and past *Sunday Times* Washington Bureau chief, foreign editor, and defense editor, had argued, "so newspapers have to seek ways of presenting their information in a lively and exciting way to their audience. That has meant not just a narrowing of the focus but a concentration on the trivial, the marginal and the irrelevant in the search for excitement."[39] Color photos, lurid images, and sensational headlines splashed across the front pages of tabloids and their more serious counterparts are what sell newspapers and advertising copy as much as commercial airtime. Accordingly, there is often the same abandonment in print as over the airwaves of any effort to understand the bigger picture. Instead, an obsession with voyeuristic detail now predominates in many newspapers. It is an outcome dictated by the same financial pressures and declining revenues that have ravaged network television news, even while the Internet and social media continue to erode both broadcast news and the news-reading public. Adams, for example, draws a comparison between his stint at the *Sunday Times* as foreign manager during the 1980s and that of one his predecessors, Ian Fleming (the creator of the fictional spy James Bond), in the 1950s. While Fleming could call on the services of 150 correspondents throughout the world, forty years later Adams had only eight at his disposal. The result, he reflected, was "that media coverage is highly selective and driven not necessarily by the importance of a story, but by the cost of covering it, or even by something as simple as who happens to be in the area at the time."[40]

Under these circumstances, news reporting is driven primarily by the imperative of speed in posting, tweeting, getting on air or into print and subsequently by the search for additional material to justify the initial expense and attention, and thereby to continue to fill a post, a tweet, a broadcast slot or a printed page. This situation is, however unwittingly, tailor-made for terrorist manipulation and contrivance. "'Don't shoot, Abdul! We're not on prime time!'" is how the late irregular warfare expert J. Bowyer Bell described terrorists' conscious efforts to play to the modern media and the media's eagerness to respond. Sadly, this jocular observation is closer to reality than exaggeration. During the 1975 seizure of OPEC (Organization of Petroleum Exporting Countries) headquarters in Vienna and kidnapping of the oil ministers, for example, Carlos "the Jackal" obligingly waited for the arrival of the television camera crews before dramatically fleeing the building with his hostages.[41] Four years later, a sullen mob outside the American embassy in Tehran, where the fifty-two hostages were being held, suddenly came to life when a Canadian Broadcasting Company camera team showed up, turned on its klieg lights, and began filming. As Alex Schmid recounts, "As soon as the cameras were on, the demonstrators began shouting 'Death to Carter', raised their fists, looked angry and burned American flags. After two minutes, the cameraman signalled the end of the 'take'. Then the same scene was done once more for the French-speaking Canadians, with the crowd shouting 'Mort a Carter.'"[42]

Cause and Effect? Terrorism, the Media, and Public Opinion

Clearly, terrorism and the media still remain bound together in an inherently symbiotic relationship, each feeding off and exploiting the other for its own purposes. The real issue, however, is not so much the relationship itself, which is widely acknowledged to exist, but whether it actually affects public opinion and government decision making, as the media's critics claim, in a manner that favors or assists terrorists. The answer is far more complex and ambiguous than the conventional wisdom on this subject suggests.

In the view most commonly, if somewhat reflexively, advanced by statesmen,[43] scholars,[44] and other critics, the media are either "the terrorists' best friends"[45] or, in former British prime minister Margaret Thatcher's well-worn metaphor, supplying "the oxygen of publicity on which [terrorists] depend."[46] The media are condemned for having "made the terrorists' task all too easy"[47] or accused of having "become the unwilling—and in some cases, willing—amplifier of the terrorists' publicity campaign."[48] Indeed,

Benjamin Netanyahu, Israel's prime minister, maintained in his 1986 book that "unreported, terrorist acts would be like the proverbial tree falling in the silent forest."[49] The obvious implication being made in all these assertions is that if the terrorists could somehow be starved of the publicity on which they thrive,[50] both their malignant influence and the frequency with which they act would be greatly reduced.[51]

This argument, while seductive in its simplicity, nonetheless ignores the fact that for all the attention and sensationalist coverage that the media lavish on terrorism, rarely is it positive. "I have seen no evidence," Lawrence K. Grossman, the president of NBC News at the time of the TWA hostage crisis, wrote in an article defending the media's coverage of that incident, "that audiences are ever taken in by the propaganda of terrorists who have blackmailed their way on to the television screen."[52] However self-serving or self-exculpatory Grossman's argument may be, it is not without foundation. Even scholars such as Walter Laqueur, who in one breath criticize the media for its unstinting coverage of terrorism, concede in the next that this has not led to more favorable public attitudes toward either terrorists or their causes.[53]

A study conducted during 1988 and 1989 by the renowned American think tank the RAND Corporation reached precisely the same conclusion. By surveying a nationally representative sample, it sought to identify empirically public perceptions of both terrorism and terrorists, and analyze how public opinion is affected by terrorist acts. The timing of the survey was particularly significant: it immediately followed a prolonged period of heightened international terrorist activity, characterized by repeated attacks on American targets abroad. These incidents (including the 1985 TWA hijacking) had also been heavily reported by the American press and broadcast media. Public awareness of the issue was therefore high. Indeed, terrorism had been a major news item throughout the five years preceding the study, and it had already been cited in a 1986 CBS News/*New York Times* opinion poll as the most important problem facing the United States by a margin of fifteen percentage points above any other problem, domestic or international. Despite the media's continual and often intense attention to terrorist activities over a period of years, however, the RAND study found that public approval for terrorists *"was effectively zero* [emphasis added]."[54]

At the same time, the study also revealed that even though the vast majority of Americans have little sympathy toward groups that sponsor or commit terrorist acts,[55] they nonetheless evince a profound and abiding fascination with both terrorists and terrorism. As the late Konrad Kellen explained, "People [may not] approve of terrorists any more than they approve of murderers. . . . But people are clearly intrigued by them."[56] This was made abundantly clear on May 5, 1986, when NBC's *Nightly News* broadcast an in-depth interview with Abul Abbas, the leader of the Palestine Liberation Front (PLF). Just seven months earlier, the PLF had shocked the world when it had seized an Italian cruise ship, the *Achille Lauro*, and then attempted to trade the vacationing passengers on board for fifty Palestinian terrorists imprisoned in Israel. In the course of the hijacking, the terrorists brutally murdered an American tourist confined to a wheelchair, Leon Klinghoffer, and cast his body into the Mediterranean. Eventually, the head of the PLO, Yasir Arafat, intervened and brokered a deal whereby the terrorists would allow the ship to dock at Alexandria and would release their hostages in return for receiving safe passage back to the PLF's base in Tunisia. U.S. Navy fighters, however, intercepted the Egypt Air plane carrying the four hijackers and forced it to land at a NATO air base in Sicily, where the terrorists were arrested by Italian police officers. The U.S. State Department subsequently announced a $250,000 reward for Abbas's capture and launched an international manhunt. In tracking down the fugitive terrorist leader and obtaining an exclusive interview with him, NBC had therefore succeeded where the U.S. government hitherto had failed. More to the point, the network disingenuously implied that its news staff had accomplished this feat entirely on their own and without Abbas's encouragement or assistance.[57] The extent of the media's symbiotic relationship with terrorism, no less than the public fascination to which both media and terrorists actively cater, could hardly have been more blatant. What was particularly striking about the NBC interview, however, was not simply the statesmanlike status that the network promiscuously accorded to a man whose hands, as the hijacking's mastermind, were arguably drenched in Klinghoffer's blood, but the preening self-importance that attended NBC's broadcast of this spectacle. "We like to interview all leaders," Grossman boasted. "I think it is important for the American people to understand, be informed and make their own judgements."[58]

Yet by no stretch of the imagination could (or should) Abbas be ranked with those world leaders whose views merit the most coveted prize on American television—a dedicated slot on a major prime-time news show. Abbas, in fact, was one of the least successful PLO commanders; his group's previous operations had featured episodes reminiscent of the Keystone Kops, with terrorists flying hot-air balloons and hang gliders, all of which had failed as miserably as the attempt to free the fifty prisoners through hijacking a luxury liner. Nevertheless, while Abbas may have been a failure as a terrorist, he certainly had a flair for a form of macabre showmanship that suited NBC and its audience's interests perfectly. In the incandescent glare of the camera's lights, the public and media fascination with terrorism transformed Abbas into the "media star of the moment" rather than the kidnapper and murderer that he really was.[59] Indeed, so far as many—perhaps most—viewers were concerned, the interview was doubtless more entertainment than news. Tasteless or inappropriate as the NBC broadcast may have been, then, it probably had little or no impact on most viewers' attitudes toward terrorists or terrorism, except perhaps to reaffirm their overwhelming negative impressions.

The phenomenon of public fascination with terrorism is by no means confined to American news audiences only. A Royal Ulster Constabulary (RUC) divisional commander quoted at a conference on terrorism and the media by his boss at the time, Chief Constable Sir John Hermon, rhetorically asked whether "a rapist in Hampshire or a burglar in Berkshire [would] be accorded the freedom through the [British] media to justify rape and burglary and be allowed to threaten more of the same."[60] The answer, as we all know, is obviously that he would not. However, the point is less the publicity showered on terrorism by the media than that terrorism patently *is* news—often in an international as well as a national context—in a way that these other crimes, mostly, are not. Perhaps Britons should have felt grateful that even after nearly forty years of violence and strife in Northern Ireland, terrorism remained so relatively infrequent an occurrence that it was still considered newsworthy.

But there is also an undeniably inherent element of drama in terrorism that seems to enable it genuinely to transcend the mundane and stimulate among audiences an almost insatiable interest, which the media of course actively encourage and feed. Thus, while the media may be guilty of constantly—perhaps at times even shamelessly—scrambling to fill a vacuum created by twenty-four-hour news channels, rolling news shows, and intense competition, the media neither exist nor function in a vacuum, and, like any business, they respond naturally to consumer demand. Whether this makes for good reporting or sound professional behavior on the part of print and broadcast journalists is another question. On this issue, too, the opinions of critics and audiences differ considerably.

As the lightning rod for much of the criticism directed at the media over its coverage of terrorism, the TWA crisis epitomizes for many the corrosive effect of terrorism on journalistic standards.[61] Reagan administration officials railed against the "media extravaganza" in Beirut that one senior political appointee claimed "gave irresponsibility and tastelessness a new meaning."[62] Even veteran newsmen, like NBC's Roger Mudd, cringed at what they too regarded as something of a "media circus."[63] Yet the American public disagreed completely. An ABC News/*Washington Post* poll conducted shortly after the TWA hostage crisis ended, for instance, found that more than two-thirds of Americans approved of the way television had reported the story,[64] while a Gallup poll from the same period revealed an even higher proportion in favor: 89 percent.[65] Nor were these strongly positive ratings ephemeral aberrations of opinion. Three-quarters of Americans surveyed a year later in a poll conducted by Gallup and the Times Mirror Corporation (which publishes the *Los Angeles Times*, among other newspapers) similarly expressed satisfaction with both television and the print media's reporting of terrorist incidents. Moreover, 71 percent of respondents regarded their country's news organizations as "highly professional."[66] These unequivocal responses, flying in the face of mostly genuinely deserved, if sometimes overheated, criticism, seem to confirm viewers' interest in terrorism stories primarily for their entertainment value—and their lack of interest in the terrorists or their broader message.

The media were further excoriated by both senior government officials and distinguished elder statesmen for the excessive attention focused on individual hostages and their families. "TV is probably going to cost the lives of a number of people in a dangerous situation like this sometime in the future,"[67] one unidentified presidential aide declared, echoing the frequently heard criticism that the intense coverage compromised administration efforts to free the hostages. However, nearly half of those surveyed in the Gallup/Times Mirror poll regarded the unrelenting attention devoted to the hostages as a positive development that ensured the hostages' safety and eventual release. As the wife of one hostage explained on a morning news show, "If we like it or not, television is a way . . . to put pressure where pressure needs to be put."[68] More than a few hostages wholeheartedly agreed. "Thank the Lord we're on our way," one declared as he boarded the flight that was to take him back to the United States, flashing the thumbs-up sign to a CNN camera crew filming his departure, and "thanks for all the coverage."[69] The former CNN reporter Jeremy Levin, who himself was kidnapped in Beirut by Hezbollah terrorists in March 1984, made the exact same point. Levin maintains that the extensive media attention focused on his plight during the eleven months he was held captive actually deterred his captors from killing him.[70] He also makes the discomforting argument that the longest hostage crisis—that of the Americans and other Western nationals (including Terry Waite, the Archbishop of Canterbury's special envoy) kidnapped by terrorists in Lebanon between 1984 and 1992—was also the one that had the least sustained media coverage.[71]

Seen in light of the above discussion, the accepted wisdom about the symbiotic relationship between terrorism and the media appears far less self-evident than is commonly assumed. While most terrorists certainly crave the attention that the media eagerly provide, the publicity that they receive cuts both ways. On the one hand, terrorists are indeed assured of the notoriety that their actions are designed to achieve, but, on the other, the public attitudes and reactions that they hope to shape by their violent actions are both less predictable and less malleable than either the terrorists or the pundits believe. For example, one of the IRA's main aims in abandoning its cease-fire in February 1996 was to convince the British public that the government was to blame for the breakdown of negotiations and thereby to put pressure on the prime minister to grant concessions to the nationalist position that the government was hitherto unwilling or unable to make. The result was equivocal—in large measure, perhaps, because of the unanimous condemnation heaped on the IRA and Sinn Fein by the British (and, arguably, the world) press for the Friday evening blast at London's Canary Wharf, which killed two people and injured hundreds of others. While 63 percent of people polled a week later thought that the government should still be willing to talk with Sinn Fein in order to find a way to restore the cease-fire, 89 percent nonetheless "overwhelmingly blamed" the IRA for wrecking the peace process. Sinn Fein and the IRA's well-oiled public relations machine in Northern Ireland were eventually able to put their spin (as noted above) on the reporting of this issue in the province. Their failure to achieve the same result on the mainland, however, was notable. As one analysis noted, "In isolation, those figures suggest television appearances since last weekend of [Gerry] Adams and other prominent Sinn Fein leaders have had little success in deflecting criticism."[72] This may also explain why the IRA was driven to escalate its bombing campaign throughout England during the weeks and months following the cease-fire's collapse. Indeed, until the change of government in May 1997, the IRA was resorting to the naked use of terrorism as a means to coerce the government back to the negotiating table, rather than to manipulate public attitudes in a manner usefully sympathetic to the nationalists' frustrations.

There are two areas in particular, however, where a clear causal relationship between terrorism and the attention it receives from the media has a negative effect on public and governmental behavior. The first is the public's perception of personal risk from terrorism, and the consequent effect on willingness to travel; the second is the time pressure imposed by the media, under which governments confronted with terrorist-created crises labor.

Action and Reaction: The Impact on Travel and Government Decision Making

When the RAND survey asked members of the American public in the late 1980s how likely they thought that they might be involved in several low-probability events, the results on terrorism were revealing. Although the majority of respondents were able accurately to gauge the relative risk involved—realizing that they were more likely to be involved in an automobile accident than a terrorist incident—the perceived difference in the likelihood of the two eventualities was far smaller than the actual difference in probabilities. For example, 71 percent thought it likely that they would be involved in a car crash—although the estimated actual probability is just 19.2 per 100,000 people. By comparison, while only 14 percent thought that they were likely to be flying on a plane that is hijacked or the victim of a terrorist bombing, the actual chances of being hijacked are fewer than one in 100,000 (no similar statistics for bombings were available). Viewed from another perspective, 47,087 persons were killed in automobile accidents in the United States during 1988 and 45,582 during 1989 (the two years during which the RAND study was conducted), while 203 Americans were killed in terrorist incidents throughout the world in 1988 (93 percent of them perishing in a single incident, the December in-flight bombing of Pan Am Flight 103 over Lockerbie), and 23 in 1989. Indeed, an American was just as likely to be killed by a dog as by a terrorist in 1989; yet nearly a third of those surveyed that year stated that they would refuse the opportunity to travel abroad because of the threat of terrorism. There is no statistical evidence whether an identical percentage had similarly concluded that it was now equally dangerous to keep dogs as pets.[73]

The distortion in perception that results in higher probabilities' being accorded to terrorism than to other life-threatening acts is in large measure doubtless a direct reflection of the disproportionate coverage accorded terrorism by the American media. Indeed, at one time during the 1980s the American television networks were devoting more attention to terrorism than to poverty, unemployment, and crime combined—despite the fact that these were arguably more important political issues since they had a far greater and more immediate impact on the daily lives of most Americans.[74] The role of media coverage in fueling viewing and reading audiences' irrational fears of terrorism was dramatically demonstrated by the wave of cancellations of travel plans by Americans immediately following the TWA hijacking. Some 850,000 people canceled their travel and holiday reservations—both foreign and domestic—because of fears of becoming enmeshed in some terrorist incident. An additional 200,000 Americans rebooked their foreign holidays to U.S. destinations, on the assumption that their own country, at least, was still safe from terrorism.[75] The attack also had severe secondary consequences for local economies in foreign countries that were dependent on the tourist trade; for example, 50 percent of American bookings to Italy and 30 percent to Greece were lost. While the reluctance of Americans to visit the country from which the ill-fated TWA flight had departed (Italy) is understandable, as perhaps are their reservations about traveling to and from a nearby country whose airports at the time were widely criticized for their poor security (Greece), it is more difficult to explain why the peaceful Netherlands experienced an only slightly less startling drop in the number of American visitors (20 percent).[76]

To put the actual terrorist threat to Americans during 1985 into perspective: 6.5 million U.S. citizens traveled abroad that year, of whom 6,000 died from a variety of natural causes, accidents, and violence. Only 17 of these 6,000 people perished as a result of terrorist-related acts.[77] The chances of dying abroad were thus only 1 in 150,000 to begin with, and an almost infinitesimally small number as far as the risk from terrorism was concerned. Yet despite these overwhelmingly low probabilities, by February 1986 a total of 1.8 million Americans had changed their plans to go on vacation outside the United States.[78] Cancellations of Greek holidays booked by Americans more than doubled from the previous year[79]—even while British and Scandinavian tourism to Greece increased by 22 percent and 25 percent, respectively.[80] The number of American visitors to Britain itself fell by an astonishing 40 percent compared to the previous year's figure.[81] Indeed, 76 percent of Americans surveyed in April 1986 (following the in-flight bombing of a TWA passenger aircraft en route from Rome to Athens and the bombing of a West Berlin discotheque by Libyan agents) stated that the threat of terrorism had made it too dangerous to travel overseas that year—compared with 67 percent who had felt that way the previous July.[82] By the end of 1986, some 80 percent of Americans who had planned to travel abroad that year had canceled[83]—despite the fact that the fears generated by the threat of terrorism were grossly divergent from the real risk.

The effects of the nexus between the news media and terrorism on decision making go far beyond the question of U.S. citizens' overseas travel plans. A third revolution in the communication of news unfolded throughout the closing decades of the twentieth century to transform not only the way the world got its news but also the manner in which political leaders make decisions. This revolution was less dependent than its two predecessors on some new major technological breakthrough, deriving more from a concatenation of technological advances that have cumulatively changed the style rather than the mechanics of news presentation. The "CNN Syndrome"—a catchphrase coined in recognition of the Atlanta-based Cable News Network—has revolutionized news broadcasting through the emergence of dedicated round-the-clock "all the news all the time" television stations on both satellite and cable. In the time since, the CNN model of 24/7 news coverage has spawned a myriad of attendant, often connected, communications outlets—Internet news providers (e.g., CNN interactive; bbc.com; aljazeera.com, etc.), automated e-mail and fax news services, and news communicated over social media that now feed a worldwide audience with an insatiable appetite for information transmitted in real time and furnish immediate access to the actual locations and the people on the spot making the news.

The lasting power of this 1990s-era expansion of the communications mass media is attested to by the multitude of television sets that can now be found in the office of virtually every functionary and politician in official Washington, D.C.—from mid-ranking civil servants to Pentagon flag officers, CIA spymasters to Commerce Department officials, congressmen to the president—their screens glowing silently throughout the day until some event of sufficient magnitude occurs to warrant both the attention of their owners and the adjustment of the volume knob upward. "Our best intelligence is invariably the media," confessed Noel Koch, the deputy assistant secretary of defense responsible for counterterrorism during the Reagan administration, even as long ago as the mid-1980s. The ultimate accolade, however, was offered by Lieutenant Colonel Oliver North, the former National Security Council aide made famous for his pivotal role in the 1986 arms-for-hostages deal, who once said that "CNN runs ten minutes ahead of NSA"—comparing the privately owned cable company to the National Security Agency, America's super-secret electronic- and signals-gathering intelligence agency.[84]

The effects of this immediacy, however, are such that television became not just an opinion shaper but a policy driver, its presenters and on-air analysts racing to define the range of options at a government's disposal or to interpret likely public reaction—and its repercussions. As the late Lloyd Cutler, adviser to President Carter during the 1979–1980 Iran hostage crisis, once explained, "If an ominous foreign event is featured on TV news, the President and his advisers feel bound to make a response in time for the next evening news program."[85] Debate is not just precipitously joined, but abruptly rushed and then quickly truncated, depriving policymakers, government officials, and military commanders of the time needed to analyze critical issues thoroughly, reach well-thought-out decisions, craft coherent responses, and act with confidence based on exhaustive deliberation.[86] Governments are consequently increasingly pressured to respond to events before they can be evaluated fully, taking their cue from the "spin" that the media give them rather than working toward decisions made on the basis of all the available information. When asked in a 1993 interview specifically about the impact of the "CNN Syndrome" on government decision making, British prime minister John Major replied: "I think it is bad for government. I think the idea that you automatically have to have a policy for everything before it happens and respond to things before you have had a chance to evaluate them isn't sensible."[87]

The Clinton administration's experience during the last months of America's involvement in Somalia is a salutary reminder of both the overpowering influence of images flashed across the television screen and the hazards of decisions made on the basis of initial impressions and incomplete information. On October 3, 1993, a U.S. military operation to arrest Somali warlord General Mohammed Farah Aideed's paymaster and chief lieutenants went disastrously awry. Fifteen U.S. Rangers were killed and seventy others were wounded. In some of the most gripping footage broadcast on American television, an injured U.S. army helicopter pilot was seen being paraded through the streets of Mogadishu by a chanting, gun-wielding Somali mob. Reacting quickly to the incident—while scrambling to preempt criticism by Congress, the media, and the American public—President Clinton announced within days the immediate dispatch of military reinforcements to Somalia, but set March 31, 1994, as the firm date for the withdrawal of all American forces there—regardless of whether the multinational UN-led humanitarian aid mission to that country had in fact been successfully completed by that date. A USA Today/CNN/Gallup poll taken shortly after the incident validated the president's fears that a majority of Americans would hold him and his administration responsible for pursuing an ill-conceived humanitarian aid mission that had now cost the lives of more than a dozen troops. Fifty-two percent of those polled thought it was a mistake to have become involved in Somalia in the first place (a decision, in fact, made by the outgoing Bush administration), with 57 percent opposing Clinton's decision to send reinforcements.[88] An ABC News poll revealed similar results.[89]

However, upon closer—and more sober—inspection, many of these results appear less conclusive. For example, according to the USA Today/CNN/Gallup poll, 50 percent of those questioned in their survey who stated that they wanted U.S. troops immediately withdrawn had watched the television coverage of the injured helicopter pilot being led by Somali militiamen past jeering crowds and had been particularly incensed by the spectacle. But among those polled who hadn't seen the broadcasts, only 33 percent favored withdrawal.[90] In addition, 49 percent of Americans surveyed in a subsequent ABC-TV poll actually disapproved of the president's decision to set a withdrawal date, compared with 45 percent who approved it,[91] while a poll conducted later that same week by the University of Maryland's Program on International Policy Attitudes found that only 28 percent of its nationwide sample favored immediate withdrawal, with 43 percent stating that they thought U.S. forces should remain in Somalia "until we have stabilized the country"—even, if necessary, beyond the stated withdrawal deadline.[92]

Accordingly, in retrospect it appears that because of the raw emotions generated by the widely televised scenes depicting the brutal treatment of the captive helicopter pilot, the president may well have been stampeded into a decision that did not necessarily reflect public opinion. John Chancellor, a former senior commentator on NBC News, once one of the towering figures of American network news, tried to distinguish between television's perennial search for dramatic footage and the responsibilities incumbent upon reporters. "You have journalism, which is thoughtful and considered," Chancellor observed, "and you have what I call 'electronics,' which is the use of our facilities to transmit pictures and words, but does not have a lot to do with journalism."[93] It is the convergence of the two that has fundamentally altered the context and content of the news, and has also at times exercised a distorted influence over both public opinion and official decision making. In this new era of mass media, where the information revolution has transformed communication worldwide as a result of breakthroughs in real-time, rapid communication, the rush to meet airtime and print deadlines, and the attendant inevitably hurried judgments and immediate decisions, may present still further opportunities for manipulation and influence by terrorists than have hitherto existed.

Conclusion

We live today in an age of sound bites and "spin," in which arresting footage or pithy phrases or tweets or Facebook posts are often valued above considered analysis and detailed exegesis—and are frequently mistaken for good journalism. One of the enduring axioms of terrorism is that it is designed to generate publicity and attract attention to the terrorists and their cause. It is, accordingly, an activity custom-tailored to mass media communication in the twenty-first century. Terrorist acts are only too easily transformed into major international media events—precisely because they are often staged specifically with this goal in mind. Their dramatic characteristics of sudden acts of violence exploding across the screen or the printed page, rapidly unfolding into crises and pitting enigmatic adversaries against the forces of law and order make these episodes as ideal for television as they are irresistible for broadsheet and tabloid journalist alike.

In Britain, the media and public fascination with terrorists is second perhaps only to that with the country's royal family. How else can one explain the small article that was featured on page 4 of the London *Times* on September 3, 1997, as part of its coverage of the Princess of Wales's tragic death, and the repetition of its content the following day as part of a larger article on page 6? Both described how Leila Khaled—the Palestinian terrorist who gained international notoriety as a result of her involvement in the in-flight hijacking of a TWA flight in 1969 and of an El Al passenger jet the following year—had been touched by the princess, to whom she dedicated a poem that she sent to the princess' two sons.[94] Apart from the fact that there could be no two people more different than a former terrorist, whose actions on those two occasions deliberately endangered the lives of hundreds of innocent airline passengers, and a woman who is remembered in part for ameliorating the suffering of the innocent and infirm, that Khaled and her thoughts should be considered newsworthy is testimony to the powerful magnetic attraction exercised by terrorists and terrorism for the media in even the most unlikely (and absurd) circumstances.

For terrorists, media coverage of their activities is, as we have seen, something of a double-edged sword, providing them with the attention and publicity that they invariably seek, but not always in a particularly useful or even helpful manner. In this respect, while the 1985 TWA hostage crisis provides a clear lesson of how terrorists exploit and prompt the media for their own advantage, the denouement of the so-called Unabomber's seventeen-year terrorist campaign arguably demonstrates the opposite. The anonymous Unabomber—the name coined by the FBI in reference to his targeting of people associated with either universities or the airline industry—who killed three people and wounded twenty-three others using simple yet ingeniously constructed homemade bombs sent through the post, had promised in June 1995 to restrict his lethal terrorist campaign provided that either the *New York Times* or the *Washington Post* printed his entire manuscript and three annual follow-up messages. As a result of the publication the following September of his 35,000-word diatribe against technology, modernity, and the destruction of the environment in the *Washington Post*,[95] information subsequently came to light that led directly to the arrest of Theodore Kaczynski, a former University of California at Berkeley mathematician, who was charged with the bombings. Had the alleged "Unabomber" not been as obsessed with publicity as he was, he might never have been unmasked and arrested. As David Rapoport has observed,

The relationship between publicity and terror is indeed paradoxical and complicated. Publicity focuses attention on a group, strengthening its morale and helping to attract recruits and sympathizers. But publicity is pernicious to the terrorist groups too. It helps an outraged public to mobilize its vast resources and produces information that the public needs to pierce the veil of secrecy all terrorist groups require.[96]

While that bizarre case was not terrorism as most commonly understood, in that the Unabomber was a lone individual acting from a frustration and animus so profound that no other person could share them, it nonetheless demonstrates the complexity of terrorism's symbiotic relationship with the media. Moreover, it poses yet another formidable challenge to the almost unthinkingly accepted conventional wisdom about this relationship and underscores the need for critical, but subtle, distinctions to be made in this area.

Chapter 7

The New Media, Terrorism, and the Shaping of Global Opinion

Bin Laden's dramatic television appearance on October 7, 2001, as recounted in chapter 4, provided stunning confirmation of just how sophisticated terrorist communications in the twenty-first century have become. In contrast to the jerky, often amateurish videos or the older Super 8 film recordings typical of even the more communications-savvy terrorists of the past, bin Laden's prerecorded statement was remarkable for both its excellent quality and its perfect timing. Professionally produced, shot, and edited, the clip was masterfully packaged and queued to go on air as soon as the anticipated U.S. air strikes commenced that fateful Sunday.[1]

For bin Laden and his followers—and no less for other terrorists around the globe—the weapons of terrorism were no longer simply the guns and bombs that they always have used. Those new weapons included the minicam and videotape; editing suite and attendant production facilities; professionally produced and mass-marketed CD-ROMs and DVDs; and, most critically, the laptop and desktop computers, CD burners and e-mail accounts, and Internet and World Wide Web access that have defined the information revolution today.

Accordingly, the art of terrorist communication has evolved to a point at which the terrorists themselves can now control the entire production process: determining the content, context, and medium over which their message is projected and targeting precisely the audience (narrowcasting)[2] or multiple audiences (broadcasting) they seek to reach. The implications of this development are enormous, challenging the monopoly on mass communication of the terrorist message that has long been exercised by commercial and state-owned broadcasting outlets. Hence, much like previous information revolutions—such as the invention of the rotary press in the mid-nineteenth century and the advances in television equipment that made possible the reporting of events in real time in the 1960s—that also profoundly affected terrorist and insurgent external communications, a new information revolution has occurred to empower these movements with the ability to shape and disseminate their own message in their own way, enabling them to completely bypass traditional, established media outlets. As Tina Brown, the doyenne of postmodern media, observed, the "conjunction of 21st-century Internet speed and 12th-century fanaticism has turned our world into a tinderbox."[3]

Violence as Communication

One of the enduring axioms of terrorism is that it is designed to generate publicity and attract attention to the terrorists and their cause. Terrorism, as was discussed in chapter 6, is widely seen as a violent act that is conceived specifically to attract attention and then, through the publicity it generates, to communicate a message.[4] The terrorist must parlay this illumination (e.g., publicity) into a more effective vehicle of elucidation (propaganda). The centrality of propaganda[5] to this communications process and its importance to terrorist and guerrilla alike are self-evident.[6] As a 1991 RAND study on this subject observed:

> Propaganda grants authority to its makers. In the first place, simply by demonstrating its ability to disseminate information that the government has banned, a guerrilla group proves that it is a viable force. Second, once a group has the people's ears and eyes it can manipulate their minds, causing them to act as they might not otherwise; or if it does not work as effectively as this, its messages at least command the attention of those who read, hear or see them. In words and pictures, those whose plans are hidden from public view can portray themselves any way they please. Furthermore, if appearing to play a particular role can win support, propaganda will help these guerrillas to become in fact the powerful forces that they claim to be.[7]

Through propaganda, terrorists seek to communicate a particular message to a particular target audience. The exact purpose of these communications can vary, depending on the message and the target audience(s) to whom it is directed. It can be didactic—designed to inform, educate, solicit support (whether material, financial, or spiritual), and ultimately rally the masses behind the terrorists or insurgents. It can be a vehicle for recruitment—meant to win new converts to the cause or replenish the ranks of depleted fighters. But it can also be deliberately coercive—conceived to promote or ensure compliance through threat or blandishment. Furthermore, its intents can transcend mere tactical coercion and seek to intimidate strategically— that is, to undermine popular confidence in government and leadership, and thereby attempt to paralyze opponents with fear by trumpeting the terrorists' ability to strike at will while underscoring the inability of the government and security forces to provide effective defense or protection. Finally, it can serve an entirely internal function—what has been termed "auto propaganda"—when communications are directed toward members of the terrorist group in order to strengthen morale, dampen dissent, or justify and legitimate or explain particularly controversial decisions or operations.[8]

In sum, propaganda is directed toward a committed audience to strengthen resolve or toward an uncommitted audience to win sympathy and support. It can be variously focused on the terrorists' or insurgents' actual or would-be constituents, the public at large, the enemy government, its bureaucratic minions and security forces, or even inwardly on the underground fighters themselves as a means to promote and enhance internal cohesion and morale.

The terrorist of the past used three principal means of facilitating this communications process:

- clandestine, rebel radio stations;
- underground newspapers, posters, flyers, and other publications; and,
- conventional, commercial, or state-owned mass media (e.g., television, radio, and the press)

Each of the above had its own attractions and limitations, dependent primarily on the degree of direct control and influence it provided the terrorist or insurgent group over a particular audience. For instance, the two means over which terrorists had the most control—their own clandestine radio stations and newspapers and other periodicals and publications—also generally had the most limited impact. They had either inherent technical and geographical constraints that inhibited reception and restricted the listening audience or publication problems that made mass production and wide distribution difficult, if not impossible.

The now totally anachronistic multimedia efforts of one of the Cold War era's more sophisticated Marxist-Leninist insurgent-cum-terrorist movements of the time, El Salvador's FMLN (Farabundo Marti Liberation Front) is a case in point. Its flagship newspaper, *Venceremos* (We will win) had a limited press run and thus a fairly narrow readership. Its usefulness, accordingly, was confined to reinforcing or guiding the political activities of already committed FMLN activists and supporters.[9] Its clandestine radio station of the same name was hardly more technically sophisticated or expansive in audience reach. Broadcasting over standard shortwave band radio transmission, with varying audio quality and mostly only to a loyal, nearby listening audience, ensured that the impact of Radio Venceremos was perennially both localized and limited.[10] Even less impressive were the external communications capabilities of the FMLN's U.S.-backed, anticommunist counterparts in neighboring Nicaragua. Radio Quince de Septiembre (Radio Fifteenth of September), the putative voice of the United States–backed Nicaraguan Contras (Nicaraguan Democratic Front), for example, was then bluntly described by one contemporary U.S. government observer as a "joke because of its basic broadcasting technology, amateurish copy, and numerically inconsequential listening audience."[11]

Given the constrained communications resources available to terrorists only one or two generations ago, it is not surprising that emphasis was often given to exploiting traditional mass media. But because of the limitations over control discussed in chapter 6, this was always at best a Hobson's choice: gaining exposure but only partially serving the terrorists' wider communication needs. By the mid-1980s, moreover, the latent romanticism of the underground fighter that at times had surfaced in some reporting was rapidly ebbing. In addition, the opportunities for terrorist exploitation were diminishing as new guidelines were imposed and more stringent self-policing was practiced in response to the wave of criticism leveled at the media.[12] Finally, for many terrorist and insurgent groups there was no escaping the fundamental bias toward the status quo evidenced by most commercial, and especially Western and state-owned, media. So long as editorial power was vested ultimately in the proestablishment, capitalist elite, many revolutionaries concluded, their message would always be diluted, misconstrued, or seized upon for its "entertainment" value rather than its didactic purposes.[13]

Then, in the 1990s, the advent of three new technological developments afforded terrorists the opportunity to break the stranglehold over mass communications hitherto enjoyed by commercial and state-owned media. These were

- the Internet,
- affordable, if not extraordinarily cheap, video production and duplication processes, and
- private, terrorist-owned television stations.

Terrorist and Insurgent Use of the Internet

Few technological innovations have had the impact of the Internet and the
World Wide Web. Beyond any doubt, in a comparatively short span of time,
they have revolutionized communications, enabling the rapid—often in real
time—pervasive, and most important, inexpensive exchange of information
worldwide. In terms of political activism, they have been something of a god-
send, providing an effective way for groups to promote what some observers
call a "global dialectic," a situation in which awakening, awareness, activism, and radicalism can be stimulated at a local level and then mobilized
into a wider process of dissent and protest.[14] "Groups of any size, from two
to millions," Dorothy E. Denning, of the Naval Postgraduate School, points
out, "can reach each other and use the Net to promote an agenda. Their
members and followers can come from any geographical region on the
Net, and they can attempt to influence foreign policy anywhere in the
world."[15] That sort of reach is one dramatic advantage that the Internet
provides; speed is another. As a human rights activist working for an East
Timor refugee NGO (nongovernmental organization) explained in a 1996
interview:

> Using "old" communications, vital information could take weeks before
> it reached us. Often we had to wait for the first refugees to arrive. Then
> their accounts were written down and sent by mail. It could take days and
> weeks before they reached Australia or the USA. So, when the "news" of
> a massacre finally arrived at the newsdesk, the so called news was already
> old. With the arrival of new media and in particular, the Internet, this
> whole process might take just a few hours.[16]

Indeed, as is described below, a variety of terrorist and insurgent groups
were quick to exploit this feature as a means of mobilizing international support and pressure, and actively enlisting international humanitarian relief
organizations and other NGOs on their behalf.

In addition to ubiquity and timeliness, the Internet has other advantages.
It can circumvent government censorship, messages can be sent anonymously

and also quickly and almost effortlessly, and it is an especially cost-effective means of mass communication.[17] It also enables terrorists to undertake what Denning has termed "perception management."[18] In other words, they can use it to portray themselves and their actions in precisely the positive light and flattering context they wish—unencumbered by the filter, editing, screening, censorship, and spin of established media.[19] The Internet also facilitates terrorist engagement in what has been referred to as "information laundering," taking an interesting or provocative video clip or sound bite, or both, and featuring them, focusing on them, and creating an "Internet buzz" about them in the hope that they will move into the mainstream press.[20] Finally, the Internet carries with it new and significantly enhanced fund-raising capabilities for otherwise illegal, underground entities. Financial contributions, in essence, are now "just a click away," with many sites providing banking details for cash transfers.[21] In this respect, the Internet has proved to be an especially beneficial communications medium for terrorists—a key means for both external propaganda and internal command and control and information purposes.

The first group to successfully harness the power of the Internet was arguably the Zapatista National Liberation Army (EZLN), known more familiarly simply as the Zapatistas.[22] The group, it should be emphasized, is *not* a terrorist organization but an insurgent movement. Nonetheless, its effective exploitation of the Internet at the beginning of the 1990s was subsequently emulated by other insurgent movements and terrorist groups alike. As the Zapatistas themselves boasted in a Web posting accessed in June 2005:

> The international circulation through the Net of the struggles of the Zapatistas in Chiapas, Mexico has become one of the most successful examples of the use of computer communications by grassroots social movements. That circulation has not only brought support to the Zapatistas from throughout Mexico and the rest of the World, but it has sparked a world wide discussion of the meaning and implications of the Zapatista rebellion for many other confrontations with contemporary capitalist economic and political policies.[23]

The EZLN's insurrection commenced on New Year's Day 1994 in Mexico's rural and southernmost state, Chiapas. The government responded as it had countless times in the past: deploying military and police force to suppress the rebellion and hunt down the EZLN guerrillas. And, like countless peasant uprisings before it, the Zapatistas' revolt was likely to go mostly unnoticed by a world preoccupied with more pressing matters than the grievances of a couple of hundred landless indigenous Indians and mestizos in a long-impoverished and largely inconsequential corner of the country. As it turned out, the Zapatistas were not to be so easily brushed aside.[24] In addition to repulsing initial government efforts to dislodge them from the five towns and one city they occupied, the Zapatistas quickly demonstrated an unusual flair for external communications.[25] Their leader, the articulate and charismatic, ski mask–clad, pipe-smoking spokesman for the group who reportedly was a former philosophy professor at Mexico City's Autonomous Metropolitan University named Rafael Sebastián Guillén Vicente, and who adopted the more alluring nom de guerre of Subcomandante Marcos, pursued a novel tactic.[26] By appealing directly to Mexican civil society and specifically to local, national, and international peace activists, human rights groups, humanitarian relief organizations, and other nongovernment entities to support the Zapatistas' struggle, the EZLN created a powerful communal force to effectively lobby the Mexican government and challenge its historical stranglehold over Chiapas. Mobilization of, and through, the Internet thus created connections with other indigenous peoples, as well as with a variety of civil society groups that together pressed the government to implement the fundamental socioeconomic and political reforms that the Zapatistas demanded. Its two to four thousand–strong fighters were thus aided by literally tens of thousands of supporters and sympathizers scattered across the globe. The EZLN also encouraged these newfound national, regional, and international allies to travel to Chiapas to observe and monitor the conflict and act as a bulwark against government abuses and human rights violations. "This was not at all a conventional way to mount an insurrection," a 1998 RAND Corporation analysis observed.

Over the next fifteen months or so, the Zapatistas' mobilization strategy proved pivotal in halting government efforts to defeat the rebellion. Legend has it that, using a laptop computer that he carried in a backpack, Subcomandante Marcos plugged into the cigarette lighter socket of a Jeep or a truck and simply dialed up to log on to the Internet, enabling him to dispatch messages in real time to activists and supporters in Mexico City, the United States, Canada, and Europe. However, as Thomas Olesen concluded in his book, *International Zapatismo*, "there is no evidence as such that either the EZLN or Subcomandante Marcos [had] direct access to the Internet through modem or cellular phones."[27] Marcos, however *indirectly*, was nonetheless able to communicate quickly and effectively to reach a larger national and international audience than pre–Internet era insurgents could ever have hoped.[28] Indeed, the group's communication strategy was critical in blunting a major 1995 government offensive. "Information flooded out of the conflict zone," one account of the information counteroffensive reported. "The smallest of details, the slightest harassment of the civilian population, was spread to thousands of sympathisers and journalists all over the world. The result saw demonstrations and protests against the army offensive and concerned reports from human rights groups."[29]

Through their pioneering use of electronic "floodgate" tools and other denial-of-service measures,[30] as well as the forging of effective connections with activists, supporters, and sympathizers around the world, the Zapatistas were able to orchestrate a campaign of e-mail and fax bombardment directed at Mexico's president at the time, Ernesto Zedillo, and his minister of the interior, Esteban Moctezuma, which successively halted the offensive. "Before, we used faxes and telephones and it took forever," one sympathetic peace activist gushed. "Now the information arrives [with the snap of a finger]. The feedback is instantaneous."[31] So successful were the Zapatistas' mobilization efforts that in January 1995, President Zedillo proclaimed a truce and agreed to enter negotiations with the EZLN. As Mexico's foreign minister, Jose Angel Gurría, later reflected: "Chiapas . . . is a place where there has not been a shot fired in the last fifteen months. . . . The shots lasted ten days and ever since the war has been a war of ink, of written word, a war on the Internet."[32] Indeed, when Mexican security forces raided a collection of EZLN safe houses in Mexico City and Veracruz, they reportedly discovered "as many computer diskettes as bullets."[33] For Marcos, the message and significance of the Zapatistas' Internet strategy was clear. "This is a new type of warfare," he declared in an interview published in a British Internet magazine in 1996.[34] The Zapatistas used Internet-based "collective manifestations" that they themselves variously called or described as "electronic civil disobedience," "net strikes," and "mail bombs." As one observer of the EZLN's networking phenomenon explains, "The idea of these computer-mediated actions is to go beyond the sending of emails to figures such as politicians. The purpose, instead, is disruptive: for example, to flood mailboxes and overwork websites to the extent that they break down or become defunct for periods of time."[35] A 1998 Internet posting by the "New York Zapatistas" advocated "electronic civil disobedience," describing it as

applying the principles and tactics of traditional civil disobedience—like trespass and blockade—to the electronic systems of communication upon which Mexican government officials and their supporters depend. . . . We therefore urge that the following tactics be used against governmental, financial, and corporate sites responsible for the ongoing genocide in Chiapas. 1) Phone Zaps: Repeated calling to disrupt normal operations. 2) Fax Jams: Repeated faxing to overload fax machines. 3) Email Jams: Massive emailing to overload email inboxes and servers. 4) Virtual Sit-Ins: trespassing and blockading of web sites.[36]

Although it is impossible to detect a direct causal connection between the Zapatistas' success and the spread of Internet usage to other insurgent and terrorist groups, it is clear that around this time they began to awake to the power of electronic communications and their distinct advantage over other, older propaganda vehicles. Among the first were the LTTE (Tamil Tigers). The group established TamilNet.com in 1995,[37] and its success subsequently spawned several additional sites, including www.eelam.com,[38] www .eelam.net, www.eelamweb.com, www.tamiltigers.net, www.cantam.com, and www.canadatamils.net.[39] These servers were based in India, the United Kingdom, Norway, Canada, and Australia, among other places—all countries with sizable, existing Tamil émigré communities. Like the Zapatistas, the Tigers' initial presence on the Internet was motivated by a desire to present an alternative news and information source to the Sri Lankan state-controlled media.[40] The Sri Lankan government's imposition of press censorship coupled with the announcement of a new, major military offensive was what had specifically prompted the creation of TamilNet. As a Tiger spokesperson explained: "We all knew what would happen if the government started a large scale offensive in the heavily populated Jaffna region. At the same time, the Sri Lankan government and its media were engaged in a massive stream of propaganda trying to justify the war against the People of Tamil Eelam."[41]

The site was conceived to mobilize the support of the 450,000-member Tamil diaspora by providing them with breaking news from Eelam, the historical Tamil homeland in the north and northeast of Sri Lanka, where the fighting between the rebels and Sri Lanka Armed Forces had mostly occurred.[42] Like the Zapatistas, the Tiger site also sought to link up with international humanitarian relief organizations and various Tamil and non-Tamil NGOs. A 2005 survey of www.eelam.com's home page, for example, revealed links to topics such as the tsunami that devastated parts of Sri Lanka's coast in December 2004 and attendant LTTE-sponsored relief efforts ("Tsunami Disaster Relief: Please Contact Your Nearest Tamils Rehabilitation Organisations Office").[43] Home pages for other Tiger sites encouraged readers to "link to us" and provided instructions on how to do so. Like that of most other terrorist and insurgent organizations' sites, the Tiger's Web presence was primarily information-oriented,[44] with navigational bars that provided background and history about the Tamil people and the LTTE's struggle. These sites often also contained a map of the historical Tamil homeland in Sri Lanka; a history tab with further information on the Tamil people's long struggle for self-determination; a biography of the Tiger's founder and leader, Velupillai Prabhakaran; audio buttons through which recordings of "VOT: Voice of the Tigers" could be downloaded and listened to; LTTE press releases; daily news clips and links to other news sources; and a gallery of photographs of alleged atrocities inflicted by the Sri Lankan military on Tamil civilians. Features included profiles of the LTTE's feared women fighters, "freedom poems," and even an interactive online quiz. Finally, as on many other terrorist sites, merchandising—serving the dual purposes of fund-raising and morale boosting cum solidarity building—occupied a prominent place on the site. A variety of terrorist kitsch, including flags, calendars, videos, books, and pamphlets, was available for sale.[45]

TamilNet scored a huge public relations coup in the summer of 1996 when it convincingly refuted Sri Lankan army claims of having repulsed a Tiger attack on an important base at Mullaitivu at the cost of only about seventy government casualties. With credible reports from LTTE cadres coming directly from the scene via satellite telephone, TamilNet posted dispatches and stories that painted a completely different picture. Not only had the camp *not* been captured, but more than a thousand Sri Lankan soldiers had already been killed in the failed assault. As one analyst of terrorist websites at that time had observed:

> It's not unusual that two parties in a war have vastly differing stories. As it turned out, the Tamil Tigers were more accurate. A week later, the Sri Lankan Army admitted to losing the camp. Twelve hundred soldiers were also lost. This was a major breakthrough for TamilNet and the alternative news channels. Newspapers such as the *Washington Post* and the *International Herald Tribune* began quoting bulletins from the LTTE statements and were extremely suspicious of the official Sri Lankan Army news dispatches.[46]

Not surprisingly, the success of the Tiger websites prompted determined government attempts to shut them down.[47] One such effort in November 1997, however, backfired completely and resulted instead in denial-of-service attacks presumably launched by the Tigers against Sri Lankan diplomatic facilities worldwide in retaliation.[48] The embassies in Seoul, Ottawa, and Washington, D.C., were reportedly the worst affected, with e-mail unavailable at each for at least a week.[49]

By 2006, almost without exception, every major (and many minor) terrorist and insurgent groups had their own websites.[50] As a researcher at the U.S. government's Foreign Broadcast and Information Service (FBIS), now known as the Open Source Center (OSC), had commented as long ago as 2000, "These days, if you're not on the web, you don't exist."[51] Indeed, according to perhaps the preeminent expert in the field of terrorist communication and the Internet, Gabriel Weimann, in 1998 fewer than half of the thirty groups that the U.S. State Department designates as Foreign Terrorist Organizations (FTOs) had websites, but by the end of the following year, nearly all of them did.[52] The presence of terrorist groups on the Internet increased dramatically over the next four years, so that by 2003 Weimann had identified 2,600 such sites.[53] Two years later, this number had nearly doubled (to 4,300),[54] and by 2013, Weimann was tracking nearly 10,000 sites.[55]

Despite the multiplicity and diversity of terrorist websites, they share a number of key characteristics. These sites are often notable for their colorful, well-designed, and visually arresting graphic content. In this respect, they seem intended particularly to appeal to a computer-savvy, media-saturated, video game–addicted generation. Most of the sites chart the terrorist group's history, its aims and objectives, and the depredations inflicted by an enemy state(s) or people(s) on the constituency it purports to represent. The sites also often contain biographies of the group's leadership, its founders, and key personalities; up-to-date news and accompanying feature stories; speeches, ideological treatises, and especially the organization's communiqués and other important statements. Ethnonationalist/separatist movements will also generally have maps of the contested territory they claim to represent or be fighting for. Virtually without exception, all sites studiously avoid focusing on or drawing any attention to either the violence or death and destruction that they are responsible for. Instead, issues such as freedom of expression and the plight of imprisoned comrades are highlighted.[56] In the case of the more sophisticated organizations, such as the LTTE and Hezbollah, multiple sites are maintained in different languages. Arab and Islamic groups, Basque and Irish national-separatist movements, religious cults, Marxist-Leninist and Maoist movements, European neo-Nazi groups, and al-Qaeda and its many affiliates and franchises could all be found on the Web.[57] Nonetheless, Arab and Islamic groups are regarded by knowledgeable observers to have long had the largest presence.[58] "That Internet usage by Islamists is growing is obvious," an article published in 1999 opined. "What is also obvious is that they will use it to promote their views, advance the strategies of the 'global Islamic movement' and organize their activities, which experience has shown are sometimes inimical to western security, and in a wider sense might also seek to subvert the security of the state."[59]

Middle East Arab terrorist organizations in particular are regarded as having been most prominently on the "cutting edge of organizational networking"; demonstrating an ability to harness information technology for offensive operations, as well as having proven adept in emulating the more typical propaganda, fund-raising, and recruiting purposes of other groups.[60]

Perhaps the preeminent group in this respect, and one of the first to harness fully the communications power of the Web, is Hezbollah. The group has often maintained as many as twenty different sites,[61] in three different languages: English, French, and Arabic.[62] Each site has a different purpose, orientation, and intended audience. The movement's Central Press Office and main Web page site, for instance, in the past could be accessed directly at www.hizbollah.org (it is no longer accessible).[63] It had the requisite background account of the struggle and history of the organization that is found on other terrorist and insurgent sites, as well as tabs presenting "statements on the resistance," "political declarations," press clips and releases, special focuses on the "occupied zone" (e.g., Israel) and on "hostages and wounded," as well as "speeches of the S.G."—that is, the movement's secretary general and spiritual leader, Sheikh Hassan Nasrallah.[64] Nasrallah, in fact, also maintains his own dedicated site containing postings in French,[65] English, and Arabic.[66] Readers were encouraged to contact the website and post their own views and opinions on the anti-Zionist struggle and alleged crimes committed by Israel and its armed forces.[67] This feature is apparently especially valued by Hezbollah. According to a group spokesman: "The service is very important for the morale of the resistance fighters. They are always very happy to know that people around the world are backing them."[68] Hezbollah in 2001 claimed that it was receiving forty thousand visitors to its sites per month.[69]

A more circuitous route was required in 2005 to find the Hezbollah Central Press Office site at http://almashriq.hiof.no/lebanon/300/320/324/324.2/hizballah, which today is actually more easily found.[70] While it is not dissimilar to the previous iteration, it does more obviously reflect the movement's redoubled bid for political legitimacy outside Lebanon.[71] For instance, the home page still features the same long statement titled "Hizballah—*social radicals* [my emphasis]," which describes the group's background and history, with an emphasis on its social welfare and political activities. Resistance, much less the movement's terrorist legacy and continuing armed operations, is prominently absent. The series of links to other Hezbollah documents, institutions, and sites that it offers includes such ostensibly benign topics as

- the movement's 1996 electoral platform,
- a 1997 message Hezbollah received from Pope John Paul II,
- the Emdad Committee for Islamic Charity,
- Al Manar TV, and
- the Al Jarha Association ("Getting by with a Little Help from a Friend: Beirut's al-Jarha Association Helps Wounded Resistance Fighters Build Themselves").

The "Hizbullah: Views and Concepts" section is similarly anodyne, address-ing issues such as "Hizbullah and Dialogue," "Hizbullah and the Political System in Lebanon," and, of course, "Hizbullah and Human Rights," among other subjects.

Other prominent Hezbollah websites include www.moqawama.org, which is still accessible and specifically focuses on attacks against Israeli tar-gets, and www.almanar.com.lb (*manar* is Arabic for "the Beacon"), the movement's television and radio station, which continues to post news re-ports, video clips, and other pro-Hezbollah panegyrics in Arabic, English, French, and Spanish.[72] Hezbollah also used the Internet and its television station, as well as other media outlets to promote and sell a video game called *Special Force* that its Central Internet Bureau claims to have labored for "two long years" to create (access to the site is now blocked).[73] "Pursue your enemy from position to position," one spot on al-Manar beckoned pro-spective purchasers. "Take part in making victory."[74] That Hezbollah intui-tively understood the market for such a game is evidenced by the claim that some ten thousand copies were reportedly sold in Lebanon, Syria, Bahrain, the United Arab Emirates, Canada, Germany, and Australia during the eight weeks following its release in March 2003.[75] An advertisement for the game, easily located on the Internet in June 2005, explained:

"SPECIAL FORCE" IS BASED ON REALITY, MEANING THAT THE GAME IS BASED ON EVENTS THAT TOOK PLACE IN A LAND CALLED LEBANON. LEBANON WAS INVADED BY "ISRAEL" IN 1978 & 1982, AND WAS FORCED TO WITHDRAW AND DID WITHDRAW IN THE YEAR 2000. AFTER THAT WE DECIDED TO PRODUCE A GAME THAT WILL BE EDUCATIONAL FOR OUR FUTURE GENER-ATIONS AND FOR ALL FREEDOM LOVERS OF THIS WORLD OF OURS.

"Special Force game," it concludes, "will render you a partner of the re-sistance."[76] Features included a training simulation, where players could hone their shooting skills by firing at targets of then Israeli prime minister Ariel Sharon and then minister of defense and former IDF chief of staff Shaul Mofaz. The qualification medal for excellent marksmanship that follows is then awarded by a simulated Sheikh Nasrallah. The game's main attraction, however, was doubtless the assaults on IDF positions and tanks that test a player's skill at avoiding land mines and snipers, and shooting down attack helicopters to accomplish the mission. "Thank you," stated the registration card that comes with *Special Force*. "The Designers of 'Special Force' are very Proud to provide you with this special product which embodies objectively the defeat of the Israeli enemy and the heroic actions taken by the heroes of the Islamic Resistance in Lebanon."[77] As Bilal Zain, a member of the game's design team, explained, through the medium of entertainment *Special Force* sought to convey Hezbollah's "values, concepts and ideas."[78] Accordingly, instructions for play were available in Arabic, English, French, and Farsi. "Be a Partner in the Victory . . . ," the liner notes on the video case state. "Fight, Resist, Destroy Your Enemy in the Game of Force and Victory."[79]

The Palestinian group Hamas has had a similarly strong presence on the Internet. Although its original website did refer to the group by name (www .hamas.org), like Hezbollah, Hamas also relied on another, more generic, moniker—in this case, "Palestinian Information Center."[80] In the past, additional links have been provided through such general information sites as the Ohio-based MSANews (originating at Ohio State University) and from groups such as the Islamic Association for Palestine.[81] Observers often cited the professionalism, excellent content, and clean and fluid English and Arabic prose found on the site. Indeed, for these reasons, Israeli authorities regarded the website as a very effective communications vehicle for the group.[82] In the past, the site has very adroitly featured interviews with the father of Muhammad al-Dura, the twelve-year-old Palestinian boy who was allegedly shot to death shortly after the al-Aqsa Intifada began in October 2000 at an Israeli–Palestinian border crossing as the father vainly attempted to shield him from the bullets flying around them,[83] along with photographs of wounded Palestinian babies in hospital and other depictions of IDF mistreatment of Palestinian youths.[84] The site also posted copies of the Hamas Covenant in what was reported to be an excellent, verbatim English translation, various communiqués of attacks and messages from Hamas's military wing, the Izz al-Din al-Qassam brigades, and a daily account or running diary of the wing's operations.[85] A more nefarious purpose was reported by observers of terrorist Internet usage: the reported communication of operational instructions through steganography—the clandestine concealment of messages and other information embedded in images and other visual displays[86]—and other activities meant to facilitate terrorist activities, including fund-raising and logistical and other support.[87]

Hamas's presence on the Internet was also maintained through sites such as IntifadaOnline.com,[88] which was active from 1988 until about a decade ago[89] and purported to "bring . . . you the Palestinian side of the story. We also advise you on how to help." Its home page once contained the familiar image of Muhammad al-Dura, wounded Palestinian babies in the hospital, Palestinian children being beaten and dragged through the street by IDF soldiers, IDF troops restraining a Palestinian teenager in a choke hold, and the ubiquitous image of a youthful Palestinian demonstrator facing an

Israeli tank. Scrolling farther down the page revealed photographs of Palestinian martyrs—including suicide bombers—and additional images of Palestinian babies injured in Israeli violence.[90] The site featured the compelling image of a Palestinian youth hurling a stone at an IDF tank, thus deliberately evoking the enduring memory of the lone Chinese pro-democracy demonstrator who faced down a Chinese tank at Tiananmen Square in 1989. Under the headline "Justice, Freedom, and Peace," alongside banners the color of the Palestinian national flag, additional links were provided to translations in twenty-two languages—including Arabic, Danish, Dutch, English, Farsi, French, German, Greek, Japanese, Korean, Malay, Norwegian, Russian, Spanish, Turkish, and Urdu.[91] Links were provided to websites providing additional news and information on the Palestinian struggle, poetry, and the websites of mainstream established news media, such as the BBC and CNN. Navigational bars also direct viewers to

- stories and pictures,
- explanations such as "Why Intifada?"
- other news items about the Intifada,
- a discussion of the nefarious "silencing of the Intifada," and
- information on how to "be part of Intifada."

The last link encouraged visitors to participate in demonstrations, write letters to their elected officials and newspapers, and boycott Israeli goods. Instructions were also given on how to add Hamas links and banners to one's own site.[92]

Until the summer of 2002, an affiliated Hamas site, www.qassam.net, actively solicited donations for the explicit purpose of purchasing AK-47 assault rifles, dynamite, and bullets with which "to assist the cause of jihad and resistance until the [Israeli] occupation is eliminated and Muslim Palestine is liberated." Donations in the amount of US$3 for bullets, US$100 per kilogram of dynamite, US$2,000 for an AK-47, and US$12,000 for a rocket-propelled grenade launcher were reportedly suggested. Prospective donors were invited to contact an address on a website that provided instructions for transferring money to a Gaza-based bank account. The name on the account and the account number were said to change every forty-eight to seventy-two hours. A message addressed to the would-be donor stated: "Dear Donor: Please tell us the field in which you prefer your money to be spent on such as: martyrdom attacks; buying weapons for the mujahadeen; training the youth; or inventing and developing missiles, mortars [and] explosives."[93]

Hamas reportedly maintained some twenty active sites at the end of 2004.[94] Among them was a site in Arabic, www.sabiroon.net, extolling terrorist operations, including suicide bombings; another for a radio station associated with Hamas (al-Aqsa Voice), at www.aqsavoice.com; and one featuring the movement's children's magazine, *al-Fateh*, at www.al-fateh .net.[95] Like Hezbollah, for a time Hamas also maintained a dedicated site for its leader, Abd al Aziz al Rantisi (www.rantisi.net), who succeeded Sheikh Yasin following his assassination in March 2004. The site for Rantisi, who was killed shortly after Yasin, was hosted by an American server.[96] It could not be accessed as of June 2005. The PIJ, Hamas's counterpart, has a considerably less extensive presence on the Internet—but at the time still maintained six sites.[97]

In addition, Muslim—but non-Arabic and non–Middle Eastern—sites have also had an active presence on the Internet. The most sophisticated have been websites of various radical Pakistani organizations such as Lashkar-e-Taiba (Army of the Pure), Harakat ul Mujahideen (Movement of Warriors), Harakat al-Ansar (Movement of the Partisans), and the London-based Hizb ut Tahrir (Party of Liberation),[98] which itself has maintained upward of twenty different sites. According to the aforementioned FBIS analysts, Hizb ut Tahrir had a "bigger presence on the Web than in life." Nonetheless, the multiplicity of its sites and the sophistication of its Web design and content have made it an important resource on radical Islamic ideology. Although the majority of the Pakistani-based groups once had relatively anemic and poorly designed sites (e.g., Hizb ul Mujahideen, Harakat al-Ansar), Lashkar-e-Taiba was always an exception. Its Web designers were not only proficient but also capable of posting content in multiple languages— English, Arabic, and Urdu.[99] Audio links on the site provided connections to Radio al-Jihad and Mercaz al-Dawa.[100] Fund-raising was a prominent feature on the Web for Lashkar and other groups, with banking details and instructions provided for direct deposits into the group's account.[101] An entreaty on the site described how the group's holy warriors were engaged in fighting the "oppressive Hindu Army in the snow covered valleys, mountains and jungles of Kashmir. These Mujadhideen best deserve your charity."[102] The site was visceral in its enmity toward what its authors defined as Islam's triumvirate of most-hated opponents: India, the United States, and Israel.[103] According to Jessica Stern, in the past one of Lashkar's sites included a "list of purported Jews working for the Clinton administration," listing staff such as Robert Nash, who was then director of presidential personnel (a non-Jewish African American), and George Tenet, the former director of the Central Intelligence Agency (a Greek American).[104]

Finally, the generic websites for radical Islamic ideology maintained more than a decade ago out of London and other places in the United Kingdom provided an additional vehicle for the dissemination of propaganda and solicitation of philanthropic contributions. Principal among these were www .azzam.com and www.kawkaz.com, which later became www.kavkaz.com. and www.kavkazcenter.com.[105] Azzam.com's real sponsor is unknown. It was posted in the name of Azzam Publications, a reference to Abdullah Azzam, the aforementioned theologian and propagandist who became bin Laden's mentor in the early 1980s and was assassinated in 1989.[106] The azzam.com site was openly dedicated to global jihad and actively solicited contributions for the Taliban and Chechen guerrillas fighting against Russian forces. A message in early 2001 stated how an "Appeal for cash donations" to the Taliban "is especially urgent." It suggested a minimum US$20,000 contribution and provided advice on how to deliver it personally to the Taliban consul general in Karachi, Pakistan.[107] This site also had long served as a mouthpiece for bin Laden and al-Qaeda.[108] Indeed, azzam.com postings in 2002 urged Muslims to come to Pakistan and Afghanistan to fight against the "Jewish-backed American Crusaders." It also provided these would-be recruits with useful practical travel information on how to unobtrusively leave one's job and how to avoid arousing suspicion from employers, diplomats issuing visas, and inquisitive border and immigration officials.[109]

The kawkaz website was similarly devoted to fund-raising for both the Taliban and the Chechens—as well as encouraging volunteers to travel to Afghanistan and Chechnya to fight for Islam. The goal of raising US$10 million per month for the Taliban was once encouraged. As large sums had already been successfully raised for the Chechens, the aforementioned FBIS analysts did not regard this pretension as entirely "unrealistic." The site contained translations in some sixteen different languages and was sophisticated in design and message. According to the FBIS analysts, the Chechen site provided an "example par excellence of where we are in a new era of propaganda."[110] It has continued to operate as www.kavkaz.org.uk and ww.kavkazcenter.com, under the banner "News—Facts—Analysis," with postings in three languages (Russian, English, and Turkish). Its main focus was on Chechnya and Chechen mujahideen issues, and in 2005 and 2006 also presented information and news about the insurgency in Iraq. Other tabs linked to a photo gallery, videos, sections titled "Analysis," "Talking Points," "Chat," and opportunities for cooperation. Among the postings on its home page were articles such as "Russians turn Chechen orphans into zombies" and "21 invaders, collaborators eliminated in Chechnya." Online polls also asked readers whether the alleged 2005 energy crisis in Moscow is the result of: (a) an "Act of sabotage," (b) "Technical problems," or (c) "Human error." In addition, there were links to at least six other sites, including www.kavkaz.tv, www.kavkazcenter.com, www.kavkazcenter.net., and www.kavkazcenter.info.[111] As one U.S. government observer of the terrorism Internet phenomenon noted in the context of the kavkaz sites, "Never in history has there been an opportunity where propaganda is so effective."[112]

Al-Qaeda, in fact, was unique among all terrorist groups in this respect: from the start, its leadership seems to have intuitively grasped the enormous communicative potential of the Internet and sought to harness this power both to further the movement's strategic aims and to facilitate its tactical operations. The priority that al-Qaeda accorded to external communications is evidenced by its pre-9/11 organizational structure. One of the original four al-Qaeda operational committees was specifically charged with media and publicity (the others were responsible for military operations, finance and business, and fatwa and Islamic study).[113] Egyptian computer experts who had fought alongside bin Laden in Afghanistan against the Red Army during the late 1980s were reportedly specifically recruited to create the extensive network of websites, e-mail capabilities, and electronic bulletin boards.[114]

The Internet has thus long facilitated three critical functions for al-Qaeda:

1. Propaganda for recruitment and fund-raising, and to shape public opinion in the Muslim world
2. Terrorist training and instruction
3. Operational planning for attacks through both e-mail communication and the access it provides to an array of useful open source information

Each assumed great importance in the immediate post-9/11 era and the loss of Afghanistan as a physical sanctuary. For al-Qaeda, the Internet became something of a virtual sanctuary, providing an effective, expeditious, and anonymous means through which the movement can continue to communicate with its fighters, followers, sympathizers, and supporters worldwide. For example, before 9/11, al-Qaeda had only one website: www.alneda.com. In 2005, the movement was present on more than fifty different sites.[115] "The more websites, the better it is for us," a jihadist statement posted on azzam .com in 2002 proclaimed. "We must make the Internet our tool."[116]

Initially, as already stated, www.alneda.com fulfilled this requirement.[117] The site, which was published in the Arabic language only (as indeed are all the hard-core jihadist sites), emphasized three core messages that remain the basic staple of al-Qaeda and other jihadi websites today:

- First, that the West is implacably hostile to Islam;
- Second, that the only way to address this threat and the only language that the West understands is violence;
- Third, that jihad, therefore, is the only option.[118]

In support of these arguments, the theory of jihad was elaborated on in great theological and legalistic detail. The obligation of all Muslims both to protect and to spread Islam by the sword was a particular focus of online treatises. In addition, summaries of news affecting the Islamic struggle against the West, al-Qaeda's own accounts of ongoing fighting and skirmishing with American and allied forces both in Afghanistan and in Pakistan, and suggested readings—including books by authors approved by al-Qaeda theoreticians—could be found on the site.[119] Lengthy justifications for the 9/11 attacks were also posted. Video clips and other messages extolling the operation were featured, accompanied by Islamic juridical arguments sanctioning the killing of innocents. Like other terrorist sites, poems glorified the sacrifices of al-Qaeda martyrs and waxed eloquent on the unrelenting defensive struggle being fought against Islam's enemies.

During the period immediately following the 9/11 attacks, when al-Qaeda suffered a series of stunning reverses, culminating in the loss of Afghanistan as a base, alneda.com also performed an invaluable morale-boosting purpose by trying to lift the spirits of al-Qaeda fighters and shore up support among its sympathizers. According to British journalist Paul Eedle, a February 2002 Internet posting contained the names and home phone numbers of eighty-four al-Qaeda fighters being held by Pakistani authorities "presumably with the aim that sympathizers would contact their families and let them know that they were alive."[120]

The alneda.com site was also used to call Muslims' attention to the alleged control, suppression, and censorship of information about the jihadist struggle by the West and established media outlets. "The U.S. enemy, unable to gain the upper hand over the mujahadeen on the battlefield," one June 2002 statement explained, "has since Sept. 11 been trying to gag the world media. The more the United States tries to stifle freedom of expression, the more determined we will become to break the silence. America will lose the media war, too."[121] Another, titled "America Nears the Abyss," compared the damage wrought to the U.S. economy by the 9/11 attacks to the struggle prosecuted by the mujahideen in Afghanistan during the 1980s that, it maintained, had set in motion the chain of events that led to the collapse of the Soviet Union and the demise of communism. The same fate, it predicted, would befall the United States, and it cited the weakening American dollar, the parlous state of the U.S. stock market, and the erosion of confidence both at home and abroad in the American economy.[122] Indeed, as previously noted, bin Laden long argued that the United States was poised on the verge of financial ruin and total collapse much as the U.S.S.R. (Union of Soviet Socialist Republics) once was—with the force of Islam ensuring America's demise much as it achieved that of the Soviet Union two decades ago. When bin Laden addressed his fighters as they fled Afghanistan in December 2001, he struck the same defiant note. "America is in retreat by the grace of God Almighty and economic attrition is continuing up to today," he declared. "But it needs further blows. The young men need to seek out the nodes of the American economy and strike the enemy's nodes."[123]

The alneda.com site continued to function sporadically throughout 2002, repeatedly moving from one Internet service provider to another to circumvent the efforts of the United States and other governments to shut it down completely. In its death throes that summer, it shifted during one eight-week period from a provider in Malaysia to one in Texas and then to one in Michigan before disappearing completely.[124] Afterward, a variety of online magazines maintained al-Qaeda's presence on the Net. The first appeared shortly after 9/11 and featured a series of articles titled "In the Shadow of the Lances." Initially written by the movement's putative spokesman, Suleimain Abu Ghaith, the first five issues were mostly theological or ideological treatises. Typical were discussions reiterating how "America does not understand dialogue. Nor peaceful coexistence. Nor appeals, nor condemnation, nor criticism. America," Abu Ghaith argued, "will only be stopped by blood."[125] In February 2003, however, as the U.S.-led invasion of Iraq loomed imminent, authorship of the series abruptly changed from Abu Ghaith, the theoretician and philosopher, to Saif al-Adel, the warrior. Al-Adel, one of the movement's most senior operational commanders and a former Egyptian Army Special Forces officer who joined al-Qaeda as a result of the 1998 merger with Ayman al-Zawahiri's Egyptian Islamic Jihad, implored jihadists to descend upon Iraq—not to support Saddam Hussein but to defend Muslims against this latest instance of U.S. and Western aggression. He also dispensed detailed, practical advice on guerrilla operations and urban warfare tactics with which to engage—and ultimately defeat—the invading American and British forces in Iraq.[126] The virtues of guerrilla warfare were again lavishly extolled in a posting that appeared on alneda.com on April 9, 2003. Clearly written sometime after American forces had entered Baghdad, it cited prominent historical cases where numerically smaller and less powerful forces using guerrilla tactics had successfully challenged larger, better-equipped adversaries. Under the caption "Guerrilla Warfare Is the Most Powerful Weapon Muslims Have, and It Is the Best Method to Continue the Conflict with the Crusader Enemy," the statement foreshadowed the prolonged insurgency in Iraq, presciently explaining how

> with guerilla warfare, the Americans were defeated in Vietnam and the Soviets were defeated in Afghanistan. This is the method that expelled the direct Crusader colonialism from most of the Muslim lands, with

Algeria the most well known. We still see how this method stopped Jewish immigration to Palestine, and caused reverse immigration of Jews from Palestine. The successful attempts of dealing defeat to invaders using guerilla warfare were many, and we will not expound on them. However, these attempts have proven that the most effective method for the materially weak against the strong is guerrilla warfare.[127]

This mixture of ideology and propaganda alongside practical guidance on guerrilla warfare and related terrorist operations came to typify al-Qaeda's Internet profile in the years immediately following the 9/11 attacks.[128] With respect to the former, a new Internet magazine named *Sawt al-Jihad* (Voice of Jihad) appeared in February 2004, published by al-Qaeda's Saudi organization. Its message was less one of attacking U.S. and other Western targets than the importance of mobilizing Muslim public opinion and support of jihad.[129] Nonetheless, according to the late Israeli analyst Reuven Paz, an editorial titled "Belief First: They Are the Heretics, the Blood of Each of Them Is the Blood of a Dog" implicitly justified the slaughter of Americans. "My fighting brother," its author, Sheikh Naser al-Najdi, wrote,

> kill the heretic; kill whoever his blood is the blood of a dog; kill those that Almighty Allah has ordered you to kill. . . .
> Bush son of Bush. . . . a dog son of a dog . . . his blood is that of a dog. . . .
> Shut your mouth and speak with your other mouth—the mouth of the defender against his attacker.[130]

In Islam, dogs are considered to be among the most impure creatures, and true believers are forbidden to even touch one. Thus, the equating of President Bush with a dog is meant to be especially damning.

With respect to practical guidance, another online publication, also published by the al-Qaeda organization in Saudi Arabia, *Mu'askar al-Battar* (Camp of the Sword) sought to provide operational information. Its first issue, published in January 2004, explained how "in order to join the great training camps you don't have to travel to other lands. Alone, in your home or with a group of your brothers, you too can begin to execute the training program. You can all join the Al-Battar Training Camp."[131] The power of this particular communications vehicle appears to have been demonstrated by the influence that the March 2004 edition had on subsequent patterns of terrorist activities in Saudi Arabia and Iraq. Reportedly written by Abdul Azziz al-Moqrin,[132] the reputed commander of al-Qaeda's operations on the Arabian Peninsula until he was killed by Saudi security forces in May 2005, it singled out economic targets, especially those connected with the region's oil industry, as priorities for attack. "The purpose of these targets," Moqrin wrote,

> is to destabilize the situation and not allow the economic recovery such as hitting oil wells and pipelines that will scare foreign companies from working there and stealing Muslim treasures. Another purpose is to have foreign investment withdrawn from local markets. Some of the benefits of those operations are the effect it has on the economic powers like the one that had happened recently in Madrid where the whole European economy was affected.[133]

In the weeks that followed, al-Moqrin's strategy seemed to bear fruit. The U.S. State Department, for instance, advised American citizens to leave Saudi Arabia. After the murder in April 2004 of five expatriate workers at a petrochemical complex in the Saudi industrial city of Yanbu, foreign companies there were reported to have evacuated employees from the country.[134] These fears acquired new urgency with the attack in May on a housing complex in Khobar, where twenty-two foreigners were killed, and the execution by beheading in June of an American defense contractor, Paul M. Johnson Jr.[135]

This same targeting guidance also explains the spate of kidnappings and tragically similar executions of foreign contractors, diplomats, and aid workers in Iraq that commenced within a week of its release. The first victim was Mohammed Rifat, a Canadian, who was seized on April 8, 2004. During the following three months, more than sixty others were kidnapped. Although the majority were eventually released, five hostages were brutally murdered—most often by beheading, with the act itself filmed and posted on jihadi websites.[136] Among the dead was a young Jewish American businessman, Nicholas Berg. Al-Moqrin had deemed as a special priority "assassinating Jewish businessmen and teach lessons to those who cooperate with them [sic]." Indeed, al-Moqrin provided additional "practical examples" of how his targeting guidance should be implemented. The preferred hierarchy of targets was:

- "American and Israeli Jews first, the British Jews and then French Jews and so on."
- "Christians: Their importance is as follows: Americans, British, Spanish, Australians, Canadians, Italians."

Within these categories, there were further distinctions:

- "Businessmen, bankers, and economists, because money is very important in this age"

- "Diplomats, politicians, scholars, analysts, and diplomatic missions"
- "Scientists, associates and experts"; "Military commander and soldiers"; and
- "Tourists and entertainment missions and anybody that was warned by mujahideen not to go to step in the lands of Moslems."[137]

Indeed, the changing nature of terrorism in the twenty-first century was perhaps best exemplified by the items recovered by Saudi security forces during a raid on an al-Qaeda safe house in Riyadh used by a cell in al-Moqrin's network just weeks later. In addition to the traditional terrorist arsenal of AK-47 assault rifles, explosives, rocket-propelled grenades, hand grenades, and thousands of rounds of ammunition that the authorities expected to find, they also discovered an array of electronic consumer goods, including video cameras, laptop computers, CD burners, and the requisite high-speed Internet connection. According to CNN investigative journalist Henry Schuster, the videos "had been part of an al Qaeda media blitz on the Web that also included two online magazines full of editorials and news digests, along with advice on how to handle a kidnapping or field-strip an AK-47 assault rifle. The videos mixed old appearances by bin Laden with slick graphics and suicide bombers' on-camera last wills and testaments. They premiered on the Internet, one after the other, and were aimed at recruiting Saudi youth."[138]

The insurgency in Iraq between 2003 and 2010 arguably became the cynosure of this process of effective, mass audience, cutting-edge communications. According to analysts at the Alexandria, Virginia–based Intel-Center, within a couple of years more than a dozen terrorist and insurgent groups—both indigenous Iraqi insurgent organizations and foreign jihadists fighting there—were producing their own compelling videos.[139] They were either sold in DVD format at souks and bazaars throughout Iraq or posted either in part or in whole on the Internet. The films variously

- depicted scenes of insurgents using roadside bombs to ambush U.S. military forces on patrol in Humvees or firing handheld surface-to-air missiles (SAMs) at U.S. military aircraft flying overhead;
- imparted practical, tactical advice to insurgents (e.g., advising insurgents "to vacate the area no later than 10 minutes after launching an attack, before US forces zero in on their position") and instruction in the use of weaponry and the planning and execution of attacks;
- transmitted the last words of kidnapped Iraqis and foreigners about to be executed[140] and, in many instances, displayed gory footage of the executions themselves;[141]
- appealed for financial contributions;[142] and,

- perhaps most important, solicited recruits from the Middle East, South and Central Asia, North Africa, Europe, and even North America to come to Iraq to become "lions from the martyr's brigade."[143]

These so-called mujahideen films were but one manifestation of a much broader and highly sophisticated communications strategy. The more prominent insurgent organizations then fighting in Iraq, for instance, had themselves established dedicated information offices that in essence functioned as online press agencies, issuing communiqués, developing and posting new content for their websites (often several times a day), and generally updating and regularly replenishing news and other features. "The Iraqi armed opposition appear to make a priority of communication," two particularly knowledgeable observers of the insurgency in that country observed,

in ways that go far beyond the unique intention of terrorising the adversary. Combatant groups produce an astonishingly large and varied range of texts and images, which it would be wrong to reduce to their most brutal types. Besides the threatening tracts there is an impressive body of strategic analysis, cold-blooded, lucid and detailed. Similarly, the most monstrous video sequences eclipse a wealth of films, sometimes of professional quality, extending from "lectures" in classical Arabic on the manufacture of explosives to "advertising" material put out by new groups making their first public appearance.

The insurgents' intent was to explain and legitimate their use of violence (employing theological arguments and treatises, for example, to differentiate between "illicit terrorism" and "licit terrorism," and thereby justify their attacks); drive a wedge between the Iraqi people and the so-called collaboration authorities (e.g., the Iraqi interim government); undermine popular confidence in the ability of the Iraqi government and Iraqi security forces and the U.S. and coalition militaries to maintain order throughout the country; and, last, to facilitate communications between and among various groups in order to forge new alliances and cooperative arrangements, however tactical or short-lived.[144]

Finally, along with propaganda and training, al-Qaeda has also made extensive use of the Internet for intelligence-gathering purposes and targeting. The so-called Manchester Manual, the compendium of terrorist tradecraft assembled by al-Qaeda sometime during the 1990s, advises explicitly that "openly and without resorting to illegal means, it is possible to gather at least 80% of information about the enemy."[145] Indeed, *The 9/11 Commission Report* cites four specific instances in which KSM and the nineteen hijackers accessed information from the Internet to plan or facilitate the 9/11 attacks.[146] An al-Qaeda computer found by American military forces in Afghanistan contained architectural models of a dam in the United States and software with which to simulate various catastrophic failures, as well as programming instructions for the digital switches that operate American power, water, transport, and communications grids.[147] In March 2005, three British al-Qaeda operatives were indicted by a U.S. federal court on charges of having carried out detailed reconnaissance of financial targets in lower Manhattan, Newark, and Washington, D.C. In addition to videotaping the Citigroup Center and the New York Stock Exchange in New York City, the Prudential Financial building in Newark, and the headquarters of the International Monetary Fund and the World Bank in Washington, D.C., the men were alleged to have amassed more than five hundred photographs of the sites—many of which had simply been downloaded from the Internet.[148]

Video Production and Duplication Processes

Al-Qaeda and other terrorist groups have also made use of a variety of contemporary technologies to project their message—including computer CD-ROMs, DVDs, and the professionally produced digital video clips. Indeed, a two-hour al-Qaeda recruitment video that bin Laden had circulated throughout the Middle East during the summer of 2001—and that Peter Bergen argues subtly presaged the September 11 attacks—is just such an example.[149] The video, with its graphic footage of infidels attacking Muslims in Chechnya, Kashmir, Iraq, Israel, Lebanon, Indonesia, and Egypt; children starving under the yoke of United Nations economic sanctions in Iraq; and, most vexatiously, the accursed presence of "Crusader" military forces in the holy land of Arabia was subsequently converted to CD-ROM and DVD formats for ease in copying onto computers and loading onto the World Wide Web for still wider, global dissemination. Titled *The Destruction of the American Destroyer USS Cole*, the DVD version, except for the misspellings, choppy English translation, and tendentious message, had a color jacket sleeve and liner notes that appeared little different from the commercial videos that one once rented or purchased at the local video store.[150] "This tape are real life scenes that potray [sic]," the liner notes stated, "with blood and tears, the sorry state of the Muslim Nation. after [sic] revealing the illness, it goes on to discribe [sic] the cure, whils [sic] giving the glad tiding and hopes for the future as a means of encouragement to remain firm and be steadfast for the sake of the future generation."[151]

Other video productions that either al-Qaeda or its affiliated groups have distributed in the decade following the 9/11 attacks evidenced the same sophisticated production capabilities and accomplished editing. A particularly revealing sign of their professionalism is the way that videos depicting scenes such as the repugnant execution in 2002 of the journalist Daniel Pearl[152] or the last will and testament of Ahmed Ibrahim al-Haznawi, one of the September 11 hijackers, are all shot with a blue background. This technique enables an editor to insert contemporary news footage or evocative images at a later time and thereby enhance or put in a particularly powerful context the video's message.[153] The video clip of Daniel Pearl's brutal execution, for example, is intercut simultaneously with footage in the left and right corners of the screen depicting the widely televised alleged shooting death in October 2000 of the Palestinian child Muhammad al-Dura, as well as similar scenes of Israeli Defense Force operations involving Palestinian civilians. The tape of al-Haznawi, one of the hijackers aboard the American Airlines flight that crashed into the Pentagon on September 11, contained a date and place name beside his reproduced signature indicating that it was recorded in Khandahar, Afghanistan, around March 2001. Broadcast first by the Qatar-based Arab language news network al-Jazeera in mid-April 2002, the clip was similarly interspersed with contemporary footage showing Ayman al-Zawahiri lauding the 9/11 attacks as a "gift from God" with additional voice-over referring to the Arab League summit in Beirut that had been held two weeks earlier.[154] Both videos—like much al-Qaeda propaganda of that era—are noteworthy for the repeated references to, and depictions of, the suffering of Muslim children, whether in Palestine, Iraq, or elsewhere. It is hard to imagine a more potent propaganda tool, recruiting vehicle, or means to justify and legitimate violence than to focus on the maltreatment and abject condition of children.

It was not surprising, therefore, to find another professionally produced al-Qaeda recruitment video circulating around the Middle East in the spring of 2002 in an effort to attract new martyrs to bin Laden's cause. The seven-minute tape, seized from an al-Qaeda member by American authorities, reportedly opens with the image of a spinning globe with still pictures of dead men floating by and the words in Arabic: "They are the ones that say, (of their brethren slain), while they themselves sit (at ease:) 'If only they had listened to us, they would not have been slain.' Say: 'Avert death from your own selves if you speak the truth.' Think not of those who are slain in Allah's way as dead. Nay, they live, finding their sustenance in the presence of their Lord."

This is then followed by footage of mujahideen in battle, with depictions of the fighters' death and beneath it text reading, "Say not the martyr had died, for he is alive and happy lodged in eternal paradise." The video goes on to show more combat scenes, followed by the images of twenty-seven martyrs shown in rapid succession with the name of each listed, where he or she is from, and where he or she died. The narrator explains that they hailed from Algeria, Chechnya, Egypt, Jordan, Kuwait, Libya, Mecca, Medina, Morocco, Najd, Pakistan, Palestine, United Arab Emirates, and Yemen, and that they perished while fighting in Afghanistan, Bosnia, Chechnya, Dagestan, Pakistan, and Tajikistan, circa the early and mid-1990s. Twelve of the martyrs are then featured in a special segment accompanied by a voice-over saying, "They rejoice in the bounty provided by Allah: And with regard to those left behind who have not yet joined them (in their bliss), the martyrs glory in the fact that on them is no fear, nor have they (cause to) grieve." The video concludes with a message of greeting from the "Black Banner Center for Islamic Information," along with accompanying contact details and the Qur'anic invocation "There is no god but Allah, and Muhammad is Allah's messenger."[155]

Al-Qaeda, however, cannot claim credit for having pioneered the filming of jihadi attacks for propaganda, recruitment, and marketing purposes. That distinction is often credited to the infamous Saudi Arabian-born commander of Chechen fighters known by the nom de guerre Khattab. Khattab reportedly began to film his group's attacks on Russian military forces under the assumption that "if they killed a few Russian soldiers in an ambush along a road the impact of the strike was limited, however if the operation was filmed and then shown to the Russian people that impact was multiplied manifold." Khattab and his men thus videotaped any assault—whether involving ambushes, roadside bombings, kidnappings, or rocket attacks—and soon had enough footage to produce a forty-minute video titled *Russian Hell 1*.[156] Khattab's successors have continued this policy. During the August 2005 siege of a school in Beslan, Ossetia, by Chechen terrorists, a hostage reported that one of the attackers had "constantly filmed us."[157]

Social Media

Utilizing a variety of freely available social networking platforms such as Facebook, Twitter, YouTube, Instagram, and, Flickr, among others, terrorist and insurgent groups today have introduced an even more direct and personally intimate form of messaging. ISIS has positioned itself at the forefront of yet another revolution in terrorist communications. Indeed, since 2014, it has produced and disseminated a succession of increasingly more heinous and grisly propaganda videos of brutal executions and similar depredations that have captured the attention of a new generation of terrorist recruits. These videos, and their unrestrained exultation of violence, have attracted many more viewers than bin Laden's and al-Zawahiri's comparatively priggish presentations recanting complex theological treatises or imparting didactic philosophical and historical lectures.[158] "Where al-Qaeda and its affiliates saw the internet as a place to disseminate material anonymously or meet in 'dark spaces,'" Robert Hannigan, the director of the UK Government Communications Headquarters (GCHQ), the British counterpart of America's National Security Agency, notes, "ISIS has embraced the web as a noisy channel in which to promote itself, intimidate people, and radicalise new recruits."[159]

ISIS has thus been remarkably effective in its use of these social media to speak to a global audience, thereby completely bypassing and thwarting the traditional media from misinterpreting or otherwise distorting its core message. A common ISIS propaganda mantra, accordingly, is, "Don't hear about us, hear from us." These social media platforms facilitate both ubiquitous and real-time communication between like-minded radicals with would-be recruits and potential benefactors—the previously cited phenomenon of narrowcasting. "Also called 'niche marketing' or 'target marketing,'" Weimann explains that "narrowcasting aims media messages at specific segments of the public, defined by characteristics such as values, preferences, demographic attributes, or location."[160] Ease, interactivity, networking, reach, frequency, usability, stability, immediacy, publicity, and permanence are among benefits to terrorist groups such as ISIS, which have quickly harnessed and exploited these technologies for their nefarious purposes. "I don't think it is far-fetched to say that the internet is a major reason why ISIS is so successful, and so worrying," an unnamed American intelligence officer commented in a May 2016 article detailing ISIS's mastery of digital media and technology.[161]

It is, accordingly, now common for ISIS foreign fighters in Syria and Iraq, for instance, to individually amass thousands of followers on platforms such as Twitter, Facebook, Instagram, and YouTube.[162] They communicate with their audiences, often on a daily basis—and sometimes multiple times each day—providing firsthand, immediate accounts of heroic battles and more mundane daily activities, thus making jihad accessible and comprehensible on a uniquely intimate and personal basis.[163] These fighters invite, motivate, animate, and summon their digital media followers and friends and other online contacts to come to Syria and Iraq, and partake of the holy war against the apostate regimes of Bashar al-Assad and Haider al-Abadi. Blatant sectarian messages coupled with divinely ordained clarion calls to resist Persian domination and decisively affect the outcome of the eternal struggle between Sunni and Shi'a—and the latter's Alawite satraps—provide additionally compelling incentives.[164] Indeed, a 2014 ISIS recruitment video circulated via social media featured heavily armed militants with distinctive British and Australian accents trumpeting the virtues of jihad and the ineluctable religious imperative of joining the caravan of martyrs. Through these voices, the group is able to tailor its messages to specific target audiences back in these fighters' own neighborhoods, schools, clubs, community centers, and mosques.[165] "[W]hereas the older versions of terrorist websites effectively were waiting for visitors to arrive," Weimann argues, "a social networking approach allows terrorists to reach their target audiences and virtually 'knock on their doors.'"[166]

ISIS's unbridled visual depictions of particularly gruesome executions and other wanton acts of violence galvanize the attention of this select audience and beseech them to join ISIS's struggle.[167] A new generation of celebrity fighters, accordingly, has been created to facilitate this process. "Ultraviolence," as Stern and Berger term this phenomenon, "sold well with the target demographic for foreign fighters—angry, maladjusted young men whose blood stirred at images of grisly beheadings and the crucifixion of so-called apostates."[168] Other types of appeals, utilizing more traditional messages intended for more mainline religious audiences are also used by ISIS to target this entirely different demographic. Familiar historical and theological references are invoked for this particular audience's consideration and specific solicitations are directed to the descendants of pious families of ancient, respected, lineage and stature. ISIS propagandists also portray the organization as messengers and executors of apocalyptic prophecies, promising the imminence of an inevitable clash between the forces of good and evil in an epic, decisive battle as part of a compelling narrative with which to target potential recruits. These themes both resonate with and have a very powerful effect on their intended audiences.[169] According to Will McCants, ISIS's eschatological arguments have infused the group with newfound momentum, producing an "inrush of foreign fighters to Syria, many of them seeking a role in the End-Time drama."[170]

For terrorists today, the advantages of these new social media are thus as profound as they are manifold. It is therefore also not surprising to find that all of al-Qaeda's most important affiliates—al-Shabaab; Ansar al-Sharia; the Abdullah Azzam Brigades; al-Qaeda in the Islamic Maghreb; al-Qaeda in the Arabian Peninsula; Jabhat al-Nusra; and the Afghan Taliban, all have Twitter accounts on which they regularly tweet. In fact, during its lethal assault on Nairobi, Kenya's Westgate shopping center in September 2013, al-Qaeda's Somali branch, al-Shabaab, provided live, ongoing commentary of the attack over Twitter.[171]

Insurgent Television

Perhaps the most startling advance in terrorist communications has been the emergence of the terrorists' own television stations. In this respect, the video production and duplication capabilities already cited that have facilitated the customization of sophisticated messages on the Internet are a product of a growing sophistication among terrorists in the television studio and the editing booth as well. Among the pioneers in this process has been Hezbollah, whose al-Manar television station, along with its news website on the Internet, has afforded this movement an unprecedented ability to shape and tailor its external communications. In this way, terrorist groups have been able to assume complete control over the content, context, footage, and voice-overs depicting their organization and its activities.

Al-Manar began broadcasting as a small terrestrial station in 1991 with limited on-air time and programming content.[172] Within a decade, however, it was transmitting via satellite on a 24/7 basis.[173] Al-Manar has provided eight news bulletins daily in Arabic and one each in English and French. In addition to its headquarters operations in Beirut, the station has maintained bureaus in Egypt, Iran, Jordan, and the United Arab Emirates (UAE) and correspondents stationed in Belgium, France, Iraq, Kosovo, Kuwait, Morocco, the Occupied Territories (Palestine), Russia, Sweden, Syria, Turkey, and, until a decade ago, even the United States.[174] Al-Manar's website describes the station's mission as

> motivated by the ambitions of participation in building a better future for the Arab and Muslim generations by focusing on the tolerant values of Islam and promoting the culture of dialogue and cooperation among the followers of the Heavenly religions and human civilizations. It focuses on highlighting the value of the human being as the center of the Godly messages which endeavor to save his dignity and freedom and develop the spiritual and moral dimensions of his personality [sic].
>
> Al-Manar avoids cheap incitement in dealing with developments and activities, and it stresses objectively on the adoption of the fair and just causes of the whole nation [sic].[175]

However, according to Avi Jorisch, the author of a detailed study of the station and its programming content,

> Today, Hizballah [sic] continues to use al-Manar as a means of publicly offering its services to Palestinians fighting for the destruction of Israel

and the total liberation of historic Palestine (e.g., all territory west of the Jordan River). . . . Accordingly, one of al-Manar's major objectives is to inspire resistance. . . .

With regard to the United States, al-Manar has broadcast anti-American propaganda since its inception, often using the same propaganda methods it employs against Israel. Various programs have focused on distorting U.S. history, lambasting U.S. Middle East policy, propagating conspiracy theories about the September 11 attacks, and demonizing the relationship between Washington and the "Zionist entity," i.e., Israel. With the start of Operation Iraqi Freedom in 2003, both Hizballah and al-Manar renewed their vitriol toward their old, reliable foe, the "Great Satan."[176]

The station's prime-time programming clearly reflects its biases. Shows such as *The Spider's House* (see the previous allusion to the significance of this Qur'anic verse with respect to Israel, in chapter 5) detailed Israel's inherent weaknesses and its inevitable defeat through the use of suicide attacks and other terrorist tactics. The same attributes and eventuality were ascribed to the United States as a result of its occupation of Iraq. *What's Next* is a talk show that has hosted guests with particularly "vitriolic anti-American views." Another show, called *Terrorists*, details the alleged depredations inflicted throughout history by Israel on the Arab world, while *My Blood and the Rifle* was a panegyric to Hezbollah's fighters, extolling their victory over Israel in south Lebanon and their heroic sacrifices.[177] That this format is tremendously appealing is indisputable. A Gallup poll of Middle Eastern audience viewing preferences for news taken in March 2002 revealed that al-Manar was the fifth most popular station watched in the past week and was ranked as the third most popular station to which viewers turn to first to catch up on current world affairs.[178] It is reportedly one of the most watched stations in the Palestine territories.[179] Lebanese television officials have boasted that al-Manar is the third most popular station in that country, and at times of crisis with Israel, it is often the first.[180]

During the 1990s, Hezbollah created field units of combat camera crews that accompanied the organization's operational units into battle to provide al-Manar with the compelling footage it required.[181] Footage of Hezbollah fighters, attired in fatigues, with body armor and helmets, carrying out textbook military assaults on Israeli positions in South Lebanon and those of their South Lebanon Army (SLA) allies were a regular feature of al-Manar's television broadcasts and Internet website from the mid-1990s until the Israeli withdrawal in May 2000.[182] As one United Nations official explained,

"For Hezbollah, 60 per cent of the success of an operation depends on getting some good footage."[183] Indeed, Hezbollah propaganda efforts, directed at Israeli audiences back home—and specifically at the mothers of IDF troops serving in southern Lebanon—are widely regarded as having been influential in generating public pressure on the Israeli government to withdraw from Lebanon.[184] "By means of the Internet," Ibrahim Nasser al-Din, a Hezbollah military leader, claimed, "Hezbollah has succeeded in entering the homes of Israelis, creating an important psychological breakthrough."[185] This quote appeared in an article published in a leading Israeli newspaper, which further reported how parents of IDF soldiers serving in Lebanon had regularly visited the Hezbollah site to get a version of the news unvarnished by Israeli military censors. "I regard these sites as a legitimate source of information," one father was quoted as saying.[186] Much as the efforts of Sri Lankan authorities to suppress news of military defeats backfired disastrously in public relations terms, the same occurred with Israel in 1999. Contradicting IDF reports that Hezbollah had returned the body of only one member of a team of Israeli marine commandos killed in a Hezbollah ambush, the group publicized on its website that the coffin contained the body parts of other soldiers as well. The statement generated a nasty confrontation between the commando's families and the IDF, with accusations of cover-up and duplicity undermining trust and confidence among the Israelis in its armed forces.[187]

Hezbollah, however, is not the only terrorist group to use its own television for propaganda and mobilization purposes. The widespread protests unleashed throughout Europe immediately following the arrest by Turkish authorities of the Kurdish terrorist leader Abdullah Ocalan in February 1999 provided further proof of the reach and rapidity with which modern communications technology could rally the masses. Within hours of the announcement of his arrest, demonstrators swarmed onto the streets of Paris, Moscow, London, Frankfurt, Milan, Bern, Sydney, and more than a dozen other cities in response to pleas issued by the PKK over both its Internet site and its London-based television station, Med-TV.[188] The television station, founded in 1995, appears to have ceased broadcasting a few years later. While it existed, Med-TV mirrored the ambitions of terrorists and insurgents throughout the globe today. "Our aim," in the words of the station manager, Sami Abdurahman, "is to present our Kurdish brothers across the world with the objective facts."[189] Or, as the American statesman Hiram W. Johnson, would have said, "The first casualty when war comes is truth."

Conclusion

In the final analysis, a terrorist movement's longevity ultimately depends on its ability to recruit new members as well as to appeal to an expanding pool of both active supporters and passive sympathizers. The role of effective communication in this process is pivotal: ensuring the continued flow of fighters into the movement, binding supporters more tightly to it, and drawing sympathizers more deeply into its orbit. "Without communication," Schmid and de Graaf presciently argued more than thirty years ago, "there can be no terrorism."[190] The revolutions in terrorist communications described in this chapter have facilitated this process in hitherto unimaginable ways. The U.S.-born master al-Qaeda propagandist of Yemeni parents, Anwar al-Awlaqi, is just such a case in point. He has shown himself to be the Salafi-Jihadi movement's preeminent recruiting sergeant—despite having been killed in an American drone strike in September 2011.

Al-Awlaqi first came to the attention of U.S. authorities during the investigations into the 9/11 attacks. As the imam of a San Diego mosque in 2000 and starting in 2001 of another in Falls Church, Virginia, he was reportedly in contact with at least two of nineteen hijackers in both locations. In addition, al-Awlaqi's telephone number was reportedly found in a cell phone belonging to Ramzi Binalshibh—a key figure in the planning and execution of the attacks.[191] Al-Awlaqi left the United States in late 2002 and moved to London, where he lived for two years until permanently relocating to Yemen in 2004. Two years later, Yemeni authorities arrested al-Awlaqi on kidnapping charges and he was detained for eighteen months. It is not clear when the American-born cleric first formally became involved with al-Qaeda's branch in Yemen, AQAP. But following his release from jail in 2007, al-Awlaqi quickly became enmeshed in its recruitment and operational activities, rapidly moving from his role as chief ideologue and propagandist to a key AQAP planner, strategist, and field commander. His fluency in English and ability to communicate in a patois accessible to youth combined with his excellent oratorical skills and charisma, provided al-Awlaqi with a platform that other radical preachers with their often halting, heavily accented English, lacked. "Jihad," he was once famously quoted as declaring, "is becoming as American as apple pie and as British as afternoon tea."[192]

Al-Awlaqi's ability to mix Islamic history with contemporary issues served as a magnet for young Anglophone recruits lacking a firm theological grounding or command of the Arabic language. His most famous statement of jihad, titled, "44 Ways to Support Jihad," has strong echoes of Sayyid Qutb's writing, which al-Awlaqi boasts was seminal to his thinking and radicalization. "44 Ways" was designed as a kind of "how-to," or DIY manual, for aspiring jihadis.[193] "Jihad is the greatest deed in Islam," al-Awlaqi declared,

> and the salvation of the ummah is in practicing it. In times like these, when Muslim lands are occupied by the kuffar, when the jails of tyrants are full of Muslim POWs, when the rule of the law of Allah is absent from this world and when Islam is being attacked in order to uproot it, Jihad becomes obligatory on [sic] every Muslim. Jihad must be practiced by the child even if the parents refuse, by the wife even if the husband objects and by the one in debt even if the lender disagrees.[194]

Al-Awlaqi's messages of radicalization and violence have reportedly been linked to more than fifty persons who since 2009 have either carried out terrorist attacks or been indicted on terrorism-related charges both in the United States and elsewhere.[195] In the aftermath of the fatal shootings of thirteen persons at Fort Hood, Texas, by a U.S. Army officer, Major Nidal Hasan, in November 2009, it was revealed that during the six months preceding the attack, al-Awlaqi and Hasan had exchanged at least sixteen e-mails. Although there is no evidence that al-Awlaqi actually ordered Hasan to carry out the attack, he did praise the shootings afterward.[196] Al-Awlaqi's fundamental message in the incident's aftermath was that, due to American's inherent evil, Muslims do not require a fatwa or need to consult an Islamic scholar to be justified in killing Americans.[197] Al-Awlaqi has been credited for his effectiveness in communicating with—and radicalizing—impressionable Muslims of a variety of ages and in a number of different places in addition to Hasan.[198] Among them have been:

- *Umar Farouk Abdulmutallab.* The so-called Underwear Bomber, who attempted to explode a bomb while in flight on Northwest Airlines Flight 253 en route from Amsterdam to Detroit on December 25, 2009.[199]
- *Faisal Shahzad.* The so-called Times Square bomber, Shahzad attempted to detonate a vehicular bomb at New York City's famed Times Square on May 1, 2010. He admitted following his arrest that he was inspired by al-Awlaqi's online sermons encouraging jihad—although Shahzad had no direct contact with the cleric.[200]
- *Roshonara Choudry.* A twenty-one-year-old student at King's College London, Choudry stated that she was inspired by al-Awlaqi's sermons when she attempted to stab to death British member of parliament Stephen Timms in revenge for his vote in support of the 2003 invasion of Iraq.[201]

- *Farooque Ahmed.* A U.S. citizen arrested in October 2011, Ahmed was charged with plotting to bomb Washington, D.C., Metrorail (subway) stations. Ahmed allegedly had in his possession a biography of al-Awlaqi and admitted listening to his online sermons. He was sentenced to twenty-three years imprisonment in April 2011.[202]
- *Abdel Hameed Shehadeh.* Another U.S. citizen, Shehadeh was arrested and charged in October 2010 with attempting to travel overseas to join the Taliban. Shehadeh had allegedly developed a website based on al-Awlaqi's that also provided hyperlinks to al-Awlaqi's site. He also discussed al-Awlaqi's beliefs with another person whom Shehadeh was trying to recruit for jihad.[203]
- *Zachary Chesser.* Also a U.S. citizen, Chesser grew up in a Northern Virginia suburb of Washington, D.C. He was arrested in 2010, and after conviction was sentenced to twenty-five years in prison for attempting to join the Somali al-Qaeda affiliate, al-Shabaab. Chesser was also charged with engaging in online propagandizing for jihad and had been in e-mail contact with al-Awlaqi. According to court documents, al-Awlaqi replied at least twice to Chesser's e-mails.[204]
- *Mohamed Alessa and Carlos Almonte.* Both men were arrested in June 2010 while attempting to fly from the United States to Somalia to join al-Shabaab. They admitted watching videos and listening to al-Awlaqi's sermons.[205]

Additional terrorists, including the persons responsible for the July 7, 2005, simultaneous suicide bomb attacks on London transport; the six men who plotted to attack the U.S. Army base at Fort Dix, New Jersey, in 2007 (known as "the Fort Dix Six"); and the "Toronto 18," the eighteen men who planned a series of bombings and shootings against the Canadian Broadcasting Corporation, the Canadian Parliament, and the Canadian Security Intelligence Service headquarters, and threatened to seize and behead the Canadian prime minister, all claimed to have been inspired by al-Awlaqi's online sermons. Then-U.S. director of National Intelligence James R. Clapper stated that al-Awlaqi was also involved in a daring 2009 plot to assassinate Prince Nayef, the Saudi Arabian official responsible for that country's counterterrorism policy and operations; for the murder of four kidnapped tourists from South Korea who were visiting Yemen in 2009; and for a plot to assassinate the British ambassador to Yemen that year as well.[206] And al-Awlaqi has been linked to the radicalization of Najibullah Zazi, whose suicide bombing plot of the New York City subway system is discussed in chapter 5.[207] Al-Awlaqi has also been described as having "turned the web into a tool for extremist indoctrination."[208] His cofounding in 2010 of

Inspire, AQAP's popular, colorful online magazine with Samir Khan, a U.S. citizen from North Carolina, arguably has made al-Awlaqi among the pre-eminent jihadi propagandists of our time.[209] Indeed, an article that appeared in the summer 2010 issue of *Inspire* titled "How to Make a Bomb in the Kitchen of Our Mom," figured prominently in the 2013 bombing of the Boston Marathon.

Al-Awlaqi has thus been supremely effective in his use of both the Internet and social media to radicalize young Muslims, especially in the United States and the United Kingdom.[210] According to a 2010 report prepared for the U.S. Congress by the Congressional Research Service, "Social networking, now inherently part of the Internet, is likely a tool that is used in the development of contacts among radicalized individuals and recruitment into violent jihadist groups. Before he died, Anwar al-Awlaki [*sic*] circulated jihadist lectures online and managed his own popular Facebook page and blog."[211]

Al-Awlaqi has also successfully employed other forms of media for his propagandistic purposes, including the aforementioned *Inspire* magazine as well as CDs with his sermons, books distributed online, a personal website (that has long since been shut down), a Facebook page (also shut down), and most significantly, through his video postings on the popular website, You-Tube.[212] He maintained a blog (which was shut down repeatedly) that contained statements inciting violence.[213] YouTube, however, became al-Awlaqi's most effective method of communication following the closing down of his personal website and Facebook page.[214] For all these reasons, al-Awlaqi has been described as the "bin Laden of the internet."[215] From the grave, he is considered to have been responsible for influencing the two brothers, Tamerlan and Dzhokhar Tsarnaev, who, as previously noted, relied on the bomb-making instructions published in *Inspire* to build the two explosive devices concealed in pressure cookers that killed three persons and injured more than two hundred fifty others at the 2013 Boston Marathon; Sayeed Farook and Tashfeen Malik, the two 2015 San Bernadino shooters; and, Omar Mateen, the Afghan-born private security guard guilty of America's worst mass killing when he killed forty-nine persons at a LGBT bar in Orlando, Florida, in May 2016.

Hence, the revolution in terrorist communications that has rapidly unfolded within the past few decades is certain to continue.[216] Terrorist reliance on "old media" for attention and exposure via mass communication will continue alongside the allure of the technological innovation and the unprecedented speed and reach of the "person-to-person" power of "new media." The implications of this phenomenon are perhaps only now beginning to be understood, given capabilities and products that are sure to become increasingly more sophisticated in quality, content, rapidity, intimacy, and transmission capacity—and more numerous and pervasive than ever. What is clear, though, is that as terrorist communications change and evolve, so will the nature of terrorism itself. While one cannot predict what new forms and dimensions terrorism will assume during the rest of the twenty-first century, this evolutionary process will not only continue, but will be abetted—and accelerated—by new communications technologies—much as has been the case over the century.

Chapter 8

The Modern Terrorist Mind-Set

Tactics, Targets, Tradecraft, and Technologies

T he wrath of the terrorist is rarely uncontrolled. Contrary to both popular belief and media depiction, most terrorism is neither crazed nor capricious. Rather, terrorist attacks are generally both premeditated and carefully planned. As shown in chapters 6 and 7, the terrorist act is specifically designed to communicate a message. But, equally important, it is also conceived and executed in a manner that simultaneously reflects the terrorist group's particular aims and motivations, fits its resources and capabilities, and takes into account the target audience at which the act is directed. The tactics and targets of various terrorist movements, as well as the weapons they favor, are therefore ineluctably shaped by a group's ideology, its internal organizational dynamics, and the personalities of its key members, as well as a variety of internal and external stimuli.

The Nexus of Ideological and Operational Imperatives

All terrorist groups seek targets that are rewarding from their point of view and employ tactics that are consonant with their overriding political aims. Whereas left-wing terrorists such as the German Red Army Faction (RAF) and the Italian Red Brigades (RB) have selectively kidnapped and assassinated people whom they blamed for economic exploitation or political repression in order to attract publicity and promote a Marxist-Leninist revolution, terrorists motivated by a religious imperative have engaged in more indiscriminate acts of violence, directed against a far wider category of targets encompassing not merely their declared enemies but anyone who does not share their religious faith. The actions of ethnonationalist/separatist groups arguably fall somewhere in between these two models. On the one hand, the violent campaigns waged by groups such as the PLO, the IRA, and the Basque separatist organization ETA have frequently been more destructive and have caused far greater casualties than those of their left-wing counterparts. On the other hand, however, their violence has largely been restricted to a specifically defined "target set," namely, the members of a specific rival or dominant ethnonationalist group.[1] Perhaps the least consequential of all these terrorist group categories (both in terms of frequency of incidents and of impact on public and governmental attitudes) has been the disparate collection of recycled Nazis, racist "political punk rockers," and other extreme right-wing elements that has emerged over the years in various European countries. But even their sporadic and uncoordinated, seemingly mindless violence—fueled as much by beer and bravado as by a discernible political agenda—is neither completely random nor unthinkingly indiscriminate. Indeed, for all these categories, the point is less their inherent differences than the fact that their tactical and targeting choices correspond to, and are determined by, their respective ideologies and attendant mechanisms of legitimation and justification, and, perhaps most critically, by their relationship with the intended audience of their violent acts.

The overriding tactical—and, indeed, ethical—imperative for left-wing terrorists, for example, has been the deliberate tailoring of their violent acts to appeal to their perceived "constituencies." In a 1978 interview, the German left-wing terrorist Michael "Bommi" Baumann denounced the hijacking of a Lufthansa passenger plane the previous year by terrorists seeking the release of imprisoned RAF members as "madness . . . you can't take your life and place it above that of children and Majorca holiday-makers and say: *My* life is valuable! That is elitarian madness, bordering on Fascism."[2] For Baumann, the deliberate involvement of innocent civilians in that terrorist operation was not only counterproductive but wrong. It was counterproductive in that it tarnished the left-wing terrorists' image as a true revolutionary vanguard—using violence to draw attention to themselves and their cause and educate the public about what the terrorists perceived as the inequities of the democratic-capitalist state. It was also wrong in itself because innocent people—no matter what the political justification—should not be the victims of terrorist acts directed against the state.

For this reason, left-wing terrorists' use of violence historically has been heavily constrained. Their self-styled crusade for social justice is typically directed against governmental or commercial institutions, or specific individuals who they believe represent capitalist exploitation and repression. They are therefore careful not to undertake actions that might alienate potential supporters or their perceived constituency. Accordingly, left-wing violence tends to be highly discriminate, selective, and limited. Individuals epitomizing the focus of the terrorists' ideological hostility—wealthy industrialists such as Hans Martin Schleyer (who was kidnapped and later murdered by the RAF in 1977) or leading parliamentarians such as Aldo Moro (who similarly was kidnapped and subsequently murdered by the RB)—are deliberately selected and meticulously targeted for their intrinsic symbolic value. "You know that we did not kidnap Moro the man, but [rather] his function," explained Mario Moretti, the leader of the RB Rome column who masterminded the operation, during his trial in November 1984. For Moretti, Moro was first and foremost a powerful symbol: a former prime minister and reigning Christian Democratic Party chief; a political wheeler-dealer par excellence; and architect of the impending historic compromise with the Italian Communist Party that would fundamentally alter the country's political landscape and further marginalize the RB. He was, in the terrorists' eyes, the "supreme manager of power in Italy" and had been for the previous twenty years, a man whom Moretti described as the "demiurge of bourgeois power." By abducting so important a leader and so profound a symbol, the RB sought to galvanize the Italian Left and thereby decisively transform the political situation in its favor.[3]

Even when less discriminate tactics such as bombing are employed, the violence is meant to be equally symbolic. That is, while the damage inflicted is real, the terrorists' main purpose is not to destroy property or obliterate tangible assets but to dramatize or call attention to a political cause. The decision-making process of the left-wing terrorist group is perhaps depicted most clearly in Baumann's description of the planning of a 1969 terrorist attack by the group known as the Tupamaros West Berlin—a precursor of both the Second of June Movement and the original RAF. Baumann and his colleagues wanted to stage an operation that would simultaneously attract attention to themselves and their cause, publicize the plight of the Palestinian people, and demonstrate the West German Left's solidarity and sympathy with the Palestinians' struggle. "We sat down and pondered what would be a story that nobody could miss, that everyone would have to talk about and everyone would have to report," Baumann recalled. "And we came up with the right answer—a bomb in the Jewish Community Centre—and on the anniversary of the 'Crystal Night'[4] during the Third Reich. . . . Though it didn't explode, the story [still] went round the world."[5] By striking on this particular date, against this specific target, with its deep—and unmistakable—symbolic significance, the group sought to draw a deliberate parallel between Israeli oppression of the Palestinians and Nazi persecution of the Jews.[6]

The use by left-wing terrorists of "armed propaganda" (i.e., violent acts with clear symbolic content) is thus a critical element in their operational calculus. It is also the principal means by which these organizations educate the masses through their self-anointed role as revolutionary vanguard. The first official "strategic resolution" of the RB, for example, stressed exactly this theme. "It is not a question of organizing the class movement within the area of armed struggle," the 1975 document stated, "but of entrenching the organization of the armed struggle and the political realization of its historical necessity within the class movement."[7] A less turgid explanation of this strategy was later offered by Patrizio Peci, leader of the group's Turin column, when he reflected how, "as crazy as it might seem, the plan in a few words was this: First phase, armed propaganda. . . . Second phase, that of armed support. . . . Third phase, the civil war and victory. In essence, we were the embryo, the skeleton of the future . . . the ruling class of tomorrow in a communist society."[8] The RAF drew similar parallels in its exegesis of the relationship between the terrorist vanguard and "the people." "Our original conception of the organization implied a connection between the urban guerrilla and the work at the base," explained the document, titled "Sur la Concepcíon de la Guerilla Urbaine":

> We would like it if each and all of us could work at the neighborhoods and factories, in socialist groups that already exist, influence discussion, experience and learn. This has proved impossible. . . .
>
> Some say that the possibilities for agitation, propaganda and organization are far from being eradicated and that only when they are, should we pose the question of arms. We say: it will not really be possible to profit from any political actions as long as armed struggle does not appear clearly as the goal of the politicization.[9]

This approach is not entirely dissimilar to that of many ethnonationalist/separatist groups. These terrorist movements also see themselves as a revolutionary vanguard—if not in classic Marxist-Leninist terms, at least as a spearhead, similarly using violence to educate fellow members of their national or ethnic group about the inequities imposed on them by the ruling government and the need for communal resistance and rebellion. As one Basque nationalist bluntly told an interviewer, "ETA is the vanguard of our revolution."[10] Accordingly, like all ethnonationalist/separatist terrorists, ETA uses demonstratively symbolic acts of violence to generate publicity and rally support by underscoring the powerlessness of the government to withstand the nationalist expression that ETA champions, and thereby to embarrass and coerce the government into acceding to the group's irredentist demands. ETA's target audience, however, is not just the local, indigenous population but often the international community as well. These groups, accordingly, recognize the need to tightly control and focus their operations in such a manner as to ensure both the continued support of their local constituencies and the sympathy of the international community. What this essentially means is that their violence must always be perceived as both purposeful and deliberate, sustained and omnipresent. Gerry Adams, the president of Sinn Fein, the Irish nationalist political party linked to the IRA, himself expressed precisely this point in an article he wrote in 1976 to commemorate the sixtieth anniversary of the 1916 Easter Uprising. "Rightly or wrongly, I am an IRA Volunteer," Adams explained,

> and, rightly or wrongly, I take a course of action as a means to bringing about a situation in which I believe the people of my country will prosper. . . . The course I take involves the use of physical force, but only if I achieve the situation where my people can genuinely prosper can my course of action be seen, by me, to have been justified.[11]

Indeed, as the veteran Northern Ireland correspondent David McKittrick points out, "Sinn Fein, in its efforts to build a political machine in both parts of Ireland, has [always] been concerned to project IRA violence as the clinical and carefully directed use of force."[12]

The more successful ethnonationalist/separatist terrorist organization will be able to determine an effective level of violence that is at once tolerable for the local populace, tacitly acceptable to international opinion, and sufficiently modulated not to provoke massive governmental crackdown and reaction. The IRA demonstrably mastered this synchronization of tactics to strategy. From the mid-1980s onward, according to Patrick Bishop and Eamonn Mallie, the organization's military high command clearly recognized that "Republican strategy required a certain level of violence—but only enough to distort the private and public life of the North, and to make sure that the military arm was properly exercised."[13] What this has often resulted in was the targeting of members of the security forces (ordinary policemen and soldiers) in preference to the terrorists' avowed enemies in some rival indigenous community. Fewer than 20 percent of the IRA's victims between 1969 and 1993, for example, were Protestant civilians,[14] and in

Spain, more than 60 percent of fatalities inflicted by the Basque ETA have been members of the Spanish security forces.[15]

Certainly, traitors, informants, and other collaborators among their own brethren are regularly targeted, but here the terrorist group must be careful to strike another balance between salutary, if sporadic, lessons that effectively intimidate and compel compliance from their own communities and more frequent and heavy-handed episodes that alienate popular support, encourage cooperation with the security forces, and therefore prove counterproductive. By the same token, highly placed government officials and security force commanders will, when the opportunity presents itself and the political conditions are propitious, be attacked. But given the combination of uncertain—and possibly undesirable—political and security repercussions, the difficulties involved in gaining access to these VIPs, and the considerable effort required of such operations, they are generally eschewed in favor of more productive, if less spectacular, operations that, moreover, conform to the terrorists' perceptions of what are regarded as legitimate or acceptable targets—however abhorrent the attacks may seem to the outside world.

The terrorist campaign is like a shark in the water: it must keep moving forward—no matter how slowly or incrementally—or die. Hence, when these more typical targets fail to sustain the momentum of a terrorist campaign, or when other, perhaps even totally unrelated, events overshadow the terrorists and shunt their cause out of the public eye, terrorists often have to resort to more violent and dramatic acts to refocus attention back on themselves. But it would be a mistake to see these acts—which often involve the bombing of public gathering places or the hijacking of airliners—as random or senseless. For example, the discussion in chapter 3 showed how, following the Palestinian terrorists' failure to mount a concerted guerrilla campaign against Israel in the occupied West Bank and Gaza Strip after the 1967 Six Day War, the PFLP began hijacking international airliners. The purpose of these operations was not necessarily wantonly to kill or otherwise harm innocent persons (in contrast to many subsequent terrorists' targeting of civil aviation) but to use the passengers as pawns in pursuit of publicity and the extraction of concessions from unsympathetic governments. As one of the group's most famous hijackers, Leila Khaled, once explained: "Look, I had orders to seize the plane, not to blow it up. . . . I care about people. If I had wanted to blow up the plane no one could have prevented me."[16]

Even when terrorists' actions are not as deliberate or discriminating, and when their purpose is in fact to kill innocent civilians, the target is still regarded as "justified" because it represents the terrorists' defined "enemy." Although incidents may be quantitatively different in the volume of death or destruction caused, they are still qualitatively identical in that a widely known "enemy" is being specifically targeted. This distinction is often accepted by the terrorists' constituents, and at times by the international community as well. The recognition that the Palestinians obtained in the wake of the 1972 Munich Olympics massacre is a particularly prominent case in point. The poignant message left behind by the terrorist team struck precisely the sympathetic chord they had intended. "We are neither killers nor bandits," their letter stated. "We are persecuted people who have no land and no homeland. . . . We are not against any people, but why should our place here be taken by the flag of the occupiers . . . why should the whole world be having fun and entertainment while we suffer with all ears deaf to us?"[17] As the PFLP's Bassam Abu Sharif explained, "For violence to become fruitful, for it to get us to our aims, it should not be undertaken without a proper political base and intention."[18] While the logic in such a case may well be contrived, there is nonetheless a clear appreciation both that violence has its limits and that, if used properly, it can pay vast dividends. In other words, the level of violence must be kept within the bounds of what the terrorists' target audience will accept.

But acts of terrorism, like battles in conventional wars, are difficult to limit and control once they are started, and often result in tragedy to civilians who are inadvertently caught up in the violence. One well-known example is the tragic bombing that occurred at Enniskillen, Northern Ireland, in November 1987, causing the deaths of eleven innocent bystanders attending a memorial ceremony and injuries to sixty-three others. The IRA was quick to describe the incident as an accident resulting from the "catastrophic consequences" of an operation against British troops gone awry.[19] In this instance, there was an acceptance that some grievous wrong had been done, albeit clothed in layers of self-serving justifications. The truth of the matter, as terrorism scholar Jacob Shapiro notes, was that by 1987, the IRA "was losing support, particularly because of the civilians who had been killed, [which] brought into question the very feasibility of making political progress through war." The IRA, accordingly, took the extraordinary step of disbanding the terrorist unit responsible for the incident, while Gerry Adams, president of the group's aboveground political arm, Sinn Féin, publicly declared that the unintended killing of civilians had to stop.[20] Eamon Collins, a former IRA terrorist who was later found murdered in mysterious circumstances, describes the organization's reaction to another botched attack that also accidentally claimed the lives of innocent civilians some years later:

> The IRA—regardless of their public utterances dismissing the condemnations of their behaviour from church and community leaders—tried to act in a way that would avoid severe censure from within the nationalist

community; they knew they were operating within a sophisticated set of informal restrictions on their behaviour, no less powerful for being largely unspoken.[21]

The Basque ETA is no different—alternately threatening and remorseful in communiqués that seek simultaneously to absolve it of responsibility for its violent deeds and to reap the rewards of introspection and self-criticism. "We claim responsibility for the failed action against a member of the Spanish police," reads one, "following the placing of an explosive charge under his car. We very much deplore the accidental injuries involuntarily caused to his neighbor . . . and we wish his prompt and complete recovery."[22]

Right-wing terrorism has often been characterized as the least discriminating, most senseless type of contemporary political violence. It has earned this reputation mostly as a result of the seemingly mindless street violence and unsophisticated attacks that have targeted immigrants, refugees, guest workers, and other foreigners in many European countries, especially in eastern Germany and other former Communist-bloc states,[23] but also from an inchoate bombing campaign that briefly convulsed Western Europe in the early 1980s. If the means of the right-wing terrorists sometimes appear haphazardly planned and often spontaneously generated, their ends are hardly less indistinct. Essentially, their ostensible goal is the destruction of the liberal-democratic state to clear the way for a renascent National Socialist (Nazi) or fascist one. But the extent to which this is simply an excuse for the egocentric pleasure derived from brawling and bombing, preening or parading in 1940s-era Nazi regalia, is difficult to judge, given that the majority of far right-wing extremist groups do not espouse any specific program of reform, preferring to hide behind vague slogans of strident nationalism, the need for racial purity, and the reassertion of governmental strength. In sum, the democratic state is somewhat reflexively assailed for its manifold weaknesses—notably its liberal social welfare policies and tolerance of diverse opinion—alongside its permitting of dark-skinned immigrants in the national labor force and of Jews and other minorities in positions of power or influence. The right-wing terrorists believe that their nation's survival is dependent upon the exorcism of these elements from its environs; only by becoming politically, racially, and culturally homogeneous can the state recover its strength and again work for its natural citizens rather than the variegated collection of interlopers and parasites who now sap the nation of its strength and greatness.

It should be noted that while violently-inclined far right European groups share many similarities with their American counterparts—racism, anti-Semitism, xenophobia, and a hatred of liberal government—they differ fundamentally in their mechanisms of legitimation and justification. Whereas some U.S. groups may be more accurately categorized as religious rather than strictly as right-wing terrorists because of the pivotal roles that liturgy, divine inferences, and clerical sanction play in underpinning and motivating their violence, the foundations of the European Far Right are avowedly secular, with neither theological imperatives nor clerics exerting any significant influence. Indeed, the ill-defined, amorphous contours of the contemporary European extreme Right's political philosophy can be summed up by the refrain from a popular song by the British white power band White Noise: "Two pints of lager and a packet of crisps. Wogs out! White Power!"[24] or the folk song composed by Gottfried Küssel, Führer of an Austrian neo-Nazi organization: "Do you see his nose, no? Do you know his nose? His nose you do not know? It is crooked and ugly? Then hit him in the face. He is a Jew, a damned Jew, bloodsucker of the European race."[25] By comparison, the lunatic and far-fetched millenarian views of American Christian white supremacists appear to be profoundly theological treatises.

It is for this reason, perhaps, that European right-wing terrorism has rarely transcended the boundaries of street brawls or the Molotov cocktail hurriedly tossed into a refugee shelter or a guest workers' dormitory—even though, of course, such crude acts of violence possess just the same tragic potential to kill and maim as much more sophisticated terrorist operations. Nonetheless, it would be a mistake to see right-wing violence as completely indiscriminate or entirely irrational. Indeed, the few occasions on which the neo-Nazis have attempted more ambitious types of operations have sent shock waves throughout the Continent. In August 1980, for instance, a powerful explosion tore through the crowded rail station in Bologna, Italy, in the midst of the summer holiday crush. At the time, the total of 84 people killed (and 180 wounded) was second only to the record 91 who had perished in a single terrorist act in the Irgun's bombing of the King David Hotel thirty-four years before. When it was followed less than a month later by a bombing at the popular Munich Oktoberfest celebration, killing 14 and injuring another 215, fears were raised of a new terrorist onslaught more lethal and indiscriminate than that waged by either the European leftist terrorist organizations or the Continent's various ethnonationalist/separatist groups. It did not materialize, however. Instead, the pattern of right-wing terrorism in Europe has remained largely the same since the 1970s: one of sporadic attacks, albeit specifically directed against particular types of targets— primarily refugee shelters and immigrant workers' hostels, anarchist houses and political party offices, and Arab and African immigrants walking along the street, as well as Jewish-owned property or businesses.

As crude and relatively unsophisticated, and indeed intellectually depraved, as this terrorist category may appear, then, right-wing violence, like all forms of terrorism, is based not on some pathological obsession to kill or beat up as many people as possible but rather on a deliberate policy of intimidating the general public into acceding to specific demands or pressures. The right-wing terrorists see themselves, if not as a revolutionary vanguard, then as a catalyst of events that will lead to the imposition of an authoritarian form of government. Thus, like other terrorist movements, they too tailor their violence to appeal to their perceived constituency—be it fellow extreme nationalists, intransigent racists and xenophobes, reactionary conservatives, or militant anticommunists—and with the exception of a handful of noteworthy but isolated, indiscriminate bombings, they seek to keep the violence they commit within the bounds of what the ruling government will tolerate without undertaking massive repressive actions against the terrorists themselves.

Moreover, the phenomenon by which terrorists consciously learn from one another, discussed in chapter 2, is evident in the case of at least some German right-wing terrorist elements, suggesting aspirations toward a more planned and coherent campaign of violence than has hitherto existed and raising the possibility of a more serious future threat. As long ago as 1981, Manfred Roeder, for a time Germany's leading neo-Nazi, advocated the emulation of left-wing terrorist targeting and tactics in hopes of endowing the movement with a clearer purpose and attainable goal. For the rightists, however, there was another factor: envy of the attention, status, and occasional tactical victories won by left-wing terrorists in groups such as the RAF, alongside the realization that indiscriminate terrorist attacks would not result in the attainment of the neo-Nazis' goals. "The RAF had brought terrorism to modern Europe," Ingo Hasselbach, one of Roeder's successors, recalled, "and even though they could not have been more opposed to our ideology, we respected them for their fanaticism and skill." Hasselbach therefore advocated for his *Kameradschaft* (Nazi "brotherhood"), before his own disillusionment forced him to break completely with the movement he had once so enthusiastically championed, a lethally discriminate campaign of terrorism mirroring that pursued by the RAF. Like the original founders of the Baader-Meinhof Group twenty years before, Hasselbach believed that his National Alternative Berlin (NA) neo-Nazi organization could not achieve its political objectives by attempting to operate as a legal political party. Accordingly, he sought to mold the group into a terrorist organization modeled on the RAF and laid plans to assassinate prominent Jews and communists, and leading politicians. "We wanted to bring neo-Nazi terrorism up to the level of that carried out by the radical Left," Hasselbach later explained,

> striking at targets that would be both better guarded and more significant— targets that would do serious damage to the democratic German state

while driving home our racial message. There was, for instance, talk of assassinating Gregor Gusi, the head of the reformed Communist Party, the PDS [East German Party of Democratic Socialism]; he was East Germany's most prominent Jew and leader of the Communists to boot. He was not only a major politician but the political representative of the former GDR [German Democratic Republic] system. We also considered hitting Ignatz Bubis, the new head of the Jewish community, as well as a number of politicians in Bonn—including the interior minister and Chancellor Kohl himself.[26]

Like other terrorist organizations, the more sophisticated right-wing groups also seek targets that are likely to advance their cause. In this respect, their terrorist acts are as calculated as those of the left-wing organizations they try to emulate. Publicity and attention are, of course, paramount aims, but at the same time, there is a conscious recognition that only if their violence is properly calculated and at least in some (however idiosyncratic) way regulated will they be able to achieve the effects they desire and the political objectives they seek.[27] As an IRA terrorist once said, "You don't bloody well kill people for the sake of killing them."[28] This is not, however, the case with many of the religious terrorist movements discussed in chapter 4. For them, though violence does still have an instrumental purpose, it is also often an end in itself—a sacred duty executed in direct response to some theological demand or imperative. A 1990 study of Lebanese Shi'a terrorists, for example, revealed that none of those in the sample were interested in influencing an actual or self-perceived constituency or in swaying popular opinion; their sole preoccupation was serving God through the fulfillment of what they deemed their divinely ordained mission.[29] Hence, for religious terrorists there are demonstrably fewer constraints on the actual infliction of violence, and the category of targets/enemies is much more open-ended. The leader of an Egyptian terrorist cell, for instance, professed absolutely no remorse when he was told that an attack he had planned against visiting Israeli Jews had instead killed nine German tourists. His matter-of-fact response was that "infidels are all the same."[30] Indeed, how else can one explain the mad plots of the American Christian white supremacists? Or the Aum sect's wanton and repeated attempts to use chemical warfare nerve agents indiscriminately in populous urban centers? Or the cataclysmic aim of the Jewish Temple Mount bombers in Israel? The willingness of religious terrorists to contemplate such wholesale acts of violence is a direct reflection of the fact that unlike their secular counterparts, they see in violence a demonstrably divine or transcendental purpose, committed in the service of or on the commandment of their own

god or religious figures; they therefore feel little need to regulate or calibrate that violence. Al-Qaeda's repeated calls for unconstrained violence
against Americans, Jews, and others clearly underscores the elasticity of the
movement's defined "enemy." "All those who oppose U.S. policy," Suleimain
Abu Ghaith suggestively warned in October 2001, should "not ride planes
or live in high buildings."[31] With only slightly more specificity, Abu Musab
al-Zarqawi, the Jordanian-born leader of Tanzim Qa'idat al-Jihad fi Bilad al-
Rafidayn (QJBR), al-Qaeda's operations arm in Iraq, attempted in May 2005
to justify the suicide terrorist attacks in that country that had claimed the
lives of Muslims and non-Muslims alike—including in some cases women
and children. "There is no doubt," Zarqawi expostulated,

> that Allah commanded us to strike the Kuffar (unbelievers), kill them, and
> fight them by all means necessary to achieve the goal. The servants of
> Allah who perform Jihad to elevate the word (laws) of Allah, are permitted
> to use any and all means necessary to strike the active unbeliever com-
> batants for the purpose of killing them, snatch their souls from their
> body, cleanse the earth from their abomination, and lift their trial and
> persecution of the servants of Allah. The goal must be pursued even if
> the means to accomplish it affect both the intended active fighters and
> unintended passive ones such as women, children and any other passive
> category specified by our jurisprudence. This permissibility extends to
> situations in which Muslims may get killed if they happen to be with or
> near the intended enemy, and if it is not possible to avoid hitting them or
> separate them from the intended Kafirs.
>
> Although spilling sacred Muslim blood is a grave offense, it is not only
> permissible but it is mandated in order to prevent more serious adversity
> from happening, stalling or abandoning Jihad that is [sic].[32]

The Organizational Dynamics of Terrorist Groups

All terrorists, however, have one trait in common: they live in the future,
for that distant—yet imperceptibly close—point in time when they will as-
suredly triumph over their enemies and attain the ultimate realization of
their political destiny. For religious groups, this future is divinely decreed
and the terrorists themselves are specifically anointed to achieve it. The inevitability of their victory is taken for granted, as a 1996 communiqué issued by the Egyptian Gamat al-Islamiya (Islamic Group) reveals. Citing the
Qur'an, the document brusquely dismisses even the possibility that its

secular opponents might succeed. "They plot and plan and God too plans," it declares, "but the best of planners is God." Therefore, the group must faithfully and resolutely "pursue its battle . . . until such time as God would grant victory—just as the Prophet Mohammed did with the Quredish [his most implacable enemies] until God granted victory over Mecca."[33]

For the secular terrorists, too, eventual victory is as inevitable as it is predetermined. Indeed, they believe that the innate righteousness of their cause itself assures success. "Our struggle will be long and arduous because the enemy is powerful, well-organised, and well-sustained from abroad," Leila Khaled wrote in her autobiography, published in 1973. "We shall win because we represent the wave of the future . . . because mankind is on our side, and above all because we are determined to achieve victory."[34] Comparatively small in number, limited in capabilities, isolated from society, and dwarfed by both the vast resources of their enemy and the enormity of their task, secular terrorists necessarily function in an inverted reality where existence is defined by the sought-after, ardently pursued future rather than the oppressive, angst-driven, and incomplete present. "You convince yourself that to reach this Utopia," the Red Brigades' Adriana Faranda later recalled of the group's collective mind-set, "it is necessary to pass through the destruction of society which prevents your ideas from being realised."[35] By ignoring the present and literally soldiering on despite hardship and adversity, terrorists are able to compensate for their abject weakness and thereby overcome the temporal apathy or hostility of a constituency whom they claim to represent. "We made calculations," Faranda's comrade-in-arms Patrizio Peci explained in his memoirs. "The most pessimistic thought that within twenty years the war would be won, some said within five, ten. All, however, thought that we were living through the most difficult moment, that gradually things would become easier."[36] The left-wing terrorists thus console themselves that the travails and isolation of life underground are but a mere transitory stage on the path to final victory.

The longevity of most modern terrorist groups, however, would suggest otherwise. David Rapoport, for example, found that from 1968 to 1992, the life expectancy of at least 90 percent of terrorist organizations was less than a year and that nearly half of the ones that make it that far cease to exist within a decade.[37] Thus, the optimistic clarion calls to battle issued by terrorist groups the world over in communiqués, treatises, and other propaganda have a distinctly hollow ring given the grim reality of their organizational life cycles. "NEVER BE DETERRED BY THE ENORMOUS DIMENSIONS OF YOUR OWN GOALS," proclaimed a communiqué issued by the left-wing French terrorist group Direct Action in 1985,[38] yet less than two years later the group had effectively been decapitated by the capture of virtually its entire leadership, and shortly afterward it fell into complete lassitude. Similarly, in 1978 the RB leader Renato Curcio bragged about a struggle that he envisioned would last forty years, but within a decade even this terrorist organization—for a time one of Europe's most formidable—had collapsed under the weight of arrests and defections.[39]

Some categories of terrorist groups admittedly have better chances of survival—and perhaps success—than others. Historically, although religious movements such as the Assassins persisted for nearly two centuries and the Thugs remained active for more than six hundred years, in modern times ethnonationalist/separatist terrorist groups have typically lasted the longest and have been the most successful. Al-Fatah, the Palestinian terrorist organization led by the late Yasir Arafat, for example, was founded in 1957. The PLO itself is now more than fifty years old. The Basque group ETA was established in 1959, while the most recent incarnation of the IRA, formally known as the Provisional Irish Republican Army, lasted for nearly forty years and was itself the successor of the older official IRA that was founded nearly a century ago, which can in turn be traced back to the various Fenian revolutionary brotherhoods that had surfaced periodically since Wolfe Tone's rebellion in 1789. Except in the immediate postwar era of massive decolonization, however, success for ethnonationalist terrorist organizations has rarely involved the actual realization of their stated long-term goals of self-determination or nationhood. More often it has amounted to a string of key tactical victories that have sustained prolonged struggles and breathed new life into faltering—and in some instances, geriatric—terrorist movements.

The resilience of these groups is doubtless a product of the relative ease with which they are able to draw sustenance and support from an existing constituency, namely, the fellow members of their ethnonationalist group or religious persuasion. This is increasingly the case with many contemporary terrorist movements motivated by a salient religious imperative and whose longevity now rivals that of their ethnonationalist/separatists counterparts. Hezbollah, for instance, was founded more than forty years ago. Hamas is nearly as old, and al-Qaeda has existed for nearly three decades. Divine ordination thus endows these groups with longevity, relevance, and a potentially perennial source of recruits. By contrast, both left- and right-wing terrorist organizations have typically had shorter life spans because they must actively proselytize among a more limited pool of the politically aware and radical, though often uncommitted, for recruits and support. The ethnonationalists derive a unique advantage from their historical longevity by being able to appeal to a collective revolutionary tradition, and even at times a predisposition to rebellion. This assures successive terrorist generations both a steady stream of recruits from their respective communities' youth and a ready pool of sympathizers and supporters among their more nostalgic elders. These groups' unique ability to replenish their ranks from within already close, tight-knit communities means that even when a continuing campaign shows signs of flagging, the torch can be smoothly passed to a new generation. Abu Iyad, Arafat's intelligence chief, can therefore dismiss as mere ephemeral impediments the cul-de-sacs and roundabouts that have long hampered the advance of the Palestinian liberation movement. "Our people will bring forth a new revolution," he wrote in 1981. "They will engender a movement much more powerful than ours, better armed and thus more dangerous to the Zionists. . . . And one day, we will have a country."[40]

The ethnonationalists' comparative success, however, may have as much to do with the clarity and tangibility of their envisioned future—the establishment (or reestablishment) of a national homeland from within some existing country—as with these other characteristics. The articulation of so concrete and comprehensible a goal is by far the most potent and persuasive rallying cry. It also makes the inevitable victory appear both palpable and readily attainable, even though the path to it might be prolonged and protracted. Few would have doubted the 1977 pledge by former deputy first minister of Northern Ireland, Martin McGuinness, that the IRA (which he claimed to have left three years earlier) would keep "blattering on until Brits leave,"[41] or Danny Morrison's declaration twelve years later that "when it is politically costly for the British to remain in Ireland, they'll go. . . . It won't be triggered until a large number of British soldiers are killed and that's what's going to happen."[42]

Left-wing terrorist movements, by comparison, appear doubly disadvantaged. Not only do they lack the sizable existing pool of potential recruits available to most ethnonationalist groups, but among all the categories of terrorists they have formulated the least clear and most ill-defined vision of the future. Prolific and prodigious though their myriad denunciations of the evils of the militarist, capitalist state may be, precious little information is forthcoming about its envisioned successor. "That is the most difficult question for revolutionaries," replied Kozo Okamoto, the surviving member of the three-man Japanese Red Army (JRA) team that staged the 1972 Lod Airport massacre, when asked about the postrevolutionary society that his group sought to create. "We really do not know what it will be like."[43] The RAF's Gudrun Ensslin similarly brushed aside all questions about the group's long-term aims. "As for the state of the future, the time after victory," she once said, "that is not our concern. . . . We build the revolution, not the socialist model."[44] This inability to articulate coherently, much less cogently, their future plans may explain why the left-wing terrorists' campaigns have historically been the least effectual.

Even when left-wing terrorists have attempted to conceptualize a concrete vision of the future, their efforts have rarely produced anything more lucid or edifying than verbose disquisitions espousing an idiosyncratic interpretation of Marxist doctrine. "We have applied the Marxist analysis and method to the contemporary scene—not transferred it, but actually applied it," Ensslin wrote in a collection of RAF statements published by the group in 1977 (and subsequently banned by the German government). Yet no further elucidation of the desired result is offered, except the belief that Marxism will be rendered obsolete when the revolution triumphs and the "capitalist system has been abolished."[45] Slightly more reflective is the exposition offered by the American radical Jane Alpert, who in her memoir explains how she and her comrades-in-arms

> believed that the world could be cleansed of all domination and submission; that perception itself could be purified of the division into subject and object; and that power playing between nations, sexes, races, ages, between animals and humans, and between individuals and groups could be brought to an end. Our revolution would create a universe in which all consciousness was cosmic, in which everyone would share the bliss we knew from acid [LSD], but untainted by fear, possessiveness, sickness, hunger, or the need for a drug to bring happiness.[46]

Nonetheless, this vision comes across as so vague and idyllic as to appear almost completely divorced from reality—an effect, perhaps, of its drug-induced influence. That drugs played a part in the formulation of other leftist terrorist strategies is an interesting, though perhaps exaggerated, sidelight. Baumann, for example, also recounts the centrality of drugs to the would-be revolution. "We said integrate dope into praxis too," he recalled. "No more separate shit, but a total unification around this thing, so that a new person is born out of the struggle."[47] It should be noted, though, that a study commissioned by the Italian secret services in the 1970s discovered (somewhat counterintuitively) that right-wing terrorists were in fact more likely to abuse[48] and, indeed, to use drugs than their left-wing counterparts. Two Italian psychiatrists conducting a related study attributed this tendency to the rightists' innate psychological instability, at least compared with Italian left-wing terrorists. "In the right-wing terrorism," wrote Drs. Franco Ferracuti and Francesco Bruno, "the individual terrorists are frequently psychopathological and the ideology is empty; in left-wing terrorism, ideology is outside of reality and terrorists are more normal and fanatical."[49]

But it would be a grave error to dismiss left-wing terrorists as either totally feckless and frivolous or completely devoid of introspection or seriousness of purpose. For them, the future was simply too large and abstract a concept to comprehend; instead, action—terrorist attacks specifically designed to effect the revolution—was embraced as a far more rewarding pursuit. Accordingly, it was Fanon, and not Marx, who arguably exerted the greater influence. For example, Susan Stern, a member of the 1970s-era American left-wing terrorist group the Weathermen, recalled the dynamic tension between thought and action that permeated the group and affected all internal debate. "Once we tore down capitalism, who would empty the garbage, and teach the children and who would decide that?" she and her comrades would often consider.

> Would the world be Communist? Would the Third World control it? Would all whites die? Would all sex perverts die? Who would run the prisons—would there be prisons? Endless questions like these were raised by the Weathermen, but we didn't have the answers. *And we were tired of trying to wait until we understood everything.*[50]

The RAF's seminal treatise, "Sur la Concepcíon de la Guerilla Urbaine," reflects the same frustration. Quoting fellow revolutionary Eldridge Cleaver, a leader of the Black Panther Party, an African American radical political organization active during the 1960s, it stated: "For centuries and generations we have contemplated and examined the shit from all sides. 'Me, I'm convinced that most things which happen in this country don't need to be analysed much longer,' said Cleaver. The RAF put the words of Cleaver into practice."[51]

Indeed, all terrorists are driven by this burning impatience, coupled with an unswerving belief in the efficacy of violence. The future that they look forward to is neither temporal nor born of the natural progression of humankind; rather, it is contrived and shaped, forged and molded, and ultimately determined and achieved by violence. "What use was there in writing memoranda?" Begin rhetorically inquired to explain the Irgun's decision to resume its revolt in 1944.

> What value in speeches? . . . No, there was no other way. If we did not fight we should be destroyed. To fight was the only way to salvation.
>
> When Descartes said: 'I think, therefore, I am,' he uttered a very profound thought. But there are times in the history of peoples when thought alone does not prove their existence. . . . There are times when everything in you cries out: your very self-respect as a human being lies in your resistance to evil.
>
> We fight, therefore we are![52]

Thirty years later, Leila Khaled similarly invoked the primacy of action over talk and bullets over words: "We must act, not just talk and memorise the arguments against Zionism," she counseled.[53] This view was echoed by Yoyes, an ETA terrorist who lost faith in the endless promises that "independence can be won by peaceful means. It's all a lie. . . . The only possibility we have of gaining our liberty is through violence."[54] As the former neo-Nazi Ingo Hasselbach recalled of his own experience: "The time for legal work and patience was through. The only thing to do was to turn our *Kameradschaft* into a real terrorist organization."[55]

For some terrorists, however, the desire for action can lead to an obsession with violence itself. Abu Nidal, for example, was once known and admired for his "fiery and unbending nationalism," whereas today he is recalled and almost universally disdained as little more than an "outlaw and killer."[56] Eamon Collins recounts a similar transformation in his PIRA-gunman cousin Mickey, who, Collins realized, had gradually "lost any sense of the wider perspective, and was just obsessively absorbed by the details of the next killing."[57] Andreas Baader is perhaps a different type altogether. From the very start of the RAF's campaign, he never wavered from his conviction that the terrorist's only "language is action."[58] Baumann, who knew Baader well, remembers the RAF's founder as a "weapons maniac, [who] later developed an almost sexual relationship with pistols (the Heckler and Koch type in particular)."[59] Indeed, according to Baader himself, "Fucking and shooting [were] the same thing."[60] Unquestionably a man of action and not words, he preferred, in the terrorist vernacular, "direct actions"—bank robberies, vandalism and arson, bombings, and armed attacks—to debate and discourse. "Let's go, then!" was Baader's immediate response, for example, when his lover and coleader Ensslin suggested that the group bomb an American military base in retaliation for the U.S. Air Force's mining of North Vietnam's Haiphong harbor in 1972. Despite being the leading figure of an organization dedicated to achieving profound political change, he had absolutely no time for politics, which he derisively dismissed as a load of "shit."[61] Baader's whole approach can be summed up in the advice he gave to a wavering RAF recruit. "Either you come along [and join the revolution and fight]," he said, "or you stay forever an empty chatterbox."[62]

Although Baader may perhaps be an extreme example of this phenomenon, action is the undeniable cynosure for all terrorists—and perhaps even more so, the thrill and heady excitement that accompany it. Far more of Peci's 222-page account of his life as a Red Brigadist, for instance, is devoted to recounting in obsessive detail the types of weapons and their technical specifications used on particular RB operations and which group members actually did the shooting than to elucidating the organization's ideological aims and political goals.[63] Baumann is particularly candid about the cathartic relief that an operation brought to a small group of individuals living underground, in close proximity to one another, constantly on the run and fearful of arrest and betrayal. The real stress, he said, came from life in the group—not from the planning and execution of attacks.[64] Others, like Stern, Collins, the RAF's Silke Maier-Witt, and the RB's Susana Ronconi, are even more explicit about the "rush" and the sense of power and accomplishment they derived from the violence they inflicted. "Nothing in my life had ever been this exciting," Stern enthused as she drifted deeper into terrorism.[65] Collins similarly recalls how he led an "action-packed existence" during his six years in the IRA, "living each day with the excitement of feeling I was playing a part in taking on the Orange State."[66] For Maier-Witt, the intoxicating allure of action was sufficient to overcome the misgivings she had about the murder of Schleyer's four bodyguards in order to kidnap the man himself. "At the time I felt the brutality of that action. . . . [But it] was a kind of excitement too because something had happened. The real thing," she consoled herself, had "started now."[67] Ronconi is the most expansive and incisive in analyzing the terrorist's psychology. "The main thing was that you felt you were able to influence the world about you, instead of experiencing it passively," thereby combining intrinsic excitement with profound satisfaction. "It was this ability to make an impact on the reality of everyday life that was important," she explained, "and obviously still is important."[68]

For the terrorist, success in having this impact is most often measured in terms of the amount of publicity and attention received. Newsprint and airtime, and more recently, the accumulation of followers on Facebook, Twitter, Instagram, and other social media are thus the coins of the realm in the terrorists' mind-set—the only tangible or empirical means they have by which to gauge their success and assess their progress. In this respect, little distinction or discrimination is made between good and bad publicity. The satisfaction of simply being noticed is often regarded as sufficient reward. "The only way to achieve results," boasted the JRA in its communiqué claiming credit for the 1972 Lod Airport massacre, in which twenty-six people were slain (including sixteen Puerto Rican Christians on a pilgrimage to the Holy Land), "is to shock the world right down to its socks."[69] The archterrorist Carlos "the Jackal" reportedly meticulously clipped and had translated newspaper accounts about him and his deeds.[70] "The more I'm talked about," Carlos once explained to his terrorist colleague—later turned apostate—Hans Joachim Klein, "the more dangerous I appear. That's all the better for me."[71] Similarly, when Ramzi Ahmed Yousef, the alleged mastermind behind the 1993 bombing of New York's World Trade Center, was apprehended in Pakistan two years later, police found in his possession two remote-control explosive devices, along with a collection of newspaper articles detailing his exploits.[72]

For Carlos and Yousef, as for many other terrorists, however, this equation of publicity and attention with success and self-gratification has the effect of locking them into an unrelenting upward spiral of violence to keep the eye of the media and the public on them.[73] Yousef, for example, planned to follow the World Trade Center bombing with the assassinations of Pope John Paul II and the prime minister of Pakistan, Benazir Bhutto, and the nearly simultaneous in-flight bombings of eleven U.S. passenger airliners. Klein in fact describes escalation as a "force of habit" among terrorists—an intrinsic product of their perennial need for validation—which in turn is routinely assessed and appraised on the basis of media coverage. The effect is that terrorists today often feel driven to undertake ever more dramatic and destructively lethal deeds to achieve the same effect that a less ambitious or bloody action may have had in the past. To their minds at least, the media and the public have become progressively inured or desensitized to the seemingly endless litany of successive terrorist incidents; thus, a continuous upward ratcheting of the violence is required to retain media and public interest and attention. As Klein once observed, the "more violent things get, the more people will respect you. The greater the chance of achieving your demands."[74] Timothy McVeigh, the convicted Oklahoma City bomber, seemed to be offering the same explanation when responding to his attorney's question about whether he could not have achieved the same effect of drawing attention to his grievances against the U.S. government without killing anyone. "That would not have gotten the point across," McVeigh reportedly replied. "We needed a body count to make our point."[75] In this respect, although the Murrah Building bombing was doubtless planned well in advance of the portentously symbolic date of April 19 deliberately chosen by McVeigh, he may nonetheless have felt driven to surpass in terms of death and destruction the previous month's dramatic and more exotic nerve gas attack on the Tokyo subway in order to guarantee that his attack too received the requisite media coverage and public attention.

The terrorists' ability to attract—and, moreover, to continue to attract—attention is most often predicated on the success of their attacks. The most feared terrorists are arguably those who are the most successful in translating thought into action: they are ruthless and efficient, demonstrating that they are able to make good on their threats and back up their demands with violence. This organizational imperative to succeed, however, in turn imposes on some terrorist groups an operational conservatism that makes an ironic contrast with their political radicalism, decreeing that they adhere to an established modus operandi that, to their minds at least, minimizes the chances of failure and maximizes the chances of success. "The main point is to select targets where success is 100% assured," the doyen of modern international terrorism, George Habash, once explained.[76] For the terrorist, therefore, solid training, sound planning, good intelligence, and technological competence are the essential prerequisites for a successful operation. "I learned how to be an effective IRA member," Collins reminisced about his two-year training and induction period: "how to gather intelligence, how to set up operations, how to avoid mistakes."[77] Similarly, in a 1970 interview, an unidentified American left-wing radical who specialized in bombings described the procedures and extreme care that governed all of his group's operations. The "first decision," he said, is

> political—determining appropriate and possible targets. Once a set of tar-
> gets is decided on, they must be reconnoitered and information gathered
> on how to approach the targets, how to place the bomb, how the security
> of the individuals and the explosives is to be protected. Then the time is
> chosen and a specific target. Next there was a preliminary run-through—
> in our case a number of practice sessions. . . . The discipline during the
> actual operation is not to alter any of the agreed-upon plans or to discuss
> the action until everyone's safe within the group again. Our desire is not
> just for one success but to continue as long as possible.[78]

Good intelligence, therefore, is as critical for the success of an operation as it is for the terrorists' own survival. Perhaps for this reason, bin Laden and his minions spent five long years planning and plotting the 1998 suicide bombings of the U.S. embassies in Nairobi, Kenya, and Dar es Salaam, Tanzania.[79] The seaborne attack on the USS *Cole* took them two years to plan, while the monumental operations that would become 9/11 began to take shape as early as 1995, when KSM first began to speculate about crashing aircraft into the World Trade Center's Twin Towers and the Central Intelligence Agency headquarters in Langley, Virginia.[80] Indeed, *Mu'askar al-Battar* (Camp al-Battar) magazine, for instance, published multiple special issues such as "Covert Work Groups," "Intelligence: How to Set-up an Intelligence Network," "Outlines for Planning a Surveillance Operation," and "Military Sciences: The Planning of Operations." Typical of the detailed instruction provided was the guidance on how the

> mujahideen need a strong Islamic Intelligence apparatus to counter the
> dangers that surround their secret operations in towns. . . . The members

of this group must be chosen with extreme care . . . [and] all members [must] be trained in the gathering of field intelligence by all methods, in the writing of intelligence reports, in photography (still and video) and in the correct evaluation of information found in the filed [*sic*] (the surveillance site) . . . [so] that if security is compromised, perhaps by the arrest of a cell member, that the remaining cell member are not endangered [*sic*].[81]

An almost Darwinian principle of natural selection also seems to affect terrorist organizations, whereby (as noted above) every new terrorist generation learns from its predecessors, thus becoming smarter, tougher, and more difficult to capture or eliminate.[82] In this respect, terrorists also analyze the "lessons" to be drawn from mistakes made by former comrades who have been either killed or apprehended. Press accounts, judicial indictments, courtroom testimony, and trial transcripts are meticulously culled for information on security force tactics and methods, which is then absorbed by surviving group members. The third generation of the RAF that emerged in the late 1980s and survived for a decade more before they decided to end their self-described "campaign of liberation" in 1998, is a classic example of this phenomenon. According to a senior German official, group members routinely studied "every court case against them to discover their weak spots." Having learned about the techniques used against them by the authorities from testimony presented by law enforcement personnel in open court (in some instances having been deliberately questioned on these matters by sympathetic attorneys), the terrorists are consequently able to undertake the requisite countermeasures to avoid detection. For example, learning that the German police could usually obtain fingerprints from the bottom of toilet seats or the inside of refrigerators, surviving RAF members began to apply a special ointment to their fingers that, after drying, prevented fingerprints and thus thwarted their identification and incrimination.[83] As a spokesperson for the Bundeskriminalamt (BKA, or Federal Investigation Department) lamented in the months immediately preceding the RAF's unilateral declaration of a cease-fire in April 1992, the "'Third Generation' learnt a lot from the mistakes of its predecessors—and about how the police works. . . . They now know how to operate very carefully."[84] Indeed, according to a former member of the group, Peter-Jürgen Brock, who in 1998 was granted parole from a life sentence for murder, the RAF had "reached maximum efficiency" in the year prior to its self-declared cease-fire.[85]

Similar accolades have also been bestowed on the IRA. At the end of his tour of duty in 1992 as general officer commanding British forces in

Northern Ireland, General Sir John Wilsey described the IRA as "an absolutely formidable enemy. The essential attributes of their leaders are better than ever before. Some of their operations are brilliant in terrorist terms."[86] By this time, too, even the IRA's once comparatively unsophisticated loyalist terrorist counterparts had absorbed the lessons of their own past mistakes and had consciously emulated the IRA to become disquietingly more professional as well. One senior Royal Ulster Constabulary (RUC) officer noted this change in the loyalist terrorists' capabilities, observing in 1991 that they too were increasingly "running their operations from small cells, on a need to know basis. They have cracked down on loose talk. They have learned how to destroy forensic evidence. And if you bring them in for questioning, they say nothing."[87]

Finally, the pre-9/11 al-Qaeda also evidenced the absorption of lessons from previous experience in order to help its operatives blend in in Western environments and avoid attracting attention. Manuals found in the movement's training camps in Afghanistan purported to provide a list of "dos and don'ts" that amounted to a "Tips for the Traveling Terrorist" list. Included among the proffered advice were such pointers as:

- Don't wear short pants that show socks when you're standing up. The pants should cover the socks, because intelligence authorities know that fundamentalists don't wear long pants. . . .
- Underwear should be the normal type that people wear, not anything that shows you're a fundamentalist.
- Not long before traveling—especially from Khartoum—the person should always wear socks and shoes to [get] rid of cracks [in the feet that come from extended barefoot walking], which take about a week to cure. . . .
- You should differentiate between men and women's perfume. If you use women's perfume, you are in trouble.[88]

This learning process was evident in the operational tradecraft of the bombers responsible for the simultaneous explosions that tore through three London subway trains and a bus on July 7, 2005. The attacks on mass transit during the morning rush hour in London have inevitably been compared with the similar incident involving the bombing of four commuter trains in Madrid, Spain, on March 11, 2004, that killed 191 people. According to counterterrorism experts, a pattern has emerged whereby "radical cells learn from each attack and refine their operations, making preventive measures and police investigations more difficult." As one German police officer lamented, "Terrorists discover our tactics and respond. The competition is continuous."[89]

The Technological Treadmill

Finally, success for the terrorists is dependent on their ability to keep one step ahead of not only the authorities but also counterterrorist technology. The terrorist group's fundamental organizational imperative to act also drives this persistent search for new ways to overcome or circumvent or defeat governmental security and countermeasures.[90] The IRA's own relentless quest to pierce the armor protecting both the security forces in Northern Ireland and the most senior government officials in England illustrates the professional evolution and increasing operational sophistication of a terrorist group. The first generation of early-1970s IRA devices were often little more than crude antipersonnel bombs, consisting of a handful of roofing nails wrapped around a lump of plastic explosive and detonated simply by lighting a fuse. Time bombs from the same era were hardly more sophisticated. Typically, they were constructed from a few sticks of dynamite and commercial detonators stolen from construction sites or rock quarries attached to ordinary battery-powered alarm clocks. Neither device was terribly reliable and often put the bomber at considerable risk. The process of placing and actually lighting the first type of device carried with it the potential to attract undesired attention while affording the bomber little time to effect the attack and make good his or her escape. Although the second type of device was designed to mitigate precisely this danger, its timing and detonation mechanism was often so crude that accidental or premature explosions were not infrequent, thus causing some terrorists to kill themselves inadvertently—what was known in Belfast as "own goals." About 120 IRA members were killed in this way between 1969 and 1996.[91]

In hopes of obviating, or at least reducing, these risks, the IRA's bomb makers invented a means of detonating bombs from a safe distance using radio controls for model aircraft, which could be purchased at hobby shops. Scientists and engineers working in the scientific research and development division of the British Ministry of Defence (MoD) in turn developed a system of electronic countermeasures and jamming techniques for the army that effectively thwarted this means of attack. Rather than abandon the tactic completely, however, the IRA began to search for a solution to the problem. In contrast to the state-of-the art laboratories, huge budgets, and academic credentials of their government counterparts, the IRA's own "R&D" department toiled in cellars beneath cross-border safe houses and the back rooms of urban tenements for five years before devising a network of sophisticated electronic switches for their bombs that would ignore or bypass the army's electronic countermeasures. Once again, the MoD scientists returned to their laboratories, emerging with a new system of electronic scanners able to detect radio emissions the moment the radio is switched on—and, critically, just tens of seconds before the bomber can actually transmit the detonation signal. The almost infinitesimal window of time provided by this early warning of impending attack was just sufficient to allow army technicians to activate a series of additional electronic measures to neutralize the transmission signal and render detonation impossible.

For a time, this mechanism proved effective. But then the IRA discovered a means to outwit even this countermeasure. Using radar detectors like those used by motorists in the United States to evade speed traps, in 1991 the group's bomb makers fabricated a detonating system that could be triggered by the same type of handheld radar gun used by police throughout the world to catch speeding drivers. Since the radar gun could be aimed at its target before being switched on, and the signal that it transmitted was nearly instantaneous, no practical means currently existed either to detect or to intercept the transmission signal. Moreover, shortly after making this breakthrough, the IRA's research and development units developed yet another means to detonate bombs, using a photo-flash "slave" unit that could be triggered from a distance of up to eight hundred meters by a flash of light. This device, which sold for between sixty and seventy pounds, is used by commercial photographers to produce simultaneous flashes during photo shoots. The IRA bombers attached the unit to the detonating system on a bomb and then simply activated it with an ordinary commercially available flashgun.

Not surprisingly, therefore, the IRA bombers earned a reputation for their innovative expertise, adaptability, and cunning. "There are some very bright people around," the British Army's chief ammunitions technical officer (CATO) in Northern Ireland commented in 1992. "I would rate them very highly for improvisation. IRA bombs are very well made."[92] A similar accolade was offered that same year by the staff officer of the British Army's 321 Explosives and Ordnance Disposal Company: "We are dealing with the first division," he said. "I don't think there is any organization in the world as cunning as the IRA. They have had twenty years at it and they have learned from their experience. We have a great deal of respect for their skills . . . not as individuals, but their skills."[93] While not yet nearly as good as the IRA, the province's loyalist terrorist groups themselves were also on a learning curve with regard to bomb-making and are said to have become increasingly adept in the construction, concealment, and surreptitious placement of bombs by the early 1990s.

In certain circumstances, even attacks that are not successful in conventionally understood military terms of casualties inflicted or assets destroyed can still be counted a success for the terrorists provided that they are technologically daring enough to garner media and public attention.[94] Although the IRA failed to kill the prime minister, Margaret Thatcher, at the Conservative Party's 1984 conference in Brighton, the technological ingenuity of the attempt, involving the bomb's placement at the conference site weeks before the event and its detonation timing device powered by a computer microchip, nonetheless succeeded in capturing the world's headlines and provided the IRA with a platform from which to warn Mrs. Thatcher and all other British leaders: "Today we were unlucky, but remember we only have to be lucky once—you will have to be lucky always."[95] Similarly, although the remote-control mortar attack staged by the IRA on No. 10 Downing Street as Mrs. Thatcher's successor, John Major, and his cabinet met at the height of the 1991 Gulf War failed to hit its intended target, it nonetheless successfully elbowed the war out of the limelight and shone renewed media attention on the terrorists, their cause, and their impressive ability to strike at the nerve center of the British government, even at a time of heightened security. "The Provies are always that step ahead of you," a senior RUC officer has noted. "They are very innovative."[96] Although the technological mastery employed by the IRA is arguably unique among terrorist organizations, experience has nonetheless demonstrated repeatedly that when confronted by new security measures, terrorists will seek to identify and exploit new vulnerabilities, adjusting their means of attack accordingly and often carrying on despite the obstacles placed in their path.

Conclusion

"All politics is a struggle for power," wrote C. Wright Mills, and "the ultimate kind of power is violence."[97] Terrorism is where politics and violence intersect in the hope of delivering power. All terrorism involves the quest for power: power to dominate and coerce, to intimidate and control, and ultimately to effect fundamental political change. Violence—or the threat of violence—is thus the sine qua non of terrorists, who are unswervingly convinced that only through violence can their cause triumph and their long-term political aims be attained. Terrorists therefore plan their operations in a manner that will shock, impress, and intimidate, ensuring that their acts are sufficiently daring and violent to capture the attention of the media and, in turn, of the public and government as well. Often erroneously seen as indiscriminate or senseless, terrorism is actually a very deliberate and planned application of violence. It may be represented as a concatenation of five individual processes, designed to achieve, sequentially, the following key objectives:

1. *Attention.* Through dramatic, attention-riveting acts of violence, terrorists seek to focus attention on themselves and their causes through the publicity they receive, most often from news media coverage.
2. *Acknowledgment.* Having attracted this attention and thrust some otherwise previously ignored or hitherto forgotten cause onto the state's—or, often more desirably, the international community's—agenda, terrorists seek to translate their newfound notoriety into acknowledgment of, and perhaps even sympathy and support for, their cause.
3. *Recognition.* Terrorists attempt to capitalize on the interest and acknowledgment that their violent acts have generated by obtaining recognition of their rights (i.e., acceptance of the justification of their cause) and of their particular organization as *the* spokesperson of the constituency whom the terrorists purport to, or in some cases actually do, represent.
4. *Authority.* Armed with this recognition, terrorists seek the authority to effect the changes in government or society, or both, that lie at the heart of their movement's struggle. This may involve a change in government or in the entire state structure, or redistribution of wealth, readjustment of geographical boundaries, assertion of minority rights, imposition of theocratic rule, etc.
5. *Governance.* Having acquired authority, terrorists seek to consolidate their direct and complete control over the state and their homeland or their people, or both.

While some terrorist movements have been successful in achieving the first three objectives, rarely in modern times has any group attained the last two. Nonetheless, all terrorists exist and function in hopes of reaching this ultimate end. For them, the future rather than the present defines their reality. Indeed, they can console themselves that in 1987 the British prime minister, Margaret Thatcher, said of the African National Congress, "Anyone who thinks it is going to run the government in South Africa is living in cloud-cuckoo land."[98] Exactly ten years after that remark was uttered, Queen Elizabeth II greeted President Nelson Mandela on his first official state visit to London.

1 Four faces of terrorism (*clockwise from top left*): Carlos "the Jackal"; Yasir Arafat; Leila Khaled; George Habash. All from author's collection.

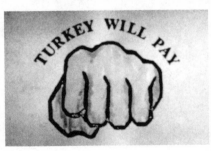

2 Symbols of terrorism (*top to bottom*): Red Army Faction (RAF); Red Brigades; Popular Front for the Liberation of Palestine (PFLP); Justice Commandos of the Armenian Genocide (JCAG). All from author's collection.

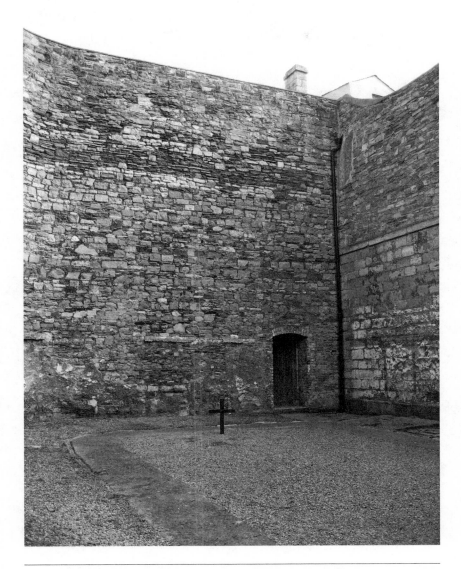

3 Courtyard of Kilmainham Gaol in Dublin, Ireland, where Patrick Pearse, a leader of the 1916 Easter Rising, was shot by firing squad. Author's collection.

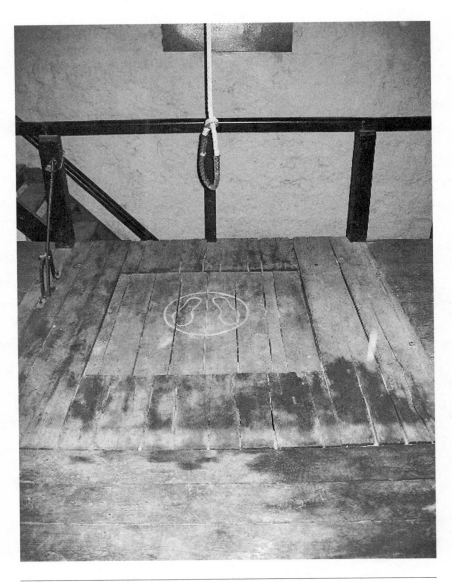

4 Gallows at Central Prison facility, Russian Compound, Jerusalem, used by the British to hang Jewish terrorists, 1947. Author's collection.

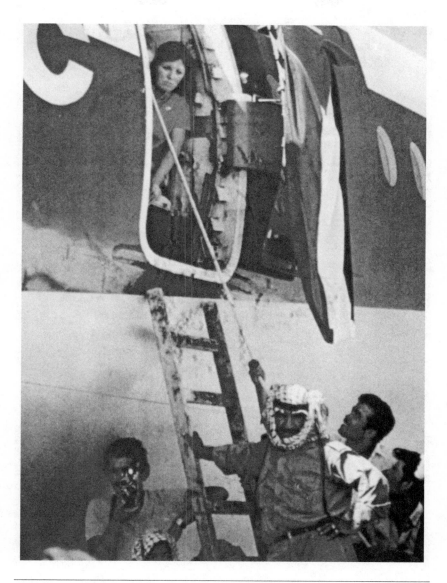

5 Popular Front for the Liberation of Palestine hijacking of BOAC airliner, Dawson's Field, Jordan, September 1970. Author's collection.

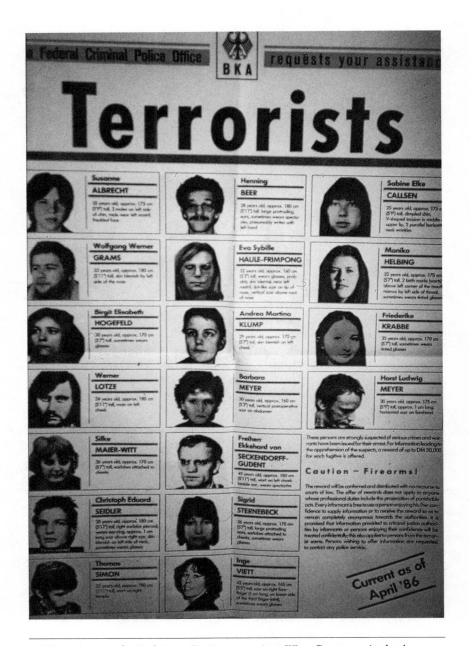

6 Wanted poster for Red Army Faction terrorists, West Germany. Author's collection.

7 Americans held hostage in Iran, 1979–1980. Author's collection.

8 The IRA (Irish Republican Army) targets London: Hyde Park, July 1982. Author's collection.

9 "Free Ireland" with Fist in Chains wall mural, Beechmount Avenue, West Belfast, Northern Ireland, 1991. Author's collection.

10 Wreckage of Pan Am Flight 103 at Lockerbie, Scotland, December 1988. Photo courtesy of Georges de Keerle/Getty Images.

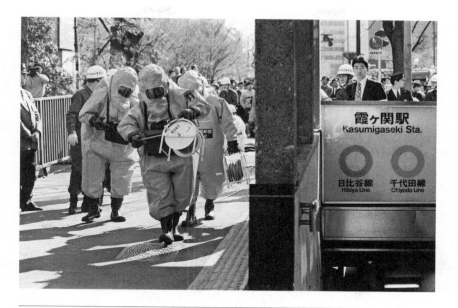

11 Tokyo nerve gas attack, March 1995. Photo courtesy of *Asahi Shimbun*/Getty Images.

12 Bombing of the Alfred P. Murrah Federal Office Building, Oklahoma City, April 1995. Photo courtesy of J. Pat Carter/Getty Images.

13 LTTE (Liberation Tigers of Tamil Eelam, or Tamil Tigers) suicide terrorist ID cards. Author's collection.

14 "The Zionist entity surely will disintegrate." Hamas poster in Arabic and Hebrew, 2004. Author's collection.

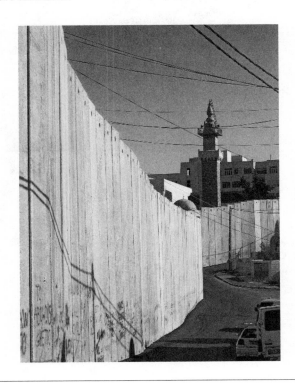

15 Section of separation barrier cutting through Abu Dis, East Jerusalem. Author's collection.

16 Osama bin Laden. Photo courtesy of Universal Images Group/Getty Images.

17 World Trade Center collapses, New York City, September 11, 2001. Photo courtesy of David Surowiecki/Getty Images.

18 Front page of the *Daily Mirror*, London, January 8, 2003. Photo courtesy of Scotland Yard and Mirrorpix.

19 The Madrid train attack on March 11, 2004. Photo courtesy of Oliver Lang/Getty Images.

20 July 7, 2005, suicide bombing of a London bus. Photo courtesy of AFP (Agence France Presse)/Getty Images.

21 U.S. Predator unmanned aerial vehicle taking off from Bagram Airfield, Afghanistan, March 2008. Author's collection.

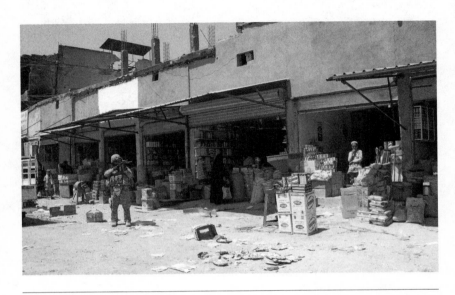

22 U.S. Army patrol in the Sadr City neighborhood of Baghdad, Iraq, August 2008. Author's collection.

Chapter 9

Terrorism Today and Tomorrow I

Force Multipliers

S tate sponsorship of terrorism did not cease with either the Soviet Union and the Warsaw Pact's demise or with the dramatic regime changes that occurred in both Iraq and Libya. Indeed, for other countries such as Iran, Syria, and Sudan—which remain on the U.S. State Department's list of state sponsors of terrorism—covert aid to these proxies continues to be viewed as an efficacious instrument to attain their respective foreign policy priorities. Meanwhile, terrorist attraction to CBRN—chemical, biological, radiological,[1] and nuclear—weapons[2] similarly is also undiminished. Accordingly, we face a two-pronged threat: on the one hand from terrorists attempting to develop capabilities spanning all four weapons categories, and on the other hand from those who are attracted to some of these weapons less for their potential lethality than because of the profoundly corrosive and unsettling psychological effects that even a limited, discrete attack using a chemical, biological, or radiological device could have on a targeted society. This chapter considers these two highly consequential force multipliers of contemporary terrorism. It first assesses the persistence and implications of ongoing state-sponsored terrorism before considering the history of terrorist attraction to CBRN weapons, the challenges that terrorists have encountered in attempting to harness these potential game-changing means of attack, and potential future terrorist intentions regarding their use.

The Emergence of Modern State-Sponsored Terrorism

Governments have long engaged in various types of illicit, clandestine activities—including the systematic use of terror—against their enemies, both domestic and foreign. The Nazis' victimization of Jews, Gypsies, communists, homosexuals, political rivals, and other "enemies of the state" in Germany, and the Serbian military's intimate involvement in fomenting anti-Hapsburg unrest in Bosnia on the eve of World War I are two clear examples of past state sponsorship of, or indeed outright use of, terrorism. But what sets these (and many other historical) cases apart from the type of state-sponsored terrorism that has emerged since the early 1980s is the way in which some governments have embraced terrorism as a deliberate instrument of foreign policy, i.e., as a cost-effective means of waging war covertly, through the use of surrogate warriors, proxies, or guns for hire.

The pivotal event in this most recent emergence of state-sponsored terrorism as a weapon of state and an instrument of foreign policy was the November 1979 seizure of fifty-two American hostages at the U.S. embassy in Tehran by a group of militant Iranian "students." For 444 days, these so-called students—who claimed to have acted independently, without government support or encouragement—held the world's most powerful country at bay. Throughout that protracted episode, they focused unparalleled worldwide media attention on both themselves and their anti-American cause, ultimately costing an American president his reelection to office. As events would later show, this incident was only the beginning of an increasingly serious and extensive state-sponsored terrorism campaign directed by the Iranian regime of Ayatollah Khomeini against the United States as well as other Western countries. Its lessons, moreover, were absorbed not only by Iran's clerical rulers, who sought to expunge Western—and especially American—influence from the Middle East, but by the leaders of the region's other pariah states (Libya, Syria, and Iraq) as well as by foreign governments elsewhere. Acts of violence, perpetrated by terrorists secretly working for governments, were shown to be a relatively inexpensive and, if executed properly, potentially risk-free means of anonymously attacking stronger enemies, thereby avoiding the threat of international punishment or reprisal. As Daniel Byman argues in his seminal work on the subject, "States sponsor terrorists as their proxies for a variety of reasons. The most important is often strategic interest: terrorists offer another means for states to influence their neighbors, topple a hostile adversary regime, counter US hegemony, or achieve other aims of state."[3]

For the terrorist, the benefits of state sponsorship were even greater. Such a relationship appreciably enhanced the capabilities and operational capacity of otherwise limited terrorist groups, placing at their disposal the resources of an established nation-state's entire diplomatic, military, and intelligence apparatus, thus greatly facilitating planning and operations. The logistical support provided by states assured the terrorists of otherwise unobtainable luxuries, such as the use of diplomatic pouches for the transport of weapons and explosives, false identification in the form of genuine passports, and the use of embassies and other diplomatic facilities as safe houses or staging bases. State sponsorship also afforded terrorists greater training opportunities; hence, some groups were transformed into entities more akin to elite commando units than to the stereotypical conspiratorial cell of anarchists wielding Molotov cocktails or radicals manufacturing crude pipe bombs. Finally, terrorists were often paid handsomely for their services, turning hitherto financially destitute entities into well-endowed organizations with investment profiles and healthy balance sheets.

For all these reasons, it was not necessary for the state-sponsored terrorist to identify with his patron's cause. Nor did he necessarily have to be the rabid ideologue, religious zealot, or extreme nationalist common to ideologically and religiously motivated groups or ethnonationalist/separatist organizations. All the state-sponsored terrorist needed to do was to be willing to perform a service for a price, as an independent mercenary—a mere "hired gun." The Abu Nidal Organization (ANO) is among the most prominent cases in point. This group, founded and led by the Palestinian terrorist Sabri al-Banna (aka Abu Nidal, "Father of the Struggle"), had been variously employed by Syria, Iraq, and Libya—three countries that regularly appeared on the U.S. State Department's list of state sponsors of terrorism from the time that it was established in 1979 until Iraq was removed in 2003 and Libya in 2006 (Syria remains on the list).[4] As ANO profited from its mercenary role, the group progressively relinquished its original revolutionary/political motivations in favor of activities devoted almost entirely to making money. The group, accordingly, had reputedly amassed a considerable fortune, initially through its for-hire terrorist activities, but subsequently from shrewd commercial and real estate investments derived from its nefarious income, including the lucrative operation of a multinational arms trading company that had been based in Poland. In 1988, ANO's assets were said to be worth an estimated $400 million. Given the vast profits involved, it is not surprising that the group's financial portfolio was administered by a separate finance directorate within the organization—with Abu Nidal himself at its head.[5] He died in 2002, having fled from Libya to Iraq, where he allegedly committed suicide rather than face continued interrogation at the hands of Saddam Hussein's feared security service.[6]

Even supposedly ideologically pure Marxist-Leninist organizations, such as the Japanese Red Army (JRA), built up a fortune during the 1980s through commissioned terrorism. The JRA, which was based in Lebanon's Bekaa Valley since its founding in 1971 by a former Meiji University student named Fusako Shigenobu, always sought outside patrons. Initially, the PFLP filled this role, with the JRA performing operations—such as the 1972 suicide machine-gun and hand-grenade attack on Israel's Lod Airport, in which twenty-six people were killed and eighty others were wounded—on the Palestinian organization's behalf. Later, the JRA was taken under the wing of the world's legendary master terrorist, Carlos "the Jackal," for whom it carried out operations including the takeover of the French embassy in The Hague in 1974 and the bombing that same year of a popular discotheque on rue St. Germain in Paris, where two people were killed and thirty-five were injured. In 1986, Shigenobu decided to diversify the JRA's income stream still further by cutting a lucrative deal with Libyan leader Muammar Qaddafi. Only a few months earlier, U.S. Air Force jets had bombed Tripoli and Benghazi in retaliation for Libya's alleged involvement in a terrorist attack on a West Berlin nightclub popular with American GIs that had killed two people and wounded some two hundred others. Qaddafi was desperate for revenge; fearing further American retaliatory air strikes were he to take direct action, he turned to the JRA for help. The group was only too happy to oblige, adopting the alias Anti-Imperialist International Brigades (AIIB) as a cover for those operations executed specifically on Libya's behalf.

The JRA mounted the first AIIB attack in June 1986, targeting the American and Japanese embassies in Jakarta, Indonesia, with remote-controlled mortars positioned in a nearby hotel room. The following year, the group commemorated the first anniversary of the U.S. air strike with an identical attack on three U.S. diplomatic facilities in Madrid. They struck again in June, detonating a car bomb outside the U.S. embassy in Rome, and shortly afterward launched rocket attacks against that same target as well as the nearby British embassy. To mark the second anniversary of the 1986 U.S. air strike, the JRA/AIIB initiated its most ambitious plan: simultaneous attacks against American military targets in the United States and Europe. The American arm of the plan, however, went seriously awry a month before the attacks were to commence when a veteran JRA terrorist, Yu Kikumura, was arrested by a New Jersey state police officer in March while en route to New York. In the backseat of Kikumura's car, the police officer found several hollowed-out fire extinguishers, packed with explosive material and roofing nails. Kikumura had planned to place these crude but effective antipersonnel bombs outside a U.S. Navy recruiting station on Thirty-Fourth Street in Manhattan.[7] Kikumura was subsequently convicted and sentenced to thirty years in prison.

The other JRA/AIIB attacks scheduled for that day in Europe, however, went as planned. A car bomb exploded outside a U.S. military club in Naples, killing five people and wounding seventeen others, while in Spain the group bombed a U.S. air base. Then, in July, the AIIB attacks suddenly ended, with a failed remote-controlled rocket attack on the U.S. embassy in Madrid. Thereafter, the JRA itself mysteriously ceased active terrorist operations, its twenty or so members supposedly having retired from terrorism to the group's base in the Bekaa Valley or to its sanctuary in North Korea to live off the sizable nest egg that Shigenobu had accumulated for herself and her followers. In 2000, however, Shigenobu returned to Japan and was promptly arrested. Six years later she was tried and sentenced to a twenty-year prison term. Shigenobu formally disbanded the group in 2002.[8]

Since state-sponsored terrorism is geared less to obtaining publicity than to pursuing specific foreign policy objectives by covertly bringing pressure to bear on the sponsor's opponents through acts of violence, it operates under fewer constraints than does ordinary terrorism. In addition, because state-sponsored terrorists do not depend on the local population for support, they need not concern themselves with the risk of alienating popular support or provoking a public backlash. Thus, the state-sponsored terrorist and his patron can engage in acts of violence that are typically more destructive and bloodier than those carried out by groups acting on their own behalf. Indeed, given the enhanced resources that state-supported groups can command, it is not surprising to find that in the 1980s identifiable state-sponsored terrorist attacks were overall eight times more lethal than those carried out by groups without state support or assistance. Among them were

- the April 1983 suicide car bomb explosion outside the U.S. embassy in Beirut that killed 69 people and was claimed by Islamic Jihad (Islamic Holy War), a cover name used by the Iranian-backed Lebanese Shi'a terrorist group Hezbollah;
- the simultaneous suicide truck bombings of the U.S. Marine headquarters at Beirut International Airport and the French paratroop headquarters in that city, which killed 241 Marines and 58 paratroopers, respectively, in October 1983, and for which Islamic Jihad/Hezbollah also took credit, boasting in a communiqué how "two martyr *mujahidin* [holy warriors] set out to inflict upon the U.S. Administration an utter defeat not experienced since Vietnam, and a similar one upon the French Administration";[9]
- the identical attack carried out by the same group on the Israeli military government building in Sidon the following month that resulted in the deaths of 67 people;

- the coordinated car bomb attacks in Karachi, Pakistan, carried out by agents of Afghanistan's secret intelligence service, WAD (Wizarat-i Amaniyyat-i Dawlati or "Ministry of State Security"), in July 1987, killing 72 people and wounding more than 250 others;
- the bomb placed by two North Korean agents on a Korean Air Lines plane en route from Baghdad to Seoul that killed all 115 people on board in November 1987;
- the sabotage of a munitions dump in Islamabad, Pakistan, in April 1988 by Afghani WAD operatives that killed more than 100 people and wounded 1,100;
- the midair explosion aboard Pan Am Flight 103 in December 1988 over Lockerbie, Scotland, that claimed the lives of all 259 passengers as well as 11 people on the ground and has been linked to two Libyan intelligence agents, acting not only with official Libyan state sanction but possibly at the behest of Iran as well; and
- the in-flight bombing of a French UTA (Union de Transports Aériens) passenger jet over Chad in August 1989 that killed 171 people and was claimed by Islamic Jihad.

State-sponsored terrorism has also been employed on a far more discriminating scale to stifle external dissent. Exiled opposition figures, political dissidents, human rights activists, journalists, political cartoonists, and others have been intimidated and, in some instances, murdered at the behest of various foreign governments. In one especially notorious case, Bulgarian agents used a poison-tipped umbrella to murder dissident exile Georgi Markov on a London bridge in 1978.[10] Libyan, Iranian, and Iraqi agents have also allegedly carried out operations against opponents of their respective regimes residing in the United States, France, Germany, Italy, Switzerland, Austria, South Africa, and the United Kingdom. In 1991, for example, an Iranian hit team, using diplomatic cover, assassinated former prime minister and outspoken critic of the Khomeini regime Shahpur Baktiar in Paris, and since 1989 Salman Rushdie, the Pakistani-born British author of *The Satanic Verses*, has lived under the fatwa (religious edict) death sentence imposed on him and his publishers for blasphemy by the Ayatollah Khomeini, in pursuit of which a group of Iranian clerics offered a $2.5 million bounty to whoever fulfills the ayatollah's decree. Thus far, the book's Japanese translator has been stabbed to death, its Norwegian publisher shot, and its Italian translator knifed, while Rushdie himself once was forced to lead a life on the run, protected around the clock by Scotland Yard's Special Branch at a cost to British taxpayers of more than one million pounds.[11] The most serious—and daring—state-sponsored terrorist incident of the 1980s was the attempt on the life of Pope John Paul II as he greeted the crowd gathered in St. Peter's Square on May 13, 1981. Although a young Turkish terrorist, Mehmet Ali Agca, was apprehended on the spot and subsequently convicted of the attack, it is widely believed that the Bulgarian secret service was behind the assassination plot—allegedly acting on instructions from KGB head and later premier of the Soviet Union Yuri Andropov.[12]

Finally, countries have supported terrorists to fulfill internal as well as external political and geostrategic priorities—sometimes simultaneously. The assistance provided by Pakistan's Inter-Services Intelligence (ISI) to Kashmiri separatist groups such as Lashkar-e-Taiba (LeT) is an especially notable example. Through LeT, the ISI first and foremost is able to prosecute a covert shadow war against India over the contested former princely state of Kashmir. Among the most egregious incidents in this campaign have been the series of bombings of Mumbai commuter trains in 2006 that killed 209 persons and injured more than 700 others, and the simultaneous assaults two years later on two luxury hotels, the central train station, a hospital, bars and cafes, a cinema, and a Jewish community center in that same city that claimed the lives of 164 persons and wounded over 300 others. At the same time, Pakistani intelligence has also regularly employed the LeT as a useful stalking horse to undermine domestic antistate religious extremists and dampen down internal political violence and unrest.[13]

A Persistent Phenomenon

Today, state sponsorship of terrorism continues—albeit with fewer countries formally designated as sponsors by the U.S. State Department. As of 2016, only three countries are listed as terrorism sponsors: Iran, Sudan, and Syria.[14] With the exception of Sudan, which was added in 1993, both Syria and Iran have remained on the list of terrorism's patron states for more than three decades. The reason, as noted above, is that neither economic sanctions in the case of both Libya and Iran nor military reprisals in Libya's case proved entirely successful in effecting positive changes to these countries' policies on terrorism. In the past, the use of military force short of outright invasion and regime change has actually been counterproductive in some instances. The aforementioned 1986 U.S. air strike against Libya, for example, is frequently cited as proof of the effectiveness of military retaliation; yet rather than deterring the Qaddafi regime from engaging in state-sponsored terrorism, it appears that it may have had precisely the opposite effect. In the first place, far from stopping Libyan-backed terrorism, the U.S.

air strike goaded the Libyan dictator to undertake even more serious and heinous acts of terrorism against the United States and its citizens. Indeed, after a brief lull, Libya not only resumed but actually increased its international terrorist activities. According to the RAND Corporation's Terrorism Incident Database, at least fifteen identifiable state-sponsored terrorist incidents occurred in 1987 and eight in 1988—including the previously cited for hire incidents perpetrated by the JRA/AIIB—and they were subsequently linked to Libya.[15] The incident involving Kikumura is especially noteworthy as evidence that Qaddafi not only continued his terrorist campaign against the United States but significantly escalated it in dispatching the veteran JRA terrorist to New York on the failed bombing mission.

The United States was not the only country to suffer continued acts of Libyan-sponsored international terrorism. In retaliation for Britain's role in allowing the U.S. warplanes that bombed Tripoli and Benghazi to take off from bases in the United Kingdom, Qaddafi deliberately increased his supply of weapons to the IRA. During the months following the air strike, the Irish terrorist group reportedly took delivery of some five to ten tons of Semtex-H plastic explosive (Semtex-H is so powerful that investigators believe that only about 8 ounces were required to bring down Pan Am Flight 103), in addition to 120 tons of other arms and explosives, including twelve SAM-7 ground-to-air missiles, stocks of RPG-7 rocket-propelled grenades, and antiaircraft and antitank guns.[16] British authorities largely credit the Libyan weapons shipments with having appreciably facilitated the IRA's terror campaign over the following months and years.

As for the air strikes sending a powerful deterrent message to other terrorists elsewhere, as the Reagan administration claimed at the time, the evidence is similarly wanting. Indeed, more terrorist attacks against American targets occurred during the three-month period following the U.S. action (fifty-three) than during the three months preceding it (forty-one).[17] In fact, the U.S. State Department admitted in the 1996 edition of its *Patterns of Global Terrorism* that Libya had continued throughout the period to provide support for the most "rejectionist" (that is, the most vehemently opposed to the Israeli-Palestinian peace process and dialogue) and extreme of the Palestinian terrorist groups, including ANO, the PIJ, and Ahmed Jibril's PFLP-GC (General Command). And as previously noted, Abu Nidal made his home—and had his organization's headquarters—in Libya for more than a decade afterward.[18]

Finally, even the oft-repeated claims of the attack's surgical precision and the immense technological sophistication of American precision-guided air-delivered ordnance fail to hold up under examination. Despite the particularly careful selection of military targets for the U.S. fighter-bombers, thirty-six civilians were killed in the air strike and ninety-three others were wounded. These civilian deaths and injuries not only were tragic in themselves but they deprived the United States of the moral high ground it often claims to occupy with respect to terrorists and terrorism, and thereby engendered further domestic and international criticism. Perhaps the most incontrovertible—and obvious, if ignored—refutation of the persuasive force of military retaliation, however, is the 1988 in-flight bombing of Pan Am Flight 103. After what has been described as "the most extensive criminal investigation in history," the joint FBI and Scottish police investigation resulted in the indictment of two Libyan employees of that country's national airline, Abdel Basset Ali al-Megrahi and Lamen Khalifa Fhimah, who were alleged to have been agents of Qaddafi's intelligence service.[19] In January 2001, a special Scottish court sitting in the Netherlands convicted al-Megrahi, who was sentenced to life imprisonment. Fhimah was acquitted of the charges against him and released.[20] Al-Megrahi, however, gained his freedom in 2009 on compassionate grounds after he received a medical diagnosis of terminal prostate cancer. He returned to a hero's welcome in Libya, where he died nearly three years later.[21]

Iran's long-standing sponsorship of terrorism has become a regular feature of the U.S. State Department's annual *Country Reports on Terrorism*. The 2015 report (the most recent year available), for instance, unambiguously assailed Iran for its "continued . . . terrorist-related activity," specifically citing

- the support Iran regularly provides to "Hizballah, Palestinian terrorist groups in Gaza, and various groups in Iraq and throughout the Middle East";
- Iran's refusal to "bring to justice senior al-Qa'ida (AQ) members it continue[s] to detain and refus[ing] to publicly identify the members in its custody";
- for having "previously allowed AQ facilitators to operate a core facilitation pipeline through Iran since at least 2009, enabling AQ to move funds and fighters to South Asia and Syria";
- for giving "weapons, funding, and training to Shia militants in Bahrain"; and
- providing "arms, financing, training, and the facilitation of primarily Iraqi, Afghan, and Pakistani Shia fighters to support the Assad regime's brutal crackdown that has resulted in the deaths of more than 250,000 people in Syria."[22]

In previous years, the State Department has also accused Iran of actively planning and facilitating the execution of attacks by both its agents and surrogates in groups such as the Lebanese Hezbollah.[23] During the 1990s, for instance, Iran was alleged to have disbursed about $100 million a year to various Islamic terrorist organizations across the world, with the lion's share going to Hezbollah.[24] Tehran has also been linked to ongoing subversive activities in several Gulf states, including a foiled 1996 coup in Bahrain. And Iran has been directly implicated in the 1992 and 1994 bombings of the Israeli embassy and a Jewish community center in Buenos Aires, respectively, which claimed the lives of a total of 114 persons and injured more than 500 others.[25]

Conclusive proof of Iran's continued sponsorship of international terrorism was revealed in a Berlin court in April 1997, when convictions were obtained for an Iranian and four Lebanese accused of the 1992 killing of three Iranian Kurdish dissidents and their translator, murders carried out on instructions from Tehran. As a result of evidence presented during the trial, which lasted nearly four years, the German authorities issued an arrest warrant for Ali Fallahian, the Iranian minister of intelligence, for his role in the murders, and accused the Iranian government's Committee for Special Operations, which reportedly comprised the highest echelon of Iran's ruling elite, including President Hashemi Rafsanjani and the country's supreme religious leader, the Ayatollah Ali Khamenei, of actually having issued orders for the dissidents' murder. Exile sources maintained that Tehran was directly responsible for the murder of at least twenty Iranian opposition figures in Europe between 1979 and 1997.[26] Nevertheless, American efforts to dissuade Iran from sponsoring terrorism have proven largely ineffective. In 1995, for example, the CIA's deputy director for intelligence testified before Congress that the U.S. economic embargo imposed the previous April had been "a failure" and would be unlikely ever to have any impact without more widespread international support. At the time, only Israel, El Salvador, and Côte d'Ivoire had answered President Clinton's call for sanctions.[27]

Even those countries on the State Department's list that may not be current, active sponsors of international terrorism nevertheless play a critical role in abetting terrorist operations. Although the degree of active involvement may ebb and flow depending on circumstances, internal or external political conditions, and timeous opportunities for expansion or consolidation, or both, these regimes' belief in this covert means of power projection is unwavering. Also, without their provision of training facilities, sanctuary, safe havens, and other passive forms of support, many terrorist groups would find it far more difficult to continue to operate. For example, although there is no evidence that either Syria or Syrian government officials have been directly involved in the planning or execution of international terrorist attacks since 1986, that country continues to provide sanctuary and assistance to terrorists. The PFLP-GC, a Palestinian faction firmly opposed to the Arab-Israeli peace process, which was implicated just before the 1988 bombing of Pan Am Flight 103 in a plot to target American and Israeli commercial aircraft flying from Europe,[28] has had its headquarters in Damascus for over half a century and continues to help prop up the Assad regime.[29] And Syria has long allowed Iran to use Damascus as a transit point for supplies destined for Hezbollah in neighboring Lebanon.[30]

At the height of the anti-American insurgency in Iraq, in June 2005 the United States had faulted Syria for permitting Iraqi insurgents—former Ba'athist Party members and regime loyalists as well as foreign fighters affiliated with Abu Musab al-Zarqawi's organization—to use that country as a cross-border base from which to mount attacks in Iraq.[31] Finally, both Syria and Iran's terrorist client Hezbollah has been blamed for the car bomb assassination of former Lebanese prime minister Rafik Hariri in February 2005 (twenty others were also killed), as well as for the subsequent murder of other outspoken Lebanese politicians and journalists opposed to Syrian domination of Lebanon.[32] And most recently Iran and Hezbollah were accused of orchestrating the 2012 bombing of a bus filled with Israeli tourists at the Black Sea resort of Burgas, which killed six persons and injured more than thirty others.[33]

For countries such as Iran and Syria, then, terrorism remains a useful and integral foreign policy tool: a clandestine weapon to be wielded whenever the situation is appropriate and the benefits are tangible, or kept sheathed when the risks of using it appear to outweigh the potential gains and the possible repercussions are likely to be counterproductive. For the state sponsor, much as for the terrorist group itself, terrorism—contrary to popular perception—is not a mindless act of fanatical or indiscriminate violence; rather, it is a purposefully targeted, deliberately calibrated method of pursuing specific objectives at acceptable cost. In this respect, the attractions of terrorists as surrogate warriors or mercenaries for various renegade regimes may in fact have increased thus far in the twenty-first century. Future aggressors may prefer to accomplish clandestinely with a handful of armed men and a limited amount of weaponry what traditionally whole armies, navies, and air forces have been deployed to achieve. Not only could such small bands facilitate the subversion and conquest of neighboring or rival states, but if such action is carried out covertly—and successfully—the state sponsor might escape identification, and hence international military response and economic sanction. Accordingly, terrorists may in the future come to be regarded by the globe's rogue states as the "ultimate fifth column"—a clandestine, cost-effective force used to wage war covertly against more powerful rivals or to subvert neighboring countries or hostile regimes.

CBRN Terrorism

From the time of the French Revolution until the late twentieth century, terrorism was practiced mostly by groups and persons inspired by ideological, ethnonationalist, or irredentist motivations. Radical leftist organizations such as the JRA, RAF, and Red Brigades, as well as ethnonationalist and separatist terrorist movements such as the PLO, IRA, and ETA, generally engaged in highly selective and mostly discriminate acts of violence. To attract attention to themselves and their causes, they chose for bombing various symbolic targets representing the source of their animus (i.e., embassies, banks, national airline carriers, etc.) or kidnapped and assassinated specific persons whom they blamed for economic exploitation or political repression. In this respect, their violence was deliberately kept within the bounds of what the terrorists believed to be the prevailing political order and their core constituency of sympathizers and supporters deemed acceptable.

Terrorists were therefore seen as being careful not to undertake actions that might foreclose negotiations with their opponents, alienate them from the global political order that the terrorist organizations sought to become a part of, or brook censure, condemnation, or worse from their actual or perceived constituency. These terrorists appeared to be cognizant of the likelihood that acts of mass destruction or unmitigated bloodshed might result not only in international and domestic revulsion and castigation but that they might also trigger severe governmental reprisals or countermeasures. In the words of James Woolsey, a former Director of Central Intelligence, terrorists used to want to acquire a "seat at the table" as opposed to today when they "seek . . . to blow up the table and kill everyone sitting there."[34]

For this reason, the violence used by left-wing movements that were among the dominant forces of terrorism throughout the latter decades of the twentieth-century was always narrowly proscribed: it was typically directed against governmental or commercial institutions or persons whom they believed represented capitalist exploitation or political repression, or both. Specific individuals—wealthy industrialists such as Hans Martin Schleyer, who was kidnapped and murdered by the RAF in 1977, or distinguished parliamentarians such as Aldo Moro, whom the Italian Red Brigades similarly abducted and executed the following year, alongside lower-ranking government officials, factory managers, or ordinary civil servants—were most often targeted. When the Left did resort to bombing, the violence was conceived in equally symbolic terms. In this sense, although the damage and destruction that often resulted were certainly not symbolic, the act itself was meant to dramatize or call attention to the terrorists' grievances or political cause by striking at targets emblematic or symbolic of the terrorists' animus and fundamental raison d'être.

This approach was not entirely dissimilar from that taken by the numerous ethnonationalist and separatist groups that were also active during that era: the PLO, IRA, and ETA, among others. Although acts of terrorism committed by this category of terrorists were frequently more destructive and caused more casualties than those of their left-wing counterparts, the same self-imposed constraints and balancing act of finding a level of violence acceptable to their actual or perceived constituents while still generally conforming to the international political community's acceptable boundaries of tolerance was clearly evident. In a broader sense, ethnonationalist and separatist terrorism was often specifically designed to appeal to international as well as internal opinion in support of the terrorists' irredentist or nationalist aims. Hence, to continue to receive the support of their constituency, gain a seat at the table, generate sympathy among the international community, and indeed forestall massive governmental countermeasures as well, these terrorists also strove to regulate and calibrate their violence. The vast majority of their targets, accordingly, were often individuals: they were confined to low-ranking government officials, ordinary soldiers or policemen, other so-called agents of the state, and members of rival communities or ethnic groups, as well as their own brethren suspected of being traitors and informants.

Finally, however radical or revolutionary these groups were politically, the vast majority were also equally conservative in their operations. In Brian Jenkins's memorable aphorism, these sorts of terrorists were said to be demonstrably more "imitative than innovative"; they had a very limited tactical repertoire that was mostly directed against a similarly narrow target set.[35] They were judged as hesitant to take advantage of new situations, let alone to create new opportunities. Accordingly, what little innovation that was observed was more in the terrorists' choice of targets—e.g., the 1985 hijacking of the Italian cruise ship the *Achille Lauro* by Palestinian terrorists as opposed to the more typical terrorist hijacking of passenger aircraft—or in the methods used to conceal and detonate explosive devices than in any particularly innovative tactics, much less in their use of unconventional weapons, whether chemical, biological, radiological, and especially, nuclear.

Although various terrorist groups—the RAF,[36] the Red Brigades, and some Palestinian organizations—had reputedly toyed with the idea of using such indiscriminately lethal weapons, none had crossed the critical threshold of actually implementing their heinous daydreams or executing their half-baked plots. For example, occasionally there were unconfirmed reports that these groups had at one time or another "recruited microbiologists, purchased bacteriological experimentation equipment and dabbled in sending toxins such as anthrax to potential victims."[37] What is known is that in 1979 in hopes of sabotaging Israel's economy, Palestinian terrorists were suspected of having poisoned some Jaffa oranges exported to Europe; then, in 1984, followers of the Bhagwan Shree Rajneesh, as discussed in chapter 4, contaminated the salad bars of ten restaurants with salmonella bacteria; and six years later, the LTTE used chlorine gas in an attack on a Sri Lankan military camp at East Kiran.[38] But until the mid-1990s, these three isolated incidents represented virtually the total extent of either actual use or serious attempts at the use by terrorists of such unconventional weapons and tactics.

Instead, most terrorists seemed almost content with the limited killing potential of their handguns and machine-guns, and the slightly higher rates that their bombs achieved. Like most people, terrorists themselves appeared to fear powerful contaminants and toxins they knew little about and were uncertain how to fabricate and safely handle, much less effectively deploy and disperse. Indeed, of the some twelve thousand incidents then recorded in the RAND Terrorism Incident Database between 1968 and 1998, perhaps only sixty or so evidenced any indication[39] of terrorists *seriously* plotting such attacks, attempting to use chemical or biological agents or intending to steal, or otherwise fabricate, their own nuclear devices.

Perhaps the main reason that terrorist use of CBRN was discounted was because terrorists, it was repeatedly argued, were fundamentally rational.[40] There were few realistic demands that terrorists could make by threatening the use of such indiscriminate weapons. There were also few objectives that terrorists sought that could not be obtained by less extreme measures than the detonation of a nuclear device or dispersal of radioactive materials,[41] or by attacks employing either biological or chemical warfare agents. In perhaps the most important book written on the subject in the 1970s, Walter Laqueur unambiguously concluded, "It can be taken for granted that most of the terrorist groups existing at present will not use this option, either as a matter of political principle or because it would defeat their purpose."[42]

The terrorists' perceived obsession with controlling events was also regarded as an important constraint.[43] "Terrorists, like war planners," one unidentified expert opined at a mid-1980s symposium on the subject of nuclear terrorism, "believe they can control what they start . . . and CB [chemical and biological agents] seems too uncontrollable."[44] Hence, this line of argument went, terrorists would forswear from using weapons that could not be discriminately directed against their enemies only, and that therefore could also harm their ethnic brethren, coreligionists, or that often declared but indistinctly amorphous constituency, the so-called people. Of equal significance was that whereas terrorists had mastered all the components of operations using conventional weapons, they were thought to be wary of venturing into such terra incognita as CBRN weapons. Like most ordinary people, it was reasoned, terrorists also harbored profound fears about dangerous radioactive and infectious substances, toxins, and gases that they knew little about and, if handled improperly, would affect them as adversely as it would their intended target(s).

Even when experts in the 1970s thought about possible terrorist use of WMD, the prevailing consensus was that terrorists would axiomatically prefer nuclear or radiological weapons over chemical or biological ones.[45] As Brian Jenkins, perhaps that era's preeminent terrorism analyst, explained in a paper presented at the same conference noted above: "Terrorists imitate governments, and nuclear weapons are in the arsenals of the world's major powers. That makes them 'legitimate.' Chemical and biological weapons also may be found in the arsenals of many nations, but their use has been widely condemned by public opinion and proscribed by treaty, although in recent years the constraints against use seem to be eroding."[46]

But most important, there was a general acceptance of the other observation made famous by Jenkins that "Terrorists want a lot of people watching and a lot of people listening and not a lot of people dead."[47] This maxim was applied directly to potential terrorist use of CBRN weapons, and in turn was often used to explain the paucity of actual known plots, much less verifiable, incidents. Writing in 1975 with reference to potential terrorist use of radiological or nuclear weapons, Jenkins argued:

Scenarios involving the deliberate dispersal of toxic radioactive material . . . do not appear to fit the pattern of any terrorist actions carried out thus far. . . . Terrorist actions have tended to be aimed at producing immediate dramatic effects, a handful of violent deaths—not lingering illness, and certainly not a population of ill, vengeance-seeking victims. . . . If terrorists were to employ radioactive contaminants, they could not halt the continuing effects of their act, not even long after they may have achieved their ultimate political objectives. It has not been the style of terrorists to kill hundreds or thousands. To make hundreds or thousands of persons terminally ill would be even more out of character.[48]

This was also the conclusion reached by a contemporary of Jenkins, the noted authority on subnational conflict, J. Bowyer Bell. He too had dismissed the possibility that terrorists might target a commercial nuclear power plant in hopes of engineering a meltdown or large-scale atmospheric release of radioactive materials on similar grounds of political expediency and logical instrumentality. "[T]here is no evidence," Bell wrote in 1978, "that terrorists have any interest in killing large numbers of people with a meltdown. The new transnational television terrorists want media exposure, not exposure of the masses to radioactive fallout. And finally, the technological capacities of organizations with sufficient military skills to launch an attack . . . are not great. The mix of motive, military and technological skills, resources, and perceived vulnerability simply does not exist."[49]

Despite the events of the mid-1980s—when a series of high-profile and particularly lethal suicide car and truck bombings were directed against American diplomatic and military targets in the Middle East (in one instance resulting in the deaths of 241 Marines)—many analysts saw no need to revise these arguments. In 1985, Jenkins, for example, again reiterated, "simply killing a lot of people has seldom been one terrorist objective. . . . Terrorists operate on the principle of the minimum force necessary. They find it unnecessary to kill many, as long as killing a few suffices for their purposes."[50] In the revised version of his earlier work, Laqueur similarly emphasized: "Groups such as the German, Italian, French, Turkish or Latin American terrorists are unlikely to use nuclear, chemical or bacteriological weapons, assuming that they have any political sense at all—an assumption that cannot always be taken for granted. They claim to act on behalf of the people, they aspire to popular support, and clearly the use of arms of mass destruction would not add to their popularity."[51]

In sum, the conventional wisdom on terrorism prior to 9/11 held that terrorists were not interested in killing, but in publicity. Violence was employed less as a means of wreaking death and destruction than as a way to appeal to and attract supporters, focus attention on the terrorists and their causes, or to attain a tangible political aim or concession—for example, the release of imprisoned brethren, some measure of political autonomy, independence for a historical homeland, or a change of government. Terrorists therefore feared that they would alienate the very audience they sought to mobilize or influence. Furthermore, use of a chemical, biological, radiological, or nuclear weapon also risked creating a crisis that governments could seize on to justify the severest repressive measures imaginable to eliminate completely any organization that dared to employ such a heinous means of attack.

The only significant modification to this thinking in terms of U.S. government counterterrorism policy did not occur until President Bill Clinton's second administration, during the final years of the twentieth century.[52] At the time, fears of the former Soviet Union's nuclear and biological weapons stockpiles falling into terrorist hands, coupled with the 1993 bombing of New York City's World Trade Center—where the attack's mastermind bragged that his intention had been to topple one of the 107-story twin towers onto the other in hopes of killing 250,000 people[53]—and the sarin nerve gas attack on the Tokyo subway two years later, galvanized fears of further terrorist employment of unconventional weapons and set in motion increased federal spending and new programs designed to counter this menace. The emergent logic behind this reversal was summed up by Laqueur, who, writing in 1996, had similarly changed his mind. "Proliferation of weapons of mass destruction does not mean that most terrorists are likely to use them in the foreseeable future," he now surmised, "but some almost certainly will, in spite of all the reasons militating against it."[54] In this respect, bin Laden's alleged development of chemical warfare agents for use against the U.S. military stationed in Saudi Arabia to defend the kingdom following the 1990/1991 Gulf War was cited by the Clinton administration to justify the controversial 1998 American cruise missile attack on the al-Shifa pharmaceutical plant in Khartoum, Sudan.[55]

Al-Qaeda's Unrealized CBRN Ambitions

Nonetheless, on the eve of the September 11, 2001, attacks, the threat of potential terrorist use of CBRN weapons remained poorly understood and efforts to counter it were necessarily inchoate. As George Tenet, the director of Central Intelligence during the four years preceding and three years following the attacks recalled in his memoirs: "We established beyond any reasonable doubt that al-Qa'ida had clear intent to acquire chemical, biological, and radiological/nuclear (CBRN) weapons, to possess not as a deterrent but to cause mass casualties in the United States. The assessment prior to 9/11 that terrorists were not working to develop strategic weapons of mass destruction was simply wrong. They were determined to have, and to use, these weapons."[56]

In particular, the implications of terrorism motivated by a religious imperative, in contrast to the secular terrorism that hitherto had dominated this phenomenon, was also as unappreciated as it was misunderstood. Thus, most thinking on terrorism in general, and potential terrorist use of CBRN weapons in particular, was still filtered through the previously described anachronistic Cold War-era prism. This meant that many of our most basic assumptions about terrorists and terrorism—and, more critically, many governmental policies—had largely ossified since terrorism had emerged as a global security problem more than thirty years before. All this changed, of course, on September 11. Long-standing assumptions that terrorists were more interested in publicity than in killing were dramatically swept aside that morning in a crescendo of death and destruction. Heightened fears were in turn generated that terrorists would henceforth readily embrace an array of deadly unconventional weapons to inflict even greater levels of lethality. As the invasion of Afghanistan by U.S. and coalition forces would subsequently demonstrate, this concern was well founded given the incontrovertible information that came to light clearly illuminating al-Qaeda's long-standing and concerted efforts to develop a diverse array of chemical, biological, and even nuclear weapons capabilities.[57] As one knowledgeable U.S. government official observed, "Al-Qaeda's WMD efforts weren't part of a single program but rather multiple compartmentalized projects involving multiple scientists in multiple locations."[58]

Indeed, bin Laden's initial interest in acquiring a nuclear weapon had commenced in 1993—less than five years after al-Qaeda's creation. An emissary's attempt to purchase uranium from South Africa was subsequently reportedly made either late the following year or early in 1994 without success.[59] Bin Laden was apparently prepared to pay $1.5 million for the uranium. Four years later, al-Qaeda operatives were still engaged in this quest when Mamdouh Mahmud Salim, a senior official in the organization, was arrested in Germany while attempting to buy enriched uranium. Bin Laden, however, appears to have been undeterred by these initial failures. Indeed, in May 1998, he issued a proclamation in the name of the "International Islamic Front for Fighting the Jews and Crusaders," titled "The Nuclear Bomb of Islam." In it, the al-Qaeda leader unambiguously declared, "it is the duty of Muslims to prepare as much force as possible to terrorize the enemies of God."[60] When a Pakistani journalist asked him several months later whether al-Qaeda was "in a position to develop chemical weapons and try to purchase nuclear material for weapons" Bin Laden replied, "In answer, I would say that acquiring weapons for the defense of Muslims is a religious duty."[61]

Evidence of bin Laden's continued interest in nuclear weaponry again surfaced just six weeks after the 9/11 attacks with the arrests of two Pakistani nuclear scientists, Sultan Bashiruddin Mahmood and Chaudiri Andul Majeed. In August 2001, the scientists had held three days of meetings with bin Laden, al-Zawahiri, and other top al-Qaeda officials at the group's secret headquarters located near Kabul, Afghanistan. Although their discussions ranged widely to include chemical and biological weapons, Mahmood told his Pakistani interrogators that bin Laden was specifically interested in nuclear weapons. Al-Qaeda supposedly had acquired some nuclear material from an affiliated jihadi movement in Central Asia, the Islamic Movement of Uzbekistan (IMU), and Mahmood's opinion was solicited on its suitability for use in an explosive device.[62] According to Harvard University political scientist Graham Allison:

> Mahmood explained to his hosts that the material in question could be used in a dirty bomb but could not produce a nuclear explosion. Al-Zawahiri and the others then sought Mahmood's help in recruiting other Pakistani nuclear experts who could provide uranium of the required purity, as well as assistance in constructing a nuclear weapon. Though Mahmood characterized the discussions as "academic," Pakistani officials indicated that Mahmood and Majeed "spoke extensively about weapons of mass destruction" and provided detailed responses to bin Laden's questions about the manufacture of nuclear, biological, and chemical weapons.[63]

The so-called "Cheney Doctrine" thus emerged as a result of these revelations. The doctrine derived from Vice President Dick Cheney's reported statement, "If there's a one percent chance that Pakistani scientists are helping al Qaeda build or develop a nuclear weapon, we have to treat it as a certainty in terms of our response."[64] What the "one percent doctrine" meant in practical terms, one observer has argued, is that, "Even if there's just a one percent chance of the unimaginable coming due, act as if it's a certainty."[65] Countering the threat of unconventional weapons proliferation thus became one of the central pillars of America's post-9/11 national security strategy, whether by rogue states arrayed in the "axis of evil" cited by President George W. Bush in his 2002 State of the Union address or by terrorists who might acquire such weapons from those same states or develop them on their own. The U.S.-led invasion of Iraq in 2003 was also one of the products of these dramatically recast perceptions of threat and vulnerability.[66]

Meanwhile, al-Qaeda's ongoing quest to develop nuclear weapons capability was again revealed in January 2002 when CNN reporters discovered a twenty-five-page document containing designs for such a device in a Kabul office the group had occupied before the U.S.-led invasion.[67] Further evidence of bin Laden's desire to acquire a nuclear weapon surfaced during 2002 and 2003, when the U.S. intelligence community learned that al-Qaeda was negotiating with Russian sources to purchase three such devices.[68] They attained further credence from the fatwa issued in May 2003 at bin Laden's request by an influential Saudi cleric. Titled "A Treatise on the Legal Status of Using Weapons of Mass Destruction Against Infidels," its author, Sheikh

Nasir bin Mahid al-Fahd, justified the killing of large numbers of civilians if the purpose of the attack was to defeat an enemy.[69]

In addition to its nuclear ambitions, al-Qaeda also actively sought to develop a variety of chemical and biological weaponry.[70] It was bin Laden's alleged development of chemical warfare agents for use against U.S. forces in Saudi Arabia, as previously mentioned, that was cited by the Clinton administration in August 1998 to justify the controversial American cruise missile attack on the al-Shifa pharmaceutical plant in Khartoum. An Egyptian physicist had reportedly been recruited to work on al-Qaeda's Sudanese chemical weapons and nuclear development programs.[71] The movement's efforts in the biological warfare realm appear to have begun in earnest with a memo written by al-Zawahiri on April 15, 1999, to Muhammad Atef, then–deputy commander of al-Qaeda's military committee. Citing articles published in *Science*, the *Journal of Immunology*, and the *New England Journal of Medicine*, as well as information gleaned from standard texts such as *Tomorrow's Weapons* (1964), *Peace or Pestilence* (1949), and *Chemical Warfare* (1924), Zawahiri outlined his thoughts on the particular attraction of biological weapons:

a) The enemy started thinking about these weapons before WWI. Despite their extreme danger, we only became aware of them when the enemy drew our attention to them by repeatedly expressing concerns that they can be produced simply with easily available materials. . . .
b) The destructive power of these weapons is no less than that of nuclear weapons.
c) A germ attack is often detected days after it occurs, which raises the number of victims.
d) Defense against such weapons is very difficult, particularly if large quantities are used. . . . I would like to emphasize what we previously discussed—that looking for a specialist is the fastest, safest, and cheapest way [to embark on a biological- and chemical-weapons program].[72]

One of the specialists thus recruited was a U.S.-trained Malaysian microbiologist named Yazid Sufaat. A former captain in the Malaysian army, Sufaat graduated from California State University in 1987 with a degree in biological sciences. He later joined al-Jemaah al-Islamiya (the "Islamic Group"), an al-Qaeda affiliate operating in Southeast Asia, and worked closely with its military operations chief, Riduan Isamuddin, better known as Hambali—and in turn with Hambali's al-Qaeda handler, Khalid Sheikh Mohammed (KSM). Sufaat had also played host to two of the 9/11 hijackers,

Khalid Almihdar and Nawaf Alhazmi, who stayed in his Kuala Lumpur condominium in January 2000. Later that year, Zacarias Moussaoui, the alleged "20th hijacker," who was sentenced in 2006 to life imprisonment by a federal district court in Alexandria, Virginia, stayed with Sufaat, too. Under KSM's direction, Hambali and Sufaat set up shop at an al-Qaeda camp in Kandahar, Afghanistan, where their efforts focused on the weaponization of anthrax.[73] Although the two made some progress, bio-warfare experts believe that on the eve of 9/11 al-Qaeda was still at least two to three years away from producing a sufficient quantity of anthrax to use as a weapon.[74] Sufaat's arrest in late 2001 did not derail al-Qaeda's bio-terror efforts. When KSM himself was apprehended two years later, he was found hiding in the Rawalpindi home of a Pakistani bacteriologist.[75]

Before 9/11, a separate team of al-Qaeda operatives reportedly had been engaged in a parallel research and development effort to produce ricin and chemical warfare agents at the movement's Derunta camp, near the eastern Afghan city of Jalalabad. The Derunta facility reportedly included laboratories and a school that trained a handpicked group of terrorists in the use of chemical and biological weapons. Its director was an Egyptian, Midhat Mursi, known as Abu Khabab al-Masri, and the school's teachers included Sufaat and a Pakistani microbiologist. When U.S. military forces overran the camp, they found castor beans (ricin is derived from castor beans) and the equipment required to transform them into the deadly toxin. Mursi and a colleague named Menad Benchellali managed to avoid capture. A U.S. drone killed Mursi in Pakistan in 2009. Benchellali, a French national of Algerian heritage, was arrested in 2002. After fleeing Afghanistan, he had initially settled in the Pankisi Gorge, an area in Georgia that borders Chechnya, but became homesick. Once back in France, Benchellali became involved in a terrorist cell that had planned to bomb the Russian embassy in Paris. Acting on information provided by French authorities following Benchellali's arrest, police in Britain and Spain detained twenty-nine suspects from North African countries suspected of ties to al-Qaeda.[76] Evidence seized by British police in the search of one suspect's apartment in London included recipes as well as ingredients for several toxins—including ricin, cyanide, and botulinum.[77] British authorities believe that the ricin production instructions had been downloaded from an American white supremacist website and then photocopied on a machine at a well-known radical London mosque.[78] A police raid the previous year on a house in Norfolk used by another cell of Northern Africans also found recipes for ricin and other poisons, along with information about explosives and instructions for making bombs.[79]

The so-called ricin plot had been orchestrated by a thirty-one-year-old Algerian national and al-Qaeda operative named Kamel Bourgass.

Conscripted into the national police, where he served for a year, Bourgass subsequently fled Algeria for Britain. He arrived illegally in Dover on the back of a truck in January 2000 and immediately made his way to London's then-notorious Finsbury Park Mosque—a well-known center of Islamist extremism, where Richard Reid (the "shoe bomber" who tried to blow up an American Airlines plane bound from Paris to Miami in December 2001 with explosives concealed in his sneaker) and Zacarias Moussaoui (the aforementioned "20th hijacker") had also worshiped. Bourgass applied for asylum using the name Nadir Habra, but his claim was rejected, and then in November 2001 was denied on appeal. Bourgass simply disappeared. According to his subsequent court testimony, Bourgass claimed to have spent the following three years working in a London pizzeria and selling clothes. He also somehow drew state welfare benefits and further supplemented his income with petty thievery. In the summer of 2002, Bourgass was arrested for shoplifting in Romford, Essex. Presenting false documentation to the police and court, he avoided identification and thus deportation by giving his name as Kamel Bourgass and not Nadir Habra—the name used on his asylum application.[80]

Coincidentally, about the same time that Bourgass was being charged with shoplifting, in July 2002 British antiterrorist police began an investigation into North African criminal networks working in Britain suspected of credit card fraud. Their attention had been drawn to these gangs by reports that the proceeds were being used to fund terrorism. Meanwhile, a parallel investigation was unfolding that same month that led to the aforementioned police raid on a house in Thetford, Norfolk, where the recipes for ricin and other poisons, referred to above, were discovered. A third, simultaneous, but unrelated, police operation, also cited above, had resulted in the arrest of an Algerian national named Mohamed Meguerba. But after making bail, Meguerba decamped to Algeria, where he was arrested by police two months later. Under interrogation, Meguerba told the Algerian authorities that he and a group of fellow expatriates in London had been planning to carry out attacks in Britain using ricin and that sufficient quantities of the biological weapon had been produced to fill two small jars of Nivea skin cream. The plot's leader, Meguerba claimed, was Bourgass.[81]

Based on information that Meguerba provided to his Algerian interrogators, in January 2003 British police raided the apartment in north London where Bourgass allegedly had made the ricin. Initial reports that small amounts of the biological agent were discovered by police in the apartment were later proven false following detailed scientific analysis. Even if no actual ricin was found, however, the means and utensils required to produce it were certainly present. In addition to four sets of recipes and instructions in Arabic for making ricin[82] as well as other toxins, along with a mortar and pestle that appeared to contain chemical residue, twenty castor beans, cherry and apple seeds, which are used in the production of cyanide, a CD-ROM containing instructions for the fabrication of homemade explosives, were seized by police. A nationwide manhunt was subsequently launched for Bourgass. Coincidentally, nine days later police staged what they believed to be a routine raid on an apartment in Manchester where illegal immigrants were thought to be living. Unaware that Bourgass himself was among the persons apprehended at the apartment, the unarmed police officers neglected to take any of the special precautions that are standard operating procedure for handling terrorist suspects, failing even to handcuff Bourgass or any of the others. Desperate to escape before he could be identified, Bourgass suddenly grabbed a kitchen knife from a table around which he and the officers were gathered, stabbing one policeman to death and wounding three others. Bourgass was convicted of murder in June 2004 and the following April of "conspiracy to commit a public nuisance by the use of poisons, and/or explosives." He was acquitted of charges of conspiracy to commit murder using ricin—as were his four indicted coconspirators from the London apartment.[83]

According to police documents and testimony given at his second trial, Bourgass plotted to target businessmen and holidaymakers using the Heathrow Express, the train that travels throughout the day between Heathrow Airport and London's Paddington Station. The plan was to surreptitiously paint or swab door handles on the train with the ricin in hopes of poisoning the victims when they touched the substance with their fingers and palms of their hands.[84] Their objective, according to prosecutors, was not necessarily to kill as much as to "cause mayhem and widespread panic."[85] However, ricin molecules are in fact too large to be easily absorbed through the skin through ordinary tactile contact. "Although the ricin might not have killed anyone," a British Home Office official later reflected, "it would still have been regarded as a major terror coup" to carry out an attack with such a weapon.[86] This was also the conclusion reached by Peter Clarke, then deputy assistant commissioner at Scotland Yard and the head of its police antiterrorist branch. "It is clear had Bourgass been allowed to continue his plot undetected some people would have been made very ill and quite possibly have died," Clarke believes. "It would have been hard to underestimate the fear and disruption this plot could have caused across the country."[87]

Significantly, the plot had a clear al-Qaeda pedigree from the start. British authorities are convinced that Bourgass left the United Kingdom at some point to travel to Afghanistan to train at an al-Qaeda facility there in order to acquire the expertise necessary to concoct and disseminate ricin and other poisons. Indeed, according to British intelligence sources, Bourgass had been singled out by al-Qaeda commanders for specialized, advanced training in the making and use of poisons.[88] Meguerba himself confessed to having received such training at an al-Qaeda facility in Afghanistan.[89] Hence, rather than the homegrown, organic radicalization problem that often is assumed to be behind many of the European terrorist attacks and plots from 2003 to the present, the evidence linking both Bourgass and Meguerba to al-Qaeda points to a more conscious and deliberate strategy of subversion and the insertion of terrorist sleepers into Western society via Muslim Diaspora communities. Equally disturbing is the realization that less than a decade earlier, the same terrorists would more likely have been sitting in a basement attempting to fabricate crude pipe bombs and other conventional, explosive devices rather than plotting to concoct and disseminate highly lethal biological agents such as ricin.

Although Mursi's 2008 death dealt a significant blow to al-Qaeda's unconventional weapons development efforts, it did not end them. In 2010, for instance, it was reported that al-Qaeda in the Arabian Peninsula (AQAP)—widely considered to be the movement's most dangerous and capable affiliate—was deeply involved in the development of ricin.[90] Three years later, Turkish authorities seized two kilos of sarin nerve gas—the same weapon used in the 1995 attack on the Tokyo subway system—and arrested twelve men linked to al-Qaeda's Syrian affiliate, Jabhat al-Nusra.[91] And in November 2013, Israeli authorities disclosed that for the previous three years they had been holding a senior al-Qaeda operative whose specialty was biological warfare. "The revelations over his alleged biological weapons links," one account noted, "comes amid concerns that Al Qaeda affiliates in Syria are attempting to procure bioweapons—and may already have done so."[92] Indeed, Syria's ongoing civil war may yet afford groups such as Jabhat al-Nusra and ISIS ample opportunity to gain access to the Bashar al-Assad regime's chemical weapons stockpiles. ISIS has already repeatedly used chemicals weapons against civilians in Syria, and in May 2013 Iraqi authorities arrested an ISIS cell that had set up two factories in Baghdad to produce sarin and mustard gas.[93]

Continuing Technical Hurdles and Challenges

A common thread in all these cases—whether involving actual al-Qaeda and ISIS operatives or others with putative links to either movement—is a strong interest in, and clear willingness to use, these highly lethal unconventional weapons. But, as recounted above, this ardor has not always been matched by the expertise and capabilities required either to fabricate or effectively disseminate them. As John Parachini, a CBRN terrorism expert at the RAND Corporation, has argued: "Demonstrating interest in something is far different both from, first, experimenting with it and, second, mastering the procedures to execute an attack. Gaining access to materials is certainly a major barrier, but it is not the only one. Delivering toxic materials to targets in sufficient quantities to kill in the same fashion as explosives is not easy."[94]

Accordingly, as mesmerizingly attractive to terrorists as these chemicals, toxins, and germs may be, they have often proven frustratingly difficult to effectively deploy and disseminate—even when in the hands of the standing armies of established nation-states.[95] Despite the extensive use of poison gas during World War I, for instance, it accounted for only 5 percent of all casualties in that epic conflict. Even in more recent times, such as during the 1980s when Iraq used chemical weapons in its war against Iran, less than 1 percent (5,000) of the 600,000 Iranians who perished were killed by gas. The wartime use of biological weapons has a similarly checkered record. On at least eleven occasions before and during World War II, the Imperial Japanese Army employed germ agents as diverse as cholera, dysentery, bubonic plague, anthrax, and paratyphoid, disseminated in both water and air. Not only did these fail to kill as many Chinese soldiers as the Japanese had hoped, but on at least one occasion—the 1942 assault on Chekiang—10,000 Japanese soldiers themselves were affected, of whom some 1,700 died. "The Japanese program's principal defect, a problem to all efforts so far," David Rapoport concluded, was "an ineffective delivery system."[96] The difficulties of using germs as weapons is further substantiated by the work of Seth Carus, a researcher at the National Defense University in Washington, D.C. Carus has compiled perhaps the most authoritative accounting of the use of biological agents by a wide range of adversaries, including terrorists, government operatives, ordinary criminals, and the mentally unstable. His exhaustive database, which begins in 1900, reveals that during the entirety of the twentieth century a grand total of 10 people were killed and fewer than 900 were made ill as a result of some 180 acts of either bio-terrorism or bio-crime. The majority of these incidents, moreover, involved the selective poisoning of specific individuals rather than the wholesale, indiscriminate attacks most often imagined.[97]

As the previously recounted experience of Aum also demonstrated, delivery remains a significant technological hurdle for even well-financed, scientifically adept terrorists, whether they are using chemical or biological weapons. On at least nine occasions, Aum attempted to disseminate botulinum toxin (*Clostridium botulinum*) or anthrax (*Bacillus anthracis*) using aerosol means; each time, the terrorists failed, either because the botulinum agents they grew and enriched were not sufficiently toxic or because the mechanical sprayers used to disseminate the anthrax spores became clogged and hence inoperative.[98] These multiple failures with biological weapons prompted the cult's scientists to concentrate on developing chemical ones instead.[99] But even the use of chemical agents in an enclosed environment such as a subway car in an underground tunnel proved problematic. Far more people would likely have died in the London subway attack from the explosive force and smoke inhalation caused by conventional bombs—as occurred in the July 7, 2005, attacks on the London Underground that killed more than fifty people—than the sarin nerve gas that claimed the lives of twelve persons—including, inadvertently, one of the perpetrators. In addition, nearly three-quarters (73.9 percent) of the nearly five thousand reported casualties from the Tokyo subway incident were in fact treated for shock, emotional upset, or some psychosomatic symptom.[100] In other words, the actual number of people physically injured or harmed in the sarin attack was far lower than is widely believed. Given the formidable challenges that states have faced in effectively using these weapons, the hurdles confronting small terrorist cells, often with no more than a modicum of training and minimal expertise, must seem Herculean.

But these constraints notwithstanding, terrorists are fully cognizant of the potentially corrosive and unsettling psychological impact that such unconventional attacks can have on society—even if such weapons fail to kill or physically harm large numbers of persons. Prominent in the terrorists' calculations must be the assumption that these weapons substantially enhance the fear and intimidation that is the stock and trade of terrorism. Doubtless present in their calculations too are the potential effects that such unconventional weapons could have in undermining public confidence and trust in the ability of the government and authorities to prevent and protect their citizens from such attacks. As Peter Clarke noted of the ricin incident, "This was a hugely serious plot because what it had the potential to do was to cause real panic, fear, disruption and possibly even death to the public."[101]

The November 2006 conviction of Dhiren Barot (also known as Issa al-Hindi or Issa al-Britani), another al-Qaeda operative who in this case planned to use a radioactive "dirty bomb" in a series of attacks on both public gathering places and key economic targets in both Britain and the United States underscores the continuing attractiveness of unconventional weapons to terrorists. According to prosecutors, Barot's motive was less wanton, homicidal killing than the creation of "injury, fear, terror and chaos."[102] Moreover, Barot and his cell's intended use of an unconventional weapon paradoxically may have been a reflection of, or to compensate for, their inability to stage a more sophisticated or lethal conventional attack.

In other words, the value of these unconventional weapons to terrorists may counterintuitively be less some ruthless act of mass destruction weapon than a more limited attack designed to inflict far-reaching damage on a targeted population or provoke a counterproductive reaction from their political representatives.

A key lesson in this respect is the October 2001 anthrax letters incidents, which demonstrated that terrorists don't have to kill three thousand people to create panic and foment widespread fear and insecurity: five people dying under mysterious circumstances is quite sufficient to unnerve an entire nation. The extended closures of the four sites of the attacks—the Hart Senate Office Building and the Brentwood postal station in Washington, D.C., another mail facility in Hamilton Township, New Jersey, and the American Media Building in Boca Raton, Florida, underscore the profound challenges of remediation and decontamination in the aftermath of such attacks. Although the Hart Building finally reopened in January 2002, the Brentwood and Hamilton Township stations were not declared fit for human occupancy until 2003 and 2004, respectively. And the American Media building did not reopen until 2007.[103] Moreover, it cost $41.7 million to decontaminate the Hart Building, where the anthrax contagion was smallest and the most contained. This sum was nearly double the initial projection of $23 million. Estimates as high as $100 million have been posited as the cost to clean up the American Media structure.[104]

Conclusion

Despite the technical constraints on potential terrorist use of CBRN weapons, compelling motives, such as those raised by religious terrorism, coupled with potential opportunity, e.g., ease of access to both the information and material required to fabricate and employ CBRN weapons, could portend both for a bloodier and more destructive era of terrorism in the future. Certainly the combination of motive and opportunity has already fueled al-Qaeda's quest to develop a range of CBRN weapons capabilities. In this respect, a combination of unforeseen developments and unexpected technological breakthroughs could launch terrorism on a higher trajectory toward greater levels of lethality and destruction, perhaps involving even CBRN weapons.

The most salient motive—as the al-Qaeda and Aum cases demonstrate—remains one involving some religious or theological imperative, whereby a group animated by a desire to decisively attack an enemy state and its population in order to deliver a stunning knockout blow or, in the case of a millenarian movement, to hasten redemption through acts of violence or to attempt to implement Armageddon by the apocalyptic use of a biological or nuclear weapon, would clearly fulfill such an objective.

In terms of opportunities, the obsolescence of the control regimes erected during the Cold War to prevent states from acquiring strategic nuclear materials and developing even very basic chemical and biological warfare capabilities has been illuminated by al-Qaeda and Aum's concerted efforts to acquire or produce chemical, biological, and even nuclear weapons. Future endeavors by other nonstate actors in this realm may well be abetted by theft or pilferage of fissile materials from existing nuclear states or as a result of direct assistance from rogue nuclear countries such as Iran, Pakistan, and North Korea.[105]

Admittedly, while much of the material that has historically appeared on the globe's black market cannot be classified as SNM (strategic nuclear material) that is suitable for the construction of a fissionable explosive device, highly toxic radioactive agents can potentially be paired with conventional explosives and turned into a crude "dirty" bomb.[106] Hence, in terms of capabilities, a combination of a large fertilizer truck bomb with even a small amount of radioactive material, for example, could not only destroy an iconic landmark, commercial building, or ordinary government facility but also render a considerable area of prime real estate, and the area surrounding it, indefinitely unusable because of radioactive contamination. The disruption to commerce and the shattering of the public's sense of security and well-being would be tremendous. Even a small "dirty bomb," detonated within an enclosed space such as an office building or a subway car and resulting in commensurately smaller loss of life and actual physical destruction, could have devastating psychological consequences, given the popular fear and anxiety it would surely provoke. In either instance, the indefinite prolongation of the terrorist incident because of the radioactive contamination caused could last for years. Not only would the primary target of the attack have been destroyed or seriously damaged, but a much larger secondary target area surrounding it would also be contaminated and therefore need to be isolated and cordoned off from further access or use. Such an attack, though using a chemical weapon rather than a radioactive one, paired with conventional explosives, has already been attempted. In April 2004, authorities in Jordan disrupted a plot orchestrated by Abu Musab al-Zarqawi to use twenty tons of chemicals and explosives to attack the prime minister's office, the General Intelligence Department's headquarters, and the U.S. embassy in Amman. An estimated eighty thousand people reportedly could have been killed or seriously injured both from the initial explosions and the chemical toxins that would have been released into the air.[107]

There is sometimes a thin line between prudence and panic. The challenge, therefore, in responding to the potential threat of terrorist use of chemical, biological, radiological, and nuclear weapons is to craft a comprehensive defense that is not only cost-effective and appropriate but also sufficiently dynamic that it can respond as effectively as possible under the most difficult circumstances. Because of the extreme consequences that potentially could result from an attack involving a nuclear bomb or radiological material, or a chemical weapon or biological agent, even the remotest likelihood of such a possibility cannot be completely dismissed as nonexistent. In this respect, a critical balance must be struck between avoiding overreaction while still adequately preparing for threats that remain highly uncertain but would nonetheless have profoundly serious consequences.

Chapter 10

Terrorism Today and Tomorrow II

New and Continuing Challenges

Terrorism today is dominated by several different trends that have become increasingly intertwined—often with unsettling consequences. In the early 1980s, the reemergence of terrorism motivated by a religious imperative set in motion profound changes in the nature, motivations, and capabilities of terrorists that are still unfolding. In addition, the appearance of a greatly expanded subculture of terrorist foreign fighters gravitating from one conflict to another across an increasingly volatile landscape of failed and failing states, lawless border zones, and ungoverned spaces has added another destabilizing dimension to a phenomenon that was already becoming more difficult to describe and neatly categorize. At one time, becoming a terrorist entailed an often circuitous and, in some cases, protracted progression of vetting, recruitment, indoctrination, training, and deployment. However, the radicalization process that characterizes contemporary terrorism is arguably both more immediate and less intimate. Inspiration, motivation, and activation now follow in rapid succession, producing increasingly lethal incidents and transforming terrorism into the more diffuse and amorphous phenomenon it has become. This concluding chapter discusses some of the implications of these trends within the context of the mercurial rise of ISIS and stubborn persistence of al-Qaeda.

Understanding Today's Terrorists

Terrorism, as chapter 8 recounted, is the ultimate personal choice. The reasons someone picks up a gun or throws a bomb represent an ineluctably deeply idiosyncratic decision born variously of grievance and frustration; religious piety, the desire for systemic socioeconomic change; irredentist conviction; or commitment to some utopian or millenarian ideal. Joining an organization in pursuit of these aims is meant to give collective meaning, and equally important, cumulative power, to this commitment. The forces that impel individuals to become terrorists are thus timeless. And perhaps most significant, they defy broad generalizations predicated on poverty, illiteracy, relative deprivation, or other socioeconomic and demographic factors that purport to explain what drives individual men and women into this realm of political violence.

"Revolution is a young man's game,"[1] the late J. Bowyer Bell wrote in 1998. His reflection, based on some forty years spent studying "active and recent undergrounds," applied to the preeminent terrorist groups of Bell's era: the young Jewish men and women who challenged Britain's rule of Palestine in the 1940s; their Muslim Algerian counterparts who a decade later undermined France's continued possession of Algeria; the Palestinian fedayeen of the 1960s and 1970s who both transformed the nature and conduct of terrorism and ushered in the modern era of global political violence in which we are still enmeshed; the teenagers in Northern Ireland who graduated from throwing stones and Molotov cocktails at British soldiers to the ranks of gun-carrying and bomb-making, bona fide members of the IRA; and the radical students—the "generation of 1968"—who manned the barricades in Paris, Berlin, Milan, and elsewhere, and subsequently formed such iconic, if mostly forgotten, leftist terrorist groups as West Germany's RAF, Italy's Red Brigades, and America's Weather Underground.

In fact, little has changed in terms of terrorism's core demographics. The average age of the nineteen September 11th hijackers, for instance, was 24.2 years, while that of Palestinian suicide bombers at the height of the Second Intifada between 2000 and 2005 was 21 years according to one research team's data and 22 years according to another.[2] The mean age of Hezbollah suicide bombers in Lebanon was in the middle—at 21.6 years.[3] The average age of Tamil Tiger suicide cadre was only slightly higher, at 21.9 years.[4] According to the "Sinjar Records," the documents pertaining to some 700 Sunni foreign fighters who joined the insurgency, cum terrorist, campaign in Iraq prosecuted by al-Qaeda in Iraq (AQI) against U.S. and coalition forces, the precursor to today's ISIS, were mostly 24 and 25 years old.[5] The average age of Taliban cadre fighting in Afghanistan is between 20 and

25 years of age;[6] while that of recruits to al-Qaeda is also reported to be about 25 years old.[7] Unmarried males in their late teens and twenties have long been the main focus of Salafist-Jihadi terrorist recruiters, but female volunteers are now actively sought as well.[8] Hence, Walter Laqueur's observation of some four decades ago remains completely germane today: the "only feature common to all terrorist movements" is that "their members have been young . . . and that hardly requires explanation."[9]

By the same token, the leadership of terrorist groups has also crystallized both historically and today at a remarkably consistent point in a fighter's life: most often in one's late twenties and early thirties. Bin Laden, for instance, was age 27 when he first arrived in Pakistan in 1984 to establish himself as a patron and supporter of the mujahideen fighting the Red Army across the border in Afghanistan. He was 30 when he led his Arab Afghan fighters in the legendary battle at Jaji in 1987, and 32 when his lack of combat experience contributed to their defeat two years later in the failed siege of Jalalabad.[10] ISIS's leader and self-proclaimed caliph, Abu Bakr al-Baghdadi, had already established himself as a competent "mid-ranking figure in the anti-US insurgency" by age 34, when he was arrested in 2005 and imprisoned at Camp Bucca, the American military detention facility near Umm Qasr, Iraq. It was there that he began the process of transforming the grievously weakened AQI organization into the powerhouse that eventually emerged nearly a decade later as ISIS.[11] Baitullah Mehsud, the late commander of Tehrik-i-Taliban Pakistan and alleged mastermind of former prime minister Benazir Bhutto's 2008 assassination, was age 35 when he was killed the following year by an American drone strike, and Maulana Fazlullah, his successor, first acquired notoriety as the "most powerful Taliban commander" in the Northwest Frontier Province's Swat Valley,[12] when he was in his early thirties.[13]

The ages of rank-and-file terrorists and their leaders have thus remained remarkably constant over time, but what about their socioeconomic backgrounds and levels of education? These factors have long figured prominently in explanations for the eruption of terrorism.[14] In the aftermath of the September 11, 2001, attacks, the debate over the root causes of this violent political phenomenon acquired both new relevance and greater urgency. A succession of global leaders seemed to fasten on poverty, illiteracy, and lack of education as the sources of worldwide terrorism.[15] "We fight against poverty because hope is an answer to terror . . . ," President George W. Bush, for example, declared before the United Nations Financing for Development Conference in March 2002. "We will challenge the poverty and hopelessness and lack of education and failed governments that too often allow conditions that terrorists can seize and try to turn to their advantage."[16] His statement was but one of a plethora of similar panaceas repeatedly provided in the wake of the September 11 attacks. World figures as diverse as the United Kingdom's Prime Minister Tony Blair, Pope John Paul II, Malaysia's Prime Minister Mahathir Mohamad, Jordan's Prime Minister Ali Abul Ragheb, and the Philippines' President Gloria Macapagal-Arroyo, as well as Nobel Peace Prize laureates Elie Wiesel, Desmond Tutu, the Dalai Lama, Kim Dae-jung, and Oscar Arias Sanchez, identified these same "root causes." These arguments remain canons of the conventional wisdom on terrorism a decade and a half later.

Yet both the historical and contemporary empirical evidence fail to support such sweeping claims.[17] According to Laqueur, none of the forty-nine countries that the United Nations designated as the least developed in the world have been plagued by terrorism. The often posited causal connection between terrorism and poverty, Laqueur believes, is explained by Western guilt, the legacy of imperialism, and a well-intentioned but misguided assumption that "it might be relatively easy to remedy this state of affairs by offering much greater support to the poor countries, to have a redivision of wealth, by providing employment and thus restoring hope."[18]

To a large extent, those historically attracted to terrorism have in fact tended to be reasonably well, if not highly, educated; financially comfortable, and in some cases, quite well off; and often gainfully employed.[19] Bin Laden, for instance, obtained degrees in economics and public administration from Saudi Arabia's King Abdul-Aziz University,[20] while al-Baghdadi has both a master's and a PhD in Islamic studies from the University of Islamic Sciences at Adhamiya, a Baghdad suburb.[21] A century ago, IRA Volunteers in West Cork, according to Peter Hart, were similarly "more likely to have jobs, trades, and an education than was typical of their peers.'[22] Menachem Begin, who as Israel's prime minister received the Nobel Peace Prize but previously commanded the Irgun during the 1940s, received his law degree from Warsaw University in 1935.[23] Yasir Arafat, Begin's Palestinian counterpart who was awarded his own Nobel Peace Prize, was employed by the Kuwaiti Public Works Department as an engineer when he founded al-Fatah, having graduated from Cairo's Fouad the First University (now Cairo University).[24] George Habash, the founder and leader of the rival PFLP, was the son of a wealthy grain merchant who received his medical degree from the American University in Beirut,[25] as did his close friend and collaborator, Wadi Haddad, who directed the PFLP's most spectacular aircraft hijackings, including the 1976 hijacking of an Air France plane to Entebbe, Uganda.[26] Leila Khaled, the Palestinian airline hijacker cum heroine of the 1970s, was herself also the product of a comparatively well-off, middle-class family.[27] While it is certainly true that the rank-and-file Palestinian fedayeen were likely to be from far less comfortable socioeconomic backgrounds, it is nonetheless clear that the Palestinian movement's leadership did not conform to the stereotype of the poor, uneducated, jobless fighter—as is the case with their terrorist counterparts across the world today.[28]

Indeed, if anything, the distinction between leader and foot soldier is arguably now even less demarcated than it once was. As Laqueur explains, for terrorists to survive, much less thrive, in today's globalized, technologically savvy, and interconnected world, they have to be "educated, have some technical competence and be able to move without attracting attention in alien societies. In brief, such a person will have to have an education that cannot be found among the poor in Pakistani or Egyptian villages or Palestinian refugee camps, only among relatively well-off town folk."[29]

This was the conclusion that Peter Bergen and Swati Pandey reached in their study of madrassas (Islamic schools) and lack of education as a putative terrorist incubator. Using a database of some 79 jihadis who were responsible for the five most serious terrorist incidents between 1993 and 2005, they found that 54 percent of the perpetrators either attended university or had obtained a university degree. The terrorists they studied "thus appear, on average, to be as well educated as many Americans"—given that only about half of the persons living in the United States have attended university.[30] They further note that two-thirds of the 25 terrorists involved in the planning and hijacking of the four aircraft on September 11, 2001, had attended university[31] and that 2 of the 79 in their database had earned PhD degrees, while two others were enrolled in doctoral programs. Finally, they observed that the most popular subjects among those who attended university was engineering, followed by medicine.[32] Echoing Laqueur's previously quoted observation, Bergen and Pandey also observed, "While madrassas may breed fundamentalists who have learned to recite the Koran in Arabic by rote, such schools do not teach the technical or linguistic skills necessary to be an effective terrorist" in today's world.[33]

That engineers have disproportionately filled the ranks of violent Islamist movements is in fact the central argument of Diego Gambetta and Steffen Hertog's book, *Engineers of Jihad: The Curious Connection Between Violent Extremism and Education*.[34] They found that 69 percent of their sample of 335 violent jihadis had attended institutes of higher education—including nearly half who studied engineering.[35] "Relative to their presence in the male population in their countries of origin," Gambetta and Hertog note: "the number of engineers among [Islamist] extremist groups is fourteen times what we would expect; and relative to graduates with other degrees they are four times more numerous than we would expect. Furthermore, the overrepresentation is evenly distributed across all groups and across all countries of origin."[36] Among the more notorious terrorists with this particular academic credential are Ramzi Ahmed Yousef, the mastermind behind the 1993 bombing of New York City's World Trade Center, who studied electrical engineering at a technical institute in Wales;[37] his uncle, Khalid Sheikh Mohammad, the architect of the 9/11 attacks, who graduated with a bachelor of science degree in mechanical engineering from a North Carolina state university;[38] and Umar Farouk Abdulmutallab, the so-called underwear bomber, the Nigerian national and son of a wealthy banker who tried to blow up a Northwest Airlines flight en route from Amsterdam to Detroit on Christmas Day 2009.[39] His mechanical engineering degree was awarded by University College London—one of Britain's top universities.[40]

The popularity of medicine as a terrorist vocation is, of course, also not new. In addition to the aforementioned Drs. Habash and Haddad, Ayman al-Zawahiri, al-Qaeda's current leader, is a trained surgeon.[41] Perhaps the best-known terrorists in recent years with medical degrees were among the eight persons arrested in Britain following the botched attempt to bomb a nightclub in central London and the dramatic, but largely ineffectual, attack on Glasgow's International Airport in June 2007.[42] Six were either doctors or medical students; the seventh person was employed as a technician in a hospital laboratory; and the eighth member of the conspiracy was neither a medical doctor nor employed in health care, but instead had earned a doctorate in design and technology.[43] By all accounts, the terrorist cell's leader, British-born Dr. Bilal Abdullah, came from a comfortable, indeed privileged, background. His family was well known and his father was a prominent doctor in Iraq, where Bilal was raised. His mother and sisters have degrees in pharmacy, and his brother is a medical doctor, too.[44]

In the annals of terrorism, Abdullah's profile is hardly unusual. Shahzad Tanweer, one of the four July 2005 London suicide bombers, drove a Mercedes,[45] as did his father, who was a prominent local businessman, and indeed, the archetype of the successful, hardworking immigrant. The elder Tanweer owned a slaughterhouse, a convenience store, and a chain of fish-and-chips shops. The son graduated from Leeds Metropolitan University, where he obtained a degree in sports science.[46] The cell's ringleader, Mohammad Siddique Khan, who was age thirty at the time of the bombings, had a business studies degree from the same university and was gainfully employed as a community worker. Although the third and youngest member of the cell, Hasib Hussain, had an undistinguished academic record and never completed his college course in business studies, according to the official British parliamentary inquiry's report of the attacks, his family's socioeconomic background, like that of Tanweer and Khan, "was not poor by the standards of the area."[47]

Omar Khyam, the mastermind behind a 2004 bombing plot of London that Scotland Yard code-named "Operation Crevice," was the son of a wealthy businessman and grew up in a comfortable, upper-middle-class environment.[48] Similarly, Ahmed Omar Saeed Sheikh, who was twenty-nine when he kidnapped and executed *Wall Street Journal* reporter Daniel Pearl in 2002,[49] attended an exclusive private school. He later was admitted to the world-renowned London School of Economics (LSE), where he studied applied mathematics, statistical theory, economics, and social psychology. Described as "handsome, tall and muscular, very bright and charming," his parents expected he would be knighted some day, not languish in prison awaiting execution.[50] Omar Khan Sharif, who, with a fellow British Muslim named Asif Hanif, staged a suicide bomb attack on a Tel Aviv seaside bar in 2003, also studied mathematics at a similarly prestigious British university—King's College, London.[51] As Ed Husain, the former British Islamic extremist recounts in his memoir, "Interestingly, neither Asif Hanif nor Omar Sharif Khan came from an unemployed, disenchanted inner-city Muslim community; both had middle-class backgrounds."[52] Indeed, Husain recalls of his experience that all the members of his radical circle were students at London's top universities, including the LSE, SOAS (the School of Oriental and African Studies), King's College, and Imperial College.[53] Abdullah Ahmed Ali, the then twenty-seven-year-old who was one of the ringleaders of the August 2006 plot to bomb simultaneously U.S. and Canadian passenger airliners departing from London's Heathrow Airport, also hardly conformed to the stereotype of the wild-eyed, fanatical, homicidal suicide bomber. A husband and father of a two-year-old son, Ali held a bachelor of science degree in computer systems engineering from a respectable British university. For all intents and purposes, he appeared to be a solidly middle-class product of a successful first-generation immigrant family.[54]

Perhaps the seminal scholarly work to debunk the conventional wisdom that links poverty and lack of education to terrorism is the 2003 article by Princeton economist Alan B. Krueger and his Australian colleague, Jitka Malecková. Surveying American white supremacists, members of the Israeli Jewish (right-wing) underground, Hezbollah fighters, and Palestinian suicide bombers, and using a variety of data and different methodological approaches, they concluded that not only is there little evidence for this causality, but in fact, persons with higher incomes and more education are more, not less, likely to join terrorist groups.[55] In the case of the Israeli Jewish underground, they found, "These Israeli extremists were disproportionately well-educated and in high-paying occupations. The list includes teachers, writers, university students, geographers, engineers, entrepreneurs, a combat pilot, a chemist and a computer programmer."[56] For Hezbollah, they determined that fewer of its members came from impoverished backgrounds compared with the general Lebanese population (28 percent versus 33 percent). They also noted that the movement's ranks included more persons who had attended secondary school than most other Lebanese had.[57] Krueger and Malecková determined that Palestinian suicide bombers were also "less likely to come from impoverished families and are much more likely to have completed high school and attended college than the general Palestinian population."[58]

This counterintuitive conclusion about Palestinian suicide bombers—given the immense poverty and deprivation that continues to define the Palestinian people's existence—is well supported by the previously cited research of UN aid worker Nasra Hassan and scholar Claude Berrebi, which were discussed in chapter 5. This misconception about suicide terrorism being a product of economic deprivation and lack of education and career opportunities has also been challenged by Ariel Merari, an Israeli psychologist and academician, who has intensively studied Palestinian suicide terrorism since 1997 and terrorism generally for some forty years. "Palestinian suicide bombers," he found, "were, on average, much better educated than the population from which they emerged." Nearly half, for instance, had attended university—compared with less than a fifth of all Palestinians.[59] Indeed, according to Ronni Shaked, the Israeli journalist and former Shabak (Israel Security Agency, or Shin-Bet) intelligence officer and expert on Hamas, "All leaders of Hamas are university graduates, some with M.A. degrees. . . . It is not a movement of poor, miserable people, but the highly educated who are using poverty to make the periphery of the movement more powerful."[60]

It would of course be wrong to conclude that all terrorist organizations are populated exclusively by the financially comfortable and better educated. Indeed, an inevitable bifurcation generally occurs across all terrorist movements whereby the top leadership and mid-level command strata are populated by the educated (or relatively well-educated) and financially well-off, while the majority of foot soldiers will be less educated and often come from more modest socioeconomic backgrounds.[61] A rule of thumb is thus that the larger the movement, the more diverse its members' socioeconomic and educational backgrounds. For example, while the leadership and first generation of the Kurdish Workers Party (PKK) comprised mostly an elite of middle-class, university-educated intellectuals, their efforts to mobilize the Kurdish population inevitably brought into the PKK's ranks recruits from the lowest economic stratum of the Kurdish minority community.[62] According to one account, the PKK's foot soldiers were a representation of "the uprooted, half-educated village and small-town youth who knew what it felt like to be oppressed, and who wanted action, not ideological sophistication."[63]

Even if AQI recruiters preferred Saudis and Kuwaitis because, according to a Syrian who oversaw their infiltration into Iraq, citizens of those two countries came "with enough money to support themselves and their Iraqi brothers," considerably less well-off Syrian, Jordanian, Egyptian, Libyan, Yemeni, Algerian, Moroccan, and Tunisian volunteers were also welcomed into the organization's ranks.[64] Among Iraqis who joined AQI, economic rather than ideological motivations predominated. Major Matt Alexander, the U.S. Air Force interrogator who obtained the intelligence that led to the killing of AQI's founder and commander, Abu Musab al-Zarqawi, and who personally conducted more than 300 interrogations of Iraqi fighters and supervised those of over a 1,000 others, concluded that economic necessity and fear of Shi'a reprisal and not fervent religious belief, much less the establishment of the caliphate, was behind the decision of the average Sunni fighting for AQI a decade ago.[65] His view is borne out by a U.S. military survey of Iraqi detainees at the height of the insurgency against the United States there. The majority were found to be "young, poorly educated men without jobs who accepted money from al-Qaida in Iraq to serve as lookouts, or to build or plant roadside bombs."[66]

The same can be said of recruits to the Afghan Taliban. Lack of education and the paucity of employment opportunities alongside the grinding poverty endemic to the country's southern provinces provides a significant attraction for young men with few other options but to join that movement. Flush with money from narcotics trafficking, the Taliban thus offers an income and elevation in status to these young men that would otherwise be unobtainable.[67] As the U.S. Navy commander of a Provincial Reconstruction Team (PRT) in Assadabad, Kunar Province, told me during a visit to Afghanistan in March 2008: "Illiteracy is very high. The majority of young males here are very impressionable. They are told their country is being conquered and Islam destroyed, women are being violated. . . . It is a very compelling message to the un-educated. And then there is the economic component to marriages, where cash or goats is the dowry. Marriage is therefore also a compelling factor in joining the Taliban, in order to have a dowry."[68]

The socioeconomic diversity evident in large terrorist movements such as the PKK, AQI, and the Taliban can also be present in small, tightly knit terrorist cells as well. While three of the four members of the cell responsible for the suicide bombings of London transportation targets on July 7, 2005, came from the same small community of Pakistani immigrants outside of Leeds and were essentially all products of the same middle-class or upper-middle-class backgrounds (albeit atypical of that area), the fourth bomber, Jermaine Lindsay was not. The Jamaican-born Lindsay, a convert to Islam, was from a broken home and appears to have grown up without the benefit of either a good education or comfortable financial circumstances. He left school while a teenager, and although he intermittently worked as a carpet fitter, Lindsay was mostly unemployed.[69] Two other British Muslims who turned to terrorism—Richard Reid and Andrew Rowe—were also converts, also hailed from Jamaica, and also had dropped out of school.[70] Both Reid, the infamous al-Qaeda shoe bomber who attempted to blow up an American Airlines flight in December 2001 while en route from Paris to Miami, and Rowe, another al-Qaeda operative implicated in the 2003 plot to attack Heathrow Airport, had previously served time in British prisons.[71] As ex-convicts from broken homes, they were arguably the antithesis of the pampered LSE student Omar Saeed Sheikh or his equally well-off counterparts such as Omar Khyam and Shahzad Tanweer.

Assad Ali Sarwar, another of the 2006 airline bombing plotters, conforms perhaps more closely to the popular stereotype of the suicide bomber than his better-educated, wealthier peers. He was seemingly adrift with little ambition and few prospects and was thus prime cannon fodder for a terrorist movement looking for someone who was himself looking for some purpose or meaning for his life. Sarwar was an unemployed university dropout who, though nearly thirty, still lived with his parents at their home. But rather than a pliable bit player in the plot, Sarwar was one of its lynchpins. It was he who was assigned both to gather information on potential targets and to obtain all the ingredients required to fabricate the homemade explosives to be used to destroy the passenger aircraft.[72]

The Singapore-based Jemaah Islamiya terrorists who in 2001 plotted a series of attacks on U.S., British, Israeli, Australian, and Singaporean targets on al-Qaeda's behalf were similarly a mixed bag of the well-off and well-educated along with those at the socioeconomic margins of society. They included businessmen and engineers with university-level degrees, as well as taxi drivers and janitors. What they did have in common—like their British counterparts—was a profoundly deep devotion to their Muslim faith alongside an all-consuming hatred of the predominantly secular country in which they lived.[73]

But, as with the individual decision to become a terrorist, there is no one path that accounts for the process of radicalization—the essential first step in the personal odyssey toward political awareness, political awakening, political extremism, and ultimately, to violence.[74] There are, however, some key commonalities.[75] According to Professor Peter Neumann, the founder and director of the International Centre for the Study of Radicalisation and Political Violence at King's College, London,

Those who are familiar with the academic literature know that over the past decade researchers have managed to identify a set of drivers that seem to be common to the majority of radicalization trajectories:

1. One is the perception of grievance—conflicted identities, injustice, oppression, or socio-economic exclusion, for example—which can make people receptive to extremist ideas.

2. Another is the adoption of an extremist narrative or ideology that speaks to the grievance and provides a compelling rationale for what needs to be done.

3. Also important are social and group dynamics, given that radicalization often happens in 'dense, small networks of friends,' and that extremist ideas are more likely to resonate if they are articulated by a credible or charismatic leader.[76]

A study of the radicalization phenomenon conducted by two American scholars, Mohammed Hafez and Creighton Mullins, similarly identified four significant factors as the driving forces behind this phenomenon:

1. grievances over discrimination, racism, lack of employment prospects and Western intervention in Muslim countries;

2. social networks exploited by radicalizers;

3. ideological narratives and theological arguments; and

4. enabling environments and support structures, including access to terrorist training opportunities and communication over social media, and the Internet.[77]

Of course, people will always be attracted to violence in different ways. The diversity of radicalized Muslims who have gravitated toward terrorism in the United States in recent years bears this out. We have seen terrorists of South Asian and North, West, and East African descent, as well as those hailing both from the Middle East and the Caribbean. They have been life-long, devout Muslims, as well as recent converts—including one Philadelphia suburban housewife who touted her petite stature and blonde hair and blue eyes as being so atypical of the stereotypical Muslim terrorist as to defy any efforts at profiling. Radicalized over the Internet, she sought to use her self-described ability to avoid detection to assassinate the Swedish artist who had drawn an offensive cartoon of the Prophet Muhammad.[78] These individuals, accordingly, seem to come from every walk of life, including marginalized people working in menial jobs, some with long criminal records or histories of juvenile delinquency, as well as people from solidly middle- and upper-middle-class backgrounds, with university and perhaps even graduate degrees and prior passions for cars, sports, rock music, and other completely secular, material interests.

Relationships formed at work, at school, on sports teams, and other recreational and religious activities, as well as over the Internet, have played an important role in their radicalization. In some instances, first generation sons and daughters of immigrants embrace an interpretation of their religion and heritage that is more political, more extreme, and more austere—and thereby demands greater personal sacrifices—than that practiced by their parents. Existing social networks are thus a principal source of recruits for terrorist organizations. Recruitment in this context occurs less as a result of a "top down"—direct process than because of "bottom up" joining. That is, people gravitate to these violent movements not in response to active organizational efforts but are instead drawn into them by friends, relatives, neighbors, coworkers, and others who are already members.[79] The odyssey of Harry Sarfo, a German national of African descent who served in both ISIS's elite special operations unit, the Quwat Khas, and in its external operations force, the Amniyat al-Kharji (also known as "Emni" or "Amni"—the respective Turkish and Arabic rendering of the word, "Amniyat," or security service), illustrates this. He recounts that the mosque he worshiped at in Bremen alone had already sent some twenty persons to Syria to fight with ISIS.[80] Hence, preexisting social ties appear to be as significant as ideological affinity and commitment to the cause in the path to terrorism.[81]

In the case of the foreign fighters recruited to AQI during the insurgency in Iraq between 2003 and 2011, this phenomenon has been widely observed. Although about a third of volunteers cited "brothers"—that is, organized, local jihadi organizations (e.g., "top down" recruitment) as the initial or primary contact that drew them to the insurgency cum terrorist campaign in Iraq, half claimed that friends, relatives, neighbors, coworkers, or schoolmates played the most important role in their decision to come fight in Iraq.[82] The late Reuven Paz, who extensively studied this phenomenon, concluded that personal networks played a salient part in the recruitment of foreign fighters by AQI. He found that friendship circles and especially close family relations played an especially key role. In at least ten cases he examined, pairs of Saudi brothers, for instance, together volunteered to fight in Iraq and were subsequently martyred.[83] Indeed, "[w]ithout these preexisting networks," Mohammed Hafez concurs in his authoritative study of suicide bombers in Iraq, "jihadists could not have mobilized so many volunteers."[84]

The Jemaah Islamiya organization in Indonesia also attracted recruits on the basis of preexisting social relationships, whether from worship at the same mosque, attendance at the same madrassa, membership of the same religious study group, or family relations.[85] Family ties, moreover, also accounted for membership in the various Islamic separatist movements long active in the Philippines.[86] Among the most prominent fighters were the three Janjalani brothers—Khadaffy, Abdurajak, and Hector.[87] In addition, a cousin was implicated in that country's deadliest terrorist attack: the 2004 bomb explosion that sank a large Filipino passenger ferryboat killed 116 passengers.[88] And the Afghan Taliban, of course, is both largely populated and led by "Kandaharis"—the Pashtun friends and relatives from the southern provinces of Kandahar, Helmand, and Oruzgan.[89]

In addition to these "friends and family" social network pathways, there is often also a group dynamic behind recruitment. In other words, a cluster of individuals previously connected in some manner—whether by a sports club, a social organization, their school, or a religious worship group—decide collectively to join a terrorist movement. Marc Sageman, for instance, points to the eight postgraduate students who were friends and attended the same Hamburg mosque and all decided to join al-Qaeda. They then made good on that commitment by traveling in two separate parties to Afghanistan for this purpose.[90] The same process has been noted in connection with AQI's recruitment of foreign volunteers for the insurgency in Iraq. Paz discovered that "[m]any of the Arabs killed in Iraq, especially the Saudis, went to Iraq in groups, consisting mainly of friends."[91] According to Hafez, preexisting networks of Saudi youths, including the members of an entire soccer team, were recruited.[92] Ami Pedahzur points to a similar phenomenon in the Israeli-occupied West Bank, where seven Palestinian players from the same Hebron soccer team became suicide bombers.[93] This is by no means a new development, however. In *The I.R.A. and Its Enemies*, Peter Hart notes how in County Cork during the late 1910s and early 1920s, soccer and Gaelic hurling teams were an important source of recruits for the IRA. "It was a small leap from playing together to marching or drilling together."[94]

Finally, the violence inflicted on Muslims around the world, and on Muslim women and children especially, have been cited by many homegrown terrorists both in the United States and other countries as a salient motivating factor in their politicization and radicalization, and may explain why the U.S.-led invasions of Iraq and Afghanistan were cited by Dzhokhar Tsarnaev as the main reasons behind his and his brother's bombing of the 2013 Boston Marathon.[95]

The Foreign Fighter Phenomenon

The multiplicity of factors that nowadays swiftly impel someone along the path of radicalization to terrorism also doubtless accounts for the tens of thousands of foreign fighters who in recent years have answered either al-Qaeda's or ISIS's clarion calls to battle in countries as diverse as Syria, Iraq, Yemen, Afghanistan, Pakistan, Somalia, Libya, and Mali. This concerted flow of fighters to these many conflicts has also raised anew concerns that the survivors will return to their native or adopted homelands to carry out terrorist attacks. The experience of the Afghan Arabs following the end of the U.S.S.R.'s occupation of Afghanistan in 1989 is often invoked to justify this grim potentiality. Rather than laying down their arms and quietly resuming their ordinary lives back home, these foreign veterans of the holy war waged against the Red Army simply continued fighting elsewhere, establishing the foundation of the al-Qaeda movement and setting in motion the concatenation of circumstances that eventually produced the September 11, 2001, attacks. Whether in the Balkans or the Caucasus, on Mindanao or in Kashmir, in Algeria and Saudi Arabia, as well as Egypt and Yemen, these "wandering mujahidin," as an especially prescient 1993 U.S. intelligence analysis termed them, infused local terrorist groups such as Egypt's Gama'at Islamiya and Islamic Jihad, Algeria's Armed Islamic Group (GIA), and al-Qaeda, with their newly acquired martial capabilities and enthusiasm for jihad.[96] In a July 2016 speech, then FBI director James Comey cited precisely this concern, explaining how "at some point there is going to be a terrorist diaspora out of Syria like we've never seen before. Not all of the Islamic State killers are going to die on the battlefield . . . and hundreds of really dangerous people . . . are going to flow primarily to Western Europe but we might as well be right next door to Western Europe, given the ease with which people can travel. . . . This is an order of magnitude greater than any diaspora we have seen before."[97]

The number of foreign recruits fighting under ISIS's aegis, Comey continued, already exceeds by more than ten the flow of foreign fighters to Iraq at even the height of the war there a decade ago.[98] And according to a report issued by the U.S. House of Representatives Homeland Security Committee in September 2015, three times as many volunteers had already arrived in Syria and Iraq that year compared with 2014.[99] Among them was Omar Abdul Azis of Indonesia—the son of Imam Samudra, one of the al-Qaeda–affiliated terrorists convicted of the 2002 Bali bombings—who died that autumn fighting for ISIS.[100] Moreover, by February 2016, the number of foreign fighters estimated by the U.S. government to have traveled either to Syria or Iraq had jumped from 25,000 to 36,500. And in July 2016, that number had climbed to 43,000. They hail from 120 countries, compared with the 80 countries cited less than a year previously by the Homeland Security Committee's report. Among them are some 7,400 citizens or residents of Europe, North America, and Australia, including more than 250

Americans.[101] As then U.S. Director of National Intelligence (DNI), General (retired) James R. Clapper, explained in his annual worldwide threat assessment presented before the U.S. Senate Armed Services Committee in February 2016, "Foreign fighters who have trained in Iraq and Syria might potentially leverage skills and experience to plan and execute attacks in the West. Involvement of returned foreign fighters in terrorist plotting increases the effectiveness and lethality of terrorist attacks." Clapper cited the November 2015 attacks in Paris, which included European citizens or residents who had returned from Syria with the skills and wherewithal to mount simultaneous assaults that claimed the lives of 137 persons and wounded more than three hundred others.[102] That this has become standard operating procedure for ISIS's external operations arm, the Amniyat al-Kharji, was revealed by the aforementioned defector, Harry Sarfo. "Many of them [ISIS foreign fighters and recruits] have returned [to Europe]," he confirmed. "Hundreds definitely."[103] U.S. intelligence and defense officials agree. According to the *New York Times*, they believe that ISIS has already sent "hundreds of operatives" into the European Union and "hundreds more" have been dispatched to Turkey.[104] If accurate, this investment of operational personnel ensures that ISIS will retain an effective international terrorist strike capability in Europe irrespective of its battlefield reverses in Syria and Iraq. Indeed, ISIS's leader, Abu Bakr al-Baghdadi, has already instructed potential foreign fighters who are unable to travel to the Caliphate to instead emigrate to other *wilayets* (Arabic for "provinces," or in this context, branches or affiliates)—where Islamic State branches are located.[105] This suggests that these other branches could develop their own external operations capabilities independent of the parent organization and present significant future threat(s)—much as al-Qaeda's franchises have over the past decade in Yemen, North Africa, and South Asia, among other places.

Accordingly, in just four years, ISIS's international cadre has already equaled even the most liberal estimates of the number of foreign fighters that the U.S. intelligence community believes had traveled to Afghanistan during the 1980s and 1990s to join al-Qaeda.[106] Viewed from another perspective, far more foreign nationals have been trained by ISIS and other radical Islamist groups in Syria than were trained by al-Qaeda in Afghanistan during the five years preceding the 9/11 attacks.[107] This recreates the same constellation of organizational capabilities and trained operatives that made al-Qaeda so dangerous in 2001. And, unlike the comparatively narrow geographical demographics of the al-Qaeda recruits two decades ago, ISIS's foreign fighters cadre includes hitherto unrepresented nationalities, such as hundreds of Latin Americans along with citizens from Mali, Benin, Bangladesh, and Trinidad and Tobago, among other atypical jihadi recruiting grounds.[108]

These numbers alone are disturbing. The vast pool of recruits drawn to Syria affords ISIS as well as Jabhat Fateh al-Sham (the Front for the Conquest of the Levant; formerly known as Jabhat al-Nusra, al-Qaeda's local affiliate), and any of the other militant Islamist groups active there, a surfeit of potential terrorists to cherry-pick and potentially dispatch back home to carry out terrorist attacks. The *9/11 Commission Report*'s conclusion in this respect regarding the repercussions of bin Laden's far more modest effort is chilling. "Thousands flowed through" bin Laden's camps before the September 11th attacks," the report states, but "no more than a few hundred seem to have become al Qaeda members." Indeed, this small number, handpicked from the larger crop, were subsequently screened, vetted, and having been deemed "worthy," were confidently provided with subsequent, specialized terrorist training that enabled them to complete their assigned missions.[109] In this respect, Stern and Berger argue in their book, *ISIS: The State of Terror*, "the soaring numbers of foreign fighters in Syria generally, and in ISIS specifically, point . . . to an increased risk of terrorism that could linger for years."[110]

As the 2015 Paris attacks demonstrated, this unprecedented pool of foreign recruits has given ISIS the capability to undertake Mumbai-style attacks, modeled on the previously mentioned simultaneous assaults and running gun battles that occurred in that Indian city in November 2008.[111] Less complex operations—such as the 2016 Brussels Airport bombing and the assault mounted by the Somali jihadi terrorist group, al-Shabaab, in September 2013 that targeted Nairobi's Westgate Shopping Center—are arguably well within the capacity of ISIS's external operations group to undertake.[112] Any notion that the potentiality to export these types of attacks to the United States by either ISIS or al-Qaeda was put to rest by the American journalist Theo Padnos (Peter Theo Curtis), who spent two years in Syria as a hostage of al-Qaeda local affiliate, which was then called Jabhat al-Nusra but was also known as the Nusra Front. Padnos relates how, "The Nusra Front higher-ups were inviting Westerners to the jihad in Syria not so much because they needed more foot soldiers—they didn't—but because they want to teach the Westerners to take the struggle into every neighborhood and subway back home."[113]

In addition to the threat from skilled, trained terrorists, there is also the prospect of continued attacks perpetrated by lone wolves or cells of individuals banding together to carry out entirely self-generated and self-directed incidents such as the December 2015 San Bernardino and June 2016 Orlando shootings, and the July 2016 attack using a truck on the Nice, France, beach-front promenade. The late ISIS commander Abu Muhammad al-Adnani's famous September 2014 summons to battle has hitherto proven far more effective than al-Qaeda's longstanding efforts to similarly animate, motivate, and inspire individuals to engage in violence in support of its aims.[114]

Fifty-four years ago, Jean-Paul Sartre warned of the "boomerang" effect in his preface to Frantz Fanon's classic treatise of revolutionary warfare, *The Wretched of the Earth*. "It is the moment of the boomerang," he wrote, a new phase "of violence; it comes back on us, it strikes us, and we do not realize any more than we did the other times that it's we that have launched it."[115] More than half a century later, we are again confronted by the "boomerang"—this time from a hard-core of battle-hardened terrorists drawn from the thousands of foreign fighters trained and commanded by both ISIS and al-Qaeda, who, according to both ISIS defector Harry Sarfo and the unnamed American senior intelligence and defense officials quoted in the same *New York Times* article, are supposedly awaiting orders to execute a variety of preplanned attacks in Europe as well as the United States.[116]

The Forever War: Al-Qaeda's Enduring Threat

Meanwhile, for more than a decade, our unalloyed triumph over al-Qaeda, and by extension, the Salafi-Jihadi terrorist movement, has been repeatedly heralded. "Al-Qa'ida's Top Primed to Collapse, US Says," trumpeted a *Washington Post* headline two weeks after Khalid Sheikh Mohammed was arrested in March 2003. "I believe the tide has turned in terms of al-Qa'ida," Congressman Porter J. Goss, then chairman of the U.S. House of Representatives Intelligence Committee and himself a former CIA case officer who became its director a year later, was quoted in that same article. "We've got them nailed," an unidentified American intelligence expert also boasted that same month, before more expansively declaring, "We're close to dismantling them."[117] Identically upbeat assessments were voiced following the nearly bloodless capture of Baghdad a month later and the failure of al-Qaeda to make good on threats of renewed attacks in retaliation for the U.S.-led invasion.[118] Citing Bush administration sources, an article in the *Washington Times* on April 24, 2003, for instance, reported the prevailing view in official Washington that al-Qaeda's "failure to carry out a successful strike during the U.S.-led military campaign to topple Saddam Hussein has raised questions about their ability to carry out major new attacks."[119] Then, in rapid succession came the March 2004 commuter train bombings in Madrid; the suicide attacks against London transportation targets the following year; and, among the most serious of the various post-9/11 al-Qaeda

Central–commanded plots, the planned in-flight suicide bombings of seven American and Canadian passenger aircraft departing from London in August 2006.[120]

The airlines plot is especially instructive in this context. Rather than selecting the softer, more accessible targets such as subway and commuter trains, hotels and tourist destinations, which conventional wisdom at the time held was all an arguably seriously degraded al-Qaeda was capable of, the intended attack was directed against perhaps the most hardened target set in the post–September 11, 2001, environment: commercial aviation. This development thus called into question some of the most fundamental assumptions about al-Qaeda's capabilities and intentions and—not least—our collective ability to deter it. In this latter respect, al-Qaeda's leadership apparently was completely unfazed by the succession of intelligence successes that led first to the arrest of the plot's initial commander, Abu Faraj al-Libi, in May 2005, and then to the death of his successor, Hamza Rabia, in a U.S. drone strike just five months later. Such was the movement's determination to attack despite its allegedly catastrophic condition that, these presumably fatal setbacks notwithstanding (e.g., one leader in custody and another dead), it reached into its supposedly exhausted bench of core fighters and appointed Abu Ubaydah al-Masri to press ahead with the operation.

Not two years later, though, similar assertions of al-Qaeda Central's demise were being voiced. Juan Zarate, the Bush administration's deputy national security advisor for combating terrorism and one of the most perceptive and knowledgeable observers of the entire al-Qaeda phenomenon, offered an unusually nuanced and balanced assessment of the movement and the core leadership in a speech presented in April 2008. Carefully calibrating recent progress in the war on terrorism against remaining challenges, Zarate nonetheless drew attention to a "number of important developments that signal that al Qaeda and the movement it represents are under greater stress and finding more opposition to its program, in particular by Muslims affected directly by al Qaeda's tactics."[121] Zarate's remarks were amplified two weeks later by an anonymous senior American counterterrorism official quoted in an interview with London's *Daily Telegraph*: "[T]he end of the global threat al Qaeda poses," he stated, "is now as visible as it is foreseeable."[122] Then there was the statement by Ryan Crocker, the then U.S. ambassador to Iraq, who told reporters on a visit to the Shi'a holy cities of Najaf and Karbala in May 2008, "You are not going to hear me say that al Qaeda is defeated, but they've never been closer to defeat than they are now."[123] And finally, under a front-page headline in the *Washington Post*, "US Cites Big Gains Against al Qaeda," then CIA director Michael Hayden ticked off a list of indicators that, he argued, portended al-Qaeda's imminent demise:

"Near strategic defeat of al Qaeda in Iraq. Near strategic defeat for al Qaeda in Saudi Arabia. Significant setbacks for al Qaeda globally . . . as a lot of the Islamic world pushes back on their form of Islam."[124]

At the time, these views fit neatly with the prevailing consensus among government officials, academicians and pundits alike that al-Qaeda had ceased to exist as an organizational entity and had become nothing more than a hollow shell—an ideology without an organization to advance it—and a leaderless entity of disparate individuals unconnected to any central authority. Bin Laden was said to be completely estranged from the movement he created, isolated from his fighters, sympathizers, and supporters, and unable to exercise any meaningful role in the movement's operations and future trajectory. Terrorism, it was argued, had therefore become primarily "bottom up" and not "top down"—to the extent that terrorist organizations themselves and the command and control functions that they had traditionally exercised were said to no longer matter. Instead, it was argued, the threat now came from self-radicalized, self-selected "lone wolves" and "bunches of guys," and not from actual, existing identifiable terrorist organizations.[125] Then the plot to stage simultaneous suicide attacks on the New York City subway system, to coincide with the eighth anniversary of the September 11, 2001, attacks, came to light the following year. The ringleader, an Afghan-born green card holder who lived in Queens, named Najibullah Zazi, testified that both he and two fellow conspirators had been trained at an al-Qaeda camp in Pakistan. Three senior Core al-Qaeda commanders— the late Rashid Rauf and Saleh al-Somali, who were respectively killed in U.S. drone strikes in 2008 and 2009, together with Adnan al-Shukrijumah, who is still at large—had overseen and directed the plot, which was also linked to two other ambitious sets of attacks planned for April 2009 in Manchester, England, and July 2010 in Scandinavia.[126] May 2010 brought additional refutation of the "bottom up" argument when a naturalized U.S. citizen of Pakistani birth named Faisal Shahzad nearly succeeded in staging a massive car bombing in the heart of New York City's Times Square. Shahzad had been recruited by a close core al-Qaeda ally, the Tehrik-e-Taliban (TTP, or Pakistani Taliban), which had also trained him in bomb making at a camp in North Waziristan before sending him back to the United States on this mission.[127] In sum, despite repeated claims about the irrelevance or impending demise of al-Qaeda, virtually every major terrorist attack or plot against either the United States or Europe—and especially in Britain—during the period between 2002 and 2009[128] either directly emanated from al-Qaeda or was undertaken by affiliated terrorist groups acting on its behalf.[129]

The daring U.S. Navy SEAL mission that killed bin Laden in May 2011 understandably gave rise to a new round of assertions of al-Qaeda's doom.

The deaths in rapid succession of such top bin Laden lieutenants as Ilyas Kashmiri, who was described by a U.S. State Department analysis of terrorism trends as "one of the most capable terrorist operatives in South Asia";[130] of al-Qaeda's reported number-two leader, Atiyah abd al-Rahman, in August 2011, and his successor, Abu Yahya al Libi, in June 2012;[131] and, as recounted in chapter 8, of Anwar al-Awlaqi, the movement's chief propagandist, recruiter, and radicalizer, in September 2011, appeared to validate this hope. Indeed, the fourfold increase in targeted assassinations undertaken by the Obama administration since it had taken office,[132] whereby more than three dozen other senior al-Qaeda leaders were killed,[133] along with the deaths of over two hundred key fighters,[134] was supposed to have set the organization, in the words of a contemporary U.S. State Department analysis, "on a path of decline that will be difficult to reverse."[135] This was also the conclusion reached by a variety of prominent American pundits, academicians, and analysts.[136]

The prevailing consensus that al-Qaeda was poised on the brink of collapse seemed to acquire greater weight in May 2012 when the U.S. Military Academy's Combating Terrorism Center (CTC) published seventeen documents seized at bin Laden's Abbottabad, Pakistan, villa during the previous year's raid.[137] "Osama bin Laden's last words show dark days for al Qaeda" was typical of the news coverage afforded the documents' release.[138] In the rush to draw inferences from this minuscule sample of the hundreds of thousands of documents removed from bin Laden's lair by the U.S. Navy SEALs who killed the al-Qaeda leader, there was no mention of the starkly different interpretation of the materials that was offered by Obama administration officials shortly after the raid. For example, an anonymous senior U.S. official quoted at the time in *ProPublica* depicted bin Laden as a hands-on "micro-manager." "The cumbersome process he had to follow for security reasons," the official explained," "did not prevent him from playing a role. . . . He was down in the weeds as far as best operatives, best targets, best timing."[139]

Intelligence analysts then dissecting bin Laden's diary had reportedly also concluded that the movement's preeminent figure had also been involved in "every recent major al Qaeda threat."[140] These included plots directed against the United States, where bin Laden urged his followers to recruit non-Muslims and minorities—especially African Americans and Latinos—for attacks that would target smaller cities in addition to New York City and Los Angeles. According to the information released immediately following the Abbottabad raid, striking on significant dates such as July 4 and the tenth anniversary of the September 11, 2001, attacks, and hitting targets such as trains and passenger aircraft, were among his exhortations to al-Qaeda planners as well as to operatives in the group's affiliated movements in Yemen, Pakistan, and Somalia, among other places.[141] An article based on interviews with senior U.S. government officials published in the *Washington Post* that same month described how bin Laden "functioned like a crime boss pulling strings from a prison cell, sending regular messages to his most trusted lieutenants and strategic advice to far-flung franchises, including al Qaeda's affiliate in Yemen."[142]

No explanation, however, was offered a year later with the U.S. Military Academy's CTC release of the Abbottabad materials to square these discrepancies. The documents in fact revealed a far more ambiguous picture than portrayed in both the CTC report and accompanying U.S. government statements. For instance, it is significant that, notwithstanding the severe limitations imposed on al-Qaeda by U.S. intelligence and military operations, especially since the escalation of American drone strikes in 2009, the movement had been able to expand appreciably beyond its South Asia base. The documents indisputably depict an al-Qaeda that in 2011 had an active presence in more places than it did on September 11, 2001.[143] Moreover, in the six years since bin Laden's killing, the movement has been able to expand still further to at least two dozen countries—compared to less than a third as many in 2008.[144]

That bin Laden may have been "out of sync" or had fraught relations with the variety of far-flung al-Qaeda affiliate organizations is therefore not entirely surprising. This was the trade-off he accepted after 2002 to ensure the movement's survival and longevity by devolving power to the local franchises. Nonetheless, bin Laden remained both determined and able to communicate his wishes to al-Qaeda's growing stable of associates. Getting them to listen was, of course, a problem familiar to any manager coping with rapid expansion. Admittedly, this led to uneven relations with some of al-Qaeda's affiliates and associates because of the cumbersome and elongated communications loop. And at times they spurned his advice and entreaties.[145] But it should be remembered that al-Qaeda itself established none of these franchises. All had already existed before choosing to align themselves with al-Qaeda; hence, as independent entities, it is unreasonable to assume that they would necessarily fall into lockstep with all of bin Laden's wishes or dictates.[146]

Nonetheless, the picture that emerged from the seized Arabic-language documents is of a leader involved in both al-Qaeda's day-to-day operations and long-term strategy.[147] Ever the policy wonk, opining on topics as diverse as the Arab Spring and the declining U.S. economy, bin Laden also retained his penchant for attempting to micromanage—however unresponsive his franchises and affiliates may or may not have been. In actual fact, the documents portray the affiliates as responsive to bin Laden on the most important, pressing issues regarding either personnel or strategy. The extent of bin Laden's influence is perhaps best illustrated by his ability to block both the promotion of the late Anwar al-Awlaqi within al-Qaeda's Yemeni affiliate, AQAP (al-Qaeda in the Arabian Peninsula),[148] and the formalization of relations between the movement's Somali arm, al-Shabaab, with al-Qaeda.[149]

From bin Laden documents reportedly leaked to the British press,[150] we also know that as far back as 2003, he had taken an interest in expanding al-Qaeda's operations to West Africa, and in fact was in direct contact with leaders of Nigeria's Boko Haram.[151] We also know that both he and his successor and cofounder of al-Qaeda, Ayman al-Zawahiri, maintained close relations with both the Afghan and Pakistani Talibans. Both men reportedly regularly conferred with the late Taliban commander Mullah Omar and discussed the opportunities that the eventual U.S. and International Assistance Force's (ISAF) withdrawal from Afghanistan would present to their respective organizations.[152] Indeed, that al-Qaeda has already taken advantage of these opportunities is evident in the October 2015 discovery of a vast al-Qaeda munitions storage complex carved into a hillside in the Shorabak District near Kandahar, where the group was stockpiling weapons and husbanding its resources in preparation for a revived terrorist campaign. Only the most inveterate optimist would believe that the Shorabak facility was the only one of its kind that al-Qaeda has built along the remote border area straddling the Durand Line.[153]

Perhaps the most remarkable bin Laden communication, however, is one dated August 27, 2010. In it, the al-Qaeda leader expresses his concerns for the safety of his fighters and followers in Pakistan—not because they might be arrested or detained by the authorities, but because of the torrential rains and flooding then afflicting that country.[154] Bin Laden, accordingly, was more fearful that his men might be affected by the weather than by any effort of the Pakistani government to apprehend them. This assertion alone speaks volumes about how amenable he and his minions found their refuge in Pakistan—a comfort level that is unlikely to have changed in the years since bin Laden was killed.

Moreover, there is little in the documents that suggests that it was terribly difficult for al-Qaeda fighters to travel from Iran to Pakistan—or, for that matter, between Afghanistan and Pakistan.[155] And there is no indication that, once in Pakistan, they had any trouble traversing Baluchistan en route to the Federally Administered Tribal Areas (FATA) or North-West Frontier Province, two of the movement's favorite haunts. Given the continuing antipathy between Pakistan and the United States, and the absence of any indication of a change in this laissez-faire policy of the Pakistani government toward al-Qaeda since bin Laden's death,[156] there is no reason to believe that al-Qaeda's freedom of movement has been inhibited in any meaningful way.

Finally, despite al-Qaeda's alleged abject decrepitude at that time and the suppositions about bin Laden somehow being "out of touch" (as well as "out of sync"), he nonetheless laid out a compelling strategy for al-Qaeda's survival that the movement appears to be pursuing today. Continuing to attack the United States was only a part of his strategic plan, which also focused on

- attriting and enervating America so that a weakened United States would be forced out of Muslim lands and therefore have neither the will nor the capability to intervene beyond the limited use of airpower and the minimal training support provided to local governments;
- taking over and controlling territory, creating the physical sanctuaries and safe havens that are al-Qaeda's lifeblood; and
- declaring "emirates" in these liberated lands that would be safe from the United States and Western intervention because of their collective enfeeblement.[157]

Although it may be tempting to dismiss bin Laden's grand plans and ambitious strategy, as former National Security Council official Mary Habeck has cogently argued: "No al Qaeda affiliate or partner (including the Taliban, al Qaeda in Iraq, or the Shabaab) has been deposed from power by an uprising of the local population alone. They have needed outside intervention in order to expel the insurgents, even when the people have hated al Qaeda's often brutal rule."[158]

Two salient conclusions thus emerge from this period of time following bin Laden's killing. First, one could draw tentative conclusions that have since been validated and which were at odds with the conventional wisdom, or at least the manner in which many analyses precipitously embraced al-Qaeda's defeat. Second, given that this contrarian view has been proven correct, the inescapable conclusion is that today al-Qaeda's demise is neither ordained nor imminent. Rather, one can make a reasonable argument that al-Qaeda has

- well-established sanctuaries in Syria, Yemen, Pakistan, Afghanistan, Libya, and Mali, among other places that it continues to use to train its forces as well as to plan and plot terrorist operations while taking advantage of new opportunities to expand and consolidate its presence wherever it is able;

- a deeper bench than has often been posited (or at least has been shown to be deeper at various critical junctures in the past when al-Qaeda's demise had also been proclaimed);[159]

- a defined and articulated strategy for the future that it is actively implementing;

- a highly capable leader in al-Zawahiri, who, since bin Laden's killing in 2011—despite predictions to the contrary—has been able not only to keep the movement alive, but also to expand its brand and forge new alliances; and

- a well-honed, long-established dexterity that enables al-Qaeda to be as opportunistic as it is instrumental, that is, capable of identifying and exploiting whatever new opportunities for expansion and consolidation may present themselves.

Moreover, much like bin Laden's killing, at the time the Arab Spring was widely believed to have provided the final nail in al-Qaeda's coffin.[160] However, while the mostly nonviolent, mass protests of the Arab Spring were successful in overturning hated despots and thus appeared to discredit al-Qaeda's long-standing message that only violence and jihad could achieve the same ends, in the years since these dramatic developments commenced, evidence has repeatedly come to light of al-Qaeda's ability to take advantage of the instability and upheaval in these same countries to reassert its relevance and revive its waning fortunes.[161] Nowhere is this more patently clear than in Syria, Libya, and Yemen. Tunisia alone appears to be the only country to have truly realized the promise of democratic reforms raised by the Arab Spring—even while it ironically provides more foreign fighters to the conflicts in Syria, Iraq, and Libya than any other Middle Eastern or North African country.[162] On the periphery of those countries most directly affected by the Arab Spring, the continued antipathy in Pakistan toward the United States, coupled with the increasing activity of militant groups there—most of whom are already closely affiliated with al-Qaeda—has already largely undermined the progress achieved in recent years against terrorism in South Asia. Indeed, al-Zawahiri's stunning announcement in September 2014 of the creation of a new al-Qaeda franchise—this time in the Indian subcontinent (AQIS)—is further proof of both the movement's revitalization and its interest in cultivating new opportunities for expansion. Taking advantage of resurgent Hindu nationalism in a country with the world's second largest Muslim population, recruits from India, along with those from Pakistan, Bangladesh, the Maldives, and Burma, are remaking al-Qaeda from its once predominant Arabian and Middle Eastern demographic to a distinctly South Asian one.[163]

Furthermore, the effects of the Arab Spring in Yemen have clearly benefited AQAP at the expense of the chronically weak central government in that country. In fact, AQAP has been able to expand its reach considerably, seizing and controlling more territory, gaining new adherents and supporters, and continuing to innovate tactically as it labors to extend its attack capabilities beyond the Arabian Peninsula. Although al-Shabaab has been weakened in Somalia as a result of its expulsion from the capital, Mogadishu, and the deaths of two key Core al-Qaeda who had both embedded in the group and had enhanced appreciably its terrorist capabilities,[164] it nonetheless also continues to present a formidable terrorist threat.

Accordingly, the instability and disorder generated by the Arab Spring created new opportunities for al-Qaeda and its allies in the region to regroup and reorganize, which also led directly to the rise of ISIS.[165] Indeed, the number of failed or failing states or ungoverned spaces now variously found in the Sahel, in the Sinai, in parts of Syria, Iraq, Libya, and elsewhere, has in fact increased in the aftermath of the changes that swept across North Africa and the Middle East in 2011. In no place is this clearer or more consequential than in Syria. The priority that Core al-Qaeda has attached to Syria may be seen in the special messages conveyed in February and June 2012, respectively, by al-Zawahiri and the late Abu Yahya al-Libi in support of the uprising against the regime of Syrian president Bashar al-Assad and calling on Muslims in Turkey, Iraq, Jordan, and Lebanon to do everything within their power to assist in the overthrow of Syria's hated minority Alawite rulers.[166]

The leading thread in the top three sites in the most relevant and important password-protected/access-controlled jihadi websites at the time—al-Shumukh al-Islam, al-Fida', and Ansar al-Mujahideen—was Syria. Typical of these was the February 14, 2012, message posted on al-Fida' that described Syria as presenting an ideal opportunity for those mujahideen who lament having missed the Afghan and Iraqi jihads. "Since the launch of the Syrian revolution and since the barbaric Nusayri [Alawite] regime began killing our people there," it stated: "[T]he mujahideen, and praise and gratitude belong to Allah, took the initiative to help those weak ones in the East and West of the earth. We ask Allah to grant them success in liberating the Muslims in Syria from the disbelieving regime. There must be weapons to stop the harm of these aggressors. The Ummah will not get out of humiliation and weakness except through Jihad."[167]

Another message, presumably from a frontline fighter who had answered that call, described how "[t]hese attacks in Syria remind me of my time in Iraq." And in March 2012, a new e-journal, *Balagh* (Message), appeared from a group calling itself the Levant News Battalion, containing religious exhortations to overthrow al-Assad and his Alawite cronies. It was posted on the al-Shumukh al-Islam online forum.[168] Pleas for financial aid to support the mujahideen fighting in Syria also regularly appeared on this same site.[169]

Al-Qaeda's intense interest in Syria is neither recent nor ephemeral. As Ed Husain has argued, "The territory in the Middle East that al Qaeda covets most is of course Saudi Arabia, but Syria is next on the list." Indeed, Syria is not known by the name Syria to al-Qaeda and its minions but rather as al Bilaad al-Shaam[170]—"The Land of the Levantine People"—treasured Muslim territory that was once administered by the Ottoman Empire as a single, unitary entity encompassing present-day Syria, Lebanon, Jordan, and Israel/Palestine. Bin Laden often referred to the events following World War I that resulted in the dismemberment of Turkey's empire and the end of both Islamic rule of Muslims and the demise of the caliphate. His famous statement on October 7, 2001, in response to the commencement of U.S. military operations to liberate Afghanistan referred specifically to the 1920 Treaty of Sèvres, which detached these Arab provinces from Muslim rule.[171] And in one of the al-Qaeda leader's major addresses before the 2003 American-led invasion of Iraq, bin Laden cited the 1916 Sykes-Picot Agreement—the secret understanding reached between France and Britain that divided the Levant and surrounding countries into French and British spheres of influence. Under this arrangement, France received Syria and Lebanon, while Britain got Palestine and Jordan—as well as Iraq.[172]

Syria has thus long been an al-Qaeda idée fixe. According to Husain, that country has even more of the characteristics of the perfect jihadi storm that Afghanistan possessed three decades ago: widespread support among the Arab world, the provision of financial assistance from wealthy Gulf supporters, a popular cause that readily attracts foreign volunteers, and a contiguous border facilitating the movements of these fighters into and out of the declared battle space. Syria, though, has several additionally compelling factors that have figured prominently in the attention al-Qaeda has focused on it:

- First, it is sacred land referred to in early Muslim scripture and history, complete with enormously evocative "end times," prophetic overtones.
- Second, in the geographical scheme of traditional Ottoman rule, it contains the al-Haram al Sharif—the "Holy Precinct" of Jerusalem, where the Dome of the Rock (from which the Prophet is reputed to have ascended to Heaven) and the al-Aqsa Mosque, Islam's third holiest shrine, are located.

- Third, the enemy—as the above-quoted al-Fida' message states—are the Nusayri: the hated Shi'a apostate Alawite minority sect whom the revered thirteenth-century Islamic theologian Ibn Taymiyah, author of the key jihadi text *The Religious and Moral Doctrine of Jihad*,[173] called on Sunnis to do battle with. "For Sunni jihadist fighters," Husain explains, "the conflict in Syria is religiously underwritten by their most important teacher."[174]
- Fourth, unlike Afghanistan, which was part of the *ummah* but distant from Arab lands, Syria offers al-Qaeda a base in the Arab heartland. As Husain notes, "This makes them relevant again to daily politics of the Middle East."[175]

Al-Qaeda's attraction to Syria is thus nothing less than irresistible. After al-Qaeda missed the opportunities to intervene or assert itself in the seismic events that initiated the Arab Spring in Tunisia and Egypt in early 2011, and saw itself at first relegated to only a supporting role in Libya, al-Zawahiri doubtless still regards the Syrian civil war as a key opportunity with which to burnish al-Qaeda's credentials and demonstrate its relevance. Even more so, Syria's geographic proximity to both neighboring Jordan and Israel realizes an al-Qaeda dream: bringing it to the borders of precisely the pro-Western, insufficiently Islamic Arab monarchy that the organization has long despised in Jordan and to the very gates of its most detested foe, Israel.[176]

Al-Qaeda's spear carrier in Syria was initially AQI.[177] But in April 2013, its commander, al-Baghdadi, asserted command over Jabhat al-Nusra, al-Qaeda's separate Syrian arm, and decreed that he was therefore changing the name of the newly amalgamated organization from the Islamic State of Iraq (ISI) to the Islamic State of Iraq and Syria.[178] Jabhat al-Nusra rejected the merger and appealed to al-Zawahiri to intervene and order its reversal.[179] The conflict intensified as al-Zawahiri's efforts to mediate the dispute collapsed. The former ISI and Jabhat al-Nusra now found themselves locked in a violent struggle with one another: prompting al-Zawahiri to formally expel ISI from the al-Qaeda network.[180] The movement's former Iraqi branch arguably also demonstrates the limitations of decapitation as a counterterrorism strategy, given that its first three commanders—al-Zarqawi, Abu Ayyub al-Masri, and Abu Abdullah al-Rashid al-Bagdadi—had all been killed (al-Zarqawi in 2006 and his two successors both in 2010). Yet since its emergence in 2014, ISIS, the group's current manifestation, proved to be more threatening and consequential than at even the height of the insurgency in Iraq between 2003 and 2011.

The al-Qaeda Movement Today and Tomorrow

Bin Laden would arguably be a happy man were he still alive. In a long-forgotten 1998 interview with a Pakistani newspaper, the al-Qaeda leader declared: "I am not afraid of death. Rather, martyrdom is my passion because martyrdom would lead to the birth of 1,000s of Osamas."[181] With the tens of thousands of foreign recruits from over a hundred countries now fighting for al-Qaeda and ISIS and their respective franchises and branches in Syria, Iraq, Libya, Afghanistan, Pakistan, Yemen, Somalia, and Mali, bin Laden's death wish has arguably been achieved.

Moreover, unlike on September 11, 2001, the threats these fighters pose are now internal as well as external. No longer it is a matter of having to infiltrate attack teams into targeted countries. Homegrown violent extremism abetted by the reach and power of contemporary social media has completely changed national security today. "We have two kinds of threats," Bernard Bajolet, the head of French intelligence presciently observed at a Washington, D.C., conference in October 2015, "an inside threat" posed by radicalized individuals living in France and "the threat from the outside, either through terrorist actions which are planned [and] ordered from outside or . . . through fighters coming back to our countries."[182]

It was, of course, the latter category that was responsible for the tragic attacks in Paris two weeks later. Indeed, that incident fulfilled yet another long-standing bin Laden edict: that the cities of Europe should run red with infidel blood. In September 2010, when the al-Qaeda leader issued that command, his orders had mostly fallen on deaf ears as none of bin Laden's followers had the capability to do so.[183] But today, with the rise of ISIS and the successful efforts of its external operations department, the Amniyat al-Khalifa, that desideratum has been satisfied—with fears of future attacks consuming both Europe and the United States.[184]

But perhaps bin Laden would have been most satisfied with the opportunity created by the Syrian civil war to rebrand al-Qaeda and thus endow it with an image of comparative moderation—in contrast to the unrestrained ISIS. Among the documents seized by U.S. Navy SEALS in bin Laden's Abbottabad villa was one from 2011 in which a supplicant expressed his concern that the al-Qaeda brand had outlived its usefulness, complaining to bin Laden that the group's name had become universally associated with violence—to the extent that its core ideological and political goals were being completely ignored. The familiarity implied in the letter, suggests that its author was raising an issue that bin Laden himself had judged important. The writer in fact offers a list of potential new names for the movement that would more accurately reflect its ideological pretensions and self-appointed role as defender of Muslims everywhere.[185] This calculated assessment of al-Qaeda's public relations shortcomings is thus very different from the desperate hand-wringing described by news accounts when the documents were released in 2012.[186]

Accordingly, bin Laden would have been very pleased that until recently al-Qaeda's Syrian wing was widely known as Jabhat al-Nusra—the very anodyne-sounding "Support Front." Rarely is it ever referred to as al-Qaeda's Syrian arm, or, it often seems, directly associated with its justly maligned parent organization. The group has now, in fact, further distanced itself from al-Qaeda with the July 2016 announcement of its severing of "external ties"—as distinct from a complete break—with al-Qaeda and its rebranding as Jabhat Fateh al-Sham.[187] This is actually a long-standing al-Qaeda gambit to portray its satraps as more independent than they are and thereby avoid the pejorative implications that a more blatant relationship raises. Al-Qaeda has repeatedly, and successfully, used this ploy numerous times in the past to mask its continued close relations with groups such as Arar al-Sham, the Afghan Taliban, al-Shabaab, Ansar al-Din, and the variety of Ansar al-Shariah entities that surfaced following the Arab Spring. The fact that regardless of what it calls itself, Jabhat al-Nusra is even more dangerous and capable than ISIS seems completely immaterial to those across the region who not only actively support and assist al-Qaeda's Syrian affiliate, but actively seek to partner with what they perversely regard as a more moderate and reasonable rival to ISIS.

These deliberate obfuscations, both to eschew the al-Qaeda name and portray its most important franchise in a more benign light than ISIS, is a reflection of a calculated strategic choice taken by al-Zawahiri at a pivotal moment of al-Qaeda's history. In 2013, he instructed the movement's fighters to avoid mass casualty operations in order not to cause the death of Muslim civilians and innocent women and children. The legacy of this edict is evident in a tweet by a Dutch fighter belonging to Jabhat al-Nusra who eagerly reminded his followers that, unlike ISIS, "Al Qaeda focuses mostly on political & military targets instead of civilians." This development thus fits neatly into al-Zawahiri's broader strategy of letting ISIS take all the heat and absorb all the blows from the coalition arrayed against it, while al-Qaeda quietly rebuilds its military strength and basks in its paradoxical cachet as "moderate extremists" in contrast to the unconstrained ISIS.[188]

Finally, and most important, bin Laden would be immensely pleased to see that the seven-stage strategy to victory first presented to him in 2005 by al-Qaeda's longtime operational chief, Saif al-Adel, is progressing toward fruition. These stages entail:

- The Awakening Stage (2000–2003), which coincided with the September 11, 2001, attacks, and is described as "Reawakening the nation by dealing a powerful blow to the head of the snake in the U.S."
- The Eye-Opening Stage (2003–2006), which unfolded after the U.S. invasion of Iraq and was allegedly designed to perpetually engage and enervate the United States and the West in a series of prolonged overseas ventures.
- The Rising Up and Standing on the Feet Stage (2007–2010) involved al-Qaeda's proactive expansion to new venues of operations, exactly as has occurred in West Africa and the Levant.
- The Recovery Stage (2010–2013), which was originally intended to allow al-Qaeda to consolidate its previous gains and catch its breath, but which ended up having to be adjusted in light of both bin Laden's killing and the exploitation of new opportunities created by the Arab Spring to topple a variety of regional apostate regimes, especially in Syria.
- The Declaration of the Caliphate Stage (2013–2016), when al-Qaeda will achieve its ultimate goal of establishing trans- or supranational Islamic rule over the Sunni Muslim world.
- The Total Confrontation Stage (2016–2020), which will occur after the caliphate has been created and an Islamic Army commences the final "fight between the believers and the non-believers."
- The final, Definitive Victory State (2020–2022), when the caliphate will ultimately triumph over the rest of the world.[189]

It is disturbing to map the accuracy of this strategic trajectory dating from 2000 to the present and to understand why al-Baghdadi was so desperate to declare the caliphate to stay on schedule in June 2014, and thus attempt to enhance his own reputation and buttress his credentials by implementing al-Qaeda's strategy—and not least by stealing its thunder.

Indeed, the apocalyptic elements of the seventh and final stage are clearly evident in both al-Qaeda's and ISIS's ideology and strategy. Their mutually apocalyptic visions ineluctably entail an eventual epic clash between Islam and the infidels prophesized to occur at Dabiq, Syria—which is the name that ISIS chose for its online magazine. Because al-Qaeda and ISIS see themselves as defending the Sunni *umma* against a myriad of aggressive predators—including apostate Iraqi and Lebanese Shi'a, Iran, the United States, and the West—this alone ensures that neither organization's aims will remain confined to the Levant and Iraq, as has often been suggested. Instead, they are patently global in ambition, given their mutual adherence to the inevitability of this impending, divinely prophesized clash.

Conclusion

For more than a decade and a half, al-Qaeda and the Salafi-Jihadi terrorist network that it spawned have defied our efforts to bring the war on terrorism begun in September 2001 to any kind of meaningful conclusion. Its longevity is as much a history of our missteps and misreading of the threat as it is our adversaries' enormous capacity for change, adaptation, and regeneration. That we now face an enemy that has transcended terrorist tactics to evidence credible hybrid military capabilities—terrorist, guerrilla, and conventional—in the cases of ISIS and Jabhat al-Nusra in Syria, as well as AQAP in Yemen, is testament to a challenge that has only become more variegated, diffuse, and complex—and, quite simply, exponentially more difficult to defeat. It is difficult to imagine a worse constellation of terrorist threats than that currently posed by both al-Qaeda and ISIS—and their piebald affiliates and associates and franchises and provinces.

Although one cannot deny the vast inroads made against al-Qaeda in recent years as a result of the developments described above, the long-established nucleus of the al-Qaeda organization has proven itself to be as resilient as it is formidable. Despite the damage and destruction and losses of key leaders and personnel that al-Qaeda has suffered since 2001, it stubbornly adheres to its fundamental raison d'être: continuing to inspire and motivate the broader radical jihadi community. The principle of jihad is the ideological bond that unites this amorphous movement, transcending its loose structure, diverse membership, and geographical separation. The requirement to engage in jihad has been relentlessly expounded, originally in video- and audiotapes of bin Laden, al-Zawahiri, and other senior al-Qaeda personalities, on jihadi websites, and by radical clerics and lay preachers speaking in mosques or addressing informal circles of adherents in more private settings.

More recently, it has been even more effectively communicated over social media by ordinary jihadis messaging in a familiar patois to their friends, relatives, classmates, teammates, and others back home via such widely used apps as Facebook, Twitter, Instagram, Telegram, and WhatsApp, among others. The struggle is described in narrow, defensive terms: extolling the duty of the faithful to defend Islam by the sword. Imitation by example is encouraged through the depiction of the sacrifices of past martyrs—especially suicide terrorists and others who perished in battle against the infidel—coupled with messages about the importance and virtues of continuous battle against Islam's enemies. "It is no secret that warding off the American enemy is the top duty after faith and that nothing should take priority over it," bin Laden originally wrote in his seminal 1996 declaration of war.[190] Indeed, similar exhortations by a new generation of mujahideen continue to resonate today, when many Muslims harbor a deep sense of humiliation and resentment over the invasions of Afghanistan and Iraq; the continued bloodletting of their coreligionists in Syria, Iraq, Yemen, Palestine, Chechnya, and Kashmir, and elsewhere;[191] and the ill treatment of detainees at Abu Ghraib and Guantánamo, alongside the plethora of other reasons jihadis have for hating the United States and the West. The expostulated theological requirement to avenge the shedding of innocent Muslim blood—and particularly that of Muslim children—was once repeatedly invoked by bin Laden.[192] Today, it is an even simpler message based on a profound sense of catharsis, empowerment, and satisfaction derived from striking a blow at a hated, predatory oppressor. Both al-Qaeda and ISIS's core propaganda messages invoke the same justifications of self-satisfying violence articulated by Frantz Fanon in the 1950s during Algeria's struggle for national liberation from France. "At the level of individuals," Fanon famously explained, "violence is a cleansing force. It frees the native from his inferiority complex and from his despair and inaction; it makes him fearless and restores self-respect."[193] These perennial calls for revenge and retribution, coupled with the terrorists' own abiding faith in the regenerative power of even a single, dramatic terrorist attack to continue to breathe new life into their struggle, ensure that the war on terrorism will be won neither easily nor soon.

Whatever the future holds for al-Qaeda and ISIS, it is indisputable that the war on terrorism will likely continue far beyond what many believed when it began more than and a decade and a half ago. In this respect, the epic battle that bin Laden launched is not over yet. His killing did not result in the collapse of the movement that he created and lives on despite his death. Embedded in al-Qaeda's DNA is the same immense patience, elongated time frames, and meticulous planning that characterized bin Laden's oversight of all its major operations from 1992 through 2011. And we can be sure that his heirs have devoted the requisite thought and effort to safeguarding bin Laden's legacy, ensuring the longevity of the movement he created, while in their minds, continuing to steer it toward victory. What they doubtless understand is that in the post–September 11, 2001, world, terrorism's power to coerce and intimidate, to force changes in our daily lives, and to influence our policies and affect how and on what we spend money has increased enormously. The age-old terrorist objectives of undermining confidence in a country's elected leaders, creating deep fissures in political systems, generating paranoia and xenophobia, and pushing liberal societies to embrace illiberal security solutions, have all materialized during recent national electoral campaigns in both the United States and Europe.

In this respect, not only the stakes have grown, but so have public fears and expectations. More and more, the measure of success in the war on terrorism is defined as the ability of intelligence agencies and law enforcement organizations to prevent, preempt, and deter attacks. Conversely, the measure of success for the terrorists has become simply the ability to act, whether organizationally or simply by inspiring someone to do so in its name or on the terrorist group's behalf. Although there is a world of difference between driving a truck through a holiday crowd on a promenade in Nice and laying waste to the World Trade Towers and severely damaging the Pentagon, the impact is no longer completely dissimilar. The tragic loss of innocent life in any attack linked to either al-Qaeda or ISIS is calculated by their respective masterminds to rekindle throughout the world the same profound fears and anxieties that the attacks on September 11, 2001, ignited. Both these terrorist groups' stature and popularity are products of the sheer resiliency of the violent Salafi-Jihadi movement, its continuing appeal, globally recognized brands of the terrorist organizations that comprise it, and the extraordinary success they have achieved and publicity they have garnered through attention-riveting attacks on either small or large scales, whether in San Bernardino and Orlando or Paris and Brussels.

Countering terrorism is akin to taking a series of time-lapse photographs. The image captured on film today is not the same as yesterday's image, nor will it be the same tomorrow.[194] Terrorism, similarly, is constantly changing and evolving—indeed, far more rapidly and consequentially during the period of time since September 11, 2001. In 2017, we face a different enemy than we confronted in 2001 and 2002, and in 2011 and 2012. We now face a two-pronged threat from al-Qaeda as well as from ISIS. Given the deep ideological commonalities between the two organizations, it is not surprising that their strategies are similar—to the point that it appears as if ISIS has arrogated for itself al-Qaeda's own decade-old seven-stage path to victory. Accordingly, the prospect of a grand bargain and reconciliation between ISIS an al-Qaeda cannot be completely discounted. ISIS's continuing setbacks and serial weakening arguably create the conditions for such a modus vivendi.[195] Efforts to re-unite have been continuous from both sides virtually from the time of ISIS's expulsion from al-Qaeda in 2014. Al-Zawahiri himself has called for unity and an end to the divisiveness that has afflicted the jihadi movement—even while he has repeatedly continued to deride al-Baghdadi and criticize what the al-Qaeda leader derisively termed an "innovative caliphate."[196] For its part, ISIS propaganda has often been respectful of al-Qaeda, referring to its soldiers, emirs, and sheikhs in a positive manner and glorifying bin Laden's and al-Awlaqi's accomplishments. And even while profoundly critical of al-Zawahiri and some al-Qaeda affiliates,

ISIS still appears to have continually kept alive the possibility of some recon-ciliation, albeit alongside ongoing invective and vituperation. Nonetheless, irrespective of how such a rapprochement or merger might actually occur, any kind of reconciliation between ISIS and al-Qaeda or re-amalgamation of the two would profoundly change the current conflict and result in a signifi-cantly escalated threat of foreign fighter terrorist operations in the West. It would certainly enhance al-Qaeda's international reach and endow it with a robust additional attack capability.

The U.S.-led war on terrorism has now lasted longer than America's par-ticipation in both world wars. It has surpassed even its active military involvement in Vietnam during the 1960s and 1970s. Like the Viet Cong guerrillas and People's Army of Vietnam main force units, both ISIS and al-Qaeda and their respective branches and affiliates have locked the U.S. and its allies into an enervating war of attrition—the preferred strategy of terrorists and guerrillas from time immemorial. In his last publicly released, videotaped statement, bin Laden revealed precisely this strategy on the eve of the 2004 presidential election. "So we are continuing this policy in bleed-ing America to the point of bankruptcy," he declared. "Allah willing, and nothing is too great for Allah. . . . This is in addition to our having experience in using guerrilla warfare and the war of attrition to fight tyrannical super-powers, as we, alongside the mujahidin, bled Russia for 10 years, until it went bankrupt and was forced to withdraw in defeat."[197]

Decisively breaking this stasis and emerging from this war of attrition must therefore be among the highest priorities in our ongoing struggle against terrorism.

Notes

1. Defining Terrorism

1. See, for example, Cecilia Kang, Craig Timberg, and Ellen Nakashima, "Sony's Hacked E-mails Expose Spats, Director Calling Angelina Jolie a 'Brat,'" *Washington Post*, December 11, 2014, and Mark Lagon and Arch Puddington, "Exploiting Terrorism as a Pretext for Repression," *Wall Street Journal*, January 28, 2015.
2. *The Oxford English Dictionary, Compact Edition* (Oxford: Oxford University Press, 1971), *s.v.* "Terrorism."
3. Ibid.
4. David Rapoport, "Terrorism," in *Routledge Encyclopedia of Government and Politics*, ed. Mary Hawkesworth and Maurice Kogan (London: Routledge, 1992), 2:1061; Adam Roberts, "Terrorism Research: Past, Present, and Future," *Studies in Conflict and Terrorism* 38, no. 1 (January 2015): 65.
5. Quoted in R. R. Palmer, *The Age of the Democratic Revolution*, vol. 2, *The Struggle* (Princeton, N.J.: Princeton University Press, 1970), 126.
6. Quoted in ibid., 124.
7. Walter Laqueur, *The Age of Terrorism* (Boston: Little, Brown, 1987), 11.
8. Quoted in *Oxford English Dictionary, Compact Edition, s.v.* "Terrorism."
9. It should be noted that the phrase "propaganda by deed" itself was popularized by Paul Brousse, the French physician turned anarchist, in the newspaper he founded and edited, *L'Avant-Garde*. See David Stafford, *From Anarchism to Reformism: A Study of the Political Activities of Paul Brousse Within the First International and the French Socialist Movement, 1870–90* (Toronto: University of Toronto Press, 1971), 76–88, 123–24. The text of the article may be found on 256–59.
10. Quoted in George Woodcock, ed., *The Anarchist Reader* (Glasgow: Fontana, 1977), 43–44.

11.   It is interesting to note that the group was staunchly opposed to terrorism in democratic, open societies such as the United States. In 1881, for example, the executive committee of Narodnaya Volya publicly denounced for this reason the alleged anarchist political motive behind the assassination of U.S. president James Garfield that year. As Grant Wardlaw explains, Narodnaya Volya believed that terrorism could be justified only in extreme circumstances, and it denounced all such actions in countries that permitted "normal political activity." See *Political Terrorism: Theory, Tactics, and Counter-measures* (Cambridge: Cambridge University Press, 1990), 23.

12.   Lavrov, quoted in Zeev Ivianski, "Fathers and Sons: A Study of Jewish Involvement in the Revolutionary Movement and Terrorism in Tsarist Russia," *Terrorism and Political Violence* 1, no. 2 (April 1989): 146.

13.   An interesting account of the assassination and the context that gave rise to Narodnaya Volya can be found in Franklin L. Ford, *Political Murder: From Tyrannicde to Terrorism* (Cambridge, Mass.: Harvard University Press, 1985), 224–30.

14.   The successor group active in 1905 has already been described. In 1887, another group, which included Vladimir Lenin's older brother, attempted to assassinate Alexander III. They too were arrested and hanged. See Vera Broido, *Apostles Into Terrorists: Women and the Revolutionary Movement in the Russia of Alexander II* (London: Maurice Temple Smith, 1977), 198–203.

15.   The anarchist, it should be noted, was neither necessarily nor exclusively violent. Indeed, many remained simply intellectuals, advocating freedom of all types, while abjuring and condemning the use of violence.

16.   Robert A. Pinkerton, "Detective Surveillance of Anarchists," *North American Review* 173, no. 5 (November 1901): 617. See also "NSA Surveillance," American Civil Liberties Union, https://www.aclu.org/issues/national-security/privacy-and-surveillance/nsa-surveillance (accessed April 18, 2016); and "Reviewing the Surveillance State," *Economist*, May 23, 2015, http://www.economist.com/news/united-states/21651817-america-argues-anew-over-how-much-snooping-nsa-can-do-reviewing-surveillance-state.

17.   For example, in addition to McKinley, anarchists attempted to assassinate the German kaiser in 1878 and murdered the president of Italy in 1894, King Umberto I of Italy in 1900, Empress Elizabeth of Austria-Hungary in 1898, and the prime ministers of Spain in 1897 and 1912, and were implicated in the 1886 Haymarket Square bombing in Chicago, as well as other incidents such as François-Claudius Ravachol's bombings of Paris's rue St. Germain in 1892 and Émile Henry's bombing of the Café Terminus in 1894.

18.   As James Joll recounts, "The violence of this propaganda and the explicit incitement contained in pamphlets like [Johann] Most's . . . *Science of Revolutionary Warfare* ('a manual of instruction in the use and preparation of Nitro-glycerine, Dynamite, Gun-cotton, Fulminating Mercury, Bombs, Fuses, Poisons, etc.') all contributed to the anarchists' being held responsible for any violent disturbances." *The Anarchists* (Boston: Little, Brown, 1964), 141.

19.   Quoted in Patrick Bishop and Eamonn Mallie, *The Provisional IRA* (London: Corgi, 1989), 21.

20.   Walter Laqueur, *Terrorism* (London: Weidenfeld and Nicolson, 1977), 106.

21. Michael Burleigh, *Blood and Rage: A Cultural History of Terrorism* (New York: HarperCollins, 2009), 3; Tim Pat Coogan, *The IRA: A History* (Niwot, Colo.: Roberts Rinehart, 1993), 11.

22. Richard English, *Armed Struggle: The History of the IRA* (Oxford: Oxford University Press, 2003), 8–9.

23. See, for example, Ingrid Bazinet, "British Ex-Detainees See Link Between Guantanamo, Iraq Torture," *Agence France Presse*, May 14, 2004; Kate Zernike and David Rhode, "Forced Nudity of Iraqi Prisoners Is Seen as a Pervasive Pattern, Not Isolated Incidents," *New York Times*, June 8, 2004; David Rose, *Guantanamo: America's War on Human Rights* (London: Faber and Faber, 2004), 97–99; and R. Jeffrey Smith, "Justice Redacted Memo on Detainees: FBI Criticism of Interrogations Was Deleted," *Washington Post*, March 22, 2005.

24. Jeremiah O'Donovan Rossa, *Irish Rebels in English Prisons: A Record of Prison Life* (New York: D & J Sadlier, 1880), 94, 121, 166, 177, 222, 304–5, 371. See also Coogan, *The IRA*, 12.

25. Quoted in Lindsay Clutterbuck, "The Progenitors of Terrorism: Russian Revolutionaries or Extreme Irish Republicans?," *Terrorism and Political Violence* 16, no. 1 (Spring 2004): 163.

26. See "O'Donovan Rossa's Dynamiters," from *Irish World*, August 28, 1880, in Walter Laqueur, ed., *Voices of Terror: Manifestos, Writings, and Manuals of Al Qaeda, Hamas, and Other Terrorists from Around the World and Throughout the Ages* (New York: Reed, 2004), 117–18.

27. See the calculator at http://www.in2013dollars.com/1877-dollars-in-2016 ?amount=23000.

28. Quoted in Clutterbuck, "The Progenitors of Terrorism," 163.

29. Burleigh, *Blood and Rage*, 13–14; Laqueur, *Terrorism*, 113.

30. Clutterbuck, "The Progenitors of Terrorism," 165.

31. Lindsay Clutterbuck, "Countering Irish Republican Terrorism in Britain: Its Origin as a Police Function" (unpublished manuscript, 2005; made available courtesy of Dr. Clutterbuck).

32. Laqueur, *Terrorism*, 69.

33. Clutterbuck, "The Progenitors of Terrorism," 169.

34. Coogan, *The IRA*, 12.

35. Clutterbuck, "Countering Irish Republican Terrorism in Britain," 10.

36. Clutterbuck, "The Progenitors of Terrorism," 176.

37. Kachig Tololyan, "Martyrdom as Legitimacy: Terrorism, Religion, and Symbolic Appropriation in the Armenian Diaspora," in *Contemporary Research on Terrorism*, ed. Paul Wilkinson and A. M. Stewart (Aberdeen: Aberdeen University Press, 1987), 90–91.

38. See Roland Gaucher, *Les Terroristes* (Paris: Editions Albin Michel, 1965), 181–89.

39. The second is Hitler's "Final Solution" involving the Jews, and the third, Pol Pot's reign of terror in Cambodia after 1975.

40. Laurence Lafore, *The Long Fuse: An Interpretation of the Origins of World War I* (London: Weidenfeld and Nicolson, 1966), 180.

41. Ibid.; Christopher Clark, *The Sleepwalkers: How Europe Went to War in 1914* (New York: HarperCollins, 2013), 26–27, 35; Imanuel Geiss, ed., *July 1914: The Outbreak of the First World War: Selected Documents* (New York: Norton, 1967), 51–52.

42.   Lafore, *The Long Fuse*, 179–80; Clark, *The Sleepwalkers*, 35, 38–40.

43.   Lafore, *The Long Fuse*, 180.

44.   Clark, *The Sleepwalkers*, 40.

45.   The names of both the Black Hand and Dmitrievich were again invoked in July 1997 in threats issued against British peacekeeping forces stationed in Bosnia as part of the NATO-led Stabilization Force, SFOR.

46.   Clark, *The Sleepwalkers*, 11–13, 15, 20, 26–27, 38.

47.   Ibid., 40, 47–49, 55; Geiss, *July 1914*, 52.

48.   Geiss, *July 1914*, 52.

49.   Ibid., 52–53. See also Vladimir Dedijer, *The Road to Sarajevo* (London: Mac-Gibbon and Kee, 1967), 393–95.

50.   Clark, *The Sleepwalkers*, 95–98, 374–75, 381–87.

51.   Roberts, "Terrorism Research," 69.

52.   Quoted in Laqueur, *The Age of Terrorism*, 66.

53.   Quoted in Alan Bullock, *Hitler: A Study in Tyranny* (New York: Harper, 1958), 239–40.

54.   Robert Conquest, *The Great Terror* (Harmondsworth: Penguin, 1971), 14.

55.   Robert C. Tucker, *Stalin in Power: The Revolution from Above, 1928–1941* (New York: Norton, 1990), 271.

56.   See the brilliant exegesis of terrorism's history of imprecise definition in Conor Gearty, *The Future of Terrorism* (London: Phoenix, 1997), 11–13.

57.   Yasir Arafat, "Address to the UN General Assembly (November 13, 1974)," in *The Israel-Arab Reader: A Documentary History of the Middle East Conflict*, ed. Walter Laqueur (New York: Bantam, 1976), 510.

58.   Claire Sterling, *The Terror Network: The Secret War of International Terrorism* (New York: Holt, Rinehart, and Winston, 1981). See also Ray S. Cline and Yonah Alexander, *Terrorism: The Soviet Connection* (New York: Crane Russak, 1984), and by far the least polemical of this genre, Roberta Goren, *The Soviet Union and Terrorism*, ed. Jillian Becker (London: Allen and Unwin, 1984).

59.   See, e.g., Brian Michael Jenkins, *New Modes of Conflict* (Santa Monica, Calif.: RAND Corporation, R-3009-DNA, June 1983), 13–14; Brian Michael Jenkins, *International Terrorism: The Other World War* (Santa Monica, Calif.: RAND Corporation, R-3302-AF, November 1985), 19–20; and David C. Martin and John Walcott, *Best Laid Plans: The Inside Story of America's War Against Terrorism* (New York: Harper and Row, 1988), 46.

60.   The term was first coined in 1991 by the French criminologist and terrorism expert Xavier Raufer.

61.   Rachel Ehrenfeld, *Narco-Terrorism* (New York: Basic Books, 1990), ix, xiii.

62.   Two particularly informative discussions about the myth of "narco-terrorism" and the political baggage the term carried with it can be found in Grant Wardlaw, "Linkages Between the Illegal Drugs Traffic and Terrorism," *Conflict Quarterly* 8, no. 3 (Summer 1988): 5–26, and Abraham H. Miller and Nicholas A. Damask, "The Dual Myths of 'Narco-Terrorism': How Myths Drive Policy," *Terrorism and Political Violence* 8, no. 1 (Spring 1996): 114–31. See also Mark Bowden, *Killing Pablo: The Hunt for the World's Greatest Outlaw* (New York: Atlantic Monthly Press, 2001).

63.   See, for example, Bowden, *Killing Pablo*.

64. Peter Lupsha, "Gray Area Phenomenon: New Threats and Policy; Dilemmas," unpublished paper quoted by Ambassador Edwin G. Corr in introduction to Max G. Manwaring, ed., *Gray Area Phenomena: Confronting the New World Disorder* (Boulder, Colo.: Westview, 1993), xiii.

65. Xavier Raufer, "Gray Areas: A New Security Threat," *Political Warfare*, no. 19 (Spring 1992): 1.

66. Bruce Hoffman, "Low-Intensity Conflict: Terrorism and Guerrilla Warfare in the Coming Decades," in *Terrorism: Roots, Impact, Responses*, ed. Lawrence Howard (New York: Praeger, 1992), 140.

67. The exact number of deaths caused by the 9/11 attacks is believed to be 2,976. Of these, the New York City Medical Examiner's Office concluded that 2,752 were killed by American Airlines Flight 11 and United Airlines Flight 75, which struck the World Trade Center towers. Forty people were killed when United Airlines Flight 93 crashed into a rural field in Somerset County, Pennsylvania, and 184 people were killed when American Airlines Flight 77 struck the Pentagon. The numbers of people seriously injured were surprisingly low and defied initially dire expectations. According to a RAND Corporation estimate, no more than about 250 people required hospitalization for one day or more as a result of the attacks. See Lloyd Dixon and Rachel Kaganoff Stern, *Compensation Losses from the 9/11 Attacks* (Santa Monica, Calif.: RAND Corporation, MG-264-ICJ, 2004), 15–16. The RAND report cites New York City Medical Examiner's Office, Office of Chief Medical Examiner, "World Trade Center Operational Statistics," April 2004, as the source from which these data were obtained. See also National Commission on Terrorist Attacks Upon the United States, *The 9/11 Commission Report: Authorized Edition* (New York: Norton, 2004), 552n188.

68. Wm. Robert Johnston, "Worst Terrorist Strikes—Worldwide," last updated July 10, 2016, http://www.johnstonsarchive.net/terrorism/wrjp255i.html. See also Brian Michael Jenkins, "The Organization Men: Anatomy of a Terrorist Attack," in *How Did This Happen? Terrorism and the New War*, ed. James F. Hoge Jr. and Gideon Rose (New York: Public Affairs, 2001), 5.

69. Some 477 people perished in a 1978 fire deliberately set by terrorists at a movie theater in Abadan, Iran. See Johnston, "Worst Terrorist Strikes—Worldwide."

70. See the White House, President George W. Bush, Office of the Press Secretary, "President Declares 'Freedom at War with Fear': Address to a Joint Session of Congress and the American People," September 20, 2001, http://www.whitehouse.gov/news/releases/2001/09/print/20010920–8.html. It is interesting to note that neither conclusive data nor complete agreement exists on this figure. A U.S. State Department publication produced shortly after the attacks, for instance, cites seventy-eight countries. See U.S. Department of State, *The Network of Terrorism* (Washington, D.C.: U.S. State Department, 2001), 6. *The New York Times, A Nation Challenged: A Visual History of 9/11 and Its Aftermath* (New York: Callaway, 2002), 234, states that among the victims were the citizens of 115 countries. A website dedicated to the victims of the 9/11 attacks, http://www.september11victims.com/september11victims/COUNTRY_CITIZENSHIP.htm, cites a much lower figure of citizens of only 36 countries.

71.   Bruce Hoffman, *Lessons of 9/11: Statement Submitted for the Committee Record to the United States Joint September 11, 2001 Inquiry Staff of the House and Senate Select Committees on Intelligence, 8 October 2002* (Santa Monica, Calif.: RAND Corporation, 2002), 2.

72.   Quoted in Ken Herman, "After the Assault: U.S. Braces for Crusade Against 'Evil,'" *Atlanta Journal-Constitution*, September 17, 2001.

73.   *Oxford English Dictionary, s.v.* "terror."

74.   Quoted in U.S. Department of State, *Patterns of Global Terrorism 2001* (Washington, D.C.: U.S. Department of State, Publication 10940, May 2002), i.

75.   White House, "President Declares 'Freedom at War with Fear,'" September 20, 2001. See also the 2002 State of the Union Address, in which President Bush stated, "Iraq continues to flaunt its hostility toward America and to support terror." White House, "The President Delivers State of the Union Address," January 29, 2002, http://www.whitehouse.gov/news/releases/2002/01/20020129–11 .html.

76.   See White House, "The President Delivers State of the Union Address," in which President Bush declared: "States like these, and their terrorist allies, constitute an axis of evil, arming to threaten the peace of the world. By seeking weapons of mass destruction, these regimes pose a grave and growing danger. They could provide these arms to terrorists, giving them the means to match their hatred. They could attack our allies or attempt to blackmail the United States. In any of these cases, the price of indifference would be catastrophic."

77.   Michael Howard, "What Friends Are For," *National Interest*, no. 69 (Fall 2002): 8.

78.   See Richard A. Clarke, *Against All Enemies: Inside America's War on Terrorism* (New York: Free Press, 2004), 30–33, 241–42, 264–65, 268–69.

79.   See the White House, "President Bush Discusses Iraq: Remarks by the President to the Pool Before and After Golf—Crawford, Texas," August 10, 2002, http://www .whitehouse.gov/news/releases/2002/08/20020810–3.html, in which the president explains: "I described them [Iraq] as the axis of evil once. I described them as an enemy until proven otherwise. They obviously, you know, desire weapons of mass destruction. I presume that he [Saddam Hussein] still views us as an enemy. I have constantly said that we owe it to our children and our children's children to free the world from weapons of mass destruction in the hands of those who hate freedom. . . . What I do believe the American people understand is that weapons of mass destruction in the hands of leaders such as Saddam Hussein are very dangerous for ourselves, our allies. They understand the concept of blackmail. They know that when we speak of making the world more safe, we do so not only in the context of al-Qaeda and other terrorist groups, but nations that have proven themselves to be bad neighbors and bad actors."

80.   Quoted in Walter Pincus, "British Intelligence Warned Blair of War," *Washington Post*, May 13, 2005.

81.   Michael Howard, "Smoke on the Horizon," *Financial Times* (London), September 7, 2002.

82.   Quoted in Bob Woodward, *Bush at War* (New York: Simon & Schuster, 2003), 94. The acute sensitivity that this particular word arouses among Muslims is

explained by medieval historian Hugh Kennedy as follows: "The word 'crusade' is used by Western politicians almost without thought to describe a war fought for idealistic and ideological motives, rather than for naked gain. For many Muslims, brought up to see themselves as innocent victims and the idea of the crusade as essentially anti-Islamic, the apparent survival of the crusading ideal is threatening and sinister." See Hugh Kennedy, "Holy Warriors: Telling the Story of the Crusades as History, Not Metaphor," *New York Times Book Review*, April 3, 2005, 24.

83. Geoffrey Nunberg, "The War of Words: 'Terror' and 'Terrorism,' " *International Herald Tribune* (Paris), July 22, 2004.

84. See, e.g., John [Johann] Most, "Advice for Terrorists," in *The Terrorism Reader*, ed. Walter Laqueur and Yonah Alexander (New York: Meridian, 1987), 100–109, and David Rapoport, "The Politics of Atrocity," in *Terrorism: Interdisciplinary Perspectives*, ed. Yonah Alexander and Seymour Maxwell Finger (New York: John Jay, 1977), 46.

85. See, e.g., the treatises written by two group members, Nikolai Morozov's "The Terrorist Struggle" and G. Tarnovski's "Terrorism and Routine," in Laqueur and Alexander, *The Terrorism Reader*, 72–79; see also Broido, *Apostles Into Terrorists*, 180.

86. See, for example, Committee for the Publication of Lehi Writings, *B'Ha'Machterot* [In the Underground] (Tel Aviv: Yair, 1959), vol. D, 45–46; ibid., vol. A, 357; ibid., vol. B, 141–44; Gerold Frank, *The Deed* (New York: Simon & Schuster, 1963), 131, 133–34; Joseph Heller, *The Stern Gang: Ideology, Politics, and Terror, 1940–1949* (London: Frank Cass, 1995), 104, 115, 125; and Yitzhak Shamir, *Summing Up: An Autobiography* (London: Weidenfeld and Nicolson, 1994), 151–52.

87. Martha Crenshaw, *Terrorism and International Cooperation*, Occasional Paper Series 11 (New York: Institute for East-West Security Studies, 1989), 5.

88. Carlos Marighela, *For the Liberation of Brazil*, trans. John Butt and Rosemary Sheed (Harmondsworth: Penguin, 1971), 62, 89.

89. Peter Bergen, *Holy War, Inc.: Inside the Secret World of Osama bin Laden* (New York: Free Press, 2001), 29.

90. As Jason Burke notes, " 'Al-Qaeda' is a messy and rough designation. . . . The word itself is critical. 'al-Qaeda' comes from the Arabic root *qaf-ayn-dal*. It can mean a base, as in a camp or a home, or a foundation, such as what is under a house. It can mean a pedestal that supports a column. It can also mean a precept, rule, principle, maxim, formula, method, model or pattern." Jason Burke, *Al-Qaeda: Casting a Shadow of Terror* (London: I. B. Tauris, 2003), 7. See also Jason Burke, "Think Again: Al Qaeda," *Foreign Policy* (May/June 2004), http://www.foreignpolicy.com.

91. Quoted in Julian Nundy, "Wounded Jackal Defends Record of Family Values," *Independent* (London), August 31, 1994.

92. Rohan Gunaratna, "Khalid Sheikh Mohammed: The Brain," *Playboy* 52, no. 6 (June 2005): 80, 170.

93. "Transcript of Bin Laden's October interview," *CNN.com*, February 5, 2002, http://edition.cnn.com/2002/WORLD/asiapcf/south/02/05/binladen.transcript/.

94. Quoted in Hala Jaber, *Hezbollah: Born with a Vengeance* (New York: Columbia University Press, 1997), 130.

95. Konrad Kellen, *On Terrorists and Terrorism* (Santa Monica, Calif.: RAND Corporation, N-1942-RC, December 1982), 10.

96. Quoted in Alison Jamieson, *Terrorism* (Hove, East Sussex: Wayland, 1991), 33.

97. See Judith Palmer Harik, *Hezbollah: The Changing Face of Terrorism* (London: I. B. Tauris, 2004), 2–5, and Amal Saad-Horayeb, *Hizbu'llah: Politics and Religion* (London: Pluto, 2002), 95–97, 145–47.

98. See Hassan M. Fattah, "Hezbollah Declares Full Support for Syria," *New York Times*, March 6, 2005, and Neal MacFarquhar, "Leader of Hezbollah Discovers a New Fray: Lebanese Politics," *New York Times*, March 13, 2005.

99. See, e.g., Crenshaw, *Terrorism and International Cooperation*, 5; Boaz Ganor, *The Counter-Terrorism Puzzle: A Guide for Decision Makers* (New Brunswick, N.J.: Transaction, 2005), 17; Brian Michael Jenkins, *The Study of Terrorism: Definitional Problems* (Santa Monica, Calif.: RAND Corporation, P-6563, December 1980), 10; Gary Sick, "The Political Underpinnings of Terrorism," in *International Terrorism: Characteristics, Causes, Controls*, ed. Charles W. Kegley Jr. (New York: St. Martin's, 1990), 52; and Paul Wilkinson, "Terrorism," in *Ideas That Shape Politics*, ed. Michael Foley (Manchester: Manchester University Press, 1994), 189.

100. Jenkins, *The Study of Terrorism*, 10.

101. Quoted in Harris O. Schoenberg, *A Mandate for Terror: The United Nations and the PLO* (New York: Shapolsky Books, 1989), 71.

102. Quoted in Frederick J. Hacker, *Crusaders, Criminals, Crazies: Terror and Terrorism in Our Time* (New York: Norton, 1976), 174.

103. Quoted in Schoenberg, *A Mandate for Terror*, 75–76.

104. Quoted in Hacker, *Crusaders, Criminals, Crazies*, 274.

105. Quoted in Abraham D. Sofaer, "Terrorism and the Law," *Foreign Affairs* 64, no. 5 (Summer 1986): 904.

106. Quoted in Albert Parry, *Terrorism: From Robespierre to Arafat* (New York: Vanguard, 1976), 552.

107. North Atlantic Assembly Papers, Subcommittee on Terrorism, *Terrorism* (Brussels: International Secretariat, January 1989), 34.

108. See UNGA (United Nations General Assembly) Resolution 52/164, http://www.unodoc.org/unodoc/terroris_convention_terrorist_bombing.html (accessed May 15, 2005).

109. See http://www.cns.miis.edu/pubs/inven/pdfs/bomb.pdf (accessed May 15, 2005).

110. Jenkins, *The Study of Terrorism*, 2.

111. For a particularly insightful discussion of this dichotomy, see Gearty, *The Future of Terrorism*, 10–11. See also "What Is Terrorism?," *Economist*, March 2, 1996, 23–25.

112. Quoted in Sofaer, "Terrorism and the Law," 904.

113. Alex P. Schmid et al., *Political Terrorism: A New Guide to Actors, Authors, Concepts, Data Bases, Theories, and Literature* (New Brunswick, N.J.: Transaction Books, 1988), 12.

114. Quoted in Christopher Dobson, *Black September: Its Short, Violent History* (London: Robert Hale, 1974, 1975), 62–63.

115. "Editorial Guidelines, in Full: War, Terror and Emergencies," *BBC News*, http://www.bbc.co.uk/guidelines/editorialguidelines/edguide/war/mandatoryreferr.shtml (accessed April 18, 2016).

116. Quoted in David Shariatmadari, "Is It Time to Stop Using the Word 'Terrorist'?," *Guardian* (London), January 27, 2015, http://www.theguardian.com/global /commentisfree/2015/jan/27/is-it-time-to-stop-using-the-word-terrorist.
117. The RAND Terrorism Incident Database.
118. "Arab Leaders Join World in Assailing Terrorists' Attack," *Los Angeles Times*, December 19, 1973.
119. "The Arab Terrorists," *New York Times*, December 18, 1973.
120. Juan de Onis, "Guerrilla Unit Attacks Cairo Proposal," *New York Times*, June 21, 1973.
121. John K. Cooley, "New Arab Unity Hits Palestinian Guerrillas," *Christian Science Monitor*, September 19, 1973; Joseph Fitchett, "Guerrillas Seeking Leverage," *Christian Science Monitor*, November 27, 1973.
122. "Syrian Clampdown on Fatah Guerrillas Told," *Los Angeles Times*, September 20, 1973.
123. Jonathan C. Randal, "Guerrillas Fear Trade-off of Interests," *Washington Post*, October 12, 1973; Jim Hoagland, "Palestinian Guerrillas Say They Reject Cease-Fire," *Washington Post*, October 23, 1973.
124. Rapoport, "The Politics of Atrocity," 46.
125. "30 More Slain by 'Terrorists' Near Algiers," *International Herald Tribune* (Paris), April 15, 1997.
126. James F. Clarity, "Obscure Doctor Again Faces Sinn Fein Chief," *International Herald Tribune* (Paris), April 15, 1997.
127. "In Our Pages: 100, 75, and 50 Years Ago—1947: Zionists' Suicide," *International Herald Tribune* (Paris), April 22, 1997.
128. "39 Killed in Jerusalem Headquarters," *Times* (London), July 23, 1946; "41 Dead, 53 Injured, 52 Missing in Terrorist Attack on Secretariat," *Palestine Post*, July 23, 1946.
129. Rapoport, "The Politics of Atrocity," 46.
130. Peter Baker and Susan B. Glasser, "Hundreds Held Hostage at School in Russia," *Washington Post*, September 2, 2004; Peter Baker and Susan B. Glasser, "Russia School Siege Ends in Carnage," *Washington Post*, September 4, 2004.
131. C. J. Chivers and Stephen Lee Meyers, "Insurgents Seize School in Russia and Hold Scores," *New York Times*, September 2, 2004.
132. C. J. Chivers and Stephen Lee Meyers, "Terror in Russia; Battle in Beslan," *New York Times*, September 4, 2004.
133. Edward Cline, "Terrorists, Period," *Washington Post*, September 11, 2004.
134. Daniel Okrent, "The War of the Words: A Dispatch from the Front Lines," *New York Times*, March 6, 2005.
135. Nicola Clark, "Why Security Breaches Have Become Relatively Rare," *New York Times*, March 30, 2016.
136. Yezid Sayigh, *Armed Struggle and the Search for State: The Palestinian National Movement, 1949–1993* (Washington: Institute for Palestine Studies and Oxford: Oxford University Press, 1997), 257.
137. Anthony Richards, *Conceptualizing Terrorism* (Oxford: Oxford University Press, 2015), 3.
138. Alex P. Schmid, ed., *The Routledge Handbook of Terrorism Research* (London: Routledge, 2011), 44.

139. Quoted in U.S. Department of State, Bureau of Counterterrorism, *Country Reports on Terrorism 2014*, United States Department of State (June 2015), 388, http://www.state.gov/documents/organization/239631.pdf.

140. FBI, "What We Investigate," https://www.fbi.gov/albuquerque/about-us/what-we-investigate (accessed April 18, 2016).

141. FBI, "Definitions of Terrorism in the U.S. Code," https://www.fbi.gov/about-us/investigate/terrorism/terrorism-definition (accessed April 18, 2016).

142. U.S. Department of Homeland Security, "Homeland Security: Countering Violent Extremism," https://www.dhs.gov/topic/countering-violent-extremism (accessed April 18, 2016).

143. U.S. Department of Defense, *Department of Defense Dictionary of Military and Associated Terms* (Washington, D.C: Joint Publication 1-02, as amended through February 16, 2016), http://www.dtic.mil/doctrine/new_pubs/jp1_02.pdf.

144. U.S. Department of State, Office of the Coordinator for Counterterrorism, *Patterns of Global Terrorism 2003* (Washington, D.C.: U.S. Department of State, Publication No. 11124, April 2004), xii.

145. Brian M. Jenkins, "International Terrorism: A New Mode of Conflict," in *International Terrorism and World Security*, ed. David Carlton and Carlo Schaerf (London: Croom Helm, 1975), 16.

146. Office of Justice Programs, NIJ (National Institute of Justice), "Terrorism," http://www.nij.gov/topics/crime/terrorism/pages/welcome.aspx (accessed April 18, 2016).

147. See, for example, the explanation in Counterterrorism Threat Assessment and Warning Unit, *Terrorism in the United States 1999* (Washington, D.C.: U.S. Department of Justice, FBI Publication No. 0308, 2000), 1, 5–7.

148. Alex P. Schmid, *Political Terrorism: A Research Guide* (New Brunswick, N.J.: Transaction Books, 1984), x.

149. Schmid et al., *Political Terrorism*, 1.

150. Schmid, *The Routledge Handbook of Terrorism Research*, 40.

151. Walter Laqueur, *Terrorism* (London: Weidenfeld and Nicolson, 1977), 7; Laqueur, *The Age of Terrorism*, 11, 142–56.

152. The "study of terrorism," Laqueur further argued, "can manage with a minimum of theory." Quoted in Schmid et al., *Political Terrorism*, 3.

153. Ibid., 6.

154. Boaz Ganor, *The Counter-Terrorism Puzzle*, 17.

155. Central Intelligence Agency (CIA), *Guide to the Analysis of Insurgency 2012* (Washington, D.C.: U.S. Government Printing Office, n.d.), 2.

156. Walter Laqueur, *Guerrilla: A Historical and Critical Study* (Boston: Little, Brown, 1976), xi.

157. Ian F. W. Beckett, *Encyclopedia of Guerrilla Warfare* (New York: Checkmark Books, 2001), xiii.

158. Laqueur, *Guerrilla*, x. Laqueur goes on to note, "What is now commonly called 'urban guerrilla' warfare is, of course, terrorism in a new dress" (xi).

159. Beckett, *Encyclopedia of Guerrilla Warfare*, ix.

160. Central Intelligence Agency, *Guide to the Analysis of Insurgency* (Washington, D.C.: U.S. Government Printing Office, n.d.), 2. This pamphlet was first published and distributed in the mid-1980s.

161. U.S. Department of State, Office of the Coordinator for Counterterrorism, *Patterns of Global Terrorism 2003*, 113.
162. Ibid., 89.
163. Ibid. At the same time, it should be emphasized that the situation in Iraq was often so fluid and opaque, with secular Ba'athists and other former regime elements, for instance, conducting insurgent attacks against U.S. and coalition forces, at times allying themselves tactically and operationally with foreign terrorists and Islamic extremists. See Bruce Hoffman, *Insurgency and Counterinsurgency in Iraq* (Santa Monica, Calif.: RAND Corporation, OP-127, 2004), 17.
164. ISIS's precursor, al-Qaeda in Iraq, is also known by its acronym, QJBR, literally, Tanzim Qa'idat al-Jihad fi Bilad al Rafidayn (Organization of Jihad's Base in the Country of the Two Rivers).
165. Michael Weiss and Hassan Hassan, *ISIS: Inside the Army of Terror* (New York: Reagan Arts, 2015), xv, 198, 212, 219, 229; Jessica Stern and J. M. Berger, *ISIS: The State of Terror* (New York: HarperCollins, 2015), 113, 234–36.
166. Weiss and Hassan, *ISIS: Inside the Army of Terror*, 235.
167. Matt Bradley, "Insurgents in Iraq Seizing Advanced Weaponry: Arms Turning Up in Battles and Military-Style Parades in Iraq and Syria," *Wall Street Journal*, July 6, 2014, http://www.wsj.com/articles/insurgents-in-iraq-seizing-advanced-weaponry-1404684313.
168. Stern and Berger, *ISIS: The State of Terror*, 45.
169. Kellen, *On Terrorists and Terrorism*, 9.
170. See Ford, *Political Murder*, 362.
171. Kellen, *On Terrorists and Terrorism*, 10.
172. See Louise Richardson, *What Terrorists Want* (New York: Random House, 2006), 5, and Paul Wilkinson, "Terrorism," in *Ideas That Shape Politics*, ed. Michael Foley (Manchester: Manchester University Press, 1994), 189.
173. See Richard Jackson, Marie Breen Smyth, and Jeroen Gunning, "Introduction: The Case for Critical Terrorism Studies," in *Critical Terrorism Studies: A New Research Agenda* (Abingdon: Routledge, 2009), 1; Richard Jackson, "Knowledge, Power and Politics in the Study of Political Terrorism," in ibid., 67; Lee Jarvis and Michael Lister, "State Terrorism Research and Critical Terrorism Studies: An Assessment," *Critical Studies on Terrorism* 7, no. 1 (2014): 43–44, 49, 57; and Gilbert Ramsay, "Why Terrorism Can, but Should Not Be Defined," *Critical Studies on Terrorism* 8, no. 2 (2015): 211–12.
174. Roberts, "Terrorism Research: Past, Present, and Future," 65.
175. Sam Raphael, "In the Service of Power: Terrorism Studies and US Intervention in the Global South," in Jackson, Smyth, and Gunning, *Critical Terrorism Studies: A New Research Agenda*, 52.
176. John Arquilla and David Ronfeldt, "A New Epoch—and Spectrum—of Conflict," in *In Athena's Camp: Preparing for Conflict in the Information Age*, ed. John Arquilla and David Ronfeldt (Santa Monica, Calif.: RAND Corporation, MR-880-OSD /RC, 1997), 3.
177. Quoted in Dan Barry and Al Baker, "Getting the Message from 'Eco-Terrorists': Mystery Group Takes Its Campaign East," *New York Times*, January 8, 2001.
178. *Igniting the Revolution: An Introduction to the Earth Liberation Front*, distributed by the North American Earth Liberation Front Press Office, Portland (n.d.).

179.   Quoted in Barry and Baker, "Getting the Message from 'Eco-Terrorists.'"

180.   Ayman al-Zawahiri, Knights Under the Prophet's Banner, translated and published in Foreign Broadcast Information Service (FBIS), "Al-Sharq Al-Awsat Publishes Extracts from Al-Jihad Leader al-Zawahiri's New Book," Document ID: GMP20020108000197, January 8, 2002, 86. See also the excerpt reprinted in Laqueur, *Voices of Terror*, 431–32.

181.   Stern and Berger, *ISIS: The State of Terror*, 97.

182.   See text of the statement in ibid., 95–96.

183.   These three concepts, most commonly used by or associated with the American white supremacist/Far Right militia movements, are discussed in chapter 4.

184.   The phrase now often used to describe al-Qaeda's vast international network appears to have been coined first by John Arquilla and David Ronfeldt. See Francis Pisani, "How to Fight the Terror Network," *Le Monde Diplomatique*, February 6, 2002, http://mondeodiplo.com/2002/06/02network.

185.   John Arquilla and David Ronfeldt, "The Advent of Netwar (Revisited)," in *Networks and Netwars: The Future of Terror, Crime, and Militancy*, ed. John Arquilla and David Ronfeldt (Santa Monica, Calif.: RAND Corporation, MR-1382-OSD, 2001), 6.

186.   John Arquilla and David Ronfeldt, "The Advent of Netwar," in Arquilla and Ronfeldt, *In Athena's Camp*, 280.

187.   See FBI, Office for Victim Assistance, *Federal Bureau of Investigation Strategic Plan 2004–2009* (Washington, D.C.: U.S. Department of Justice, 2004), originally accessed at http://www.fbi.gov/publications/strategicplan/strategicplantext.htm.

2. The End of Empire and the Origins of Contemporary Terrorism

1.   B. H. Liddell Hart, *History of the Second World War* (New York: Paragon, 1979), 233.

2.   See, e.g., General George Grivas's observations concerning the impact of these promises on postwar Greek-Cypriot nationalist aspirations, in Charles Foley, ed., *The Memoirs of General Grivas* (London: Longmans, 1964), 12.

3.   David Thomson, *Europe Since Napoleon* (Harmondsworth: Penguin, 1978), 778.

4.   Text of the "Joint Declaration by the President and the Prime Minister, August 12, 1941," in Winston S. Churchill, *The Second World War*, vol. 3, *The Grand Alliance* (London: Reprint Society, 1956), 352.

5.   Winston S. Churchill, *The Second World War*, vol. 4, *The Hinge of Fate* (London: Reprint Society, 1956), 705.

6.   Quoted in Alistair Horne, *A Savage War of Peace: Algeria 1954–1962* (Harmondsworth: Penguin, 1977), 42.

7.   Quoted in Foley, *The Memoirs of General Grivas*, 13.

8.   See Bruce Hoffman, *Anonymous Soldiers: The Struggle for Israel 1917–1947* (New York: Knopf, 2015 and Vintage, 2016).

9.   Menachem Begin, *The Revolt: Story of the Irgun* (Jerusalem: Steimatzky, 1977), 52.

10.   Quoted in Bruce Hoffman, "Jewish Terrorist Activities and the British Government in Palestine, 1939 to 1947" (D.Phil. thesis, Oxford University, 1986), 327–28.

11.   Begin, *The Revolt*, 52–54.

12.   Ibid., 56.

13.   Carlos Marighela, *For the Liberation of Brazil*, trans. John Butt and Rosemary Sheed (Harmondsworth: Penguin, 1971), 61–97.

14.   Begin, *The Revolt*, 52.

15.   Hansard, *House of Commons*, vol. 441, col. 2342 (Oliver Stanley), August 12, 1947.

16.   Begin, *The Revolt*, 54–55.

17.   See texts of 80th Congress, House Joint Resolution 196, introduced by Andrew Somers on May 15, 1947, and Senate Resolution 149, introduced by Warren Magnusson et al. on July 17, 1947, in Isaac Zaar, *Rescue and Liberation: America's Part in the Birth of Israel* (New York: Bloch, 1954), 230, 243, and House Joint Resolution 237, introduced by Somers on July 11, 1947, quoted in Hoffman, "Jewish Terrorist Activities," 370.

18.   Quoted in Michael J. Cohen, *Palestine and the Great Powers, 1945–1948* (Princeton, N.J.: Princeton University Press, 1982), 250.

19.   Elizabeth Monroe, "Mr Bevin's 'Arab Policy,'" in Albert Hourani, ed., *St. Antony's Papers no. 11: Middle Eastern Affairs No. 2* (London: Chatto and Windus, 1961), 34.

20.   For details of UNSCOP's visit and deliberations, see Jorge García-Granados, *The Birth of Israel: The Drama as I Saw It* (New York: Knopf, 1948). García-Granados was the Guatemalan representative on the committee.

21.   The special committee issued its report on August 31, 1947, and unanimously recommended that Palestine should be granted its independence. See "Summary of the Report of UNSCOP," in Walter Laqueur, ed., *The Israel-Arab Reader: A Documentary History of the Middle East Conflict* (New York: Bantam, 1976), 108–12.

22.   Arthur Creech Jones to Elizabeth Munro [sic], October 23 and November 30, 1961, boxes 32/3 and 32/6, Letters, Creech Jones Papers, Rhodes House, Oxford.

23.   "Only Thus" was the Irgun's motto. See "Speech of the Commander-in-Chief of the Irgun Zvai Le'umi, 15 May 1948," in Eli Tavin and Yonah Alexander, eds., *Psychological Warfare and Propaganda: Irgun Documentation* (Wilmington, Del.: Scholarly Resources, 1982), 240–41.

24.   Foley, *The Memoirs of General Grivas*, 47.

25.   Quoted in Horne, *A Savage War of Peace*, 95.

26.   Foley, *The Memoirs of General Grivas*, 208.

27.   Quoted in Horne, *A Savage War of Peace*, 95.

28.   General Grivas, *Guerrilla Warfare and Eoka's Struggle*, trans. A. A. Pallis (London: Longmans, 1964), 19.

29.   Foley, *The Memoirs of General Grivas*, appendix 1, 204.

30.   Ibid., 31.

31.   Grivas, *Guerrilla Warfare and Eoka's Struggle*, 19.

32.   Ibid., 38.

33.   Foley, *The Memoirs of General Grivas*, 53.

34.   Ibid., 56–57; Michael Dewar, *Brush Fire Wars: Minor Campaigns of the British Army since 1945* (New York: St. Martin's, 1984), 80.

35.   Foley, *The Memoirs of General Grivas*, 71.

36.   Charles Foley and W. I. Scobie, *The Struggle for Cyprus* (Stanford, Calif.: Hoover Institution, 1975), 160.

37.   Quoted in Alan Hart, *Arafat: A Political Biography. The Definitive Biography Written in Co-operation with Yasser Arafat* (London: Sidgwick and Jackson,

1994), 112–13. See also John K. Cooley, *Green March, Black September: The Story of the Palestinian Arabs* (London: Frank Cass, 1973), 91; David Hirst, *The Gun and the Olive Branch* (London: Futura, 1977), 273, 276, 306–7; Edgar O'Ballance, *Arab Guerilla Power* (London: Faber, 1974), 23, 26; and Zeev Schiff and Raphael Rothstein, *Fedayeen: The Story of the Palestinian Guerrillas* (London: Valentine, Mitchell, 1972), 8 and 60.

38. Nelson Mandela, *Long Walk to Freedom* (London: Abacus, 1994), 326, 355.
39. Quoted in Roland Gaucher, *Les Terroristes* (Paris: Editions Albin Michel, 1965), 262.
40. Quoted in Horne, *A Savage War of Peace*, 186.
41. Quoted in ibid., 194.
42. Quoted in George Armstrong Kelly, *Lost Soldiers: The French Army and Empire in Crisis, 1947–1962* (Cambridge, Mass.: MIT Press, 1965), 201.
43. Florence Beauge, "'If France Recognized and Condemned These Practices, I Would Take That as a Step Forward,'" *Le Monde* (Paris), November 23, 2000.
44. Florence Beauge, "'I Am Resolute on Torture . . . I Myself Have Proceeded with Summary Executions . . .'" *Le Monde* (Paris), November 23, 2000.
45. Paul Aussaresses, *The Battle of the Casbah: Terrorism and Counter-Terrorism in Algeria, 1955–1957* (New York: Enigma Books, 2002), 126.
46. Ibid., 129.

3. The Internationalization of Terrorism

1. Quoted in Alex P. Schmid and Janny de Graaf, *Violence as Communication: Insurgent Terrorism and the Western News Media* (Beverly Hills, Calif.: Sage, 1982), 32.
2. Between 1968 and 1980, Palestinian groups were responsible for 331 incidents, compared with the 170 incidents attributed to the next most active group, the anti-Castro Cuban terrorist movements, and Irish and Turkish groups were in third position with 115 incidents each (RAND Chronology of Terrorism Incidents: see note 14).
3. Michael B. Oren, *Six Days of War: June 1967 and the Making of the Modern Middle East* (Oxford: Oxford University Press, 2002), 2.
4. Quoted in David Hirst, *The Gun and the Olive Branch* (London: Futura, 1977), 304.
5. Quoted in Schmid and de Graaf, *Violence as Communication*, 30.
6. Simon Reeve, *One Day in September: The Story of the 1972 Munich Olympics Massacre* (London: Faber and Faber, 2000), 95–103.
7. Abu Iyad with Eric Rouleau, *My Home, My Land: A Narrative of the Palestinian Struggle*, trans. Linda Butler Koseoglu (New York: Times Books, 1981), 111–12.
8. John K. Cooley, *Green March, Black September: The Story of the Palestinian Arabs* (London: Frank Cass, 1973), 126; Hirst, *The Gun and the Olive Branch*, 311. The American ABC network alone had four hundred broadcast staff present. See James W. Hoge, "The Media and Terrorism," in *Terrorism: The Media and the Law*, ed. Abraham Miller (New York: Transnational, 1982), 96.
9. Peter Taylor, *States of Terror: Democracy and Political Violence* (London: Penguin, 1993), 8.

10. Guy R. Sanan, "Olympic Security, 1972–1996: Threat, Response, and International Cooperation" (PhD diss., St. Andrews University, 1997), 77.

11. Quoted in Christopher Dobson and Ronald Payne, *The Carlos Complex: A Study in Terror* (London: Coronet/Hodder and Stoughton, 1978), 17–18.

12. *Al-Sayad* (Beirut), September 13, 1972, quoted in Sanan, "Olympic Security 1972–1996," 77. The same communiqué, attributed to George Habash, is quoted in part in Taylor, *States of Terror*, 8.

13. Schmid and de Graaf, *Violence as Communication*, 31.

14. The RAND Terrorism Incident Database defined and categorized terrorist incidents to help analysts, policymakers, and practitioners understand general trends in the threat. It was based on more than forty years of research by analysts at the RAND Corporation who had both regional expertise and relevant language skills. The database was divided into two different data sets. The incidents collected between 1968 and 1998 account only for international terrorism. International terrorism includes incidents in which the perpetrators go abroad to strike their targets, select domestic targets associated with a foreign state, or create an international incident by attacking airline passengers or equipment. This data set had been continuously maintained since 1972 by the RAND Corporation, in Santa Monica, California, between 1994 and 1998 by the Centre for the Study of Terrorism and Political Violence at St. Andrews University, Scotland, in association with RAND, and between 1998 and 2009 by RAND alone. The more recent database (2001 to 2009) includes both international and domestic terrorist incidents. Domestic terrorism is defined as incidents perpetrated by local nationals against a purely domestic target. See "Terrorism Update: Understanding the Terrorism Database," in Oklahoma City National Memorial Institute for the Prevention of Terrorism, *MIPT Quarterly Bulletin* (First Quarter 2002), 4n, and RAND Database of Worldwide Terrorism Incidents, http://www.rand.org/nsrd/projects/terrorism-incidents.html (accessed April 25, 2005).

15. "Interview with ASALA," *Panorama Magazine* (Milan), September 1, 1980, 62–65.

16. Armenian Secret Army for the Liberation of Armenia, *The Reality* (Armenian Secret Army for the Liberation of Armenia, n.d.), 4; reprinted as "Booklet Giving History of ASALA's Existence Gives New Insight Into the Revolutionary Movement," *Armenian Reporter* (New York), January 10, 1985.

17. Moorad Mooradian, "Terrorists Speak: Interviews with ASALA Members" (unpublished manuscript, n.d.), 15–16.

18. "Armenians Turning to Terrorism," *Los Angeles Times*, January 25, 1981.

19. "The Portrait of an Armenian Terrorist Leader," *Le Matin* (Paris), quoted in "French Paper Provides Information on ASALA Leader Hagopian," *Mamara* (Istanbul), January 16, 1985.

20. Gerard Chaliand and Yves Ternon, *The Armenians: From Genocide to Resistance*, trans. Tony Berrett (London: Zed, 1983), 6.

21. Andrew Corsun, *Research Papers on Terrorism: Armenian Terrorism, 1975–1980* (Washington, D.C.: Office of Security Threat Analysis Group, U.S. Department of State, 1982), 1.

22. Mark Armen Ayanian and John Z. Ayanian, "Armenian Political Violence on American Network News: An Analysis of Content," *Armenian Review* 40, no. 1–157 (Spring 1987): 28.

23.   Alex P. Schmid and Janny de Graaf, *Insurgent Terrorism and the Western News Media: An Exploratory Analysis with a Dutch Case Study* (Leiden: Center for the Study of Social Conflicts [COMT], Dutch State University, The Netherlands, November 1980), quoted in Brian Michael Jenkins, *The Psychological Implications of Media-Covered Terrorism* (Santa Monica, Calif.: RAND Corporation, P-6627, June 1981), 7.

24.   "The Palestinians of the 1990s," *Foreign Report* (London), no. 2202 (April 2, 1992).

25.   Quoted in I. Fetscher and G. Rohrmoser, *Analysen zum Terrorismus* [Analyses on the subject of terrorism], vol. 1, *Ideologien und Strategien* [Ideologies and strategies] (Bonn: Westdeutscher Verlag, 1981), 301.

26.   Christoph Wackerngel, "Transcript of a Talk by Christoph Wackerngel," September 14, 1995 (unpublished manuscript), 1.

27.   Eileen MacDonald, *Shoot the Women First* (New York: Random House, 1991), 210.

28.   Michael "Bommi" Baumann, *Terror or Love? Bommi Baumann's Own Story of His Life as a West German Urban Guerrilla*, trans. Helene Ellenbogen and Wayne Parker (New York: Grove, 1979), 19–20. The book was originally published in Germany in 1971 under the title *Wie alles anfing* [How it all began].

29.   Klein had first gained notoriety for his role in the 1975 seizure of the OPEC ministers' meeting in Vienna masterminded by the infamous Carlos "the Jackal," the Venezuelan terrorist Ilich Ramirez Sanchez. Seriously wounded during the attack, in 1978 Klein broke with his former comrades and completely disavowed armed struggle as a means to achieve political change.

30.   Quoted in Jean Marcel Bougereau, "Memoirs of an International Terrorist: Conversations with Hans Joachim Klein," in *The German Guerrilla: Terror, Reaction, and Resistance* (Sanday, Orkney: Cienfuegos, n.d.), 12. See also the similar statements on 9, 14, and 15.

31.   See especially "CHANGE YOUR HATRED INTO ENERGY" (issued by the BLACK FRONT); "SHALOM & NAPALM" (issued by the BLACK RATS, T.W.); and "STATION TW," quoted in Baumann, *Terror or Love?*, 56–57, 67–69. For the wider influence of the Vietnam War on German terrorism, see especially the communiqués claiming credit for the attempted assassination of the American commander in chief of NATO (and future secretary of state) General Alexander Haig in Obourg, Belgium, on June 25, 1979, and the "Hunger Strike Declaration of 4 December 1984 by Imprisoned Members of the Red Army Faction," both quoted in Dennis Pluchinsky, "Western Europe's Red Terrorists: The Fighting Communist Organizations," in *Europe's Red Terrorists: The Fighting Communist Organizations*, ed. Yonah Alexander and Dennis Pluchinsky (London: Frank Cass, 1992), 24, 62.

32.   Quoted in Stefan Aust, *The Baader-Meinhof Group: The Inside Story of a Phenomenon* (London: Bodley Head, 1987), 366.

33.   Baumann, *Terror or Love?*, 60. See also p. 59 and the "SHALOM & NAPALM" communiqué on pp. 67–68.

34.   Baumann, *Terror or Love?*, 5.

35.   David C. Rapoport, "The International World as Some Terrorists Have Seen It: A Look at a Century of Memoirs," *Journal of Strategic Studies* 10, no. 4 (December 1987): 45.

36. David Th. Schiller, "From a National to an International Response," in *Combating the Terrorists: Democratic Responses to Political Violence*, ed. H. H. Tucker (New York: Facts on File, 1988), 188.

37. James Adams, *The Financing of Terror* (New York: Simon & Schuster, 1986), 49.

38. Ibid., 243.

39. Ibid., 104.

40. Iyad, *My Home, My Land*, 221.

41. Christopher Walker, "£194m 'Missing' as Arafat Seeks Aid from Britain," *Times* (London), July 14, 1997.

4. Religion and Terrorism

1. "Broadcast by Usama bin Ladin (October 7, 2001), Al-Jazira Television. Translation by BBC News," in *Anti-American Terrorism and the Middle East: A Documentary Reader*, ed. Barry Rubin and Judith Colp Rubin (Oxford: Oxford University Press, 2002), 249–51.

2. Quoted in John Kifner, "Israelis Investigate Far Right: May Crack Down on Speech," *New York Times*, November 8, 1995.

3. Institute for Economics and Peace (IEP), *Global Terrorism Index 2016: Measuring and Understand the Impact of Terrorism* (Sydney, New York, and Mexico City: Institute for Economics and Peace, November 2016), 4, http://economicsand peace.org/wp-content/uploads/2015/11/Global-Terrorism-Index-2016.pdf.

4. See Gregory Crouch, "Suspect in Killing of Dutch Filmmaker Maintains His Silence," *New York Times*, July 12, 2005; Gregory Crouch, "Man on Trial in Dutch Killing Says He'd Do 'Same Again,'" *New York Times*, July 13, 2005; Associated Press, "Extremist Admits to the Slaying of Dutch Filmmaker," *Washington Post*, July 13, 2005.

5. *Oxford English Dictionary, Compact Edition* (Oxford: Oxford University Press, 1971), *s.v.* "zealot."

6. See David C. Rapoport, "Fear and Trembling: Terrorism in Three Religious Traditions," *American Political Science Review* 78, no. 3 (September 1984): 668–72, and Walter Laqueur, *The Age of Terrorism* (Boston: Little, Brown, 1987), 7–8.

7. *Oxford English Dictionary, s.v.* "thug."

8. Rapoport, "Fear and Trembling," 660–64. If one accepts that upwards of a million people may have been murdered by the Thugs, then on average they killed 833.333 people a year.

9. *Oxford English Dictionary, s.v.* "assassin."

10. Rapoport, "Fear and Trembling," 659.

11. Numbers of active, identifiable terrorist groups from 1968 to the present are derived from the RAND Terrorism Incident Database.

12. Bureau of Counterterrorism, "Foreign Terrorist Organizations," U.S. Department of State: Diplomacy in Action (2016), http://www.state.gov/j/ct/rls/other /des/123085.htm (accessed May 5, 2016).

13. Mark Juergensmeyer, "Terror Mandated by God," *Terrorism and Political Violence* 9, no. 2 (Summer 1997): 20.

14. Murray Sayle, "Martyrdom Complex," *New Yorker*, May 13, 1996.

15. Nicholas D. Kristof, "Japanese Cult Planned U.S. Attack," *International Herald Tribune* (Paris), March 24, 1997; Robert Whymant, "Cult Planned Gas Raids on America," *Times* (London), March 29, 1997.

16. The hijackers' plans were foiled, however, after the French authorities learned of their intentions and ordered commandos to storm the aircraft after it had landed for refueling in Marseilles.

17. RAND Terrorism Incident Database.

18. According to the RAND Terrorism Incident Database, between 1982 and 1989 Shi'a terrorist groups committed 247 terrorist incidents and were responsible for 1,057 deaths.

19. According to the RAND Terrorism Incident Database, there were a total of 11,769 terrorist attacks recorded between 1998 and 2004. Al-Qaeda was responsible for 22 of those incidents but caused a total of 3,457 fatalities.

20. Imam Khomeini, *Islam and Revolution*, trans. Hamid Algar (London: KPI, 1981), 286–87.

21. Quoted in Amir Taheri, *Holy Terror: The Inside Story of Islamic Terrorism* (London: Sphere, 1987), 7–8.

22. Hezbollah was the product of several splits within the Lebanese Shi'a movement. Its origins can be traced back to 1974, when a Lebanese Shi'a cleric, Imam Musa al-Sadr, who had studied in the Iranian holy city of Qom, organized the "Movement of the Underprivileged" to advance Shi'a interests and improve the community's lowly socioeconomic conditions. This movement was subsequently reorganized as the principal Shi'a political party in Lebanon, Amal, which formed its own militia during the civil war that racked Lebanon a year later. In 1979, however, al-Sadr vanished during a visit to Libya. The disappearance of the imam created a vacuum within Amal that made the party fertile ground for Iranian influence and rendered the movement susceptible to the fundamentalist call of the revolution that had brought Khomeini to power earlier that year. Nabih Berri, a lawyer, was appointed head of Amal the following year. Hussein Mussawi, the person quoted above and the alleged mastermind behind the terrorist campaign against Libya to recover the imam, was named Berri's deputy and commander of the militia. A fanatical supporter of Khomeini, Mussawi sought to place Amal in the vanguard of a regional revolution based on the new Iranian Islamic Republic. Berri, on the other hand, clung to a moderate line and advocated a new deal for the Shi'a community within the confines of the existing Lebanese state structure. By this time, however, the radicalization of the Shi'a in Lebanon had gone far beyond the narrow nationalist and social aims of Amal. In 1981, Mussawi broke with Berri and founded his own organization, Islamic Amal. Shortly after, another faction split from Amal and under the leadership of Abbas Mussawi (a nephew of Hussein) and the "spiritual guidance" of Sheikh Muhammed Hussein Fadlallah, it soon came to be known as Hezbollah. Like Islamic Amal, Hezbollah embraced Khomeini's summons for a pan-Islamic revolt designed to turn Lebanon into an Iranian-style Islamic republic.

23. "Open Letter from the Party of God to the Disinherited of Lebanon and the World Revealing the Way and the Intentions Which Are Their Own on the Occasion of the First Anniversary of Ragheb Harb, Symbol of the Islamic Resistance and Exemplary Martyr," issued by Hezbollah, Beirut, Lebanon, February 16, 1985.

24. Ayatollah Muhammed Hussein Fadl Allah [sic], "Islam and Violence in Political Reality," *Middle East Insight* 4, nos. 4–5 (1986): 4–13. See also the quote from Fadlallah's book *Invisible Armies* in Alison Jamieson, *Terrorism* (Hove, East Sussex: Wayland, 1991), 33:

   > We don't see ourselves as terrorists, because we don't believe in terrorism. . . . We don't see resisting the occupier as a terrorist action. We see ourselves as mujihadeen who fight a Holy War for the people. Faith, whether religious or political, is all. To the individual terrorist, or supporter of terrorism, a murder can be an expression of the defence of freedom; a car-bomb which kills civilians can be a blow struck in a war of liberation; a kidnapping and murder can be a step towards justice. The intensity of conviction that justifies one man's justice at any price almost inevitably means that the freedom or justice of others will be ignored, or at worst trampled and destroyed.

25. Quoted in Laura Marlowe, "A Fiery Cleric's Defense of Jihad," *Time*, January 15, 1996.

26. Quoted in Hala Jaber, *Hezbollah: Born with a Vengeance* (New York: Columbia University Press, 1997), 23.

27. See H. A. R. Gibb, *Islam* (Oxford: Oxford University Press, 1978), 71, and Malise Ruthven, *A Fury for God: The Islamist Attack on America* (London: Granta, 2002), xvii.

28. Quoted in draft copy of the *United States Department of Defense Commission on the Beirut International Airport (BIA) Terrorist Act of October 23, 1983* (known as "The Long Commission" in reference to its chairman, retired admiral Robert L. J. Long, U.S. Navy, n.d.), 38.

29. Armed Islamic Group communiqué, containing a twelve-page interview with Antar Zouabri, September 1996.

30. Hamas was founded in 1987 by Sheikh Amid Ibrahim Yassin. Its estimated $70 million annual budget is derived mostly from contributions by Iran and Saudi Arabia, although Palestinians and Arabs in countries throughout the world (including the United States and Britain) also donate funds to the movement. In addition to its violent activities, Hamas provides social services to Palestinian communities in the Gaza Strip and West Bank, including schools, medical assistance, and related welfare activities. In this respect, Hamas is consciously emulating the success of both the PLO and Hezbollah in providing social services while simultaneously waging a violent terrorist campaign.

31. Quoted in Anti-Defamation League of B'nai B'rith, *ADL Special Background Report: Hamas, Islamic Jihad, and the Muslim Brotherhood: Islamic Extremists and the Terrorist Threat to America* (New York: Anti-Defamation League of B'nai B'rith, 1993), 4.

32. As Fathi Shiqaqi, the general secretary of Palestine Islamic Jihad, whom it is believed was assassinated by the Israeli secret services in Malta in 1995, once explained: "Our struggle with the enemy in Palestine is meant to open every possible form of jihad, including suicide attacks. The enemy thought he had closed the Palestine file when he signed the Oslo Agreements and thus could eliminate us. That requires us to make a special effort to foil his plot. That is why suicide bombers are important." Quoted in Rafi Yisra'eli, "Islamikaze: Suicide Terrorism Examined," *Nativ* (Tel Aviv), January–April 1997, 3.

33. Imad Saluji, quoted in Mark Juergensmeyer, "The Worldwide Rise of Religious Nationalism," *Journal of International Affairs* 50, no. 1 (Summer 1996): 1.

34. Quoted in Yisra'eli, "Islamikaze," 3.

35. Quoted in *ADL Special Background Report: Hamas, Islamic Jihad, and the Muslim Brotherhood*, 4.

36. T. E. Lawrence, *Seven Pillars of Wisdom* (Harmondsworth: Penguin Books, 1977), 23.

37. "Text of Bin Laden Remarks: 'Hypocrisy Rears Its Ugly Head,'" *Washington Post*, October 8, 2001.

38. Neal MacFarquhar, with Jim Rutenberg, "Bin Laden, in a Taped Speech, Says Attacks in Afghanistan Are a War Against Islam," *New York Times*, November 4, 2001, B2.

39. See Anonymous, *Through Our Enemies' Eyes: Osama bin Laden, Radical Islam, and the Future of America* (Dulles, Va.: Brassey's, 2002), 55–59. This book, written by Michael Scheuer, a veteran Central Intelligence Agency analyst who headed its bin Laden Unit in the late 1990s, is without doubt the preeminent work on bin Laden and al-Qaeda.

40. Quoted in Yonah Alexander and Michael S. Swetnam, *Usama bin Laden's al-Qaida: Profile of a Terrorist Network* (Ardsley, N.Y.: Transnational, 2001), appendix 1A, 1–2, 19.

41. Quoted in ibid., appendix 1A, 21.

42. Quoted in ibid., appendix 1B, 1.

43. Ruthven, *A Fury for God*, xxii.

44. Quoted in Alexander and Swetnam, *Usama bin Laden's al-Qaida*, appendix 1B, 1–2.

45. Quoted in Ben Venzke and Aimee Ibrahim, *The al-Qaeda Threat: An Analytical Guide to al-Qaeda's Tactics and Targets* (Alexandria, Va.: Tempest, 2003), 158–59.

46. Anonymous, *Through Our Enemies' Eyes*, 53–54, 69–70, 72.

47. Quoted in Venzke and Ibrahim, *The al-Qaeda Threat*, 160.

48. U.S. Department of State, *Patterns of Global Terrorism 2001* (Washington, D.C.: U.S. Department of State, Publication 10940, May 2002), 105.

49. National Commission on Terrorist Attacks Upon the United States, *The 9/11 Commission Report: Authorized Edition* (New York: Norton, 2004), 49–51.

50. Gibb, *Islam*, 2–3, 10–11. See also Ruthven, *A Fury for God*, xvi, xix.

51. Counter Terrorism Center, *Counter Terrorism 2005* (Washington, D.C.: Central Intelligence Agency, 2004), 214.

52. See Rohan Gunaratna, *Inside Al Qaeda: Global Network of Terrorism* (London: Hurst, 2002), 26.

53. Quoted in Alexander and Swetnam, *Usama bin Laden's al-Qaida*, 2.

54. Ayman al-Zawahiri, *Knights Under the Prophet's Banner: Meditations on the Jihadist Movement*, translated and published in FBIS (Foreign Broadcast Information Service), "Al-Sarq Al-Aswat Publishes Extracts from Al-Jihad Leader Al-Zawahiri's New Book," Document ID GMP20020108000197, December 2, 2001, 87.

55. Jason Burke, "Think Again: Al Qaeda," *Foreign Policy* (May/June 2004), http://www.foreign policy.com. This concept of the "far and near" enemies was first articulated by al-Zawahiri in an article titled "The Way to Jerusalem Passes

Through Cairo," published in *Al-Mujahideen*, April 1995. See Montasser Al-Zayyat, *The Road to Al-Qaeda: The Story of Bin Laden's Right-Hand Man* (London: Pluto, 2004), 62.

56. Quoted in National Commission on Terrorist Attacks Upon the United States, *The 9/11 Commission Report*, 47.

57. Quoted in U.S. Department of State, *The Network of Terrorism* (Washington, D.C.: U.S. Department of State, 2001), 8.

58. Quoted in ibid.

59. Loretta Napoleoni, *The Islamic Phoenix* (New York: Seven Stories, 2014), Kindle Location 365.

60. Michael Weiss and Hassan Hassan, *ISIS: Inside the Army of Terror* (New York: Reagan Arts, 2015), 116.

61. Jessica Stern and J. M. Berger, *ISIS: The State of Terror* (New York: Harper-Collins, 2015), 95, 97, 116, 194, 215–17, and Weiss and Hassan, *ISIS: Inside the Army of Terror*, xiv, 158, 189.

62. David Cook, *Understanding Jihad* (Berkeley: University of California Press, 2005), 128–30, and Omar Nasiri, *Inside the Jihad: My Life with Al Qaeda—A Spy's Story* (New York: Basic, 2006), 151.

63. Peter Bergen, *Holy War, Inc.: Inside the Secret World of Osama bin Laden* (New York: Free Press, 2001), 52.

64. Abdel Bari Atwan, *The Secret History of al Qaeda* (Berkeley: University of California Press, 2006), 73; Steve Coll, *Ghost Wars: The Secret History of the CIA, Afghanistan, and bin Laden, from the Soviet Invasion to September 10, 2001* (New York: Penguin, 2004), 155; Nasiri, *Inside the Jihad*, 151. See also Sayyid Qutb, *Milestones: Ma'alim fi'l-tareeq* [Literally, "Milestones Along the Way" or "Signposts Along the Way"], ed. A. B. al-Mehri (Birmingham, England: Maktabah, n.d.).

65. Olivier Roy, *Globalized Islam: The Search for a New Ummah* (New York: Columbia University Press, 2004), 295.

66. Lawrence Wright, *The Looming Tower: Al-Qaeda and the Road to 9/11* (New York: Alfred A. Knopf, 2006), 95, and Nasiri, *Inside the Jihad*, 151.

67. Atwan, *The Secret History of al Qaeda*, 42, 70, 73; Coll, *Ghost Wars*, 85; Fawaz A. Gerges, *The Far Enemy: Why Jihad Went Global* (Cambridge: Cambridge University Press, 2005), 13, 134; Gilles Kepel, *Jihad: The Trail of Political Islam* (London: I.B. Tauris, 2006), 144; Gilles Kepel, *The War for Muslim Minds: Islam and the West* (Cambridge, Mass.: Bellknap, 2004), 172; Michael Scheuer, *Through Our Enemies' Eyes: Osama bin Laden, Radical Islam, and the Future of America* (Washington, D.C.: Potomac, 2006), 41, 43; Wright, *The Looming Tower*, 95.

68. Wright, *The Looming Tower*, 96.

69. Ibid., 179; Peter L. Bergen, *The Osama bin Laden I Know: An Oral History of al Qaeda's Leader* (New York: Free Press, 2006), 42; Kepel, *The War for Muslim Minds*, 84.

70. Cook, *Understanding Jihad*, 129–31; Wright, *The Looming Tower*, 102–3.

71. Abdullah Azzam, *Defence of Muslim Lands* (London: Maktabah, 2002); Abdullah Azzam, *Join the Caravan* (London: Azzam, 2001); Abdullah Azzam, *The Lofty Mountain* (London: Azzam, n.d.).

72. "ISIS Spokesman Vows 'Defeat' for America, Calls for Killing Westerners in New Audio Message," TRR2014092201178788, *Hanin Network Forums* (Arabic), September 22, 2014.

73. Quoted in Shaykh Muhammad Ibn Haadee al-Madkhalee, "The Reality of Daesh (ISIS)," August 24, 2015, http://www.miraathpublications.net/en/the-reality-of -daesh-ISIS/.

74. David Ignatius, "The Islamic State Is Still on the Rise," *Washington Post*, February 4, 2016, https://www.washingtonpost.com/opinions/the-islamic-state-is-still -on-the-rise/2016/02/04/e631bdea-cb82-11e5-88ff-e2d1b4289c2f_story.html.

75. Kahane was assassinated in New York City in November 1990 by El Sayyid A. Nosair, one of the men convicted of conspiring to bomb the World Trade Center (while he was serving a prison term in connection with Kahane's assassination), as well as the follow-on plot to blow up bridges and tunnels linking New York with New Jersey in hopes of obtaining the release of the Trade Center bombers.

76. See, e.g., books such as *Never Again! A Program for Survival* (Los Angeles: Nash, 1971) and *They Must Go* (New York: Grosset and Dunlap, 1981), and pamphlets such as *Viewpoint Kahane: There Is No More Tal* (n.d.) and *Uncomfortable Questions for Comfortable Jews* (n.d.).

77. His "Rabbi Kahane Speaks" column was regularly featured in the American-Jewish newspaper the *Jewish Press*.

78. See Ami Pedahzur, *The Israeli Response to Jewish Extremism and Violence: Defending Democracy* (Manchester: Manchester University Press, 2002), 34–37, and Ehud Sprinzak, *Brother Against Brother: Violence and Extremism in Israeli Politics from Altalena to the Rabin Assassination* (New York: Free Press, 1999), 2–3.

79. Kahane, *Never Again!*, 110.

80. Ehud Sprinzak, "Violence and Catastrophe in the Theology of Rabbi Meir Kahane: The Ideologization of Mimetic Desire," in *Violence and the Sacred in the Modern World*, ed. Mark Juergensmeyer (London: Frank Cass, 1992), 51, 64–66. In his book, written at the height of the Algerian war, Fanon, a psychiatrist, wrote of the "liberating" effects of violence on the oppressed. See Frantz Fanon, *The Wretched of the Earth* (London: Penguin, 1990).

81. Quoted in Janet L. Dolgin, *Jewish Identity and the JDL* (Princeton, N.J.: Princeton University Press, 1977), 69.

82. *New York Times*, May 15, 1980, quoted in Bruce Hoffman, "The Jewish Defense League," *Terrorism, Violence, and Insurgency Journal* 5, no. 1 (Summer 1984): 13.

83. Kahane, speaking at California State University at Northridge, California, March 1988 (attended by author).

84. Ibid.

85. Kahane, *They Must Go*, 272 (emphasis in original).

86. Ehud Sprinzak, *The Ascendance of Israel's Radical Right* (Oxford: Oxford University Press, 1991), 98–99.

87. Ehud Sprinzak, "Fundamentalism, Terrorism, and Democracy: The Case of the Gush Emunim Underground," Wilson Center Occasional Paper no. 4 (Washington, D.C.: Smithsonian Institution, 1986), 11.

88. See Thomas L. Friedman, "Jewish Terrorists Freed by Israel," *New York Times*, December 9, 1984; Grace Halsell, "Why Bobby Brown of Brooklyn Wants to Blow Up Al Aqsa," *Arabia*, August 1984; Martin Merzer, "Justice for All in Israel?," *Miami Herald*, May 17, 1985; and "Jail Term of Jewish Terrorist Reduced," *Jerusalem Post* (international edition), October 12, 1985. The information per-

taining to the terrorists' desire to provoke a cataclysmic holy war between Muslims and Jews was verified by an American law enforcement officer, involved with the investigation of Jewish terrorist incidents in the United States and knowledgeable about the Jerusalem incident, in conversation with the author.

89. Sprinzak, "Fundamentalism, Terrorism, and Democracy," 11–13.
90. Pedahzur, *The Israeli Response to Jewish Extremism and Violence*, 84.
91. Quoted in Joel Greenberg, "Israeli Police Question Two Rabbis in Rabin Assassination," *New York Times*, November 22, 1995.
92. Michael Karpin and Ina Friedman, *Murder in the Name of God: The Plot to Kill Yitzhak Rabin* (New York: Metropolitan, 1998), 4. See also Pedahzur, *The Israeli Response to Jewish Extremism and Violence*, 5–6, 94–95, 253–58, 281.
93. Quoted in Greenberg, "Israeli Police Question Two Rabbis in Rabin Assassination."
94. Quoted in Marie Colvin, "Rabbi Calls for Suicide Bombings," *Sunday Times* (London), April 13, 1997.
95. Stewart Bell, *Cold Terror: How Canada Nurtures and Exports Terrorism Around the World* (Toronto: John Wiley, 2007), 24.
96. Mark Juergensmeyer, *Terror in the Mind of God* (Berkeley: University of California Press, 2000), 98; Paul Wallace, "Political Violence and Terrorism in India," in *Terrorism in Context*, ed. Martha Crenshaw (University Park: Pennsylvania State University Press, 2007), 363.
97. National Archives and Records Administration (NARA), Ronald Reagan Library, Simi Valley, Calif., "Near East and South Asia Affairs Directorat [*sic*]," NSC (National Security Council) Records, Box 90583-90585, Iraq, 1983 [2 of 4], OA 90583 containing declassified Directorate of Intelligence, *Terrorism Review* (Washington, D.C.: Central Intelligence Agency, November 1986), 20; Mark Juergensmeyer, *The New Cold War? Religious Nationalism Confronts the Secular State* (Berkeley: University of California Press, 1993), 163. See also Ian Grieg, "The Punjab: Plagued by Terror," *Conflict International*, July 1992, and Wallace, "Political Violence and Terrorism in India," 363–65.
98. K. P. S. Gill, *Punjab: The Knights of Falsehood* (New Delhi: Har-Anandp, 2001), 76.
99. Eleanor Nesbitt, "Sikh Sants and Their Establishments in India and Abroad," in *The Oxford Handbook of Sikh Studies* ed. Pashura Singh and Louis E. French (Oxford: Oxford University Press, 2014), 363; Directorate of Intelligence, *Terrorism Review*, 19; Juergensmeyer, *The New Cold War?*, 94.
100. Quoted in Juergensmeyer, *Terror in the Mind of God*, 98.
101. Ibid., 92, 164, and Mark Juergensmeyer, "Sacrifice and Cosmic War," in *Violence and the Sacred in the Modern World* (London: Frank Cass, 1992), 106.
102. Quoted in Juergensmeyer, *Terror in the Mind of God*, 172, and Walter Laqueur, *The New Terrorism: Fanaticism and the Arms of Mass Destruction* (New York: Oxford University Press, 1999), 153.
103. Juergensmeyer, *Terror in the Mind of God*, 95–96.
104. Quoted in ibid., 203.
105. Grieg, "The Punjab: Plagued by Terror."
106. Juergensmeyer, *Terror in the Mind of God*, 98, and Kim Bolan, *Loss of Faith: How the Air-India Bombers Got Away with Murder* (Toronto: M&S, 2005), 31.

107.   Gill, *Punjab: The Knights of Falsehood*, 9. See also Wallace, "Political Violence and Terrorism in India," 385–86; William K. Stevens, "Indian Government Takes Over a State Swept by Religious Strife," *New York Times*, October 7, 1983; William K. Stevens, "Mrs. Gandhi Says Terrorism Will End," *New York Times*, October 15, 1983.

108.   Stanley A. Kochanek and Robert L. Hardgrave, *India: Government and Politics in a Developing Nation*, 7th ed. (Boston: Thomson, 2008), 175; Directorate of Intelligence, *Terrorism Review*, 19; Juergensmeyer, *The New Cold War?*, 95; Nesbitt, "Sikh Sants and Their Establishments in India and Abroad," 363; Wallace, "Political Violence and Terrorism in India," 385–88.

109.   Michael T. Kaufman, "Sikh Separatists Hijack Indian Jetliner to Pakistan," *New York Times*, September 30, 1981; Bell, *Cold Terror*, 24; Directorate of Intelligence, *Terrorism Review*, 20.

110.   Quoted in Bell, *Cold Terror*, 23–25.

111.   See *The Government of Canada Response to the Commission of Inquiry Into the Investigation of the Bombing of Air India Flight 182* (Ottawa: Public Safety Canada, December 8, 2015), https://www.publicsafety.gc.ca/cnt/rsrcs/pblctns/rspns-cmmssn/index-en.aspx.

112.   The domestic terrorist incident responsible for the largest number of deaths was the fire deliberately set by terrorists at a movie theater in Abadan, Iran, in 1979 that claimed the lives of 477 persons. See Richard Falkenrath, Robert D. Newman, and Bradley A. Thayer, *America's Achilles' Heel: Nuclear, Biological, and Chemical Terrorism and Covert Attack* (Cambridge, Mass.: MIT Press 1998), 47, table 1.

113.   See Bell, *Cold Terror*, 37.

114.   Bolan, *Loss of Faith*, 31.

115.   Gill, *Punjab: The Knights of Falsehood*, 5.

116.   Directorate of Intelligence, *Terrorism Review*, 19.

117.   Grieg, "The Punjab: Plagued by Terror."

118.   Gill, *Punjab: The Knights of Falsehood*, 5.

119.   The assault came at the end of a fifty-one-day standoff between the Branch Davidian cult, led by Reverend David Koresh, and agents of both the Bureau of Alcohol, Tobacco, and Firearms (BATF) and the FBI. The crisis began when BATF agents attempted to arrest Koresh and some of his followers on charges of illegal possession of firearms (specifically of converting single-shot AR-15 assault rifles into full automatic machine guns). There had also been reports of the cult's bizarre sexual practices and abuse of its members' children that had prompted increased law enforcement interest in the Davidians' Mount Carmel compound. Koresh believed that he was God's special messianic messenger, sent to earth, he claimed, to "reveal the hidden meaning of the entire biblical prophetic corpus." Through his charismatic and persuasive personality, Koresh inculcated in his followers a sense of imminent redemption and apocalyptic visions that culminated in the deaths of Koresh and his followers on April 19, 1993. See James D. Tabor and Eugene V. Gallagher, *Why Waco? Cults and the Battle for Religious Freedom in America* (Berkeley: University of California Press, 1995).

120.   In 1992, one U.S. marshal was killed attempting to arrest Randy Weaver for the sale of illegal sawed-off shotguns. Weaver's son was shot to death in the initial confrontation, and his wife was subsequently killed by an FBI sniper before the

tense standoff was defused six days later. The incident became a cause célèbre for the militias and other extremist groups and is widely believed to have "lit the fuse" for the 1995 Oklahoma City bombing.

121. See Lou Michel and Dan Herbeck, *American Terrorist: Timothy McVeigh and the Oklahoma City Bombing* (New York: Regan, 2001), 166–69.

122. Quoted in Associated Press, "McVeigh Aimed to Spark Revolt, Ex-Buddy Says," *International Herald Tribune* (Paris), May 13, 1997.

123. Arie Perliger, *Challengers from the Sidelines: Understanding America's Violent Far-Right* (West Point, N.Y.: Combatting Terrorism Center, November 2012), 28.

124. Linda Thompson, "Waco, Another Perspective," *American Justice Foundation* (n.d.), http://www.skeptictank.org/files/waco/ltstory2.htm (accessed May 5, 2016).

125. Mike German, "Behind the Lone Terrorists, a Pack Mentality," *Washington Post*, June 5, 2005; Perliger, *Challengers from the Sidelines*, 69.

126. Quoted in Keith Schneider, "Fearing a Conspiracy, Some Heed a Call to Arms," *New York Times*, November 14, 1994.

127. Quoted in Jo Thomas, "Militias Hold a Congress, and Not a Gun Is Seen," *New York Times*, November 1, 1994.

128. Michigan Militia, http://www.michiganmilitia.com (accessed May 5, 2016).

129. The U.S. Anti-Defamation League of B'nai B'rith, one of the most authoritative of the groups monitoring the militia phenomenon, puts the number of active members at a considerably lower figure of fifteen thousand people in forty states (see Anti-Defamation League of B'nai B'rith, *ADL Special Report: The Militia Movement in America* [New York: Anti-Defamation League of B'nai B'rith, 1995], 1), while the Southern Poverty Law Center (SPLC) reported some 809 militia organizations that were active in all fifty states plus the District of Columbia (see *False Patriots: The Threat of Antigovernment Extremists* [Montgomery, Ala.: SPLC, 1996], 58–68). Meanwhile, another authority, Paul de Armond, the director of the Public Good, a Washington State grassroots community organization, claimed that the total number of militia members plus other Americans involved in the wider Christian white supremacist movement exceeded five million (Paul de Armond, "The Anti-Democratic Movement—More Than Militias," August 1995, http://www.nwcitizen.com/publicgood).

130. "Antigovernment Militia Groups Grew by More Than One-Third in Last Year," SPLC website, January 4, 2016, https://www.splcenter.org/news/2016/01/04/antigovernment-militia-groups-grew-more-one-third-last-year. See also Kurt Eichenwald, "Right-Wing Extremists Are a Bigger Threat to America Than ISIS," *Newsweek*, February 12, 2016, http://www.newsweek.com/2016/02/12/right-wing-extremists-militants-bigger-threat-america-isis-jihadists-422743.html; Jaeh Lee, Brandon Ellington, and Gabrielle Canon, "The Rise of Violent Right-Wing Extremism, Explained," *Mother Jones*, June 30, 2015, http://www.motherjones.com/politics/2015/06/right-wing-extremism-explainer-charleston-mass-shooting-terrorism; Perliger, *Challengers from the Sidelines*, 69–70; and Richard Reed, "Life, Liberty, and the Pursuit of Anyone Who Gets in the Way: Lessons from a Comparative Analysis of U.S. Militias and Ulster Loyalists," *Studies in Conflict and Terrorism* 36, no. 9 (September 2013): 758.

131. There is reportedly also a "bridge" faction, believed to consist of extreme right-wing Mormons associated with the racist (but not anti-Semitic) splinter of the

Far Right Libertarian Party, known as the Constitution Party, attempting to reconcile these two factions. I am indebted to Paul de Armond, of the Public Good in Bellingham, Washington State, for drawing my attention to these critical distinctions and providing me with information on these groups.

132. Quoted in David Harrison, "Jackboot Stamp of the New Right," *Observer* (London), April 23, 1995. See also Anti-Defamation League of B'nai B'rith, "Militia of Montana," Extremism in America (2005), http://archive.adl.org/learn/ext_us/ mom.html?xpicked=3 (accessed May 5, 2016); and Perliger, *Challengers from the Sidelines*, 66.

133. See John Carlin, "DIY Apocalypse," *Independent* (London), April 30, 1995, and Timothy Egan, "Trying to Explain Contacts with Paramilitary Groups," *New York Times*, May 2, 1995.

134. "Militia of Montana: Statement of Purpose," http://www.militiaofmontana.com (accessed May 5, 2016).

135. "Montana Militia Community," Facebook, https://www.facebook.com/ Montana-Militia-192651084206745/info?tab=page_info (accessed May 5, 2016).

136. Quoted in John Carlin, "'We Need Blood to Cleanse Us,'" *Independent* (London), May 2, 1995.

137. Gritz's millenarian preparatory plans suffered a grievous setback when he was arrested on kidnapping charges in Connecticut involving his part in an ugly child custody battle.

138. Rebecca Boone, "Once a Hotbed: 'Bo' Gritz and His Anti-government Followers Have Left," *Salt Lake Tribune*, August 30, 2004, http://archive.sltrib.com /article.php?id=2400556&itype=NGPSID; Nicholas K. Geranios, "'Almost Heaven' Survivalist Community Pines for Its Founder," *Los Angeles Times*, November 19, 1999, http://articles.latimes.com/1999/nov/14/local/me-33373.

139. Lorna Thackeray, "The Freeman Standoff," *Billings Gazette*, March 25, 2006, http://billingsgazette.com/news/state-and-regional/montana/the-freemen -standoff/article_52ea8d8f-c28e-5170-8b65-8c5f71ea4fe9.html.

140. Quoted in Sam Howe Verhovek, "Showdown at the 'Republic of Texas' Ends in Surrender," *International Herald Tribune* (Paris), May 5, 1997.

141. "Texas Constitutional Militia: Rights of the People; Citizens of a Founded Republic Working Towards Our Nation" (n.d.), http://www.rightsofthepeople. com/guns/militia/militia_texas_constitutional_militia.php (accessed May 5, 2016).

142. Quoted in Harrison, "Jackboot Stamp of the New Right."

143. The group's name is believed to be derived from the "Operation American Viper"—a sixty-eight-page "war plan" cum strategy document that is circulated among U.S. militias, inciting them to revolution and guerrilla war against the "global conspiracy" orchestrated by the U.S. federal government and the United Nations in league with international bankers, Jews, and others. See Steven A. Holmes, "U.S. Charges 12 in Arizona Plot to Blow Up Government Office," *New York Times*, July 2, 1996.

144. James Brooke, "Agents Seize Arsenal of Rifles and Bomb-Making Material in Arizona Militia Inquiry," *New York Times*, July 3, 1996; "Volatile Mix in Viper Militia: Hatred Plus a Love for Guns," *New York Times*, July 4, 1996; "As Trial Nears for Militia, Some Charges Are Dropped," *New York Times*, October 9, 1996.

145. McVeigh, however, claims that he used 5,400 pounds (108 fifty-pound bags) of ammonium nitrate that he bought for $540. He paid about $3,000 for the racing fuel. See James Brooke, "Newspaper Says McVeigh Described Role in Bombing," *New York Times*, March 1, 1997.

146. Richard A. Serrano and Edith Stanley, "2 Georgia Militia Group Members Face Bomb Counts," *Los Angeles Times*, April 27, 1996.

147. "Threats from Within," *Washington Post*, April 19, 2005.

148. Lois Romano, "Domestic Extremist Groups Weaker but Still Worrisome," *Washington Post*, April 19, 2005.

149. "Guilty: Father and Son Convicted of Murder of Bank Security Guard," Associated Press, September 27, 2005, http://www.securityinfowatch.com/news /10594789/guilty-father-and-son-convicted-of-murder-of-bank-security-guard.

150. International Security Program, "Deadly Attacks Since 9/11: Homegrown Extremists," New America Foundation (n.d.), http://securitydata.newamerica.net/ extremists/deadly-attacks.html (accessed May 5, 2016).

151. Associated Press, "Man Accused of Possessing Lethal Toxin Hangs Himself," *Los Angeles Times*, December 24, 1995.

152. Karl Vick, "Man Gets Hands on Bubonic Plague Germs, but That's No Crime," *Washington Post*, December 30, 1995.

153. Associated Press, "Man Accused of Possessing Lethal Toxin Hangs Himself"; John Kifner, "Antiterrorism Law Used in Poison Smuggling Case," *New York Times*, December 23, 1995; John Kifner, "Man Arrested in Poison Case Kills Himself in Jail Cell," *New York Times*, December 24, 1995.

154. Eichenwald, "Right-Wing Extremists Are a Bigger Threat"; "Feds: Militia Plot Involved D.C. Ricin Attack," *CBS News*, November 2, 2011, http://www.cbsnews .com/news/feds-militia-plot-involved-dc-ricin-attack/; "Ricin Terror Plot Suspects Appear in Ga. Court," November 2, 2011, http://www.cbsnews.com/news /ricin-terror-plot-suspects-appear-in-ga-court/.

155. Perliger, *Challengers from the Sidelines*, 3.

156. Charles Kurzman and David Schanzer, *Law Enforcement Assessment of the Violent Extremism Threat* (Durham, N.C.: Triangle Center on Terrorism and Homeland Security, June 25, 2015), 3–4, http://sites.duke.edu/tcths/files/2013/06 /Kurzman_Schanzer_Law_Enforcement_Assessment_of_the_Violent_Extremist _Threat_final.pdf.

157. Charles Kurzman and David Schanzer, "The Growing Right-Wing Terror Threat," *New York Times*, June 16, 2015.

158. International Security Program, "Deadly Attacks Since 9/11: Homegrown Extremists."

159. See, respectively, Polly Mosendz, "Dylann Roof Confesses: Says He Wanted to Start 'Race War,'" *Newsweek*, June 19, 2015, http://www.newsweek.com/dylann -roof-confesses-church-shooting-says-he-wanted-start-race-war-344797, and Victor Gerhard, "Payback's a Bitch," Vanguard News Network: No Jews. Just Right (n.d.), http://www.vanguardnewsnetwork.com/v1/index117.htm (accessed May 5, 2016).

160. Quoted in Tim Kelsey, "The Oklahoma Suspect Awaits Day of Reckoning," *Sunday Times* (London), April 21, 1996.

161. See James Corcoran, *Bitter Harvest: The Birth of Paramilitary Terrorism in the Heartland* (New York: Penguin, 1995).

162. Quoted in Flo Conway and Jim Siegelman, "Identity and the Militia," *Arkansas Democrat-Gazette* (Little Rock), December 3, 1995.

163. Quoted in Kelsey, "The Oklahoma Suspect Awaits Day of Reckoning." See also German, "Behind the Lone Terrorists, a Pack Mentality."

164. "Legal Action: Keenan v. Aryan Nations," SPLC website, http://www.splcenter .org/legal/docket/files.jsp?cdrID=30&sortID=3 (accessed May 5, 2016).

165. Bob Moser, "Alabama Getaway," SPLC website, http://www.splcenter.org/legal /intel/intelreport/article.jsp?aid=506 (accessed May 5, 2016).

166. Aryan Nations website, http://www.aryan-nation.org, April 2005.

167. Ibid., http://www.aryan-nation.org/holyorder.Jihad.htm, April 2005.

168. "Rest in Peace, Richard Girnt Butler (February 23, 1918–September 8, 2004)," aryan-nations.org, accessed at: http://www.aryan-nations.org (accessed May 5, 2016).

169. *This Is Aryan Nations* brochure distributed by the Aryan Nations (n.d.). This document can also be accessed from the World Wide Web at http://www .stormfront.org/aryan_nations/platform.html (accessed May 5, 2016).

170. Aryan Nations, *Calling Our Nation*, no. 53 (n.d.), 2. This document can also be accessed from the World Wide Web at http://www.stormfront.org/aryan_nations /platform.html (accessed May 5, 2016).

171. "To Our New People," open letter from Reverend Richard G. Butler, Aryan Nations (n.d.).

172. *This Is Aryan Nations.*

173. *Washington Post*, December 26, 1984, quoted in Bruce Hoffman, *Terrorism in the United States and the Potential Threat to Nuclear Facilities* (Santa Monica, Calif.: RAND Corporation, R-3351-DOE, January 1986), 42.

174. Roy B. Masker, "An All White Nation? Why Not?," *Calling Our Nation*, no. 53 (n.d.): 23.

175. See Rodney Bowers, "White Radicals Charged with Sedition," *Arkansas Gazette* (Little Rock), April 25, 1987.

176. Joseph M. Melnachak, "A Chronicle of Hate: A Brief History of the Radical Right in America," *Terrorism, Violence, and Insurgency Report* 6, no. 4 (n.d.): 41–42. This was also confirmed to the author by an FBI agent present at the raid.

177. Andrew MacDonald, *The Turner Diaries* (Arlington, Va.: National Alliance/ National Vanguard Books, 1985). For a biography of MacDonald/Pierce see Michael Janofsky, "One Man's Journey from Academia to Extremism," *New York Times*, July 5, 1995.

178. *New York Times*, December 27, 1984, quoted in Hoffman, *Terrorism in the United States*, 42.

179. McVeigh, quoted in interviews with Patrick E. Cole, "'I'm Just Like Anyone Else,'" *Time*, April 15, 1996, and Kelsey, "The Oklahoma Suspect Awaits Day of Reckoning."

180. Quoted in Conway and Siegelman, "Identity and the Militia."

181. Quoted in Anti-Defamation League of B'nai B'rith, *Hate Groups in America: A Record of Bigotry and Violence* (New York: Anti-Defamation League of B'nai B'rith, 1982), 52.

182. Quoted in ibid., 51, 53.

183. Carlin, "DIY Apocalypse."

184. Paul de Armond, "Christian Patriots at War with the State," Public Good home page, http://www.nwcitizen.com/publicgood (accessed May 5, 2016).

185. Among the congregants of Peters's church in Laporte, Colorado, were members of the 1980s terrorist group "the Order"; Jeffrey Kaplan, "Right-Wing Violence in North America," *Terrorism and Political Violence* 7, no. 1 (Spring 1995): 54; Conway and Siegelman, "Identity and the Militia."

186. See Morris Dees, with James Corcoran, *Gathering Storm: America's Militia Threat* (New York: HarperCollins, 1996), 1–2 and passim, and Paul de Armond, "Leaderless Resistance: The Two-Pronged Movement Consolidates Under Identity," Public Good home page, http://www.nwcitizen.com/publicgood.

187. Louis Beam, Leaderless Resistance (text from Cyberspace Minuteman BBS 312-275–6326), quoted in Tom Burghardt, "Leaderless Resistance and the Oklahoma City Bombing," Public Good home page, http://www.nwcitizen.com/publicgood.

188. *Field Manual Section 1: Principles Justifying the Arming and Organizing of a Militia* (Wisc.: Free Militia, 1994), 78, quoted in ibid.

189. Quoted in de Armond, "Leaderless Resistance."

190. Abby Ohlheiser and Elahe Izadi, "Police: Austin Shooter Was a 'Homegrown American Extremist,'" *Washington Post*, December 1, 2014.

191. Quoted in James Ridgeway, "Arms and the Men: Are Far Right Militia Cells Using Robbery to Fund Their Cause?," *Village Voice* (New York), May 9, 1995.

192. Ibid.; James Brooke, "Arrests Add to Idaho's Reputation as a Magnet for Supremacists," *New York Times*, October 27, 1996; Loretta J. Ross, "Using the Bible to Justify Killing," *Baltimore Sun*, August 8, 1994; personal communication with Paul de Armond, August 1997.

193. Quoted in "Klanwatch, a Project of the Southern Poverty Law Center," *Intelligence Report* (Montgomery, Ala.), no. 84 (November 1996): 1, 4.

194. See http://www.amazon.com/Vigilantes-Christendom-History-Phineas-Priesthood/dp/1881867056 (accessed May 5, 2016).

195. See Perliger, *Challengers from the Sidelines*, 36–39.

196. Quoted in Ross, "Using the Bible to Justify Killing."

197. "Spokane Robbery Document" on Public Good home page, http://www.nwcitizen.com/publicgood.

198. Leonard Doyle, "US Militias Show Way for British Fascists," *Independent* (London), April 27, 1995.

199. Personal communication with Paul de Armond, April 1996.

200. Anne Lise Fimreite, Peter Lango, Per Laegreid, and Lise H. Rykkja, "After Oslo and Utøya: A Shift in the Balance Between Security and Liberty in Norway?," *Studies in Conflict and Terrorism* 36, no. 10 (October 2013): 839–56.

201. German, "Behind the Lone Terrorists, a Pack Mentality."

202. Henry Schuster, "Lone Wolves: Solitary Threats Harder to Hunt," http://www.cnn.com/2005/US/02/01/schuster.column/index.html (accessed May 5, 2016).

203. See Henry Schuster, "Why Did Rudolph Do It? Question Lingers After Plea Deal Reached," CNN, http://www.cnn.com/2005/US/04/11/schuster.column/index.html (accessed May 5, 2016); and Shalila Dewan, "Bomber Offers Guilty Pleas, and Defiance," *New York Times*, April 14, 2005.

204. Reed, "Life, Liberty, and the Pursuit of Anyone Who Gets in the Way," 758.

205. Federal Bureau of Investigation, "Domestic Terrorism: The Sovereign Citizen Movement," April 13, 2010, https://www.fbi.gov/news/stories/2010/april/sovereign citizens_041310/domestic-terrorism-the-sovereign-citizen-movement.

206. FBI Counterterroism Analysis Section, "Sovereign Citizens: A Growing Threat to Law Enforcement," *FBI Law Enforcement Bulletin* (Washington, D.C.: Federal Bureau of Investigation, September 2011), https://leb.fbi.gov/2011/september /sovereign-citizens-a-growing-domestic-threat-to-law-enforcement; "Sovereign Citizens Movement," SPLC website (n.d.), https://www.splcenter.org/fighting -hate/extremist-files/ideology/sovereign-citizens-movement (accessed May 5, 2016); Caitlin Dickson, "Sovereign Citizens Are America's Top Cop-Killers," *Daily Beast*, November 25, 2014, http://www.thedailybeast.com/articles/2014/11 /25/sovereign-citizens-are-america-s-top-cop-killers.html.

207. FBI, "Domestic Terrorism: The Sovereign Citizen Movement."

208. Dickson, "Sovereign Citizens Are America's Top Cop-Killers"; SPLC, "Sovereign Citizens Movement."

209. FBI Counterterrorism Analysis Section, "Sovereign Citizens: A Growing Threat to Law Enforcement."

210. SPLC, "Sovereign Citizens Movement," and personal correspondence with Professor David Brannan, Center for Homeland Defense and Security, Naval Postgraduate School, Monterey, Calif., April 20, 2016. See also Morris Dees and J. Richards Cohen, "White Supremacists Without Borders," *New York Times*, June 22, 2015.

211. Quoted in Mary Thornton, "Oregon Guru Disavows Rajneeshism, Vows to Survive Investigations," *Washington Post*, October 20, 1985; Peter H. King, "Guru Revels in Revelation of a 'Paradise' Defiled," *Los Angeles Times*, September 22, 1985.

212. W. Seth Carus, "The Rajneeshees" (1984), in *Toxic Terror: Assessing Terrorist Use of Chemical and Biological Weapons*, ed. Jonathan B. Tucker (Cambridge, Mass.: MIT Press, 2000), 131. The two most complete and authoritative accounts of this incident are W. Seth Carus, "The Rajneeshees," 115–37, and Judith Miller, Stephen Engelberg, and William Broad, *Germs: Biological Weapons and America's Secret War* (New York: Simon & Schuster, 2001), 15–33.

213. Miller, Engelberg, and Broad, *Germs*, 32–33.

214. In revising this discussion of Aum Shinrikyo, I benefited from the research and translations from original Japanese sources provided by Ms. Mayuka Yamazaki, a graduate student in the Security Studies Program at Georgetown University, Washington, D.C.

215. Manabu Watanabe, "Religion and Violence in Japan Today: A Chronological and Doctrinal Analysis of Aum Shinrikyo," *Terrorism and Political Violence* 10, no. 4 (Winter 1998): 83.

216. Quoted in David E. Kaplan and Andrew Marshall, *The Cult at the End of the World: The Incredible Story of Aum* (London: Hutchinson, 1996), 7–12.

217. Shoichi Okawa, "Aum Shinrikyo," http://www.guardian.co.uk/cults/a-z-cults/a _cults.html (accessed May 5, 2016).

218. Kaplan and Marshall, *The Cult at the End of the World*, 18.

219. "Aum Shinrikyo Special Edition: Expanded Leveraging 'Supernatural Power,'" *Asahi Shimbun* (Tokyo), May 21, 1998.

220. See National Police Agency, "Aum Shinrikyo," *Shoten* (Tokyo), no. 269, chap. 2, http://www.npa.go.jp/kousi/biki2/seco2/seco2_09.htm (accessed April 28, 2005); Andrew Pollack, "Japanese Sect May Struggle to Get by Without Its Leader," *New York Times*, May 17, 1995; and Alessandra Stanley, "Russians Shut Down Branch of Japanese Sect," *New York Times*, March 30, 1995.

221. William J. Broad, "Seismic Blast: Bomb or Quake?," *New York Times*, January 23, 1997.

222. Quoted in James Walsh, "Shoko Asahara: The Making of a Messiah," *Time*, April 3, 1995.

223. Quoted in National Police Agency, "Aum Shinrikyo: An Alarming Report on the Terrorist Group's Organization and Activities," *Shoten* (Tokyo), no. 252 (1995): 6.

224. "Special Edition: The First Aum Case Will Start on April 24th," *Yomiuri Shimbun* (Tokyo), April 20, 1996.

225. Quoted in Kaplan and Marshall, *The Cult at the End of the World*, 16–17.

226. Quoted in Nicholas D. Kristof with Sheryl WuDunn, "The Seer Among the Blind: Japanese Sect Leader's Rise," *New York Times*, March 26, 1995.

227. "Special Edition: 1998 Aum Case—Matsumoto [Asahara] Was a Ringleader," *Yomiuri Shimbun* (Tokyo), December 31, 1998.

228. Quoted in James K. Campbell, "Excerpts from Research Study 'Weapons of Mass Destruction and Terrorism: Proliferation by Non-State Actors'" (paper presented at the International Conference on Aviation Safety and Security in the 21st Century, White House Commission on Aviation Safety and Security and George Washington University, Washington, D.C., January 13–15, 1997), 14.

229. See David Van Biema, "Prophet of Poison," *Time*, April 3, 1995.

230. Quoted in Juergensmeyer, "The Worldwide Rise of Religious Nationalism," 17.

231. Quoted in Kaplan and Marshall, *The Cult at the End of the World*, 85. See also "Special Edition: Summary of Aum Case," *Yomiuri Shimbun* (Tokyo), June 14, 1996.

232. Watanabe, "Religion and Violence in Japan Today," 82.

233. "Aum Shinrikyo Special Edition: Targeted Elites—They Were Brainwashed and Became Aum's Robot," *Asahi Shimbun* (Tokyo), May 28, 1995. See also Robert Jay Lifton, *Destroying the World to Save It: Aum Shinrikyo, Apocalyptic Violence, and the New Global Terrorism* (New York: Metropolitan Books, 1999), 30.

234. Haruki Murakami, *Underground* (Tokyo: Kodansha bunko, 1999), 35.

235. Lifton, *Destroying the World to Save It*, 28–31.

236. Mayuka Yamazaki, "Aum Shinrikyo" (unpublished manuscript, April 2005), 4.

237. Broad, "Seismic Blast: Bomb or Quake?"

238. Okawa, "Aum Shinrikyo."

239. As a result of the raids on Aum facilities in March 1995, Japanese police found a notebook belonging to a senior Aum executive listing this weaponry and associated purchase and production costs. See "Aum Shinrikyo Special Edition: Transforming Into a 'Terrorist' Cult," *Asahi Shimbun* (Tokyo), June 16, 1996.

240. "Aum Shinrikyo Special Edition: Targeted Elites."

241. Richard Lloyd Parry, "Sect's Poisons 'Could Kill 4.2m,'" *Independent on Sunday* (London), March 26, 1995; Andrew Pollack, "Japanese Police Say They Found Germ-War Material at Cult Site," *New York Times*, March 29, 1995.

242. National Police Agency, "Aum Shinrikyo," 11.

243. "Special Edition: Examination of Aum's Other Crime—Illegal Drug Production," *Yomiuri Shimbun* (Tokyo), February 28, 1996.

244. Reuters, "Tokyo Cult Leader Said to Have Made Gas Confession," *Times* (London), October 5, 1995.

245. Jonathan Annells and James Adams, "Did Terrorists Kill with Deadly Nerve Gas Test?," *Sunday Times* (London), March 19, 1995. It is interesting to note that this news account was published only a day before the nerve gas attack on the Tokyo underground took place.

246. Watanabe, "Religion and Violence in Japan Today," 82.

247. "Special Edition: The Arrest of Guru Shoko Asahara, and the History of Asahara's Analects," *Yomiuri Shimbun* (Tokyo), May 16, 1995.

248. National Police Agency, *Keisatsu Hakusyo 1996* (Police White Paper 1996), http://www.pdc.npa.go.jp/halusyo/h08/h080101.html (accessed April 28, 2005).

249. Testimony by a former member of Aum in "Special Edition: 1998 Aum Case—Matsumoto [Asahara] Was a Ringleader," *Yomiuri Shimbun* (Tokyo), December 31, 1998.

250. "Special Edition: The First Aum Case Will Start on April 24th."

251. Ibid.; National Police Agency, *Keisatsu Hakusyo* (Police White Paper 2000), chap. 5, http://www.pdc.npa.go.jp/hakusyo/h12h120500.html (accessed April 28, 2005).

252. Joyu was not implicated in the cult's violence and was convicted only of charges involving fraudulent real estate transactions. Accordingly, he served only a brief prison term. Lifton, *Destroying the World to Save It*, 31.

253. See Aleph's website, http://www.aleph.to/info/2000c.html#991201 (accessed April 28, 2005).

254. See ibid., http://www.aleph.to/news/200503.html#01 (accessed April 28, 2005).

255. See, for example, "No Flames, No Guns in Montana," *New York Times*, June 15, 1996; David Johnston, "Surrender Is a Victory for a Strategy of Patience," *New York Times*, June 13, 1996; Brad Knickerbocker, "Patience Is a Virtue in Freeman Standoff," *Christian Science Monitor*, June 14, 1996; and Lucinda Franks, "Annual of Law Enforcement: Don't Shoot—In the New FBI, Patience Comes First," *New Yorker*, July 22, 1996, http://www.threatlink.com/pr/articles/Don20Shoot.pdf't%.

256. See Pew Research Center for People and the Press, "Summary of Findings: A Year After the Iraq War—Mistrust of America in Europe Even Higher, Muslim Anger Persists," March 16, 2004, http://people-press.org/reports/display.php3?ReportID=206.

257. See "Biden Says Prison at Guantanamo Bay Should Be Closed," *Washington Post*, June 6, 2005; Seymour M. Hersh, *Chain of Command: The Road from 9/11 to Abu Ghraib* (New York: HarperCollins, 2004), 1–72; and David Rose, *Guantanamo: America's War on Human Rights* (London: Faber and Faber, 2004).

258. "Interview with Usama bin Ladin (December 27, 2001)," in Rubin and Colp Rubin, *Anti-American Terrorism and the Middle East*, 266.

259. Bruce Stokes, "Do Muslims Around the World Really Hate the United States?," *Foreign Policy*, December 15, 2015, http://foreignpolicy.com/2015/12/15/do-muslims-around-the-world-really-hate-the-united-states/.

260. Office of the Press Secretary, The White House, "Fact Sheet: The White House Summit on Countering Violent Extremism," February 18, 2015, https://www

.whitehouse.gov/the-press-office/2015/02/18/fact-sheet-white-house-summit
-countering-violent-extremism. See also Kim Ghattas, "Talking Loud and Saying Nothing," foreignpolicy.com, August 4, 2015, http://foreignpolicy.com/2015
/08/04/four-problems-with-obama-countering-violent-extremism-cve-isis/,
and Muqtedar Khan, "Countering Violent Extremism: The War on Terror, Reset,"
huffingtonpost.com, April 18, 2016, http://www.huffingtonpost.com/muqtedar
-khan/countering-violent-extrem_1_b_9713132.html.

261. Bruce Hoffman, "Old Madness, New Methods: Revival of Religious Terrorism
Begs for Broader U.S. Policy," *RAND Review* 22, no. 2 (Winter 1998): 12–17.

5. Suicide Terrorism

1. That there has been a significant rise in the incidence of suicide terrorism since
9/11 is not disputed by scholars. See, for instance, Robert A. Pape, "The Strategic Logic of Suicide Terrorism," *American Political Science Review* 97, no. 3 (August 2003): 343–61, and Robert A. Pape, *Dying to Win: The Strategic Logic of
Suicide Terrorism* (New York: Random House, 2005), as well as Mia A. Bloom,
Dying to Kill: The Allure of Suicide Terror (New York: Columbia University
Press, 2005). The role of religion behind this increase, however, is debated. Pape
argues in his seminal article that "religious fanaticism does not explain why the
world leader in suicide terrorism is the Tamil Tigers in Sri Lanka," while conceding that "although religious motives may matter, modern suicide terrorism
is not limited to Islamic Fundamentalism" ("The Strategic Logic of Suicide Terrorism," 343). In his book, however, Pape is more explicit, writing that the "presumed connection between suicide terrorism and Islamic fundamentalism is
misleading. . . . There is little connection between suicidal terrorism and Islamic
fundamentalism, or any of the world's religions. In fact, the leading instigators
of suicide attacks are the Tamil Tigers" (*Dying to Win*, 1–2). While I fully agree
with Pape on the point that the Tigers are responsible for the largest number of
suicide terrorist attacks between 1968 and 2001, they are not, however, the driving force behind the increasing use of this tactic *since* 9/11. Moreover, Pape is not
accurate in categorizing the Tamil Tigers as a "Marxist Leninist" group. They are
more appropriately described as an ethnonationalist/separatist movement. Furthermore, as is discussed below, while the Tigers are not a religious terrorist
organization, they nonetheless share some characteristics more commonly seen
in religious cults than in their secular ethnonationalist/separatist counterparts.
For a particularly incisive critique of Pape's fundamental arguments about suicide terrorism, see Bloom, *Dying to Kill*, 83–84.

2. National Consortium for the Study of Terrorism and Responses to Terrorism
(START), University of Maryland, Global Terrorism Database, https://www
.start.umd.edu/gtd/ (accessed March 2, 2017).

3. The RAND Terrorism Incident Database; Bloom, *Dying to Kill*, 2.

4. Yoram Schweitzer, Ariel Levin, and Einav Yogev, *Suicide Attacks in 2014: The
Global Picture* (Tel Aviv: Institute for National Security Studies, INSS Insight
No. 653, January 6, 2015), http://www.inss.org.il/?id=4538&articleid=8514. See
also Amos Harel, "Number of Suicide Bombings Around the World Surged 94%

in 2014 Amid Rise of ISIS," *Haaretz*, January 4, 2015, http://www.haaretz.com /israel-news/.premium-1.635193; and Avi Issachaoff, "2016 Was Deadliest Year Ever for Suicide Bombings Worldwide," *Times of Israel*, January 6, 2017, http:// www.timesofisrael.com/2016-was-deadliest-year-ever-for-suicide-bombings -worldwide/.

5.   START, Global Terrorism Database, https://www.start.umd.edu/gtd/, March 2, 2017; RAND Terrorism Incident Database; and Israeli Security Agency, "Se-curity Seminar on Combating the Threat of Suicide Bombers," Washington, D.C.: Israeli Embassy, September 16, 2003.

6.   START, Global Terrorism Database, https://www.start.umd.edu/gtd/ (accessed March 2, 2017).

7.   Pape, "The Strategic Logic of Suicide Terrorism," 345–47. See also Bruce Hoff-man, "The Logic of Suicide Terrorism: Lessons from Israel that America Must Learn," *Atlantic Monthly* 291, no. 5 (June 2003): 40–47.

8.   Rashmi Singh, *Hamas and Suicide Terrorism: Multi-causal and Multi-level Approaches* (Abingdon: Routledge, 2011), 13.

9.   See Yoram Schweitzer, "Suicide Terrorism: Development and Main Charac-teristics," in *Countering Suicide Terrorism: An International Conference*, International Policy Institute for Counter-Terrorism at the Interdisciplinary Center, Herzilya (Jerusalem: Gefen, 2001), 76.

10. Shaul Mishal and Reuben Aharoni, *Speaking Stones: Communiqués from the In-tifada Underground* (Syracuse, N.Y.: Syracuse University Press, 1994), xiii. The First (and less violent) Palestinian Intifada is most commonly said to have erupted in 1987 and ended in 1993 with the signing of the Oslo Accords. The al-Aqsa Intifada takes its name from the mosque on the al-Haram al-Sharif (Holy Precinct or Noble Sanctuary), the thirty-five-acre plaza built atop the site of the destroyed Jewish Second Temple where both the mosque and the Dome of the Rock are located. The name for the uprising is derived from the riots there that followed Ariel Sharon's well-publicized visit to the Temple Mount (the Jewish name for the Holy Precinct) in September 2000. See James Bennet, "Jerusalem Holy Site a Tense Crossroads Again," *New York Times*, August 29, 2003, and David Eshel, "The Al-Aqsa Intifada: Tactics and Strategies," *Jane's Intelligence Review*, May 2001, 36.

11. Nasra Hassan, "Letter from Gaza: An Arsenal of Believers," *New Yorker*, Novem-ber 19, 2001, 39.

12. RAND Terrorism Incident Database.

13. Singh, *Hamas and Suicide Terrorism*, 14.

14. See Yosri Fouda and Nick Fielding, *Masterminds of Terror: The Truth Behind the Most Devastating Terrorist Attack the World Has Ever Seen* (New York: Arcade, 2003), 136; Rohan Gunaratna, "Khalid Sheikh Mohammed: The Brain," *Playboy* 52, no. 6 (June 2005): 168; and National Commission on Terrorist At-tacks Upon the United States, *The 9/11 Commission Report: Authorized Edition* (New York: Norton, 2004), 156.

15. *The 9/11 Commission Report*, 235.

16. Quoted in Fouda and Fielding, *Masterminds of Terror*, 141.

17. Ibid., 99.

18. *The 9/11 Commission Report*, 154.

19. Ibid., 172.

20. al-Jazeera.net, "Arab World—Full Transcript of bin Laden's Speech," November 1, 2004, http://englishaljazeera.net/NR/exeres/79C6AF22–98FB-4A1C -B21F-2BC36E87F61F.htm.
21. *The 9/11 Commission Report*, 498n127.
22. "Militant Islamist: Attack on Cole Cost 10,000 Dollars," *Deutsche Presse-Agentur* (Nicosia), November 12, 2000.
23. *The 9/11 Commission Report*, 212–13.
24. "Videotape of a Private Meeting (December 13, 2001: Usama Bin Ladin)," in *Anti-American Terrorism and the Middle East: A Documentary Reader*, ed. Barry Rubin and Judith Colp Rubin (Oxford: Oxford University Press, 2002), 245.
25. "Ayman al-Zawahiri Interview September 2002 Audio Interview by Unknown Interviewer," quoted in Ben Venzke and Aimee Ibrahim, *The al-Qaeda Threat: An Analytical Guide to al-Qaeda's Tactics and Targets* (Alexandria, Va.: Tempest, 2003), 173.
26. See "Americans and 9/11: The Personal Toll," Pew Research Center for the People and the Press Survey Reports, September 5, 2002, http://people-press.org /reports/dislay.php3?PageID=633, and "Introduction. One Year Later: New Yorkers More Troubled, Washingtonians More on Edge," Pew Research Center for the People and the Press Survey Reports, September 5, 2002, http:// peoplepress.org/reports/display.php3?PageID=160.
27. Quoted in John Miller, "Interview: Osama Bin Laden (May 1998)," http://www .pbs.org/wgbh/pages/frontline/shows/binladen/who/interview.html.
28. See, for example, the excerpts from bin Laden statements collected in the chapter titled "Martyrdom" in Venzke and Ibrahim, *The al-Qaeda Threat*, 169–72.
29. "Osama bin Laden Interview March 1997 Peter Arnett Interview for CNN," quoted in Venzke and Ibrahim, *The al-Qaeda Threat*, 170.
30. "Sulaiman Abu Ghaith Video 9 October 2001 Video Aired on al-Jazeera," quoted in Venzke and Ibrahim, *The al-Qaeda Threat*, 171.
31. "Ayman al-Zawahiri Interview September 2002 Audio Interview by Unknown Interviewer," quoted in Venzke and Ibrahim, *The al-Qaeda Threat*, 173.
32. The Reporters, Writers, and Editors of *Der Spiegel* Magazine, *Inside 9–11: What Really Happened* (New York: St. Martin's, 2001), 304.
33. "Suicide Note (September 18, 2001): Muhammad Atta," in Rubin and Colp Rubin, *Anti-American Terrorism and the Middle East*, 236.
34. "Pre-Attack Videotape (Summer 2001): Ahmad Al-Haznawi Al-Ghamidi," in Rubin and Colp Rubin, *Anti-American Terrorism and the Middle East*, 276.
35. See Shaul Mishal and Avraham Sela, *The Palestinian Hamas: Vision, Violence, and Coexistence* (New York: Columbia University Press, 2000), 66.
36. Although the idea to use suicide terrorist tactics originated with the PIJ in 1988, Hamas was the first Palestinian group to actually carry out such an attack.
37. The suicide attack unit controlled by both al-Fatah, the Palestinian terrorist group founded by PLO leader and Palestine Authority (PA) head Yasir Arafat in 1957 and still closely linked to him and its popular militia, the Tanzim. See Dani Naveh et al., Minister of Parliamentary Affairs, *The Involvement of Arafat, PA Senior Officials, and Apparatuses in Terrorism Against Israel, Corruption, and Crime* (Jerusalem: Ministry of Foreign Affairs, 2002).

38.   Principally, the Popular Front for the Liberation of Palestine (PFLP) and the Popular Front for the Liberation of Palestine-General Command (PFLP-GC), both of whose headquarters are located in Damascus.

39.   No precise, widely accepted total is easily accessible. Dr. Rohan Gunaratna claims that the total was 168 as of the year 2000 (see Rohan Gunaratna, "Suicide Terrorism: A Global Threat," *Jane's Intelligence Review*, October 20, 2000, http://www.janes.com/security/international_security/news/usscole/jir001020_1_n.shtml). A *New York Times* article, however, puts the total at 220 attacks (see Amy Waldman, "Suicide Bombing Masters: Sri Lankan Rebels," *New York Times*, January 14, 2003). The Tigers themselves claim that as of 1999, the LTTE had conducted 147 suicide attacks. However, this figure does not include operations involving nonmilitary targets—including politicians and other prominent people, ordinary civilians, and infrastructure and economic targets (see Rohan Gunaratna, "The LTTE and Suicide Terrorism," *Frontline*, February 2000, 5–8). It is interesting to note that while a private study undertaken by a serving Sri Lankan Armed Forces officer does not cite total incident numbers, this officer has tallied the number of Tamil suicide cadre killed. As LTTE suicide attacks are mainly (but not exclusively) executed by one perpetrator only, the total of 239 LTTE Black Tigers (special suicide cadre) killed in action that this officer claims (including 60 male Black Tigers and 18 female Tigers who died in land attacks and 115 and 46, respectively, in maritime operations) dovetails with the Gunaratna and Waldman figures. See "LTTE Declared Total Numbers of Killed During the Last 20 Years" (unpublished manuscript, n.d.).

40.   See, for example, Radika Coomaraswamy, "Women of the LTTE: The Tiger's and Women's Emancipation," *Frontline* (Chennai, India), January 10, 1997, 61–64; Dexter Filkins, "Sri Lanka Women at War: Tamil Rebel Group Is Now One-Third Female," *International Herald Tribune* (Paris), March 13, 2000; Rohan Gunaratna, "Suicide Terrorism," 53; and Jenny Kay, "Dying for Their Cause," *Eva* (London), June 1998, 18–19.

41.   The LTTE maintains so-called Baby Brigade and Tiger Cub units composed of children reputedly as young as thirteen to fifteen years old who are groomed for later service in the movement's elite military units. See Barbara Crossette, "Sri Lanka's Army Is Hitting Last Guerrilla Group," *New York Times*, May 2, 1991; Barbara Crossette, "Tamil Rebels Said to Recruit Child Soldiers," *New York Times*, July 17, 2000; Celia W. Dugger, "Rebels Without a Childhood in Sri Lanka War," *New York Times*, September 10, 2000; Guy Goodwin-Gill and Ilene Cohn, *Child Soldiers: The Role of Children in Armed Conflict* (Oxford: Clarendon, 1994), 29, 31, 40; Rohan Gunaratna, "Tiger Cubs and Childhood Fall as Casualties in Sri Lanka," *Jane's Intelligence Review* (July 1998), 32–37; and Lindsay Murdoch, "Reign of Terror by Sir Lanka's Pol Pot," *Sydney Morning Herald* (Australia), June 15, 1995.

42.   See, for example, Anthony Foster, "An Emerging Threat Shapes Up as Terrorists Take to the High Seas," *Jane's Intelligence Review*, July 1998, 44, and Rohan Gunaratna, "Sea Tiger Success Threatens the Spread of Copycat Tactics," *Jane's Intelligence Review*, March 2001, 12–16.

43.   Using so-called ultralights (small, single-pilot aircraft also known as microlights), a special LTTE unit reportedly planned to attack the Sri Lankan prime

minister's official residence at Temple Trees on the Galle Road in Colombo. This airborne option was pursued after attempts to target the residence by ground attack were deterred by heavy security surrounding the compound. Interview with retired Sri Lankan Air Force officer, subsequently confirmed by Sri Lankan authorities, December 1997. See also Chris Kamalendran, "LTTE's Aircraft: Yes, No," *Sunday Times* (Colombo), December 6, 1998, and Rohan Gunaratna, "Case Study: The Liberation Tigers of Tamil Eelam," *Jane's Intelligence Review*, October 2001, 8.

44. The Sherut Ha-Bitachon Ha-Klali, also known as the Shabak or Shin Bet. According to their figures, 61 suicide bombings occurred between 1993 and September 2000, and 145 between October 2000 and September 2002. See Amos Harel, "Shin Bet: 145 Suicide Bombers since the Start of the Intifada," *Ha'aretz*, September 29, 2002.

45. For a detailed discussion of suicide terrorism's instrumental purpose in this respect, see Bruce Hoffman and Gordon H. McCormick, "Terrorism, Signaling, and Suicide Attack," *Studies in Conflict and Terrorism* 27, no. 4 (July/August 2004): 243–81.

46. Tamara Herath, *Women in Terrorism: The Case of the LTTE* (New Delhi: Sage, 2012), 127.

47. Rosemarie Skaine, *Female Suicide Bombers* (Jefferson, N.C.: McFarland, 2006), 51.

48. See Rohan Gunaratna, *War and Peace in Sri Lanka* (Sri Lanka: Institute of Fundamental Studies, 1987), 16–18, and Rohan Gunaratna, "The Conflict in Sri Lanka, 1982–Present" (unpublished paper prepared as part of a project on how terrorism escalates conducted at the Centre for the Study of Terrorism and Political Violence, University of St. Andrews [Scotland]), March 1997, 1–2. See also Patrick Brogan, *The Fighting Never Stopped* (New York: Vintage, 1990), 228–29, and Mackenzie Briefing Notes, "Funding Terror: The Liberation Tigers of Tamil Eelam and Their Criminal Activities in Canada and the Western World" (Toronto: Mackenzie Centre, December 1995), 2.

49. The renaming added insult to injury for the country's Tamil population, as "Lanka" refers to the island's ancient Sinhalese name, ignoring the Tamil minority, and the word *sri* meaning "auspicious" or "resplendent" in the Sinhalese language. See Christine Niven et al., *Sri Lanka: A Lonely Planet Travel Survival Kit* (Victoria, Australia: Lonely Planet, 1996), 9–10.

50. Gunaratna, *War and Peace in Sri Lanka*, 27.

51. Interviews with LTTE suicide cadre, Colombo, Sri Lanka, December 1997 and February 2003.

52. Brogan, *The Fighting Never Stopped*, 228.

53. Interview with LTTE suicide cadre, Colombo, Sri Lanka, December 1997.

54. The adoption of the tiger as the TNT's—and subsequently the LTTE's—identifying symbol was meant to evoke the powerful Cholas dynasty of ancient times, which had once conquered Sri Lanka and other parts of Asia and had used the tiger as its symbol as well. See Rohan Gunaratna, "The Rebellion in Sri Lanka: Sparrow Tactics to Guerrilla Warfare (1971–1996)" (unpublished manuscript, n.d.), 10.

55. Significantly, attention was drawn precisely to this LTTE policy in a 1988 analysis by the U.S. Department of Defense. Included in a synopsis of the LTTE's

"political objectives" was "Eliminate moderate Tamils and other Tamil militant groups that compete with the LTTE for influence and power within the Sri Lankan Tamil community." See U.S. Department of Defense, *Terrorist Group Profiles* (Washington, D.C.: U.S. Government Printing Office, 1988), 120.

56. Gunaratna, "The Rebellion in Sri Lanka," 11, and Rohan Gunaratna, *Implications of the Sri Lankan Tamil Insurgency* (Colombo: Alumni Association of the Bandaranaike Centre for International Studies/London: International Foundation of Sri Lankans United Kingdom, 1997), 8–9.

57. "Masked Gunmen Kill Jaffna Mayor," *Daily News* (Colombo), July 28, 1975.

58. For a list of these groups, see Gunaratna, *War and Peace in Sri Lanka*, 27.

59. Gunaratna, "The Rebellion in Sri Lanka," 13.

60. Interview with LTTE suicide cadre, Colombo, Sri Lanka, December 1997. See also, for example, "Three Former TULF MPs Shot Dead in Jaffna," *The Hindu* (Chennai), April 9, 1985; K. P. Sunil, "The Midnight Massacre," *Illustrated Weekly of India*, June 8, 1986; "Amir, Yoheswaran Shot Dead, Siva Serious," *Daily News* (Colombo), July 14, 1989; and "Yogasangari—MP Killed in Madras," *Daily News* (Colombo), June 21, 1990.

61. Interview with former senior LTTE cadre, Colombo, Sri Lanka, December 1997.

62. Manoj Joshi, "On the Razor's Edge: The Liberation Tigers of Tamil Eelam," *Studies in Conflict and Terrorism* 19, no. 1 (January–March 1996): 21.

63. See Gunaratna, *Implications of the Sri Lankan Tamil Insurgency*, 10–12, and Gunaratna, *War and Peace in Sri Lanka*, 32–33.

64. Interview with LTTE suicide cadre, Colombo and Batticaloa, Sri Lanka, December 1997. See also Sri Lankan Armed Forces briefing, "Suicide Terrorism in Sri Lanka," n.d., slide 5.

65. Quoted in Charu Lata Joshi, "Ultimate Sacrifice—Sri Lanka: Suicide Bombers," *Far Eastern Economic Review*, June 1, 2000, www.feer.com/00601/p64current .html.

66. Interviews conducted with former LTTE cadre in Colombo, Jaffna, and Batticoloa, Sri Lanka, December 1997. See also Rohan Gunaratna, "Suicide Terrorism in Sri Lanka and India: LTTE Suicide Capability, Likely Trends, and Response" (unpublished manuscript, expanded version of a paper presented at the First International Conference on Countering Suicide Terrorism, Herzilya, Israel, February 20–23, 2000), 1.

67. Gunaratna, *War and Peace in Sri Lanka*, 20.

68. In discussions with his followers, Prabhakaran had reportedly often cited Hezbollah's 1983 attack on the Marine barracks as the main inspiration for the group's use of suicide attack. Interview with former senior LTTE cadre, Colombo, Sri Lanka, December 1997 and February 2003.

69. Quoted in Gunaratna, "The LTTE and Suicide Terrorism."

70. Quoted in Waldman, "Suicide Bombing Masters."

71. The LTTE's reputation and prowess were greatly enhanced by its success in compelling the 1990 withdrawal of the Indian Peace Keeping Force (IPKF) sent to restore order in the predominantly Tamil northern and northeastern parts of the island. After three years of persistent LTTE attack and harassment, the

Indians left Sri Lanka—a singularly dramatic achievement for any terrorist group or insurgent movement, given India's military power and prowess.

72. See "The Black Tiger Unit of the LTTE" (unpublished report written by a Sri Lankan Army intelligence officer known to the author), 1, and Waldman, "Suicide Bombing Masters."

73. Gunaratna, "Suicide Terrorism in Sri Lanka and India," 9.

74. Quoted in Kay, "Dying for Their Cause," 19. See also, Peng Wang, "Women in the LTTE: Birds of Freedom or Cogs in the Wheel?," *Journal of Politics and Law* 4, no. 1 (March 2011): 100–101.

75. Quoted in Charu Lata Joshi, "Ultimate Sacrifice—Sri Lanka."

76. A photocopy of such a card is in the author's possession. It dates from the 1998–1999 time period. See also interviews with senior Sri Lankan intelligence officials, Colombo, Sri Lanka, February 2003.

77. Interviews conducted with former LTTE cadre in Colombo, Jaffna, and Batticoloa, Sri Lanka, December 1997. See also Gunaratna, "Suicide Terrorism in Sri Lanka and India," 9.

78. Waldman, "Suicide Bombing Masters."

79. Interviews conducted with former LTTE cadre in Colombo, Jaffna, and Batticoloa, Sri Lanka, December 1997. See also Filkins, "Sri Lanka Women at War."

80. Interviews conducted with former LTTE cadre in Colombo, Jaffna, and Batticoloa, Sri Lanka, December 1997. See also Gunaratna, "Suicide Terrorism in Sri Lanka and India," 9.

81. Ibid.

82. Sea-borne operations have included surface attacks involving Jet Skis, high-speed rubber rafts, and specially designed radar-evading vessels constructed of fiberglass, as well as minisubmarines and other underwater propulsion devices along with underwater demolition missions carried out by well-trained frogmen. See Rohan Gunaratna, "Maritime Terrorism: Future Threats and Responses" (briefing presented to the International Research Group on Political Violence and Terrorism, Washington, D.C., May 2001), and Gunaratna, "Suicide Terrorism in Sri Lanka and India," 1. According to one account, Sea Tiger attacks had destroyed a third of the Sri Lankan Navy. Al-Qaeda's sea-borne attack on the USS *Cole* in Aden harbor in October 2000 is believed to have been copied from Sea Tiger assaults. See Waldman, "Suicide Bombing Masters."

83. Interview conducted with former LTTE cadre in Colombo, December 1997.

84. Skaine, *Female Suicide Bombers*, 50, 93, and V. G. Rajan, *Women Suicide Bombers: Narratives of Violence* (New York: Routledge, 2011), 84. See also Riaz Hassan, *Life as a Weapon: The Global Rise of Suicide Bombings* (New York: Routledge, 2011), 165–67.

85. "Sri Lanka Terrorist Groups," *South Asia Terrorism Portal—Institute for Conflict Management*, February 14, 2016, at:http://www.satp.org/satporgtp/countries/srilanka/terroristoutfits/index.html.

86. Herath, *Women in Terrorism*, 127.

87. Interview, Colombo, Sri Lanka, February 2003.

88. The U.S. Department of State classifies the LTTE as a terrorist organization, explaining that the group "has an integrated battlefield insurgent strategy with a terrorist program that targets not only key personnel in the countryside but

also senior Sri Lankan political and military leaders in Colombo." See U.S. Department of State, Office of the Coordinator for Counterterrorism, *Patterns of Global Terrorism 1996* (Washington, D.C.: U.S. Department of State, Publication 10433, April 1997), 54. The LTTE was also classified as a terrorist group by the U.S. Department of Defense in its *Terrorist Group Profiles*, 120–21.

89.   Christopher Thomas, "Appeal for Calm as Tamils Deny Train Bombing," *Times* (London), July 26, 1996.

90.   Gunaratna, "The LTTE and Suicide Terrorism."

91.   "Sri Lanka Say Leader of Rebels Has Died," *New York Times*, May 18, 2009, http://www.nytimes.com/2009/05/19/world/asia/19lanka.html?_r=2&ref=liberation_tigers_of_tamil_eelam.

92.   Among the best-known, if not most significant, of these groups are al-Fatah, the Palestinian guerrilla group founded by Yasir Arafat in 1957; the PFLP, established in 1967; the PFLP-GC, established in 1967; and at least ten other secular organizations. See Directorate of Intelligence, Central Intelligence Agency, *Palestinian Organizations: A Reference Aid* (Washington, D.C.: Central Intelligence Agency, LDA 90–11155, March 1990).

93.   The Gaza percentage is likely to be even higher given the militancy and more entrenched religious orientation of its Palestinian population.

94.   The Muslim Brotherhood was founded in Egypt by Hassan al-Banna in 1929. Its goal is to "impose the laws of Islam upon the social, political and constitutional life of the Muslim nations." See Evyatar Levine and Yaacov Shimoni, eds., *Political Dictionary of the Middle East in the Twentieth Century* (London: Weidenfeld and Nicolson, 1972), 262–63.

95.   See Ziad Abu-Amr, "Hamas: A Historical and Political Background," *Journal of Palestinian Studies* 23, no. 4 (Summer 1993): 10; Phyllis Bennis, *From Stones to Statehood: The Palestinian Uprising* (New York: Olive Branch Press, 1990), 27; Singh, *Hamas and Suicide Terrorism*, 47; and Michael Theodoulu, "New Attacks Feared After Defiant Vow by Hamas," *Times* (London), August 22, 1995.

96.   Interview with Roni Shaked, *Yedioth Ahronoth* (Tel Aviv) reporter and an expert on Hamas. See also Joe Stork, *Erased in a Moment: Suicide Bombing Attacks Against Israeli Civilians* (New York: Human Rights Watch, October 2002), 64.

97.   Rex Brynen and Neil Caplan, "Israel and Palestine: Implications of the Intifada," in *Echoes of the Intifada: Regional Repercussions of the Palestinian-Israeli Conflict*, ed. Rex Brynen (Boulder, Colo.: Westview, 1991), 7.

98.   Mishal and Sela, *The Palestinian Hamas*, 50.

99.   In recent years, however, Hamas has conceded that a *hudna*—a cease-fire or truce—with Israel is permissible.

100.   Quoted in Mishal and Aharoni, *Speaking Stones*, 31.

101.   Brynen and Caplan, "Israel and Palestine," 7.

102.   Mishal and Sela, *The Palestinian Hamas*, 56–57.

103.   Mishal and Aharoni, *Speaking Stones*, 26.

104.   Hisham H. Ahmad, *Hamas; from Religious Salvation to Political Transformation: The Rise of Hamas in Palestinian Society* (Jerusalem: Passia, 1994), 51.

105.   Ali Jarbawi and Roger Heacock, "The Deportations and the Palestinian-Israeli Negotiations," *Journal of Palestinian Studies* 22, no. 3 (Spring 1993): 32.

106.   Mishal and Sela, *The Palestinian Hamas*, 57.

107. Ibid., 64.

108. The unit is named after a Syrian-born sheikh who became an iconic figure in the history of the Palestinian nationalist resistance movement. Sheikh al-Qassam was the spiritual head of a collection of villages in the area around Haifa during the 1920s and 1930s, populated mostly by landless peasants who had been displaced by the Zionists. A militant nationalist and devout Muslim, al-Qassam organized a Palestinian guerrilla unit that in 1931 began to raid Jewish settlements in the Jezreel Valley. In a clash with British police in November 1935, al-Qassam was killed. The loss of their leader did not deter al-Qassam's followers, who continued fighting, setting the stage for the countrywide revolt against British rule, known as the Arab Rebellion, which erupted the following year and continued until 1939. See Y. Porath, *The Palestinian Arab National Movement, 1929–1939: From Riots to Rebellion* (London: Frank Cass, 1977), 132–39. See also Abu-Amr, "Hamas," 6, and Stork, *Erased in a Moment*, 65n158.

109. Mishal and Sela, *The Palestinian Hamas*, 65.

110. Stork, *Erased in a Moment*, 73.

111. Jarbawi and Heacock, "The Deportations and the Palestinian-Israeli Negotiations," 32. See also Mishal and Sela, *The Palestinian Hamas*, 96–97.

112. The deportees included, for example, Dr. Ab al-Azziz al-Rantisi, Husayn Abu Kuwik (a West Bank union official), Fadil Salih (an imam), and Hasan Yusuf (a schoolteacher). See Abu-Amr, "Hamas," 26, and Ahmad, *Hamas from Religious Salvation to Political Transformation*, 77.

113. Scott Atran, "Genesis of Suicide Terrorism," *Science* 299 (March 7, 2003): 1535. See also Stork, *Erased in a Moment*, 73.

114. Mishal and Sela, *The Palestinian Hamas*, 65–66.

115. Jarbawi and Heacock, "The Deportations and the Palestinian-Israeli Negotiations," 40.

116. Ehud Ya'ari, "The Metamorphosis of Hamas," *Jerusalem Report*, January 14, 1993, 25.

117. The two Security Council resolutions in essence call for Israel to return to the boundaries that existed before the 1967 Six Days' War and therefore for Israeli withdrawal from the West Bank and the Gaza Strip in return for the unqualified recognition by both Israel and Palestinians of one another's legitimate right to statehood. Jeffrey Michels, "National Vision and the Negotiation of Narratives: The Oslo Agreement," *Journal of Palestinian Studies* 24 (Autumn 1994): 37.

118. Abu-Amr, "Hamas," 13, and Mishal and Sela, *The Palestinian Hamas*, 66–67.

119. Mishal and Sela, *The Palestinian Hamas*, 67.

120. Boaz Ganor, "Suicide Attacks in Israel," in *Countering Suicide Terrorism: An International Conference*, International Policy Institute for Counter-Terrorism, ed. Boaz Ganor (Jerusalem: Gefen, 2001), 136.

121. Mark Juergensmeyer, "The Worldwide Rise of Religious Nationalism," *Journal of International Affairs* 50, no. 1 (Summer 1996): 7.

122. Abu-Amr, "Hamas," 13.

123. See Walter Laqueur, *The New Terrorism: Fanaticism and the Arms of Mass Destruction* (Oxford: Oxford University Press, 1999), 139, and Walter Laqueur, *No End to War: Terrorism in the Twenty-first Century* (New York: Continuum, 2003), 107.

124. Singh, *Hamas and Suicide Terrorism*, 55.
125. Stork, *Erased in a Moment*, 66n158.
126. "Record of Suicide Attacks," *Times* (London), March 5, 1996.
127. Ehud Sprinzak, "Rational Fanatics," *Foreign Policy*, no. 120 (September/October 2000): 71. See also, Singh, *Hamas and Suicide Terrorism*, 52.
128. Ganor, "Suicide Attacks in Israel," 136, and Theodoulu, "New Attacks Feared After Defiant Vow by Hamas."
129. BBC Summary of World Broadcasts, July 23, 2000, quoted in Pape, "The Strategic Logic of Suicide Terrorism," 355.
130. Mishal and Sela, *The Palestinian Hamas*, 66.
131. Shiqaqi reportedly borrowed the distinction used by Hezbollah between suicide and martyrdom. While Islam disdains suicide, it extols martyrdom: hence, Shiqaqi's formulation that "Allah may cause to be known those who believe and may make some of you martyrs, and Allah may purify those who believe and may utterly destroy the disbelievers . . . [however] no one can die except by Allah's leave." Quoted in Atran, "Genesis of Suicide Terrorism,"1535.
132. Singh, *Hamas and Suicide Terrorism*, 52.
133. According to a Hamas activist, in the early 1990s Ayyash sent a letter to the Hamas leadership that reportedly argued, "We paid a high price when we used only slingshots and stones. We need to exert more pressure, make the cost of the occupation that much more expensive in human lives, that much more unbearable." Quoted in Hassan, "Letter from Gaza," 38.
134. Ayyash was assassinated with a small bomb concealed in a mobile telephone. For the most complete account of Ayyash and Israel's hunt for him, see Samuel M. Katz, *The Hunt for the Engineer: How Israeli Agents Tracked the Hamas Master Bomber* (New York: Fromm, 1999). See also Marie Colvin and Andy Goldberg, "Israel on Alert for Wave of 'Sleeper' Bombers," *Sunday Times* (London), March 10, 1996.
135. "Record of Suicide Attacks," *Times* (London), March 5, 1996.
136. See Serge Schmemann, "Bus Bombing Kills Five in Jerusalem, 100 Are Wounded," *New York Times*, August 22, 1995.
137. Quoted in Israel Shahak, "Hamas and Arafat: The Balance of Power," *Middle East International*, no. 468 (February 4, 1996): 17.
138. Quoted in Serge Schmemann, "Terror Isn't Alone as a Threat to Middle East Peace," *Jerusalem Post*, March 4, 1996.
139. Sprinzak, "Rational Fanatics," 71, and Singh, *Hamas and Suicide Terrorism*, 58.
140. Mishal and Sela, *The Palestinian Hamas*, 50, and Singh, *Hamas and Suicide Terrorism*, 53.
141. From *al-Quds* (East Jerusalem), October 12, 1995, quoted in Mishal and Sela, *The Palestinian Hamas*, 71.
142. "Database of Terrorism Attacks Against Israel, 1948–Present," maintained by the National Security Studies Center (NSSC), Haifa University, Mt. Carmel, Haifa, Israel. Information courtesy of Dr. Ami Pedahzur and Mr. Arie Perliger of the NSSC staff.
143. See, for example, Singh, *Hamas and Suicide Terrorism*, 53.
144. See Yariv Tsfati and Gabriel Weimann, "www.terrorism.com: Terror on the Internet," *Studies in Conflict and Terrorism* 25, no. 5 (September/October 2011): 315–16. See also Edward Lucas, "Deadly Image Which Could Give Hezbollah

the Edge," *Scotsman* (Edinburgh), April 14, 2000; Bill Maxwell, "Good Women Help Bring War's End," *Albany Times Union*, June 5, 2000; and Tanya Willmer, "Soldiers' Mothers Pray Their Own Battle Over After Israel Ends Its Vietnam," *Agence France Presse*, May 24, 2000.

145. Pape, "The Strategic Logic of Suicide Terrorism," 355.
146. BBC Summary of World Broadcasts, November 3, 2001, quoted in ibid.
147. BBC Summary of World Broadcasts, July 23, 2000, quoted in Pape, "The Strategic Logic of Suicide Terrorism," 355.
148. See General (Ret.) Amnon Lipkin-Shahak, introduction to *Countering Suicide Terrorism*, 5, where he writes: "I believe that these [suicide] attacks were motivated by desperation."
149. Quoted in Sprinzak, "Rational Fanatics," 68.
150. Abdallah Shami, interviewed on Israeli television Channel 1 on December 9, 1994, quoted in Rafi Yisra'eli, "Islamikaze: Suicide Terrorism Examined," *Nativ* (Tel Aviv), January–April 1997, 3.
151. Quoted in Hassan, "Letter from Gaza," 38.
152. "Hamas' Mishal: Jihad Palestinians' Sole Option," *Al-Zaman*, November 23, 2000, FBIS-NES, Document ID: GMP 20001123000110, 4.
153. Quoted in Sprinzak, "Rational Fanatics," 68.
154. Quoted in Anders Strindberg, "'The Ultimate Sacrifice': The Social and Political Dynamics of Suicide Operations in Palestine," *MIPT Quarterly Bulletin* (Second Quarter, 2002): 4.
155. Quoted in Hassan, "Letter from Gaza," 39.
156. Quoted in ibid.
157. Quoted in ibid., 38.
158. Yassin was assassinated in 2004 by the Israeli Air Force in what the Israeli authorities described as a "targeted killing."
159. Quoted in Burhan Wazis, "Suicide Bombing Is Democratic Right, Says the 'Soul' of Hamas," *Observer* (London), August 19, 2001.
160. Quoted in Thomas L. Friedman, "Strategy of Suicide Bombings," *New York Times*, March 31, 2002.
161. Quoted in Jeffrey Goldberg, "The Martyr Strategy: What Does the New Phase of Terrorism Signify?," *New Yorker*, July 9, 2001.
162. Quoted in Ari Shavit, "The Enemy Within," *Ha'aretz Friday Magazine*, August 20, 2002, 3, http://www.freeman.org/m_online/sept02/shavit.htm.
163. Interview with senior IDF officers, the Kirya, Tel Aviv, Israel, December 2002.
164. Singh, *Hamas and Suicide Terrorism*, 18.
165. See, for example, the poster jointly produced by Hamas and the al-Aqsa Martyrs Brigade (circa 2002–2003) of three martyrs, two of whom are brothers (also in the author's collection).
166. For another discussion of this phenomenon, see Mark Juergensmeyer, *Terror in the Mind of God* (Berkeley: University of California Press, 2000), 166.
167. One such announcement, for a young Palestinian suicide terrorist, proclaimed, "The Wedding of the Martyr Ali Khadr Al-Yassini to the Black-Eyed in Eternal Paradise"—one of the reputed seventy-two virgins whom Muslim martyrs are promised in Heaven—in *Al-Hayat Al-Jadida*, which was described as an "Arafat controlled paper." See Joseph Lelyveld, "All Suicide Bombers Are Not Alike: A Journey to Gaza, Cairo, and Hamburg in Search of What Really Made

Sept. 11 Possible," *New York Times Magazine*, October 28, 2001, 51. It should be noted that an important recruiting incentive is indeed the promise—allegedly according to Islamic mythology—that the would-be martyr would feel no pain in the commission of his sacred act and would then ascend immediately to a glorious heaven, described as a place replete with "rivers of milk and wine . . . lakes of honey, and the services of 72 virgins," where the martyr will see the face of Allah and later be joined by seventy chosen relatives. See "Wedded to Death in a Blaze of Glory—Profile: The Suicide Bomber," *Sunday Times* (London), March 10, 1996, and Christopher Walker, "Palestinian 'Was Duped Into Being Suicide Bomber,'" *Times* (London), March 27, 1997.

168.   Hassan, "Letter from Gaza," 39.

169.   Gal Luft, "The Palestinian H-Bomb: Terror's Winning Strategy," *Foreign Affairs* 81, no. 4 (July/August 2002): 6.

170.   Hamza Hendawi, "Cult Evolves Around Suicide Bombers," Associated Press, April 28, 2002, http://www.news.findlaw.com/ap_stories/i/1107/4–28–2002 /20020428102000255505.html.

171.   Lelyveld, "All Suicide Bombers Are Not Alike," 50.

172.   See the series of martyrdom videos collected and distributed by the Intel-Center, *Hamas Audio/Video Files*, vol. 1 (Alexandria, Va.: www.intelcenter.com, n.d.), and Singh, *Hamas and Suicide Terrorism*, 66.

173.   Lelyveld, "All Suicide Bombers Are Not Alike," 51.

174.   Quoted in Hendawi, "Cult Evolves Around Suicide Bombers."

175.   Ibid. Lelyveld cites a 78 percent approval. See Lelyveld, "All Suicide Bombers Are Not Alike," 50.

176.   Anti-Defamation League of B'nai B'rith, "Arab Leaders Glorify Suicide Terror-ism," April 17, 2002, http://www.adl.org/israel/Israel-suicide-terror.asp.

177.   This clip was shown to participants at the International Policy Institute for Counter-Terrorism's (ICT) Third International Conference, Herzilya, Israel, September 7–10, 2003.

178.   FBIS, Near East/South Asia, "Israel: Palestinian Television Broadcasts Clip En-couraging Martyrdom," *Ma'ariv* (Tel Aviv) (Hebrew), August 11, 2003, 8.

179.   Itmar Marcus, "PA Music Video Promising 'Maidens of Paradise' to Shahids—2 Days Before Suicide Bombings," *Palestinian Media Watch Multi-media Bulle-tin*, August 12, 2003, http://www.pmw.org.il.

180.   Anti-Defamation League of B'nai B'rith, "Arab Leaders Glorify Suicide Terrorism."

181.   See the Qur'an, for example, Sura 4, verse 29: "And do not kill yourselves; verily God is compassionate unto you," http://lexicorient.com/eo/texts/Qur'an/Qur'an004 .htm (accessed April 30, 2005), and especially the treatise by Brother Abu Ruqaiyah, "The Islamic Legitimacy of the 'Martyrdom Operations,'" originally published in the sixteenth issue of *Nida'ul Islam*, December–January 1996–97, http://www.islam.org.au/articles/16martyrdom.htm.

182.   Eyad Sarraj, "The Making of a Suicide Bomber," March 10, 1996, e-mail dated March 23, 1997, sent by news@baraka.baraka.org. Dr. Reuven Paz, one of Isra-el's leading authorities on Islamic terrorism, has advanced the same argument. See Reuven Paz, "The Islamic Legitimacy of Suicide Terrorism," in *Countering Suicide Terrorism*, 87–88.

183.   Hassan, "Letter from Gaza," 38.

184. Mouin Rabbani, "Suicide Attacks Fueled by Alienation and Futility," *Philadelphia Inquirer Commentary*, April 3, 2001, http://inq.philly.com/content/inquirer/2001/04/03/opinion/RABBANI03.htm.

185. Ruqaiyah, "The Islamic Legitimacy of the 'Martrydom Operations.'"

186. According to journalist Joyce M. Davis, other leading Islamic authorities, such as Mohammed Sayed Tantawi of al Azhar University in Cairo and Sheikh Hamed al-Midawi, a cleric at Jerusalem's al-Aqsa mosque and the chairman of the (Muslim) Legal Appeals Court in that city, "believe Islamic teachings clearly support suicide bombings, but only against Israeli military targets. Suicide bombings are merely a form of jihad, one of the pillars of Islam, these jurists say. And they say Palestinian suicide bombers are helping to defend their land from Israeli aggression." See Joyce M. Davis, *Martyrs: Innocence, Vengeance, and Despair in the Middle East* (New York: Palgrave/Macmillan, 2003), 113.

187. Quoted in Mark Juergensmeyer, *The New Cold War? Religious Nationalism Confronts the Secular State* (Berkeley: University of California Press, 1993), 153.

188. Quoted in Rafi Yisra'eli, "Islamikaze: Suicide Terrorism Examined."

189. Quoted in Davis, *Martyrs*, 113.

190. "Wedded to Death in a Blaze of Glory," and Walker, "Palestinian 'Was Duped Into Being Suicide Bomber.'"

191. Yisra'eli, "Islamikaze," 3.

192. Lance Corporal Eddie DiFranco, quoted in David C. Martin and John Walcott, *Best Laid Plans: The Inside Story of America's War Against Terrorism* (New York: Harper and Row, 1988), 125.

193. The Israeli secret service reportedly planted a small bomb comprising an estimated two ounces of plastic explosive in a cellular phone used by Ayyash that was detonated by radio signal on January 5, 1996, when he answered a telephone call from his father. See Joel Greenberg, "Slaying Blended Technology and Guile," *New York Times*, January 10, 1996, and Serge Schmemann, "Palestinian Believed to Be Bombing Mastermind Is Killed," *New York Times*, January 6, 1997.

194. "Hamas Issues Statement on Ayyash Killing," al-Quds Palestinian Radio (in Arabic), 1755 GMT, January 5, 1996.

195. Quoted in Harvey W. Kushner, "Suicide Bombers: Business as Usual," *Studies in Conflict and Terrorism* 19, no. 4 (October–December 1996): 335.

196. Quoted in Lelyveld, "All Suicide Bombers Are Not Alike," 50.

197. Davis, *Martyrs*, 154.

198. Quoted in Barbara Victor, *Army of Roses: Inside the World of Palestinian Women Suicide Bombers* (New York: Rodale, 2003), 111–12.

199. *Al Hayat al Jadida*, September 17, 1999, quoted in Aluma Solnick, "The Joy of the Mothers of Palestinian 'Martyrs,'" *MEMRI: Inquiry and Analysis Series*, no. 61 (June 25, 2001): 1, www.memri.org.

200. Hassan, "Letter from Gaza," 39.

201. *Jerusalem Post Internet Edition*, September 6, 2001, quoted in Steven Stalinsky, "Palestinian Authority Sermons, 2000–2003," *MEMRI Special Report*, no. 24 (December 26, 2003), http://www.memri.org.

202. Davis, *Martyrs*, 154. See also Ibn Warraq, "Virgins? What Virgins?," *Guardian* (London), January 12, 2002, http://www.guardian.co.uk/saturday_review/story/0%2C3605%2C631332%2C00.html.

203. Davis, *Martyrs*, 154. See also *Al Hayat Al Jadida* (Palestine Authority), September 17, 1999, quoted in Solnick, "The Joy of the Mothers of Palestinian 'Martyrs,'" 1, and *The Jerusalem Post Internet Edition*, September 6, 2001, quoted in Stalinsky, "Palestinian Authority Sermons, 2000–2003," 2.

204. As one analyst notes of the 1995–1996 Hamas suicide bombing campaign: "The bombings were not directed to effect change in Israel; rather, they were intended to undermine the PA." See Ori Slonim, "The Hamas and Terror: An Alternative Explanation for the Use of Violence," *Strategic Assessment* 2, no. 3 (Ramat Aviv: Jaffee Center for Strategic Studies at Tel Aviv University, December 1999): 17.

205. See Naveh et al., *The Involvement of Arafat, PA Senior Officials, and Apparatuses in Terrorism Against Israel, Corruption, and Crime*. See also Matthew Levitt, "Designating the Al-Aqsa Martyrs Brigades," *Peacewatch*, no. 371 (Washington, D.C.: Washington Institute for Near East Policy, March 25, 2002), 1–2, and Stork, *Erased in a Moment*, 77–79.

206. See Hassan, "Letter from Gaza," 39. See also William Drozdiak, "Extremes Squeeze Arafat as Hamas's Power Swells," *International Herald Tribune* (Paris), August 25, 1997, and Neal MacFarquhar, "Portrait of a Suicide Bomber: Devout, Apolitical, and Angry," *New York Times*, March 18, 1996.

207. Luft, "The Palestinian H-Bomb," 4–5.

208. The *Karine-A* was intercepted in the Red Sea on January 3, 2002, by Israeli commandos and the Israeli Navy while en route from Iran to Gaza. See Gal Luft, "Special Policy Forum Report: The *Karine-A* Affair: A Strategic Watershed in the Middle East?," *Peacewatch*, no. 361 (Washington, D.C.: Washington Institute for Near East Policy, January 30, 2002), 1–2; David Makovsky, "The Seizure of Gaza-Bound Arms: Political Implications," *Peacewatch*, no. 358 (Washington, D.C.: Washington Institute for Near East Policy, January 8, 2002), 1–2; Robert Satloff, "*Karine-A*: Strategic Implications of Iranian-Palestinian Collusion," *Policywatch*, no. 539 (Washington, D.C.: Washington Institute for Near East Policy, January 15, 2002), 1–2; and "Caught Red-Handed: The Inside Story of an Arms Shipment," *Jane's Foreign Report*, no. 2672 (January 17, 2002): 1.

209. Among the injured was a Woodmere, Long Island, resident named Mark Sokolow, who on September 11 had escaped unharmed from the second tower of the World Trade Center, only to find himself enmeshed in another life-threatening terrorist incident, this time in Jerusalem.

210. Database of Terrorism Attacks Against Israel, 1948–Present, maintained by the National Security Studies Center, Haifa University, Mt. Carmel, Haifa, Israel.

211. See, for example, Sarraj, "The Making of a Suicide Bomber," and Rabbani, "Suicide Attacks Fueled by Alienation and Futility."

212. Hassan, "Letter from Gaza," 38.

213. Claude Berrebi, "Evidence About the Link Between Education, Poverty and Terrorism Among Palestinians," *Peace Economics, Peace Science and Public Policy* 13, no. 1 (2007): 30.

214. Lou Michel and Dan Herbeck, *American Terrorist: Timothy McVeigh and the Oklahoma City Bombing* (New York: Regan, 2001), 102, 144–45, 332, 358.

215. United States District Court Eastern District of New York, United States of America v. Adis Medunjanin, Abid Nasser, Adnan El Shukrijumah, Tariq Ur Rehman, and FNU LNU, July 7, 2010. See also Duncan Gardham, "Manchester Bomb Plot Students Were Planning Co-ordinated Attacks in New York and

Scandinavia," *Daily Telegraph* (London), December 16, 2010, http://www.tele graph.co.uk/news/worldnews/northamerica/usa/8205200/Manchester-bomb -plot-students-were-planning-co-ordinated-attacks-in-New-York-and-Scandi navia.html; Nic Robertson, Paul Cruickshank, and Tim Lister, "Document Shows Origins of 2006 Plot for Liquid Bombs on Planes," *CNN World*, April 30, 2012, http://www.cnn.com/2012/04/30/world/al Qaeda-documents/index.html?iref =allsearch.

216. Matt Apuzzo and Adam Goldman, *Enemies Within: Inside the NYPD's Secret Spying Unit and Bin Laden's Final Plot Against America* (New York: Simon & Schuster, 2013), 2–3.

217. Quoted in Daniel Pipes, *Militant Islam Reaches America* (New York: Norton, 2002), 201–2.

218. Quoted in MacNeil/Lehrer Productions, *Transcript of "The News Hour with Jim Lehrer,"* August 1, 1997.

219. Interviews and discussions with senior Israeli military, intelligence, and law enforcement officers in Tel Aviv, Jerusalem, Haifa, and Herzilya during December 2002, July 2003, and September 2003.

220. Margot Dudevitch, "2003 Terror Report: 50% Decrease in Israeli Casualties," *Jerusalem Post*, January 9, 2004. See also Patrick Bishop, "Have the Suicide Bombers Been Defeated?," *Daily Telegraph* (London), May 26, 2004.

221. Interview with senior Israel Defense Officer responsible for counterterrorism planning and operations, Tel Aviv, December 2002. Moreover, both Israelis and Palestinians "agree that the main factor in the decline in activity is Israel's success in killing or capturing leaders of the most militant [Palestinian terrorist] groups." See Bishop, "Have the Suicide Bombers Been Defeated?"

222. The New York City Police Department (NYPD) has already developed and implemented in the New York metropolitan area an ambitious program precisely along these lines. Discussions with and presentations by NYPD Intelligence Division officers, November 2003 and February 2004.

223. Ehud Sprinzak, "Outsmarting Suicide Terrorists," *Christian Science Monitor*, October 24, 2000.

224. Interview with NYPD officer, February 2004.

225. Ayman al-Zawahiri, *Knights Under the Prophet's Banner: Meditations on the Jihadist Movement*, translated and published in FBIS, "Al-Sarq Al-Aswat Publishes Extracts from Al-Jihad Leader al-Zawahiri's New Book" (Document ID GMP20020108000197, December 2, 2001), 90–91.

226. Jessica Stern and J. M. Berger, *ISIS: The State of Terror* (New York: HarperCollins, 2015), 94, 97.

227. "Al-Qaeda Firebrand Threatens New Attacks on US, Taunts Bush: Television," *Agence France Presse*, February 24, 2004.

6. The Old Media, Terrorism, and Public Opinion

1. Frederick J. Hacker, *Crusaders, Criminals, Crazies: Terror and Terrorism in Our Time* (New York: Norton, 1976), xi.

2. Quoted in Gerald McKnight, *The Mind of the Terrorist* (London: Michael Joseph, 1974), 168.

3. Anthony Richards, *Conceptualizing Terrorism* (Oxford: Oxford University Press, 2015), 57.

4. Brian Michael Jenkins, "International Terrorism: A New Mode of Conflict," in *International Terrorism and World Security*, ed. David Carlton and Carlo Schaerf (London: Croom Helm, 1975), 16.

5. J. Bowyer Bell, "Terrorist Scripts and Live-Action Spectaculars," *Columbia Journalism Review* 17, no. 1 (1978): 50.

6. Tony Atwater, "Network Evening News Coverage of the TWA Hostage Crisis," *Terrorism and the News Media Research Project* (Boston: Emerson College, n.d.), 5.

7. Ibid., 7.

8. John Dillin, "NBC News President Defends, but Revises, Terrorism Coverage," *Christian Science Monitor*, August 5, 1985.

9. ABC dispatched forty people, NBC sent twenty-five, and CBS sent twenty. See Roderick Townley and John Weisman, "The Reporters' Rat Race: Danger, Chaos, and Rumors of Payoffs," *TV Guide*, September 21, 1985.

10. Atwater, "Network Evening News Coverage of the TWA Hostage Crisis," 6.

11. Eleanor Randolph, "Networks Turn Eye on Themselves," *Washington Post*, June 30, 1985.

12. Quoted in Fred Barnes, "Shiite Spin Control," *New Republic* (Washington, D.C.), July 15 and 22, 1985, 12.

13. Quoted in Edwin Diamond, "The Coverage Itself—Why It Turned Into 'Terrorvision,'" *TV Guide*, September 21, 1985, 13.

14. Quoted in ibid., 10.

15. Quoted in A. P. Schmid, "Terrorism and the Media: The Ethics of Publicity," *Terrorism and Political Violence* 1, no. 4 (October 1989): 564.

16. Joseph Fromm, "TV: Does It Box in [the] President in a Crisis?," *U.S. News and World Report*, July 5, 1985.

17. Walter Mears, quoted in Randolph, "Networks Turn Eye on Themselves."

18. Quoted in Walter Laqueur, *The Age of Terrorism* (Boston: Little, Brown, 1987), 125.

19. Diamond, "The Coverage Itself," 10, 12.

20. As part of the deal, West German television was forced to broadcast footage of each of the five freed terrorists being released and boarding the aircraft that would take them to freedom, as well as present communiqués prepared by the Second of June terrorist group. Daniel Schorr, "The Encouragement of Violence," in *Terrorism: How the West Can Win*, ed. Benjamin Netanyahu (New York: Avon, 1986), 114.

21. Notes from the International Seminar on Terrorism and the Mass Media held in Sicily, April 3–5, 1981; archival material in the RAND Terrorism Incident Database.

22. Henry McDonald, "How the BBC Dances to an IRA Tune," *Sunday Times* (London), January 19, 1997.

23. Followed by Israel, France, Britain, Germany, the former Soviet Union/Russia, Turkey, Cuba, Spain, and Iran. RAND Terrorism Incident Database.

24. Including the geographical scope and diversity of America's overseas commercial interests, its numerous military bases on foreign soil, and the United States'

stature as the leader of the free world during the Cold War and as the lone remaining superpower today.

25. Quoted in Laqueur, *The Age of Terrorism*, 125.

26. Grant Wardlaw, *Political Terrorism: Theory, Tactics, and Counter-measures*
     (Cambridge: Cambridge University Press, 1990), 80.

27. Ibid.

28. Jeffrey Z. Rubin and Nehemia Friedland, "Theater of Terror," *Psychology Today*
     20, no. 3 (March 1986): 24.

29. Barnes, "Shiite Spin Control," 10.

30. David C. Martin and John Walcott, *Best Laid Plans: The Inside Story of America's
     War Against Terrorism* (New York: Harper and Row, 1988), 189.

31. Garrick Utley, "The Shrinking of Foreign News," *Foreign Affairs* 76, no. 2
     (March/April 1997): 6.

32. Quoted in James Adams, "The Role of the Media," in *Ethnic Conflict and Re-
     gional Instability: Implications for U.S. Policy and Army Roles and Missions*,
     ed. Robert L. Pfaltzgraff Jr. and Richard H. Schultz Jr. (Carlisle, Pa.: U.S. Army
     Strategic Studies Institute, 1994), 163.

33. Utley, "The Shrinking of Foreign News," 2.

34. Ibid., 6.

35. T. E. Pattern and R. D. McClure, *The Unseeing Eye: The Myth of Television Power
     in National Elections* (New York: G. P. Putnam's Sons, 1976), quoted in Sandra
     Wurth-Hough, "Network News Coverage of Terrorism: The Early Years," *Ter-
     rorism* 6, no. 3 (Summer 1983): 410.

36. Tom Shales, "America's Ordeal by Television," *Washington Post*, July 2, 1985.

37. Burns W. Roper, *Public Perceptions of Television and Other Mass Media: A
     Twenty Year Review, 1959–1978* (New York: Roper Organization, 1979), 1–5,
     quoted in Mark Armen Ayanian and John Z. Ayanian, "Armenian Political Vio-
     lence on American Network News: An Analysis of Content," *Armenian Review*
     40, no. 1–157 (Spring 1987): 16.

38. See Aryanian and Ayanian, "Armenian Political Violence on American Network
     News," 28–29.

39. Adams, "The Role of the Media," 162.

40. Ibid., 166.

41. Neil Hickey, "Terrorism and Television," *TV Guide*, July 31, 1976, 6.

42. Schmid, "Terrorism and the Media," 559.

43. In addition to Kissinger and Brzezinksi, mentioned above, the U.S. attorney gen-
     eral at the time, Edwin Meese, Secretary of Defense Caspar Weinberger, and
     the U.S. State Department legal adviser Abraham D. Sofaer also called for
     greater press restraint in the aftermath of the TWA hostage crisis.

44. See, e.g., the discussions in Yonah Alexander and Richard Latter, eds., *Terror-
     ism and the Media* (McLean, Va.: Brassey's, 1990), and Netanyahu, *Terrorism*,
     109–29, 229–39.

45. Laqueur, *The Age of Terrorism*, 121.

46. Quoted in R. W. Apple Jr., "Meese Suggests Press Code on Terrorism," *New York
     Times*, July 18, 1985.

47. Paul Wilkinson, "Terrorism and Propaganda," in Alexander and Latter, *Terror-
     ism and the Media*, 30.

48. Margaret Thatcher, quoted in Karen DeYoung, "U.S. Considering Talks on Hijacking Coverage," *Washington Post*, July 18, 1985.

49. Netanyahu, *Terrorism: How The West Can Win*, 109.

50. Ibid.

51. Perhaps the most far-reaching legislation enacted in this regard was the ban imposed by Britain between 1988 and 1994 on the broadcast of all interviews with terrorists or their supporters. According to the home secretary at the time the ban was introduced, Douglas Hurd, this extreme measure was not an attempt to impose censorship of the media but simply to deny members of the IRA, Sinn Fein, and other paramilitary groups "this easy platform for those who use it to propagate terrorism" (*Guardian* [London], October 20, 1988). Its effects, however, were perhaps more farcical than efficacious. Although the terrorists or spokespeople themselves were prevented from appearing on air, their statements were nonetheless still broadcast—by actors "standing in" for the proscribed individuals, in essence, reading scripts prepared by the terrorists. The result went beyond even the obvious circumvention and dilution of the legislation's intent, but mocked the government—completely destroying its efforts to control the dissemination of terrorist views. For a contrasting view, see the analysis in Shane Kingston, "Terrorism, the Media, and the Northern Ireland Conflict," *Studies in Conflict and Terrorism* 18, no. 3 (July–September 1995): 203–32.

52. Lawrence K. Grossman, "Television and Terrorism: A Common Sense Approach," *TVI Report* 6, no. 4 (1986): 3.

53. Laqueur, *The Age of Terrorism*, 127.

54. Theo Downes-LeGuin and Bruce Hoffman, *The Impact of Terrorism on Public Opinion, 1988 to 1989* (Santa Monica, Calif.: RAND Corporation, MR-225-F.F/RC, 1993), 16.

55. It should be noted, however, that a small percentage of the respondents who expressed relevant ethnic identification with a specific group were found to have slightly more ambivalent attitudes (mainly Jewish Americans and Irish Americans, respectively, with regard to the Jewish Defense League and the IRA). Ibid.

56. Konrad Kellen, quoted in ibid.

57. Philip Geyelin, "NBC: How to Protect a Terrorist," *Washington Post*, May 19, 1986.

58. Quoted in ibid. See also the editorial by Mortimer B. Zuckerman, the chairman and editor in chief of *U.S. News & World Report*, "Playing the Terrorists' Game," *U.S. News & World Report*, June 9, 1986.

59. As John O'Sullivan of the *Daily Telegraph* (London) remarked in a 1985 interview, "We mishandle [terrorists] because . . . we treat them in effect as politicians rather than . . . criminals." "Do Terrorists Need Television, TV Guide Asks," *United Press International*, February 18, 1985.

60. Quoted in Sir John Hermon, "The Police, the Media, and the Reporting of Terrorism," in Alexander and Latter, *Terrorism and the Media*, 39.

61. See Martin and Walcott, *Best Laid Plans*, 188–92.

62. Abraham D. Sofaer, quoted in DeYoung, "U.S. Considering Talks on Hijacking Coverage."

63. Quoted in Diamond, "The Coverage Itself."

64. Margaret Genovese, "Terrorism: Newspapers Grapple with the Extraordinary Challenges of Covering Worldwide Terrorist Incidents," *Presstime* (New York), August 1986.

65. Grossman, "Television and Terrorism," 1.

66. Donald Bremner, "Media Given Mixed Reviews on Terrorism," *Los Angeles Times*, September 26, 1986.

67. Quoted in Fromm, "TV: Does It Box in [the] President in a Crisis?"

68. Quoted in Barnes, "Shiite Spin Control," 12.

69. Quoted in Fromm, "TV: Does It Box in [the] President in a Crisis?"

70. Patrick Clawson, "Why We Need More but Better Coverage of Terrorism," *Orbis* 80, no. 4 (Winter 1987): 702. It should be noted, however, that Sir Geoffrey Jackson, the British ambassador to Uruguay who was kidnapped by the Tupamaros in 1971 and held for eight months, maintains that the absence of media publicity was critical in the terrorists' decision to release him.

71. Martin and Walcott, *Best Laid Plans*, 191.

72. "Public Support Adams Talks," *Sunday Times* (London), February 18, 1996.

73. Downes-LeGuin and Hoffman, *The Impact of Terrorism on Public Opinion*, 14–15. Information on dog bites provided courtesy of Dr. Andrew Rowan, researcher at Tufts University, Medford, Massachusetts.

74. See David Rapoport, "Terrorism," in *Routledge Encyclopedia of Government and Politics*, ed. Mary Hawkesworth and Maurice Kogan (London: Routledge, 1992), 2:1073.

75. Graham Norton, "The Terrorist and the Traveller: A Gulf Aftermath Assessment," *World Today* (London), May 1991, 81.

76. Desmond Balmer, "U.S. Tourists React to Terrorism Fear," *New York Daily News*, March 2, 1986.

77. Stuart I. Feiler, "Terrorism: Is Tourism Really the Target?," *Hotel and Restaurants International*, October 1986.

78. Survey conducted by the U.S. Travel Data Center (a national nonprofit travel and tourism trade organization), cited in Harvey J. Iglarsh, "Fear of Flying: Its Economic Costs," *Terrorism* 10, no. 1 (Winter 1987): 46.

79. Feiler, "Terrorism: Is Tourism Really the Target?"

80. Ralph Blumenthal, "Peak Season of American Travel to Europe Ends Showing Little Recovery," *New York Times*, September 14, 1986.

81. Norton, "The Terrorist and the Traveller," 81.

82. ABC News/*Washington Post* poll, cited in "Views on National Security," *National Journal* (Washington, D.C.), October 25, 1986.

83. Norton, "The Terrorist and the Traveller," 81.

84. Quoted in Martin and Walcott, *Best Laid Plans*, 191.

85. Quoted in Fromm, "TV: Does It Box in [the] President in a Crisis?"

86. Adams, "The Role of the Media," 164–65.

87. Thomas Plate and William Tuohy, "Los Angeles Times Interview: John Major—Even Under Fire, Britain's Prime Minister Holds His Own," *Los Angeles Times*, June 20, 1993.

88. Tom Squiteri, "U.S.: Return Our Men," *USA Today* (Washington, D.C.), October 6, 1993.

89. B. Drummond Ayres Jr., "The Somalia Mission: Voices," *New York Times*, October 9, 1993.

90. Everett Carl Ladd, "U.S. Public and Somalia," *Christian Science Monitor*, October 15, 1993.
91. American Broadcasting Companies, Inc., *Nightline* (ABC), October 7, 1993.
92. Cited in Benjamin C. Schwarz, *Casualties, Public Opinion, and U.S. Military Intervention: Implications for U.S. Regional Deterrence Strategies* (Santa Monica, Calif.: RAND Corporation, MR-431-A/AF, 1994), 24.
93. Quoted in Fromm, "TV: Does It Box in [the] President in a Crisis?"
94. See "Khaled Tribute," *Times* (London), September 3, 1997, and Christopher Walker, "Arabs Are Convinced Car Crash Was a Murder Plot," *Times* (London), September 4, 1997.
95. See "Unabomber Manifesto," *Washington Post*, September 19, 1995.
96. David Rapoport, "The Media and Terrorism: Implications of the Unabomber Case," editorial in *Terrorism and Political Violence* 8, no. 1 (Spring 1996): viii.

7. The New Media, Terrorism, and the Shaping of Global Opinion

1. Mohammed El-Nawawy and Adel Iskandar, *Al-Jazeera: The Story of the Network That Is Rattling Governments and Redefining Modern Journalism* (Cambridge, Mass.: Westview, 2003), 143, 146–47.
2. Gabriel Weimann, *Terrorism in Cyberspace: The Next Generation* (Washington, D.C.: Woodrow Wilson Center Press/New York: Columbia University Press, 2015), 11, 53–61, 129.
3. Tina Brown, "Death by Error," *Washington Post*, May 19, 2005.
4. Alex P. Schmid and Janny de Graaf, *Violence as Communication: Insurgent Terrorism and the Western News Media* (Beverly Hills, Calif.: Sage, 1982), 9.
5. For the purposes of this study, the definition of propaganda used is that of the Institute for Propaganda Analysis, cited in Jacques Ellul, *Propaganda: The Formation of Men's Attitudes*, trans. Konrad Kellen and Jean Lerner (New York: Knopf, 1965), xi–xii: "Propaganda is the expression of opinion or actions carried out deliberately by individuals or groups with a view to influencing the opinions or actions of other individuals or groups for predetermined ends and through psychological manipulations."
6. As Ellul notes, "Propaganda is made, first of all, because of a will to action, for the purpose of effectively arming policy and giving irresistible power to its decisions." Ibid., x.
7. Christina Meyer, *Underground Voices: Insurgent Propaganda in El Salvador, Nicaragua, and Peru* (Santa Monica, Calif.: RAND Corporation, N-3299-USDP, 1991), 2.
8. See Bonnie Cordes, "When Terrorists Do the Talking: Reflections on Terrorist Literature," in ""Inside Terrorist Organizations," ed. David C. Rapoport, special issue, *Journal of Strategic Studies* 10, no. 4 (December 1987): 164.
9. Meyer, *Underground Voices*, 9–10.
10. Ibid., 11–12.
11. Quoted in Stephen Engelberg, "Contras to Start New Radio Station, *New York Times*, November 5, 1986.

12. Yariv Tsfati and Gabriel Weimann, "www.terrorism.com: Terror on the Internet," *Studies in Conflict and Terrorism* 25, no. 5 (September/October 2001): 316.

13. See Schmid and de Graaf, *Violence as Communication*, 223–24; Edward Herman and Gerry O'Sullivan, *The "Terrorism" Industry* (New York: Pantheon, 1989), 191–93, 218; and Dorothy E. Denning, "Activism, Hacktivism, and Cyber-Terrorism: The Internet as a Tool for Influencing Foreign Policy," http://www.nautilus.org/info-policy/workshop/papers/denning.html (accessed April 16, 2002), 4.

14. "Militant Islamic Political Activism on the Worldwide Web" (seminar by two analysts with the Foreign Broadcast Information Service, presented at the RAND Corporation Washington, D.C., Office, December 19, 2000).

15. Denning, "Activism, Hacktivism, and Cyberterrorism," 3.

16. Charles Schreiner, coordinator of East Timor Action Network, quoted in Roy Krovel, "www.guerrilla.net," *Internet Today* (London), no. 25 (November 1996): 23.

17. Denning, "Activism, Hacktivism, and Cyberterrorism," 4; David C. Benson, "Why the Internet Is Not Increasing Terrorism," *Security Studies* 23, no. 2 (2014): 298; and Office of the Director of National Intelligence, *Declassified Key Judgments of the National Intelligence Estimate, "Trends in Global Terrorism: Implications for the United States,"* dated April 2006, http://www.au.af.mil/au/awc/awcgate/dni/declass_nie_key_jdgmnts06apr.pdf.

18. Dorothy Denning, "Information Warfare and Cyber-Terrorism" (Women in International Security [WIIS] seminar, Washington, D.C., December 15, 1999).

19. As two observers have noted with respect to the perception management conducted by terrorists on the Web: "It is not surprising that networked terrorists have already begun to leverage IT for perception management and propaganda to influence public opinion, recruit new members, and generate funding. Getting a message out and receiving extensive news media exposure are important components of terrorist strategy, which ultimately seeks to undermine the will of an opponent. In addition to such traditional media as television or print, the Internet now offers terrorist groups an alternative way to reach out to the public, often with much more direct control over the message." Michele Zanini and Sean J. A. Edwards, "The Networking of Terror in the Information Age," in *Networks and Netwars: The Future of Terror, Crime, and Militancy*, ed. John Arquilla and David Ronfeldt (Santa Monica, Calif.: RAND Corporation, MR-1382-OSD, 2001), 43.

20. "Militant Islamic Political Activism on the Worldwide Web."

21. Ibid.

22. For a detailed examination and analysis of the EZLN, see Thomas Olesen, *International Zapatismo: The Construction of Solidarity in the Age of Globalization* (London: Zed, 2005), and David F. Ronfeldt et al., *The Zapatista Social Netwar in Mexico* (Santa Monica, Calif.: RAND Corporation, MR-994-A, 1998).

23. "An Accion Zapatista Report—Zapatistas in Cyberspace: A Guide to Analysis and Resources," http://www.eco.utexas.edu/faculty/Cleaver/zapsincyber.html (accessed June 14, 2005). The EZLN's seven-year-old website could still be accessed as of 2002 at http://www.utexas.edu/students/nave (note the server's U.S.-based location at a Texas university site). Today, its official site can be

accessed as of June 14, 2005 at "Zapatista Network: A Clearinghouse of Zapatista Information and Support Worldwide." Another site, "EZLN—¡Ya Basta!"
[Enough already], at http://www.ezln.org (accessed June 15, 2005), is not an
official EZLN site, but according to Olesen, it "was the first website devoted
entirely to the issues of the EZLN and Chiapas." See Olesen, *International
Zapatismo*, 190.

24. Note that in the global crackdown on terrorist fund-raising and related support
activities that followed the September 11, 2001, attacks, the sites of many of the
better-known terrorist and insurgent groups prominently featured on the Web
either closed down completely or became accessible only on a sporadic basis.
These include al-Qaeda's www.alneda.com, Hezbollah's www.hizbollah.org, and
Hamas's www.hamas.org, among others (accessed August 1, 2002).

25. Tim Golden, "Mexico's New Offensive: Erasing Rebel's Mystique," *New York
Times*, February 11, 1995.

26. Ronfeldt et al., *The Zapatista Social Netwar in Mexico*, 2.

27. Olesen, *International Zapatismo*, 190.

28. Ibid., 3; Tod Robberson, "Loaded Guns and Diskettes: Rebels Win Hearts and
Minds on Internet," *International Herald Tribune* (Paris), February 21, 1995, and
Krovel, "www.guerrilla.net," 23.

29. Krovel, "www.guerrilla.net," 23.

30. "Militant Islamic Political Activism on the Worldwide Web."

31. Quoted in Robberson, "Loaded Guns and Diskettes."

32. Quoted in Ronfeldt et al., *The Zapatista Social Netwar in Mexico*, 4.

33. Robberson, "Loaded Guns and Diskettes."

34. Quoted in Krovel, "www.guerrilla.net," 23.

35. Olesen, *International Zapatismo*, 84–85.

36. Quoted in ibid., 85.

37. Krovel, "www.guerrilla.net," 23.

38. Accessed June 14, 2005.

39. Rohan Gunaratna, *International and Regional Security Implications of the
Sri Lankan Tamil Insurgency* (St. Albans, Herts: International Foundation
of Sri Lankans, 1997), 53–58. See also Denning, "Activism, Hacktivism, and
Cyberterrorism," 8, and Tsfati and Weimann, "www.terrorism.com: Terror on the
Internet."

40. Reuters, "Propaganda to the People," Wired News.com, http://www.wired.com
/news/print/0,1294,11363,00.html (accessed April 11, 2002).

41. Quoted in Krovel, "www.guerrilla.net," 24.

42. Gunaratna, *International and Regional Security Implications of the Sri Lankan
Tamil Insurgency*, 58.

43. Accessed June 14, 2005.

44. See the excellent content analysis of terrorist websites in Tsfati and Weimann,
"www.terrorism.com: Terror on the Internet," 319–21.

45. See http://www.eelam.web.com/ (accessed regularly between July and August
2002).

46. Krovel, "www.guerrilla.net," 25.

47. Ibid., 24.

48. Thailif Deen, "Tigers Try Electronic Terrorism," *Daily News* (Colombo), November 22, 1997.

49. Thailif Deen, "Tigers Try Electronic Terrorism," *Daily News* (Colombo), November 22, 1997.

50. Zanini and Edwards, "The Networking of Terror in the Information Age," 43.

51. "Militant Islamic Political Activism on the Worldwide Web."

52. Gabriel Weimann, *Terror on the Internet: The New Arena, the New Challenges* (Washington, D.C.: U.S. Institute of Peace, 2006), 15.

53. Weimann, *Terrorism in Cyberspace: The Next Generation*, 10.

54. Weimann, *Terror on the Internet*, 15.

55. Weimann, *Terrorism in Cyberspace*, 10.

56. Weimann, *Terror on the Internet*, 49–50.

57. A survey conducted by two Israeli academicians, which examined sites in 1998 and again in 2002, showed that Hamas, Hezbollah, the Shining Path, Kahane Lives, the Basque separatist group ETA, the IRA, Aum Shinrikyo, the FARC, the ELN (Ejército de Liberación Nacional), Peru's MRTA (Movimiento Revolucionario Túpac Amaru; Tupac Amaru), the Turkish Marxist group DHKP/C (Devrimci Halk Kurtuluş Partisi-Cephesi), the PKK, the IMU (Islamic Movement of Uzbekistan), Egypt's Islamic Group, the Popular Front for the Liberation of Palestine, Palestine Islamic Jihad, and the Cold War dinosaur the Japanese Red Army, in addition to the EZLN and the LTTE, had a presence on the Internet. See Tsfati and Weimann, "www.terrorism.com: Terror on the Internet," 328–30. See also Peter Victor, "Fascists Take to the Keyboards," The Independent on Sunday (London), April 7, 1995; Agence France Presse, "Eta Driven from Internet," Times (London), February 20, 1996; "Intelligence Battle in Cyberspace," Intelligence Newsletter, no. 263 (April 27, 1995): 3; and www.alneda.com (al-Qaeda's website) (accessed August 12, 2002).

58. "Militant Islamic Political Activism on the Worldwide Web"; Michael Whine, "Islamist Organizations on the Internet," *Terrorism and Political Violence* 11, no. 1 (Spring 1999): 125–26; Zanini and Edwards, "The Networking of Terror in the Information Age," 29.

59. Whine, "Islamist Organizations on the Internet," 131.

60. Zanini and Edwards, "The Networking of Terror in the Information Age," 29.

61. Whine, "Islamist Organizations on the Internet," 125–26.

62. "Militant Islamic Political Activism on the Worldwide Web."

63. Efforts to access these and all other Hezbollah sites, except for the al-Manar television site (www.manartv.com.lb/news/aspx and www.manar.com), in June 2005 proved unsuccessful.

64. See www.hizbollah.org/english (accessed July and August 2002).

65. Reportedly, only one other terrorist or insurgent group, Algeria's Islamic Salvation Party (Front Islamique du Salut; FIS), regularly posts content in French. See "Militant Islamic Political Activism on the Worldwide Web."

66. Ibid.

67. Zanini and Edwards, "The Networking of Terror in the Information Age," 26.

68. Quoted in Whine, "Islamist Organizations on the Internet," 126.

69. Charles Pillar, "Terrorists Taking Up Cyberspace: Web Sites Have Become Inexpensive, Easily Accessible Tools for Giving Instructions to Operatives and Raising Funds," *Los Angeles Times*, February 9, 2001.

70. http://almashriq.hiof.no/lebanon/300/320/324/324.2/hizballah/ (accessed June 15, 2005).

71. Ibid.
72. Accessed June 9, 2016. See also Zanini and Edwards, "The Networking of Terror in the Information Age," 43; Denning, "Activism, Hacktivism, and Cyberterrorism," 7–8; Julia Scheeres, "Blacklisted Groups Visible on Web," Wired News. com, http://www.wired.com/news/print/0,1283,47616,00.html (accessed April 19, 2002); and James Kitfield, "The Hezbollah Model," National Journal 34, no. 20 (May 18, 2002).
73. Badih Chayban, "Hizbullah Rolls Out New Computer Game: Special Force Lets Players Use Sharon for Target Practice," Daily Star (Beirut), March 3, 2003, http://www.specialforce.net/english/news/dailystart.htm.
74. Quoted in Mariam Karouny, "Hizbollah Computer Game Recalls Israeli Battles," Reuters Technology, March 18, 2003, http://www.specialforce.net/english/news/reuters.htm.
75. Daniel J. Wakin, "Video Game Mounts Simulated Attacks Against Israeli Targets," New York Times, May 18, 2003.
76. See http://www.specialforce.net/english/indexeng.htm (accessed June 15, 2005).
77. Registration Card No. 336070, Special Force Version 1 (n.d.).
78. Quoted in Wakin, "Video Game Mounts Simulated Attacks Against Israeli Targets."
79. Back cover, Special Force Version 1 (n.d.).
80. See, for example, http://www.palestine-info.com (accessed January 2002 and June 15, 2005). See also Scheeres, "Blacklisted Groups Visible on Web." The affiliated www.qassam.net was closed down in 2002.
81. See, for example, http://www.msanews-list (accessed August 2002). MSANews has also included links to, and communiqués from, other radical Islamic groups such as the FIS, GIA, etc. See also Whine, "Islamist Organizations on the Internet," 127.
82. "Militant Islamic Political Activism on the Worldwide Web."
83. Doubts about the authenticity of this entire episode have been raised. See especially James Fallows, "Who Shot Mohammed Al-Dura?," Atlantic Monthly 291, no. 5 (June 2003): 49–56.
84. See, for example, http://www.palestine-info.com (accessed January 2002).
85. Whine, "Islamist Organizations on the Internet," 128. See also the discussion in Tsfati and Weimann, "www.terrorism.com: Terror on the Internet," 319–20.
86. Bin Laden and al-Qaeda have also been alleged to employ this means to communicate secretly over the Internet. See Reuters, "Extremists Post Hidden Messages," Wired News.com, February 6, 2001, http://www.wired.com/news/print/0,1294,41650,00.html; Declan McCullagh, "Bin Laden: Steganography Master?," Wired News.com, February 7, 2001, http://www.wired.com/news/print/0,1283,41658,00.html; Jack Kelley, "Terror Groups Hide Behind Web Encryption: Officials Say Sites Disguise Activities," USA Today, February 6, 2001; and Jack Kelley, "Militants Wire Web with Links to Jihad," USA Today, July 10, 2002.
87. See Whine, "Islamist Organizations on the Internet," 128, and Zanini and Edwards, "The Networking of Terror in the Information Age," 37.
88. http://www.IntifadaOnline.com (accessed August 2002 and June 15, 2005).
89. "Special Information Bulletin: Marketing of Terrorism Through the Internet," Intelligence and Terrorism Information Center at the Center for Special Stud-

ies (C.S.S.), November 2004, http://www.intelligence.org.il/eng/sib/1_05/n_t
.htm.

90.   This image has regularly been featured on these sites since 2000.

91.   http://www.IntifadaOnline.com (accessed June 15, 2005). See also, for example,
      http://www.palestine-info.com (accessed January 2002).

92.   http://www.IntifadaOnline.com (accessed October 2000, January 2001, Au-
      gust 2002, and June 15, 2005).

93.   Quoted in Kelley, "Militants Wire Web with Links to Jihad."

94.   "Special Information Bulletin: Marketing of Terrorism Through the Internet,"
      November 2004, and Part 2, December 2004, http://www.intelligence.org.il/eng
      /sib/1_05/n_t.htm.

95.   Only www.sabiroon.net could be accessed on June 9, 2016.

96.   Weimann, *Terror on the Internet*, 80.

97.   Only two—http://www.qudsway.com and http://www.palestineway.com—
      could be accessed on June 16, 2005.

98.   Accessed at http://www.hizb-ut-tahrir.info/english/index.html, June 15, 2005.

99.   www.lashkar-e-taiba.net (accessed February 2001).

100. "Militant Islamic Political Activism on the Worldwide Web."

101. Jessica Eve Stern, "Pakistan's Jihad Culture," *Foreign Affairs* 79, no. 6 (Novem-
      ber/December 2000): 120. See also Naill McKay, "Do Terrorists Troll the Net?,"
      Wired News.com, http://www.wired.com/news/print/0,1294,15812,00.html
      (accessed April 16, 2002); Pillar, "Terrorists Taking Up Cyberspace"; Scheeres,
      "Blacklisted Groups Visible on Web"; and Zanini and Edwards, "The Networking
      of Terror in the Information Age," 38.

102. Quoted in Pillar, "Terrorists Taking Up Cyberspace."

103. www.lashkar-e-taiba.net (accessed February 2001).

104. Stern, "Pakistan's Jihad Culture," 124.

105. Accessed June 9, 2016.

106. "Militant Islamic Political Activism on the Worldwide Web."

107. Quoted in Pillar, "Terrorists Taking Up Cyberspace."

108. Peter Bergen, *Holy War, Inc.: Inside the Secret World of Osama bin Laden* (New
      York: Free Press, 2001), 38.

109. Quoted in Kelley, "Militants Wire Web with Links to Jihad."

110. "Militant Islamic Political Activism on the Worldwide Web."

111. Accessed June 15, 2005.

112. "Militant Islamic Political Activism on the Worldwide Web."

113. Rohan Gunaratna, *Inside Al-Qa'ida: Global Network of Terrorism* (London:
      Hurst), 57. Its director was known by the nom de guerre Abu Reuter—an obvi-
      ous reference to the famous global news wire service.

114. Zanini and Edwards, "The Networking of Terror in the Information Age," 37.

115. Weimann, *Terror on the Internet*, 64.

116. "Information Security News: Militants Wire Web with Links to Jihad," *Info-Sec
      News*, July 11, 2002, quoted in ibid., 27.

117. See www.alneda.com, www.swithun.demon.co.uk/markaz/homepage02jul22
      .htm (accessed August 12, 2002).

118. Paul Eedle, "Terrorism.com," *Guardian* (London), July 17, 2002.

119. Presentation made by British journalist Paul Eedle, "The Language of Jihad" at
      the third annual conference of the Centre for the Study of Terrorism and

Political Violence, Symposium on Islamic Extremism and Terrorism in the Greater Middle East, St. Andrews University, St. Andrews, Scotland, June 8, 2002.

120. Eedle, "Terrorism.com."

121. Quoted in Kelley, "Militants Wire Web with Links to Jihad."

122. Eedle, "Terrorism.com."

123. Translation by, and personal communication with, Eedle, July 31, 2002.

124. Kelley, "Militants Wire Web with Links to Jihad." Discussion and communications between the author and British journalist Paul Eedle, July and August 2002.

125. Quoted in Eedle, "Terrorism.com."

126. See "Al-Qa'ida Organization Addresses a Message to Iraqi, Islamic Peoples (Internet) www.alfjr.com in Arabic," March 5, 2003 (posting by "Ayn al-Haqiqah," titled "The al-Qa'ida Organization Writes a Letter to the Iraqi People" in the Issues of the Islamic Nation section of the chat room of http://www.alfjr.com, March 5, 2003). See also Ben Venzke and Aimee Ibrahim, *Al-Qaeda's Advice for Mujahideen in Iraq: Lessons Learned in Afghanistan*, vol. 1.0 (Alexandria, Va.: IntelCenter, April 14, 2003).

127. *MEMRI Special Dispatch—Jihad and Terrorism Studies*, no. 493 (April 11, 2003), quoting http://www.cubezero.nt/vhsvideo/imagis/?subject=2&rec=1043.

128. Reuven Paz, "Who Wants to Email Al-Qaeda?," *Occasional Paper, PRISM (Project for the Study of Islamist Movements)* 1, no. 8 (October 2003); *Occasional Paper, PRISM (Project for the Study of Islamist Movements)* 2, no. 2 (July 2004), http:www.e-prism.org/images/PRISM_vol_2_no_2.doc.

129. Weimann, *Terror on the Internet*, 41.

130. Quoted in Reuven Paz, "Sawt al-Jihad: New Indoctrination of Qa'idat al-Jihad," *Occasional Paper, PRISM (Project for the Study of Islamist Movements)* 1, no. 8 (October 2003), http:www.e-prism.org/images/PRISM_no_9.doc.

131. Quoted in Weimann, *Terror on the Internet*, 105.

132. Moqrin was reportedly killed by Saudi security forces in Riyadh on June 18, 2004.

133. IntelCenter, *Al-Qaeda Targeting Guidance* (Alexandria, Va.: IntelCenter/ Tempest, April 1, 2004), 1:6–9.

134. See the following articles by Neal MacFarquhar in the *New York Times*: "As Terrorists Strike Arab Targets, Escalation Fears Arise," April 30, 2004; "Firm Pulls 100 from Saudi Arabia After 5 Deaths," May 2, 2004; "After Attack, Company's Staff Plans to Leave Saudi Arabia," May 3, 2004. See also Kim Ghattas and Roula Khalaf, "Shooting Spree in Saudi City Spreads Jitters Among Western Companies," *Financial Times* (London), May 3, 2004.

135. Craig Whitlock, "Islamic Radicals Behead American in Saudi Arabia," *Washington Post*, June 19, 2004.

136. See Sean Young, "Online Co. Shuts Down Site with Beheading," *Yahoo! News*, May 14, 2004, http://www.crime-research.org/news/14.05.2004/270; John F. Burns, "Video Appears to Show Insurgents Kill a Downed Pilot," *New York Times*, April 23, 2005; and Jonathan Finer and Anthony Faiola, "Insurgents Say They Have Killed Japanese: Video May Show Body of Hostage," *Washington Post*, May 29, 2005.

137. IntelCenter, *Al-Qaeda Targeting Guidance*, 1:6–9.

138. Henry Schuster, "Studios of Terror: Al Qaeda's Media Strategy," http://www.cnn
     .com/2005/WORLD/MCAST/02/15/schuster.column/index.html (accessed Feb-
     ruary 15, 2005).
139. They include al-Qaeda, Ansar al-Islam, Ansar al-Sunnah, Islamic Army in Iraq,
     Salafist Group for Call and Combat (GSPC), Sout al-Jihad in Iraq, Organization
     of Jihad's Base in the Country of the Two Rivers (Tanzim Qa'idat al-Jihad fi
     Bilad al-Rafidayn; QJBR), the al-Haramain Brigades, the Taliban, and groups in
     Chechnya, Bosnia, Kashmir, and Indonesia. See IntelCenter, *Evolution of Jihadi
     Video (EJV)*, (Alexandria, Va.: IntelCenter/Tempest, May 11, 2005), 1:5.
140. Awadh al-Taee and Steve Negus, "Now Showing (Despite Official Warnings):
     'Mujahideen Movie,'" *Financial Times* (London), February 16, 2005.
141. See, for example, Finer and Faiola, "Insurgents Say They Have Killed Japanese,"
     and John F. Burns, "Rebels Kill Egyptian Diplomat, Adding Pressure on Others
     in Iraq," *New York Times*, July 8, 2005.
142. David E. Kaplan, "National Security Watch: Eurolefties Fund Iraq Insurgency,"
     U.S. News & World Report, June 23, 2005, http://www.usnews.com/usnews/news
     /articles/050623/23euroleft.htm.
143. Quoted in Susan B. Glasser, "'Martyrs' in Iraq Mostly Saudis: Web Sites Track
     Suicide Bombings," *Washington Post*, May 15, 2005.
144. David Baran and Mathieu Guidère, "Sons et images de l'opposition irakienne"
     [Sound and pictures of the Iraqi opposition], *Le Monde Diplomatique* (Paris),
     May 2005. An infelicitous translation, titled "Iraq: A Message from the Insur-
     gents" was also published by *Le Monde Diplomatique*'s English edition. See also
     Robert F. Worth, "Jihadists Take Stand on Web, and Some Say It's Defensive,"
     New York Times, March 13, 2005.
145. *Declaration of Jihad Against the Country's Tyrants—Military Series* (n.d.). Also
     known as the Manchester Manual, this document was obtained by British po-
     lice during a March 2000 raid of an al-Qaeda safe house in Manchester. It was
     found on a computer left behind by Abu Anas al-Libi, a key al-Qaeda operative
     wanted in connection with the 1998 East Africa embassy bombings, who fled
     Britain and is believed to be still at large. A version of the manual can be accessed
     at http://www.au.af.mil/au/awc/awcgate/terrorism/alqaida_manual/manualpart1
     _1.pdf (accessed March 6, 2017).
146. National Commission on Terrorist Attacks Upon the United States, *The
     9/11 Commission Report: Authorized Edition* (New York: Norton, 2004), 157,
     164, 495.
147. Barton Gellman, "Cyber-Attacks by Al-Qaeda Feared: Terrorists at Threshold
     of Using Internet as Tool of Bloodshed, Experts Say," *Washington Post*, June 27,
     2002.
148. Dan Eggen, "Indictment Cites Plans to Target Financial Hubs: 3 Britons' Extra-
     dition to Be Sought," *Washington Post*, April 13, 2005.
149. Bergen, *Italy War, Inc.*, 27.
150. Intended, in the version the author acquired, most likely for British Muslims in
     the United Kingdom.
151. *The Destruction of the American Destroyer USS Cole*, DVD version, produced
     by the Assahab (the Cloud) Foundation (n.d.).
152. See http://prohosters.com/pearl/#ogr or the link to the execution clip found on
     the site www.ogrish.com (accessed April 15, 2005).

153. Eedle, "The Language of Jihad." Also, further discussion and communication between the author and Eedle in July and August 2002.

154. Howard Schneider and Walter Pincus, "Bin Laden Video Includes Sept. 11 Praise," *Washington Post*, April 16, 2002.

155. Transcript of video, April 3, 2002, 9.

156. IntelCenter, *EJV*, 1:4.

157. Quoted in Peter Finn and Peter Baker, "Hostages Were Helpless in the Face of Chaos," *Washington Post*, September 5, 2005.

158. Michael Weiss and Hassan Hassan, *ISIS: Inside the Army of Terror* (New York: Reagan Arts, 2015), 179.

159. Robert Hannigan, "The Web Is a Terrorists's Command-and-Control Network of Choice," *Financial Times* (London), November 4, 2014, http://www.ft.com/intl/cms/s/2/c89b6c58-6342-11e4-8a63-00144feabdco.html#axzz3I6l8Haho.

160. Weimann, *Terrorism in Cyberspace*, 53.

161. Quoted in Sheera Frenkel, "Everything You Ever Wanted to Know About How ISIS Uses the Internet," *BuzzFeed*, May 12, 2016, https://www.buzzfeed.com/sheerafrenkel/everything-you-ever-wanted-to-know-about-how-isis-uses-the-i?utm_term=.dejrLb930#.fv4DYvgm1.

162. Daniel Byman, *Al Qaeda, the Islamic State, and the Global Jihadist Movement: What Everyone Needs to Know* (New York: Oxford University Press, 2015), 179.

163. Michael S. Schmidt, "Canadian Killed in Syria Lives On as Pitchman for Jihadis," *New York Times*, July 15, 2014, http://www.nytimes.com/2014/07/16/world/middleeast/isis-uses-andre-poulin-a-canadian-convert-to-islam-in-recruitment-video.html?_r=0.

164. Ronan Farrow, "Like. Share. Kill. Social Media Companies Are Ignoring How Terrorists Exploit Their Services," *Wall Street Journal*, July 13, 2014.

165. Maria Abi-Habib, "Jihadists Step Up Recruitment Drive," *Wall Street Journal*, June 26, 2014.

166. Weimann, *Terrorism in Cyberspace*, 128.

167. William McCants, *The ISIS Apocalypse: The History, Strategy, and Doomsday Vision of The Islamic State* (New York: St. Martin's Press, 2015), 153.

168. Jessica Stern and J. M. Berger, *ISIS: The State of Terror* (New York: HarperCollins, 2015), 72. See also, Farrow, "Like. Share. Kill."

169. Weiss and Hassan, *ISIS: Inside the Army of Terror*, 175.

170. McCants, *The ISIS Apocalypse*, 126.

171. Gabriel Weimann, *New Terrorism and New Media* (Washington, D.C.: Wilson Center and Commons Lab, Research Series, 2014), 2:8.

172. It was initially on air only six hours a day. See Kitfield, "The Hezbollah Model."

173. See the "About Us" description at http://www.manartv.com.lb/aboutUS.aspx?Language.=en (accessed June 20, 2005).

174. Avi Jorisch, *Beacon of Hatred: Inside Hizballah's Al-Manar Television* (Washington, D.C.: Washington Institute for Near East Policy, 2004), xiv.

175. "About Us" description at http://www.manartv.com.lb/aboutUS.aspx?Language=en.

176. Jorisch, *Beacon of Hatred*, xiv. This report is noteworthy for an accompanying CD-ROM with video clips of fifty-seven actual al-Manar broadcasts to illustrate

its central arguments. See especially pp. 52–61 for discussions of al-Manar's anti-American and Iraq coverage.

177. Ibid., xv.
178. According to the Gallup poll, in response to the question of television stations watched in the last seven days, the rankings were MBC, 37.1 percent of total audience; LBC, 26.6 percent; Abu Dhabi, 25.8 percent; Future TV, 21.1 percent; and al-Manar, 16.0 percent. In response to the question of which television channel is turned to first to catch up on current world affairs, the rankings were al-Jazeera, 43.2 percent; MBC, 7.7 percent; and al-Manar, 5.4 percent. Personal communication between the author and an analyst in the U.S. State Department's Policy Planning Staff responsible for monitoring Middle Eastern media, August 12, 2002.
179. Kitfield, "The Hezbollah Model."
180. Jorisch, *Beacon of Hatred*, xiii.
181. Zanini and Edwards, "The Networking of Terror in the Information Age," 42.
182. Hezbollah video clips obtained by the author in 1999 that were packaged on the al-Manar website and related Hezbollah sites, for fund-raising purposes. See also Kitfield, "The Hezbollah Model."
183. Quoted in Edward Lucas, "Deadly Image Which Could Give Hezbollah the Edge," *Scotsman* (Edinburgh), April 14, 2000.
184. See ibid.; Tanya Willmer, "Soldiers' Mothers Pray Their Own Battle Over After Israel Ends Its Vietnam," *Agence France Presse*, May 24, 2000; and Bill Maxwell, "Good Women Help Bring War's End," *Albany Times Union*, June 5, 2000.
185. Quoted from the Hezbollah website, which appeared in the Israeli daily newspaper *Yediot Aharonot* on December 16, 1998, and is cited by Tsfati and Weimann, "www.terrorism.com: Terror on the Internet," 315.
186. Quoted in Tsfati and Weimann, "www.terrorism.com: Terror on the Internet," 325.
187. Ibid., 325–26; "Hizbullah's Cyber-Success," *Foreign Report* (London), no. 2527 (January 14, 1999): 4–5.
188. Alessandra Stanley, "Top Kurd's Arrest Unleashes Rioting All Across Europe," *New York Times*, February 17, 1999; Thomas W. Lippman, "Capture of Kurd Spurs Rage in Europe," *Washington Post*, February 17, 1999.
189. Amberin Zaman, "Swords Into Rabbit Ears," *Washington Post*, February 4, 1999.
190. Schmid and de Graaf, *Violence as Communication*, 9.
191. Bobby Ghosh, "How Dangerous Is the Cleric Anwar al-Awlaqi?," *Time*, January 13, 2010, http://www.time.com/time/world/article/0,8599,1953426,00.html.
192. Quoted in Scott Shane and Souad Mekhennet, "Imam's Path from Condemning Terror to Preaching Jihad," *New York Times*, May 8, 2010, http://www.nytimes.com/2010/05/09/world/09awlaki.html?pagewanted=all. See also Christopher Heffelfinger, Scott Shane, and Christopher Boucek, Carnegie Endowment for International Peace—Transcript, "The Rise of Anwar al-Awlaki," June 1, 2010, http://www.carnegieendowment.org/events/?fa=eventDetail&id=2920.
193. Ghosh, "How Dangerous Is the Cleric Anwar al-Awlaki?"
194. Quoted in "Anwar al Awlaqi: '44 Ways to Support Jihad,'" *The NEFA Foundation*, February 5, 2009.

195. Peter Bergen and David Sterman, "The Man Who Inspired the Boston Bomb-ings," cnn.com, April 11, 2014, http://www.cnn.com/2014/04/11/opinion/bergen -boston-bombing-awlaki-jihadists/.

196. Dennis MacEoin, "Anwar al-Awlaki: "I Pray That Allah Destroys America," *Middle East Quarterly* 17, no. 2 (Spring 2010): 13–19, http://www.meforum.org /2649/anwar-al-awlaki-pray-allah-destroys-america.

197. Jerome P. Bjelopera and Mark A. Randol, *American Jihadist Terrorism: Com-bating a Complex Threat—CRS Report for Congress* (Washington, D.C., Septem-ber 20, 2010, CRS 7-5700, R41416), 72; Eric Schmitt and Eric Lipton, "Focus on Internet Imams as Recruiters for al-Qaeda," *New York Times*, January 1, 2010, http://www.nytimes.com/2010/01/01/us/01imam.html.

198. Christopher Heffelfinger, Scott Shane, and Christopher Boucek, "The Rise of Anwar al-Awlaqi."

199. Bjelopera and Randol, *American Jihadist Terrorism*, 15; MacEoin, "Anwar al-Awlaqi: 'I Pray That Allah Destroys America'"; Schmitt and Lipton, "Focus on Internet Imams as Recruiters for al-Qaeda"; and Robert F. Worth, "Cleric in Yemen Admits Meeting Airliner Plot Suspect, Journalist Says," *New York Times*, February 1, 2010.

200. Bjelopera and Randol, *American Jihadist Terrorism*, 15; Shane and Mekhennet, "Imam's Path from Condemning Terror to Preaching Jihad"; Yochi J. Dreazen and Evan Perez, "Suspect Cites Radical Imam's Writings," *Wall Street Journal*, May 2010.

201. Gordon Rayner, John Bingham, and Duncan Gardham, "Roshonara Choudry: Model Student Inflamed by a Web Preacher Stabbed MP 'to Avenge Iraqis,'" *Daily Telegraph* (London), November 3, 2010; "Woman Jailed for Life for Attack on MP Stephen Timms," BBC Mobile News, November 3, 2010, http://www.bbc .co.uk/news/uk-england-london-11682732.

202. Bjelopera and Randol, *American Jihadist Terrorism*, 14.

203. Ibid., 15.

204. Ibid., 15, 72.

205. Ibid., 15.

206. Bobby Ghosh, "How Dangerous Is the Cleric Anwar al-Awlaqi?," *Time*, Janu-ary 13, 2010, http://www.time.com/time/world/article/0,8599,1953426,00.html; Scott Shane, "Born in U.S., a Radical Cleric Inspires Terror Against West," *New York Times*, November 18, 2009.

207. Bergen and David Sterman, "The Man Who Inspired the Boston Bombings."

208. Shane, "Born in U.S., a Radical Cleric Inspires Terror Against West."

209. Ghosh, "How Dangerous Is the Cleric Anwar al-Awlaqi?"

210. Warren Richey, "Anwar al-Awlaqi: ACLU Wants Militant Cleric Taken Off US 'Kill List,'" *Christian Science Monitor*, August 31, 2010.

211. Bjelopera and Randol, *American Jihadist Terrorism*, 19.

212. Ghosh, "How Dangerous Is the Cleric Anwar al-Awlaqi?"

213. Ibid.

214. Schmitt and Lipton, "Focus on Internet Imams as Recruiters for al-Qaeda."

215. Ghosh, "How Dangerous Is the Cleric Anwar al-Awlaqi?"

216. Office of the Director of National Intelligence, *Declassified Key Judgments of the National Intelligence Estimate, "Trends in Global Terrorism: Implications for the United States,"* dated April 2006.

8. The Modern Terrorist Mind-Set: Tactics, Targets, Tradecraft, and Technologies

1. Peter H. Merkl, prologue to *Political Violence and Terror*, ed. Peter H. Merkl (Berkeley: University of California Press, 1986), 8.
2. Quoted in Peter Neuhauser, "The Mind of a German Terrorist," *Encounter* 51, no. 3 (September 1978): 81.
3. Quoted in Richard Drake, *The Aldo Moro Murder Case* (Cambridge, Mass.: Harvard University Press, 1995), 118–19.
4. On the night of November 10, 1938, German storm troopers destroyed virtually every synagogue in Germany and set fire to some seven thousand Jewish businesses. About thirty thousand Jews were arrested and forced into concentration camps. The event takes its name—Kristallnacht—from the broken plate-glass windows of the Jewish-owned stores.
5. Neuhauser, "The Mind of a German Terrorist," 83–84.
6. Baumann's vignette, like the previously discussed 1972 Munich Olympics operation, again underscores how even attacks that fail to achieve their ostensible objective (the successful detonation of a bomb and attendant damage and destruction caused) can nonetheless still accomplish a terrorist group's immediate objectives and therefore just as effectively serve its wider intentions.
7. Quoted in Alison Jamieson, *The Heart Attacked: Terrorism and Conflict in the Italian State* (London: Marion Boyars, 1989), 89.
8. Patrizio Peci, *Io, l'infame* [I, the scoundrel] (Milan: Arnoldo Mondadori, 1983), 46.
9. "RAF Philosophy," in *The German Guerrilla: Terror, Reaction, and Resistance* (Sanday, Orkney: Cienfuegos, n.d.), 98–99.
10. Quoted in Eileen MacDonald, *Shoot the Women First* (New York: Random House, 1991), 11.
11. Quoted in Peter Taylor, *Provos: The IRA and Sinn Fein* (London: Bloomsbury, 1997), 201.
12. David McKittrick, *Despatches from Belfast* (Belfast: Blackstaff, 1989), 77.
13. Patrick Bishop and Eamonn Mallie, *The Provisional IRA* (London: Heinemann, 1987; paperback ed., London: Corgi, 1989), 387.
14. Robert W. White, "The Irish Republican Army: An Assessment of Sectarianism," *Terrorism and Political Violence* 9, no. 1 (Spring 1997): 44.
15. "But Basques Aren't Irish," *Economist*, July 20, 1996.
16. Quoted in Gerald McKnight, *The Mind of the Terrorist* (London: Michael Joseph, 1974), 26.
17. Quoted in Christopher Dobson, *Black September: Its Short, Violent History* (London: Robert Hale, 1974, 1975), 95.
18. Quoted in McKnight, *The Mind of the Terrorist*, 26.
19. Quoted in Howell Raines, "With Latest Bomb, IRA Injures Its Own Cause," *New York Times*, November 15, 1987.
20. Jacob Shapiro, *The Terrorist's Dilemma: Managing Violent Covert Organizations* (Princeton, N.J.: Princeton University Press, 2013), 187–88. See also Richard English, *Armed Struggle: The History of the IRA* (Oxford: Oxford University Press, 2003), 260.
21. Eamon Collins, with Mick McGovern, *Killing Rage* (London: Granta, 1997), 296.
22. Quoted in MacDonald, *Shoot the Women First*, 5.

23.   See, for example, the compelling autobiographical account of the German neo-Nazi Ingo Hasselbach (with Tom Reiss), *Führer-Ex: Memoirs of a Former Neo-Nazi* (London: Chatto and Windus, 1996).

24.   Quoted in Bill Buford, *Among the Thugs* (London: Mandarin, 1992), 154.

25.   Hasselbach, *Führer-Ex*, 119.

26.   Ibid., 274–75.

27.   See Shapiro, *The Terrorist's Dilemma*, 3, 5–6, 11, 188.

28.   Quoted in McKnight, *The Mind of the Terrorist*, 179.

29.   Ayla H. Schbley, "Religious Terrorists: What They Aren't Going to Tell Us," *Terrorism* 13, no. 3 (Summer 1990): 240.

30.   Quoted in Agence France Presse, "Bomber 'Wanted to Kill Jews,'" *Times* (London), October 15, 1997.

31.   "Sulaimain Abu Ghaith—Statement—13 October 2001," quoted in Ben Venzke and Aimee Ibrahim, *The al-Qaeda Threat: An Analytical Guide to al-Qaeda's Tactics and Targets* (Alexandria, Va.: Tempest, 2003), 109.

32.   "Zarqawi Statement May 20, 2005, Part 1" (English translation), *Jihad Unspun 2005*, May 26, 2005, http://www.jihadunspun.com/newsarchive/article_internal .php?article=102833&list=/newsarchive/index.php&.

33.   Islamic Group in Egypt, "Statement on U.S. Sentencing of Sheikh Rahman," January 19, 1996.

34.   Leila Khaled, *My People Shall Live: The Autobiography of a Revolutionary* (London: Hodder and Stoughton, 1973), 209.

35.   Quoted in Jamieson, *The Heart Attacked*, 271.

36.   Peci, *Io, l'infame*, 46.

37.   David Rapoport, "Terrorism," in *Routledge Encyclopedia of Government and Politics*, ed. Mary Hawkesworth and Maurice Kogan (London: Routledge, 1992), 2:1067.

38.   Quoted in Bonnie Cordes, "When Terrorists Do the Talking: Reflections on Terrorist Literature," in ""Inside Terrorist Organizations," ed. David C. Rapoport, special issue, *Journal of Strategic Studies* 10, no. 4 (December 1987): 155.

39.   Quoted in "Inside the Red Brigades," *Newsweek*, May 15, 1978.

40.   Abu Iyad with Eric Rouleau, *My Home, My Land: A Narrative of the Palestinian Struggle*, trans. Linda Butler Koseoglu (New York: Times Books, 1981), 226.

41.   Quoted in David Blundy, "Inside the IRA," *Sunday Times* (London), July 3, 1977.

42.   Quoted in M. L. R. Smith, *Fighting for Ireland? The Military Strategy of the Irish Republican Movement* (London: Routledge, 1995), 224.

43.   Quoted in Patricia G. Steinhoff, "Portrait of a Terrorist: An Interview with Kozo Okamoto," *Asian Survey* 16, no. 9 (September 1976): 844–45.

44.   Quoted in I. Fetscher and G. Rohrmoser, *Analysen zum Terrorismus* [Analyses on the subject of terrorism], vol. 1, *Ideologien und Strategien* [Ideologies and strategies] (Bonn: Westdeutscher Verlag, 1981), 327.

45.   Gudrun Ensslin, "Statement of 19 January 1976," in *Red Army Faction, Texte der RAF* [RAF texts] (Malmö, Sweden: Verlag Bo Cavefors, 1977), 345.

46.   Jane Alpert, *Growing Up Underground* (New York: William Morrow, 1981), 141, 175.

47.   Michael "Bommi" Baumann, *Terror or Love? Bommi Baumann's Own Story of His Life as a West German Urban Guerrilla*, trans. Helene Ellenbogen and Wayne Parker (New York: Grove Press, 1979), 49.

48. Anonymous, "Notes for the First Analysis of the Phenomenon of Terrorism of the Right" (unpublished study commissioned by the Italian secret services, n.d.), 2.

49. Franco Ferracuti and Francesco Bruno, "Psychiatric Aspects of Terrorism in Italy" (unpublished study commissioned by the Italian secret services, n.d.), 18, 20.

50. Susan Stern, *With the Weathermen: The Personal Journey of a Revolutionary Woman* (Garden City, N.Y.: Doubleday, 1975), 90 (emphasis added). In her memoir, Alpert describes similar discussions and frustrations giving way to action. See *Growing Up Underground*, 140–41, 155.

51. "RAF Philosophy," 99–100. Alpert similarly recalls how her lover and fellow terrorist, Sam Melville, quickly reached the point at which he was fed up with talk and ready for action: "Sam, after a few days, dispensed with theorizing and got down to what interested him: hideouts, disguises, dynamite, plastique, secret communiques." See Alpert, *Growing Up Underground*, 155.

52. Menachem Begin, *The Revolt: Story of the Irgun* (Jerusalem: Steimatzky, 1977), 46.

53. Khaled, *My People Shall Live*, 110.

54. Quoted in Peter Taylor, *States of Terror: Democracy and Political Violence* (London: Penguin, 1993), 159.

55. Hasselbach, *Führer-Ex*, 272.

56. Patrick Seale, *Abu Nidal: A Gun for Hire* (New York: Random House, 1992), 57. See also, Shapiro, *The Terrorist's Dilemma*, 11, 45–46, 48, 76, 270.

57. Collins, *Killing Rage*, 177.

58. Quoted in Michael Seufert, "Dissension Among the Terrorists: Killing People Is Wrong," *Encounter* 51, no. 3 (September 1978): 84.

59. Neuhauser, "The Mind of a German Terrorist," 82–83. Heckler and Koch is a leading German weapons manufacturer, producing "top of the line" handguns, submachine guns, and other small arms.

60. Quoted in Stefan Aust, *The Baader-Meinhof Group: The Inside Story of a Phenomenon* (London: Bodley Head, 1987), 97.

61. Quoted in Jillian Becker, *Hitler's Children: The Story of the Baader-Meinhof Gang* (London: Panther Books, 1978), 90.

62. Quoted in ibid., 244.

63. Observation by Dr. Sue Ellen Moran, a RAND consultant, in April 1985.

64. Neuhauser, "The Mind of a German Terrorist," 85.

65. Stern, *With the Weathermen*, 41.

66. Collins, *Killing Rage*, 363.

67. Quoted in Taylor, *States of Terror*, 125.

68. Quoted in MacDonald, *Shoot the Women First*, 198.

69. Quoted in McKnight, *The Mind of the Terrorist*, 180.

70. Klein specifically recalls that when the German newsmagazine *Der Spiegel* serialized a book about Carlos written by an English journalist—presumably Colin Smith's *Carlos: Portrait of a Terrorist* (London: Andre Deutsch, 1976)—he "kept all the articles and had them translated." Jean Marcel Bougereau, "Memoirs of an International Terrorist: Conversations with Hans Joachim Klein," in *The German Guerrilla: Terror, Reaction, and Resistance* (Sanday, Orkney: Cienfuegos, n.d.), 38.

71. Quoted in Bougereau, "Memoirs of an International Terrorist: Conversations with Hans Joachim Klein," 36.

72. James Bone and Alan Road, "Terror by Degree," *The Times Magazine* (London), October 18, 1997.

73. See, e.g., David Hearst, "Publicity Key Element of Strategy," *Guardian* (London), July 31, 1990, and David Pallister, "Provos Seek to 'Play Havoc with British Nerves and Lifestyle,'" *Guardian* (London), July 31, 1990.

74. Quoted in Bougereau, "Memoirs of an International Terrorist," 12, 39.

75. Quoted in James Brooke, "Newspaper Says McVeigh Described Role in Bombing," *New York Times*, March 1, 1997. See also the extended discussion of McVeigh's motivation in this respect in Lou Michel and Dan Herbeck, *American Terrorist: Timothy McVeigh and the Oklahoma City Bombing* (New York: Regan, 2001), 169.

76. Quoted in Oriana Fallaci, "Interview with George Habash," *Life Magazine*, June 12, 1970.

77. Collins, *Killing Rage*, 65–66.

78. Quoted in "Bombs Blast a Message of Hate," *Life Magazine*, March 27, 1970.

79. Peter Bergen, *Holy War, Inc.: Inside the Secret World of Osama bin Laden* (New York: Free Press, 2001), 86, 132; National Commission on Terrorist Attacks Upon the United States, *The 9/11 Commission Report: Authorized Edition* (New York: Norton, 2004), 261.

80. *The 9/11 Commission Report*, 152–53.

81. Abdul Azziz al-Moqrin, "Covert Work Groups," *Mu'askar al-Battar* [Camp al-Battar], no. 6; Saif al-Adel, "Outlines for Planning a Surveillance Operation," *Camp al-Battar*, no. 9; Saif al-Adel, "Military Sciences: The Planning of Operations," *Camp al-Battar*, no. 11; and Saif al-Adel, "Intelligence: How to Set-up an Intelligence Network," *Camp al-Battar*, no. 20; www.mawsuat.com /index.html (accessed June 14, 2005).

82. David Omand, *Securing the State* (New York: Columbia University Press, 2010), 16.

83. See Frederick Kempe, "Deadly Survivors: The Cold War Is Over but Leftist Terrorists in Germany Fight On," *Wall Street Journal*, December 27, 1991.

84. Quoted in Adrian Bridge, "German Police Search for Red Army Faction Killers," *Independent* (London), April 6, 1991.

85. Quoted in Kempe, "Deadly Survivors."

86. Quoted in Edward Gorman, "How to Stop the IRA," *Times* (London), January 11, 1992.

87. Quoted in William E. Schmidt, "Protestant Gunmen Are Stepping Up the Violence in Northern Ireland," *New York Times*, October 29, 1991.

88. Alan Cullison, "Inside Al-Qaeda's Hard Drive," *Atlantic Monthly* 294, no. 2 (September 2004): 61.

89. Keith Johnson et al., "British Police Fear More Attacks by Terrorists: Lack of Clues, Hard Leads Suggests Bombers Learned from Madrid-Blast Arrests," *Wall Street Journal*, July 8, 2005.

90. Omand, *Securing the State*, 262.

91. "Terrorists Killed by Their Own Devices," *Independent* (London), February 20, 1996.

92.   Quoted in Ian Graham, "Official: IRA Using 'Bigger, Better' Bombs," *London Press Association*, January 23, 1992.

93.   Quoted in Edward Gorman, "Bomb Disposers Mark 21 Years in Ulster," *Times* (London), November 7, 1992.

94.   See, e.g., Maria McGuire, *To Take Arms: A Year in the Provisional IRA* (London: Macmillan, 1973), 62.

95.   Quoted in "Outrage Not a Reason for Inaction," *Manchester Guardian* (international edition), October 21, 1984.

96.   Interview, North Armagh, Northern Ireland, August 1992.

97.   C. Wright Mills, *The Power Elite* (London: Oxford University Press, 1956), 171.

98.   Quoted in "Don't Spoil the Party," *Economist*, July 13, 1996.

9. Terrorism Today and Tomorrow I: Force Multipliers

1.   Radiological terrorism involves *contamination* with readily available radioactive materials, such as those used in medicine and commerce, as compared with nuclear terrorism, which implies an explosion caused by the chain reaction created by fissionable materials.

2.   For reasons of clarity and precision, the term CBRN is preferred to the more commonly used yet potentially misleading term "weapons of mass destruction," or WMD. With the exception of nuclear weapons, none of these unconventional weapons by itself is, in fact, capable of wreaking mass destruction, at least not in structural terms. Indeed, the terminology "weapons of mass casualties" may be a more accurate depiction of the potentially lethal power that could be unleashed by chemical, biological, or nonexplosive radiological weapons. The distinction is more than rhetorical; it is critical to understanding the vastly different levels of technological skills and capabilities, weapons expertise, production requirements, and dissemination or delivery methods needed to undertake an effective attack using either chemical or biological weapons in particular. See Advisory Panel to Assess Domestic Response Capabilities for Terrorism Involving Weapons of Mass Destruction, *First Annual Report to the President and the Congress* (Washington, D.C.: RAND Corporation, December 15, 1999), ii–iii.

3.   Daniel Byman, *Deadly Connections: States That Sponsor Terrorism* (Cambridge: Cambridge University Press, 2005), 4.

4.   This list of state sponsors of terrorism was mandated by the Export Administration Act of 1979 to identify and report to Congress "countries that have repeatedly provided state support for international terrorism." See U.S. Department of State, Office of the Coordinator for Counterterrorism, *Patterns of Global Terrorism 1996* (Washington, D.C.: U.S. Department of State, Publication 10433, April 1997), v, and U.S. Department of State, Bureau of Counterterrorism and Countering Violent Extremism, "Chapter 3: State Sponsors of Terrorism," *Country Reports on Terrorism 2015*, http://www.state.gov/j/ct/rls/crt/2015/257520.htm (accessed May 11, 2016).

5.   Patrick Seale, *Abu Nidal: A Gun for Hire* (New York: Random House, 1992), 202–5.

6.   Robert Fisk, "Abu Nidal, Notorious Palestinian Mercenary, 'Was a US Spy,'" *Independent*, October 24, 2008, http://www.independent.co.uk/news/world/middle-east/abu-nidal-notorious-palestinian-mercenary-was-a-us-spy-972812.html.

7.   Counter Terrorist Unit, *New Jersey State Police: Kikumura Investigation—A Case Study* (PowerPoint presentation, n.d.).

8.   Justin McCurry, "Founder of Japan's Red Army in Final Appeal for Freedom," *Guardian*, December 12, 2008, https://www.theguardian.com/world/2008/dec/13/japan-fusako-shigenobu-red-army.

9.   Quoted in Magnus Ranstorp, *Hizb'allh in Lebanon: The Politics of the Western Hostage Crisis* (Basingstoke: Macmillan, 1997), 38.

10.   The sharpened tip of the umbrella contained ricin, a poison derived from castor beans that is ranked third in toxicity, behind only plutonium (which is used in thermonuclear weapons) and botulism. Before he died, Markov told doctors that a man had bumped into him on Westminster Bridge and had casually apologized for poking Markov with his umbrella. Traces of the poison pellet concealed in the umbrella were discovered in Markov's thigh. See Christopher Andrew and Oleg Gordievsky, *KGB: The Inside Story* (New York: HarperCollins, 1990), 64–65.

11.   Michael Binyon and Michael Theodoulou, "Bounty on Rushdie Raised to $2.5M," *Times* (London), February 13, 1997. In 1992, the bounty had been raised to $2 million. See Reuters, "$2 Million Reward for Death of Rushdie Repeated by Iran," *New York Times*, June 18, 1992.

12.   For the most detailed accounts of the plot to kill the pope, who as a staunch Polish nationalist, head of the Roman Catholic Church, and ardent proponent of civil liberties and religious freedoms, had supposedly incurred the unswerving enmity of the Kremlin. See Paul B. Henze, *The Plot to Kill the Pope* (New York: Scribner's, 1983), and Claire Sterling, *The Time of the Assassins* (New York: Holt, Rinehart, and Winston, 1983). For a different interpretation, see Ugur Mumcu, *Papa-Mafya-Agca* [Pope, mafia, Agca] (Ankara: Tekin Yayinevi, 1984).

13.   C. Christine Fair, *Fighting for the End: The Pakistan Army's Way of War* (Oxford: Oxford University Press, 2014), 16–17, 217, 227, 243–60.

14.   U.S. Department of State, "State Sponsors of Terrorism," http://www.state.gov/j/ct/list/c14151.htm (accessed May 11, 2016).

15.   See Karen Gardela and Bruce Hoffman, *The RAND Chronology of International Terrorism for 1987* (Santa Monica, Calif.: RAND Corporation, R-4006-RC, 1991), 7.

16.   See "IRA: The Libyan Connection," *Economist*, March 31, 1990. See also James Adams and Liam Clarke, "War Without End," *Sunday Times*, June 17, 1990; Edward Gorman, "Libyan Arms Shipments Allow IRA to Maintain Campaign of Violence," *Times*, March 7, 1991; Robert Cottrell, "French Court Told of Huge Libyan Arms Run by IRA," *Independent*, January 8, 1991; and David McKittrick, "Voyage Into Business of Terror," *Independent*, January 12, 1991.

17.   Gardela and Hoffman, *The RAND Chronology of International Terrorism for 1987*, 6.

18.   U.S. Department of State, Office of the Coordinator for Counterterrorism, *Patterns of Global Terrorism 1996*, 25.

19.   A 193-count federal grand jury indictment presented in Washington, D.C., charged the two Libyans with specifically executing the bombing of Pan Am Flight 103 by placing a suitcase containing the bomb on board a flight originating

in Malta that would be subsequently transferred to the ill-fated Pan Am aircraft. See U.S. District Court for the District of Columbia, United States of America v. Abdel Basset Ali al-Megrahi and Lamen Khalifa Fhimah, November 14, 1991.

20. Marlise Simons, "Lockerbie Bomber Loses Appeal and Begins Sentence," *New York Times*, March 15, 2002.

21. "Lockerbie Bomber Abdelbaset al-Megrahi Dies in Tripoli," *BBC News*, May 20, 2012, http://www.bbc.com/news/world-africa-18137896.

22. U.S. Department of State, Bureau of Counterterrorism and Countering Violent Extremism, "Chapter 3: State Sponsors of Terrorism." *Country Reports on Terrorism 2015*.

23. U.S. Department of State, Office of the Coordinator for Counterterrorism, *Patterns of Global Terrorism 1996*, 23–24.

24. Douglas Jehl, "Iran Tells the Europeans That It Doesn't Back Terrorism," *New York Times*, March 8, 1996.

25. Ronen Bergman, *The Secret War with Iran: The 30-Year Clandestine Struggle Against the World's Most Dangerous Terrorist Power* (New York: Free Press, 2008), 170–84. See also Alexei Barrionuevo, "Inquiry on 1994 Blast at Argentina Jewish Center Gets New Life," *New York Times*, July 17, 2009, http://www.nytimes.com/2009/07/18/world/americas/18argentina.html.

26. William Drozdiak, "EU Recalls Envoys as Iran Is Found Guilty of Terror," *International Herald Tribune* (Paris), April 11, 1997. See also Roya Hakakian, *Assassins of the Turquoise Palace* (New York: Grove, 2011).

27. Quoted in Tom Rhodes, "Sanctions on Iran 'a Failure,'" *Times*, October 13, 1995.

28. The remaining questions regarding the PFLP-GC and Syria's involvement in the Pan Am Flight 103 bombing are documented in Roy Rowan, "Pan Am 103: Why Did They Die?," *Time*, April 27, 1992. See also David Hoffman, "Reports Renew Suspicions of Iran, Syria Bomb Link," *Washington Post*, April 26, 1992; Kathy Evans and Richard Norton-Taylor, "Spain Checks Syrian Link to Lockerbie," *Times*, June 6, 1992; and David Twersky, "The Risks of Cozying Up to Syria," *New York Times*, July 28, 1992.

29. Jonathan Steele, "How Yarmouk Refugee Camp Became the Worst Place in Syria," *Guardian*, March 5, 2015, https://www.theguardian.com/news/2015/mar/05/how-yarmouk-refugee-camp-became-worst-place-syria.

30. U.S. Department of State, Office of the Coordinator of Counterterrorism, *Country Reports on Terrorism 2004*, 90. See also John Ward Anderson, "7 Arrested in Tel Aviv Bombing: Syrian-Based Leaders of Islamic Jihad Assert Responsibility," *Washington Post*, February 27, 2005.

31. See, for example, Eric Schmitt, "Don't Aid Zarqawi, U.S. Warns Iraqi Neighbors," *New York Times*, June 2, 2005; John Hendren, "Rumsfeld Tells Nations Not to Help Zarqawi," *Los Angeles Times*, June 2, 2005; John F. Burns, "Iraq's Ho Chi Minh Trail," *New York Times*, June 5, 2005; Ghaith Abdul-Ahad, "Outside Iraq but Deep in the Fight: A Smuggler of Insurgents Reveals Syria's Influential, Changing Role," *Washington Post*, June 8, 2005; and Steven R. Weisman, "White House Escalates Its Campaign to Isolate Syria," *New York Times*, June 23, 2005.

32. See, for example, Steven R. Weisman, "U.S. Has 'Credible' Word of Syrian Plot to Kill Lebanese," *New York Times*, June 10, 2005; Sam F. Ghattas, "Syria Foes to Control Lebanon's Parliament," *Washington Post*, June 21, 2005; and John

402 9. Terrorism Today and Tomorrow I

Kifner, "Anti-Syria Alliance Claims Victory in Lebanese Voting," *New York Times*, June 20, 2005.

33. "Hezbollah Linked to Burgas Bus Bombing," *BBC News*, February 5, 2015, http://www.bbc.com/news/world-europe-21342192.

34. R. James Woolsey, *Testimony Before the U.S. House of Representatives, Committee on National Security*, February 12, 1998, https://www.loyola.edu/departments/academics/political-science/strategic-intelligence/intel/19980212woolsey.html.

35. Brian Michael Jenkins, *International Terrorism: The Other World War* (Santa Monica, Calif.: RAND Corporation, R-3302-AF, November 1985), 12.

36. For example, it was reported in 1979 that German Red Army Faction terrorists were being trained in the use of bacteriological weapons at Palestinian camps in Lebanon. Additional information about the group's reputed interests in this respect came to light as a result of a police raid of an RAF safe house in Paris that uncovered a miniature laboratory containing a culture of *Clostridium botulinum*, used to create a botulinum toxin, alongside earlier threats by the group to poison water supplies in twenty German towns if three radical lawyers were not permitted to defend an imprisoned RAF member. Subsequent investigation, however, revealed that these efforts likely never occurred. For the most authoritative account and analysis, see Terence Taylor and Tim Trevan, "The Red Army Faction (1980)," in *Toxic Terror: Assessing Terrorist Use of Chemical and Biological Weapons*, ed. Jonathan B. Tucker (Cambridge, Mass.: MIT Press, 2000), 107–13.

37. See "Violence: A Buyer's Market," *Jane's Defence Weekly*, May 12, 1990, 909–11. A similar report is detailed in W. Seth Carus, *Bioterrorism and Biocrimes: The Illicit Use of Biological Agents in the 20th Century* (Washington, D.C.: Center for Counterproliferation Research, National Defense University, March 1999), 175–76.

38. The attack—like Aum's five years later—was relatively crude, thus again suggesting the impediments to mounting more sophisticated operations employing CBRN weapons. In this instance, several large drums of the chemical were transported from a nearby paper mill and positioned around the camp's perimeter. When the wind currents were judged right, the attackers released the gas, which wafted into the camp. The use of this weapon was verified personally by the author, who visited the destroyed encampment in December 1997 and saw the drums of chlorine gas used in the attack, which had been left on the outskirts of the camp. It was further confirmed in the course of in-depth interviews with more than a dozen serving or retired senior Sri Lankan military commanders (including an officer who was present at the East Kiran camp when the attack occurred), intelligence officials, police officers, and captured LTTE cadre conducted in Colombo, Jaffna, and Batticaloa, Sri Lanka, by the author in December 1997 and January 2000. See Bruce Hoffman, "The First Non-State Use of a Chemical Weapon in Warfare: The Tamil Tigers' Assault on East Kiran," *Small Wars and Insurgencies* 20, no. 3 (September 2009): 463–77.

39. Admittedly, these were only those incidents or plots that we both *definitely* knew about and that had also been reported in open, published sources.

40. See, for example, the studies conducted by the RAND Corporation during the 1970s for Sandia National Laboratories, and in particular, Gail Bass et al., *Motivations and Possible Actions of Potential Criminal Adversaries of U.S. Nuclear*

Programs (Santa Monica, Calif.: RAND Corporation, R-2554-SL, February 1980).

41.   See, for example, the discussion in Peter deLeon, Bruce Hoffman, and Konrad Kellen, *The Threat of Nuclear Terrorism: A Reexamination* (Santa Monica, Calif.: RAND Corporation, N-2706, January 1988), 4–6.

42.   Walter Laqueur, *Terrorism* (London: Weidenfeld and Nicolson, 1977), 231.

43.   Jeffrey D. Simon, *Terrorists and the Potential Use of Biological Weapons: A Discussion of Possibilities* (Santa Monica, Calif.: RAND Corporation, R-3771-AFMIC, December 1989), 12.

44.   Robert L. Beckman, "Rapporteur's Summary," in *Nuclear Terrorism: Defining the Threat*, ed. Paul Leventhal and Yonah Alexander (Washington, D.C.: Pergamon-Brassey's, 1986), 13.

45.   Ibid.

46.   Brian M. Jenkins, "Is Nuclear Terrorism Plausible?," in Alexander and Leventhal, *Nuclear Terrorism*, 31.

47.   Brian Michael Jenkins, "International Terrorism: A New Mode of Conflict," in *International Terrorism and World Security*, ed. David Carlton and Carlo Schaerf (London: Croom Helm, 1975), 15.

48.   Brian Jenkins, "Will Terrorists Go Nuclear?," California Seminar on Arms Control and Foreign Policy, paper no. 64 (Los Angeles: Crescent, 1975), also published under the same title as P-5541 (November 1975) in the RAND Corporation Paper series, 6–7.

49.   J. Bowyer Bell, *A Time of Terror: How Democratic Societies Respond to Revolutionary Violence* (New York: Basic Books, 1978), 121.

50.   Brian Michael Jenkins, *The Likelihood of Nuclear Terrorism* (Santa Monica, Calif.: RAND Corporation, P-7119, July 1985), 6.

51.   Walter Laqueur, *The Age of Terrorism* (Boston: Little, Brown, 1987), 319.

52.   See, for instance, "Remarks by the President [William Jefferson Clinton] to 17th Annual Legislative Conference of the International Association of Fire Fighters," Washington, D.C., March 15, 1999, 3, http://www.usia.gov/topical/ pol/terror /99031502.html, where President Clinton explained:

> Since 1996, the number of weapons of mass destruction threats called in to fire fighters, police and the FBI has increased fivefold. The threat comes not just from conventional weapons, like the bomb used in Oklahoma City, but also from chemical weapons, like the nerve gas agent that killed 12, but injured thousands in Tokyo, in the subway, just four years ago; and even from biological weapons that could spread deadly disease before anyone even realized that attack has occurred. I have been stressing the importance of this issue, now, for some time. As I have said repeatedly, and I want to say again to you, I am not trying to put any American into a panic over this, but I am determined to see that we have a serious, deliberate, disciplined, long-term response to a legitimate potential threat to the lives and safety of the American people.

53.   Direct examination of Brian Parr, United States of America v. Ramzi Ahmed Yousef and Eyad Ismoil, S1293CR.180 (KTD), October 22, 1997, 4721, cited in John V. Parachini, "The World Trade Center Bombers (1993)," in *Toxic Terror: Assessing Terrorist Use of Chemical and Biological Weapons*, ed. Jonathan B. Tucker (Cambridge, Mass.: MIT Press, 2000), 202n78. In fact, excluding visitors,

only approximately fifty thousand persons actually worked in each tower. See Dennis Cauchon, "For many on Sept. 11, survival was no accident," *USA Today*, December 20, 2001, http://usatoday30.usatoday.com/news/sept11/2001/12/19/usatcov-wtcsurvival.htm.

54. Walter Laqueur, "Postmodern Terrorism," *Foreign Affairs* 75, no. 5 (September/October 1996): 34.

55. See the contemporary accounts of the explanation for the strike by Barbara Crossette et al., "U.S. Says Iraq Aided Production of Chemical Weapons in Sudan," *New York Times*, August 25, 1998; Michael Evans, "Iraqis Linked to Sudan Plant," *Times* (London), August 25, 1998; James Risen, "New Evidence Ties Sudanese to Bin Laden, U.S. Asserts," *New York Times*, October 4, 1998; and Gregory L. Vistica and Daniel Klaidman, "Tracking Terror," *Newsweek*, October 19, 1998. See also the "insider" account published by two members of President Clinton's National Security Council staff, Daniel Benjamin and Steven Simon, *The Age of Sacred Terror* (New York: Random House, 2002), 259–62, 353–65.

56. George Tenet, *At the Center of the Storm: My Years at the CIA* (New York: HarperCollins, 2007), 260.

57. John Parachini, "Putting WMD Terrorism Into Perspective," *Washington Quarterly* 26, no. 4 (Autumn 2003): 44.

58. E-mail correspondence with author, November 17, 2013.

59. See Graham Allison, *Nuclear Terrorism: The Ultimate Preventable Catastrophe* (New York: Times Books, 2004), 3; Peter Bergen, "The Bin Laden Trial: What Did We Learn?," *Studies in Conflict and Terrorism* 24, no. 6 (November/December 2001): 431; Tenet, *At the Center of the Storm*, 261; Benjamin Weiser, "U.S. Says Bin Laden Aide Tried to Get Nuclear Material," *New York Times*, September 26, 1998; and Michael Grunwald, "U.S. Says Bin Laden Sought Nuclear Arms," *Washington Post*, September 26, 1998.

60. "A Muslim Bomb, December 1998" (bin Laden interview with) in Bruce Lawrence, ed., *Messages to the World: The Statements of Osama Bin Laden* (London: Verso, 2005), 72. See also Ben Venzke and Aimee Ibrahim, *The al-Qaeda Threat: An Analytical Guide to al-Qaeda's Tactics and Targets* (Alexandria, Va.: Tempest, 2003), 52. Tenet, *At the Center of the Storm*, 261.

61. "Osama bin Laden—Interview—23 December 1998, Rahimullah Yusufzai Interview," in Venzke and Ibrahim, *The al-Qaeda Threat*, 53.

62. Tenet, *At the Center of the Storm*, 262–64, 268, and Allison, *Nuclear Terrorism*, 20–23.

63. Allison, *Nuclear Terrorism*, 23.

64. Quoted in Ron Suskind, *The One Percent Doctrine: Deep Inside America's Pursuit of Its Enemies Since 9/11* (New York: Simon & Schuster, 2006), 62, and in Tenet, *At the Center of the Storm*, 264.

65. Suskind, *The One Percent Doctrine*, 62.

66. Report of a Committee of Privy Counsellors, *The Report of the Iraq Inquiry (Chilcot Report): Executive Summary* (London: Williams Lea Group on behalf of the Controller of Her Majesty's Stationery Office, HC 264, July 6, 2016), 10, http://www.iraqinquiry.org.uk/media/246416/the-report-of-the-iraq-inquiry_executive-summary.pdf.

67. CNN, "Live from Afghanistan—Was Al Qaeda Working on a Super Bomb?," January 24, 2004, http://www.isis-online.org/publications/terrorism/transcript.html.

68. Tenet, *At the Center of the Storm*, 272.

69. See ibid., 274; Dafna Linzer, "Nuclear Capabilities May Elude Terrorists, Experts Say," *Washington Post*, December 29, 2004; and "Bin Laden Seeking Nukes," *Toronto Star*, November 24, 2004.

70. Tenet, *At the Center of the Storm*, 102, 260; John Parachini, "Putting WMD Terrorism Into Perspective," *Washington Quarterly* 26, no. 4 (Autumn 2003): 44; and Edward M. Spiers, *A History of Chemical and Biological Weapons* (London: Reaktion Books, 2010), 141–43.

71. See Crossette et al., "U.S. Says Iraq Aided Production of Chemical Weapons in Sudan"; Michael Evans, "Iraqis Linked to Sudan Plant"; James Risen, "New Evidence Ties Sudanese to Bin Laden, U.S. Asserts"; and Gregory L. Vistica and Daniel Klaidman, "Tracking Terror." See also Benjamin and Simon, *The Age of Sacred Terror*, and the account in Tenet, *At the Center of the Storm*, 102.

72. Quoted in Alan Cullison, "Inside Al-Qaeda's Hard Drive," *Atlantic Monthly* 294, no. 2 (September 2004): 62. See also Spiers, *A History of Chemical and Biological Weapons*, 141.

73. Tenet, *At the Center of the Storm*, 260; Alan Sipress, "Key Player in Nuclear Trade Ring Found Hospitable Base in Malaysia," *Washington Post*, February 24, 2004; Spiers, *A History of Chemical and Biological Weapons*, 141; and Judith Miller, "U.S. Has New Concerns About Anthrax Readiness," *New York Times*, December 28, 2003.

74. Eric Lipton, "Qaeda Letters Are Said to Show Pre-9/11 Anthrax Plans," *New York Times*, May 21, 2005.

75. Barton Gellman, "Al Qaeda Near Biological, Chemical Arms Production," *Washington Post*, March 23, 2003.

76. Ibid.; Spiers, *A History of Chemical and Biological Weapons*, 141; and Joby Warrick, "An Al Qaeda 'Chemist' and the Quest for Ricin," *Washington Post*, May 5, 2004.

77. Alan Cowell, "One Conviction in Plot to Spread Deadly Toxins, but 8 Go Free," *New York Times*, April 13, 2005.

78. Information provided by British authorities.

79. Duncan Campbell and Rosie Cowan, "Ricin Plot: Terror Trail That Led from Algeria to London," *Guardian*, April 14, 2005.

80. See "The Many Names of Danger Man Bourgass," *Manchester Evening News*, April 15, 2005; "Pack of Lies Told by a Ruthless Killer," *Manchester Evening News*, April 15, 2005; "Ricin Plot: The Bourgass Case—How the Parties Compare," *Guardian*, April 15, 2005; Neville Dean and Nick Allen, "Mosque's Terrorist Roll Call," *Press Association Newswire*, February 7, 2006; Spiers, *A History of Chemical and Biological Weapons*, 142; and John Steele and Sue Clough, "How Jihad Network's Tentacles Reached the Back Streets of Gloucester," *Daily Telegraph* (London), April 14, 2005.

81. "CHRONOLOGY—Britain's Thwarted Chemical Attack Plot," Reuters, April 14, 2005. See also Rosie Cowan and Duncan Campbell, "Detective Murdered by an Obsessive Loner," *Guardian*, April 14, 2005; Karen McVeigh, "Killer and the

Chemical Weapons Factory in a Kitchen," *Scotsman* (Edinburgh), April 14, 2005; Kate Southern, "Terror Plot Man Had Wood Green Base," *Newsquest Media Group Newspapers*, April 15, 2005; "Terror Police Find Deadly Poison," *BBC News World Edition*, January 7, 2003, http://www.bbc.co.uk/2/hi/uk_news/2636099.stm; and James Tourgout, "Killer Was on the Run in Weymouth," *Newsquest Media Group Newspapers*, April 15, 2005.

82. During the trial, evidence was presented that scientists working at the British Ministry of Defence's chemical warfare laboratories at Porton Down in Wiltshire were able to produce enough ricin and cyanide using Bourgass's recipes to kill hundreds of people if properly employed. McVeigh, "Killer and the Chemical Weapons Factory in a Kitchen, April 14, 2005.

83. Ibid. See also Ben English, "Plot to Poison London," *Herald Sun* (Victoria, Australia), April 15, 2005, and "Man Admits UK-US Terror Bomb Plot," *BBC News*, October 12, 2006, http://newsvote.bbc.co.uk/mpapps/pagetools/print/news.bbc.co.uk/2/hi/uk_news/6044.

84. Michael Isikoff and Mark Hosenball, "Terror Watch: What Ricin? Colin Powell and British Authorities Pointed to a Poison Lot as Justification for the War on Iraq. But a Jury Says the Case Didn't Add Up," *Newsweek Web Exclusive*, April 13, 2005.

85. Southern, "Terror Plot Man Had Wood Green Base."

86. Quoted in Roddy Ashworth, "Ricin Gang Targeted Heathrow Express," *The Express on Sunday*, April 17, 2005.

87. Southern, "Terror Plot Man Had Wood Green Base."

88. Jenny Booth, "Profile: True Identity of Ricin Plotter Remains a Mystery," *Times*, April 13, 2005, http://www.timesonline.co.uk/printFriendly/0,,1-2-1567904-2,00.html. See also Rosie Cowan and Duncan Campbell, "Detective Murdered by an Obsessive Loner," *Guardian*, April 14, 2005; McVeigh, "Killer and the Chemical Weapons Factory in a Kitchen"; and Tourgout, "Killer Was on the Run in Weymouth."

89. McVeigh, "Killer and the Chemical Weapons Factory in a Kitchen."

90. Eric Schmitt and Thom Shanker, *Counterstrike: The Untold Story of America's Secret Campaign Against Al Qaeda* (New York: Henry Holt, 2011), 225–26.

91. See, among other credible reports, Karen Hodgson, "Threat Matrix: Reports Claim Al Nusrah Front Members in Turkey Were Planning Sarin Gas Attacks," *Long War Journal*, May 31, 2013, http://www.longwarjournal.org/threat-matrix/archives/2013/05/on_may_30_the_turkish-print.php.

92. Yishai Karov and Ari Soffer, "Revealed: Israel Holding Senior Al Qaeda Operative," *Israel National News*, November 17, 2013, http://www.israelnationalnews.com/News/News.aspx/174122#.UolAzSeIiuI.

93. Ted Thornhill, "Has ISIS Looted Chemical Weapons from a Former Iraqi Nerve Agent Factory That the US Failed to Destroy," *Daily Mail*, October 15, 2014, http://www.dailymail.co.uk/news/article-2793731/will-rusting-chemical-weapons-cache-ignored-americans-fall-isis-hands-iraq-claims-2-500-rockets-containing-deadly-sarin-hands-terrorists.html.

94. John Parachini, "Putting WMD Terrorism Into Perspective," *Washington Quarterly* 26, no. 4 (Autumn 2003): 39.

95. Spiers, *A History of Chemical and Biological Weapons*, 23–24.

96. David C. Rapoport, "Terrorism and Weapons of the Apocalypse," *National Security Studies Quarterly* 5, no. 3 (Summer 1999): 52–54.

97. W. Seth Carus, "Bioterrorism and Biocrimes: The Illicit Use of Biological Agents Since 1900," working paper (Washington, D.C.: Center for Counterproliferation Research, National Defense University, February 2001, Revision), v, 10, 11, 21.

98. Two attempts were made with anthrax and seven with botulinum toxin. W. Seth Carus, *Bioterrorism and Biocrimes: The Illicit Use of Biological Agents in the Twentieth Century* (Washington, D.C.: Center for Counterproliferation Research, National Defense University, March 1999), 62.

99. Chemical attacks are, however, arguably easier to detect and to contain (e.g., localize), because biological infection occurs without notice and is usually followed by an incubation period during which victims unknowingly spread the contagion.

100. Anthony G. Macintyre et al., "Weapons of Mass Destruction: Events with Contaminated Casualties—Effective Planning for Health Care Facilities, *Journal of the American Medical Association*, no. 263 (January 2000): 242–49.

101. Quoted in "Police Killer and His Plot to Poison Britain," *Scotsman* (Edinburgh), April 14, 2005, http://www.scotsman.com/news/uk/police-killer-and -his-plot-to-poison-britain-1-707843.

102. "Man Admits UK-US Terror Bomb Plot," *BBC News*, October 12, 2006, http:// newsvote.bbc.co.uk/mpapps/pagetools/print/news.bbc.co.uk/2/hi/uk_news /6044. See also Alan Cowell, "British Muslim Sentenced in Terror Attacks," *New York Times*, November 8, 2006.

103. Gretel Sarmiento, "Former AMI Building Declared Free of Anthrax Contamination," *Palm Beach Post*, February 8, 2007, http://www.ph.ucla.edu/epi/bioter /formeramibldganthraxfree.html.

104. Leonard A. Cole, *The Anthrax Letters: A Medical Detective Story* (Washington, D.C.: Joseph Henry, 2003), 215–17.

105. See Graham T. Allison et al., *Avoiding Nuclear Anarchy: Containing the Threat of Loose Russian Nuclear Weapons and Fissile Material* (Cambridge, Mass.: MIT Press, 1996), 57–61; Bruce Hoffman, with David Claridge, "Illicit Trafficking in Nuclear Materials," *Conflict Studies*, nos. 314/315 (London: Research Institute for the Study of Conflict and Terrorism, January/February 1999); and Robert S. Litwak, *Rogue States and U.S. Foreign Policy: Containment After the Cold War* (Washington, D.C.: Woodrow Wilson Center Press, 2000), 158–238.

106. Spiers, *A History of Chemical and Biological Weapons*, 175.

107. Video prepared by the General Intelligence Directorate, Hashemite Kingdom of Jordan (n.d.). See also Jamal Halaby, "Zarqawi Among 13 Indicted by Jordan in Plot: Officials Say Militants Planned to Attack Premier's Office, U.S. Embassy in Amman," *Washington Post*, October 18, 2004.

10. Terrorism Today and Tomorrow II: New and Continuing Challenges

1. J. Bowyer Bell, *The Dynamics of the Armed Struggle* (London: Frank Cass, 1998), viii.

2. Efraim Benmelech and Claude Berrebi, "Human Capital and the Productivity of Suicide Bombers," *Journal of Economic Perspectives* 21, no. 3 (Summer 2007): 224, 230, and Ariel Merari, *Driven to Death: Psychological and Social Aspects*

of Suicide Terrorism (Oxford: Oxford University Press, 2010), 69. See also Jodi Wilgoren, "After the Attacks: The Hijackers: A Terrorist Profile Emerges That Confounds the Experts," *New York Times*, September 15, 2001.

3. Merari, *Driven to Death*, 69. See also Alan B. Krueger and Jitka Malecková, "Education, Poverty and Terrorism: Is There a Causal Connection?," *Journal of Economic Perspectives* 17, no. 4 (Fall 2003): 131–33.

4. Robert Pape, *Dying to Win: The Strategic Logic of Suicide Terrorism* (New York: Random House, 2005), 208.

5. Joseph Felter and Brian Fishman, *Al-Qa'ida's Foreign Fighters in Iraq: A First Look at the Sinjar Records* (West Point, N.Y.: U.S. Military Academy, Combating Terrorism Center, 2007), 16.

6. Antonio Giustozzi, *Koran, Kalashnikov, and Laptop: The Neo-Taliban Insurgency in Afghanistan* (New York: Columbia University Press, 2008), 38.

7. Marc Sageman, *Leaderless Jihad: Terror Networks in the Twenty-First Century* (Philadelphia: University of Pennsylvania Press, 2008), 58.

8. Neil Ferguson and Eve Binks, "Understanding Radicalization and Engagement in Terrorism Through Religious Conversion Motifs," *Journal of Strategic Security* 8, nos. 1–2 (Spring/Summer 2015): 17.

9. Walter Laqueur, *Terrorism* (London: Weidenfeld and Nicolson, 1977), 20.

10. Peter Bergen, *The Osama bin Laden I Know: An Oral History of al Qaeda's Leader* (New York: Free Press, 2006), 2, 49–53, 87–92. See also Steve Coll, *The Bin Ladens: An Arabian Family in the American Century* (New York: Penguin, 2008), 302.

11. Martin Chulov, "Abu Bakr al-Baghdadi Emerges from Shadows to Rally Islamist Followers," *Guardian*, July 6, 2014, https://www.theguardian.com/world/2014/jul/06/abu-bakr-al-baghdadi-isis; Tim Arango and Eric Schmitt, "U.S. Actions in Iraq Fueled Rise of a Rebel," *New York Times*, August 10, 2014, http://www.nytimes.com/2014/08/11/world/middleeast/us-actions-in-iraq-fueled-rise-of-a-rebel.html?_r=0; and Anthony Shadid, "Iraqi Insurgent Group Names New Leaders," *New York Times*, May 16, 2010, http://atwar.blogs.nytimes.com/2010/05/16/iraqi-insurgent-group-names-new-leaders/?_php=true&_type=blogs&_r=0.

12. Jane Perlez and Ismail Khan, "Taliban Truce Seems in Flux in Pakistan," *New York Times*, February 2, 2009.

13. "In the Face of Chaos," *Economist*, February 21, 2009, 28.

14. See Walter Laqueur, *The Age of Terrorism* (Boston: Little, Brown, 1987), 7; Walter Laqueur, *The New Terrorism: Fanaticism and the Arms of Mass Destruction* (New York: Oxford University Press, 1999), 8; and Claude Berrebi, "Evidence About the Link Between Education, Poverty and Terrorism Among Palestinians," *Peace Economics, Peace Science and Public Policy* 13, no. 1 (2007): 5–7.

15. See, for instance, Scott Atran, "Who Wants to Be a Martyr," *New York Times*, May 5, 2003; "Poverty 'Fuelling Terrorism,'" *BBC News*, March 22, 2002; and Nicholas D. Kristof, "Behind the Terrorists," *New York Times*, May 7, 2002.

16. *Online Newshour*, "President Bush's Speech at the United Nations Financing for Development Conference," Monterrey, Mexico, March 22, 2002, PBS.org, http://www.pbs.org/newshour/updates/march02/bush_3-22.html.

17. See Eli Berman, *Radical, Religious and Violent: The New Economics of Terrorism* (Cambridge, Mass.: MIT Press, 2009), 152–53; Alan B. Krueger, *What Makes*

a Terrorist (Princeton, N.J.: Princeton University Press, 2007), 1–3, 6–7; John Horgan, *Walking Away from Terrorism: Accounts of Disengagement from Radical and Extremist Movements* (London: Routledge, 2009), 3; Jytte Klausen et al., "Toward a Behavioral Model of 'Homegrown' Radicalization Trajectories," *Studies in Conflict and Terrorism* 39, no. 1 (January 2016): 79; Alan B. Krueger and David D. Laitin, "*Kto Kogo*? A Cross-Country Study of the Origins and Targets of Terrorism," (unpublished paper, January 18, 2007), 5, http://krueger.princeton.edu/files/terrorism4.pdf; Tim Krieger and Daniel Meirerrieks, "What Causes Terrorism?," *Public Choice* 147, no. 3 (2011): 10; and Fernanda Llussa and Jose Tavares, "Economics and Terrorism: What We Know, What We Should Know, and the Data We Need," in *Terrorism, Economic Development, and Political Openness*, ed. Philip Keefer and Norman Loayza (New York: Cambridge University Press, 2008), 237–38.

18. Walter Laqueur, *No End to War: Terrorism in the Twenty-First Century* (New York: Continuum, 2003), 18.

19. Ibid.

20. Peter Bergen, *Holy War, Inc.: Inside the Secret World of Osama bin Laden* (New York: Free Press, 2001), 47.

21. Chulov, "Abu Bakr al-Baghdadi Emerges from Shadows to Rally Islamist Followers."

22. Peter Hart, *The I.R.A. and Its Enemies: Violence and Community in Cork, 1916–1923* (Oxford: Oxford University Press, 2000), 131. See also p. 155.

23. Frank Gervasi, *The Life and Times of Menachem Begin: Rebel to Statesman* (New York: G.P. Putnam's Sons, 1979), 88, and Eitan Haber, *Menachem Begin: The Legend and the Man* (New York: Delacorte, 1978), 37.

24. Alan Hart, *Arafat: A Political Biography; The Definitive Biography Written in Cooperation with Yasser Arafat* (London: Sidgwick and Jackson, 1994), 61, 106.

25. Edmund L. Andrews and John Kifner, "George Habash, Palestinian Terrorism Tacticians, Dies at 82," *New York Times*, January 27, 2008.

26. "Palestinian Biography: Wadi Haddad," *Palestine History.com*, http://www.palestinehistory.com/biography/palestine/palbio53.htm (accessed February 10, 2010).

27. Laqueur, *No End to War*, 16.

28. This conforms to the observation about the differences between leaders and foot soldiers joining contemporary jihadi movements described by Peter Nesser, "Joining Jihadi Terrorist Cells in Europe: Exploring Motivational Aspects of Recruitment and Radicalization," in *Understanding Violent Radicalisation: Terrorist and Jihadist Movements in Europe*, ed. Magnus Ranstorp (London: Routledge, 2010), 88.

29. Ibid., 17.

30. The five most serious terrorist incidents between 1993 and 2005 were the 1993 World Trade Center bombing; the 1998 bombings of the U.S. embassies in Kenya and Tanzania; the September 11, 2001, attacks; the 2002 Bali, Indonesia, nightclub bombings; and the 2005 bombings of London transport targets. See Peter Bergen and Swati Pandey, "The Madrassa Scapegoat," *Washington Quarterly* 29, no. 2 (Spring 2006): 117–18.

31. Peter Bergen and Swati Pandey, "The Madrassa Myth," *New York Times*, June 14, 2005.

32. Bergen and Pandey, "The Madrassa Scapegoat," 118. These findings dovetail with those of *Leaderless Jihad: Terror Networks in the Twenty-First Century* (Philadelphia: University of Pennsylvania Press, 2008), 58–59, and *Understanding Terror Networks* (Philadelphia: University of Pennsylvania Press, 2004), 74–78.

33. Bergen and Pandey, "The Madrassa Myth."

34. Diego Gambetta and Steffen Hertog, *Engineers of Jihad: The Curious Connection Between Violent Extremism and Education* (Princeton, N.J.: Princeton University Press, 2016), viii, 3–7.

35. Ibid., 8–11. See also 24–26, 33, 67–70, 128.

36. Ibid., 32.

37. "Swansea Student Links to Bin Laden," *BBC News*, September 18, 2001, http://news.bbc.co.uk/2/hi/uk_news/wales/1549539.stm.

38. Susan Candiotti et al., "Suspected 9/11 Mastermind Graduated from U.S. University," *CNN.com/U.S.*, December 19, 2002, http://edition.cnn.com/2002/US/South/12/19/al.qaeda.aggie/.

39. Adam Nossiter, "Lonely Trek to Radicalism for Terror Suspect," *New York Times*, January 16, 2010, http://www.nytimes.com/2010/01/17/world/africa/17abdulmutallab.html?hp.

40. David Berreby, "Idea Lab: Engineering Terror," *New York Times Sunday Magazine*, September 10, 2010, http://www.nytimes.com/2010/09/12/magazine/12FOB-IdeaLab-t.html?scp=1&sq=Berreby&st=cse&_r=0.

41. Lawrence Wright, *The Looming Tower: Al-Qaeda and the Road to 9/11* (New York: Alfred A. Knopf, 2006), 42.

42. Duncan Campbell et al., "Mastermind Based Abroad Suspected of Guiding Plot," *Guardian*, July 4, 2007, and Kevin Sullivan and Karla Adam, "Terrorism Threat Level in Britain Is Lowered," *Washington Post*, July 5, 2007.

43. The terrorists were Dr. Mohammed Asha, age 26; Dr. Mohammed Haneef, age 27 (cousin of Kafeel Ahmed); Dr. Sabeel Ahmed, 26; wife of Asha; two unidentified trainee MDs, ages 28 and 25; and Khafeel Ahmed, PhD, age 27. It was Abduallah and Khafeel Ahmed, the brother of Sabeel, who crashed a Jeep Cherokee into Glasgow Airport. "Bomb Plot: Arrests and Releases," *BBC News*, October 5, 2007, http://news.bbc.co.uk/2/hi/uk_news/6264230.stm. See also Serge F. Kovaleski and Alan Cowell, "London Bombers Sped to Glasgow, Authorities Say," *New York Times*, July 6, 2007; Karla Adam and Kevin Sullivan, "Glasgow Suspect Angered by Iraq War, Relative Says," *Washington Post*, July 6, 2007, http://www.washingtonpost.com/wp-dyn/content/article/2007/07/05/AR2007070501862.html; Victoria Burnett and Alissa J. Rubin, "Doctor Accused in Glasgow Attack Described as Loner Angry About the Iraq War," *New York Times*, July 5, 2007; and Raymond Bonner, Jane Perlez, and Eric Schmitt, "British Inquiry of Failed Plots Points to Iraq's Qaeda Group," *New York Times*, December 14, 2007.

44. Quoted in Adam and Sullivan, "Glasgow Suspect Angered by Iraq War, Relative Says."

45. Craig Whitlock, "Trail from London to Leeds Yields Portraits of 3 Bombers: Identities Revealed, but Motives Still a Mystery," *Washington Post*, July 15, 2005.

46. Intelligence and Security Committee, *Report Into the London Terrorist Attacks on 7 July 2005: Presented to Parliament by the Prime Minister by Command of Her Majesty*, Cmd 6785, May 2006, 13–14. See also Paul Stokes and Nick Britten,

"The Cricket-Loving Terrorist Whose Father Runs the Local Chip Shop," *Daily Telegraph* (London), July 14, 2005, and Ian Herbert and Arifa Akbar, "Shahzad Tanweer: 'I Cannot Begin to Explain This. He Was Proud to Be British,'" *Independent*, July 14, 2005.

47. Intelligence and Security Committee, *Report Into the London Terrorist Attacks on 7 July 2005*, 13–14.

48. Assaf Moghadam, *The Globalization of Martyrdom: Al Qaeda, Salafi Jihad, and the Diffusion of Suicide Attacks* (Baltimore: Johns Hopkins University Press, 2008), 218.

49. Ibid., 3, and Bernard-Henri Lévy, *Who Killed Daniel Pearl?* (Hoboken, N.J.: 2003), 84.

50. Sageman, *Leaderless Jihad*, 3–7.

51. Shiv Malik, "NS Profile—Omar Sharif," *New Statesman*, April 24, 2006, http://www.newstatesman.com/200604240017.

52. Ed Husain, *The Islamist: Why I Joined Radical Islam in Britain, What I Saw Inside and Why I Left* (London: Penguin, 2007), 263–64.

53. Ibid., 132.

54. Sean O'Neill, "The Eight in the Dock: The Men Who Appeared at Woolwich Crown Court Over a Six-Month Period in the Liquid Bomb Trial Which Finished Yesterday," *Times* (London), September 9, 2008, http://143.252.148.161/tol/news/uk/crime/article4707712.ece.

55. Krueger and Malecková, "Education, Poverty and Terrorism," 119–44.

56. Ibid., 137.

57. Ibid., 131–33.

58. Ibid., 135. See also Berrebi, "Evidence About the Link Between Education, Poverty and Terrorism Among Palestinians."

59. Merari, "Driven to Death," 74–75.

60. Interview with the author, Jerusalem, December 17, 2002.

61. See, for instance, Andreas Freytag et al., "The Origins of Terrorism: Cross-Country Estimates of Socio-economic Determinants of Terrorism," *European Journal of Political Economy*, no. 27 (2011): 514.

62. Paul J. White, *Primitive Rebels or Revolutionary Modernizers? The Kurdish National Movement in Turkey* (London: Zed Books, 2001), 155–56.

63. Martin van Bruinessen, *Kurdish Ethno-nationalism Versus Nation-Building States* (Istanbul: Isis, 2000), 235.

64. Quoted in Mohammed Hafez, *Suicide Bombers in Iraq: The Strategy and Ideology of Martyrdom* (Washington, D.C.: USIP, 2007), 174–75. See also Felter and Fishman, *Al-Qa'ida's Foreign Fighters in Iraq*, 7–8, and Reuven Paz, "Arab Volunteers Killed in Iraq: An Analysis," *PRISM Series of Global Jihad* 3, no. 1 (March 2005): 5, http://www.e-prism.org/pages/4/index.htm.

65. Alexander interrogated over 300 detainees himself and supervised the interrogations of some 1,000 others. Matthew Alexander, with John R. Bruning, *How to Break A Terrorist: The U.S. Interrogators Who Used Brains, Not Brutality to Take Down the Deadliest Man in Iraq* (New York: Free Press, 2008), 124, 219–20.

66. Tom Bowman, "U.S. Offers Training, Pay as It Frees Iraqi Detainees," *Morning Edition, NPR News*, May 16, 2008, http://www.npr.org/templates/story/story.php?storyId=90506939.

67. Giustozzi, *Koran, Kalashnikov, and Laptop*, 40. See also Nasreen Ghufran, "Afghanistan in 2007: A Bleeding Wound," *Asian Survey* 48, no. 1 (January/February 2008): 155, 163.
68. Interview with author, PRT commander of A. O. Saber, in Asadabad, Kunar, Afghanistan, March 8, 2008.
69. Intelligence and Security Committee, *Report Into the London Terrorist Attacks on 7 July 2005*, 17–18; Lisette Alvarez, "New Muslim at 15, Terror Suspect at 19," *New York Times*, July 18, 2005; and Alison Pargeter, *The New Frontiers of Jihad: Radical Islam in Europe* (Philadelphia: University of Pennsylvania Press, 2008), 175–76.
70. Pargeter, *The New Frontiers of Jihad*, 175–76.
71. See Olga Craig et al., "What Drove a Boy from Bromley to Become a Suicide Bomber?," *Sunday Telegraph* (London), December 30, 2001; Paul Harris, Nick Paton Walsh, and Burhan Wazir, "The Making of a Terrorist: How a Petty Thief Turned Into a Human Timebomb," *Guardian*, December 30, 2001; and David Leppard, "Al-Qaeda's Heathrow Jet Plot Revealed," *Sunday Times* (London), October 9, 2005.
72. Peter Walker and Vikram Dodd, "Video Tirades That Sealed Case Against Liquid Bomb Plotters," *Guardian*, September 8, 2008, http://en.europenews.dk/Video-tirades-that-sealed-case-against-liquid-bomb-plotters-98106.html.
73. Briefings presented to the author by the Ministry of Home Affairs, Singapore, June 2002 and September 2003. See also, Ministry of Home Affairs, *White Paper: The Jemaah Islamiyah Arrests and the Threat of Terrorism*, Cmd. 2 of 2003, Presented to Parliament by Command of the President of the Republic of Singapore, January 7, 2003, 15.
74. Jamie Bartlett and Carl Miller, "The Edge of Violence: Towards Telling the Difference Between Violent and Non-Violent Radicalization," *Terrorism and Political Violence* 24, no. 1 (2012): 2; Randy Borum, "Radicalization Into Violent Extremism I: A Review of Social Science Theories," *Journal of Strategic Security* 4, no. 4 (Winter 2011): 57; Anja Dalgaard-Nielsen, "Violent Radicalization in Europe: What We Know and What We Do Not Know," *Studies in Conflict and Terrorism* 33, no. 9 (September 2010): 810; and Mohammed Hafez and Creighton Mullins, "The Radicalization Puzzle: A Theoretical Synthesis of Empirical Approaches to Homegrown Extremism," *Studies in Conflict and Terrorism* 38, no. 11 (November 2015): 960–61.
75. Anne Aly and Jason-Leigh Striegher, "Examining the Role of Religion in Radicalization to Violent Islamist Extremism," *Studies in Conflict and Conflict* 35, no. 12 (December 2012): 849–52; John Horgan, "From Profiles to Pathways and Roots to Routes: Perspectives from Psychology on Radicalization Into Terrorism," *Annals of the American Academy of Political and Social Science* 618 (July 2008): 84, 92–93.
76. Peter Neumann, *Briefing Note—Radicalisation, CVE, and Counter-Radicalisation: Core Issues and Questions* (London: International Center for the Study of Radicalisation [ICSR], King's College London, August 8, 2015), 1.
77. Hafez and Mullins, "The Radicalization Puzzle," 962–70. See also the similar arguments and approach of Quintan Wiktorowicz, "Joining the Cause: Al-Muhajiroun and Radical Islam," in *Radicalization: Critical Concepts in Mili-*

tary, Strategic, and Security Studies, ed. Peter Neumann (London: Routledge, 2015), 126–32.

78. Caroline Joan S. Picart, "'Jihad Cool/Jihad Chic': The Roles of the Internet and Imagined Relations in the Self-Radicalization of Colleen LaRose (Jihad Jane)," Societies 5 (2015): 367–73.

79. Sageman, Leaderless Jihad, 86–87, and Sageman, Understanding Terror Networks, 103–13.

80. Rukmini Callimachi, "How a Secretive Branch of ISIS Built a Global Network of Killers," New York Times, August 3, 2016, http://www.nytimes.com/2016/08 /04/world/middleeast/isis-german-recruit-interview.html?utm_source =Sailthru&utm_medium=email&utm_campaign=New%20Campaign&utm _term=*Situation%20Report&_r=0.

81. Cited in Hafez, Suicide Bombers in Iraq, 22.

82. Brian Fishman, ed., Bombers, Bank Accounts, & Bleedout: Al-Qa'ida's Road in and Out of Iraq (West Point, N.Y.: U.S. Military Academy, Combating Terrorism Center, 2008), 45–46.

83. Paz, "Arab Volunteers Killed in Iraq," 5.

84. Hafez, Suicide Bombers in Iraq, 23.

85. Noor Huda Ismail, "The Role of Kinship in Indonesia's Jemaah Islamiya," Terrorism Monitor (Jamestown Foundation, Washington, D.C.) 4, no. 11, (June 2, 2006), http://www.jamestown.org/single/?no_cache=1&tx_ttnews%5Btt _news%5D=791.

86. See Anthony Davis, "Resilient Abu Sayyaf Resists Military Pressure," Jane's Intelligence Review, September 1, 2003, and "Philippines Terrorism: The Role of Militant Islamic Converts," International Crisis Group, December 19, 2005, http://www.crisisgroup.org/en/regions/asia/south-east-asia/philippines/110 -philippines-terrorism-the-role-of-militant-islamic-converts.aspx.

87. Zachary Abuza, Balik-Terrorism: The Return of Abu Sayyaf (Carlisle, Pa.: U.S. Army War College Strategic Studies Institute, September 2005), 7.

88. "Super Ferry 14 Bombing Solved, Says Arroyo," Asian Journal (Los Angeles), June 25–27, 2008.

89. Ahmed Rashid, Taliban: Militant Islam, Oil and Fundamentalism in Central Asia (New Haven, Conn.: Yale University Press, 2001), 35. See also Richard H. Schultz Jr. and Andrea J. Dew, Insurgents, Terrorists, and Militias: The Warriors of Contemporary Combat (New York: Columbia University Press, 2006), 51.

90. Sageman, Leaderless Jihad, 86–87, and Sageman, Understanding Terror Networks, 110, 113.

91. Paz, "Arab Volunteers Killed in Iraq," 5.

92. Hafez, Suicide Bombers in Iraq, 177.

93. Ami Pedahzur, Suicide Terrorism (Cambridge: Polity, 2005), 132.

94. Hart, The I.R.A. and Its Enemies, 210.

95. "Officials: Bombing Suspect Angry Over U.S. Wars Against Muslims," CBS News, April 24, 2013, http://www.cbsnews.com/news/officials-bombing-suspect -angry-over-us-wars-against-muslims/.

96. Gina Bennett, "The Wandering Mujahidin: Armed and Dangerous," Weekend Edition, United States Department of State Bureau of Intelligence and Research, August 21–22, 1993, http://www.nationalsecuritymom.com/3/Wandering

Mujahidin.pdf, and National Commission on Terrorist Attacks Upon the United States, *The 9/11 Commission Report: Authorized Edition* (New York: Norton, 2004), 58.

97.   Quoted in Rachel Revesz, "FBI Director: Crushing Isis in Syria Risks Releasing 'Terrorist Diaspora' Into the West," *Independent*, July 29, 2016, http://www .independent.co.uk/news/world/americas/isis-more-attacks-read-fbi-director -james-comey-terrorist-diaspora-fordham-syria-iraq-a7162426.html. See also the similar comments by Comey from 2014, quoted in Sari Horwitz and Adam Gold-man, "FBI Director: Number of Americans Traveling to Fight in Syria Increas-ing," *Washington Post*, May 2, 2014, https://www.washingtonpost.com/world /nationalsecurity/fbi-director-number-of-americans-traveling-to-fight-in-syria -increasing/2014/05/02/6fa3d84e-d222-11e3-937f-d3026234b51c_story.html.

98.   Joseph Goldstein, "F.B.I. Chief Sees an ISIS 'Diaspora,'" *New York Times*, July 29, 2016.

99.   U.S. House of Representatives Homeland Security Committee, *Final Report of the Task Force on Combating Terrorist and Foreign Fighter Travel*, Septem-ber 2015, 6, 12, https://homeland.house.gov/wp-content/uploads/2015/09/Task ForceFinalReport.pdf.

100.   "Imam Samudra's Son Killed in Syria," *Jakarta Post Online*, October 16, 2015, http://www.thejakartapost.com/news/2015/10/16/imam-samudra-s-son-killed -syria.html. See also "Indonesia: Sons of Jihadists Flock to Syria," *Jakarta Post Online*, March 30, 2015, http://www.thejakartapost.com/news/2015/03/31/sons -jihadists-flock-syria.html.

101.   Eric Schmitt, "U.S. Secures Vast Trove of Intelligence on Islamic State," *New York Times*, July 29, 2016.

102.   James R. Clapper, *Statement for the Record: Worldwide Threat Assessment of the US Intelligence Community*, Senate Armed Services Committee, February 9, 2016, 5, https://www.dni.gov/index.php/newsroom/testimonies/217-congressional -testimonies-2016/1313-statement-for-the-record-worldwide-threat-assessment-of -the-u-s-ic-before-the-senate-armed-services-committee-2016.

103.   Rukmini Callimachi, "How ISIS Built the Machinery of Terror Under Europe's Gaze," *New York Times*, March 29, 2016, https://www.nytimes.com/2016/03/29 /world/europe/isis-attacks-paris-brussels.html.

104.   Rukmini Callimachi, "How a Secretive Branch of ISIS Built a Global Network of Killers," *New York Times*, August 3, 2016; and Jean-Charles Brisard and Kevin Jackson, "The Islamic State's External Operations And The French-Belgian Nexus," *CTC Sentinel* 9, no. 11 (November/December 2016): 8–15.

105.   Abu Bakr al-Baghdadi, "This Is What Allah and His Messenger Had Promised Us," Islamic State Fuqran Media Foundation, November 2, 2016.

106.   "Estimates of the number of non-Afghan volunteers range from 4,000 to 25,000, with Arab fighters making up the majority." Bennett, "The Wandering Mujahi-din," 1–2.

107.   "U.S. intelligence estimates the total number of fighters who underwent in-struction in Bin Laden-supported camps in Afghanistan from 1996 through 9/11 at 10,000 to 20,000." *The 9/11 Commission Report*, 67.

108.   Brian Dodwell, Daniel Milton, and Don Rassler, *The Caliphate's Global Work-force: An Inside Look At the Islamic State's Foreign Fighter Paper Trail* (West Point, NY: U.S. Military Academy, Combating Terrorism Center, April 2016),

9; and Frances Robles, "Trying to Stanch Trinidad's Flow of Young Recruits to ISIS," *New York Times*, February 21, 2017.

109.   *The 9/11 Commission Report*, 67.

110.   Jessica Stern and J. M. Berger, *ISIS: The State of Terror* (New York: HarperCollins, 2015), 99.

111.   Cathy Scott-Clark and Adrian Levy, *The Siege: 68 Hours Inside the Taj Hotel* (London: Penguin, 2013).

112.   Callimachi, "How ISIS Built the Machinery of Terror Under Europe's Gaze."

113.   Theo Padnos, "My Captivity," *New York Times Magazine*, October 29, 2014, http://www.nytimes.com/2014/10/28/magazine/theo-padnos-american-journalist-on-being-kidnapped-tortured-and-released-in-syria.html?_r=0.

114.   Caleb Weiss, "Islamic State Spokesman Again Threatens West in New Speech," *Threat Matrix: A Blog of the Long War Journal*, September 21, 2014, http://www.longwarjournal.org/archives/2014/09/islamic_state_spokesman_again.php.

115.   Jean-Paul Sartre, preface to Frantz Fanon's *The Wretched of the Earth* (London: Penguin, 1990), 17.

116.   Callimachi, "How ISIS Built the Machinery of Terror Under Europe's Gaze."

117.   Quoted in Dana Priest and Susan Schmidt, "Al-Qa'ida's Top Primed to Collapse, U.S. Says," *Washington Post*, March 16, 2003.

118.   See, for example, CNN, "Alleged bin Laden Tape a Call to Arms," http://cnn.com/2003/WORLD/meast/02/11/sprj.irq.wrap (accessed March 3, 2003); and bin Laden's statement, "We want to let you know and confirm to you that this war of the infidels that the US is leading with its allies . . . we are with you and we will fight in the name of God."

119.   David R. Sands, "Al-Qa'ida's Credibility 'On the Line' as War in Iraq Winds Down," *Washington Times*, April 24, 2003. See also Dennis Pluchinsky, "Al-Qa'ida Identity Crisis," *Washington Times*, April 28, 2003.

120.   While both the 2005 London bombings and the 2006 airline bomb have been conclusively linked to Core al-Qaeda, its links to the Madrid attack—though suspected—have never satisfactorily been established. See, for instance, Fernando Reinares, "The Evidence of al-Qa'ida's Role in the 2004 Madrid Attack," *CTC Sentinel* 5, no. 3 (March 2012), http://www.ctc.usma.edu/posts/the-evidence-of-al-qaidas-role-in-the-2004-madrid-attack, and Fernando Reinares, "The Madrid Bombings and Global Jihadism," *Survival* 52, no. 2 (April/May 2010): 83–104.

121.   Juan Zarate, "Winning the War on Terror: Marking Success and Confronting Challenges," text of prepared remarks at the Washington Institute for Near East Policy, Washington, D.C., April 23, 2008, http://www.washingtoninstitute.org/templateC07.php?CID=393.

122.   Alex Spillius, "Demise of al-Qa'eda in Sight, US Official Says," *Telegraph.co.uk| Print version*, May 15, 2008, www.telegraph.co.uk/news/newstopics/uselection2008/democrats/1957428/ Demise-of-al-Qa'eda-in-sight,-US-official-says.html.

123.   Ross Colvin, "Violence in Iraq Falls to Lowest Level in 4 Years," *Reuters*, May 24, 2008, http://www.reuters.com/article/homepageCrisis/idUSCOL462053._CH_.2400.

124.   Joby Warrick, "U.S. Cites Big Gains Against al-Qadea: Group Is Facing Setbacks Globally, CIA Chief Says," *Washington Post*, May 30, 2008.

125.   See, in particular, Scott Shane, "Terrorism Experts Say Focus on al Qaeda Misses a Broader Threat," *New York Times*, August 13, 2006, and the debate in

Bruce Hoffman, "The Myth of Grass-Roots Terrorism: Why Osama bin Laden Still Matters," *Foreign Affairs* 87, no. 3 (May/June 2008): 133–38. See also Marc Sageman and Bruce Hoffman, "Does Osama Still Call the Shots?," *Foreign Affairs* 87, no. 4 (July/August 2008): 163–66.

126. United States District Court Eastern District of New York, United States of America v. Adis Medunjanin, et al., July 7, 2010. See also Nic Robertson, Paul Cruickshank, and Tim Lister, "Document Shows Origins of 2006 Plot for Liquid Bombs on Planes," CNNWorld, April 30, 2012, http://www.cnn.com/2012/04/30/world/al Qaeda-documents/index.html?iref=allsearch. See also Matt Apuzzo and Adam Goldman, *Enemies Within: Inside the NYPD's Secret Spying Unit and Bin Laden's Final Plot Against America* (New York: Simon & Schuster, 2013).

127. U.S. Department of Justice, Office of Public Affairs, "Faisal Shahzad Pleads Guilty in Manhattan Federal Court to 10 Federal Crimes Arising from Attempted Car Bombing in Times Square," June 21, 2010, http://www.justice.gov/opa/pr/2010/June/10-ag-721.html.

128. See, for instance, the November 2006 landmark speech by then–director general of the British Security Service, or MI5, Dame Eliza Manningham-Buller. She explained how upward of thirty terrorist plots and attacks in the United Kingdom "linked back to al Qaeda in Pakistan and through those links al Qaeda gives guidance and training to its largely British foot soldiers here on an extensive and growing scale." Quoted in "Extracts from MI5 Chief's Speech," *BBC News*, November 10, 2006, http://newsvote.bbc.co.uk/mpapps/pagetools/print/news.bbc.co.uk/2/hl/news/6135000.stm.

129. See the exhaustive case studies of these plots collected in Bruce Hoffman and Fernando Reinares, eds., *The Evolution of the Global Terrorist Threat from 9/11 to Osama bin Laden's Death* (New York: Columbia University Press, October 2014).

130. U.S. Department of State, Bureau of Counterterrorism, *Country Reports on Terrorism 2011* (Washington, D.C.: U.S. Department of State Publication, April 2012), 5, http://www.state.gov/documents/organization/195768.pdf.

131. Siobhan Gorman, "CIA Kills al Qaeda's No. 2," *Wall Street Journal*, June 6, 2012; Declan Walsh and Eric Schmitt, "Drone Strike Killed No. 2 in al Qaeda, U.S. Officials Say," *New York Times*, June 5, 2012; and Joby Warrick and Greg Miller, "Al Qaeda's No. 2 Leader Killed in U.S. Airstrike," *Washington Post*, June 5, 2012.

132. Jonathan Masters, "Backgrounder: Targeted Killings," Council on Foreign Relations, April 30, 2012, http://www.cfr.org/counterterrorism/targeted-killings/p9627.

133. Counterterrorism Strategy Initiative, "The Year of the Drone: Leaders Killed" (New America Foundation, 2012), http://counterterrorism.newamerica.net/about/militants.

134. John Yoo, "Obama, Drones and Thomas Aquinas," *Wall Street Journal*, June 8, 2012.

135. U.S. Department of State, *Country Reports on Terrorism 2011*, 5.

136. See, for instance, Peter Bergen, "Time to Declare Victory: Al Qaeda Is Defeated," *CNN: Security Clearance*, June 27, 2012, http://security.blogs.cnn.com/2012/06/27/time-to-declare-victory-al-qaeda-is-defeated-opinion/; Fawaz Gerges, *Obama and the Middle East: The End of America's Moment* (New York: Palgrave Macmillan, 2012), 203–7, 221–25; Thomas F. Lynch III, *The 80 Percent Solution:*

The Strategic Defeat of bin Laden's al Qaeda and Implications for South Asian Security (Washington, D.C.: New America Foundation, February 2012); the Soufan Group, "The Many Faces of al Qaeda," September 5, 2012, http://soufan group.us4.list-manage.com/track/click?u=3fe77a4916f69c37ee2ac1cbe&id =f32f943f7e&e=8e25f1caae; and Clint Watts, "What If There Is No al Qaeda? Preparing for Future Terrorism" (Philadelphia, Pa.: Foreign Policy Research Institute, July 2012), http://www.fpri.org/enotes/2012/201207.watts.alQaeda .html.

137. Nelly Lahoud et al., *Letters from Abbottabad: Bin Laden Sidelined?* (West Point, N.Y.: U.S. Military Academy, Combating Terrorism Center, May 3, 2012).

138. "Osama bin Laden's Last Words Show Dark Days for al Qaeda," *CBS World News*, May 3, 2012, http://www.cbsnews.com/8301-202_162-57426970/osama -bin-ladens-last-words-show-dark-days-for-al Qaeda/. See also, for instance, Peter Baker, "Recovered Bin Laden Letters Show a Divided al Qaeda," *New York Times*, May 3, 2012; Ben Fenton, Johanna Kassel, and Richard McGregor, "Bin Laden Papers Reveal al Qaeda Rifts," *Financial Times* (London), May 3, 2012; and Greg Miller and Peter Finn, "New Osama bin Laden Documents Released," *Washington Post*, May 3, 2012.

139. Sebastian Rotella, "New Details in the bin Laden Docs: Portrait of a Fugitive Micro-Manager," *ProPublica*, May 11, 2011, http://www.propublica.org/article /bin-laden-documents-portrait-of-a-fugitive-micro-manager.

140. "Osama Bin Laden Diary 'Planned Attacks'—US Officials," *BBC News*, May 12, 2011, http://www.bbc.co.uk/news/world-us-canada-13370524.

141. Greg Miller and Karen DeYoung, "Bin Laden's Preoccupation with U.S. Said to Be Source of Friction with Followers," *Washington Post*, May 12, 2011, and Kimberley Dozier, "Officials: Bin Laden Eyed Small Cities as Targets," Associated Press, May 12, 2011, http://news.yahoo.com/s/ap/us_bin_laden.

142. Miller and DeYoung, "Bin Laden's Preoccupation with U.S. Said to Be Source of Friction with Followers."

143. See Mary Habeck, all from *Foreign Policy—Shadow Government: Notes from the Loyal Opposition*, http://shadow.foreignpolicy.com/blog/69526: "Evaluating the War with al Qaeda" (Parts 1–4, March 2, 2012–April 17, 2012), "What Does al Qaeda Want?" (March 6, 2012), "Evaluating the War with al Qaeda" (March 15, 2012), "Answering Objections: Is al Qaeda Really Dead, Part One?" (April 19, 2012), "Al Qaeda: Alive and Kicking" (May 8, 2012), and "Can We Declare the War on al Qaeda Over?" (June 27, 2012). See also Seth G. Jones, "Al Qaeda Is Far from Defeated," *Wall Street Journal*, April 29, 2012; Seth G. Jones, "Think Again: al Qaeda," *Foreign Policy*, May/June 2012, http://www.foreignpolicy.com/ articles/2012/04/23/think_again_al_qaeda?print=yes&hidecomments=yes&pa ge=full; and Bruce Riedel, "Al Qaeda's Arab Comeback: Capitalizing on Chaos in Syria, Mali," *The Daily Beast*, July 30, 2012, http://www.thedailybeast.com /articles/2012/07/30/al Qaeda-s-arab-comeback-capitalizing-on-chaos-in-syria -mali.html.

144. Peter Bergen et al., *Jihadist Terrorism: A Threat Assessment* (Washington, D.C., September 2013), 5, http://cdn.bipartisanpolicy.org/wp-content/uploads/sites /default/files/Jihadist%20Terrorism-A%20Threat%20Assesment_0.pdf.

145. AQAP, for instance, did not follow bin Laden's advice to avoid seizing territory and controlling the populace in areas of Yemen it controlled. See U.S.

Special Operations Command (SOCOM), SOCOM-2012-0000016 and SOCOM-2012-0000018; Lahoud et al., *Letters from Abbottabad*, 2.

146. Daniel Byman, "Splitting al-Qa'ida and Its Affiliates," *Foreign Policy: The AfPak Channel*, July 30, 2012, http://afpak.foreignpolicy.com/posts/2012/07/30/splitting_al_qaida_and_its_affiliates.

147. See U.S. Special Operations Command, SOCOM-2012-0000005, SOCOM-2012-0000006, SOCOM-2012-0000010, SOCOM-2012-0000016, SOCOM-2012-0000017, and SOCOM-2012-0000019.

148. U.S. Special Operations Command, SOCOM-2012-0000013, and Lahoud et al., *Letters from Abbottabad*, 19.

149. U.S. Special Operations Command, SOCOM-2012-0000006.

150. The first of the released CTC documents curiously begins with the serial number SOCOM-2012-0000003: both 0000001 and 0000002 are missing. No explanation is offered for this discrepancy. The author is indebted to Dr. Mary Habeck, formerly of the U.S. National Security Staff, for pointing this out.

151. Jason Burke, "Bin Laden Files Show al-Qaida and Taliban Leaders in Close Contact," *Guardian*, April 29, 2012, http://www.guardian.co.uk/world/2012/apr/29/bin-laden-al-qaida-taliban-contact.

152. Ibid., and Michael Semple, "The Taliban Need Help to Break Their al-Qaida Ties," *Guardian*, April 30, 2012, http://www.guardian.co.uk/commentisfree/2012/apr/30/taliban-al-qaida-ties.

153. Dan Lamothe, "'Probably the Largest' al-Qaeda Training Camp Ever Destroyed in Afghanistan," *Washington Post*, October 30, 2015, https://www.washingtonpost.com/news/checkpoint/wp/2015/10/30/probably-the-largest-al-qaeda-training-camp-ever-destroyed-in-afghanistan/, and Bill Roggio and Thomas Joscelyn, "US Military Strikes Large al Qaeda Training Camps in Southern Afghanistan," *Long War Journal*, October 13, 2015, http://www.longwarjournal.org/archives/2015/10/us-military-strikes-large-al-qaeda-training-camps-in-southern-afghanistan.php.

154. U.S. Special Operations Command, SOCOM-2012-0000003.

155. Ibid.

156. See, for instance, Missy Ryan, "Pentagon Withholds $300 Million in Military Aid to Pakistan," *Washington Post*, August 3, 2016, https://www.washingtonpost.com/world/national-security/pentagon-withholds-300-million-in-military-aid-to-pakistan/2016/08/03/25845d54-5986-11e6-9aee-8075993d73a2_story.html.

157. See U.S. Special Operations Command, SOCOM-2012-0000016, SOCOM-2012-0000017, and SOCOM-2012-0000019.

158. Habeck, "Can We Declare the War on al Qaeda Over?"

159. See Gorman, "CIA Kills al Qaeda's No. 2."

160. See, for example, Gerges, *Obama and the Middle East*, 222–25.

161. See, for instance, al-Zawahiri's series of messages of "Hope and Glad Tidings to Our People in Egypt," in "Zawahiri Releases Ninth Episode in Series on Egypt, Current Events," February 29, 2012, text and translation provided in *SITE Monitoring Service—Jihadist Threat*, as well as Lahoud et al., *Letters from Abbottabad*, 3, 48, 50.

162. U.S. House of Representatives Homeland Security Committee, *Final Report of the Task Force on Combating Terrorist and Foreign Fighter Travel*, 11–12.

163. See Ellen Barry, "Al Qaeda Opens New Branch on Indian Subcontinent," *New York Times*, September 4, 2014, http://www.nytimes.com/2014/09/05/world/asia/al-qaeda-announces-new-branch-on-indian-subcontinent.html?nytmobile =0; Rupam Jain Nair, "5-Indian States on Alert After al Qaeda Announces Local Wing," *Reuters Africa*, September 4, 2014, http://af.reuters.com/article/commoditiesNews/idAFL3N0R51YH20140904?sp=true; Bill Roggio, "Al Qaeda in the Indian Subcontinent Incorporates Regional Jihadi Groups," *Long War Journal*, September 5, 2014, http://www.longwarjournal.org/archives/2014/09/analysis_al_qaeda_in.php.

164. Saleh Nabhan was killed by U.S. commandos in September 2009 and Fazul Abdullah Mohammed was shot at a military checkpoint in Mogadishu in June 2011.

165. U.S. Special Operations Command, SOCOM-2012-0000010. See also Lahoud et al., *Letters from Abbottabad*, 3, 4, 9, 16.

166. "Zawahiri Issues Video in Support of Syrian Uprising," February 11, 2012, and "Libi Speaks on the Plight of Syrians in New Video," June 12, 2012, text and translation provided by *SITE Monitoring Service—Jihadist Threat*. See also "Syria Uprising: al Qaeda's al-Zawahiri Lends Support," *BBC News*, February 12, 2012, http://www.bbc.co.uk/news/world-middle-east-17002573.

167. "Jihadists Discuss Jihad in Syria," February 14, 2012, text and translation provided by *SITE Monitoring Service—Jihadist Threat*.

168. "Jihadists Launch a Syria-Focused Periodical, 'Balagh,'" March 13, 2012, text and translation provided by *SITE Monitoring Service—Jihadist Threat*.

169. "Jihadists Urge Financial Support for Jihad in Syria," *SITE Monitoring Service—Jihadist Threat*, March 2, 2012.

170. Ed Husain, "Syria; Why al Qaeda Is Winning," *National Review Online*, August 23, 2012, http://www.nationalreview.com/articles/314685/syria-why-al Qaeda-winning-ed-husain. See also Radwan Mortada, "Bilad al-Sham: Jihad's Newest Hot Spot," *al Akhbar English*, June 26, 2012.

171. James S. Robbins, "Bin Laden's Vision Thing: Is bin Laden Saying That This Whole Thing Is Warren G. Harding's Fault?," *National Review.com*, October 8, 2001, http://old.nationalreview.com/comment/comment-robbins100801.shtml.

172. Osama bin Laden, "Among a Band of Knights, February 14, 2003," in *Messages to the World: The Statements of Osama Bin Laden*, ed. Bruce Lawrence (London: Verso, 2005), 186–87.

173. See Shaykh ul-Islaam Taqi-ud-Deen Ahmad ibn Taymiyyah, *The Religious and Moral Doctrine of Jihad* (Birmingham, England: Maktabah al Ansaar, 2001).

174. Husain, "Syria: Why al Qaeda Is Winning."

175. Ibid.

176. Ibid.; Dina Temple-Raston, "al-Qaida Eyes Opportunities in Syria," *All Things Considered—National Public Radio*, March 12, 2012, http://www.npr.org/2012/03/12/148467185/al-qaida-leader-eyes-opportunities-in-syria; and Eric Schmitt, "Sunni Extremists May Be Aiding al Qaeda's Ambitions in Syria, Analysts Say," *New York Times*, February 15, 2012.

177. See, for example, Iraqi foreign minister Hoshyar Zebari's statement quoted in Associated Press, "Iraq Says al-Qaida Fighters Flowing into Syria, Dangerous New Element in Fight Against Assad," *Washington Post*, July 5, 2012, and Rod Nordland, "al Qaeda Taking Deadly New Role in Syria Conflict, *New York Times*, July 24, 2012.

178.   Aaron Zelin, "Al-Qaeda Announces an Islamic State in Syria," *Washington Institute*, April, 2013, http://www.washingtoninstitute.org/policy-analysis/view/al-qaeda-announces-an-islamic-state-in-syria.

179.   Stern and Berger, *ISIS: The State of Terror*, 42.

180.   Ibid., 43.

181.   Quoted in Anonymous, *Through Our Enemies' Eyes: Osama Bin Laden, Radical Islam, and the Future of America* (Washington, D.C.: Brassey's, 2002), 6, 31.

182.   Greg Miller and Craig Whitlock, "Caught Between Internal and External Terror Threats, France Struggles to Cope," *Washington Post*, November 14, 2015, https://www.washingtonpost.com/world/national-security/caught-between-internal-and-external-terror-threats-france-struggles-to-cope/2015/11/14/c5e9fab0-8b00-11e5-9a07-453018f9a0ec_story.html.

183.   Bill Roggio and Thomas Joscelyn, "Report: Osama bin Laden Ordered Mumbai-Style Attacks in Europe," *Long War Journal*, October 1, 2010, http://www.longwarjournal.org/archives/2010/10/report_osama_bin_lad_1.php. See also Duncan Gardham and Robert Crilly, "Bin Laden 'Personally Approved' Attacks on Europe," *Daily Telegraph* (London), October 1, 2010; "Osama bin Laden's Nod Was Sought for Mumbai-Style Attacks in Europe: Report," *Economic Times*, March 1, 2015, http://articles.economictimes.indiatimes.com/2015-03-01/news/59642323_1_osama-bin-laden-abbottabad-mumbai-style-attacks; Dina Temple-Raston, "Bin Laden Told Partners to Plan Mumbai-Like Attacks," NPR, September 30, 2010, http://www.npr.org/templates/story/story.php?storyId=130242602.

184.   See Callimachi, "How ISIS Built the Machinery of Terror Under Europe's Gaze," and Callimachi, "How a Secretive Branch of ISIS Built a Global Network of Killers."

185.   U.S. Special Operations Command, SOCOM-2012-0000009.

186.   U.S. Special Operations Command, SOCOM-2012-0000012.

187.   Lisa Barrington and Suleiman Al-Khalidid, "Al Qaeda Offered to Break Ties with Its Branch in Syria as a 'Sacrifice' to Preserve Its Unity," *Business Insider*, July 28, 2016, http://www.businessinsider.com/al-qaeda-offers-to-break-with-nusra-in-syria-2016-7; Dania Akkad, "Nusra Confirms Split with al-Qaeda 'to Protect Syrian Revolution,'" *Middle East Eye*, July 28, 2016, http://www.middleeasteye.net/news/nusra-front-announces-official-split-al-qaeda-520293064; Sarah El Deeb, "Syria Nusra Front Leader Claims to Cut Ties with al-Qa'ida," *Washington Post*, July 28, 2016, https://www.washingtonpost.com/world/middle_east/al-qaida-central-appears-to-ok-split-with-syrian-branch/2016/07/28/865fa322-54c2-11e6-b652-315ae5d4d4dd_story.html; and "Syrian Nusra Front Announces Split from al-Qaeda," *BBC News*, July 29, 2016, http://www.bbc.com/news/world-middle-east-36916606.

188.   Eric Schmitt and David E. Sanger, "As U.S. Focuses on ISIS and the Taliban, Al Qaeda Re-emerges," *New York Times*, December 29, 2016, http://www.nytimes.com/2015/12/30/us/politics/as-us-focuses-on-isis-and-the-taliban-al-qaeda-re-emerges.html?_r=0.

189.   Bill Roggio, "The Seven Phases of the Base," *Long War Journal*, August 15, 2005, http://www.longwarjournal.org/archives/2005/08/the_seven_phase.php, and Yassin Musharbash, "The Future of Terrorism: What al Qaida Really Wants," *Spiegel Online International*, August 12, 2005, http://www.spiegel.de/international/the-future-of-terrorism-what-alqaida-really-wants-a-369448.html.

190. "Declaration of War Against the Americans Occupying the Land of the Two Holy Places," in *Usama bin Laden's al-Qaida: Profile of a Terrorist Network*, ed. Yonah Alexander and Michael S. Swetnam (Ardsley, N.Y.: Transnational, 2001), appendix 1A, p. 19.

191. See, for example, "Text of Bin Laden Remarks: 'Hypocrisy Rears Its Ugly Head,'" *Washington Post*, October 8, 2001.

192. Ibid. See also Anonymous, *Through Our Enemies' Eyes*, 47, 197.

193. Fanon, *The Wretched of the Earth*, 74.

194. Analogy made by the renowned French terrorism expert and criminologist Xavier Raufer, April 2003.

195. See Bruce Hoffman, "The Coming ISIS-al Qaeda Merger: It's Time to Take the Threat Seriously," *Foreign Affairs—Snapshot*, March 29, 2016, https://www.foreignaffairs.com/articles/2016-03-29/coming-isis-al-qaeda-merger.

196. "Zawahiri Calls Fighters to Unite, Attacks IS for Creating and Maintaining Division," SITE Intelligence Group, August 29, 2016, https://news.siteintelgroup.com/Jihadist-News/zawahiri-calls-fighters-to-unite-attacks-is-for-creating-and-maintaining-division.html.

197. "Full Transcript of bin Laden's Speech," al-Jazeera.com, November 1, 2004, http://www.aljazeera.com/archive/2004/11/200849163336457223.html.

Bibliography

Books, Articles, Reports, Statements, and Other Documents

Abdul-Ahad, Ghaith. "Outside Iraq but Deep in the Fight: A Smuggler of Insurgents Reveals Syria's Influential, Changing Role." *Washington Post*, June 8, 2005.

Abi-Habib, Maria. "Jihadists Step Up Recruitment Drive." *Wall Street Journal*, June 26, 2014.

Abu-Amr, Ziad. "Hamas: A Historical and Political Background." *Journal of Palestinian Studies* 23, no. 4 (Summer 1993): 5–19.

Abuza, Zachary. *Balik-Terrorism: The Return of Abu Sayyaf.* Carlisle, Pa.: U.S. Army War College Strategic Studies Institute, September 2005.

"An Accion Zapatista Report—Zapatistas in Cyberspace: A Guide to Analysis and Resources." http://www.eco.utexas.edu/faculty/Cleaver/zapsincyber.html. Accessed June 14, 2005.

Adam, Karla and Kevin Sullivan. "Glasgow Suspect Angered by Iraq War, Relative Says." *Washington Post*, July 6, 2007. http://www.washingtonpost.com/wp-dyn/content /article/2007/07/05/AR2007070501862.html.

Adams, James. *The Financing of Terror.* New York: Simon & Schuster, 1986.

——. "The Role of the Media." In *Ethnic Conflict and Regional Instability: Implications for U.S. Policy and Army Roles and Mission*, edited by Robert L. Pfaltzgraff Jr. and Richard H. Schultz, 161–69. Carlisle, Pa.: U.S. Army Strategic Studies Institute, 1994.

——. *Secret Armies: Inside the American, Soviet, and European Special Forces.* New York: Atlantic Monthly, 1987.

Adams, James and Liam Clarke. "War Without End." *Sunday Times* (London), June 17, 1990.

Advisory Panel to Assess Domestic Response Capabilities for Terrorism Involving Weapons of Mass Destruction. *First Annual Report to the President and the Congress.* Washington, D.C.: RAND Corporation, December 15, 1999.

Agence France Presse. "Al-Qaeda Firebrand Threatens New Attacks on US, Taunts Bush: Television." February 24, 2004.

——. "Bomber 'Wanted to Kill Jews.'" *Times* (London), October 15, 1997.

——. "Eta Driven from Internet." *Times* (London), February 20, 1996.

Ahmad, Hisham H. *Hamas: From Religious Salvation to Political Transformation; The Rise of Hamas in Palestinian Society.* Jerusalem: Passia, 1994.

Akkad, Dania. "Nusra Confirms Split with al-Qaeda 'to Protect Syrian Revolution.'" *Middle East Eye,* July 28, 2016. http://www.middleeasteye.net/news/nusra-front-announces-official-split-al-qaeda-520293064.

al-Adel, Saif. "Intelligence: How to Set-up an Intelligence Network." *Camp al-Battar Magazine,* no 20, (2003). www.mawsuat.com/index.html. Accessed June 14, 2005.

——. "Military Sciences: The Planning of Operations." *Camp al-Battar Magazine,* no. 11 (2003). www.mawsuat.com/index.html. Accessed June 14, 2005.

——. "Outlines for Planning a Surveillance Operation." *Camp al-Battar Magazine,* no. 9, 2003. www.mawsuat.com/index.html. Accessed June 14, 2005.

Al-Arabi al-Jadid. "Iraqi, Syrian Sources Say ISIL Executes 30 Prominent Members for 'Treason,' 'Desertion.'" December 24, 2014.

Alden, Robert. "Terrorism Issue Taken Up at UN." *New York Times,* November 10, 1972.

Alexander, Matthew, with John R. Bruning. *How to Break a Terrorist: The U.S. Interrogators Who Used Brains, Not Brutality to Take Down the Deadliest Man in Iraq.* New York: Free Press, 2008.

Alexander, Yonah and Richard Latter, eds. *Terrorism and the Media.* McLean, Va.: Brassey's, 1990.

Alexander, Yonah and Michael S. Swetnam. *Usama bin Laden's al-Qaida: Profile of a Terrorist Network.* Ardsley, N.Y.: Transnational, 2001.

al-Jazeera.com. "Full transcript of bin Laden's speech." November 1, 2004. http://www.aljazeera.com/archive/2004/11/200849163336457223.html.

al-Jazeera.net. "Arab World—Full Transcript of bin Laden's Speech." November 1, 2004. http://englishaljazeera.net/NR/exeres/79C6AF22−98FB-4A1C-B21F-2BC36E87F61F.htm.

Allen-Mills, Tony. "McVeigh Trial Leaves Militia Riddle Unsolved." *Sunday Times* (London), June 15, 1997.

——. "Real-Life Rambo Meets His Match in Schoolyard." *Sunday Times* (London), October 6, 1996.

Allison, Graham. *Nuclear Terrorism: The Ultimate Preventable Catastrophe.* New York: Times Books, 2004.

Allison, Graham T., Owen R. Cote Jr., Richard A. Falkenrath, and Steven E. Miller. *Avoiding Nuclear Anarchy: Containing the Threat of Loose Russian Nuclear Weapons and Fissile Material.* Cambridge, Mass.: MIT Press, 1996.

Al-Madkhalee, Shaykh Muhammad Ibn Haadee. "The Reality of Daesh (ISIS)." August 24, 2015. http://www.miraathpublications.net/en/the-reality-of-daesh-ISIS/.

al-Moqrin, Abdul Azziz. "Covert Work Groups." *Mu'askar al-Battar,* no. 6 (2003). www.mawsuat.com/index.html. Accessed June 14, 2005.

Alpert, Jane. *Growing Up Underground.* New York: William Morrow, 1981.

"Al-Qa'ida Leader Begins 'Islamic Spring Series,' Calls ISIL Amir 'Renegade,' Praises Al-Nusrah Front." Twitter, September 9, 2015, TRN2015091004392901.

Al-Qa'ida Organization Addresses a Message to Iraqi, Islamic Peoples (Internet) www .alfjr.com in Arabic." Posting by "Ayn al-Haqiqah," March 5, 2003, titled "The al-Qa'ida Organization Writes a Letter to the Iraqi People" in "Issues of the Islamic Nation" section of chat room at http://www.alfjr.com.

Al-Sharq al-Awsat (London). "Syrian Activist Says ISIL Executed All Members of Cell Plotted Coup." December 23, 2014.

Al-Taee, Awadh and Steve Negus. "Now Showing (Despite Official Warnings): 'Mujahideen Movie.'" *Financial Times* (London), February 16, 2005.

Alvarez, Lisette. "New Muslim at 15, Terror Suspect at 19." *New York Times*, July 18, 2005.

Aly, Anne and Jason-Leigh Striegher. "Examining the Role of Religion in Radicalization to Violent Islamist Extremism." *Studies in Conflict and Terrorism* 35, no. 12 (December 2012): 849–62.

Al-Zaman. "Hamas' Mishal: Jihad Palestinians' Sole Option." November 23, 2000, FBIS-NES, Document ID: GMP 20001123000110.

al-Zawahiri, Ayman. *Knights Under the Prophet's Banner: Meditations on the Jihadist Movement.* Translated and published in FBIS (Foreign Broadcast Information Service), "Al-Sarq Al-Aswat Publishes Extracts from Al-Jihad Leader al-Zawahiri's New Book." Document ID GMP20020108000197, December 2, 2001.

Al-Zayyat, Montasser. *The Road to Al-Qaeda: The Story of Bin Laden's Right-Hand Man.* London: Pluto, 2004.

Ambler, John Steward. *The French Army in Politics, 1945–1962.* Columbus: Ohio State University Press, 1966.

American Broadcasting Companies (ABC). *Nightline.* October 7, 1993.

American Civil Liberties Union. "NSA Surveillance." https://www.aclu.org/issues /national-security/privacy-and-surveillance/nsa-surveillance. Accessed June 10, 2016.

Ana al-Muslim Network. "ISIL Executes Members of 'Awakening Forces' Cell Tasked with Planting Bombs in Ar Raqqah." February 2, 2015, TRN2015020241516372.

Anderson, John Ward. "7 Arrested in Tel Aviv Bombing: Syrian-Based Leaders of Islamic Jihad Assert Responsibility." *Washington Post*, February 27, 2005.

Andrew, Christopher and Oleg Gordievsky. *KGB: The Inside Story.* New York: Harper-Collins, 1990.

Andrews, Edmund L. and John Kifner. "George Habash, Palestinian Terrorism Tacticians, Dies at 82." *New York Times*, January 27, 2008.

Annells, Jonathan and James Adams. "Did Terrorists Kill with Deadly Nerve Gas Test?" *Sunday Times* (London), March 19, 1995.

Anonymous. *Imperial Hubris: Why the West Is Losing the War on Terror.* Washington, D.C.: Brassey's, 2004.

——. "Notes for the First Analysis of the Phenomenon of Terrorism of the Right." Unpublished study commissioned by the Italian secret services. N.d.

——. *Through Our Enemies' Eyes: Osama bin Laden, Radical Islam, and the Future of America.* Washington, D.C.: Brassey's, 2002.

Anti-Defamation League of B'nai B'rith. *ADL Special Background Report: Hamas, Islamic Jihad, and the Muslim Brotherhood: Islamic Extremists and the Terrorist Threat to America.* New York: Anti-Defamation League of B'nai B'rith, 1993.

——. *ADL Special Report: The Militia Movement in America.* New York: Anti-Defamation League of B'nai B'rith, 1995.

——. "Arab Leaders Glorify Suicide Terrorism." April 17, 2002. http://www.adl.org/israel /Israel-suicide-terror.asp.

——. "Extremism in America: National Alliance." http://www.adl.org/learn/ext_us?N_ Alliance.asp?LEARN_Cat=Extremism&Lean_SubCat=Extremism_in_America& picked=3&item=na. Accessed May 5, 2016.

——. *Hate Groups in America: A Record of Bigotry and Violence.* New York: Anti-Defamation League of B'nai B'rith, 1982.

——. "Militia of Montana." Extremism in America (2005). http://archive.adl.org/learn/ ext_us/mom.html?xpicked=3. Accessed May 5, 2016.

"Anwar al Awlaqi: '44 Ways to Support Jihad.'" *The NEFA Foundation*, February 5, 2009.

Apple, R. W., Jr. "Meese Suggests Press Code on Terrorism." *New York Times*, July 18, 1985.

Apuzzo, Matt and Adam Goldman. *Enemies Within: Inside The NYPD's Secret Spying Unit and Bin Laden's Final Plot Against America.* New York: Simon & Schuster, 2013.

Arango, Tim and Eric Schmitt. "U.S. Actions in Iraq Fueled Rise of a Rebel." *New York Times*, August 10, 2014. http://www.nytimes.com/2014/08/11/world/middleeast/us -actions-in-iraq-fueled-rise-of-a-rebel.html?_r=0.

Armed Islamic Group communiqué, containing a twelve-page interview with Antar-Zouabri. September 1996.

Armenian Secret Army for the Liberation of Armenia. *The Reality.* Armenian Secret Army for the Liberation of Armenia, n.d.

Armond, Paul de. "The Anti-Democratic Movement—More than Militias." The Public Good home page. August 1995. http://www.nwcitizen.com/publicgood.

——. "Christian Patriots at War with the State." The Public Good home page. June 1997. http://www.nwcitizen.com/publicgood.

——. "Leaderless Resistance: The Two-Pronged Movement Consolidates Under Identity." Public Good home page. June 1997. http://www.nwcitizen.com/publicgood.

Arnold, Guy. *Revolutionary and Dissident Movements.* Harlow: Longman, 1991.

Arquilla, John and David Ronfeldt. "The Advent of Netwar." In *In Athena's Camp: Preparing for Conflict in the Information Age*, edited by John Arquilla and David Ronfeldt, 275–94. Santa Monica, Calif.: RAND Corporation, MR-880-OSD/RC, 1997.

——. "The Advent of Netwar (Revisited)." In *Networks and Netwars: The Future of Terror, Crime, and Militancy*, edited by John Arquilla and David Ronfeldt, 1–25. Santa Monica, Calif.: RAND Corporation, MR-1382-OSD, 2001.

——. "A New Epoch—and Spectrum—of Conflict." In *In Athena's Camp: Preparing for Conflict in the Information Age*, edited by John Arquilla and David Ronfeldt, 1–24. Santa Monica, Calif.: RAND Corporation, MR-880-OSD/RC, 1997.

Aryan Nations. *Calling Our Nation*, no. 53 (n.d.). http://www.stormfront.org/aryan _nations/platform.html. Accessed June 2, 2005.

——. "Rest in Peace, Richard Girnt Butler (February 23, 1918–September 8, 2004)." http://www.aryan-nations.org. Accessed May 5, 2016.

Aryan Nations website. http://www.aryan-nation.org. Accessed April 2005.

Asahi Shimbun (Tokyo). "Aum Shinrikyo Special Edition: Expanded Leveraging 'Supernatural Power.'" May 21, 1998.

——. "Aum Shinrikyo Special Edition: Targeted Elites—They Were Brainwashed and Became Aum's Robot." May 28, 1995.

——. "Aum Shinrikyo Special Edition: Transforming Into a 'Terrorist' Cult." June 16, 1996.

Asian Journal (Los Angeles). "Super Ferry 14 Bombing Solved, Says Arroyo." June 25–27, 2008.

Asprey, Robert B. *War in the Shadows: The Guerrilla in History.* Vol. 2. New York: Doubleday, 1975.

Associated Press. "Expert Warns of al-Qaida-Linked Groups." Associated Press, January 7, 2004. http://www.ap.org.

——. "Extremist Admits to the Slaying of Dutch Filmmaker." *Washington Post*, July 13, 2005.

——. "Guilty: Father and Son Convicted of Murder of Bank Security Guard." September 27, 2005. http://www.securityinfowatch.com/news/10594789/guilty-father-and -son-convicted-of-murder-of-bank-security-guard.

——. "Iraq Says al-Qaida Fighters Flowing Into Syria, Dangerous New Element in Fight Against Assad." *Washington Post*, July 5, 2012.

——. "Man Accused of Possessing Lethal Toxin Hangs Himself." *Los Angeles Times*, December 24, 1995.

——. "McVeigh Aimed to Spark Revolt, Ex-Buddy Says." *International Herald Tribune* (Paris), May 13, 1997.

——. "Purported al-Qaida Tape Warns of Attacks." December 19, 2003. http://www.ap.org.

——. "Saudis Discover al-Qaida Training Camps." January 15, 2004. http://www.ap.org.

Associated Press and Agence France Presse. "Cult 'Studied Deadly Ebola Virus.'" *New York Times*, April 25, 1995.

Aston, Clive C. *A Contemporary Crisis: Political Hostage-Taking and the Experience of Western Europe.* Westport, Conn.: Greenwood, 1982.

Atran, Scott. "Genesis of Suicide Terrorism." *Science* 299 (March 2003): 1534–39.

——. "Who Wants to Be a Martyr." *New York Times*, May 5, 2003.

Atwan, Abdel Bari. *The Secret History of al Qaeda.* Berkeley: University of California Press, 2006.

Atwater, Tony. "Network Evening News Coverage of the TWA Hostage Crisis." *Terrorism and the News Media Research Project.* Boston: Emerson College, n.d.

Aussaresses, Paul. *The Battle of the Casbah: Terrorism and Counter-Terrorism in Algeria, 1955–1957.* New York: Enigma Books, 2002.

Aust, Stefan. *The Baader-Meinhof Group: The Inside Story of a Phenomenon.* London: Bodley Head, 1987.

Ayanian, Mark Armen and John Z. Ayanian. "Armenian Political Violence on American Network News: An Analysis of Content." *Armenian Review* 40, nos. 1–157 (Spring 1987): 13–29.

Ayres, B. Drummond, Jr. "The Somalia Mission: Voices." *New York Times*, October 9, 1993.

Azzam, Abdullah. *Defence of Muslim Lands.* London: Maktabah, 2002.

——. *Join the Caravan.* London: Azzam, 2001.

——. *The Lofty Mountain.* London: Azzam, n.d.

Baker, Peter. "Recovered Bin Laden Letters Show a Divided al Qaeda." *New York Times*, May 3, 2012.

Baker, Peter and Susan B. Glasser. "Hundreds Held Hostage at School in Russia." *Washington Post*, September 2, 2004.

——. "Russia School Siege Ends in Carnage." *Washington Post*, September 4, 2004.

Balmer, Desmond. "U.S. Tourists React to Terrorism Fear." *New York Daily News*, March 2, 1986.

Baran, David and Mathieu Guidère. "Sons et images de l'opposition irakienne" [Sound and pictures of the Iraqi opposition]. *Le Monde Diplomatique* (Paris), May 2005.

Barber, Noel. *The War of the Running Dogs: How Malaya Defeated the Communist Guer-rillas 1948–60*. London: Fontana, 1972.

Barkun, Michael. "Millenarian Aspects of 'White Supremacist' Movements." *Terrorism and Political Violence* 1, no. 4 (October 1989): 409–34.

——. "Millenarian Groups and Law Enforcement Agencies: The Lessons of Waco." *Terrorism and Political Violence* 6, no. 1 (Spring 1994): 75–95.

——. "Racist Apocalypse: Millennialism on the Far Right." *American Studies* 31 (1990): 121–40.

Barnaby, Frank. "Nuclear Accidents Waiting to Happen." *World Today* (London) 52, no. 4 (April 1996).

Barnes, Fred. "Shiite Spin Control." *New Republic* (Washington, D.C.), July 15 and 22, 1985.

Barrington, Lisa and Suleima Al-Khalidid. "Al Qaeda Offered to Break Ties with Its Branch in Syria as a 'Sacrifice' to Preserve Its Unity." *Business Insider*, July 28, 2016. http://www.businessinsider.com/al-qaeda-offers-to-break-with-nusra-in-syria-2016-7.

Barrionuevo, Alexei. "Inquiry on 1994 Blast at Argentina Jewish Center Gets New Life." *New York Times*, July 17, 2009.

Barry, Dan and Al Baker. "Getting the Message from 'Eco-Terrorists': Mystery Group Takes Its Campaign East." *New York Times*, January 8, 2001.

Barry, Ellen. "Al Qaeda Opens New Branch on Indian Subcontinent." *New York Times*, September 4, 2014. http://www.nytimes.com/2014/09/05/world/asia/al-qaeda-announces-new-branch-on-indian-subcontinent.html?nytmobile=0.

Bartlett, Jamie and Carl Miller. "The Edge of Violence: Towards Telling the Difference Between Violent and Non-Violent Radicalization." *Terrorism and Political Violence* 24, no. 1 (2012): 1–21.

Bauer, Yehuda. *From Diplomacy to Resistance: A History of Jewish Palestine, 1939–1945*. New York: Atheneum, 1973.

Baumann, Michael "Bommi." *Terror or Love? Bommi Baumann's Own Story of His Life as a West German Urban Guerrilla*. Translated by Helene Ellenbogen and Wayne Parker. New York: Grove, 1979.

Bazinet, Ingrid. "British Ex-Detainees See Link Between Guantanamo, Iraq Torture." *Agence France Press*, May 14, 2004.

BBC News. "Bomb Plot: Arrests and Releases." October 5, 2007. http://news.bbc.co.uk/2/hi/uk_news/6264230.stm.

——. "Editorial Guidelines, in Full: War, Terror and Emergencies." http://www.bbc.co.uk/guidelines/editorialguidelines/edguide/war/mandatoryreferr.shtml. Accessed April 18, 2016.

——. "Extracts from MI5 Chief's Speech." November 10, 2006. http://newsvote.bbc.co.uk/mpapps/pagetools/print/news.bbc.co.uk/2/hl/new s/6135000.stm.

——. "Hezbollah Linked to Burgas Bus Bombing." February 5, 2015. http://www.bbc.com/news/world-europe-21342192.

——. "Lockerbie Bomber Abdelbaset al-Megrahi Dies in Tripoli." May 20, 2012. http://www.bbc.com/news/world-africa-18137896.

——. "Osama Bin Laden Diary 'Planned Attacks'—US Officials." May 12, 2011. http://www.bbc.co.uk/news/world-us-canada-13370524.

——. "Poverty 'Fuelling Terrorism.'" March 22, 2002. http://news.bbc.co.uk/2/hi/1886617.stm.

——. "Swansea Student Links to Bin Laden." September 18, 2001. http://news.bbc.co.uk/2/hi/uk_news/wales/1549539.stm.

——. "Syrian Nusra Front Announces Split from al-Qaeda." July 29, 2016. http://www
.bbc.com/news/world-middle-east-36916606.

——. "Syria Uprising: al Qaeda's al-Zawahiri Lends Support." February 12, 2012. http://
www.bbc.co.uk/news/world-middle-east-17002573.

——. "Woman Jailed for Life for Attack on MP Stephen Timms." November 3, 2010.
http://www.bbc.co.uk/news/uk-england-london-11682732.

Beauge, Florence. "'I Am Resolute on Torture . . . I Myself Have Proceeded with Summary Executions . . .'" *Le Monde* (Paris), November 23, 2000.

——. "'If France Recognized and Condemned These Practices, I Would Take That as a
Step Forward.'" *Le Monde* (Paris), November 23, 2000.

Becker, Jillian. *Hitler's Children: The Story of the Baader-Meinhof Gang*. London: Panther Books, 1978.

Beckett, Ian F. W. *Encyclopedia of Guerrilla Warfare*. New York: Checkmark Books,
2001.

Beckman, Robert L. "Rapporteur's Summary." In *Nuclear Terrorism: Defining the Threat*,
edited by Paul Leventhal and Yonah Alexander, 5–24. Washington, D.C.: Pergamon-
Brassey's, 1986.

Begin, Menachem. *The Revolt: Story of the Irgun*. Jerusalem: Steimatzky, 1977.

——. *White Nights: The Story of a Prisoner in Russia*. Jerusalem: Steimatzky, 1977.

Bell, J. Bowyer. *The Dynamics of the Armed Struggle*. London: Frank Cass, 1998.

——. *The Secret Army: The IRA, 1916–1979*. Dublin: Poolbeg, 1989.

——. "Terrorist Scripts and Live-Action Spectaculars." *Columbia Journalism Review* 17,
no. 1 (1978): 47–50.

——. *Terror Out of Zion: The Violent and Deadly Shock Troops of Israeli Independence,
1929–1949*. New York: St. Martin's, 1977.

——. *A Time of Terror: How Democratic Societies Respond to Revolutionary Violence*.
New York: Basic Books, 1978.

Bell, Stewart. *Cold Terror: How Canada Nurtures and Exports Terrorism Around the
World*. Toronto: John Wiley, 2007.

Benjamin, Daniel and Steven Simon. *The Age of Sacred Terror*. New York: Random House,
2002.

Benmelech, Efraim and Claude Berrebi. "Human Capital and the Productivity of Suicide
Bombers." *Journal of Economic Perspectives* 21, no. 3 (Summer 2007): 223–38.

Bennet, James. "Jerusalem Holy Site a Tense Crossroads Again." *New York Times*, August 29, 2003.

Bennett, Gina. "The Wandering Mujahidin: Armed and Dangerous." *Weekend Edition:
United States Department of State Bureau of Intelligence and Research*, August 21–22,
1993. http://www.nationalsecuritymom.com/3/WanderingMujahidin.pdf.

Bennett, Will. "Simple Bombs Improved but Lack Accuracy." *Independent* (London), February 8, 1991.

——. "Terrorists Keep Changing Tactics to Elude Security Forces." *Independent* (London), December 17, 1991.

Bennis, Phyllis. *From Stones to Statehood: The Palestinian Uprising*. New York: Olive
Branch, 1990.

Benson, "David C. "Why the Internet Is Not Increasing Terrorism." *Security Studies* 23,
no. 2 (2014): 293–328.

Bergen, Peter. "The Bin Laden Trial: What Did We Learn?" *Studies in Conflict and Terrorism* 24, no. 6 (November/December 2001): 429–34.

——. *Holy War, Inc.: Inside the Secret World of Osama bin Laden.* New York: Free Press, 2001.

——. *The Osama bin Laden I Know: An Oral History of al Qaeda's Leader.* New York: Free Press, 2006.

——. "Time to Declare Victory: Al Qaeda Is Defeated." *CNN: Security Clearance* (blog), June 27, 2012. http://security.blogs.cnn.com/2012/06/27/time-to-declare-victory-al-qaeda-is-defeated-opinion/.

Bergen, Peter, Bruce Hoffman, Michael Hurley, and Errol Southers. *Jihadist Terrorism: A Threat Assessment.* Washington, D.C. http://cdn.bipartisanpolicy.org/wp-content/uploads/sites/default/files/Jihadist%20Terrorism-A%20Threat%20Assesment_0.pdf. Accessed June 1, 2016.

Bergen, Peter and Swati Pandey. "The Madrassa Scapegoat." *Washington Quarterly* 29, no. 2 (Spring 2006): 117–25.

Bergen, Peter and David Sterman. "The Man Who Inspired the Boston Bombings." CNN, April 11, 2014. http://www.cnn.com/2014/04/11/opinion/bergen-boston-bombing-awlaki-jihadists/.

Bergman, Ronen. *The Secret War with Iran: The 30-Year Clandestine Struggle Against the World's Most Dangerous Terrorist Power.* New York: Free Press, 2008.

Berman, Eli. "Hamas, Taliban and the Jewish Underground: An Economist's View of Radical Religious Militias." Working Paper 10004. Cambridge, Mass.: National Bureau of Economic Research, September 2003. http://www.nber.org/papers/w10004.

——. *Radical Religious and Violent: The New Economics of Terrorism.* Cambridge, Mass.: MIT Press, 2009.

Bernstein, Richard. "Chemist Can't Pinpoint Bomb Contents at Trial." *New York Times,* January 12, 1994.

Berrebi, Claude. "Evidence About the Link Between Education, Poverty and Terrorism Among Palestinians." *Peace Economics, Peace Science and Public Policy* 13, no. 1 (2007): 1–36.

Berreby, David. "Idea Lab: Engineering Terror." *New York Times Sunday Magazine,* September 10, 2010. http://www.nytimes.com/2010/09/12/magazine/12FOB-IdeaLab-t.html?scp=1&sq=Berreby&st=cse&_r=0.

bin Laden, Osama. "Among a Band of Knights, February 14 2003." In *Messages to the World: The Statements of Osama Bin Laden,* edited by Bruce Lawrence, 186–206. London: Verso, 2005.

Binyon, Michael and Michael Theodoulou. "Bounty on Rushdie Raised to $2.5M." *Times* (London), February 13, 1997.

Bishop, Patrick. "Have the Suicide Bombers Been Defeated?" *Daily Telegraph* (London), May 26, 2004.

Bishop, Patrick and Eamonn Mallie. *The Provisional IRA.* London: Heinemann, 1987; paperback edition, London: Corgi, 1989.

Bjelopera, Jerome P. and Mark A. Randol. *American Jihadist Terrorism: Combating a Complex Threat—CRS Report for Congress.* Washington, D.C., September 20, 2010. CRS 7-5700, R41416.

"The Black Tiger Unit of the LTTE." Unpublished report. N.d.

Bloom, Mia A. *Dying to Kill: The Allure of Suicide Terror.* New York: Columbia University Press, 2005.

Blumenthal, Ralph. "Peak Season of American Travel to Europe Ends Showing Little Recovery." *New York Times,* September 14, 1986.

Blundy, David. "Inside the IRA." *Sunday Times* (London), July 3, 1977.

Bolan, Kim. *Loss of Faith: How the Air-India Bombers Got Away with Murder.* Toronto: M&S, 2005.

Bone, James and Alan Road. "Terror by Degree." *Times Magazine* (London), October 18, 1997.

Bonner, Raymond, Jane Perlez, and Eric Schmitt. "British Inquiry of Failed Plots Points to Iraq's Qaeda Group." *New York Times*, December 14, 2007.

Booklet Giving History of ASALA's Existence Gives New Insight Into the Revolutionary Movement." *Armenian Reporter* (New York), January 10, 1985.

Boone, Rebecca. "Once a Hotbed: 'Bo' Gritz and His Anti-government Followers Have Left." *Salt Lake Tribune*, August 30, 2004. http://archive.sltrib.com/article.php?id=2400556&itype=NGPSID.

Borum, Randy. "Radicalization Into Violent Extremism I: A Review of Social Science Theories." *Journal of Strategic Security* 4, no. 4 (Winter 2011): 7–36.

Bougereau, Jean Marcel. "Memoirs of an International Terrorist: Conversations with Hans Joachim Klein." In *The German Guerrilla: Terror, Reaction, and Resistance.* Sanday, Orkney: Cienfuegos, n.d.

Bowden, Mark. *Black Hawk Down: A Story of Modern War.* Boston: Atlantic Monthly, 1999.

——. *Killing Pablo: The Hunt for the World's Greatest Outlaw.* New York: Atlantic Monthly, 2001.

Bowers, Rodney. "White Radicals Charged with Sedition." *Arkansas Gazette* (Little Rock), April 25, 1987.

Bowman, Tom. "U.S. Offers Training, Pay as It Frees Iraqi Detainees." *Morning Edition*, NPR News, May 16, 2008. http://www.npr.org/templates/story/story.php?storyId=90506939.

Bradley, Matt. "Insurgents in Iraq Seizing Advanced Weaponry: Arms Turning Up in Battles and Military-Style Parades in Iraq and Syria." *Wall Street Journal*, July 6, 2014. http://www.wsj.com/articles/insurgents-in-iraq-seizing-advanced-weaponry-1404684313.

Bremner, Donald. "Media Given Mixed Reviews on Terrorism." *Los Angeles Times*, September 26, 1986.

Bridge, Adrian. "German Police Search for Red Army Faction Killers." *Independent* (London), April 6, 1991.

Brinton, Crane. *The Anatomy of Revolution.* New York: Vintage, 1965.

British Broadcasting Corporation (BBC). "Bosnia Serb 'Black Hand' Group Threatens to Kill Peace Force." *BBC Summary of World Broadcasts*, July 17, 1997.

——. "Leaflet in Banja Luka Vows Revenge on British Forces 'Soon.'" *BBC Summary of World Broadcasts*, July 19, 1997.

Broad, William J. "Seismic Blast: Bomb or Quake?" *New York Times*, January 23, 1997.

Brogan, Patrick. *The Fighting Never Stopped.* New York: Vintage, 1990.

Broido, Vera. *Apostles Into Terrorists: Women and the Revolutionary Movement in the Russia of Alexander II.* London: Maurice Temple Smith, 1977.

Brooke, James. "Agents Seize Arsenal of Rifles and Bomb-Making Material in Arizona Militia Inquiry." *New York Times*, July 3, 1996.

——. "Armed Group Under Siege Has Sown Anger and Hate." *New York Times*, March 31, 1996.

——. "Arrests Add to Idaho's Reputation as a Magnet for Supremacists." *New York Times*, October 27, 1996.

——. "As Trial Nears for Militia, Some Charges Are Dropped." *New York Times*, October 9, 1996.

——. "Newspaper Says McVeigh Described Role in Bombing." *New York Times*, March 1, 1997.

——. "Volatile Mix in Viper Militia: Hatred Plus a Love for Guns." *New York Times*, July 4, 1996.

Brown, Tina. "Death by Error." *Washington Post*, May 19, 2005.

Bruinessen, Martin van. *Kurdish Ethno-nationalism Versus Nation-Building States*. Istanbul: Isis, 2000.

Brynen, Rex and Neil Caplan. "Israel and Palestine: Implications of the Intifada." In *Echoes of the Intifada: Regional Repercussions of the Palestinian-Israeli Conflict*, edited by Rex Brynen, 5–12. Boulder, Colo.: Westview, 1991.

Buford, Bill. *Among the Thugs*. London: Mandarin, 1992.

Bullock, Alan. *Hitler: A Study in Tyranny*. New York: Harper, 1958.

Burghardt, Tom. "Leaderless Resistance and the Oklahoma City Bombing." Public Good home page. http://www.nwcitizen.com/publicgood. Accessed June 25, 1997.

Burke, Jason. *Al-Qaeda: Casting a Shadow of Terror*. London: I. B. Tauris, 2003.

——. "Bin Laden Files Show al-Qaida and Taliban Leaders in Close Contact." *Guardian*, April 29, 2012. http://www.guardian.co.uk/world/2012/apr/29/bin-laden-al-qaida -taliban-contact.

——. "Think Again: Al Qaeda." *Foreign Policy*, May/June 2004. http://www.foreignpolicy .com.

Burleigh, Michael. *Blood and Rage: A Cultural History of Terrorism*. New York: Harper-Collins, 2009.

Burnett, Victoria and Alissa J. Rubin. "Doctor Accused in Glasgow Attack Described as Loner Angry About the Iraq War." *New York Times*, July 5, 2007.

Burns, John F. "Iraq's Ho Chi Minh Trail." *New York Times*, June 5, 2005.

——. "Rebels Kill Egyptian Diplomat, Adding Pressure on Others in Iraq." *New York Times*, July 8, 2005.

——. "Video Appears to Show Insurgents Kill a Downed Pilot." *New York Times*, April 23, 2005.

Butler, Reverend Richard G. "To Our New People." *Aryan Nations* (n.p., n.d.).

Byford-Jones, W. *Grivas and the Story of EOKA*. London: Robert Hale, 1959.

Byman, Daniel. *Al Qaeda, the Islamic State, and the Global Jihadist Movement: What Everyone Needs to Know*. New York: Oxford University Press, 2015.

——. *Deadly Connections: States That Sponsor Terrorism*. Cambridge: Cambridge University Press, 2005.

——. "Splitting al-Qa'ida and Its Affiliates." *Foreign Policy: The AfPak Channel*, July 30, 2012. http://afpak.foreignpolicy.com/posts/2012/07/30/splitting_al_qaida_and_its _affiliates.

Callimachi, Rukmini. "How a Secretive Branch of ISIS Built a Global Network of Killers." *New York Times*, August 3, 2016. http://www.nytimes.com/2016/08/04/world /middleeast/isis-german-recruit-interview.html?utm_source=Sailthru&utm _medium=email&utm_campaign=New%20Campaign&utm_term=*Situation%20 Report&_r=0.

——. "How ISIS Built the Machinery of Terror Under Europe's Gaze." *New York Times*, March 29, 2016. https://www.nytimes.com/2016/03/29/world/europe/isis-attacks -paris-brussels.html.

Campbell, Duncan, Severin Carrell, Helen Carter, Barbara McMahon, Karen McVeigh, Hugh Muir, Richard Norton-Taylor, Alexandra Topping, and Alan Travis. "Mastermind Based Abroad Suspected of Guiding Plot." *Guardian*, July 4, 2007.

Campbell, Duncan and Rosie Cowan. "Ricin Plot: Terror Trail That Led from Algeria to London." *Guardian* (London), April 14, 2005.

Campbell, James K. "Excerpts from Research Study 'Weapons of Mass Destruction and Terrorism: Proliferation by Non-State Actors.'" Paper presented at the International Conference on Aviation Safety and Security in the 21st Century, White House Commission on Aviation Safety and Security and George Washington University, Washington, D.C., January 13–15, 1997.

——. "Excerpts from Research Study 'Weapons of Mass Destruction and Terrorism: Proliferation by Non-State Actors.'" *Terrorism and Political Violence* 9, no. 2 (Summer 1997): 24–50.

Candiotti, Susan, Maria Ressa, Justine Redman, and Henry Schuster. "Suspected 9/11 Mastermind Graduated from U.S. University." CNN, December 19, 2002. http:// edition.cnn.com/2002/US/South/12/19/al.qaeda.aggie/.

Carlin, John. "DIY Apocalypse." *Independent* (London), April 30, 1995.

——. "'We Need Blood to Cleanse Us.'" *Independent* (London), May 2, 1995.

Carr, Caleb. "Terrorism as Warfare: The Lessons of Military History." *World Policy Journal* 13, no. 4 (Winter 1996–67): 1–12.

Carruthers, Susan L. *Winning Hearts and Minds: British Governments, the Media, and Colonial Counter-Insurgency, 1944–1960*. London: Leicester University Press, 1995.

Carus, W. Seth. *Bioterrorism and Biocrimes: The Illicit Use of Biological Agents in the 20th Century*. Washington, D.C.: Center for Counterproliferation Research, National Defense University, March 1999.

——. "Bioterrorism and Biocrimes: The Illicit Use of Biological Agents since 1900." Working paper. Washington, D.C.: Center for Counterproliferation Research, National Defense University, February 2001 revision.

——. "The Rajneeshees (1984)." In *Toxic Terror: Assessing Terrorist Use of Chemical and Biological Weapons*, edited by Jonathan B. Tucker, 115–38. Cambridge, Mass.: MIT Press, 2000.

Carver, Michael. *War Since 1945*. London: Weidenfeld and Nicolson, 1980.

Cauchon, Dennis. "For Many on Sept. 11, Survival was No Accident." *USA Today*, December 20, 2001. http://usatoday30.usatoday.com/news/sept11/2001/12/19/usatcov -wtcsurvival.htm.

"Caught Red-Handed: The Inside Story of an Arms Shipment." *Jane's Foreign Report*, no. 2672 (January 17, 2002): n.p.

CBS News. "Officials: Bombing Suspect Angry Over U.S. Wars Against Muslims." April 24, 2013. http://www.cbsnews.com/news/officials-bombing-suspect-angry-over -us-wars-against-muslims/.

CBS World News. "Osama bin Laden's Last Words Show Dark Days for al Qaeda." May 3, 2012. http://www.cbsnews.com/8301-202_162-57426970/osama-bin-ladens-last-words -show-dark-days-for-al Qaeda/.

Central Intelligence Agency (CIA). *Guide to the Analysis of Insurgency*. Washington, D.C.: U.S. Government Printing Office, n.d.

——. *Guide to the Analysis of Insurgency 2012*. Washington, D.C.: U.S. Government Printing Office, n.d.

Chaliand, Gerard and Yves Ternon. *The Armenians: From Genocide to Resistance*. Translated by Tony Berrett. London: Zed, 1983.

Chayban, Badih. "Hizbullah Rolls Out New Computer Game: Special Force Lets Players Use Sharon for Target Practice." *Daily Star* (Beirut), March 3, 2003. http://www.specialforce.net/english/news/dailystart.htm.

Chivers, C. J. and Stephen Lee Meyers. "Insurgents Seize School in Russia and Hold Scores." *New York Times*, September 2, 2004.

——. "Terror in Russia: Battle in Beslan." *New York Times*, September 4, 2004.

Chulov, Martin. "Abu Bakr al-Baghdadi Emerges from Shadows to Rally Islamist Followers." *Guardian*, July 6, 2014. https://www.theguardian.com/world/2014/jul/06/abu-bakr-al-baghdadi-isis.

Churchill, Winston S. *The Second World War*. Vol. 3, *The Grand Alliance*. London: Reprint Society, 1956.

——. *The Second World War*. Vol. 4, *The Hinge of Fate*. London: Reprint Society, 1956.

Clapper, James R. Director of National Intelligence, *Statement for the Record: Worldwide Threat Assessment of the US Intelligence Community*. Senate Armed Services Committee, February 9, 2016. http://www.armed-services.senate.gov/imo/media/doc/Clapper_02-09-16.pdf.

Clarity, James F. "Obscure Doctor Again Faces Sinn Fein Chief." *International Herald Tribune* (Paris), April 15, 1997.

Clark, Christopher. *The Sleepwalkers: How Europe Went to War in 1914*. New York: HarperCollins, 2013.

Clark, Nicola. "Why Security Breaches Have Become Relatively Rare." *New York Times*, March 30, 2016.

Clarke, Richard A. *Against All Enemies: Inside America's War on Terrorism*. New York: Free Press, 2004.

Clarke, Thurston. *By Blood and Fire: The Attack on the King David Hotel*. New York: Putnam, 1981.

Clawson, Patrick. "Why We Need More but Better Coverage of Terrorism." *Orbis* 80, no. 4 (Winter 1987): 701–10.

Cline, Edward. "Terrorists, Period." *Washington Post*, September 11, 2004.

Cline, Ray S. and Yonah Alexander. *Terrorism: The Soviet Connection*. New York: Crane Russak, 1984.

Clutterbuck, Lindsay. "Countering Irish Republican Terrorism in Britain: Its Origin as a Police Function." Unpublished manuscript, 2005, 154–81.

——. "The Progenitors of Terrorism: Russian Revolutionaries or Extreme Irish Republicans?" *Terrorism and Political Violence* 16, no. 1 (Spring 2004): 154–81.

CNN. "Alleged bin Laden Tape a Call to Arms." http://cnn.com/2003/WORLD/meast/02/11/sprj.irq.wrap. Accessed June 2, 2005.

——. "Live from Afghanistan—Was Al Qaeda Working on a Super Bomb?" January 24, 2004. http://www.isis-online.org/publications/terrorism/transcript.html.

——. "Transcript of Bin Laden's October *Interview*." February 5, 2002. http://edition.cnn.com/2002/WORLD/asiapcf/south/02/05/binladen.transcript/.

Cohen, Michael J. *Palestine and the Great Powers, 1945–1948*. Princeton, N.J.: Princeton University Press, 1982.

Cohen-Almagor, Raphael. "Vigilant Jewish Fundamentalism: From the JDL to Kach (or 'Shalom Jews, Shalom Dogs')." *Terror and Political Violence* 4, no. 1 (Spring 1992): 44–66.

Cole, Leonard A. *The Anthrax Letters: A Medical Detective Story*. Washington, D.C.: Joseph Henry, 2003.

Cole, Patrick E. "'I'm Just Like Anyone Else.'" *Time*, April 15, 1996.

Coll, Steve. *The Bin Ladens: An Arabian Family in the American Century*. New York: Penguin, 2008.

——. *Ghost Wars: The Secret History of the CIA, Afghanistan, and bin Laden, from the Soviet Invasion to September 10, 2001*. New York: Penguin, 2004.

Collins, Eamon, with Mick McGovern. *Killing Rage*. London: Granta, 1997.

Colvin, Marie. "Rabbi Calls for Suicide Bombings." *Sunday Times* (London), April 13, 1997.

Colvin, Marie and Andy Goldberg. "Israel on Alert for Wave of 'Sleeper' Bombers." *Sunday Times* (London), March 10, 1996.

Colvin, Ross. "Violence in Iraq Falls to Lowest Level in 4 Years." *Reuters*, May 24, 2008. http://www.reuters.com/article/homepageCrisis/idUSCOL462053._CH_.2400.

Committee for the Publication of Lehi Writings. *B'Ha'Machterot* [In the underground]. Vols. A, B, and D. Tel Aviv: Yair, 1959.

Conquest, Robert. *The Great Terror*. Harmondsworth: Penguin, 1971.

Conway, Flo and Jim Siegelman. "Identity and the Militia." *Arkansas Democrat-Gazette* (Little Rock), December 3, 1995.

Coogan, Tim Pat. *The IRA: A History*. Niwot, Colo.: Roberts Rinehart, 1993.

Cook, David. *Understanding Jihad*. Berkeley: University of California Press, 2005.

Cooley, John K. *Green March, Black September: The Story of the Palestinian Arabs*. London: Frank Cass, 1973.

——. "New Arab Unity Hits Palestinian Guerrillas." *Christian Science Monitor*, September 19, 1973.

Coomaraswamy, Radika. "Women of the LTTE: The Tiger's and Women's Emancipation." *Frontline* (Chennai, India), January 10, 1997.

Corbett, Robert. *Guerrilla Warfare from 1939 to the Present Day*. London: Orbis, 1986.

Corcoran, James. *Bitter Harvest: The Birth of Paramilitary Terrorism in the Heartland*. New York: Penguin, 1995.

Cordes, Bonnie. "When Terrorists Do the Talking: Reflections on Terrorist Literature." In "Inside Terrorist Organizations," edited by David C. Rapoport. Special issue, *Journal of Strategic Studies* 10, no. 4 (December 1987): 150–71.

Corr, Ambassador Edwin G. Introduction to *Gray Area Phenomena: Confronting the New World Disorder*, edited by Max G. Manwaring, xiii–xx. Boulder, Colo.: Westview, 1993.

Corsun, Andrew. *Research Papers on Terrorism: Armenian Terrorism, 1975–1980*. Washington, D.C.: Office of Security Threat Analysis Group, U.S. Department of State, 1982.

Cottrell, Robert. "French Court Told of Huge Libyan Arms Run by IRA." *Independent* (London), January 8, 1991.

Counter Terrorism Center. *Counter Terrorism 2005*. Washington, D.C.: Central Intelligence Agency, 2004.

Counterterrorism Strategy Initiative. "The Year of the Drone: Leaders Killed." New America Foundation, 2012. http://counterterrorism.newamerica.net/about/militants. Accessed June 12, 2016.

Counterterrorism Threat Assessment and Warning Unit. *Terrorism in the United States 1999*. Washington, D.C.: U.S. Department of Justice, FBI Publication #0308, 2000.

——. *Terrorism in the United States 2000/2001*. Washington, D.C.: U.S. Department of Justice, FBI Publication #0308, 2002.

Cowell, Alan. "Berlin Court Says Top Iran Leaders Ordered Killings." *New York Times*, April 11, 1997.

——. "One Conviction in Plot to Spread Deadly Toxins, but 8 Go Free." *New York Times*, April 13, 2005.

——. "Two More Held in Rabin Slaying; Israeli Police See a Conspiracy." *New York Times*, November 10, 1995.

Craig, Gordon. *Germany, 1866–1945*. Oxford: Clarendon, 1978.

Craig, Olga, Charles Laurence, Rajeev Syal, and Daniel Foggo. "What Drove a Boy from Bromley to Become a Suicide Bomber?" *Sunday Telegraph* (London), December 30, 2001.

Creech Jones Papers. Rhodes House, Oxford. Boxes 32/3 and 32/6, Letters.

Crenshaw, Martha. *Terrorism and International Cooperation*. Occasional Paper Series 11. New York: Institute for East-West Security Studies, 1989.

Crossette, Barbara. "Sri Lanka's Army Is Hitting Last Guerrilla Group." *New York Times*, May 2, 1991.

——. "Tamil Rebels Said to Recruit Child Soldiers." *New York Times*, July 17, 2000.

Crossette, Barbara, Judith Miller, Steven Lee Myers, and Tim Weiner. "U.S. Says Iraq Aided Production of Chemical Weapons in Sudan." *New York Times*, August 25, 1998.

Crouch, Gregory. "Man on Trial in Dutch Killing Says He'd Do 'Same Again.'" *New York Times*, July 13, 2005.

——. "Suspect in Killing of Dutch Filmmaker Maintains His Silence." *New York Times*, July 12, 2005.

Cullison, Alan. "Inside Al-Qaeda's Hard Drive." *Atlantic Monthly* 294, no. 2 (September 2004).

Daily News (Colombo). "Amir, Yoheswaran Shot Dead, Siva Serious." July 14, 1989.

——. "Masked Gunmen Kill Jaffna Mayor." July 28, 1975.

——. "Yogasangari—MP Killed in Madras." June 21, 1990.

Dalgaard-Nielsen, Anja. "Violent Radicalization in Europe: What We Know and What We Do Not Know." *Studies in Conflict and Terrorism* 33, no. 9 (September 2010): 797–814.

Davis, Anthony. "Resilient Abu Sayyaf Resists Military Pressure." *Jane's Intelligence Review*, September 1, 2003.

Davis, Joyce M. *Martyrs: Innocence, Vengeance, and Despair in the Middle East*. New York: Palgrave/Macmillan, 2003.

Davis, Uri, Andrew Mack, and Ira Yuval-Davis. Introduction to *Israel and the Palestinians*, edited by Uri Davis, Andrew Mack, and Ira Yuval-Davis. London: Ithaca, 1975.

Declaration of Jihad Against the Country's Tyrants—Military Series. http://www.au.af.mil/au/awc/awcgate/terrorism/alqaida_manual/manualpart1_1.pdf. Accessed March 6, 2017.

"Declaration of War Against the Americans Occupying the Land of the Two Holy Places." In *Usama bin Laden's al-Qaida: Profile of a Terrorist Network*, edited by Yonah Alexander and Michael S. Swetnam, Appendix 1A, 1–22. Ardsley, N.Y.: Transnational, 2001.

Dedijer, Vladimir. *The Road to Sarajevo*. London: MacGibbon and Kee, 1967.

Deen, Thailif. "Tigers Try Electronic Terrorism." *Daily News* (Colombo), November 22, 1997.

Dees, Morris, with James Corcoran. *Gathering Storm: America's Militia Threat*. New York: HarperCollins, 1996.

Dees, Morris and J. Richards Cohen. "White Supremacists Without Borders." *New York Times*, June 22, 2015.

deLeon, Peter, Bruce Hoffman, and Konrad Kellen. *The Threat of Nuclear Terrorism: A Reexamination*. Santa Monica, Calif.: RAND Corporation, N-2706, January 1988.

Denning, Dorothy E. "Activism, Hacktivism, and Cyberterrorism: The Internet as a Tool for Influencing Foreign Policy." http://www.nautilus.org/info-policy/workshop/papers /denning.html. Accessed April 16, 2002.

Department of Defense Dictionary of Military and Associated Terms. http://www.dtic .mil/doctrine/jel/dodict/data/t/05373.html. Accessed April 25, 2016.

Dettmer, Jamie. "Has ISIS Lost Its Head? Power Struggle Erupts with Al-Baghdadi Seriously Wounded." *Daily Beast*, May 10, 2015. http://www.thedailybeast.com/articles/2015 /05/10/has-isis-lost-its-head-power-struggle-erupts-with-al-baghdadi-partially -paralyzed.html.

——. "ISIS and Al Qaeda Ready to Gang Up on Obama's Rebels." *Daily Beast*, November 11, 2014. http://www.thedailybeast.com/articles/2014/11/11/al-qaeda-s-killer-new -alliance-with-isis.html.

Dettmer, Jamie and Edward Gorman. "Seven Dead in IRA 'Human' Bomb Attacks." *Times* (London), October 25, 1990.

Deutsche Presse-Agentur (Nicosia). "Militant Islamist: Attack on Cole Cost 10,000 Dollars." November 12, 2000.

Dewan, Shalila. "Bomber Offers Guilty Pleas, and Defiance." *New York Times*, April 14, 2005.

Dewar, Michael. *Brush Fire Wars: Minor Campaigns of the British Army Since 1945*. New York: St. Martin's, 1984.

DeYoung, Karen. "U.S. Considering Talks on Hijacking Coverage." *Washington Post*, July 18, 1985.

Diamond, Edwin. "The Coverage Itself: Why It Turned Into 'Terrorvision.'" *TV Guide*, September 21, 1985.

Dickson, Caitlin. "Sovereign Citizens Are America's Top Cop-Killers." *Daily Beast*, November 25, 2014. http://www.thedailybeast.com/articles/2014/11/25/sovereign-citizens -are-america-s-top-cop-killers.html.

Dillin, John. "NBC News President Defends, but Revises, Terrorism Coverage." *Christian Science Monitor*, August 5, 1985.

Directorate of Intelligence, Central Intelligence Agency. *Palestinian Organizations: A Reference Aid*. Washington, D.C.: Central Intelligence Agency, LDA 90-11155, March 1990.

"Discussion Paper on Preventing Terrorism: U.S. Government Prevention Capabilities." Unpublished manuscript. July 23, 1996.

Dixon, Lloyd and Rachel Kaganoff Stern. *Compensation Losses from the 9/11 Attacks*. Santa Monica, Calif.: RAND Corporation, MG-264-ICJ, 2004.

Dobson, Christopher. *Black September: Its Short, Violent History*. London: Robert Hale, 1974, 1975.

Dobson, Christopher and Ronald Payne. *The Carlos Complex: A Study in Terror*. London: Coronet/Hodder and Stoughton, 1978.

——. *Terror! The West Strikes Back*. London: Macmillan, 1982.

Dolgin, Janet L. *Jewish Identity and the JDL*. Princeton, N.J.: Princeton University Press, 1977.

Downes-LeGuin, Theo and Bruce Hoffman. *The Impact of Terrorism on Public Opinion, 1988 to 1989*. Santa Monica, Calif.: RAND Corporation, MR-225-FF/ RC, 1993.

Doyle, Leonard. "US Militias Show Way for British Fascists." *Independent* (London), April 27, 1995.

Dozier, Kimberly. "Officials: Bin Laden Eyed Small Cities as Targets." Associated Press, May 12, 2011. http://news.yahoo.com/s/ap/us_bin_laden.

Drake, Richard. *The Aldo Moro Murder Case*. Cambridge, Mass.: Harvard University Press, 1995.

Dreazen, Yochi J. and Evan Perez. "Suspect Cites Radical Imam's Writings." *Wall Street Journal*, May 6, 2010.

Drozdiak, William. "EU Recalls Envoys as Iran Is Found Guilty of Terror." *International Herald Tribune* (Paris), April 11, 1997.

——. "Extremes Squeeze Arafat as Hamas's Power Swells." *International Herald Tribune* (Paris), August 25, 1997.

Dudevitch, Margot. "2003 Terror Report: 50% Decrease in Israeli Casualties." *Jerusalem Post*, January 9, 2004.

Dugger, Celia W. "Rebels Without a Childhood in Sri Lanka War." *New York Times*, September 10, 2000.

Dunn, Ross and Tom Rhodes. "The Stalking Assassin Who Killed Rabin at Third Try." *Times* (London), November 6, 1995.

Economic Times. "Osama bin Laden's Nod Was Sought for Mumbai-Style Attacks in Europe: Report." March 1, 2015. http://articles.economictimes.indiatimes.com/2015 -03-01/news/59642323_1_osama-bin-laden-abbottabad-mumbai-style-attacks.

Economist. "But Basques Aren't Irish." July 20, 1996.

——. "Don't Spoil the Party." July 13, 1996.

——. "In the Face of Chaos." February 21, 2009.

——. "IRA: The Libyan Connection." March 31, 1990.

——. "Reviewing the Surveillance State." May 23, 2015. http://www.economist.com/news /united-states/21651817-america-argues-anew-over-how-much-snooping-nsa-can -do-reviewing-surveillance-state.

——. "What Is Terrorism?" March 2, 1996.

Eddy, Paul. "Cover Story: True Detective Stories." *Sunday Times Magazine* (London), August 10, 1997.

Eedle, Paul. "Terrorism.com." *Guardian* (London), July 17, 2002.

Egan, Timothy. "Trying to Explain Contacts with Paramilitary Groups." *New York Times*, May 2, 1995.

Eggen, Dan. "Indictment Cites Plans to Target Financial Hubs: 3 Britons' Extradition to Be Sought." *Washington Post*, April 13, 2005.

Ehrenfeld, Rachel. *Narco-Terrorism*. New York: Basic Books, 1990.

Eichenwald, Kurt. "Right-Wing Extremists Are a Bigger Threat to America than ISIS." *Newsweek*, February 12, 2016. http://www.newsweek.com/2016/02/12/right-wing -extremists-militants-bigger-threat-america-isis-jihadists-422743.html.

Eickelman, Dale F. "Trans-State Islam and Security." In *Transnational Religion and Fading States*, edited by Susanne Rudolph Hoeber and James Piscatori, 27–46. Boulder, Colo.: Westview, 1996.

El Deeb, Sarah. "Al-Qaida Reportedly Plans Big New Attack." Associated Press, May 8, 2003.

——. "Syria Nusra Front Leader Claims to Cut Ties with al-Qa'ida." *Washington Post*, July 28, 2016. https://www.washingtonpost.com/world/middle_east/al-qaida-central -appears-to-ok-split-with-syrian-branch/2016/07/28/865fa322-54c2-11e6-b652-315ae5 d4d4dd_story.html.

Electronic newsletter of the Orion Group. April 24, 2003.

Ellul, Jacques. *Propaganda: The Formation of Men's Attitudes*. Translated by Konrad Kellen and Jean Lerner. New York: Knopf, 1965.

El-Nawawy, Mohammed and Adel Iskandar. *Al-Jazeera: The Story of the Network That Is Rattling Governments and Redefining Modern Journalism*. Cambridge, Mass.: Westview, 2003.

Engel, Pamela. "ISIS Finances Are Taking a Serious Hit, and It's Hurting Morale Inside the Terrorist Group." *Business Insider*, April 4, 2016. http://www.businessinsider.com /isis-finances-declining-2016-4.

Engelberg, Stephen. "Contras to Start New Radio Station." *New York Times*, November 5, 1986.

English, Richard. *Armed Struggle: The History of the IRA*. Oxford: Oxford University Press, 2003.

Ensslin, Gudrun. "Statement of 19 January 1976." In *Texte der RAF* [RAF texts], by the Red Army Faction. Malmö, Sweden: Verlag Bo Cavefors, 1977.

Eshel, David. "The Al-Aqsa Intifada: Tactics and Strategies." *Jane's Intelligence Review*, May 2001.

Evans, Kathy and Richard Norton-Taylor. "Spain Checks Syrian Link to Lockerbie." *Times* (London), June 6, 1992.

Evans, Michael. "Iraqis Linked to Sudan Plant." *Times* (London), August 25, 1998.

"EZLN—¡Ya Basta!" [Enough already]." http://www.ezln.org. Accessed June 15, 2005.

Fadl Allah [*sic*], Ayatollah Muhammed Hussein. "Islam and Violence in Political Reality." *Middle East Insight* 4, nos. 4–5 (1986).

Fair, C. Christine. *Fighting for the End: The Pakistan Army's Way of War*. Oxford: Oxford University Press, 2014.

Fallaci, Oriana. "Interview with George Habash." *Life Magazine*, June 12, 1970.

Fallows, James. "Who Shot Mohammed Al-Dura?" *Atlantic Monthly* 291, no. 5 (June 2003).

Fanon, Frantz. *The Wretched of the Earth*. London: Penguin, 1990.

Farrow, Ronan. "Like. Share. Kill. Social Media Companies Are Ignoring How Terrorists Exploit Their Services." *Wall Street Journal*, July 13, 2014.

Fattah, Hassan M. "Hezbollah Declares Full Support for Syria." *New York Times*, March 6, 2005.

FBI (Federal Bureau of Investigation). "Definitions of Terrorism in the U.S. Code." https:// www.fbi.gov/about-us/investigate/terrorism/terrorism-definition. Accessed April 18, 2016.

——. "Domestic Terrorism: The Sovereign Citizen Movement." April 13, 2010. https:// www.fbi.gov/news/stories/2010/april/sovereigncitizens_041310/domestic-terrorism -the-sovereign-citizen-movement.

——. "What We Investigate." https://www.fbi.gov/albuquerque/about-us/what-we-inves tigate. Accessed April 18, 2016.

FBI Counterterrorism Analysis Section. "Sovereign Citizens: A Growing Threat to Law Enforcement." *FBI Law Enforcement Bulletin*. Washington, D.C.: Federal Bureau of

Investigation, September 2011. https://leb.fbi.gov/2011/september/sovereign-citizens
-a-growing-domestic-threat-to-law-enforcement.

FBI Office for Victim Assistance. *Strategic Plan 2004–2009.* Washington, D.C.: U.S. Department of Justice, 2004. http://www.fbi.gov/publications/strategicplan/strategic
plantext.htm.

FBIS (Foreign Broadcast Information Service), Near East/South Asia. "Israel: Palestinian Television Broadcasts Clip Encouraging Martyrdom." [In Hebrew.] *Ma'ariv* (Tel Aviv), August 11, 2003.

Feiler, Stuart I. "Terrorism: Is Tourism Really the Target?" *Hotel and Restaurants International,* October 1986.

Felter, Joseph and Brian Fishman. *Al-Qa'ida's Foreign Fighters in Iraq: A First Look at the Sinjar Records.* West Point, N.Y.: U.S. Military Academy, Combating Terrorism Center, 2007.

Fenton, Ben, Johanna Kassel, and Richard McGregor. "Bin Laden Papers Reveal al Qaeda Rifts." *Financial Times* (London), May 3, 2012.

Ferguson, Neil and Eve Binks. "Understanding Radicalization and Engagement in Terrorism Through Religious Conversion Motifs." *Journal of Strategic Security* 8, nos. 1–2 (Spring/Summer 2015): 16–26.

Ferracuti, Franco and Francesco Bruno. "Psychiatric Aspects of Terrorism in Italy." Unpublished study commissioned by the Italian secret services. N.d.

Fetscher, I. and G. Rohrmoser. *Analysenzum Terrorismus* [Analyses on the subject of terrorism]. Vol. 1, *Ideologien und Strategien* [Ideologies and strategies]. Bonn: Westdeutscher Verlag, 1981.

Filkins, Dexter. "Sri Lanka Women at War: Tamil Rebel Group Is Now One-Third Female." *International Herald Tribune* (Paris), March 13, 2000.

Fimreite, Anne Lise, Peter Lango, Per Laegreid, and Lise H. Rykkja. "After Oslo and Utøya: A Shift in the Balance Between Security and Liberty in Norway?" *Studies in Conflict and Terrorism* 36, no. 10 (October 2013): 839–56.

Finer, Jonathan and Anthony Faiola. "Insurgents Say They Have Killed Japanese: Video May Show Body of Hostage." *Washington Post,* May 29, 2005.

Finn, Peter and Peter Baker. "Hostages Were Helpless in the Face of Chaos." *Washington Post,* September 5, 2005.

Fishman, Brian, ed. *Bombers, Bank Accounts, and Bleedout: Al-Qa'ida's Road in and Out of Iraq.* West Point, N.Y.: U.S. Military Academy, Combating Terrorism Center, 2008.

Fisk, Robert. "Abu Nidal, Notorious Palestinian Mercenary, 'Was a US Spy.'" *Independent,* October 24, 2008. http://www.independent.co.uk/news/world/middle-east/abu
-nidal-notorious-palestinian-mercenary-was-a-us-spy-972812.html.

Fiskhoff, Sue. "Gentle, Kind, and Full of Religious Fervor." *Jerusalem Post,* February 27, 1994.

Fitchett, Joseph. "Guerrillas Seeking Leverage." *Christian Science Monitor,* November 27, 1973.

Foley, Charles. *Island in Revolt.* London: Longmans, 1962.

——, ed. *The Memoirs of General Grivas.* London: Longmans, 1964.

Foley, Charles and W. I. Scobie. *The Struggle for Cyprus.* Stanford, Calif.: Hoover Institution Press, 1975.

Ford, Franklin L. *Political Murder: From Tyrannicde to Terrorism.* Cambridge, Mass.: Harvard University Press, 1985.

Foreign Report (London). "The Palestinians of the 1990s." No. 2202 (April 2, 1992).

——. "Yeltsin Adds to Kremlin Power." No. 2365 (August 24, 1995).

Foster, Anthony. "An Emerging Threat Shapes Up as Terrorists Take to the High Seas." *Jane's Intelligence Review*, July 1998.

Fouda, Yosri and Nick Fielding. *Masterminds of Terror: The Truth Behind the Most Devastating Terrorist Attack the World Has Ever Seen.* New York: Arcade, 2003.

Frank, Gerold. *The Deed.* New York: Simon & Schuster, 1963.

Frankel, Glenn and Craig Whitlock. "London Probe Extends Abroad: Egyptian Arrested, Pakistani Sought." *Washington Post*, July 16, 2005.

Franks, Lucinda. "Annual of Law Enforcement: Don't Shoot—In the New FBI, Patience Comes First." *New Yorker*, July 22, 1996. http://www.threatlink.com/pr/articles/Don't%20Shoot.pdf.

Frenkel, Sheera. "Everything You Ever Wanted to Know About How ISIS Uses the Internet." *BuzzFeed*, May 12, 2016. https://www.buzzfeed.com/sheerafrenkel/everything-you-ever-wanted-to-know-about-how-isis-uses-the-i?utm_term=.dejrLb930#.fv4DYvgm1.

Freytag, Andreas, Jens Kruger, Daniel Meierrieks, and Friedrich Schneider. "The Origins of Terrorism: Cross-Country Estimates of Socio-economic Determinants of Terrorism." *European Journal of Political Economy*, no. 27 (2011): S5–S16.

Friedman, Thomas L. "Jewish Terrorists Freed by Israel." *New York Times*, December 9, 1984.

——. "Strategy of Suicide Bombings." *New York Times*, March 31, 2002.

Fromm, Joseph. "TV: Does It Box in [the] President in a Crisis?" *U.S. News & World Report*, July 5, 1985.

Gambetta, Diego and Steffen Hertog. *Engineers of Jihad: The Curious Connection Between Violent Extremism and Education.* Princeton, N.J.: Princeton University Press, 2016.

Ganor, Boaz. *The Counter-Terrorism Puzzle: A Guide for Decision Makers.* New Brunswick, N.J.: Transaction, 2005.

——. "Suicide Attacks in Israel." In *Countering Suicide Terrorism: An International Conference.* International Policy Institute for Counter-Terrorism. Edited by Boaz Ganor, 134–45. Jerusalem: Gefen, 2001.

García-Granados, Jorge. *The Birth of Israel: The Drama as I Saw It.* New York: Knopf, 1948.

Gardela, Karen and Bruce Hoffman. *The RAND Chronology of International Terrorism for 1986.* Santa Monica, Calif.: RAND Corporation, R-3890-RC, 1990.

——. *The RAND Chronology of International Terrorism for 1987.* Santa Monica, Calif.: RAND Corporation, R-4006-RC, 1991.

Gardham, Duncan. "Manchester Bomb Plot Students Were Planning Co-ordinated Attacks in New York and Scandinavia." *Daily Telegraph* (London), December 16, 2010. http://www.telegraph.co.uk/news/worldnews/northamerica/usa/8205200/Manchester-bomb-plot-students-were-planning-co-ordinated-attacks-in-New-York-and-Scandinavia.html.

Gardham, Duncan and Robert Crilly. "Bin Laden 'Personally Approved' Attacks on Europe." *Daily Telegraph* (London), October 1, 2010.

Gaucher, Roland. *Les Terroristes.* Paris: Editions Albin Michel, 1965.

Gearty, Conor. *The Future of Terrorism.* London: Phoenix, 1997.

Geiss, Imanuel, ed. *July 1914: The Outbreak of the First World War—Select Documents.* New York: Norton, 1967.

Gellman, Barton. "Al Qaeda Near Biological, Chemical Arms Production." *Washington Post*, March 23, 2003.

——. "Cyber-Attacks by Al-Qaeda Feared: Terrorists at Threshold of Using Internet as Tool of Bloodshed, Experts Say." *Washington Post*, June 27, 2002.

General Intelligence and Security Service. *Recruitment for the Jihad in the Netherlands: From Incident to Trend.* The Hague: Ministry of the Interior and Kingdom Relations, December 2002.

Genovese, Margaret. "Terrorism: Newspapers Grapple with the Extraordinary Challenges of Covering Worldwide Terrorist Incidents." *Presstime* (New York), August 1986.

Geranios, Nicholas K. "'Almost Heaven' Survivalist Community Pines for Its Founder." *Los Angeles Times*, November 19, 1999. http://articles.latimes.com/1999/nov/14/local /me-33373.

Gerges, Fawaz A. *The Far Enemy: Why Jihad Went Global.* Cambridge: Cambridge University Press, 2005.

——. *Obama and the Middle East: The End of America's Moment.* New York: Palgrave Macmillan, 2012.

Gerhard, Victor. "Payback's a Bitch." Vanguard News Network. http://www.vanguardnews network.com/v1/index117.htm. Accessed May 5, 2016.

German, Mike. "Behind the Lone Terrorists, a Pack Mentality." *Washington Post*, June 5, 2005.

Gervasi, Frank. *The Life and Times of Menachem Begin: Rebel to Statesman.* New York: G. P. Putnam's Sons, 1979.

Geyelin, Philip. "NBC: How to Protect a Terrorist." *Washington Post*, May 19, 1986.

Ghattas, Kim. "Talking Loud and Saying Nothing." foreignpolicy.com, August 4, 2015. http://foreignpolicy.com/2015/08/04/four-problems-with-obama-countering -violent-extremism-cve-isis/.

Ghattas, Kim and Roula Khalaf. "Shooting Spree in Saudi City Spreads Jitters Among Western Companies." *Financial Times* (London), May 3, 2004.

Ghattas, Sam F. "Syria Foes to Control Lebanon's Parliament." *Washington Post*, June 21, 2005.

Ghosh, Bobby. "How Dangerous Is the Cleric Anwar al-Awlaqi?" *Time*, January 13, 2010. http://www.time.com/time/world/article/0,8599,1953426,00.html.

Ghufran, Nasreen. "Afghanistan in 2007: A Bleeding Wound." *Asian Survey* 48, no. 1 (January/February 2008).

Gibb, H. A. R. *Islam.* Oxford: Oxford University Press, 1978.

Gibbons-Neff, Thomas. "Number of Foreign Fighters Entering Iraq and Syria Drops by 90 Percent, Pentagon Says." *Washington Post*, April 26, 2016. https://www.washington post.com/news/checkpoint/wp/2016/04/26/number-of-foreign-fighters-entering -iraq-and-syria-drops-by-90-percent-pentagon-says/.

Gill, K. P. S. *Punjab: The Knights of Falsehood.* New Delhi: Har-Anandp, 2001.

Giustozzi, Antonio. *Koran, Kalashnikov, and Laptop: The Neo-Taliban Insurgency in Afghanistan.* New York: Columbia University Press, 2008.

Glasser, Susan B. "'Martyrs' in Iraq Mostly Saudis: Web Sites Track Suicide Bombings." *Washington Post*, May 15, 2005.

——. "Review May Shift Terror Policies." *Washington Post*, May 29, 2005.

Goldberg, Jeffrey. "The Martyr Strategy: What Does the New Phase of Terrorism Signify?" *New Yorker*, July 9, 2001.

Golden, Tim. "Mexico's New Offensive: Erasing Rebel's Mystique." *New York Times*, February 11, 1995.

Goldstein, Joseph. "F.B.I. Chief Sees an ISIS 'Diaspora.'" *New York Times*, July 29, 2016.

Goodwin-Gill, Guy and Ilene Cohn. *Child Soldiers: The Role of Children in Armed Conflict*. Oxford: Clarendon, 1994.

Goren, Roberta. *The Soviet Union and Terrorism*. Edited by Jillian Becker. London: Allen and Unwin, 1984.

Gorman, Edward. "Bomb Disposers Mark 21 Years in Ulster." *Times* (London), November 7, 1992.

——. "How to Stop the IRA." *Times* (London), January 11, 1992.

——. "Libyan Arms Shipments Allow IRA to Maintain Campaign of Violence." *Times* (London), March 7, 1991.

Gorman, Siobhan. "CIA Kills al Qaeda's No. 2." *Wall Street Journal*, June 6, 2012.

The Government of Canada Response to the Commission of Inquiry Into the Investigation of the Bombing of Air India Flight 182. Ottawa: Public Safety Canada, December 8, 2015. https://www.publicsafety.gc.ca/cnt/rsrcs/pblctns/rspns-cmmssn/index-en .aspx.

Graham, Ian. "Official: IRA Using 'Bigger, Better' Bombs." *London Press Association*, January 23, 1992.

Greenberg, Joel. "Israeli Police Question Two Rabbis in Rabin Assassination." *New York Times*, November 22, 1995.

——. "Slaying Blended Technology and Guile." *New York Times*, January 10, 1996.

Grivas, General. *Guerrilla Warfare and Eoka's Struggle*. Translated by A. A. Pallis. London: Longmans, 1964.

Grossman, Lawrence K. "Television and Terrorism: A Common Sense Approach." *TVI Report* 6, no. 4 (1986).

Grunwald, Michael. "U.S. Says Bin Laden Sought Nuclear Arms." *Washington Post*, September 26, 1998.

Gunaratna, Rohan. "Case Study: The Liberation Tigers of Tamil Eelam." *Jane's Intelligence Review*, October 2001.

——. "The Conflict in Sri Lanka, 1982–Present." Unpublished paper prepared as part of a project on how terrorism escalates, conducted at the Centre for the Study of Terrorism and Political Violence, University of St. Andrews, Scotland, March 1997.

——. *Implications of the Sri Lankan Tamil Insurgency*. Colombo: Alumni Association of the Bandaranaike Centre for International Studies; London: International Foundation of Sri Lankans United Kingdom, 1997.

——. *Inside Al Qaeda: Global Network of Terrorism*. London: Hurst, 2002.

——. *International and Regional Security Implications of the Sri Lankan Tamil Insurgency*. St. Albans, Herts: International Foundation of Sri Lankans, 1997.

——. "Khalid Sheikh Mohammed: The Brain." *Playboy* 52, no. 6 (June 2005).

——. "The LTTE and Suicide Terrorism." *Frontline*, February 2000.

——. "The Rebellion in Sri Lanka: Sparrow Tactics to Guerrilla Warfare (1971–1996)." Unpublished manuscript. N.d.

——. "Sea Tiger Success Threatens the Spread of Copycat Tactics." *Jane's Intelligence Review*, March 2001.

——. "Suicide Terrorism: A Global Threat." *Jane's Intelligence Review*, October 20, 2000. http://www.janes.com/security/international_security/news/usscole/jir001020_1_n .shtml.

——. "Suicide Terrorism in Sri Lanka and India: LTTE Suicide Capability, Likely Trends, and Response." Unpublished manuscript. Expanded version of a paper presented at the First International Conference on Countering Suicide Terrorism, Herzilya, Israel, February 20–23, 2000.

——. "Tiger Cubs and Childhood Fall as Casualties in Sri Lanka." *Jane's Intelligence Review*, July 1998.

——. *War and Peace in Sri Lanka*. Sri Lanka: Institute of Fundamental Studies, 1987.

Habeck, Mary. "Al Qaeda: Alive and Kicking." *Foreign Policy—Shadow Government: Notes from the Loyal Opposition*, May 8, 2012. http://shadow.foreignpolicy.com/blog/69526.

——. "Answering Objections: Is al Qaeda Really Dead, Part One?" *Foreign Policy—Shadow Government: Notes from the Loyal Opposition*, April 19, 2012. http://shadow.foreignpolicy.com/blog/69526.

——. "Can We Declare the War on al Qaeda Over?" *Foreign Policy—Shadow Government: Notes from the Loyal Opposition*, June 27, 2012. http://shadow.foreignpolicy.com/blog/69526.

——. "Evaluating the War with al Qaeda." *Foreign Policy—Shadow Government: Notes from the Loyal Opposition*, March 2, 2012–April 17, 2012. http://shadow.foreignpolicy.com/blog/69526.

——. "Evaluating the War with al Qaeda." *Foreign Policy—Shadow Government: Notes from the Loyal Opposition*, March 15, 2012. http://shadow.foreignpolicy.com/blog/69526.

——. "What Does al Qaeda Want?" *Foreign Policy—Shadow Government: Notes from the Loyal Opposition*, March 6, 2012. http://shadow.foreignpolicy.com/blog/69526.

Haber, Eitan. *Menachem Begin: The Legend and the Man*. New York: Delacorte, 1978.

Hacker, Frederick J. *Crusaders, Criminals, Crazies: Terror and Terrorism in Our Time*. New York: Norton, 1976.

Hafez, Mohammed. *Suicide Bombers in Iraq: The Strategy and Ideology of Martyrdom*. Washington, D.C.: USIP, 2007.

Hafez, Mohammed and Creighton Mullins. "The Radicalization Puzzle: A Theoretical Synthesis of Empirical Approaches to Homegrown Extremism." *Studies in Conflict and Terrorism* 38, no. 11 (November 2015): 958–75.

Hakakian, Roya. *Assassins of the Turquoise Palace*. New York: Grove, 2011.

Halaby, Jamal. "Zarqawi Among 13 Indicted by Jordan in Plot: Officials Say Militants Planned to Attack Premier's Office, U.S. Embassy in Amman." *Washington Post*, October 18, 2004.

Halsell, Grace. "Why Bobby Brown of Brooklyn Wants to Blow Up Al Aqsa." *Arabia*, August 1984.

"Hamas Issues Statement on Ayyash Killing." Al-Quds Palestinian Radio (in Arabic), 1755 GMT, January 5, 1996.

Hannigan, Robert. "The Web Is a Terrorists's Command-and-Control Network of Choice." *Financial Times* (London), November 4, 2014. http://www.ft.com/intl/cms/s/2/c89b6c58-6342-11e4-8a63-00144feabdco.html#axzz3I6l8Haho.

Hansard. *House of Commons*. 5th series, Parliamentary Debates. London, House of Commons.

Harel, Amos. "Number of Suicide Bombings Around the World Surged 94% in 2014 Amid Rise of ISIS." *Ha'aretz*, January 4, 2015. http://www.haaretz.com/israel-news/.premium-1.635193.

——. "Shin Bet: 145 Suicide Bombers since the Start of the Intifada." *Ha'aretz*, September 29, 2002.

Harik, Judith Palmer. *Hezbollah: The Changing Face of Terrorism*. London: I. B. Tauris, 2004.

Harris, Paul, Nick Paton Walsh, and Burhan Wazir. "The Making of a Terrorist: How a Petty Thief Turned Into a Human Timebomb." *Guardian*, December 30, 2001.

Harrison, David. "Jackboot Stamp of the New Right." *Observer* (London), April 23, 1995.

Hart, Alan. *Arafat: A Political Biography. The Definitive Biography Written in Cooperation with Yasser Arafat*. London: Sidgwick and Jackson, 1994.

Hart, Peter. *The I.R.A. and Its Enemies: Violence and Community in Cork, 1916–1923*. Oxford: Oxford University Press, 2000.

Hassan, Nasra. "Letter from Gaza: An Arsenal of Believers." *New Yorker*, November 19, 2001.

Hassan, Riaz. *Life as a Weapon: The Global Rise of Suicide Bombings*. New York: Routledge, 2011.

Hasselbach, Ingo, with Tom Reiss. *Führer-Ex: Memoirs of a Former Neo-Nazi*. London: Chatto and Windus, 1996.

Hays, Tom and Larry Neumeister. "Trade Center Bombers Get Life in Prison." Associated Press, May 25, 1994.

Hearst, David. "'Human Bomb' Fails to Explode." *Guardian* (London), November 24, 1990.

——. "IRA Mines Gap in Army Security." *Guardian* (London), April 10, 1990.

——. "Publicity Key Element of Strategy." *Guardian* (London), July 31, 1990.

Hedges, Chris and Joel Greenberg. "West Bank Massacre: Before Killing, a Final Prayer and a Final Taunt." *New York Times*, February 28, 1994.

Heffelfinger, Christopher, Scott Shane, and Christopher Boucek. Carnegie Endowment for International Peace—Transcript, "The Rise of Anwar al-Awlaki," June 1, 2010. http://www.carnegieendowment.org/events/?fa=eventDetail&id=2920.

Heggoy, Alf Andrew. *Insurgency and Counterinsurgency in Algeria*. Bloomington: Indiana University Press, 1972.

Heller, Joseph. *The Stern Gang: Ideology, Politics, and Terror, 1940–1949*. London: Frank Cass, 1995.

Hendawi, Hamza. "Cult Evolves Around Suicide Bombers." Associated Press, April 28, 2002. http://www.news.findlaw.com/ap_stories/i/1107/4–28–2002/20020428102000255505.html.

Hendren, John. "Rumsfeld Tells Nations Not to Help Zarqawi." *Los Angeles Times*, June 2, 2005.

Henze, Paul B. *The Plot to Kill the Pope*. New York: Scribner's, 1983.

Herath, Tamara. *Women in Terrorism: The Case of the LTTE*. New Delhi: Sage, 2012.

Herbert, Ian and Arifa Akbar. "Shahzad Tanweer: 'I Cannot Begin to Explain This. He Was Proud to Be British.'" *Independent*, July 14, 2005.

Herman, Edward and Gerry O'Sullivan. *The "Terrorism" Industry*. New York: Pantheon, 1989.

Herman, Ken. "After the Assault: U.S. Braces for Crusade Against 'Evil.'" *Atlanta Journal-Constitution*, September 17, 2001.

Hermon, Sir John. "The Police, the Media, and the Reporting of Terrorism." In *Terrorism and the Media*, edited by Yonah Alexander and Richard Latter, 37–46. McLean, Va.: Brassey's, 1990.

Hersh, Seymour M. *Chain of Command: The Road from 9/11 to Abu Ghraib*. New York: HarperCollins, 2004.

Hezbollah. "Open Letter from the Party of God to the Disinherited of Lebanon and the World Revealing the Way and the Intentions Which Are Their Own on the Occasion of the First Anniversary of Ragheb Harb, Symbol of the Islamic Resistance and Exemplary Martyr." Beirut, Lebanon, February 16, 1985.

Hickey, Neil. "Terrorism and Television." *TV Guide*, July 31, 1976.

The Hindu (Chennai). "Three Former TULF MPs Shot Dead in Jaffna." April 9, 1985.

Hirst, David. *The Gun and the Olive Branch*. London: Futura, 1977.

"Hizbullah's Cyber-Success." *Foreign Report* (London), no. 2527 (January 14, 1999).

Hoagland, Jim. "Palestinian Guerrillas Say They Reject Cease-fire." *Washington Post*, October 23, 1973.

——. "A Shifting Focus on Terrorism." *Washington Post*, April 24, 2005.

Hodgson, Karen. "Threat Matrix: Reports Claim Al Nusrah Front Members in Turkey Were Planning Sarin Gas Attacks." *Long War Journal*, May 31, 2013. http://www.longwarjournal.org/threat-matrix/archives/2013/05/on_may_30_the_turkish-print.php.

Hodson, Peregrine. "Japanese Disband Aum Cult." *Times* (London), December 15, 1995.

Hoffman, Bruce. *Anonymous Soldiers: The Struggle for Israel 1917–1947*. New York: Knopf, 2015/Vintage, 2016.

——. "The Bombing of the King David Hotel." *Midstream* 29, no. 7 (August/September 1983): 61–62.

——. "The Coming ISIS–al Qaeda Merger: It's Time to Take the Threat Seriously." *Foreign Affairs—Snapshot*, March 29, 2016. https://www.foreignaffairs.com/articles/2016-03-29/coming-isis-al-qaeda-merger.

——. "The Contrasting Ethical Foundations of Terrorism in the 1980s." *Terrorism and Political Violence* 1, no. 3 (July 1989): 361–77.

——. "Creatures of the Cold War: The JRA." *Jane's Intelligence Review*, February 1997.

——. "The First Non-State Use of a Chemical Weapon in Warfare: The Tamil Tigers' Assault on East Kiran." *Small Wars and Insurgencies* 20, no. 3 (September 2009): 463–77.

——. "'Holy Terror': The Implications of Terrorism Motivated by a Religious Imperative." *Studies in Conflict and Terrorism* 18, no. 4 (Winter 1995): 271–84.

——. *Insurgency and Counterinsurgency in Iraq*. Santa Monica, Calif.: RAND Corporation, OP-127, 2004.

——. "The Jewish Defense League." *Terrorism, Violence, and Insurgency Journal* 5, no. 1 (Summer 1984): 10–15.

——. "Jewish Terrorist Activities and the British Government in Palestine 1939 to 1947." DPhil thesis, Oxford University, 1986.

——. *Lessons of 9/11: Statement Submitted for the Committee Record to the United States Joint September 11, 2001 Inquiry Staff of the House and Senate Select Committees on Intelligence, 8 October 2002*. Santa Monica, Calif.: RAND Corporation, 2002.

——. "The Logic of Suicide Terrorism: Lessons from Israel That America Must Learn." *Atlantic Monthly* 291, no. 5 (June 2003).

——. "Low-Intensity Conflict: Terrorism and Guerrilla Warfare in the Coming Decades." In *Terrorism: Roots, Impact, Responses*, edited by Lawrence Howard, 139–54. New York: Praeger, 1992.

——. "The Myth of Grass-Roots Terrorism: Why Osama bin Laden Still Matters." *Foreign Affairs* 87, no. 3 (May/June 2008); 133–38.

——. "Old Madness, New Methods: Revival of Religious Terrorism Begs for Broader U.S. Policy." *RAND Review* 22, no. 2 (Winter 1998).

——. "Recent Trends and Future Prospects of Iranian Sponsored International Terrorism." In *Middle Eastern Terrorism: Current Threats and Future Prospects*, edited by Yonah Alexander, 41–82. New York: G. K. Hall, 1994.

——. *Recent Trends and Future Prospects of Terrorism in the United States.* Santa Monica, Calif.: RAND Corporation, R-3618, April 1986.

——. "Right-Wing Terrorism in Europe." *Conflict* 5, no. 3 (Fall 1984): 185–210.

——. "Right-Wing Terrorism in Europe since 1980." *Orbis* 28, no. 1 (Spring 1984); 16–27.

——. *Right-Wing Terrorism in Germany.* Research Report no. 13. London: Institute of Jewish Affairs, December 1986.

——. "Right-Wing Terrorism in the United States." *Violence, Aggression, Terrorism Journal,* no. 1 (Winter 1987).

——. *Terrorism in the United States and the Potential Threat to Nuclear Facilities.* Santa Monica, Calif.: RAND Corporation, R-3351-DOE, January 1986.

——. "Why Terrorists Don't Claim Credit." *Terrorism and Political Violence* 9, no. 1 (Spring 1997): 1–6.

Hoffman, Bruce, with David Claridge. "Illicit Trafficking in Nuclear Materials." *Conflict Studies,* nos. 314/315. London: Research Institute for the Study of Conflict and Terrorism, January/February 1999.

Hoffman, Bruce and Reinares Fernando, eds. *The Evolution of the Global Terrorist Threat from 9/11 to Osama bin Laden's Death.* New York: Columbia University Press, October 2014.

Hoffman, Bruce and Donna Kim Hoffman. "Chronology of International Terrorism 1995." *Terrorism and Political Violence* 8, no. 3 (Autumn 1996): 87–127.

Hoffman, Bruce and Gordon H. McCormick. "Terrorism, Signaling, and Suicide Attack." *Studies in Conflict and Terrorism* 27, no. 4 (July/August 2004): 243–81.

Hoffman, David. "Reports Renew Suspicions of Iran, Syria Bomb Link." *Washington Post,* April 26, 1992.

Hoge, James W. "The Media and Terrorism." In *Terrorism: The Media and the Law,* edited by Abraham Miller, 89–105. New York: Transnational, 1982.

Holmes, Steven A. "U.S. Charges 12 in Arizona Plot to Blow Up Government Office." *New York Times,* July 2, 1996.

Horgan, John. "From Profiles to Pathways and Roots to Routes: Perspectives from Psychology on Radicalization Into Terrorism." *Annals of the American Academy of Political and Social Science* 618 (July 2008): 80–94.

——. *Walking Away from Terrorism: Accounts of Disengagement from Radical and Extremist Movements.* London: Routledge, 2009.

Horne, Alistair. *A Savage War of Peace: Algeria 1954–1962.* Harmondsworth: Penguin, 1977.

Horwitz, Sari and Adam Goldman. "FBI Director: Number of Americans Traveling to Fight in Syria Increasing." *Washington Post,* May 2, 2014. https://www.washingtonpost.com/world/nationalsecurity/fbi-director-number-of-americans-traveling-to-fight-in-syria-increasing/2014/05/02/6fa3d84e-d222-11e3-937f-d3026234b51c_story.html.

Howard, Michael. "Smoke on the Horizon." *Financial Times* (London), September 7, 2002.

——. "What Friends Are For." *National Interest,* no. 69 (Fall 2002): 8–10.

Huband, Mark and David Buchan. "Al-Qaeda May Have Access to 18,000 'Potential Operatives,' Says Think-Tank." *Financial Times* (London), May 26, 2004.

Hurwitz, Harry. *Menachem Begin.* Johannesburg: Jewish Herald, 1977.

Husain, Ed. *The Islamist: Why I Joined Radical Islam in Britain, What I Saw Inside and Why I Left.* London: Penguin, 2007.

——. "Syria: Why al Qaeda Is Winning." *National Review Online*, August 23, 2012. http://www.nationalreview.com/articles/314685/syria-why-al Qaeda-winning-ed-husain.

Hyams, Edward. *Terrorists and Terrorism*. New York: St. Martin's, 1974.

Ibrahim, Youssef M. "Muslim Edicts Take on New Force." *New York Times*, February 12, 1995.

Iglarsh, Harvey J. "Fear of Flying: Its Economic Costs." *Terrorism* 10, no. 1 (Winter 1987): 45–50.

Ignatius, David. "The Islamic State Is Still on the Rise." *Washington Post*, February 4, 2016. https://www.washingtonpost.com/opinions/the-islamic-state-is-still-on-the-rise/2016/02/04/e631bdea-cb82-11e5-88ff-e2d1b4289c2f_story.html.

Independent (London). "Terrorists Killed by Their Own Devices." February 20, 1996.

Institute for Economics and Peace (IEP). *Global Terrorism Index 2016: Measuring and Understanding the Impact of Terrorism*. Sydney, New York, and Mexico City: Institute for Economics and Peace, November 2016. http://economicsandpeace.org/wp-content/uploads/2015/11/Global-Terrorism-Index-2016.pdf.

Institute for Palestine Studies, International Studies Section. *Who Is Menachem Begin? A Documentary Sketch*. Beirut: Institute for Palestine Studies, 1977.

IntelCenter. *Al-Qaeda Targeting Guidance*. Vol. 1.0. Alexandria, Va.: IntelCenter/Tempest, April 1, 2004.

——. *Evolution of Jihadi Video* (EJV). Vol. 1.0. Alexandria, Va.: IntelCenter/Tempest, May 11, 2005.

Intelligence and Security Committee. *Report Into the London Terrorist Attacks on 7 July 2005: Presented to Parliament by the Prime Minister by Command of Her Majesty*, Cmd 6785, May 2006.

Intelligence and Terrorism Information Center at the Center for Special Studies (C.S.S.). "Special Information Bulletin: Marketing of Terrorism Through the Internet." November 2004. http://www.intelligence.org.il/eng/sib/1_05/n_t.htm. Accessed June 16, 2005.

"Intelligence Battle in Cyberspace." *Intelligence Newsletter*, no. 263 (April 27, 1995).

International Crisis Group. "Philippines Terrorism: The Role of Militant Islamic Converts." December 19, 2005. http://www.crisisgroup.org/en/regions/asia/south-east-asia/philippines/110-philippines-terrorism-the-role-of-militant-islamic-converts.aspx.

International Herald Tribune (Paris). "In Our Pages: 100, 75, and 50 Years Ago—1947: Zionists' Suicide." April 22, 1997.

——. "Luxor Attackers Sought Cleric's Release in U.S.: Tourists Stream Home." November 19, 1997.

——. "30 More Slain by 'Terrorists' Near Algiers." April 15, 1997.

International Institute for Strategic Studies. *Strategic Survey 2003/4*. Oxford: Oxford University Press, 2004.

International Security Program. "Deadly Attacks Since 9/11: Homegrown Extremists." New America Foundation. http://securitydata.newamerica.net/extremists/deadly-attacks.html. Accessed May 12, 2016.

Issachaoff, Avi. "2016 Was Deadliest Year Ever for Suicide Bombings Worldwide." *Times of Israel*, January 6, 2017. http://www.timesofisrael.com/2016-was-deadliest-year-ever-for-suicide-bombings-worldwide/.

"ISIL Captures Cell of Foreign Elements Planning Attacks Against Emirs, Shaykhs in Al-Raqqah." Twitter, December 22, 2014, TRR2014122203827855.

"ISIS Spokesman Vows 'Defeat' for America, Calls for Killing Westerners in New Audio Message." TRR2014092201178788. *Hanin Network Forums* (Arabic), 22 September 2014.

Islamic Group in Egypt. "Statement on U.S. Sentencing of Sheikh Rahman." January 19, 1996.

Ismail, Noor Huda. "The Role of Kinship in Indonesia's Jemaah Islamiya." *Terrorism Monitor* (Jamestown Foundation, Washington, D.C.) 4, no. 11 (June 2, 2006). http://www.jamestown.org/single/?no_cache=1&tx_ttnews%5Btt_news%5D=791.

"IS's Abu Jihad Slams Caucasus Emirate and Gives More Details of 'Truce Request' Meeting in Raqqah." December 14, 2014, LIL2015012643223960.

Ivianskii, Zeev. "Fathers and Sons: A Study of Jewish Involvement in the Revolutionary Movement and Terrorism in Tsarist Russia." *Terrorism and Political Violence* 1, no. 2 (April 1989): 137–55.

Iwanski, Len. "All 16 Remaining Freemen Surrender Peacefully." Associated Press, June 14, 1996.

Iyad, Abu, with Eric Rouleau. *My Home, My Land: A Narrative of the Palestinian Struggle*. Translated by Linda Butler Koseoglu. New York: Times Books, 1981.

Jaber, Hala. *Hezbollah: Born with a Vengeance*. New York: Columbia University Press, 1997.

Jackson, Richard, et al. "Introduction: The Case for Critical Terrorism Studies." In *Critical Terrorism Studies: A New Research Agenda*, 1–10. Abingdon: Routledge, 2009.

——. "Knowledge, Power and Politics in the Study of Political Terrorism." In *Critical Terrorism Studies: A New Research Agenda*, 66–84. Abingdon: Routledge, 2009.

Jakarta Post Online. "Imam Samudra's Son Killed in Syria." October 16, 2015. http://www.thejakartapost.com/news/2015/10/16/imam-samudra-s-son-killed-syria.html.

——. "Indonesia: Sons of Jihadists Flock to Syria." March 30, 2015. http://www.thejakartapost.com/news/2015/03/31/sons-jihadists-flock-syria.html.

Jamieson, Alison. *The Heart Attacked: Terrorism and Conflict in the Italian State*. London: Marion Boyars, 1989.

——. *Terrorism*. Hove, East Sussex: Wayland, 1991.

Janke, Peter. *Guerrilla and Terrorist Organisations: A World Directory and Bibliography*. New York: Macmillan, 1983.

Janofsky, Michael. "For Aryan Congress Stridency and Scrutiny." *New York Times*, July 23, 1995.

——. "One Man's Journey from Academia to Extremism." *New York Times*, July 5, 1995.

Jarbawi, Ali and Roger Heacock. "The Deportations and the Palestinian-Israeli Negotiations." *Journal of Palestinian Studies* 22, no. 3 (Spring 1993): 32–45.

Jarvis, Lee and Michael Lister. "State Terrorism Research and Critical Terrorism Studies: An Assessment." *Critical Studies on Terrorism* 7, no. 1 (2014): 43–61.

Jehl, Douglas. "Iran Tells the Europeans That It Doesn't Back Terrorism." *New York Times*, March 8, 1996.

——. "Iraq May Be Prime Place for Training of Militants, C.I.A. Report Concludes." *New York Times*, June 22, 2005.

Jenkins, Brian Michael. "International Terrorism: A New Mode of Conflict." In *International Terrorism and World Security*, edited by David Carlton and Carlo Schaerf, 13–49. London: Croom Helm, 1975.

——. *International Terrorism: The Other World War.* Santa Monica, Calif.: RAND Corporation, R-3302-AF, November 1985.

——. *The Likelihood of Nuclear Terrorism.* Santa Monica, Calif.: RAND Corporation, P-7119, July 1985.

——. *New Modes of Conflict.* Santa Monica, Calif.: RAND Corporation, R-3009-DNA, June 1983.

——. "The Organization Men: Anatomy of a Terrorist Attack." In *How Did This Happen? Terrorism and the New War,* edited by James F. Hoge Jr. and Gideon Rose, 1–14. New York: Public Affairs, 2001.

——. *The Psychological Implications of Media-Covered Terrorism.* Santa Monica, Calif.: RAND Corporation, P-6627, June 1981.

——. *The Study of Terrorism: Definitional Problems.* Santa Monica, Calif.: RAND Corporation, P-6563, December 1980.

——. *Will Terrorists Go Nuclear?* Santa Monica, Calif.: RAND Corporation, P-5541, November 1975.

Jerusalem Post (international edition). "Jail Term of Jewish Terrorist Reduced." October 12, 1985.

"Jihadists Discuss Jihad in Syria." Text and translation provided by *SITE Monitoring Service—Jihadist Threat,* February 14, 2012.

"Jihadists Launch a Syria-Focused Periodical, 'Balagh.'" Text and translation provided by *SITE Monitoring Service—Jihadist Threat,* March 13, 2012.

"Jihadists Urge Financial Support for Jihad in Syria." Text and translation provided by *SITE Monitoring Service—Jihadist Threat,* March 2, 2012.

Johnson, Keith, et al. "British Police Fear More Attacks by Terrorists: Lack of Clues, Hard Leads Suggests Bombers Learned from Madrid-Blast Arrests." *Wall Street Journal,* July 8, 2005.

Johnston, David. "Bomber Is Called Killer Who Is Not on a Political Mission." *New York Times,* November 6, 1995.

——. "Surrender Is a Victory for a Strategy of Patience." *New York Times,* June 13, 1996.

Johnston, David and David E. Sanger. "New Generation of Leaders Is Emerging for Al-Qa'ida." *New York Times,* August 10, 2004.

Joint Inquiry Into Intelligence Community Activities Before and After the Terrorist Attacks of September 11, 2001. *Report of the U.S. Senate Select Committee on Intelligence and U.S. House Permanent Select Committee on Intelligence Together with Additional Views.* December 2002.

Joll, James. *The Anarchists.* Boston: Little, Brown, 1964.

——. *Europe since 1870: An International History.* New York: Harper and Row, 1973.

Jones, Seth G. "Al Qaeda Is Far from Defeated." *Wall Street Journal,* April 29, 2012.

——. "Think Again: al Qaeda." *Foreign Policy,* May/June 2012. http://www.foreignpolicy.com/articles/2012/04/23/think_again_al_qaeda?print=yes&hidecomments=yes&page=full.

Jorisch, Avi. *Beacon of Hatred: Inside Hizballah's Al-Manar Television.* Washington, D.C.: Washington Institute for Near East Policy, 2004.

Joshi, Charu Lata. "Ultimate Sacrifice—Sri Lanka: Suicide Bombers." *Far Eastern Economic Review,* June 1, 2000. http://www.feer.com/00601/p64current.html.

Joshi, Manoj. "On the Razor's Edge: The Liberation Tigers of Tamil Eelam." *Studies in Conflict and Terrorism* 19, no. 1 (January–March 1996): 19–42.

Juergensmeyer, Mark. *The New Cold War? Religious Nationalism Confronts the Secular State*. Berkeley: University of California Press, 1993.

——. *Terror in the Mind of God*. Berkeley: University of California Press, 2000.

——. "Terror Mandated by God." *Terrorism and Political Violence* 9, no. 2 (Summer 1997): 16–23.

——, ed. *Violence and the Sacred in the Modern World*. London: Frank Cass, 1992.

——. "The Worldwide Rise of Religious Nationalism." *Journal of International Affairs* 50, no. 1 (Summer 1996): 1–20.

Jureidini, Paul A. *Case Studies in Insurgency and Revolutionary Warfare, Algeria 1954–1962*. Washington, D.C.: American University, 1963.

Kahane, Rabbi Meir. *Never Again! A Program for Survival*. Los Angeles: Nash, 1971.

——. *They Must Go*. New York: Grosset and Dunlap, 1981.

Kamalendran, Chris. "LTTE's Aircraft: Yes, No." *Sunday Times* (Colombo), December 6, 1998.

Kang, Cecilia, Craig Timberg, and Ellen Nakashima. "Sony's Hacked E-mails Expose Spats, Director Calling Angelina Jolie a 'Brat.'" *Washington Post*, December 11, 2014.

Kaplan, David E. "National Security Watch: Eurolefties Fund Iraq Insurgency." *U.S. News & World Report*, June 23, 2005. http://www.usnews.com/usnews/news/articles/050623/23euroleft.htm.

Kaplan, David E. and Andrew Marshall. *The Cult at the End of the World: The Incredible Story of Aum*. London: Hutchinson, 1996.

Kaplan, Jeffrey. "Right-Wing Violence in North America." *Terrorism and Political Violence* 7, no. 1 (Spring 1995): 44–95.

Karouny, Mariam. "Hizbollah Computer Game Recalls Israeli Battles." *Reuters Technology*, March 18, 2003. http://www.specialforce.net/english/news/reuters.htm.

Karov, Yishai and Ari Soffer. "Revealed: Israel Holding Senior Al Qaeda Operative." *Israel National News*, November 17, 2013. http://www.israelnationalnews.com/News/News .aspx/174122#.UolAzSeIiuI.

Karpin, Michael and Ina Friedman. *Murder in the Name of God: The Plot to Kill Yitzhak Rabin*. New York: Metropolitan, 1998.

Kaufman, Michael T. "Sikh Separatists Hijack Indian Jetliner to Pakistan." *New York Times*, September 30, 1981.

Katz, Samuel M. *The Hunt for the Engineer: How Israeli Agents Tracked the Hamas Master Bomber*. New York: Fromm, 1999.

Kay, Jenny. "Dying for Their Cause." *Eva* (London), June 1998.

Kedward, Roderick. *The Anarchists: The Men Who Shocked an Era*. London: BPC Unit 25, 1971.

Kellen, Konrad. *On Terrorists and Terrorism*. Santa Monica, Calif.: RAND Corporation, N-1942-RC, December 1982.

Kelley, Jack. "Militants Wire Web with Links to Jihad." *USA Today*, July 10, 2002.

——. "Terror Groups Hide Behind Web Encryption: Officials Say Sites Disguise Activities." *USA Today*, February 6, 2001.

Kelly, George Armstrong. *Lost Soldiers: The French Army and Empire in Crisis, 1947–1962*. Cambridge, Mass.: MIT Press, 1965.

Kelsey, Tim. "The Oklahoma Suspect Awaits Day of Reckoning." *Sunday Times* (London), April 21, 1996.

Kempe, Frederick. "Deadly Survivors: The Cold War Is Over but Leftist Terrorists in Germany Fight On." *Wall Street Journal*, December 27, 1991.

Kennedy, Hugh. "Holy Warriors: Telling the Story of the Crusades as History, Not Metaphor." *New York Times Book Review*, April 3, 2005.

Kenworthy, Tom. "Peaceful End Sought to Siege of Montana 'Freemen.'" *Washington Post*, March 30, 1996.

Keppel, Gilles. *Jihad: The Trail of Political Islam*. London: I.B. Tauris, 2006.

——. *The Revenge of God: The Resurgence of Islam, Christianity, and Judaism in the Modern World*. Cambridge, U.K.: Polity, 1995.

——. *The War for Muslim Minds: Islam and the West*. Cambridge, Mass.: Belknap, 2004.

Kessler, Glen. "Old Data, New Credibility Issues." *Washington Post*, August 4, 2004.

Khaled, Leila. *My People Shall Live: The Autobiography of a Revolutionary*. London: Hodder and Stoughton, 1973.

Khan, Muqtedar. "Countering Violent Extremism: The War on Terror, Reset." *Huffington Post*, April 18, 2016. http://www.huffingtonpost.com/muqtedar-khan/countering -violent-extrem_1_b_9713132.html.

Khomeini, Imam. *Islam and Revolution*. Translated by Hamid Algar. London: KPI, 1981.

Kifner, John. "Anti-Syria Alliance Claims Victory in Lebanese Voting." *New York Times*, June 20, 2005.

——. "Antiterrorism Law Used in Poison Smuggling Case." *New York Times*, December 23, 1995.

——. "Israelis Investigate Far Right: May Crack Down on Speech." *New York Times*, November 8, 1995.

——. "Man Arrested in Poison Case Kills Himself in Jail Cell." *New York Times*, December 24, 1995.

——. "A Son of Israel: Rabin's Assassin." *New York Times*, November 19, 1995.

——. "Zeal of Rabin's Assassin Linked to Rabbis of the Religious Right." *New York Times*, November 12, 1995.

King, Neil, Jr. "Moving Target: Fighting Terrorism Is Far More Perilous than It Used to Be." *Wall Street Journal Europe*, August 25, 1998.

King, Peter H. "Guru Revels in Revelation of a 'Paradise' Defiled." *Los Angeles Times*, September 22, 1985.

Kingston, Shane. "Terrorism, the Media, and the Northern Ireland Conflict." *Studies in Conflict and Terrorism* 18, no. 3 (July–September 1995): 203–31.

Kitfield, James. "The Hezbollah Model." *National Journal* 34, no. 20 (May 18, 2002).

Kitson, Frank. *Low-Intensity Operations*. London: Faber, 1971.

"Klanwatch, a Project of the Southern Poverty Law Center (Montgomery, Alabama)." *Intelligence Report* (Montgomery, Alabama), nos. 84 and 85 (November 1996 and Winter 1997).

Klausen, Jytte, et al. "Toward a Behavioral Model of 'Homegrown' Radicalization Trajectories." *Studies in Conflict and Terrorism* 39, no. 1 (January 2016): 67–83.

Knapp, Wilfrid. *A History of War and Peace, 1939–1965*. London: Royal Institute of International Affairs and Oxford University Press, 1967.

Knickerbocker, Brad. "Patience Is a Virtue in Freeman Standoff." *Christian Science Monitor*, June 14, 1996.

Kochanek, Stanley A. and Hardgrave, Robert L., eds. *India: Government and Politics in a Developing Nation*. 7th ed. Boston: Thomson, 2008.

Koust, Hal, ed. *Cyprus, 1946–1968*. New York: Facts on File, 1970.

Kovaleski, Serge F. and Alan Cowell. "London Bombers Sped to Glasgow, Authorities Say." *New York Times*, July 6, 2007.

Kramer, Martin. "Sacrifice and Fratricide in Shiite Lebanon." In *Violence and the Sacred in the Modern World*, edited by Mark Juergensmeyer, 30–47. London: Frank Cass, 1992.

Krieger, Tim and Daniel Meirerrieks. "What Causes Terrorism?" *Public Choice* 147, no. 3 (2011): 3–27.

Kristof, Nicholas D. "Behind the Terrorists." *New York Times*, May 7, 2002.

——. "In Shrine of Japan Cult, Police Find Laboratory." *New York Times*, March 11, 1995.

——. "Japanese Cult Planned U.S. Attack." *International Herald Tribune* (Paris), March 24, 1997.

Kristof, Nicholas D., with Sheryl WuDunn. "The Seer Among the Blind: Japanese Sect Leader's Rise." *New York Times*, March 26, 1995.

Krovel, Roy. "www.guerrilla.net." *Internet Today* (London), no. 25 (November 1996).

Krueger, Alan B. *What Makes a Terrorist*. Princeton, N.J.: Princeton University Press, 2007.

Krueger, Alan B. and David D. Laitin. *"Kto Kogo?* A Cross-Country Study of the Origins and Targets of Terrorism." Unpublished paper. January 18, 2007. http://krueger.princeton.edu/files/terrorism4.pdf.

Krueger, Alan B. and Jitka Malecková. "Education, Poverty and Terrorism: Is There a Causal Connection?" *Journal of Economic Perspectives* 17, no. 4 (Fall 2003): 119–44.

Kupperman, Robert H. and Darrel Trend. *Terrorism: Threat, Reality, Response*. Stanford, Calif.: Hoover Institution Press, 1979.

Kurzman, Charles and David Schanzer. "The Growing Right-Wing Terror Threat." *New York Times*, June 16, 2015.

——. *Law Enforcement Assessment of the Violent Extremism Threat*. Durham, N.C.: Triangle Center on Terrorism and Homeland Security, June 25, 2015. http://sites.duke.edu/tcths/files/2013/06/Kurzman_Schanzer_Law_Enforcement_Assessment_of_the_Violent_Extremist_Threat_final.pdf.

Kushner, Harvey W. "Suicide Bombers: Business as Usual." *Studies in Conflict and Terrorism* 19, no. 4 (October–December 1996): 329–37.

Ladd, Everett Carl. "U.S. Public and Somalia." *Christian Science Monitor*, October 15, 1993.

Lafore, Lawrence. *The Long Fuse: An Interpretation of the Origins of World War I*. London: Weidenfeld and Nicolson, 1966.

Lagon, Mark and Arch Puddington. "Exploiting Terrorism as a Pretext for Repression." *Wall Street Journal*, January 28, 2015.

Lahoud, Nelly, et al. *Letters from Abbottabad: Bin Laden Sidelined?* West Point, N.Y.: U.S. Military Academy, Combating Terrorism Center, May 3, 2012.

Lamothe, Dan. " 'Probably the Largest' al-Qaeda Training Camp Ever Destroyed in Afghanistan." *Washington Post*, October 30, 2015. https://www.washingtonpost.com/news/checkpoint/wp/2015/10/30/probably-the-largest-al-qaeda-training-camp-ever-destroyed-in-afghanistan/.

Lapping, Brian. *End of Empire*. New York: St. Martin's, 1985.

Laqueur, Walter. *The Age of Terrorism*. Boston: Little, Brown, 1987.

——. *Guerrilla: A Historical and Critical Study*. Boston: Little, Brown, 1976.

——, ed. *The Israel-Arab Reader: A Documentary History of the Middle East Conflict*. New York: Bantam, 1976.

——. *The New Terrorism: Fanaticism and the Arms of Mass Destruction.* Oxford: Oxford University Press, 1999.

——. *No End to War: Terrorism in the Twenty-First Century.* New York: Continuum, 2003.

——. "Postmodern Terrorism." *Foreign Affairs* 75, no. 5 (September/October 1996): 24–36.

——. "Reflections on Terrorism." *Foreign Affairs* 65, no. 1 (Fall 1986): 86–100.

——. *Terrorism.* London: Weidenfeld and Nicolson, 1977.

——, ed. *Voices of Terror: Manifestos, Writings, and Manuals of Al Qaeda, Hamas, and Other Terrorists from Around the World and Throughout the Ages.* New York: Reed, 2004.

Laqueur, Walter and Yonah Alexander, eds. *The Terrorism Reader.* New York: Meridian, 1987.

Lawrence, T. E. *Seven Pillars of Wisdom.* Harmondsworth: Penguin Books, 1977.

Lee, Jaeh, Brandon Ellington, and Gabrielle Canon. "The Rise of Violent Right-Wing Extremism, Explained." *Mother Jones*, June 30, 2015. http://www.motherjones.com /politics/2015/06/right-wing-extremism-explainer-charleston-mass-shooting -terrorism.

Lelyveld, Joseph. "All Suicide Bombers Are Not Alike: A Journey to Gaza, Cairo, and Hamburg in Search of What Really Made Sept. 11 Possible." *New York Times Magazine*, October 28, 2001.

Leppard, David. "Al-Qaeda's Heathrow Jet Plot Revealed." *Sunday Times* (London), October 9, 2005.

Leventhal, Paul and Yonah Alexander, eds. *Nuclear Terrorism: Defining the Threat.* Washington, D.C.: Pergamon-Brassey's, 1986.

Levine, Evyatar and Yaacov Shimoni, eds. *Political Dictionary of the Middle East in the Twentieth Century.* London: Weidenfeld and Nicolson, 1972.

Levitt, Matthew. "Designating the Al-Aqsa Martyrs Brigades." *Peacewatch*, no. 371. Washington, D.C.: Washington Institute for Near East Policy, March 25, 2002.

Lévy, Bernard-Henri. *Who Killed Daniel Pearl?* Hoboken, N.J.: Melville House, 2003.

Lewis, Bernard. *The Assassins: A Radical Sect in Islam.* London: Al Saqi Books, 1985.

"Libi Speaks on the Plight of Syrians in New Video." Text and translation provided by *SITE Monitoring Service—Jihadist Threat*, June 12, 2012.

Liddell Hart, B. H. *History of the Second World War.* New York: Paragon, 1979.

Life Magazine. "Bombs Blast a Message of Hate." March 27, 1970.

Lifton, Robert Jay. *Destroying the World to Save It: Aum Shinrikyo, Apocalyptic Violence, and the New Global Terrorism.* New York: Metropolitan Books, 1999.

Linzer, Dafna. "Nuclear Capabilities May Elude Terrorists, Experts Say." *Washington Post*, December 29, 2004.

Lipkin-Shahak, General (Ret.) Amnon. Introduction to *Countering Suicide Terrorism: An International Conference*, International Policy Institute for Counter-Terrorism, edited by Boaz Ganor, 5–9. Jerusalem: Gefen, 2001.

Lippman, Thomas W. "Capture of Kurd Spurs Rage in Europe." *Washington Post*, February 17, 1999.

Lipton, Eric. "Qaeda Letters Are Said to Show Pre-9/11 Anthrax Plans." *New York Times*, May 21, 2005.

Lister, Tim. "Is ISIS Going Broke?" CNN, March 9, 2016. http://www.cnn.com/2016/03 /04/middleeast/isis-finance-broke-lister/.

Litwak, Robert S. *Rogue States and U.S. Foreign Policy: Containment After the Cold War.* Washington, D.C.: Woodrow Wilson Center Press, 2000.

Llussa, Fernanda and Jose Tavares. "Economics and Terrorism: What We Know, What We Should Know, and the Data We Need." In *Terrorism, Economic Development, and Political Openness*, edited by Philip Keefer and Norman Loayza, 233–54. New York: Cambridge University Press, 2008.

Long, David E. *The Anatomy of Terrorism*. New York: Free Press, 1990.

Los Angeles Times. "Al-Qa'ida Trained at Least 70,000 in Terrorist Camps, Senator Says." July 14, 2003.

——. "Arab Leaders Join World in Assailing Terrorists' Attack." December 19, 1973.

——. "Armenians Turning to Terrorism." January 25, 1981.

——. "Syrian Clampdown on Fatah Guerrillas Told." September 20, 1973.

Love, Kennett. *Suez: The Twice-Fought War*. New York: McGraw-Hill, 1969.

"LTTE Declared Total Numbers of Killed During the Last 20 Years." Unpublished manuscript. N.d.

Lucas, Edward. "Deadly Image Which Could Give Hezbollah the Edge." *Scotsman* (Edinburgh), April 14, 2000.

Luft, Gal. "The Palestinian H-Bomb: Terror's Winning Strategy." *Foreign Affairs* 81, no. 4 (July/August 2002): 2–7.

——. "Special Policy Forum Report: The *Karine-A* Affair: A Strategic Watershed in the Middle East?" *Peacewatch*, no. 361. Washington, D.C.: Washington Institute for Near East Policy, January 30, 2002.

Luttwak, Edward and Dan Horowitz. *The Making of the Israeli Army*. New York: Penguin, 1975.

Lynch, Thomas F., III. *The 80 Percent Solution: The Strategic Defeat of bin Laden's al Qaeda and Implications for South Asian Security*. Washington, D.C.: New America Foundation, February 2012.

MacDonald, Andrew. *The Turner Diaries*. Arlington, Va.: National Alliance/National Vanguard Books, 1985.

MacDonald, Eileen. *Shoot the Women First*. New York: Random House, 1991.

MacEoin, Dennis. "Anwar al-Awlaki: 'I Pray That Allah Destroys America.'" *Middle East Quarterly* 17, no. 2 (Spring 2010). http://www.meforum.org/2649/anwar-al-awlaki-pray-allah-destroys-america.

MacFarquhar, Neal. "After Attack, Company's Staff Plans to Leave Saudi Arabia." *New York Times*, May 3, 2004.

——. "As Terrorists Strike Arab Targets, Escalation Fears Arise." *New York Times*, April 30, 2004.

——. "Firm Pulls 100 from Saudi Arabia After 5 Deaths." *New York Times*, May 2, 2004.

——. "Leader of Hezbollah Discovers a New Fray: Lebanese Politics." *New York Times*, March 13, 2005.

——. "Portrait of a Suicide Bomber: Devout, Apolitical, and Angry." *New York Times*, March 18, 1996.

MacFarquhar, Neal, with Jim Rutenberg. "Bin Laden, in a Taped Speech, Says Attacks in Afghanistan Are a War Against Islam." *New York Times*, November 4, 2001.

Macintyre, Anthony G., George W. Christopher, Edward Eitzen Jr., Robert Gum, Scott Weir, Craig Deatley, Kevin Tonat, and Joseph A. Barbera. "Weapons of Mass Destruction: Events with Contaminated Casualties—Effective Planning for Health Care Facilities." *JAMA (Journal of the American Medical Association)*, no. 263 (January 2000): 242–49.

Mackenzie Briefing Notes. "Funding Terror: The Liberation Tigers of Tamil Eelam and Their Criminal Activities in Canada and the Western World." Toronto: Mackenzie Centre, December 1995.

MacNeil/Lehrer Productions. *Transcript of "The News Hour with Jim Lehrer."* August 1, 1997.

Maddox, Browne. "Texan Militia at War with US." *Times* (London), February 22, 1997.

Makovsky, David. "The Seizure of Gaza-Bound Arms: Political Implications." *Peacewatch*, no. 358. Washington, D.C.: Washington Institute for Near East Policy, January 8, 2002.

Malik, Shiv. "NS Profile—Omar Sharif." *New Statesman*, April 24, 2006. http://www.newstatesman.com/200604240017.

Manchester Guardian (international edition). "Outrage Not a Reason for Inaction." October 21, 1984.

Mandela, Nelson. *Long Walk to Freedom.* London: Abacus, 1994.

Manwaring, Max G., ed. *Gray Area Phenomena: Confronting the New World Disorder.* Boulder, Colo.: Westview, 1993.

Marcus, Itmar. "PA Music Video Promising 'Maidens of Paradise' to Shahids—2 Days Before Suicide Bombings." *Palestinian Media Watch Multi-media Bulletin*, August 12, 2003. http://www.pmw.org.il.

Marcus, Raine. "Amir: I Wanted to Kill Rabin." *Jerusalem Post*, March 8, 1996.

Marighela, Carlos. *For the Liberation of Brazil.* Translated by John Butt and Rosemary Sheed. Harmondsworth: Penguin, 1971.

Marlowe, Laura. "A Fiery Cleric's Defense of Jihad." *Time*, January 15, 1996.

Mamara (Istanbul). "French Paper Provides Information on ASALA Leader Hagopian." January 16, 1985.

Martin, David C. and John Walcott. *Best Laid Plans: The Inside Story of America's War Against Terrorism.* New York: Harper and Row, 1988.

Masker, Roy B. "An All White Nation? Why Not?" *Calling Our Nation* (Aryan Nations), no. 53 (n.d.).

Masters, Jonathan. "Backgrounder: Targeted Killings." Council on Foreign Relations, April 30, 2012. http://www.cfr.org/counterterrorism/targeted-killings/p9627.

Maxwell, Bill. "Good Women Help Bring War's End." *Albany Times Union*, June 5, 2000.

McCants, William. *The ISIS Apocalypse: The History, Strategy, and Doomsday Vision of the Islamic State.* New York: St. Martin's, 2015.

McCartney, C. A. *The Habsburg Empire, 1790–1918.* London: Weidenfeld and Nicolson, 1969.

McCullagh, Declan. "Bin Laden: Steganography Master?" Wired News.com, February 7, 2001. http://www.wired.com/news/print/0,1283,41658,00.html.

McCurry, Justin. "Founder of Japan's Red Army in Final Appeal for Freedom." *Guardian*, December 12, 2008. https://www.theguardian.com/world/2008/dec/13/japan-fusako-shigenobu-red-army.

McDonald, Henry. "How the BBC Dances to an IRA Tune." *Sunday Times* (London), January 19, 1997.

McFadden, Robert D. "Mail Bomber Links an End to Killings to His Manifesto." *New York Times*, June 30, 1995.

McGee, Jim and Rachel Stassen-Berger. "5th Suspect Arrested in Bombing." *Washington Post*, March 26, 1993.

McGuire, Maria. *To Take Arms: A Year in the Provisional IRA.* London: Macmillan, 1973.

McKay, Naill. "Do Terrorists Troll the Net?" Wired News.com. http://www.wired.com/news/print/0,1294,15812,00.html. Accessed April 16, 2002.

McKittrick, David. *Despatches from Belfast*. Belfast: Blackstaff, 1989.

——. "Voyage Into Business of Terror." *Independent* (London), January 12, 1991.

McKnight, Gerald. *The Mind of the Terrorist*. London: Michael Joseph, 1974.

Melnachak, Joseph M. "A Chronicle of Hate: A Brief History of the Radical Right in America." *Terrorism, Violence, and Insurgency Report* 6, no. 4 (n.d.).

MEMRI Special Dispatch—Jihad and Terrorism Studies, no. 493 (April 11, 2003), quoting http://www.cubezero.nt/vhsvideo/imagis/?subject=2&rec=1043.

Merari, Ariel. *Driven to Death: Psychological and Social Aspects of Suicide Terrorism*. Oxford: Oxford University Press, 2010.

Merkl, Peter H. Prologue to *Political Violence and Terror*, edited by Peter H. Merkl. Berkeley: University of California Press, 1986.

Merzer, Martin. "Justice for All in Israel?" *Miami Herald*, May 17, 1985.

Meyer, Christina. *Underground Voices: Insurgent Propaganda in El Salvador, Nicaragua, and Peru*. Santa Monica, Calif.: RAND Corporation, N-3299-USDP, 1991.

Meyer, Josh and Greg Miller. "Fresh Details Back Threats." *Los Angeles Times*, August 3, 2004.

Michel, Lou and Dan Herbeck. *American Terrorist: Timothy McVeigh and the Oklahoma City Bombing*. New York: Regan, 2001.

Michels, Jeffrey. "National Vision and the Negotiation of Narratives: The Oslo Agreement." *Journal of Palestinian Studies* 24 (Autumn 1994).

Mikolus, Edward F. *Transnational Terrorism: A Chronology of Events, 1968–1979*. Westport, Conn.: Greenwood, 1980.

Mikolus, Edward F., Todd Sandier, and Jean M. Murdock. *International Terrorism in the 1980s: A Chronology of Events*. Ames: Iowa State University Press, 1989.

"Militant Islamic Political Activism on the Worldwide Web." Seminar by two analysts with the Foreign Broadcast Information Service, presented at the RAND Corporation Washington, D.C., Office, December 19, 2000.

Militia of Montana. "Statement of Purpose." http://www.militiaofmontana.com. Accessed May 12, 2016.

Miller, Abraham H. and Nicholas A. Damask. "The Dual Myths of 'Narco-Terrorism': How Myths Drive Policy." *Terrorism and Political Violence* 8, no. 1 (Spring 1996): 114–31.

Miller, Greg and Karen DeYoung. "Bin Laden's Preoccupation with U.S. Said to Be Source of Friction with Followers." *Washington Post*, May 12, 2011.

Miller, Greg and Peter Finn. "New Osama bin Laden Documents Released." *Washington Post*, May 3, 2012.

Miller, Greg and Craig Whitlock. "Caught Between Internal and External Terror Threats, France Struggles to Cope." *Washington Post*, November 14, 2015. https://www.washingtonpost.com/world/national-security/caught-between-internal-and-external-terror-threats-france-struggles-to-cope/2015/11/14/c5e9fab0-8b00-11e5-9a07-453018f9a0ec_story.html.

Miller, John. "Interview: Osama Bin Laden (May 1998)." http://www.pbs.org/wgbh/pages/frontline/shows/binladen/who/interview.html.

Miller, Judith. "U.S. Has New Concerns About Anthrax Readiness." *New York Times*, December 28, 2003.

Miller, Judith, Stephen Engelberg, and William Broad. *Germs: Biological Weapons and America's Secret War.* New York: Simon & Schuster, 2001.

Miller, Reuben. "Game Theory and Hostage-Taking Incidents: A Case Study of the Munich Olympics." *Conflict Quarterly* 10, no. 1 (Winter 1990).

Mills, C. Wright. *The Power Elite.* London: Oxford University Press, 1956.

Mishal, Shaul and Reuben Aharoni. *Speaking Stones: Communiqués from the Intifada Underground.* Syracuse, N.Y.: Syracuse University Press, 1994.

Mishal, Shaul and Avraham Sela. *The Palestinian Hamas: Vision, Violence, and Coexistence.* New York: Columbia University Press, 2000.

Mitchell, Alison. "Fingerprint Evidence Grows in World Trade Center Blast." *New York Times,* May 20, 1993.

Moghadam, Assaf. *The Globalization of Martyrdom: Al Qaeda, Salafi Jihad, and the Diffusion of Suicide Attacks.* Baltimore, Md.: Johns Hopkins University Press, 2008.

Monroe, Elizabeth. "Mr. Bevin's 'Arab Policy.'" In *Middle Eastern Affairs, No. 2,* edited by Albert Hourani, 9–48. St. Antony's Papers, No. 11. London: Chatto and Windus, 1961.

"Montana Militia Community." Facebook. https://www.facebook.com/Montana-Militia -192651084206745/info?tab=page_info. Accessed May 12, 2016.

Mooradian, Moorad. "Terrorists Speak: Interviews with ASALA Members." Unpublished manuscript. N.d.

Moore, Jack. "ISIS Replace Injured Leader Baghdadi with Former Physics Teacher." *Newsweek,* April 22, 2015. http://www.newsweek.com/isis-replace-injured-leader-baghdadi -former-physics-teacher-324082.

Morris, Benny. *The Birth of the Palestinian Refugee Problem, 1947–1949.* Cambridge: Cambridge University Press, 1987.

——. *Israel's Border Wars, 1949–1956: Arab Infiltration, Israeli Retaliation, and the Countdown to the Suez War.* Oxford: Clarendon, 1993.

Mortada, Radwan. "Bilad al-Sham: Jihad's Newest Hot Spot." *al Akhbar English,* June 26, 2012.

Mosendz, Polly. "Dylann Roof Confesses: Says He Wanted to Start 'Race War.'" *Newsweek,* June 19, 2015. http://www.newsweek.com/dylann-roof-confesses-church -shooting-says-he-wanted-start-race-war-344797.

Moser, Bob. "Alabama Getaway." Southern Poverty Law Center. http://www.splcenter.org /legal/intel/intelreport/article.jsp?aid=506. Accessed May 5, 2016.

Mosher, Andy. "Abducted Egyptian Envoy Killed in Iraq." *Washington Post,* July 8, 2005.

Mumcu, Ugur. *Papa-Mafya-Agca* [Pope, mafia, Agca]. Ankara: TekinYayinevi, 1984.

Murakami, Haruki. *Underground.* Tokyo: Kodansha bunko, 1999.

Murdoch, Lindsay. "Reign of Terror by Sri Lanka's Pol Pot." *Sydney Morning Herald* (Australia), June 15, 1995.

Musharbash, Yassin. "The Future of Terrorism: What al Qaida Really Wants." *Spiegel Online International,* August 12, 2005. http://www.spiegel.de/international/the-future -of-terrorism-what-alqaida-really-wants-a-369448.html.

"A Muslim Bomb, December 1998." In *Messages to the World: The Statements of Osama Bin Laden,* edited by Bruce Lawrence, 65–94. London: Verso, 2005.

Nair, Rupam Jain. "5-Indian States on Alert After al Qaeda Announces Local Wing." *Reuters Africa,* September 4, 2014. http://af.reuters.com/article/commoditiesNews /idAFL3N0R51YH20140904?sp=true.

Nakashima, Ellen. "Thai Officials Probe Tie to Al-Qa'ida in Attacks." *Washington Post,* January 9, 2004.

Napoleoni, Loretta. *The Islamic Phoenix*. New York: Seven Stories, 2014.

Nasiri, Omar. *Inside the Jihad: My Life with Al Qaeda—A Spy's Story*. New York: Basic, 2006.

National Archives and Records Administration (NARA). Ronald Reagan Library, Simi Valley, Calif., "Near East and South Asia Affairs Directorat [sic]," NSC (National Security Council) Records, Box 90583-90585, Iraq, 1983 [2 of 4], OA 90583, containing declassified Directorate of Intelligence, *Terrorism Review*. Washington, D.C.: Central Intelligence Agency, November 1986.

——. U.S. Office of Strategic Services, Washington, D.C. RG 226 OSS R&A Report no. 2612, "The Objectives and Activities of the Irgun Zvai Leumi," October 13, 1944; OSS Report XL 18461, "Biographical Information—Menachem Begin," September 11, 1945.

National Commission on Terrorist Attacks Upon the United States. *The 9/11 Commission Report: Authorized Edition*. New York: Norton, 2004.

National Consortium for the Study of Terrorism and Responses to Terrorism (START). University of Maryland, Global Terrorism Database. https://www.start.umd.edu/gtd/.

National Institute of Justice (NIJ), Office of Justice Programs. "Terrorism." http://www .nij.gov/topics/crime/terrorism/pages/welcome.aspx. Accessed April 5, 2016.

National Journal (Washington, D.C.). "Views on National Security." October 25, 1986.

National Police Agency (Japan). "Aum Shinrikyo." *Shoten* (Tokyo), no. 269, chap. 2. http// :www.npa.go.jp/kousi/biki2/seco2/seco2_09.htm. Accessed April 28, 2005.

——. "Aum Shinrikyo: An Alarming Report on the Terrorist Group's Organization and Activities." *Shoten* (Tokyo), no. 252 (1995).

——. *Keisatsu Hakusyo* (Police White Paper 2000), chap. 5. http://www.pdc.npa.go.jp /hakusyo/h12h120500.html. Accessed April 28, 2005.

——. *Keisatsu Hakusyo 1996* (Police White Paper 1996). http://www.pdc.npa.go.jp /hakusyo/h08/h080101.html. Accessed April 28, 2005.

Naveh, Dani, et al. Israeli Minister of Parliamentary Affairs. *The Involvement of Arafat, PA Senior Officials, and Apparatuses in Terrorism Against Israel, Corruption, and Crime*. Jerusalem: Ministry of Foreign Affairs, 2002.

Nesbitt, Eleanor. "Sikh Sants and Their Establishments in India and Abroad." In *The Oxford Handbook of Sikh Studies*, edited by Pashura Singh and Louis E. French, 360–71. Oxford: Oxford University Press, 2014.

Nesser, Peter. "Joining Jihadi Terrorist Cells in Europe: Exploring Motivational Aspects of Recruitment and Radicalization." In *Understanding Violent Radicalisation: Terrorist and Jihadist Movements in Europe*, edited by Magnus Ranstorp, 87–114. London: Routledge, 2010.

Netanyahu, Benjamin, ed. *Terrorism: How the West Can Win*. New York: Avon, 1986.

Neuhauser, Peter. "The Mind of a German Terrorist." *Encounter* 51, no. 3 (September 1978).

Neumann, Peter. *Briefing Note—Radicalisation, CVE, and Counter-Radicalisation: Core Issues and Questions*. London: International Center for the Study of Radicalisation (ICSR), King's College London, August 8, 2015.

Newsweek. "Inside the Red Brigades." May 15, 1978.

New York Times. A Nation Challenged: A Visual History of 9/11 and Its Aftermath. New York: Callaway, 2002.

——. "The Arab Terrorists." December 18, 1973.

——. "Islamic Group Says It Set Off Dagestan Blast." July 3, 2005.

——. "No Flames, No Guns in Montana." June 15, 1996.

——. "Sri Lanka Say Leader of Rebels Has Died." May 18, 2009. http://www.nytimes.com
    /2009/05/19/world/asia/19lanka.html?_r=2&ref=liberation_tigers_of_tamil_eelam.

Niv, David. *Ma'archot Ha-Irgun Ha-Zvai Ha-Leumi* [Battle for freedom: The Irgun Zvai
    Leumi]. Vol. 3. Tel Aviv: Klausner Institute, 1975.

Niven, Christine, John Noble, Susan Forsyth, and Tony Wheeler. *Sri Lanka: A Lonely
    Planet Travel Survival Kit.* Victoria, Australia: Lonely Planet, 1996.

Nordland, Rod. "al Qaeda Taking Deadly New Role in Syria Conflict. *New York Times,*
    July 24, 2012.

North Atlantic Assembly Papers, Sub-Committee on Terrorism. *Terrorism.* Brussels: In-
    ternational Secretariat, January 1989.

Norton, Graham. "The Terrorist and the Traveller: A Gulf Aftermath Assessment." *World
    Today* (London), May 1991.

Nossiter, Adam. "Lonely Trek to Radicalism for Terror Suspect." *New York Times,*
    January 16, 2010. http://www.nytimes.com/2010/01/17/world/africa/17abdulmutallab
    .html?hp.

Notes from the International Seminar on Terrorism and the Mass Media, held in Sicily,
    April 3–5, 1981.

Nunberg, Geoffrey. "Bin Laden's Low-Tech Weapon." *New York Times,* April 18, 2004.

——. "The War of Words: 'Terror' and 'Terrorism.'" *International Herald Tribune*
    (Paris), July 22, 2004.

Nundy, Julian. "Wounded Jackal Defends Record of Family Values." *Independent* (London),
    August 31, 1994.

O'Ballance, Edgar. *Arab Guerrilla Power.* London: Faber, 1974.

O'Donovan Rossa, Jeremiah. *Irish Rebels in English Prisons: A Record of Prison Life.* New
    York: D & J Sadlier, 1880.

Office of the Director of National Intelligence. *Declassified Key Judgments of the National
    Intelligence Estimate, "Trends in Global Terrorism: Implications for the United States."*
    April 2006. http://www.au.af.mil/au/awc/awcgate/dni/declass_nie_key_jdgmnts06
    apr.pdf.

Office of the Press Secretary, The White House. "Fact Sheet: The White House Summit
    on Countering Violent Extremism." February 18, 2015. https://www.whitehouse.gov
    /the-press-office/2015/02/18/fact-sheet-white-house-summit-countering-violent
    -extremism.

Ohlheiser, Abby and Elahe Izadi. "Police: Austin Shooter Was a 'Homegrown American
    Extremist.'" *Washington Post,* December 1, 2014.

Okawa, Shoichi. "Aum Shinrikyo." *Guardian,* March 25, 1995. http://www.guardian.co
    .uk/cults/a-z-cults/a_cults.html.

Okrent, Daniel. "The War of the Words: A Dispatch from the Front Lines." *New York
    Times,* March 6, 2005.

Olesen, Thomas. *International Zapatismo: The Construction of Solidarity in the Age of
    Globalization.* London: Zed, 2005.

Omand, David. *Securing the State.* New York: Columbia University Press, 2010.

One Hundred Seventh Congress of the United States of America. *Homeland Security Act
    of 2002.* January 23, 2002, 0. HR 5005-7. http://www.dhs.gov/dhspublic/public/display
    ?theme=46&content=410.

O'Neill, Sean. "The Eight in the Dock: The Men Who Appeared at Woolwich Crown
    Court Over a Six-Month Period in the Liquid Bomb Trial Which Finished Yesterday."

Times (London), September 9, 2008. http://143.252.148.161/tol/news/uk/crime/article
4707712.ece.

Onis, Juan de. "Guerrilla Unit Attacks Cairo Proposal." *New York Times,* June 21, 1973.

Online Newshour. "President Bush's Speech at the United Nations Financing for Development Conference," Monterrey, Mexico, March 22, 2002, PBS.org. http://www.pbs.org/newshour/updates/march02/bush_3-22.html.

Oren, Michael B. *Six Days of War: June 1967 and the Making of the Modern Middle East.* Oxford: Oxford University Press, 2002.

Oxford English Dictionary, Compact Edition. Oxford: Oxford University Press, 1971.

Padnos, Theo. "My Captivity." *New York Times,* October 29, 2014. http://www.nytimes.com/2014/10/28/magazine/theo-padnos-american-journalist-on-being-kidnapped-tortured-and-released-in-syria.html?_r=0.

Palestine Post. "41 Dead, 53 Injured, 52 Missing in Terrorist Attack on Secretariat." July 23, 1946.

Pallister, David. "Provos Seek to 'Play Havoc with British Nerves and Lifestyle.'" *Guardian* (London), July 31, 1990.

Palmer, A.W. *A Dictionary of Modern History.* Harmondsworth: Penguin, 1962.

Palmer, R. R. *The Age of the Democratic Revolution.* Vol. 2, *The Struggle.* Princeton, N.J.: Princeton University Press, 1970.

——. *Twelve Who Ruled: The Year of the Terror in the French Revolution.* Princeton, N.J.: Princeton University Press, 1973.

——. *The World of the French Revolution.* New York: Harper Torchbooks, 1971.

Panorama Magazine (Milan). "Interview with ASALA." September 1, 1980.

Pape, Robert A. *Dying to Win: The Strategic Logic of Suicide Terrorism.* New York: Random House, 2005.

——. "The Strategic Logic of Suicide Terrorism." *American Political Science Review* 97, no. 3 (August 2003): 343–61.

Pappe, Ilan. *The Making of the Arab-Israeli Conflict, 1947–1951.* London: I. B. Tauris, 1994.

Parachini, John V. "Putting WMD Terrorism Into Perspective." *Washington Quarterly* 26, no. 4 (Autumn 2003): 37–50.

——. "The World Trade Center Bombers (1993)." In *Toxic Terror: Assessing Terrorist Use of Chemical and Biological Weapons,* edited by Jonathan B. Tucker, 185–206. Cambridge, Mass.: MIT Press, 2000.

Pargeter, Alison. *The New Frontiers of Jihad: Radical Islam in Europe.* Philadelphia: University of Pennsylvania Press, 2008.

Parry, Albert. *Terrorism: From Robespierre to Arafat.* New York: Vanguard, 1976.

Parry, Richard Lloyd. "Sect's Poisons 'Could Kill 4.2m.'" *Independent on Sunday* (London), March 26, 1995.

Paz, Reuven. "Arab Volunteers Killed in Iraq: An Analysis." *PRISM Series of Global Jihad* 3, no. 1 (March 2005). http://www.e-prism.org/pages/4/index.htm.

——. "The Islamic Legitimacy of Suicide Terrorism." In *Countering Suicide Terrorism: An International Conference,* International Policy Institute for Counter-Terrorism, edited by Boaz Ganor, 86–96. Jerusalem: Gefen, 2001.

——. "Sawt al-Jihad: New Indoctrination of Qa'idat al-Jihad." *Occasional Paper, PRISM (Project for the Study of Islamist Movements)* 1, no. 8 (October 2003). http:www.e-prism.org/images/PRISM_no_9.doc.

——. "Who Wants to Email Al-Qaeda?" *Occasional Paper, PRISM (Project for the Study of Islamist Movements)* 1, no. 8 (October 2003); *Occasional Paper, PRISM (Project for the Study of Islamist Movements)* 2, no. 2 (July 2004). http:www.e-prism.org/images /PRISM_vol_2_no_2.doc.

Peci, Patrizio. *Io, l'infame* [I, the scoundrel]. Milan: Arnoldo Mondadori, 1983.

Pedahzur, Ami. *The Israeli Response to Jewish Extremism and Violence: Defending Democracy.* Manchester: Manchester University Press, 2002.

——. *Suicide Terrorism.* Cambridge: Polity, 2005.

Perlez, Jane and Ismail Khan. "Taliban Truce Seems in Flux in Pakistan." *New York Times*, February 2, 2009.

Perliger, Arie. *Challengers from the Sidelines: Understanding America's Violent Far-Right.* West Point, N.Y.: Combatting Terrorism Center, November 2012.

Pew Research Center for the People and the Press Survey Reports. "Americans and 9/11: The Personal Toll." September 5, 2002. http://people-press.org/reports/display.php3 ?PageID=633.

——. "Introduction. One Year Later: New Yorkers More Troubled, Washingtonians More on Edge." September 5, 2002. http://people-press.org/reports/display.php3 ?PageID.=160.

——. "Summary of Findings: A Year After the Iraq War—Mistrust of America in Europe Even Higher, Muslim Anger Persists." March 16, 2004. http:people-press.org/reports /display.php3?ReportID=206.

Phillips, John and Eve-Ann Prentice. "Tehran Opponent Is Shot Dead in Rome." *Times* (London), March 17, 1994.

Picart, Caroline Joan S. "'Jihad Cool/Jihad Chic': The Roles of the Internet and Imagined Relations in the Self-Radicalization of Colleen LaRose (Jihad Jane)." *Societies* 5 (2015).

Pillar, Charles. "Terrorists Taking Up Cyberspace: Web Sites Have Become Inexpensive, Easily Accessible Tools for Giving Instructions to Operatives and Raising Funds." *Los Angeles Times*, February 9, 2001.

Pincus, Walter. "Al-Qa'ida Releases Tape Predicting U.S. Defeat." *Washington Post*, September 10, 2004.

——. "British Intelligence Warned Blair of War." *Washington Post*, May 13, 2005.

Pincus, Walter and John Mintz. "Pakistani-U.S. Raid Uncovered Terrorist Cell's Surveillance Data." *Washington Post*, August 2, 2004.

Pinkerton, Robert A. "Detective Surveillance of Anarchists." *North American Review*, 173, no. 5 (November 1901): 609–17.

Pipes, Daniel. *Militant Islam Reaches America.* New York: Norton, 2002.

Pisani, Francis. "How to Fight the Terror Network." *Le Monde Diplomatique*, February 6, 2002. http://mondeodiplo.com/2002/06/02network.

Plate, Thomas and William Tuohy. "Los Angeles Times Interview: John Major—Even Under Fire, Britain's Prime Minister Holds His Own." *Los Angeles Times*, June 20, 1993.

Pluchinsky, Dennis. "Al-Qa'ida Identity Crisis." *Washington Times*, April 28, 2003.

——. "Western Europe's Red Terrorists: The Fighting Communist Organizations." In *Europe's Red Terrorists: The Fighting Communist Organizations*, edited by Yonah Alexander and Dennis Pluchinsky, 16–54. London: Frank Cass, 1992.

Pollack, Andrew. "Earlier Victims' Horrors Revived." *New York Times*, March 22, 1995.

——. "Japanese Police Say They Found Germ-War Material at Cult Site." *New York Times*, March 29, 1995.

——. "Japanese Sect May Struggle to Get by Without Its Leader." *New York Times*, May 17, 1995.

Porath, Y. *The Palestinian Arab National Movement, 1929–1939: From Riots to Rebellion.* London: Frank Cass, 1977.

Potter, William C. "Before the Deluge? Assessing the Threat of Nuclear Leakage from the Post-Soviet States." *Arms Control Today*, October 1995.

Priest, Dana and Walter Pincus. "New Target and Tone: Message Shows Al-Qa'ida's Adaptability." *Washington Post*, April 16, 2004.

Priest, Dana and Susan Schmidt. "Al-Qa'ida's Top Primed to Collapse, U.S. Says." *Washington Post*, March 16, 2003.

Public Good. "Spokane Robbery Document." June 24, 1997. http://www.nwcitizen.com /publicgood.

Purver, Ron. "Chemical Terrorism in Japan." Unpublished manuscript by the Canadian Security Intelligence Service, Ottawa, Canada, June 1995.

Quandt, William B. "Political and Military Dimensions of Contemporary Palestinian Nationalism." In *The Politics of Palestinian Nationalism*, edited by William B. Quandt, Fuad Jabber, and Ann Moseley Lesch, 43–154. Berkeley: University of California Press, 1974.

Qur'an. http://lexicorient.com/eo/texts/Qur'an/Qur'an004.htm. Accessed May 12, 2016.

Qutb, Sayyid. *Milestones: Ma'alim fi'l-tareeq* [Literally, "Milestones along the way" or "Signposts along the way"], edited by A. B. al-Mehri. Birmingham, England: Maktabah, n.d.

Rabbani, Mouin. "Suicide Attacks Fueled by Alienation and Futility." *Philadelphia Inquirer Commentary*, April 3, 2001. http://inq.philly.com/content/inquirer/2001/04/03 /opinion/RABBANI03.htm.

"RAF Philosophy." In *The German Guerrilla: Terror, Reaction, and Resistance.* Sanday, Orkney: Cienfuegos, n.d.

Raines, Howell. "With Latest Bomb, IRA Injures Its Own Cause." *New York Times*, November 15, 1987.

Rajan, V. G. *Women Suicide Bombers: Narratives of Violence.* New York: Routledge, 2011.

Ramsay, Gilbert. "Why Terrorism Can, but Should Not Be Defined." *Critical Studies on Terrorism* 8, no. 2 (2015): 211–28.

Randal, Jonathan C. "Guerrillas Fear Trade-off of Interests." *Washington Post*, October 12, 1973.

Randolph, Eleanor. "Networks Turn Eye on Themselves." *Washington Post*, June 30, 1985.

Ranstorp, Magnus. *Hizb'allah in Lebanon: The Politics of the Western Hostage Crisis.* Basingstoke: Macmillan, 1997.

Raphael, Sam. "In the Service of Power: Terrorism Studies and US Intervention in the Global South." In *Critical Terrorism Studies: A New Research Agenda*, edited by Richard Jackson et al., 49–65. Abingdon: Routledge, 2009.

Rapoport, David C. "Fear and Trembling: Terrorism in Three Religious Traditions." *American Political Science Review* 78, no. 3 (September 1984): 658–77.

——. "The International World as Some Terrorists Have Seen It: A Look at a Century of Memoirs." *Journal of Strategic Studies* 10, no. 4 (December 1987): 32–58.

——. "The Media and Terrorism: Implications of the Unabomber Case." Editorial in *Terrorism and Political Violence* 8, no. 1 (Spring 1996): 7–9.

——. "The Politics of Atrocity." In *Terrorism: Interdisciplinary Perspectives*, edited by Yonah Alexander and Seymour Maxwell Finger, 17–33. New York: John Jay, 1977.

——. "Terrorism." In *Routledge Encyclopedia of Government and Politics*, edited by Mary Hawkesworth and Maurice Kogan, 2:1061–82. London: Routledge, 1992.

——. "Terrorism and Weapons of the Apocalypse." *National Security Studies Quarterly* 5, no. 3 (Summer 1999): 49–69.

Rashid, Ahmed. *Taliban: Militant Islam, Oil and Fundamentalism in Central Asia*. New Haven, Conn.: Yale University Press, 2001.

Raufer, Xavier. "Gray Areas: A New Security Threat." *Political Warfare*, no. 19 (Spring 1992).

Ravitch, Norman. "The Armenian Massacre." *Encounter* 57, no. 6 (December 1981).

Rayner, Gordon, John Bingham, and Duncan Gardham. "Roshonara Choudry: Model Student Inflamed by a Web Preacher Stabbed MP 'to Avenge Iraqis.'" *Daily Telegraph* (London), November 3, 2010.

Reed, Richard. "Life, Liberty, and the Pursuit of Anyone Who Gets in the Way: Lessons from a Comparative Analysis of U.S. Militias and Ulster Loyalists." *Studies in Conflict and Terrorism* 36, no. 9 (September 2013): 756–76.

Reeve, Simon. *One Day in September: The Story of the 1972 Munich Olympics Massacre*. London: Faber and Faber, 2000.

Reinares, Fernando. "The Evidence of al-Qa'ida's Role in the 2004 Madrid Attack." *CTC Sentinel* 5, no. 3 (March 2012). http://www.ctc.usma.edu/posts/the-evidence-of-al -qaidas-role-in-the-2004-madrid-attack.

——. "The Madrid Bombings and Global Jihadism." *Survival* 52, no. 2 (April/May 2010): 83–104.

"Remarks by the President [William Jefferson Clinton] to 17th Annual Legislative Conference of the International Association of Fire Fighters." Washington, D.C., March 15, 1999. http://www.usia.gov/topical/pol/terror/99031502.html.

The Reporters, Writers, and Editors of *Der Spiegel* Magazine. *Inside 9–11: What Really Happened*. New York: St. Martin's, 2001.

Report of a Committee of Privy Counsellors. *The Report of the Iraq Inquiry (Chilcot Report): Executive Summary*. London: Williams Lea Group on behalf of the Controller of Her Majesty's Stationery Office, HC 264, July 6, 2016. http://www.iraqinquiry.org .uk/media/246416/the-report-of-the-iraq-inquiry_executive-summary.pdf.

Republic of Singapore, Ministry of Home Affairs. *White Paper: The Jemaah Islamiyah Arrests and the Threat of Terrorism*. Cmd. 2 of 2003, Presented to Parliament by Command of the President of the Republic of Singapore, January 7, 2003.

Ressa, Maria A. *Seeds of Terror: An Eyewitness Account of Al-Qaeda's Newest Center of Operations in Southeast Asia*. New York: Free Press, 2003.

Reuters. "Aum Cult Gas Cache." *International Herald Tribune* (Paris), December 13, 1996.

——. "Extremists Post Hidden Messages." Wired News.com, February 6, 2001. http:// www.wired.com/news/print/0,1294,41650,00.html. Accessed April 11, 2002.

——. "Propaganda to the People." Wired News.com. http://www.wired.com/news/print /0,1294,11363,00.html. Accessed April 11, 2002.

——. "Tokyo Cult Leader Said to Have Made Gas Confession." *Times* (London), October 5, 1995.

——. "$2 Million Reward for Death of Rushdie Repeated by Iran." *New York Times*, June 18, 1992.

Revesz, Rachel. "FBI Director: Crushing Isis in Syria Risks Releasing 'Terrorist Diaspora' Into the West." *Independent*, July 29, 2016. http://www.independent.co.uk/news/world /americas/isis-more-attacks-read-fbi-director-james-comey-terrorist-diaspora -fordham-syria-iraq-a7162426.html.

Rhodes, Tom. "Federal US Faces War with 'Army of God.'" *Times* (London), April 7, 1997.

Richards, Anthony. *Conceptualizing Terrorism*. Oxford: Oxford University Press, 2015.

Richardson, Louise. "Sanctions on Iran 'a Failure.'" *Times* (London), October 13, 1995.

——. *What Terrorists Want*. New York: Random House, 2006.

Richey, Warren. "Anwar al-Awlaqi: ACLU Wants Militant Cleric Taken Off US 'Kill List.'" *Christian Science Monitor*, August 31, 2010.

Ridgeway, James. "Arms and the Men: Are Far Right Militia Cells Using Robbery to Fund Their Cause?" *Village Voice* (New York), May 9, 1995.

Riedel, Bruce. "Al Qaeda's Arab Comeback: Capitalizing on Chaos in Syria, Mali." *Daily Beast*, July 30, 2012. http://www.thedailybeast.com/articles/2012/07/30/al Qaeda-s-arab -comeback-capitalizing-on-chaos-in-syria-mali.html.

Risen, James. "New Evidence Ties Sudanese to Bin Laden, U.S. Asserts." *New York Times*, October 4, 1998.

Robberson, Tod. "Loaded Guns and Diskettes: Rebels Win Hearts and Minds on Internet." *International Herald Tribune* (Paris), February 21, 1995.

Robbins, James S. "Bin Laden's Vision Thing: Is bin Laden Saying That This Whole Thing Is Warren G. Harding's Fault?" *National Review.com*, October 8, 2001. http://old .nationalreview.com/comment/comment-robbins100801.shtml.

Roberts, Adam. "Terrorism Research: Past, Present, and Future." *Studies in Conflict and Terrorism* 38, no. 1 (January 2015): 62–74.

Roberts, Brad, ed. *Terrorism with Chemical and Biological Weapons: Calibrating Risks and Responses*. Alexandria, Va.: Chemical and Biological Arms Control Institute, 1997.

Robertson, Nic, Paul Cruickshank, and Tim Lister. "Document Shows Origins of 2006 Plot for Liquid Bombs on Planes." CNN, April 30, 2012. http://www.cnn.com/2012 /04/30/world/al Qaeda-documents/index.html?iref=allsearch.

Roggio, Bill. "Al Qaeda in the Indian Subcontinent Incorporates Regional Jihadi Groups." *Long War Journal*, September 5, 2014. http://www.longwarjournal.org/archives/2014 /09/analysis_al_qaeda_in.php.

——. "The Seven Phases of the Base." *Long War Journal*, August 15, 2005. http://www .longwarjournal.org/archives/2005/08/the_seven_phase.php.

Roggio, Bill and Thomas Joscelyn. "Report: Osama bin Laden Ordered Mumbai-Style Attacks in Europe." *Long War Journal*, October 1, 2010. http://www.longwarjournal .org/archives/2010/10/report_osama_bin_lad_1.php.

——. "US Military Strikes Large al Qaeda Training Camps in Southern Afghanistan." *Long War Journal*, October 13, 2015. http://www.longwarjournal.org/archives/2015/10 /us-military-strikes-large-al-qaeda-training-camps-in-southern-afghanistan.php.

Romano, Lois. "Domestic Extremist Groups Weaker but Still Worrisome." *Washington Post*, April 19, 2005.

Ronfeldt, David F., John Arquilla, Graham E. Fuller, and Melissa Fuller. *The Zapatista Social Netwar in Mexico*. Santa Monica, Calif.: RAND Corporation, MR-994-A, 1998.

Rose, David. "Devices Reveal IRA Know-How." *Guardian* (London), May 18, 1990.

——. *Guantanamo: America's War on Human Rights*. London: Faber and Faber, 2004.

Ross, Loretta J. "Anti-abortionists and White Supremacists Make Common Cause." *The Progressive* (New York), October 1994.

——. "Using the Bible to Justify Killing." *Baltimore Sun*, August 8, 1994.

Rotella, Sebastian. "New Details in the bin Laden Docs: Portrait of a Fugitive Micro-Manager." *ProPublica*, May 11, 2011. http://www.propublica.org/article/bin-laden -documents-portrait-of-a-fugitive-micro-manager.

Rowan, Roy. "Pan Am 103: Why Did They Die?" *Time*, April 27, 1992.

Roy, Olivier. *Globalized Islam: The Search for a New Ummah*. New York: 2004.

Rubin, Barry, and Judith Colp Rubin, eds. *Anti-American Terrorism and the Middle East: A Documentary Reader*. Oxford: Oxford University Press, 2002.

Rubin, Jeffrey Z., and Nehemia Friedland. "Theater of Terror." *Psychology Today* 20, no. 3 (March 1986).

Ruqaiyah, Brother Abu. "The Islamic Legitimacy of the 'Martyrdom Operations.'" Originally published in *Nida'ul Islam*, no. 16 (December/January 1996–97). http://www.islam.org.au/articles/16martyrdom.htm.

Ruthven, Malise. *A Fury for God: The Islamist Attack on America*. London: Granta, 2002.

Ryan, Missy. "Pentagon Withholds $300 Million in Military Aid to Pakistan." *Washington Post*, August 3, 2016. https://www.washingtonpost.com/world/national-security/pentagon-withholds-300-million-in-military-aid-to-pakistan/2016/08/03/25845d54-5986-11e6-9aee-8075993d73a2_story.html.

Saad-Horayeb, Amal. *Hizbu'llah: Politics and Religion*. London: Pluto, 2002.

Sageman, Marc. *Leaderless Jihad: Terror Networks in the Twenty-First Century*. Philadelphia: University of Pennsylvania Press, 2008.

——. *Understanding Terror Networks*. Philadelphia: University of Pennsylvania Press, 2004.

Sageman, Marc and Bruce Hoffman. "Does Osama Still Call the Shots?" *Foreign Affairs* 87, no. 4 (July/August 2008): 163–66.

Sanan, Guy R. "Olympic Security, 1972–1996: Threat, Response, and International Cooperation." PhD diss., St. Andrews University, 1997.

Sands, David R. "Al-Qa'ida's Credibility 'on the Line' as War in Iraq Winds Down." *Washington Times*, April 24, 2003.

Sarmiento, Gretel. "Former AMI Building Declared Free of Anthrax Contamination." *Palm Beach Post*, February 8, 2007. http://www.ph.ucla.edu/epi/bioter/formeramibldg anthraxfree.html.

Sarraj, Eyad. "The Making of a Suicide Bomber." March 10, 1996, e-mail dated March 23, 1997, sent by news@baraka.baraka.org.

Sartre, Jean-Paul. Preface to Frantz Fanon's *The Wretched of the Earth*. London: Penguin, 1990.

Satloff, Robert. "*Karine-A*: Strategic Implications of Iranian-Palestinian Collusion." *Policywatch*, no. 539. Washington, D.C.: Washington Institute for Near East Policy, January 15, 2002.

Sayigh, Yezid. *Armed Struggle and the Search for State: The Palestinian National Movement, 1949–1993*. Washington, D.C.: Institute for Palestine Studies/Oxford: Oxford University Press, 1997.

Sayle, Murray. "Martyrdom Complex." *New Yorker*, May 13, 1996.

Schbley, Ayla H. "Religious Terrorists: What They Aren't Going to Tell Us." *Terrorism* 13, no. 3 (Summer 1990).

Scheeres, Julia. "Blacklisted Groups Visible on Web." Wired News.com. http://www.wired.com/news/print/0,1283,47616,00.html. Accessed April 19, 2002.

Schere, Peter. "RAF Concentrates on New Target Spectrum." *Die Welt*, December 18, 1991.

Scheuer, Michael. *Through Our Enemies' Eyes: Osama bin Laden, Radical Islam, and the Future of America*. Washington, D.C.: Potomac, 2006.

Schiff, Zeev and Raphael Rothstein. *Fedayeen: The Story of the Palestinian Guerrillas*. London: Valentine, Mitchell, 1972.

Schiller, David Th. "From a National to an International Response." In *Combating the Terrorists: Democratic Responses to Political Violence*, edited by H. H. Tucker, 185–202. New York: Facts on File, 1988.

Schmemann, Serge. "Bus Bombing Kills Five in Jerusalem, 100 Are Wounded." *New York Times*, August 22, 1995.

——. "Palestinian Believed to Be Bombing Mastermind Is Killed." *New York Times*, January 6, 1997.

——. "Police Say Rabin Killer Led Sect That Laid Plans to Attack Arabs." *New York Times*, November 11, 1995.

——. "Terror Isn't Alone as a Threat to Middle East Peace." *Jerusalem Post*, March 4, 1996.

Schmid, Alex P., ed. *Political Terrorism: A Research Guide*. New Brunswick, N.J.: Transaction Books, 1984.

——. *The Routledge Handbook of Terrorism Research*. London: Routledge, 2011.

——. "Terrorism and the Media: The Ethics of Publicity." *Terrorism and Political Violence* 1, no. 4 (October 1989), 539–65.

Schmid, Alex P. and Janny de Graaf. *Violence as Communication: Insurgent Terrorism and the Western News Media*. Beverly Hills, Calif.: Sage, 1982.

Schmid, Alex P., Albert J. Jongman et al. *Political Terrorism: A New Guide to Actors, Authors, Concepts, Data Bases, Theories, and Literature*. New Brunswick, N.J.: Transaction Books, 1988.

Schmidt, Michael S. "Canadian Killed in Syria Lives on as Pitchman for Jihadis." *New York Times*, July 15, 2014. http://www.nytimes.com/2014/07/16/world/middleeast/isis -uses-andre-poulin-a-canadian-convert-to-islam-in-recruitment-video.html?_r=0.

Schmidt, William E. "Protestant Gunmen Are Stepping Up the Violence in Northern Ireland." *New York Times*, October 29, 1991.

Schmitt, Eric. "Don't Aid Zarqawi, U.S. Warns Iraqi Neighbors." *New York Times*, June 2, 2005.

——. "Sunni Extremists May Be Aiding al Qaeda's Ambitions in Syria, Analysts Say." *New York Times*, February 15, 2012.

——. "U.S. Secures Vast Trove of Intelligence on Islamic State." *New York Times*, July 29, 2016.

Schmitt, Eric and Eric Lipton. "Focus on Internet Imams as Recruiters for al-Qaeda." *New York Times*, January 1, 2010. http://www.nytimes.com/2010/01/01/us/01imam .html.

Schmitt, Eric and David E. Sanger. "As U.S. Focuses on ISIS and the Taliban, Al Qaeda Re-emerges." *New York Times*, December 29, 2016. http://www.nytimes.com/2015/12/30/us /politics/as-us-focuses-on-isis-and-the-taliban-al-qaeda-re-emerges.html?_r=0.

Schmitt, Eric and Thom Shanker. *Counterstrike: The Untold Story of America's Secret Campaign Against Al Qaeda*. New York: Henry Holt, 2011.

Schneider, Howard and Walter Pincus. "Bin Laden Video Includes Sept. 11 Praise." *Washington Post*, April 16, 2002.

Schneider, Keith. "Fearing a Conspiracy, Some Heed a Call to Arms." *New York Times*, November 14, 1994.

Schoenberg, Harris O. *A Mandate for Terror: The United Nations and the PLO*. New York: Shapolsky Books, 1989.

Schorr, Daniel. "The Encouragement of Violence." In *Terrorism: How the West Can Win*, edited by Benjamin Netanyahu, 114–16. New York: Avon, 1986.

Schultz, Richard H., Jr., and Andrea J. Dew. *Insurgents, Terrorists, and Militias: The Warriors of Contemporary Combat*. New York: Columbia University Press, 2006.

Schuster, Henry. "Lone Wolves: Solitary Threats Harder to Hunt." CNN, April 28, 2005. http://www.cnn.com/2005/US/02/01/schuster.column/index.html.

——. "Studios of Terror: Al Qaeda's Media Strategy." CNN. http://www.cnn.com/2005/WORLD/MCAST/02/15/schuster.column/index.html. Accessed February 15, 2005.

——. "Why Did Rudolph Do It? Question Lingers After Plea Deal Reached." CNN, April 28, 2005. http://www.cnn.com/2005/US/04/11/schuster.column/index.html.

Schwarz, Benjamin C. *Casualties, Public Opinion, and U.S. Military Intervention: Implications for U.S. Regional Deterrence Strategies*. Santa Monica, Calif.: RAND Corporation, MR-431-A/AF, 1994.

Schweitzer, Yoram. "Suicide Terrorism: Development and Main Characteristics." In *Countering Suicide Terrorism: An International Conference*. International Policy Institute for Counter-Terrorism at the Interdisciplinary Center, Herzilya. Jerusalem: Gefen, 2001.

Schweitzer, Yoram, Ariel Levin, and Einav Yogev. *Suicide Attacks in 2014: The Global Picture*. Tel Aviv: Institute for National Security Studies, INSS Insight No. 653, January 6, 2015. http://www.inss.org.il/?id=4538&articleid=8514.

Scotsman (Edinburgh). "Photoflash Bomb Threat to the Public." March 16, 1994.

——. "Police Killer and His Plot to Poison Britain." April 14, 2005. http://www.scotsman.com/news/uk/police-killer-and-his-plot-to-poison-britain-1-707843.

Scott-Clark, Cathy and Adrian Levy. *The Siege: 68 Hours Inside the Taj Hotel*. London: Penguin, 2013.

Seale, Patrick. *Abu Nidal: A Gun for Hire*. New York: Random House, 1992.

Segev, Tom. *1949: The First Israelis*. New York: Free Press, 1986.

Semple, Michael. "The Taliban Need Help to Break Their al-Qaida Ties." *Guardian*, April 30, 2012. http://www.guardian.co.uk/commentisfree/2012/apr/30/taliban-al-qaida-ties.

September 11 Victims. http://www.september11victims.com/september11victims/COUNTRY_CITIZENSHIP.htm. Accessed March 1, 2016.

Serrano, Richard A. and Edith Stanley, "2 Georgia Militia Group Members Face Bomb Counts, *Los Angeles Times*, April 27, 1996.

Seufert, Michael. "Dissension Among the Terrorists: Killing People Is Wrong." *Encounter* 51, no. 3 (September 1978).

Shadid, Anthony. "Iraqi Insurgent Group Names New Leaders." *New York Times*, May 16, 2010. http://atwar.blogs.nytimes.com/2010/05/16/iraqi-insurgent-group-names-new-leaders/?_php=true&_type=blogs&_r=0.

Shahak, Israel. "Hamas and Arafat: The Balance of Power." *Middle East International*, no. 468 (February 4, 1996).

Shales, Tom. "America's Ordeal by Television." *Washington Post*, July 2, 1985.

Shamir, Yitzhak. *Summing Up: An Autobiography*. London: Weidenfeld and Nicolson, 1994.

Shane, Scott. "Born in U.S., a Radical Cleric Inspires Terror Against West." *New York Times*, November 18, 2009.

Shane, Scott. "Terrorism Experts Say Focus on al Qaeda Misses a Broader Threat." *New York Times*, August 13, 2006.

Shane, Scott and Souad Mekhennet. "Imam's Path from Condemning Terror to Preaching Jihad." *New York Times*, May 8 2010. http://www.nytimes.com/2010/05/09/world/09awlaki.html?pagewanted=all.

Shannon, Don. "Gromyko Indirectly Supports U.S. in U.N. Drive Against Terrorism." *Los Angeles Times*, September 27, 1972.

Shariatmadari, David. "Is It Time to Stop Using the Word 'Terrorist'?" *Guardian* (London), January 27, 2015. http://www.theguardian.com/global/commentisfree/2015/jan/27/is-it-time-to-stop-using-the-word-terrorist.

Shavit, Ari. "The Enemy Within." *Ha'aretz Friday Magazine*, August 20, 2002. http:www.freeman.org/m_online/sept02/shavit.htm.

Sheridan, Michael. "Iranians 'Landing Gulf Infiltrators.'" *Independent* (London), April 8, 1995.

Shirer, William L. *The Rise and Fall of the Third Reich: A History of Nazi Germany.* New York: Simon & Schuster, 1960.

Sick, Gary. "The Political Underpinnings of Terrorism." In *International Terrorism: Characteristics, Causes, Controls*, edited by Charles W. Kegley Jr., 51–54. New York: St. Martin's, 1990.

Simon, Jeffrey D. *Terrorists and the Potential Use of Biological Weapons: A Discussion of Possibilities.* Santa Monica, Calif.: RAND Corporation, R-3771-AFMIC, December 1989.

Simons, Marlise. "Lockerbie Bomber Loses Appeal and Begins Sentence." *New York Times*, March 15, 2002.

Singh, Rashmi. *Hamas and Suicide Terrorism: Multi-causal and Multi-level Approaches.* Abingdon: Routledge, 2011.

Sipress, Alan. "Key Player in Nuclear Trade Ring Found Hospitable Base in Malaysia." *Washington Post*, February 24, 2004.

SITE Intelligence Group. "Zawahiri Calls Fighters to Unite, Attacks IS for Creating and Maintaining Division." August 29, 2016. https://news.siteintelgroup.com/Jihadist-News/zawahiri-calls-fighters-to-unite-attacks-is-for-creating-and-maintaining-division.html.

SITE Intelligence Group: Jihadist Threat. "Zawahiri Incites Lone-Wolf Attacks in the U.S. and West, Urges Fighters in Iraq, Syria to Cooperate with IS Against Enemy Alliance." September 14, 2015.

Skaine, Rosemarie. *Female Suicide Bombers.* Jefferson, N.C.: McFarland, 2006.

Skierka, Volker. "Modern Nazis: A More Devious Version." *Stuttgarter Zeitung*, December 12, 1981.

Slonim, Ori. "The Hamas and Terror: An Alternative Explanation for the Use of Violence." *Strategic Assessment* (Ramat Aviv: Jaffee Center for Strategic Studies at Tel Aviv University) 2, no. 3 (December 1999).

Smith, Colin. *Carlos: Portrait of a Terrorist.* London: Andre Deutsch, 1976.

Smith, Dan, Kristin Ingstad Sandberg, Pavel Baev, and Wenche Hauge. *The State of War and Peace Atlas.* London: Penguin, 1997.

Smith, Michael. "IRA Use of Radar Guns in Bombings Described." *Daily Telegraph* (London), May 20, 1991.

Smith, M. L. R. *Fighting for Ireland? The Military Strategy of the Irish Republican Movement.* London: Routledge, 1995.

Smith, R. Jeffrey. "Justice Redacted Memo on Detainees: FBI Criticism of Interrogations Was Deleted." *Washington Post*, March 22, 2005.

Sofaer, Abraham D. "Terrorism and the Law." *Foreign Affairs* 64, no. 5 (Summer 1986): 901–22.

Sofer, Sasson. *Begin: An Anatomy of Leadership*. Oxford: Blackwell, 1988.

Solnick, Aluma. "The Joy of the Mothers of Palestinian 'Martyrs.'" *MEMRI: Inquiry and Analysis Series*, no. 61 (June 25, 2001). http://www.memri.org.

Soufan Group. "The Many Faces of al Qaeda." September 5, 2012. http://soufangroup.us4 .list-manage.com/track/click?u=3fe77a4916f69c37ee2ac1cbe&id=f32f943f7e&e =8e25f1caae.

South Asia Terrorism Portal—Institute for Conflict Management. "Sri Lanka Terrorist Groups." February 14, 2016. http://www.satp.org/satporgtp/countries/shrilanka /terroristoutfits/index.html.

Southern Poverty Law Center (SPLC). "Antigovernment Militia Groups Grew by More than One-Third in Last Year." January 4, 2016. https://www.splcenter.org/news/2016 /01/04/antigovernment-militia-groups-grew-more-one-third-last-year.

——. *False Patriots: The Threat of Antigovernment Extremists*. Montgomery, Ala.: Southern Poverty Law Center, 1996.

——. "Legal Action: Keenan v. Aryan Nations." http://www.splcenter.org/legal/docket /files.jsp?cdrID=30&sortID=3. Accessed May 5, 2005.

——. "Sovereign Citizens Movement." https://www.splcenter.org/fighting-hate/extremist -files/ideology/sovereign-citizens-movement. Accessed May 5, 2016.

Spiers, Edward M. *A History of Chemical and Biological Weapons*. London: Reaktion Books, 2010.

Spillius, Alex. "Demise of al-Qa'eda in Sight, US Official Says." *Telegraph*, May 15, 2008. www.telegraph.co.uk/news/newstopics/uselection2008/democrats/1957428/Demise -of-al-Qa'eda-in-sight,-US-official-says.html. Accessed May 12, 2011.

Sprinzak, Ehud. *The Ascendance of Israel's Radical Right*. Oxford: Oxford University Press, 1991.

——. *Brother Against Brother: Violence and Extremism in Israeli Politics from Altalena to the Rabin Assassination*. New York: Free Press, 1999.

——. "Fundamentalism, Terrorism, and Democracy. The Case of the Gush Emunim Underground." Wilson Center Occasional Paper no. 4. Washington, D.C.: Smithsonian Institution, 1986.

——. "Outsmarting Suicide Terrorists." *Christian Science Monitor*, October 24, 2000.

——. "Rational Fanatics." *Foreign Policy*, no. 120 (September/October 2000): 66–73.

——. "Violence and Catastrophe in the Theology of Rabbi Meir Kahane: The Ideologization of Mimetic Desire." In *Violence and the Sacred in the Modern World*, edited by Mark Juergensmeyer, 48–70. London: Frank Cass, 1992.

Squiteri, Tom. "U.S.: Return Our Men." *USA Today* (Washington, D.C.), October 6, 1993.

Stafford, David. *From Anarchism to Reformism: A Study of the Political Activities of Paul Brousse Within the First International and the French Socialist Movement, 1870–90*. Toronto: University of Toronto Press, 1971.

Stalinsky, Steven. "Palestinian Authority Sermons, 2000–2003." *MEMRI Special Report*, no. 24 (December 26, 2003). http://www.memri.org.

Stanley, Alessandra. "Russians Shut Down Branch of Japanese Sect." *New York Times*, March 30, 1995.

——. "Top Kurd's Arrest Unleashes Rioting All Across Europe." *New York Times*, February 17, 1999.

Statement for the Record Before the Senate Select Committee on Intelligence, January 28, 1998. http://www.fbi.gov/congress/98archives/threats.htm.

Steele, Jonathan. "How Yarmouk Refugee Camp Became the Worst Place in Syria." *Guardian*, March 5, 2015. https://www.theguardian.com/news/2015/mar/05/how-yarmouk-refugee-camp-became-worst-place-syria.

Steinhoff, Patricia G. "Portrait of a Terrorist: An Interview with Kozo Okamoto." *Asian Survey* 16, no. 9 (September 1976).

Sterling, Claire. *The Terror Network: The Secret War of International Terrorism*. New York: Holt, Rinehart, and Winston, 1981.

——. *The Time of the Assassins*. New York: Holt, Rinehart, and Winston, 1983.

Stern, Jessica Eve. "The Covenant, the Sword, and the Arm of the Lord (1985)." In *Toxic Terror: Assessing Terrorist Use of Chemical and Biological Weapons*, edited by Jonathan B. Tucker, 139–58. Cambridge, Mass.: MIT Press, 2000.

——. "Pakistan's Jihad Culture." *Foreign Affairs* 79, no. 6 (November/December 2000): 115–26.

Stern, Jessica and J. M. Berger. *ISIS: The State of Terror*. New York: HarperCollins, 2015.

Stern, Susan. *With the Weathermen: The Personal Journey of a Revolutionary Woman*. Garden City, N.Y.: Doubleday, 1975.

Stevens, William K. "Indian Government Takes Over a State Swept by Religious Strife." *New York Times*, October 7, 1983.

——. "Mrs. Gandhi Says Terrorism Will End." *New York Times*, October 15, 1983.

Stokes, Bruce. "Do Muslims Around the World Really Hate the United States?" *Foreign Policy*, December 15, 2015. http://foreignpolicy.com/2015/12/15/do-muslims-around-the-world-really-hate-the-united-states/.

Stokes, Paul and Nick Britten. "The Cricket-Loving Terrorist Whose Father Runs the Local Chip Shop." *Daily Telegraph* (London), July 14, 2005.

Stork, Joe. *Erased in a Moment: Suicide Bombing Attacks Against Israeli Civilians*. New York: Human Rights Watch, October 2002.

Straus, Julius. "Serb Attack on British Base." *Daily Telegraph* (London), July 18, 1997.

Strindberg, Anders. "'The Ultimate Sacrifice': The Social and Political Dynamics of Suicide Operations in Palestine." *MIPT Quarterly Bulletin* (Second Quarter, 2002).

Studemann, Frederick, et al. "Five Arrested as London Bomb Attack Probe Widens to Egypt and Pakistan." *Financial Times* (London), July 16–17, 2005.

Sullivan, Kevin. "Japan Cult Survives While Guru Is Jailed." *Washington Post*, September 28, 1997.

Sullivan, Kevin and Karla Adam. "Terrorism Threat Level in Britain Is Lowered." *Washington Post*, July 5, 2007.

Sunday Times (London). "IRA Bomb-Making Guide on Internet." February 9, 1997.

——. "Israelis Discover Mass Murder Plot." November 26, 1995.

——. "Public Support Adams Talks." February 18, 1996.

——. "Wedded to Death in a Blaze of Glory—Profile: The Suicide Bomber." March 10, 1996.

Sunday Times Insight Team. *Siege! Princes Gate, London, April 30–May 5, 1980*. London: Hamlyn, 1980.

Sunil, K. P. "The Midnight Massacre." *Illustrated Weekly of India*, June 8, 1986.

Suro, Robert. "FBI Walks a Fine Line in Its Pursuit of Militia Extremists." *International Herald Tribune* (Paris), November 12, 1996.

Suskind, Ron. *The One Percent Doctrine: Deep Inside America's Pursuit of Its Enemies Since 9/11*. New York: Simon & Schuster, 2006.

Suwayd, Rami. "Efforts Fail for Truce Between Al-Nusrah and Da'ish in Aleppo." *Al-Arabi al-Jadid* (London), LIR2014111656912977, November 11, 2014.

Sverdlik, Alan. "Georgia Militia Members Who Conspired Against ATF Found Guilty." *Washington Post*, November 1, 1996.

Swain, Jon. "Algeria Dies Death of a Thousand Cuts." *Sunday Times* (London), April 6, 1997.

Tabor, James D. "Bible Scholar Claims Branch Davidian Disaster Could Have Been Avoided." *Religious Studies News* (Society of Biblical Literature/American Academy of Religion), September 1995.

Tabor, James D. and Eugene V. Gallagher. *Why Waco? Cults and the Battle for Religious Freedom in America*. Berkeley: University of California Press, 1995.

Taheri, Amir. *Holy Terror: The Inside Story of Islamic Terrorism*. London: Sphere, 1987.

Talbott, John. *The War Without a Name: France in Algeria, 1954–1962*. London: Faber, 1980.

Talmadge, Eric. "Tokyo Police Avert Cyanide Catastrophe." *Sunday Times* (London), May 7, 1995.

Tavin, Eli and Yonah Alexander, eds. *Psychological Warfare and Propaganda: Irgun Documentation*. Wilmington, Del.: Scholarly Resources, 1982.

Taylor, Peter. *Provos: The IRA and Sinn Fein*. London: Bloomsbury, 1997.

——. *States of Terror: Democracy and Political Violence*. London: Penguin, 1993.

Taymiyyah, Shaykhul-IslaamTaqi-ud-Deen Ahmad ibn. *The Religious and Moral Doctrine of Jihad*. Birmingham, England: Maktabah al Ansaar, 2001.

Temple-Raston, Dina. "Al-Qaida Eyes Opportunities in Syria." *All Things Considered—National Public Radio*, March 12, 2012. http://www.npr.org/2012/03/12/148467185/al-qaida-leader-eyes-opportunities-in-syria.

——. "Bin Laden Told Partners to Plan Mumbai-Like Attacks." National Public Radio, September 30, 2010. http://www.npr.org/templates/story/story.php?storyId=13024 2602.

Tendler, Stewart. "A Crude and Lethal Weapon to Thwart the Security Forces." *Times* (London), February 8, 1991.

Tenet, George. *At the Center of the Storm: My Years at the CIA*. New York: HarperCollins, 2007.

"Terrorism Update: Understanding the Terrorism Database." In *MIPT Quarterly Bulletin* (Oklahoma City National Memorial Institute for the Prevention of Terrorism) (First Quarter 2002).

Terrorist Research and Analytical Center, National Security Division, Federal Bureau of Investigation. *Terrorism in the United States 1995*. Washington, D.C.: U.S. Department of Justice, 1996.

Texas Constitutional Militia. "Rights of the People: Citizens of a Founded Republic Working Towards Our Nation." http://www.rightsofthepeople.com/guns/militia/militia_texas_constitutional_militia.php. Accessed May 5, 2016.

Thackeray, Lorna. "The Freeman Standoff." *Billings Gazette*, March 25, 2006. http://billingsgazette.com/news/state-and-regional/montana/the-freemen-standoff/article_52ea8d8f-c28e-5170-8b65-8c5f71ea4fe9.html.

Theodoulu, Michael. "New Attacks Feared After Defiant Vow by Hamas." *Times* (London), August 22, 1995.

This Is Aryan Nations. http://www.stormfront.org/aryan_nations/platform.html. Accessed June 25, 1997.

Thomas, Christopher. "Appeal for Calm as Tamils Deny Train Bombing." *Times* (London), July 26, 1996.

Thomas, Jo. "Militias Hold a Congress, and Not a Gun Is Seen." *New York Times*, November 1, 1994.

Thompson, Linda. "Waco, Another Perspective." *American Justice Foundation* (n.d.). http://www.skeptictank.org/files/waco/ltstory2.htm. Accessed May 12, 2016.

Thomson, David. *Europe Since Napoleon*. Harmondsworth: Penguin, 1978.

Thornhill, Ted. "Has ISIS Looted Chemical Weapons from a Former Iraqi Nerve Agent Factory That the US Failed to Destroy?" *Daily Mail*, October 15, 2014. http://www.daily mail.co.uk/news/article-2793731/will-rusting-chemical-weapons-cache-ignored -americans-fall-isis-hands-iraq-claims-2-500-rockets-containing-deadly-sarin-hands -terrorists.html.

Thornton, Mary. "Oregon Guru Disavows Rajneeshism, Vows to Survive Investigations." *Washington Post*, October 20, 1985.

Times (London). "Khaled Tribute." September 3, 1997.

——. "Record of Suicide Attacks." March 5, 1996.

——. "Satanic Verses Publisher Is Shot in Oslo Suburb." October 12, 1993.

——. "Syria to Remain on US Terrorism List." February 17, 1992.

——. "39 Killed in Jerusalem Headquarters." July 23, 1946.

Toloyan, Kachig. "Martyrdom as Legitimacy: Terrorism, Religion, and Symbolic Appropriation in the Armenian Diaspora." In *Contemporary Research on Terrorism*, edited by Paul Wilkinson and A. M. Stewart, 89–103. Aberdeen: Aberdeen University Press, 1987.

Toronto Star. "Bin Laden Seeking Nukes." November 24, 2004.

Townley, Roderick and John Weisman. "The Reporters' Rat Race: Danger, Chaos, and Rumors of Payoffs." *TV Guide*, September 21, 1985.

Traynor, Ian. " 'Iran Terrorism' Trail Comes to Climax." *Guardian* (London), April 10, 1997.

Trinquier, Roger. *Modern Warfare: A French View of Counterinsurgency*. Translated by Daniel Lee. New York: Praeger, 1964.

Tsfati, Yariv, and Gabriel Weimann. "www.terrorism.com: Terror on the Internet." *Studies in Conflict and Terrorism* 25, no. 5 (September/October 2011): 317–32.

Tucker, Jonathan B. "Chemical/Biological Terrorism: Coping with a New Threat." *Politics and the Life Sciences* 15, no. 2 (1997): 167–83.

Tucker, Robert C. *Stalin in Power: The Revolution from Above, 1928–1941*. New York: Norton, 1990.

"Tunisia: Ansar al-Sharia Head Urges, Then Retracts Call to Al-Zawahiri to Pledge Allegiance to ISIL." Twitter, January 6, 2016, TRR2016010669491211; Twitter in English, Arabic, January 6, 2016.

Twersky, David. "The Risks of Cozying Up to Syria." *New York Times*, July 28, 1992.

United Nations General Assembly Resolution 52/164. http://www.unodoc.org/unodoc /terroris_convention_terrorist_bombing.html. Accessed May 15, 2005.

United Press International. "Do Terrorists Need Television, TV Guide Asks." February 18, 1985.

United States District Court Eastern District of New York, United States of America v. Adis Medunjanin, Abid Nasser, Adnan El Shukrijumah, Tariq Ur Rehman, and FNU LNU, 7 July 2010.

U.S. Department of Defense. *Department of Defense Dictionary of Military and Associated Terms*. Washington, D.C: Joint Publication 1-02, as amended through February 16, 2016. http://www.dtic.mil/doctrine/new_pubs/jp1_02.pdf.

——. *Terrorist Group Profiles*. Washington, D.C.: U.S. Government Printing Office, 1988.

——. *United States Department of Defense Commission on the Beirut International Airport (BIA) Terrorist Act of October 23, 1983* (known as "The Long Commission" in reference to its chairman, retired Admiral Robert L. J. Long, U.S. Navy). N.d.

U.S. Department of Homeland Security. "Homeland Security: Countering Violent Extremism." https://www.dhs.gov/topic/countering-violent-extremism. Accessed April 18, 2016.

U.S. Department of Justice, Office of Public Affairs. "Faisal Shahzad Pleads Guilty in Manhattan Federal Court to 10 Federal Crimes Arising from Attempted Car Bombing in Times Square." *US Department of Justice*, June 21, 2010. http://www.justice.gov/opa/pr/2010/June/10-ag-721.html.

U.S. Department of State. Bureau of Counterterrorism. *Country Reports on Terrorism 2011*. Washington, D.C.: U.S. Department of State Publication, April 2012. http://www.state.gov/documents/organization/195768.pdf.

——. *Libya's Continuing Responsibility for Terrorism*. Washington, D.C.: U.S. Department of State, November 1991.

——. *The Network of Terrorism*. Washington, D.C.: U.S. Department of State, 2001.

——. *Patterns of Global Terrorism 1996*. Washington, D.C.: U.S. Department of State, Publication 10433, April 1997.

——. *Patterns of Global Terrorism 2001*. Washington, D.C.: U.S. Department of State, Publication 10940, May 2002.

——. *Patterns of Global Terrorism 2003*. Washington, D.C.: U.S. Department of State, Publication 11124, April 2004.

U.S. Department of State, Bureau of Counterterrorism. *Country Reports on Terrorism 2014*. June 2015. http://www.state.gov/documents/organization/239631.pdf.

U.S. Department of State, Bureau of Counterterrorism and Countering Violent Extremism. "Chapter 3: State Sponsors of Terrorism." In *Country Reports on Terrorism 2015*. http://www.state.gov/j/ct/rls/crt/2015/257520.htm. Accessed May 11, 2016.

——. "Foreign Terrorist Organizations." Diplomacy in Action (2016). http://www.state.gov/j/ct/rls/other/des/123085.htm. Accessed May 11, 2016.

U.S. Department of State, Bureau of Public Affairs, Office of Public Communication. *Fact Sheet: Additional Information on the Bombing of Pan Am Flight 103*. Washington, D.C.: U.S. Department of State, November 15, 1991.

U.S. Department of State, Office of the Coordinator for Counterterrorism. *Country Reports on Terrorism 2004*. April 2005. http://www.state.gov/s/ct/rls/c14813.htm.

U.S. Departments of the Army and the Air Force. *Military Operations in Low Intensity Conflict*. Field Manual 100–20/Air Force Pamphlet 3–20. Washington, D.C.: Headquarters, Departments of the Army and the Air Force, 1990.

U.S. District Court, Southern District of New York, 1734HA01. United States of America v. Mokhtar Haouri, S4 00 Cr. 15 (JFK), June 3, 2001.

U.S. District Court for the District of Columbia. United States of America v. Abdel Basset Ali al-Megrahi and Lamen Khalifa Fhimah. November 14, 1991.

U.S. House of Representatives Homeland Security Committee. *Final Report of the Task Force on Combating Terrorist and Foreign Fighter Travel*. September 2015. https://homeland.house.gov/wp-content/uploads/2015/09/TaskForceFinalReport.pdf.

U.S. Special Operations Command, SOCOM-2012-0000003.
——. SOCOM-2012-0000005.
——. SOCOM-2012-0000006.
——. SOCOM-2012-0000009.
——. SOCOM-2012-0000010.
——. SOCOM-2012-0000012.
——. SOCOM-2012-0000013.
——. SOCOM-2012-0000016.
——. SOCOM-2012-0000017.
——. SOCOM-2012-0000018.
——. SOCOM-2012-0000019.
Utley, Garrick. "The Shrinking of Foreign News." *Foreign Affairs* 76, no. 2 (March/ April 1997): 2–10.
Van Biema, David. "Prophet of Poison." *Time*, April 3, 1995.
Venzke, Ben and Aimee Ibrahim. *Al-Qaeda's Advice for Mujahideen in Iraq: Lessons Learned in Afghanistan.* Vol. 1.0. Alexandria, Va.: IntelCenter, April 14, 2003.
——. *The al-Qaeda Threat: An Analytical Guide to al-Qaeda's Tactics and Targets.* Alexandria, Va.: Tempest, 2003.
Verhovek, Sam Howe. "Showdown at the 'Republic of Texas' Ends in Surrender." *International Herald Tribune* (Paris), May 5, 1997.
Vick, Karl. "Man Gets Hands on Bubonic Plague Germs, but That's No Crime." *Washington Post*, December 30, 1995.
Victor, Barbara. *Army of Roses: Inside the World of Palestinian Women Suicide Bombers.* New York: Rodale, 2003.
Victor, Peter. "Fascists Take to the Keyboards." *The Independent on Sunday* (London), April 7, 1995.
Vidal-Naquet, P. *Torture: Cancer of Democracy—France and Algeria, 1954–1962.* London: Penguin, 1963.
Viewpoint Kahane: *There Is No More Tal.* N.d.
——. *Uncomfortable Questions for Comfortable Jews.* N.d.
Vistica, Gregory L. and Daniel Klaidman. "Tracking Terror." *Newsweek*, October 19, 1998.
Wackerngel, Christoph. "Transcript of a Talk by Christoph Wackerngel." Unpublished manuscript. September 14, 1995.
Wakin, Daniel J. "Video Game Mounts Simulated Attacks Against Israeli Targets." *New York Times*, May 18, 2003.
Wald, Matthew L. "Figuring What It Would Take to Take Down a Tower." *New York Times*, March 21, 1993.
Waldman, Amy. "Suicide Bombing Masters: Sri Lankan Rebels." *New York Times*, January 14, 2003.
Walker, Christopher. "Arabs Are Convinced Car Crash Was a Murder Plot." *Times* (London), September 4, 1997.
——. "Bahrain Arrests 29 in Move to Foil 'Iranian-Backed Coup.'" *Times* (London), June 4, 1996.
——. "Hamas Calls for Uprising by Muslim Worshippers." *Times* (London), October 4, 1996.
——. "Hamas Urges Suicide Attack." *Times* (London), January 11, 1997.
——. "Handing Back of 'Biblical Land' Angers Militants." *Times* (London), November 6, 1995.

——. "Intelligence Experts See Hand of Tehran in Oslo Shooting." *Times* (London), October 13, 1993.

——. "£194m 'Missing' as Arafat Seeks Aid from Britain." *Times* (London), July 14, 1997.

——. "Palestinian 'Was Duped Into Being Suicide Bomber.'" *Times* (London), March 27, 1997.

——. "Rabin Killer 'Trained by Shin Bet.'" *Times* (London), November 21, 1995.

——. "Rabin Killing 'Part of Plot Backed by West Bank Rabbis.'" *Times* (London), November 10, 1995.

Walker, Peter and Vikram Dodd. "Video Tirades That Sealed Case Against Liquid Bomb Plotters." *Guardian*, September, 2008. http://en.europenews.dk/Video-tirades-that -sealed-case-against-liquid-bomb-plotters-98106.html.

Walker, Tom. "British Base Is Attacked as Bosnia Serbs Vow Revenge." *Times* (London), July 18, 1997.

Wallis, William. "Kenya Terror Attacks 'Planned from Somalia.'" *Financial Times*, November 5, 2003.

Walsh, Declan and Schmitt, Eric. "Drone Strike Killed No. 2 in al Qaeda, U.S. Officials Say." *New York Times*, June 5, 2012.

Walsh, James. "Shoko Asahara: The Making of a Messiah." *Time*, April 3, 1995.

Walsh, Mary Williams. "German Court Finds Iran's Leaders Ordered Slayings." *Los Angeles Times*, April 11, 1997.

Wang, Peng. "Women in the LTTE: Birds of Freedom or Cogs in the Wheel?" *Journal of Politics and Law* 4, no. 1 (March 2011): 100–108.

Wardlaw, Grant. "Linkages Between the Illegal Drugs Traffic and Terrorism." *Conflict Quarterly* 8, no. 3 (Summer 1988): 5–26.

Warraq, Ibn. "Virgins? What Virgins?" *Guardian* (London), January 12, 2002. http://www .guardian.co.uk/saturday_review/story/0%2C3605%2C631332%2C00.html.

Warrick, Joby. "An Al Qaeda 'Chemist' and the Quest for Ricin." *Washington Post*, May 5, 2004.

——. "U.S. Cites Big Gains Against al-Qadea: Group Is Facing Setbacks Globally, CIA Chief Says." *Washington Post*, May 30, 2008.

Warrick, Joby and Greg Miller. "Al Qaeda's No. 2 Leader Killed in U.S. Airstrike." *Washington Post*, June 5, 2012.

Warrick, Joby and Joe Stephens. "Before Attack, U.S. Expected Different Hit: Chemical, Germ Agents Focus of Preparations." *Washington Post*, October 2, 2001.

——. *Political Terrorism: Theory, Tactics, and Counter-measures*. Cambridge: Cambridge University Press, 1990.

Washington Post. "Biden Says Prison at Guantanamo Bay Should Be Closed." June 6, 2005.

——. "Text of Bin Laden Remarks: 'Hypocrisy Rears Its Ugly Head.'" October 8, 2001.

——. "Threats from Within." April 19, 2005.

——. "Unabomber Manifesto." September 19, 1995.

Watanabe, Manabu. "Religion and Violence in Japan Today: A Chronological and Doctrinal Analysis of Aum Shinrikyo." *Terrorism and Political Violence* 10, no. 4 (Winter 1998): 80–100.

Watt, Nicholas. "IRA's 'Russian Roulette' Detonator." *Times* (London), March 16, 1994.

Watts, Clint. "What If There Is No al Qaeda? Preparing for Future Terrorism." Philadelphia: Foreign Policy Research Institute, July 2012. http://www.fpri.org/enotes/2012 /201207.watts.alQaeda.html.

Wazis, Burhan. "Suicide Bombing Is Democratic Right, Says the 'Soul' of Hamas." *Observer* (London), August 19, 2001.

Weimann, Gabriel. *Terrorism in Cyberspace: The Next Generation.* Washington, DC: Woodrow Wilson Center Press/New York: Columbia University Press, 2015.

——. *Terror on the Internet: The New Arena, the New Challenges.* Washington, D.C.: U.S. Institute of Peace, 2006.

Weiser, Benjamin. "U.S. Says Bin Laden Aide Tried to Get Nuclear Material." *New York Times*, September 26, 1998.

Weisman, Steven R. "U.S. Has 'Credible' Word of Syrian Plot to Kill Lebanese." *New York Times*, June 10, 2005.

——. "White House Escalates Its Campaign to Isolate Syria." *New York Times*, June 23, 2005.

Weiss, Michael and Hassan Hassan. *ISIS: Inside the Army of Terror.* New York: Reagan Arts, 2015.

Welch, Craig. "Three Guilty in Valley Bombings." *Spokesman-Review* (Spokane, Wash.), July 24, 1997.

Wheeler-Bennett, John. *Munich: Prologue to Tragedy.* London: Macmillan, 1948.

Whine, Michael. "Islamist Organizations on the Internet." *Terrorism and Political Violence* 11, no. 1 (Spring 1999): 123–32.

White, Paul J. *Primitive Rebels or Revolutionary Modernizers? The Kurdish National Movement in Turkey.* London: Zed Books, 2001.

White, Robert W. "The Irish Republican Army: An Assessment of Sectarianism." *Terrorism and Political Violence* 9, no. 1 (Spring 1997): 20–56.

White House. "Fact Sheet on Combating Terrorism: Presidential Decision Directive 62." May 22, 1998. http://cns.miis.edu/research/cbw/pdd-62.htm.

——. "President Bush Discusses Iraq: Remarks by the President to the Pool Before and After Golf—Crawford, Texas." August 10, 2002. http://www.whitehouse.gov/news/releases/2002/08/20020810–3.html.

——. "The President Delivers State of the Union Address." January 29, 2002. http://www.whitehouse.gov/news/releases/2002/01/20020129–11.html.

White House, President George W. Bush, Office of the Press Secretary. "President Declares 'Freedom at War with Fear': Address to a Joint Session of Congress and the American People." September 20, 2001. http://www.whitehouse.gov/news/releases/2001/09/print/20010920–8.html.

Whitlock, Craig. "Islamic Radicals Behead American in Saudi Arabia." *Washington Post*, June 19, 2004.

——. "Terror Probes Find 'the Hands, but Not the Brains.'" *Washington Post*, July 12, 2005.

——. "Trail from London to Leeds Yields Portraits of 3 Bombers: Identities Revealed, but Motives Still a Mystery." *Washington Post*, July 15, 2005.

Whymant, Robert. "Cult Planned Gas Raids on America." *Times* (London), March 29, 1997.

Wiktorowicz, Quintan. "Joining the Cause: Al-Muhajiroun and Radical Islam." In *Radicalization: Critical Concepts in Military, Strategic, and Security Studies*, edited by Peter Neumann, 115–42. London: Routledge, 2015.

Wilgoren, Jodi. "After the Attacks: The Hijackers; A Terrorist Profile Emerges That Confounds the Experts." *New York Times*, September 15, 2001.

Wilkinson, Paul. *The New Fascists.* London: Grant McIntyre, 1981.

——. "Terrorism." In *Ideas That Shape Politics*, edited by Michael Foley, 188–98. Manchester: Manchester University Press, 1994.

——. "Terrorism and Propaganda." In *Terrorism and the Media*, edited by Yonah Alexander and Richard Latter, 26–33. McLean, Va.: Brassey's, 1990.

Williams, Phil and Paul N. Woessner. "Nuclear Material Trafficking: An Interim Assessment." *Transnational Organized Crime* 1, no. 2 (Summer 1995): 1–23.

Willmer, Tanya. "Soldiers' Mothers Pray Their Own Battle Over After Israel Ends Its Vietnam." *Agence France Presse*, May 24, 2000.

Woessner, Paul N. "Recent Developments: Chronology of Nuclear Smuggling Incidents, July 1991–May 1995." *Transnational Organized Crime* 1, no. 2 (Summer 1995): 288–329.

Wolf, John B. "The Palestine Resistance Movement." *Current History* 60 (1971).

Woodcock, George, ed. *The Anarchist Reader*. Glasgow: Fontana, 1977.

Woodward, Bob. *Bush at War*. New York: Simon & Schuster, 2003.

Woolsey, R. James. *Testimony Before the U.S. House of Representatives, Committee on National Security*, February 12, 1998. https://www.loyola.edu/departments/academics/political-science/strategic-intelligence/intel/19980212woolsey.html.

WorldTribune.com. "U.S.: Al Qaida Is 70 Percent Gone, Their 'Days Are Numbered.'" January 23, 2004.

Worth, Robert F. "Cleric in Yemen Admits Meeting Airliner Plot Suspect, Journalist Says." *New York Times*, February 1, 2010.

——. "Jihadists Take Stand on Web, and Some Say It's Defensive." *New York Times*, March 13, 2005.

Wright, Lawrence. *The Looming Tower: Al-Qaeda and the Road to 9/11*. New York: Alfred A. Knopf, 2006.

Wright, Robin. "Iran Supplies Lebanese Radicals Through Syria, U.S. Aides Say." *International Herald Tribune* (Paris), December 14–15, 1996.

Wright, Robin and Ronald J. Ostrow. "Pan Am 103 Clue Leads to Libyans." *Los Angeles Times*, June 24, 1991.

Wurth-Hough, Sandra. "Network News Coverage of Terrorism: The Early Years." *Terrorism* 6, no. 3 (Summer 1983): 403–21.

Ya'ari, Ehud. "The Metamorphosis of Hamas." *Jerusalem Report*, January 14, 1993.

Yamazaki, Mayuka. "Aum Shinrikyo." Unpublished manuscript. April 2005.

Yisra'eli, Rafi. "Islamikaze: Suicide Terrorism Examined." *Nativ* (Tel Aviv), January–April 1997.

Yomiuri Shimbun (Tokyo). "Special Edition: The Arrest of Guru Shoko Asahara, and the History of Asahara's Analects." May 16, 1995.

——. "Special Edition: Examination of Aum's Other Crime—Illegal Drug Production." February 28, 1996.

——. "Special Edition: The First Aum Case Will Start on April 24th." April 20, 1996.

——. "Special Edition: 1998 Aum Case—Matsumoto [Asahara] Was a Ringleader." December 31, 1998.

——. "Special Edition: Summary of Aum Case." June 14, 1996.

Yoo, John. "Obama, Drones and Thomas Aquinas." *Wall Street Journal*, June 8, 2012.

Young, Sean. "Online Co. Shuts Down Site with Beheading." *Yahoo! News*, May 14, 2004. http://www.crime-research.org/news/14.05.2004/270.

Zaar, Isaac. *Rescue and Liberation: America's Part in the Birth of Israel*. New York: Bloch, 1954.

Zaman, Amberin. "Swords Into Rabbit Ears." *Washington Post*, February 4, 1999.

Zanini, Michele and Sean J. A. Edwards. "The Networking of Terror in the Information Age." In *Networks and Netwars: The Future of Terror, Crime, and Militancy*, edited by John Arquilla and David Ronfeldt, 29–60. Santa Monica, Calif.: RAND Corporation, MR-1382-OSD, 2001.

Zarate, Juan. "Winning the War on Terror: Marking Success and Confronting Challenges." Text of prepared remarks at the Washington Institute for Near East Policy, Washington, D.C., April 23, 2008. http://www.washingtoninstitute.org/templateC07 .php?CID=393.

"Zarqawi Statement May 20, 2005, Part 1." English translation by *Jihad Unspun*, May 26, 2005. http://www.jihadunspun.com/newsarchive/article_internal.php?article =102833&list=/newsarchive/index.php&.

"Zawahiri Issues Video in Support of Syrian Uprising." Text and translation provided by *SITE Monitoring Service—Jihadist Threat*, February 11, 2012.

Zelin, Aaron. "Al-Qaeda Announces an Islamic State in Syria." *Washington Institute*, April 2013. http://www.washingtoninstitute.org/policy-analysis/view/al-qaeda -announces-an-islamic-state-in-syria.

Zernike, Kate and David Rhode. "Forced Nudity of Iraqi Prisoners Is Seen as a Pervasive Pattern, Not Isolated Incidents." *New York Times*, June 8, 2004.

Zonis, Marvin and Daniel Brumberg. "Behind Beirut Terrorism." *New York Times*, October 8, 1984.

Zuckerman, Mortimer B. "Playing the Terrorists' Game." *U.S. News & World Report*, June 9, 1986.

Briefings and Conference and Seminar Presentations

Boetcher, Mike. "Al-Qa'ida's Nuclear Weapons Program." Presentation at the Centre for the Study of Terrorism and Political Violence Symposium on Islamic Extremism and Terrorism in the Greater Middle East, University of St. Andrews, St. Andrews, Scotland, June 7–8, 2002.

Counter Terrorist Unit. *New Jersey State Police: Kikumura Investigation—A Case Study*. N.d.

Denning, Dorothy. "Information Warfare and Cyber-Terrorism." Women in International Security (WIIS) seminar, Washington, D.C., December 15, 1999.

Eedle, Paul. "The Language of Jihad." Presentation at the Centre for the Study of Terrorism and Political Violence Symposium on Islamic Extremism and Terrorism in the Greater Middle East, University of St. Andrews, St. Andrews, Scotland, June 7–8, 2002.

Gunaratna, Rohan. "Maritime Terrorism: Future Threats and Responses." Briefing presented to the International Research Group on Political Violence and Terrorism, Washington, D.C., May 2001.

Israeli Security Agency. "Security Seminar on Combating the Threat of Suicide Bombers." Israeli Embassy, Washington, D.C., September 16, 2003.

Sri Lankan Armed Forces. "Suicide Terrorism in Sri Lanka." N.d.

Videos, DVDs, and CD-ROMs

The Destruction of the American Destroyer USS Cole. DVD version, produced by the Assahab (the Cloud) Foundation. N.d.

Igniting the Revolution: An Introduction to the Earth Liberation Front. Distributed by the
     North American Earth Liberation Front Press Office, Portland, Oregon. N.d.
IntelCenter. *Hamas Audio/Video Files.* Vol. 1. Alexandria, Va.: www.intelcenter.com, n.d.
prohosters.com/pearl/#ogr, or the link to the execution clip found at www.ogrish.com.
Special Force Version 1. Registration Card No 336070 and Back Cover. N.d.
Video prepared by the General Intelligence Directorate, Hashemite Kingdom of
     Jordan. N.d.

Index